The Collected Works of

Langston Hughes

Volume 5

The Plays to 1942:
Mulatto to *The Sun Do Move*

Projected Volumes in the Collected Works

The Poems: 1921–1940

The Poems: 1941–1950

The Poems: 1951–1967

The Novels: *Not without Laughter*
and *Tambourines to Glory*

The Plays to 1942: *Mulatto* to *The Sun Do Move*

The Gospel Plays, Operas, and Other
Late Dramatic Work

The Early Simple Stories

The Later Simple Stories

Essays on Art, Race, Politics, and World Affairs

Fight for Freedom and Other Writings on Civil Rights

Works for Children and Young Adults: Poetry,
Fiction, and Other Writing

Works for Children and Young Adults: Biographies

Autobiography: *The Big Sea*

Autobiography: *I Wonder as I Wander*

The Short Stories

The Translations

An Annotated Bibliography of the
Works of Langston Hughes

The Collected Works of

Langston Hughes

Volume 5

The Plays to 1942:
Mulatto to *The Sun Do Move*

Edited with an Introduction
by Leslie Catherine Sanders,
with Nancy Johnston

University of Missouri Press
Columbia and London

Copyright © 2002 by Ramona Bass and Arnold Rampersad,
Administrators of the Estate of Langston Hughes
Introduction copyright © 2002 by Leslie Catherine Sanders
Chronology copyright © 2001 by Arnold Rampersad
University of Missouri Press, Columbia, Missouri 65201
Printed and bound in the United States of America
All rights reserved
5 4 3 2 1   06 05 04 03 02

Library of Congress Cataloging-in-Publication Data

Hughes, Langston, 1902–1967
   [Works. 2001]
   The collected works of Langston Hughes / edited with an introduction by Leslie Catherine
Sanders, with Nancy Johnston
      p.   cm.
   Includes bibliographical references and indexes.
   ISBN 0–8262-1369-3 (v. 5 : alk. paper)
   1. African Americans—Literary collections.   I. Sanders, Leslie Catherine.   II. Johnston,
Nancy.   III. Title.
PS3515.U274   2001
818'.5209—dc21   00066601

⊗™This paper meets the requirements of the
American National Standard for Permanence of Paper
for Printed Library Materials, Z39.48, 1984.

Designer: Kristie Lee
Typesetter: BOOKCOMP, Inc.
Printer and binder: Thomson-Shore, Inc.
Typefaces: Galliard, Optima

Lines from *The Collected Poems of Langston Hughes* by Langston Hughes, copyright © 1994
   by The Estate of Langston Hughes. Used by permission of Alfred A. Knopf, a division of
   Random House, Inc.

812.52
Hug

Contents

Acknowledgments   ix

Chronology   xi

Introduction   1

A Note on the Text   15

Mulatto: A Play of the Deep South (1930)   17

Mule Bone: A Comedy of Negro Life (1930)   51

Scottsboro, Limited: A One-Act Play (1931)   116

Harvest (1934)   130

Angelo Herndon Jones (1935)   184

Little Ham (1935)   196

Soul Gone Home (1936)   266

Mother and Child: A Theatre Vignette (1936)   271

Emperor of Haiti (Troubled Island) (1936)   278

When the Jack Hollers; or Careless Love: A Negro-Folk
   Comedy in Three Acts (1936)   333

Joy to My Soul: A Farce Comedy in Three Acts (1937)   407

Front Porch (1938)   481

Don't You Want to Be Free? A Poetry Play from Slavery through
   the Blues to Now—and then some! With Singing, Music,
   and Dancing (1938)   538

Six Satires (1938)   574

The Sun Do Move (1942)   591

Notes   649

Acknowledgments

This project was begun in collaboration with the late George Houston Bass. I hope he would be pleased by the results. Many people have helped bring this volume to fruition, and I thank them. For typing, checking, and text comparisons, Karen Bernard, Tess Chakkalakal, Susan Goldberg, Chandra Hodgson, Evelyn Marrast, Peggy Pasternak, Peter Sinema, Michael Wiebe, and especially Christine Kim. For help and editing counsel, Lesley Higgins. For their endless helpfulness and courtesy, the staff at the Beinecke Library, especially Steve Jones and Timothy Young. For permission to publish *When the Jack Hollers,* Harold Ober Associates; for *Hurrah, America,* Maranantha Quick; and for *Harvest,* Pete Steffens. For her careful editing, Jane Lago of the University of Missouri Press. Thanks also to Yale University, Beinecke Library, for a Visiting Fellowship, and to the Social Science and Humanities Research Council of Canada for a major grant in support of this project.

The University of Missouri Press recognizes that the *Collected Works* would not have been possible without the support and assistance of Patricia Powell, Chris Byrne, and Wendy Schmalz of Harold Ober Associates, representing the estate of Langston Hughes, and of Arnold Rampersad and Ramona Bass, co-executors of the estate of Langston Hughes.

The University of Missouri Press offers its grateful acknowledgment to Eugene Davidson for his generous assistance in the publication of this volume of *The Collected Works of Langston Hughes.*

Chronology
By Arnold Rampersad

1902 James Langston Hughes is born February 1 in Joplin, Missouri, to James Nathaniel Hughes, a stenographer for a mining company, and Carrie Mercer Langston Hughes, a former government clerk.

1903 After his father immigrates to Mexico, Langston's mother takes him to Lawrence, Kansas, the home of Mary Langston, her twice-widowed mother. Mary Langston's first husband, Lewis Sheridan Leary, died fighting alongside John Brown at Harpers Ferry. Her second, Hughes's grandfather, was Charles Langston, a former abolitionist, Republican politician, and businessman.

1907 After a failed attempt at a reconciliation in Mexico, Langston and his mother return to Lawrence.

1909 Langston starts school in Topeka, Kansas, where he lives for a while with his mother before returning to his grandmother's home in Lawrence.

1915 Following Mary Langston's death, Hughes leaves Lawrence for Lincoln, Illinois, where his mother lives with her second husband, Homer Clark, and Homer Clark's young son by another union, Gwyn "Kit" Clark.

1916 Langston, elected class poet, graduates from the eighth grade. Moves to Cleveland, Ohio, and starts at Central High School there.

1918 Publishes early poems and short stories in his school's monthly magazine.

1919 Spends the summer in Toluca, Mexico, with his father.

1920 Graduates from Central High as class poet and editor of the school annual. Returns to Mexico to live with his father.

1921 In June, Hughes publishes "The Negro Speaks of Rivers" in *Crisis* magazine. In September, sponsored by his father, he enrolls at Columbia University in New York. Meets W. E. B. Du Bois, Jessie Fauset, and Countee Cullen.

1922 Unhappy at Columbia, Hughes withdraws from school and breaks with his father.

1923 Sailing in June to western Africa on the crew of a freighter, he visits Senegal, the Gold Coast, Nigeria, the Congo, and other countries.

1924 Spends several months in Paris working in the kitchen of a night-club.

1925 Lives in Washington for a year with his mother. His poem "The Weary Blues" wins first prize in a contest sponsored by *Opportunity* magazine, which leads to a book contract with Knopf through Carl Van Vechten. Becomes friends with several other young artists of the Harlem Renaissance, including Zora Neale Hurston, Wallace Thurman, and Arna Bontemps.

1926 In January his first book, *The Weary Blues,* appears. He enrolls at historically black Lincoln University, Pennsylvania. In June, the *Nation* weekly magazine publishes his landmark essay "The Negro Artist and the Racial Mountain."

1927 Knopf publishes his second book of verse, *Fine Clothes to the Jew,* which is condemned in the black press. Hughes meets his powerful patron Mrs. Charlotte Osgood Mason. Travels in the South with Hurston, who is also taken up by Mrs. Mason.

1929 Hughes graduates from Lincoln University.

1930 Publishes his first novel, *Not without Laughter* (Knopf). Visits Cuba and meets fellow poet Nicolás Guillén. Hughes is dismissed by Mrs. Mason in a painful break made worse by false charges of dishonesty leveled by Hurston over their play *Mule Bone.*

1931 Demoralized, he travels to Haiti. Publishes work in the communist magazine *New Masses.* Supported by the Rosenwald Foundation, he tours the South taking his poetry to the people. In Alabama, he visits some of the Scottsboro Boys in prison. His brief collection of poems *Dear Lovely Death* is privately printed in Amenia, New York. Hughes and the illustrator Prentiss Taylor publish a verse pamphlet, *The Negro Mother.*

1932 With Taylor, he publishes *Scottsboro, Limited,* a short play and four poems. From Knopf comes *The Dream Keeper,* a book of previously published poems selected for young people. Later, Macmillan brings out *Popo and Fifina,* a children's story about Haiti written with Arna Bontemps, his closest friend. In June, Hughes sails to Russia in a band of twenty-two young African

Americans to make a film about race relations in the United States. After the project collapses, he lives for a year in the Soviet Union. Publishes his most radical verse, including "Good Morning Revolution" and "Goodbye Christ."

1933 Returns home at midyear via China and Japan. Supported by a patron, Noël Sullivan of San Francisco, Hughes spends a year in Carmel writing short stories.

1934 Knopf publishes his first short story collection, *The Ways of White Folks*. After labor unrest in California threatens his safety, he leaves for Mexico following news of his father's death.

1935 Spends several months in Mexico, mainly translating short stories by local leftist writers. Lives for some time with the photographer Henri Cartier-Bresson. Returning almost destitute to the United States, he joins his mother in Oberlin, Ohio. Visits New York for the Broadway production of his play *Mulatto* and clashes with its producer over changes in the script. Unhappy, he writes the poem "Let America Be America Again."

1936 Wins a Guggenheim Foundation fellowship for work on a novel but soon turns mainly to writing plays in association with the Karamu Theater in Cleveland. Karamu stages his farce *Little Ham* and his historical drama about Haiti, *Troubled Island*.

1937 Karamu stages *Joy to My Soul*, another comedy. In July, he visits Paris for the League of American Writers. He then travels to Spain, where he spends the rest of the year reporting on the civil war for the *Baltimore Afro-American*.

1938 In New York, Hughes founds the radical Harlem Suitcase Theater, which stages his agitprop play *Don't You Want to Be Free?* The leftist International Workers Order publishes *A New Song*, a pamphlet of radical verse. Karamu stages his play *Front Porch*. His mother dies.

1939 In Hollywood he writes the script for the movie *Way Down South*, which is criticized for stereotyping black life. Hughes goes for an extended stay in Carmel, California, again as the guest of Noël Sullivan.

1940 His autobiography *The Big Sea* appears (Knopf). He is picketed by a religious group for his poem "Goodbye Christ," which he publicly renounces.

1941 With a Rosenwald Fund fellowship for playwriting, he leaves California for Chicago, where he founds the Skyloft Players. Moves on to New York in December.

1942   Knopf publishes his book of verse *Shakespeare in Harlem*. The Skyloft Players stage his play *The Sun Do Move*. In the summer he resides at the Yaddo writers' and artists' colony, New York. Hughes also works as a writer in support of the war effort. In November he starts "Here to Yonder," a weekly column in the Chicago *Defender* newspaper.

1943   "Here to Yonder" introduces Jesse B. Semple, or Simple, a comic Harlem character who quickly becomes its most popular feature. Hughes publishes *Jim Crow's Last Stand* (Negro Publication Society of America), a pamphlet of verse about the struggle for civil rights.

1944   Comes under surveillance by the FBI because of his former radicalism.

1945   With Mercer Cook, translates and later publishes *Masters of the Dew* (Reynal and Hitchcock), a novel by Jacques Roumain of Haiti.

1947   His work as librettist with Kurt Weill and Elmer Rice on the Broadway musical play *Street Scene* brings Hughes a financial windfall. He vacations in Jamaica. Knopf publishes *Fields of Wonder*, his only book composed mainly of lyric poems on nonracial topics.

1948   Hughes is denounced (erroneously) as a communist in the U.S. Senate. He buys a townhouse in Harlem and moves in with his longtime friends Toy and Emerson Harper.

1949   Doubleday publishes *Poetry of the Negro, 1746–1949*, an anthology edited with Arna Bontemps. Also published are *One-Way Ticket* (Knopf), a book of poems, and *Cuba Libre: Poems of Nicolás Guillén* (Anderson and Ritchie), translated by Hughes and Ben Frederic Carruthers. Hughes teaches for three months at the University of Chicago Lab School for children. His opera about Haiti with William Grant Still, *Troubled Island*, is presented in New York.

1950   Another opera, *The Barrier*, with music by Jan Meyerowitz, is hailed in New York but later fails on Broadway. Simon and Schuster publishes *Simple Speaks His Mind*, the first of five books based on his newspaper columns.

1951   Hughes's book of poems about life in Harlem, *Montage of a Dream Deferred*, appears (Henry Holt).

1952   His second collection of short stories, *Laughing to Keep from Crying*, is published by Henry Holt. In its "First Book" series for children, Franklin Watts publishes Hughes's *The First Book of Negroes.*

1953 In March, forced to testify before Senator Joseph McCarthy's subcommittee on subversive activities, Hughes is exonerated after repudiating his past radicalism. *Simple Takes a Wife* appears.

1954 Mainly for young readers, he publishes *Famous American Negroes* (Dodd, Mead) and *The First Book of Rhythms.*

1955 Publishes *The First Book of Jazz* and finishes *Famous Negro Music Makers* (Dodd, Mead). In November, Simon and Schuster publishes *The Sweet Flypaper of Life,* a narrative of Harlem with photographs by Roy DeCarava.

1956 Hughes's second volume of autobiography, *I Wonder as I Wander* (Rinehart), appears, as well as *A Pictorial History of the Negro* (Crown), coedited with Milton Meltzer, and *The First Book of the West Indies.*

1957 *Esther,* an opera with composer Jan Meyerowitz, has its premiere in Illinois. Rinehart publishes *Simple Stakes a Claim* as a novel. Hughes's musical play *Simply Heavenly,* based on his Simple character, runs for several weeks off and then on Broadway. Hughes translates and publishes *Selected Poems of Gabriela Mistral* (Indiana University Press).

1958 *The Langston Hughes Reader* (George Braziller) appears, as well as *The Book of Negro Folklore* (Dodd, Mead), coedited with Arna Bontemps, and another juvenile, *Famous Negro Heroes of America* (Dodd, Mead). John Day publishes a short novel, *Tambourines to Glory,* based on a Hughes gospel musical play.

1959 Hughes's *Selected Poems* published (Knopf).

1960 *The First Book of Africa* appears, along with *An African Treasury: Articles, Essays, Stories, Poems by Black Africans,* edited by Hughes (Crown).

1961 Inducted into the National Institute of Arts and Letters. Knopf publishes his book-length poem *Ask Your Mama: 12 Moods for Jazz. The Best of Simple,* drawn from the columns, appears (Hill and Wang). Hughes writes his gospel musical plays *Black Nativity* and *The Prodigal Son.* He visits Africa again.

1962 Begins a weekly column for the *New York Post.* Attends a writers' conference in Uganda. Publishes *Fight for Freedom: The Story of the NAACP,* commissioned by the organization.

1963 His third collection of short stories, *Something in Common,* appears from Hill and Wang. Indiana University Press publishes

Five Plays by Langston Hughes, edited by Webster Smalley, as well as Hughes's anthology *Poems from Black Africa, Ethiopia, and Other Countries.*

1964   His musical play *Jericho–Jim Crow,* a tribute to the civil rights movement, is staged in Greenwich Village. Indiana University Press brings out his anthology *New Negro Poets: U.S.A.,* with a foreword by Gwendolyn Brooks.

1965   With novelists Paule Marshall and William Melvin Kelley, Hughes visits Europe for the U.S. State Department. His gospel play *The Prodigal Son* and his cantata with music by David Amram, *Let Us Remember,* are staged.

1966   After twenty-three years, Hughes ends his depiction of Simple in his Chicago *Defender* column. Publishes *The Book of Negro Humor* (Dodd, Mead). In a visit sponsored by the U.S. government, he is honored in Dakar, Senegal, at the First World Festival of Negro Arts.

1967   His *The Best Short Stories by Negro Writers: An Anthology from 1899 to the Present* (Little, Brown) includes the first published story by Alice Walker. On May 22, Hughes dies at New York Polyclinic Hospital in Manhattan from complications following prostate surgery. Later that year, two books appear: *The Panther and the Lash: Poems of Our Times* (Knopf) and, with Milton Meltzer, *Black Magic: A Pictorial History of the Negro in American Entertainment* (Prentice Hall).

The Collected Works of
Langston Hughes

Volume 5

The Plays to 1942:
Mulatto to *The Sun Do Move*

Introduction

You've taken my blues and gone—
You sing 'em on Broadway
And you sing 'em in Hollywood Bowl,
You mixed 'em up with symphonies
And you fixed 'em
So they don't sound like me.
Yep, you done taken my blues and gone.
You also took my spirituals and gone.

You put me in *Macbeth* and *Carmen Jones*
And in all kinds of *Swing Mikados*
And in everything but what's about me—
But someday somebody'll
Stand up and talk about me—
Black and beautiful—
And sing about me,
And put on plays about me!
I reckon it'll be
Me myself!

Yes, it'll be me.

"Note on Commercial Theater"[1]

Langston Hughes is loved and celebrated for the brilliance with which he gives voice to "the low-down folk," especially the ordinary African Americans who flowed into northern American cities—New York, Cleveland, Chicago, and points in between—over the course of the twentieth century. Virtually all his life Hughes sought to bring those folks, their stories, and their performance of life to the stage, and even to provide stages for them. Hughes's great love of theater began in his childhood, encouraged by his mother, who had theatrical ambitions for herself. She took him to plays and involved him in amateur theatrical events. One of his earliest publications was a play for children, *The Gold Piece,* and from the late 1920s on, Hughes always had at least one dramatic iron in

1. Langston Hughes, *Selected Poems of Langston Hughes* (New York: Vintage, 1970), 190.

the fire. Theater was his love and his torment. He wrote to James Baldwin, in 1953, "If you want to die, be disturbed, maladjusted, neurotic, and psychotic, disappointed, and disjointed, just write plays!"[2] Yet, over his career, Hughes's engagement with the theater included venues ranging from Broadway and off-Broadway to community theaters such as Karamu House in Cleveland, and churches, union halls, and libraries in Harlem and elsewhere. Hughes's plays were welcomed by African American collegiate and community groups, eager for work "about them" at a time when such scripts were scarce.

"Terrific 'box office' and good, too," is the way Hughes at one point described his theatrical criteria to his lifelong friend and sometime collaborator Arna Bontemps. Less flippantly, he wrote in a draft of his 1931 application to the Rosenwald Fund, "[T]here is a great need of spiritually-true dramas for the Negro theatre."[3] For Hughes, these goals were not contradictory; moreover, all of them also arose out of his determination, expressed in his 1940 poem "Note on Commercial Theater," to render the stage a place of and for authentic black expression.

The theatrical world that Hughes encountered in the 1920s, when he first began writing for the stage, was inimical to "spiritually-true Negro drama," whether in a tragic or a comic mode, despite a vogue for black musicals, in particular. An exception to this absence was the acclaimed 1917 New York performances of the white playwright Ridgely Torrence's poignant *Three Plays for a Negro Theater,* notable for its serious treatment of black themes and its use of a black cast in dramatic roles. This production seemed to presage change. However, more generally, serious stage representations of African American life, or even serious portraits of African Americans, were rare. Moreover, plays intended as sympathetic portrayals of African American life, or as "serious" uses of the black figure, often employed troubling images. For example, the central black character in Eugene O'Neill's *The Emperor Jones* is commonly interpreted as representing the primitive unconscious, a connection as deeply dependent on racist stereotype as is the entire construction of the character. Comedy presented other difficulties. Minstrelsy's grotesque

2. Hughes to James Baldwin, July 25, 1953, Langston Hughes Papers, James Weldon Johnson Collection, Yale Collection of American Literature, Beinecke Rare Book and Manuscript Library. Hereafter referred to as Langston Hughes Papers.

3. Hughes to Arna Bontemps, January 17, 1938, in *Arna Bontemps–Langston Hughes Letters, 1925–1967,* ed. Charles H. Nichols (New York: Dodd, Mead, 1980), 27; draft of letter, Hughes to Nathan Levin, August 13, 1931, re: Rosenwald fund, Langston Hughes Papers.

images overshadowed the popular genre of black musical comedy, including those works by African American writers and composers. Low comedy, reminiscent of minstrelsy and borrowing from its conventions, marked early black Broadway productions, such as *In Dahomey* (1902) and *The ShooFly Regiment* (1907), and later, throughout the twenties, black revues, such as the popular *Shuffle Along,* which dominated Broadway in 1921, when Hughes first arrived in Harlem.

African American cultural leaders of the Harlem Renaissance encouraged the development of black theater, as they did the other arts. In 1926, in the pages of the *Crisis,* W. E. B. Du Bois called for the development of a Little Theater movement in black communities, stipulating that the plays be "about us," "by us," "for us," and "near us."[4] The nascent American folk play movement, influenced by the 1911 American tour of the Irish Abbey Players and the work of W. B. Yeats and John Millington Synge in creating a theater capable of depicting the Irish folk, was recommended as a model by the so-called dean of the New Negro movement, Alain Locke, and his Howard University colleague Montgomery Gregory. Both saw the folk play as a genre capable of expressing what they called, somewhat ambiguously, "the Drama of Negro Life."[5] However, this genre, too, generated its own problematic stereotypes. At least in the hands of such white dramatists as Eugene O'Neill, Paul Green, and Paul Connelly, black characters in folk plays often had a tenuous hold on reason, easily succumbed to superstition, and suffered patiently. Even well-intentioned playwrights typically deployed an array of damaging dramatic stereotypes and assumptions in their folk plays depicting black life.

It was in this context that Langston Hughes's career in theater began. As in his other artistic endeavors, in writing for the stage Hughes tackled virtually every form. His plays range from the relatively conventional dramatic realism of his tragedies, *Mulatto* (1930), *Emperor of Haiti* (1936), and *Front Porch* (1938), and the comedies, *Little Ham* (1935) and *Joy to My Soul* (1937), to the agitprop of *Scottsboro Limited* (1931), the episodic narrative of his chronicle plays such as *Don't You Want to Be Free?* (1938) and *The Sun Do Move* (1942), and finally his various gospel plays, written in the 1960s, which stage a traditional African American church service

4. W. E. B. Du Bois, "Krigwa Players Little Negro Theatre: The Story of a Little Theatre Movement," *The Crisis* 32 (July 1926): 134–36.

5. Alain Locke, "Introduction: The Drama of Negro Life," in *Plays of Negro Life: A Source-Book of Native American Drama,* ed. Alain Lock and Montgomery Gregory (New York: Harper and Brothers, 1927).

as a theatrical event. Hughes also wrote libretti; song lyrics; radio, film, and television scripts; and scripts for dance choreography. In addition, even during his lifetime, others created theater out of his poems and Simple stories.

From the beginning, Hughes understood the radical nature of his undertaking in the theater, for although his theatrical influences were many, his models for "authentic" African American theater were very few. In developing his own theatrical styles, Hughes particularly gained ideas and inspiration from the theater he encountered during his eight months in Moscow and his travels in Soviet Central Asia in 1932–1933, as well as from American theater in its many manifestations.[6] His central and quite specific purpose, however, remained constant: reclaiming cultural forms, redeeming black images, and telling black stories. Finally, Hughes sought a complete revisioning of theatrical possibility, desiring to make the stage a fruitful site for the representation and reenactment of African American life.

Sharing this aim, and—for a short but formative period of Hughes's artistic development—joining him in it, was Zora Neale Hurston; they first planned to collaborate on "real" Negro folk opera in 1926. Of all the Harlem Renaissance writers, Hughes and Hurston were the ones most dedicated to the folk, and most anxious that their representation on the American stage express the spirit of the folk rather than parody it. The period of Hughes's friendship and collaboration with Hurston gave him the opportunity to work with the folk materials Hurston collected— rather than with an imagined or imaginatively reconstructed folk—and with someone who was also deeply engaged by how to render these materials into theater. Their only theatrical collaboration, *Mule Bone* (1930), ended their friendship; nonetheless, Hughes clearly learned as much as he contributed to their "Negro Folk Comedy."

Thematically, *Mulatto* and *Mule Bone*, Hughes's first two full-length plays, signal preoccupations that would mark much of his later work. *Mulatto* is a social drama, a harrowing, melodramatic story of patricide and suicide. Set in the South of the period, its theme is the claim to rightful place and legacy by the son of a white plantation owner and his black housekeeper. The familial conflict central to *Mulatto* certainly had personal resonance for Hughes. However, the play's representation of

6. Leslie Sanders, " 'Interesting Ways of Staging Plays': Hughes and Russian Theatre," *Langston Hughes Review* 15:1 (spring 1997): 4–12.

southern racism at its most vicious, and of the mulatto figure as evoking the two-ness of which W. E. B. Du Bois spoke, also offers a precise critique and corrective of Paul Green's *In Abraham's Bosom,* especially its representation of the mulatto son and his black mother. The dignity and eloquence of Hughes's characters, even in extremity, are in marked contrast to the inarticulate desperation of both mother and son in the final moments of Green's tragedy. Beyond all else, of course, *Mulatto* is an uncompromising condemnation of American racism, and a warning about the fate of a nation so bitterly divided and so abusive of its black citizens. The play was eventually made into an opera entitled *The Barrier,* and both the play and the opera were translated into many languages. *Mulatto* is one of Hughes's best-known plays, although it is one of his few tragedies.

Mule Bone: A Comedy of Negro Life, the play that Hughes wrote with Zora Neale Hurston—and over which they "fell out" over authorship— represents the other central preoccupation of Hughes's work in the theater, that of bringing the folk to dramatic life. The authors shared the sense that characteristic folk expression is most aptly represented, re-created, and recorded in performance, whether on stage or in "speakerly" texts, and both not only shared but also developed an understanding of the performative nature of African American folk culture. Through his collaboration with Hurston, Hughes came to recognize the possibility of embedding plot, or drama, in the ways of the folk. In his comedies, Hughes sought to replace the routines of minstrelsy and black vaudeville with the laughter that is woven throughout characteristic black expression; that is, he sought to replace comic routine with the kind of humor that comprises not foolishness but a worldview. One might say that a preoccupation of his work in comedy is to create a space for African American laughter on the American stage.

During the 1930s, a period when there were few scripts, particularly few full-length plays, for black actors and black theater groups, Hughes provided material on subjects new to the American stage. As in much of his poetry and fiction, in theater Hughes focused on the urban folk and the history that had sent them "goin' down the road" of the Great Migration. Lacking a reservoir of collected folk materials like those available for depicting the lives of rural black folk, Hughes turned to his own observations of Harlem life, much of which also informed his own poetry, and sometimes to his poems themselves. His eclectic portraits of urban black folk challenged conventional comic portraits of black migrants as unable to handle the city; rather, his various stagings of the black working class documented the transition and adaptation of a folk worldview to the modern urban life.

The twelve years represented in this volume, between the completion of *Mulatto* (1930) and that of *The Sun Do Move* (1942), cover a period of intense dramatic activity. Hughes wrote ten full-length plays, three of which are collaborations: *Mule Bone* (with Zora Neale Hurston, 1930), *Harvest* (with Ella Winter and Ann Hawkins, 1934), and *When the Jack Hollers* (with Arna Bontemps, 1936). In addition, he wrote several shorter plays: *Scottsboro, Limited* and *Angelo Herndon Jones* on expressly political themes; the quirky *Mother and Child* (1936); the bittersweet *Soul Gone Home* (1936); and several short sketches written principally as openers for other plays, of which only a selection is included in this volume. He also completed two operas during this period—*Troubled Island,* with the composer William Grant Still, and *De Organizer,* with James P. Johnson—as well as a film script, *Way Down South,* with Clarence Muse.

Several opportunities particularly spurred Hughes's extraordinary productivity during this time. His stay at Jasper Deeter's Hedgerow Theatre in Rose Valley, Pennsylvania, during the summer and fall of 1930, where he completed *Mulatto,* introduced him to all facets of theater, and to actors at work, including the great Rose McClendon, for whom he wrote the role of Cora, the mother in *Mulatto*. His exposure, during his trip to the Soviet Union in 1932–1933, to the entire range of Moscow theater, and its most important directors, especially Vsevolod Meyerhold, Konstantin Stanislavski, and Nikolai Okhlopkov, just at the end of the theater's most brilliant period, and the equally exciting folk theater he encountered in his travels in the USSR, gave him a wealth of theatrical ideas and models. Finally, the frequent opportunity to have his plays produced, either by Cleveland's Gilpin Players of Karamu House or by companies he founded himself—the Harlem Suitcase Theatre, the New Negro Theatre in Los Angeles, and the Skyloft Players in Chicago—helped him develop a sense of what works on stage.

However, these different venues also seemed to dictate contradictory senses of theatrical purpose, as well as somewhat contradictory politics. In the formally conventional plays Hughes wrote for the Gilpin Players, he sought both to entertain and to instruct. The tragedies written for Karamu, *Troubled Island* and *Front Porch,* depict issues dividing the African American community rather than focusing on white oppression. Hughes's comedies for Karamu Theatre allude to social issues affecting African Americans and while celebrating the community also critique it, albeit gently and only as commentary underlying comic romance. Yet during the same period, and beginning with *Scottsboro, Limited* (1931), Hughes was also engaged by the forms and function of radical theater, particularly agitprop, with its twofold purpose of agitation and propaganda, its eschewal of scenery, costume, and prop, and its use of rhythmic language, choreographed movement, audience participation, and a call to action. Biographer Arnold Rampersad, and others who have written on Hughes in the theater, often posit a dichotomy between Hughes's hope for "terrific box office" and his radical experimentation, or between his commercial and overtly political aims. Certainly Hughes always desired a "hit"; he supported himself by his writing and always hoped his work would be lucrative. Moreover, as his "Note on Commercial Theater" indicates, it is into the commercial theater that he expected to intervene. Yet it is important to remember that during the 1930s in the United States, radical theater, and conventional theater on social themes, was also lucrative; for example, the work of Clifford Odets, Maxwell Anderson, Lillian Hellman, and John Steinbeck found success on mainstream stages. Even after Hughes began to distance himself from the Left at the end of the decade, he adapted aspects of radical theater as a medium for the staging of African American historical narratives, the first of which was *Don't You Want to Be Free?* The formal qualities of radical theater became, in Hughes's hands, a way of re-creating the ways in which African Americans have created, out of nothing, a rich and vibrant culture, whose verbal and musical forms of self-expression mourn and resist the oppression that has marked their lives, while proclaiming and celebrating their survival. Conventional theater, in his hands, too, was altered, both in terms of the subject matter he brought to the stage and through the ways in which he challenged and unsettled the usual and traditional representations of African American life. Especially during this period, Hughes had black audiences in mind, audiences who would not need to be informed about oppression and its effects, but who did need to investigate how they had made their way in the American world, and who desired to be entertained and instructed in their own theaters.

In 1935 Rowena Jelliffe, Karamu House's founder and director, invited Hughes to become playwright-in-residence for the Gilpin Players, at that time the premier black theater company in the United States. Hughes had known Rowena and her husband, Russell Jelliffe, since his high school years in Cleveland, when he conducted art classes in their newly founded settlement house. It was Rowena Jelliffe who, in January 1931, told Hughes that she was preparing to produce a play she had just received entitled *Mule Bone,* with Hurston cited as the sole author. In the same year, Hughes offered *Mulatto* to the Gilpin Players, but they found it too controversial. However, in 1935, the Gilpin Players had become more confident about their plays of African American life. Jelliffe's invitation provided him an assured venue for his work and helped to compensate Hughes for the terrible reviews to which *Mulatto* had just opened on Broadway. Ironically, despite those reviews, the Broadway *Mulatto*—whose script was substantially altered by producer Martin Jones in ways that Hughes found deeply offensive—was to run for more than a year and then to tour. It would be two decades, however, before another Hughes play would reach Broadway.

With Karamu House, Hughes was assured access not only to a black company but also to a black audience for his plays.[7] The schedule at Karamu was grueling. In just four years, the Gilpin Players premiered three Hughes comedies, *Little Ham, When the Jack Hollers,* and *Joy to My Soul,* and three dramas, *Troubled Island, Mulatto* (using Hughes's original text), and *Front Porch.* They also revived both *Little Ham* and *Joy to My Soul* several times. This intense exposure provided Hughes with the discipline—and the reality—of preparing a script for performance, and with appreciative audiences, if not always appreciative reviews.

For Karamu, Hughes produced plays that were radical in their representation of black characters and black life, although conventionally realistic in their form. His first play for Karamu, *Little Ham,* may be described as an urban *Mule Bone.* In *Little Ham,* the Paradise Shining Parlor in Harlem and a comic plot concerning a love triangle provide space and structure within which the "comic contrasts and humorous moves"—as the program notes to the first Karamu production describe them—of the urban folk are displayed. Working with a black theater company, and writing with a black audience in mind, Hughes felt free to indulge the comic spirit and to suggest, rather than to analyze or belabor, the sorrows and limitations of African American life. He assumes that the attitude of "laughing to keep from crying" will be understood by his audience, and that the fact of oppression need not be the primary focus of the play. Emblematic of this attitude, in *Little Ham* the

7. Although the subscription audience at Karamu during Hughes's tenure there was mostly white, the theater ran "Neighborhood Nights" so that community members, who could little afford the price of admission, would be able to attend. See Reuben Silver, "A History of the Karamu Theatre of Karamu House, 1915–1960" (Ph.D. diss., Ohio State University, 1961), 205–6.

white-controlled numbers racket underpins the local economy depicted in the play, representing the arbitrariness of black fortune in a way that is mindful of the power relations in the real world. *Little Ham* was extremely well received, *Variety* even speculating on the possibility of a Broadway run.[8]

Karamu followed the highly successful *Little Ham* with *When the Jack Hollers,* set in the Mississippi Delta and depicting southern black sharecroppers and their equally poor white neighbors. In *When the Jack Hollers,* racism and exploitation are satirized and comically rendered; the play concludes with the unmasking of the Ku Klux Klan and the suggestion that black and white sharecroppers make common cause of their condition. The following season, Karamu premiered its third Hughes comedy, *Joy to My Soul,* a madcap farce in which an array of hucksters and poseurs fleece an innocent country bumpkin, son of a black Texas oil rancher. Buster Whitehead has come to meet his fiancée, whom he wooed through a Lonely Hearts column. He falls in love instead with the equally innocent and good cigarette girl, while the Grand Lodge of Knights and Ladies of the Sphinx parade around holding a convention and various minor characters disclose and resolve their own complex relationships. Originally set in Cleveland, in the Grand Harlem Hotel, *Joy to My Soul* is both satiric and sentimental. The reviews were ambivalent. Hughes wrote his friend Toy Harper concerning the play's reception: "The Negroes liked it, but the whites didn't get lots of it, never having stopped in a cullud hotel."[9] Although offhand, this comment aptly defines Hughes's desire to extend the arena of African American comedy for African American audiences, who feared that comic portrayals only reinforced negative stereotypes. It was a daring project, not always entirely successful, and often misunderstood.

In the same season, Karamu premiered Hughes's historical drama *Troubled Island.*[10] Set in Haiti, with which Hughes had a long fascination, and which he had visited in 1931, *Troubled Island* depicts the rise and fall of Jean-Jacques Dessalines, the most revered figure in Haitian history. Hughes accounts for Dessalines's failure in ways instructive to

8. Arnold Rampersad, *The Life of Langston Hughes, Volume 1, 1902–1941: "I, Too, Sing America"* (New York: Oxford University Press, 1986), 325.

9. Hughes to Toy Harper, April 20, 1937, Langston Hughes Papers.

10. The play has also been performed as *Drums of Haiti* and *Emperor of Haiti.* Now it is known by the latter title, and the title *Troubled Island* is reserved for the opera Hughes wrote with African American composer William Grant Still during the mid-1930s.

an African American audience. Betrayed by the mulatto class, Dessalines is vulnerable, in Hughes's analysis, because he has alienated himself from the people, symbolized by his slave wife, Azelia, whom he abandons in his rise to power. Hughes's only conventional history play, *Troubled Island* responded, in part, to a call by the historian Carter Woodson for popular education about black history. Its success at Karamu encouraged Hughes, with composer William Grant Still, to begin work on the libretto of an opera by the same name.

Hughes's final play written expressly for the Gilpin Players was *Front Porch*. It is an uncharacteristic work for Hughes because it is set in a middle-class, integrated neighborhood and takes up prejudices of color, class, and labor politics among bourgeois blacks. Hughes's tragic resolution to *Front Porch* signals his harsh judgment of black bourgeois rigidity, prejudice, and myopia, and of the bourgeoisie in general. As performed, however, the play's resolution was comic because Hughes, working from New York, was so slow in getting scenes to the rehearsal that Rowena Jelliffe was compelled to compose her own resolution.

Hughes's work for Karamu during the thirties was naturalistic in both form and content. Also naturalistic in style were three plays that were not performed. *Harvest,* written with Ella Winter and Ann Hawkins, and included in this collection for historical interest, was never quite completed. Essentially, it is documentary theater, concerned with the 1933 farmworkers' strike in the San Joaquin Valley in California, which occurred while Hughes was living in Carmel. The play suggests forms of staging that Hughes had encountered in the Soviet Union, but large parts of it are drawn from newspaper clippings and possibly from interviews he and Ella Winter conducted with participants, an aspect of documentary theater well known in the United States. It is anomalous in the Hughes dramatic canon, but an important document, nonetheless.

Angelo Herndon Jones, also never produced, centers on the figure of Angelo Herndon, represented by a large poster in the center of the stage. Herndon, a Communist organizer, was imprisoned in Georgia for inciting a riot of black and white unemployed workers. Herndon never appears in the play, although his voice is heard offstage; instead the play depicts the plight of the impoverished: two streetwalkers, two unemployed workers, and a mother and daughter who are evicted from their room, only to be reinstated by a band of black and white comrades. In this play Hughes's engagement with the Left during the decade elicited a different idiom, one that would provide him a more congenial form for his theatrical intentions. Finally, Hughes's harsh tragicomedy

Soul Gone Home depicts a wry and bitter exchange between a mother and her son, who has just died. Sad and moving, the play unfolds the abyss of loveless parenting in desperate straits.

In his naturalistic plays, Hughes sought to bring to conventional stages the lives and concerns of African Americans. His association with the Left introduced him to particular uses of the theater, and to radical styles of staging, that were to make a lasting imprint on his work. In 1931, Hughes wrote *Scottsboro, Limited* to publicize and to protest the Scottsboro case, in which nine young black men were convicted of a patently false multiple rape charge in Huntsville, Alabama. A verse play, *Scottsboro, Limited* was performed in Los Angeles, San Francisco, Paris, and Moscow. It is vintage agitprop: it uses a minimum of props, delineates the situation it seeks to analyze concisely, depends on rhythmic language and choreographed movement for effect, and concludes with an audience call for action. When Hughes turned to writing for theater companies he formed himself, he resurrected and reformulated these dramatic techniques, using them to present narratives of African American history and to call for change.

In 1938, with the help of his friend Louise Thompson Patterson, Hughes formed the Harlem Suitcase Theatre and wrote for it *Don't You Want to Be Free?*—a play chronicling what Hughes called the "emotional history" of African Americans.[11] Regarding the play, Hughes recorded in his second autobiography, *I Wonder as I Wander*, that in Moscow,

> I acquired a number of interesting ways of staging plays, some of which I later utilized in directing my own Negro history play, *Don't You Want to Be Free?*, done in Harlem without a stage, curtains, or sets. . . . This play of mine, before arena staging became popular in New York, intrigued Negro audiences for more than a year, chalking up a record run in Harlem of 135 performances.[12]

11. Hughes uses this phrase in a cover note that he always inserted in requested copies of *Don't You Want to Be Free?* Langston Hughes Papers.

12. Langston Hughes, *I Wonder as I Wander* (1956; New York: Hill and Wang, 1964), 200. Earlier in this section, entitled "Theater of Whirling Seats," he credits Meyerhold and Oklopkov especially for inspiring his staging; however, his familiarity with agitprop predates his trip to Moscow and indicates his familiarity with the form as introduced to the United States in late 1929 by the Prolet-Buehne, a German-language group directed by a Communist émigré, John Bonn, that performed at meetings throughout New York and was America's first known mobile theater group.

Clearly the style of *Don't You Want to Be Free?* was well suited to the challenge of establishing theaters that had little access to resources—for example, the word *suitcase* indicated a limit on props to what a suitcase could hold. More important, however, is the way in which agitprop style emphasized body and voice, black speakers and narrative arts of various kinds, and, in Hughes's hands, the imaginative power of African Americans to create a world through their unique modes of speech, music, and song. So compelling did Hughes find this form that he repeatedly altered *Don't You Want to Be Free?* over the next fifteen years in order to provide updated versions of African American history to the many community and collegiate theater groups that requested permission to stage the play. Moreover, it inspired the play he began working on in the late 1930s and finally brought to the Skyloft Players in Chicago, his second theater company, *The Sun Do Move.*

The Sun Do Move chronicles a family's tribulations in slavery and its escape to freedom. It takes its title from the famous sermon of John Jasper (1812–1901), first preached in 1878, in which the preacher meditates on Josh. 10:13: "So the sun stood still and the moon halted until a nation had taken its vengeance," wrestling with the contradictions between what science postulates about the firmament, what the eye can see, and what the Bible says.[13] Both sermon and play assert and celebrate the triumph of faith over empirical knowledge and material fact. The possibility of freedom for the slaves in *The Sun Do Move,* like Jasper's insistence on the truth of God's word, is a triumph of faith over human circumstance and history. Hughes proposes in his notes that the play be done without scenery or interruption, with spirituals providing the transitions between episodes. This play marked Hughes's first venture into what later would become a theatrical preoccupation: bringing to the stage the compelling drama of African American religious practice.

Thus, in his major work during this period Hughes investigated a wide range of genres and of representational possibilities. Increasingly he moved toward incorporating into his work traditional African American cultural forms and voices, and toward devising plays that would dramatize them. Yet the satiric also enticed him: the comic sketches he wrote to be performed with *Don't You Want to Be Free?* signify on white American cultural practices and performances in ways that reflect the same common sense that he celebrated in *The Big Sea,* when describing

13. Hughes and Bontemps published the sermon in their coedited *Book of Negro Folklore* (New York: Dodd, Mead and Co., 1958).

the Harlem spectators of *The Emperor Jones*. As Jules Bledsoe ran naked through the forest, Hughes records, the audience howled: "Them ain't no ghosts, fool . . . come on out o' tha jungle—back to Harlem where you belong."[14] A counterpoint to Hughes's "Note on Commercial Theater," the spectators' commentary, too, crystallized Hughes's intentions for the theater he was so active in creating. This first period of Hughes's engagement with the theater reveals him as profound in his understanding of what it will take to make the American stage hospitable to spiritually true dramas of African American life. The truth he sought to bring to the stage was tragic and comic, loving and judgmental, despairing and inspirational, and it ushered in a new era for African American theater.

14. Langston Hughes, *The Big Sea* (1940; New York: Hill and Wang, 1963), 258.

A Note on the Text

"[S]ure, make any little corrections or changes you feel needful in the plays," Hughes wrote to Webster Smalley, the editor of *Five Plays by Langston Hughes*. "All of them have gone through so many revisions and production changes that it is a wonder they are as consistent as they are."[15]

Judging from the papers in the James Weldon Johnson Collection in the Beinecke Library at Yale University, the repository of Hughes's papers, and the source of the plays presented here, Hughes characteristically worked from an initial typed draft of a manuscript, making changes and then having the updated draft retyped. The drafts usually are dated only by the date he claims for copyright, and so it is sometimes difficult to ascertain their sequence. Moreover, throughout Hughes's career, he returned to earlier plays to update and revise them, but these later revised versions are not necessarily marked with the date of the revision. Also, it is clear that the cover sheets for some of the plays in the James Weldon Johnson Collection are more recent than the version of the plays beneath. Hughes observed to Webster Smalley that neither Samuel French nor the Dramatist Guild Play Service would handle Negro plays because "they say there is not a wide enough market for them in the amateur or little theatre field—so colored playwrights must have to pay fifty or sixty dollars every time they have their scripts retyped to send anywhere."[16] Because typescripts were precious, when Hughes responded to a request for a play, he would, it seems, add a cover sheet with new information for the recipient. There are no coherent typescripts in the Beinecke that are clearly performance scripts. Unless otherwise indicated, all manuscripts are in the Langston Hughes Papers, James Weldon Johnson Collection, Beinecke Library, Yale University.

Given the complexity of the state of Hughes's manuscripts, to say nothing of the general difficulties involved in selecting a definitive text for any play, I have been unable to follow a general rule for choosing which version of each play to reproduce. In this volume, for plays that

15. Hughes to Webster Smalley, July 31, 1961, Langston Hughes Papers.
16. Hughes to Smalley, July 23, 1957, Langston Hughes Papers.

have been performed, every effort has been made to select a text for reproduction that reflects if not the initial then at least an early performance, if a coherent early text is available. Some plays unperformed during the period covered by this volume have been included because they are of historical importance or interest. The rationale for each text printed here will form part of the introductions to the individual plays.

The format for all of the plays has been standardized here. However, except as noted, the only alterations to the original texts themselves are silent corrections of typographical and spelling errors.

Mulatto
A Play of the Deep South

1930

Written during the summer of 1930, *Mulatto* is Langston Hughes's first full-length play. It appears to have come to him quickly; its painful and melodramatic depictions of father-son conflict, the power of class and whiteness, the legacy of slavery, and the vicious oppression of African Americans in the South were all preoccupations taken up in his earlier work. Many commentators have noted Hughes's personal investment in his narratives of father-son conflict, and the metaphorical relation of miscegenated family and nation.

The play also seeks to correct the dramatic representation of lynching in such plays as the 1927 Pulitzer Prize–winning *In Abraham's Bosom*, by Paul Green, in which lynching is the inevitable and unchallenged—although not thereby justified—fate of Abe McCranie, the impetuous and irascible central character. The plots of the two works are similar in many ways, but in Hughes's play the black characters are articulate, rational, and courageous. Not usually understood as an antilynching play, *Mulatto* is set in Georgia and was written in a year when that state led the nation in lynchings. Cora's accusations that the Colonel is in the mob seeking the son who murdered him speak eloquently to the horrifying internecine dimensions of Southern brutality. (In 1961, Hughes wrote regarding some revisions his editor, Webster Smalley, had proposed: "*Mulatto* might be left timeless, since they still behave like that in the backwoods of Georgia. In the big towns, of course, individual sit-ins like Bert's have grown to mass-sit-ins. Otherwise, no difference.")[1]

Opening on October 24, 1935, at the Vanderbilt Theatre, *Mulatto* ran on Broadway for more than a year and toured for two seasons. The Broadway *Mulatto* was, however, greatly altered by the producer, Martin Jones, who sensationalized an already shocking story. Among other changes, in his version Sallie misses the train and is raped by Talbot in the final scene. No text for the Broadway *Mulatto* has surfaced.

The version of *Mulatto* printed here is dated by Hughes's covering remarks as 1942, although the copyright is given as 1932. The cover

17

sheet reads: "From the short story 'Father and Son' in *The Ways of White Folks*. Original first version of 'Mulatto,' written at Hedgerow Theatre, Maryland Rose Valley, in which no girl is raped. That was added by Mr. Martin Jones for the Broadway production. Langston Hughes, Dec. 28, 1942." On the title page he adds, "This play might also be called 'The Colonel's Son.'" The comment about the short story is puzzling because "Father and Son" was most certainly written later than the play; however, Hughes did, at one point, recommend the short story to Martin Jones, to give him a better sense of the play. The manuscript is actually a photocopy of a typescript on which Hughes pasted minor revisions. The photocopy on which the changes are made is dated 1945 by the Beinecke Library. Internal evidence places the original as having been written between 1934 and 1938. This version differs from the version published in *Five Plays by Langston Hughes* in several ways, most notably in the last lines of the final scene. It is this version, probably minus the changes on this photocopy, that was the basis for several of the play's translations.

Characters

COLONEL THOMAS NORWOOD, plantation owner, a still vigor-
    ous man of about sixty, nervous, refined, quick-tempered, and com-
    manding; a widower who is the father of four living mulatto children
    by his Negro housekeeper
CORA LEWIS, a brown woman in her forties who has kept the house
    and been the mistress of Colonel Norwood for some thirty years
WILLIAM LEWIS, the oldest son of Cora Lewis and the Colonel; a fat,
    easy-going, soft-looking mulatto of twenty-eight; married
SALLIE LEWIS, the seventeen year old daughter, very light with sandy
    hair and freckles, who could pass for white
ROBERT LEWIS, eighteen, the youngest boy; strong and well built;
    a light mulatto with ivory-yellow skin and proud thin features like
    his father's; as tall as the Colonel, with the same grey-blue eyes, but
    with curly black hair instead of brown; of a fiery, impetuous temper—
    immature and wilful—resenting his blood and the circumstances of
    his birth
MR. FRED HIGGINS, a close friend of Colonel Norwood's; a county
    politician; fat and elderly, conventionally Southern
SAM, an old Negro retainer, a personal servant of the Colonel's

LIVONIA, the cook
BILLY, the small son of William Lewis; a chubby brown kid
TALBOT, the overseer
MOSE, a black chauffeur, driver for Mr. Higgins
A STOREKEEPER
A WHITE UNDERTAKER
THE UNDERTAKER'S HELPER, voice off-stage only
THE LEADER OF THE MOB

Act I

TIME: *The present. An afternoon in early fall.*

THE SETTING: *The living room of the Big House on a plantation in Georgia. Rear center of the room, a vestibule with double doors lead-ing to the porch; at each side of the doors, a large window with lace curtains and green shades; at left, broad flight of stairs leading to the second floor; near the stairs, down-stage, a door-way leading to the dining room and kitchen; opposite, at right of stage, a door to the library. The room is furnished in the long out-dated horse-hair and walnut style of the nineties: a crystal chandelier, a large old-fashioned rug, a marble-topped table, upholstered chairs. At the right there is a small cabinet. It is a very clean, but somewhat shabby and rather depressing room. The windows are raised. The late afternoon sunlight streams in.*

ACTION: *As the curtain rises the stage is empty. The door at the right opens and COLONEL NORWOOD enters, crossing the stage toward the stairs, his watch in his hand. Looking up, he shouts:*

NORWOOD: Cora! Oh, Cora!

CORA: *(Heard above)* Yes, sir, Colonel Tom.

NORWOOD: I want to know if that child of yours means to leave here this afternoon?

CORA: *(At head of steps now)* Yes, sir, she's goin' directly. I's gettin' her ready now, packin' up an' all. 'Course, she wants to tell you goodbye 'fore she leaves.

NORWOOD: Well, send her down here. Who's going to drive her to the railroad? That train leaves at three—and it's after two now. You ought to know you can't drive ten miles in no-time.

CORA: *(Above)* Her brother's gonna drive her. Bert. He ought to be back here most any minute now with the Ford.

NORWOOD: *(Stopping on his way back to the library)* Ought to be *back* here? Where's he gone?

CORA: *(Coming downstairs nervously)* Why, he driv in town 'fore dinner, Colonel Tom. Said he were lookin' for some tubes or somethin'nother by de mornin' mail for de radio he's been riggin' up out in de shed.

NORWOOD: Who gave him permission to be driving off in the middle of the morning? I bought that Ford to be used when I gave orders for it to be used, not . . .

CORA: Yes, sir, Colonel Tom, but. . . .

NORWOOD: But what? *(Pausing. Then deliberately)* Cora, if you want that hard-headed yellow son of yours to get along around here, he'd better listen to me. He's no more than any other black buck on this plantation—due to work like the rest of 'em. I don't take such a performance from nobody under me—driving off in the middle of the day to town, after I've told him to keep his back in that cotton. How's Talbot gonna keep the rest of them darkies working right if that boy's allowed to set that kind of an example? Just because Bert's your son, and I've been damn fool enough to send him off to Atlanta for five or six years, he thinks he has a right to privileges, acting as if he owned the place since he's been back here this summer.

CORA: But, Colonel Tom. . . .

NORWOOD: Yes, I know what you're going to say. I don't give a damn about him. There's no nigger-child of mine, yours, ours—no darkie—going to disobey me. I put him in that field to work, and he'll stay on this plantation till I get ready to let him go. I'll tell Talbot to use the whip on him, too, if he needs it. If it hadn't been that he's yours, he'd-a had a taste of it the other day. Talbot's damn good overseer, and no saucy, lazy nigras stay on this plantation and get away with it. *(To Cora)* Get on back upstairs and see about getting Sallie out of here. Another word from you and I won't send your *(Sarcastically)* pretty little half-white daughter anywhere, either. Schools for darkies! Huh! If you take that boy of yours for an example, they do 'em more harm than good. He's learned nothing in 'em but impudence, and he'll stay here on this place and work for me awhile before he gets back to any more schools. *(NORWOOD starts across the room)*

CORA: Yes, sir, Colonel Tom. *(Hesitating)* But he's just young, sir. And he was mighty broke up when you said last week he couldn't go back to de school. *(COLONEL NORWOOD turns and looks at Cora commandingly. Understanding, SHE murmurs:)* Yes, sir. *(She starts upstairs, but turns back)* Can't I run and fix you a cool drink, Colonel Tom?

NORWOOD: No, damn you! Sam'll do it.

CORA: *(Sweetly)* Go set down in de cool, then Colonel. 'Tain't good for you to be goin' on this way in de heat. I'll talk to Robert maself soon's he comes in. He don't mean nothin'—just smart and young and kinder careless, Colonel Tom, like ma mother said you used to be when you was eighteen.

NORWOOD: Get on upstairs, Cora. Do I have to speak again? Get on! *(He pulls the cord of the servant's bell)*

CORA: *(On the steps)* Does you still be in the mind to tell Sallie goodbye?

NORWOOD: Send her down here as I told you. *(Impatiently)* Where's Sam? Send him here first. *(Fuming)* Looks like he takes his time to answer that bell. You colored folk are running the house to suit yourselves nowadays.

CORA: *(Coming downstairs again and going toward door under the steps)* I'll get Sam for you.

> *(CORA exits left. NORWOOD paces nervously across the floor. Goes to the window and looks out down the road. Takes a cigar from his pocket, sits in a chair with it unlighted, scowling. Rises, goes toward servants' bell and rings it again violently as SAM enters, out of breath)*

NORWOOD: What the hell kind of a tortoise race is this? I suppose you were out in the sun somewhere sleeping?

SAM: No, sah, Colonel Norwood. Just tryin' to get Miss Sallie's valises down to de yard so's we can put 'em in de Ford, sah.

NORWOOD: *(Out of patience)* Huh! Darkies waiting on darkies! I can't get service in my own house. Very well. *(Loudly)* Bring me some whiskey and soda, and ice in a glass. Is that damn frigidaire working right? Or is Livonia still too thick-headed to know how to run it? Any ice cubes in the thing?

SAM: Yes, sah, Colonel, yes, sah. *(Backing toward door left)* 'Scuse me please, sah, but *(As NORWOOD turns toward library)* Cora say for me to ask you is it all right to bring that big old trunk what you give Sallie down by de front steps. We ain't been able to tote it down them narrer little back steps, sah. Cora, say, can we bring it down de front way through here?

NORWOOD: No other way? *(SAM shakes his head)* Then pack it on through to the back, quick. Don't let me catch you carrying any of

Sallie's baggage out that front door here. You-all'll be wanting to go in and out the front way next. *(Turning away, complaining to himself)* Darkies have been getting mighty fresh in this part of the country since the war. The damn German's should've . . . . . . *(To Sam)* Don't take that trunk out that front door.

SAM: *(Evilly, in a cunning voice)* I's seen Robert usin' de front door—when you ain't here, and he comes up from de cabin to see his mammy.

> *(SALLIE, the daughter, appears at the top of the stairs, but hesitates about coming down.)*

NORWOOD: Oh, you have, have you? Let me catch him and I'll break his young neck for him. *(Yelling at Sam)* Didn't I tell you some whiskey and soda an hour ago?

> *(SAM exits left. SALLIE comes shyly down the stairs and approaches her father. She is dressed in a little country-style coat-suit ready for traveling. Her features are Negroid, although her skin is very light. COLONEL NORWOOD gazes down at her without saying a word as she comes meekly toward him.)*

SALLIE: *(Half-frightened)* I just wanted to tell you goodbye, Colonel Norwood, and thank you for letting me go back to school another year, and for letting me work here in the house all summer where mama was. *(NORWOOD says nothing. The girl continues in a strained voice as if making a speech)* You mighty nice to us colored folks certainly, and mama says you the best white man in Georgia. *(Still NORWOOD says nothing. The girl continues)* You been mighty nice to your—I mean to us colored children, letting my sister and me go off to school. The principal says I'm doing pretty well and next year I can go to Normal and learn to be a teacher. *(Raising her eyes)* You reckon I can, Colonel Tom?

NORWOOD: Stand up straight and let me see how you look. *(Backing away)* Hum-m-m! Getting kinder grown, ain't you? Do they teach you in that colored school to have good manners, and not to be afraid of work, *and to respect white folks*?

SALLIE: Yes, sir, I been taking up cooking and sewing, too.

NORWOOD: Well, that's good. As I recall it, that school turned your sister out a right smart cook. Cora tells me she's got a job in some hotel in Chicago. I'm thinking about you going on up there with her in a year or two. You're getting too old to be around here, and too womanish. *(He puts his hand on her arms as if feeling her flesh)*

SALLIE: *(Drawing back slightly)* But I want to live down here with mama. I want to teach school in that there empty school house by the Cross Roads what hasn't had no teacher for five years.

(SAM has been standing with the door cracked, overhearing the conversation. He enters with whiskey and soda on a tray. He places it on the table, right. NORWOOD sits down, leaving the girl standing, as SAM pours out a drink for him)

NORWOOD: Don't get that into your head, now. There's been no teacher there for years—and there won't be any teacher there, either. Cotton teaches these pickininnies enough around here. Some of 'em 's too smart as it is. The only reason I did have a teacher there was to get you young ones o' Cora's educated. I gave you-all a chance and I hope you appreciate it. *(He takes a long drink)* Don't know why I did it. No other white man in these parts ever did it, as I know of. *(To SAM)* Get out of here! *(SAM exits left)* Guess I couldn't stand to see Cora's kids working around here dumb as the rest of these no-good darkies—need a dozen of 'em to chop one row of cotton, or to keep a house clean. Or maybe I didn't want to see Talbot eyeing you gals. *(Taking another drink)* Anyhow, I'm glad you and Bertha turned out right well. Yes, hum-m-m! *(Straightening up)* You know I tried to do something for those brothers of yours, too, but William's stupid as an ox—good for work, though—and that Robert's just an impudent, hard-headed yellow young fool. I'm gonna break his damn neck for him if he don't watch out. Or else put Talbot on him.

SALLIE: *(Suddenly frightened)* Please, sir, don't put the overseer on Bert, Colonel Tom. He was the smartest boy at school, Bert was. On the football team too. Please, sir, Colonel Tom. Let brother work here in the house, or somewhere else where Talbot can't hit him. He ain't used. . . .

NORWOOD: *(Rising)* Telling me what to do, heh? *(Staring at her sternly)* I'll use the back of my hand across *your* face if you don't hush. *(He takes another drink. The noise of a Ford is heard outside)* Bert now, I reckon. He's to take you to the railroad line, and while you're riding with him, you better put some sense into his head. And tell him I want to see him as soon as he gets back here.

(CORA enters left with a bundle and an umbrella. SAM and WILLIAM come downstairs with a big square trunk, and exit hurriedly left)

SALLIE: Yes, sir, I'll tell him.

CORA: Colonel Tom, Sallie ain't got much time now. *(To the girl)* Come on, chile. Bert's here. Yo' big brother and Sam and Livonia and everybody's all waiting at de back door to say good-bye. And your baggage is being packed in. *(Noise of another car is heard outside)* Who else is that there coming up de drive? *(CORA looks out the window)* Mr. Higgins' car, Colonel Tom. Reckon he's coming to see you . . . Hurry up out o' this front room, Sallie. Here, take these things o' your'n *(Hands her the bundle and parasol)* while I opens de door for Mr. Higgins. *(In a whisper)* Hurry up chile! Get out!

   (NORWOOD turns toward the front door as CORA goes to open it)

SALLIE: *(Shyly to her father)* Goodbye, Colonel Tom.

NORWOOD: *(His eyes on the front door, scarcely noticing the departing Sallie, he motions:)* Yes, yes, goodbye! Get on now! *(CORA opens the front door as her daughter exits left.)* Well, well! Howdy do, Fred. Come in, come in!

   (CORA holds the outer door of the vestibule wide as FRED HIG-GINS enters with rheumatic dignity, supported on the arm of his chauffeur, MOSE, a very black Negro in a slouchy uniform. CORA closes the door and exits left hurriedly, following SALLIE)

NORWOOD: *(Smiling)* How's the rheumatix today? Women or licker or heat must've made it worse—from the looks of your speed!

HIGGINS: *(Testily, sitting down puffing and blowing in a big chair)* I'm in no mood for fooling, Tom, not now. *(To Mose)* All right. *(The CHAUFFEUR exits front. HIGGINS continues angrily)* Norwood, that damned yellow nigger buck of yours that drives that new Ford tried his best just now to push my car off the road, then got in front of me and blew dust in my face for the last mile coming down your gate, trying to beat me in here—which he did. Such a deliberate piece of impudence I don't know if I've ever seen out of a nigger before in all the sixty years I've lived in this country. *(The noise of the Ford is heard going out the drive, and the cries of the NEGROES shouting farewells to Sallie. HIGGINS listens indignantly)* What kind of crazy coons have you got on your place, anyhow? Sounds like a black Baptist picnic to me. *(Pointing to the window with his cane)* Tom, listen to that.

NORWOOD: *(Flushing)* I apologize to you, Fred, for each and every one of my darkies. *(SAM enters with more ice and another glass)* Permit me to offer you a drink. I realize I've got to tighten down out here.

HIGGINS: Mose tells me that was Cora's boy in that Ford—and that young black fool's what I was coming here to talk to you about today. That boy. He's not gonna be around here long—not the way he's acting. The white folks in town'll see to that. And knowing he's one of your yard niggers, Norwood, I thought I ought to come and talk to you. The white folks at the Junction aren't intending to put up with him much longer. And I don't know what good the jail would do him once he got in there.

NORWOOD: *(Tensely)* What do you mean, Fred—jail? Don't I always take care of the folks on my plantation without any help from the Junction's police force? Talbot can do more with an unruly black buck than your marshall.

HIGGINS: Warn't lookin' at it that way, Tom. I was thinking how weak the doors to that jail is. They've broke 'em down and lynched four niggers to my memory since it's been built. After what happened this morning, you better keep that yellow fool out o' town from now on. It might not be safe for him around there—today, nor no other time.

NORWOOD: What the hell? *(Perturbed)* He went in just now to take his sister to the depot. Damn it, I hope no ruffians'll break up that new Ford. What was it, Fred, about this morning?

HIGGINS: You haven't heard? Why, it's all over town already. He sassed out Miss Wilson in the Post Office over a bunch of radio tubes that come by mail.

NORWOOD: He did, heh?

HIGGINS: Seems like the stuff was sent C.O.D. and got here all smashed up, so he wouldn't take it. Paid his money first before he saw the box was broke. Then wanted the money order back. Seems like the Post Office can't give money orders back—rule against it. The nigger started to argue, and the girl at the window—Miss Wilson—got scared and yelled for some of the mail clerks. And they threw Bert out of the office, that's all. But that's enough. Lucky nothing more didn't happen. *(Indignantly)* That fellow needs a damn good beating—talking back to a white woman—and I'd like to give it to him myself, the way he kicked the dust up in my eyes all the way down the road coming out here. He was mad, I reckon. That's one yellow buck don't know his place, Tom, and it's your fault he don't—sending 'em off to be educated.

NORWOOD: Well, by God, I'll show him. I wish I'd have known it before he left here just now.

HIGGINS: Well, he's sure got mighty aggravating ways for a buck his color to have. Drives down the main street and don't stop for nobody, white or black. Comes in my store and if he ain't waited on as quick as the white folks are, he walks out and tells the clerk his money's good as a white man's any day. Said last week standing out on my store front that he wasn't *all* nigger no how; said his name was Norwood—not Lewis, like the rest of the family—and part of your plantation here would be his when you passed out—and all that kind o' stuff, boasting to the wall-eyed coons listening to him.

NORWOOD: *(Astounded)* Well, I'll be damned!

HIGGINS: Now, Tom, you know that don't go 'round these parts o' Georgia, nor nowhere else in the South. A darkie's got to keep in his place down here. Ruinous to other niggers hearing that talk, too. All this war propaganda on the radio about freedom and democracy— why the niggers think it's meant for them! And that Eleanor Roosevelt, she ought to be muzzled! She's driving our niggers crazy— your boy included! Crazy! Ain't been no race trouble in our county for three years—since the Deekin's lynching—but I'm telling you, Norwood, you better see that that boy goes away from here. I'm speaking on the quiet, but I can see ahead. And what happened this noon about them radio tubes wasn't none too good.

NORWOOD: A black ape! I—I. . . . *(Beside himself with rage)*

HIGGINS: You been too good to your darkies, Norwood. That's what's the matter with you. And then the whole county suffers with a lot of impudent black bucks who take lessons from your crowd. Folks been kicking about that, too. Guess you know it. Maybe that's the reason you didn't get that nomination for committeeman a few years back.

NORWOOD: Maybe 'tis, Higgins. *(Rising and pacing the room)* God damn niggers! *(Furiously)* Everything turns on niggers, niggers, niggers! No wonder Yankees call this the Black Belt! *(He pours a large drink of whiskey)*

HIGGINS: *(Soothingly)* Well, let's change the subject. Hand me my glass, there, too.

NORWOOD: Pardon me, Fred. *(He puts ice in his friend's glass and passes him the bottle)*

HIGGINS: Tom, you get excited too easy for warm weather . . . Don't ever show niggers they got you going, though. I think sometimes that's where you make your mistake. Keep calm, keep calm—and then you can command. Best plantation manager I ever had never raised his voice to a nigger—and they were scared to death of him.

NORWOOD: Have a smoke. *(Pushes cigars toward Higgins)*

HIGGINS: *(Lighting a cigar)* You ought've married again, Tom—brought a white woman out here on this damn place o' yours. A woman could help you run things. Women have soft ways, but they can keep things humming. Nothing but blacks in the house—a man gets soft like niggers are inside. *(Puffing at cigar)* And living with a nigger woman! Of course, I know we all have 'em—I didn't know you could make use of a white girl till I was past twenty. Thought too much o' white women for that—but I've given many a yellow gal a baby in my time. *(Long puff at cigar)* But for a man's own house you need a wife, not a black woman.

NORWOOD: Reckon you're right, Fred, but it's too late to marry again now. *(Shrugging his shoulders)* Let's get off of darkies and women for awhile. How's crops? *(Sitting down)* How's politics going?

HIGGINS: Well, I guess you know the Republicans is trying to stir up trouble for us lately in Washington. I wish the South had more Bilbo's and Rankin's there. But say, by the way, Lawyer Hotchkiss wants to see us both about that budget money next week. He's got some real Canadian stuff at his office, in his filing case, too—brought back from his vacation last summer. Taste better'n this old colored mountain juice we get around here. Not meaning to insult your drinks, Tom, but just remarking. I serve the same as you myself, 1890 Label and all.[2]

NORWOOD: *(Laughing)* I'll have you know, sir, that this is pre-war licker, sir!

HIGGINS: Hum-m-m! Well, it's got me feelin' better'n I did when I come in here—whatever it is. *(Puffs at his cigar)* Say, how's your cotton this year?

NORWOOD: Doin' right well, specially down in the South field. Why not drive out that road when you leave and take a look at it? I'll ride down with you. I want to see Talbot, anyhow.

HIGGINS: Well, let's be starting. I got to be back at the Junction by four o'clock. Promised to let that boy of mine have the car to drive over to Thomasville for a dance tonight.

NORWOOD: One more shot before we go. *(He pours out drinks)* The young ones must have their fling, I reckon. When you and I grew up down here it used to be a carriage and the best pair of black horses when you took the ladies out—now it's an automobile. That's a good lookin' new car of yours, too.

HIGGINS: Right nice.

NORWOOD: Been thinking about getting a new one myself, but money's been kinder tight this year, and conditions are none too good yet either. Reckon that's why everybody's so restless. *(He walks toward stairs calling)* Cora! Oh, Cora!. . . . . . . If I didn't have a few thousand put away, I'd feel the pinch myself. *(As CORA appears on the stairs)* Bring me my glasses up there by the side of my bed . . . Better whistle for Mose, hadn't I, Higgins? He's probably round back with some of his women. *(Winking)* You know I got nice black women in this yard.

HIGGINS: Oh, no, not Mose. I got my darkies trained to stay in their places—right where I want 'em—while they're working for me. Just open the door and tell him to come in here and help me out.

(NORWOOD goes to the door and calls the chauffeur. MOSE enters and assists his master out to the car. CORA appears with the glasses, goes to the vestibule and gets the Colonel's hat and cane which she hands him)

NORWOOD: *(To Cora)* I want to see that boy o' yours soon as I get back. That won't be long, either. And tell him to put up that Ford of mine.

CORA: Yes, sir, I'll have him waiting here. *(In a whisper)* It's hot weather, Colonel Tom. Too much of this licker makes your heart upset. It ain't good for you, you know. *(NORWOOD pays her no attention as he exits toward the car. The noise of the departing motor is heard. CORA begins to tidy up the room. She takes a glass from a side table. She picks up a doily that was beneath the glass and looks at it long and lovingly. Suddenly she goes to the door left and calls toward the kitchen.)* William, you William. Com'ere, I want to show you something. Make haste, son. *(As CORA goes back toward the table, her eldest son, WILLIAM, enters carrying a five year old boy)* Look here at this purty doily yo' sister made this summer while she been here. She done learned all about sewing and making purty things at school. Ain't it nice, son?

WILLIAM: Sho' is. Sallie takes after you, I reckon. She's a smart little critur, ma. *(Sighs)* De lawd knows, I was dumb at school. *(To his child)* Get down, Billy, you's too heavy. *(He puts the boy on the floor)* This here sewin's really fine.

BILLY: *(Running toward the big upholstered chair and jumping up and down on the springy seat)* Gityap! I's a mule driver! Haw! Gee!

CORA: You Billy, get out that chair 'fore I skins you alive. Get on into de kitchen, sah.

BILLY: I'm playin' horsie, grandma. *(Jumps up in the chair)* Horsie! Horsie!

CORA: Get! That's de Colonel's favorite chair. If he knows any little darkie's been jumpin' on it, he raise sand. Get on now.

BILLY: Ole Colonel's ma grandpa, ain't he? Ain't he ma white grandpa?

WILLIAM: *(Snatching the child out of the chair)* Boy, I'm gonna fan yo' hide if you don't hush!

CORA: Sh-s-s! You Bill, hush yo' mouth! Chile, where you hear that? *(To her son)* Some you-all been talking too much in front o' this chile. *(To the baby)* Honey, go on in de kitchen till yo' daddy come. Get a cookie from 'Vonia and set down on de back porch.

    (LITTLE BILLY exits left.)

WILLIAM: Ma, you know it 'twarn't me told him. Bert's the one been goin' all over de plantation since he come back from Atlanta tellin' folks right out we's Colonel Norwood's chilluns.

CORA: *(Catching her breath)* Huh!

WILLIAM: He comes down to my shack tellin' Billy and Marybell they got a white man for grandpa. He's gonna get my chilluns in trouble sho—like he got himself in trouble when Colonel Tom whipped him.

CORA: Ten or 'leven years ago, warn't it?

WILLIAM: And Bert's *sho'* in trouble now. Can't go back to the school, like he could-a if he'd-a had any sense. You can't fool with white folks—and de Colonel ain't never liked Bert since that there first time he beat him, neither.

CORA: No, he ain't. *(Musing sadly in a low voice)* Time Bert was 'bout seven, warn't it? Just a little bigger'n yo' Billy.

WILLIAM: Yes.

CORA: Went runnin' up to Colonel Tom out in de horse stables when de Colonel was showin' off his horses—I 'members so well—to fine white company from in town. Lawd, that boy's always been foolish! He went runnin' up and grabbed a-holt de Colonel and yelled right in front o' de white folks' faces, "O, papa, Cora say de dinner's ready, papa!" Ain't never called him papa before, and I don't know where he got it from. And Colonel Tom knocked him right backwards under de horse's feet.

WILLIAM: And when de company were gone, he beat that boy unmerciful.

CORA: I thought sho he were gonna kill ma chile that day. And he were mad at me, too, for months. Said I was teachin' you chilluns who they pappy were. Up till then Bert been his favorite little colored chile round here.

WILLIAM: Sho' had.

CORA: But he never liked him no more. That's why he sent him off to school so soon to stay, winter and summer, all these years. I had to beg and plead to have him home this summer—But I's sorry now I ever got that boy back here again. Lawd! Lawd! I's sorry!

WILLIAM: He's sho' growed more like de Colonel all de time, ain't he? Till Bert thinks he's a real white man himself now. Look at de first thing he did when he come home, he ain't seen de Colonel in six years—and Bert sticks out his hand fo' to shake hands with him!

CORA: Lawd! That chile!

WILLIAM: Just like white folks! And de Colonel just turns his back and walks off. Can't blame him. He ain't used to such doings from colored folks. God knows what's got into Bert since he come back. He's acting like a fool—just like he was a boss man round here. Won't even say 'Yes, sir' and 'No, sir' no more to de white folks. Talbot asked him warn't he gonna work in de field this mornin'. Bert say "No!" and turn and walk away. White man so mad, I could see him nearly foam at de mouth. If he warn't yo' chile, ma, he'd been knocked in de head fo' now.

CORA: You's right.

WILLIAM: And you can't talk to him. I tried to tell him something de other day, but he just laughed at me, and said we's all just old scared niggers on this plantation. Says he ain't no nigger, no how. He's a Norwood. He's half-white, and he's gonna act like it. *(In amazement at his brother's daring) And this is Georgia, too!*

CORA: I's scared to death for de boy, Willie. I don't know what to do. De Colonel say he won't send him off to Atlanta no mo'. Say he's mo' sassy and impudent now than any nigger he ever seed. Bert never has been like you was, and de girls, quiet and sensible like you knowed you *had* to be. *(She sits down)* De Colonel say he's gonna make Bert stay here now until the Draft Board call him, and make him work on this plantation like de rest of his niggers. He's gonna show him what color he is. Like that time when he beat him for callin' him 'papa'. He say he's gwine to teach him his place and make de boy know where he belongs. Seems like me nor you can't show him. Colonel Tom has to take him in hand, or these white folks'll kill him around here and then—Oh, my God!

WILLIAM: A nigger's just got to know his place in de South, that's all, ain't he, ma?

CORA: Yes, son. That's all, I reckon.

WILLIAM: And ma brother's one damn fool nigger. Don't seems like he knows nothin'. He's gonna ruin us all round here. Makin' it bad for everybody.

CORA: Oh, Lawd, have mercy! *(Beginning to cry)* I don't know what to do. De way he's acting to these white folks can't go on. Way he's acting to de Colonel can't last. Somethin's gonna happen to ma chile. I had a bad dream last night, too, and I looked out and seed de moon all red with blood. I seed a path o' livin' blood cross this house, I tell you, in my sleep. Oh, Lawd have mercy! *(Sobbing)* Oh, Lawd, help me in ma troubles. *(The noise of the returning Ford is heard outside. CORA looks up, rises, and goes to the window)* There's de chile now, Willie. Run out to de back door and tell him I wants to see him. Bring him in here where Sam and Livonia and de rest of 'em won't hear ever'thing we's sayin'. I got to talk to ma boy. He's ma baby boy, and he don't know de way.

> *(Exit WILLIAM through the door left. CORA is wiping her eyes and pulling herself together when the front door is flung open with a bang and ROBERT enters)*

ROBERT: *(Running to his mother and hugging her teasingly)* Hello, ma! Your daughter got off, and I've come back to keep you company in the parlor! Bring out the cookies and lemonade. *Mr.* Norwood's here.

CORA: *(Beginning to sob anew)* Take yo' hands off me, boy! Why don't you mind? Why don't you mind me?

ROBERT: *(Suddenly serious, backing away)* Why, mama, what's the matter? Did I scare you. Your eyes are all wet! Has somebody been telling you 'bout this morning?

CORA: *(Not heeding his words)* Why don't you mind me, son? Ain't I told you and told you not to come in that front door, never? *(Suddenly angry)* Will somebody have to beat it into you? What't got wrong with you when you was away at that school? What am I gonna do?

ROBERT: *(Carelessly)* Oh, I knew the Colonel wasn't here. I passed him and old man Higgins on the road down by the South patch.

He wouldn't even look at me when I waved at him. *(Half-playfully)* Any-how, isn't this my old man's house? Ain't I his son and heir? *(Grandly)* Am I not Mr. Norwood, Junior? *(Strutting around.)*

CORA: *(Utterly serious)* I believes you goin' crazy, Bert. I believes you wants to get us all killed or run away or something awful like that. I believes . . .

    (WILLIAM enters left.)

WILLIAM: Where's Bert? He ain't come round back. *(Seeing his brother in the room)* How'd you get in here?

ROBERT: *(Grinning)* Houses have front doors.

WILLIAM: Oh, usin' de front door like de white folks, heh? You gwine do that once too much.

ROBERT: Yes, like de white folks. What's a front door for, you rabbit-hearted coon?

WILLIAM: Rabbit-hearted coon's better'n a dead coon any day.

ROBERT: I wouldn't say so. Besides you and me's only half-coons, anyhow, big boy. And I'm gonna act like my white half, not my black half. Get me, Kid?

WILLIAM: Well, you ain't gonna act like it long here in de middle o' Georgy. And you ain't gonna act like it when de Colonel's around, either.

ROBERT: Oh, no? My stay down here'll be short and sweet, boy, short and sweet. The old man won't send me away to school no more—so you think I'm gonna stay and work in the fields? Like fun! I might stay here awhile and teach some o' you darkies to think like men, maybe—till it gets too much for the old Colonel—but no more bowing down to white folks for me.

CORA: Hush, son!

ROBERT: Certainly not right on my own old man's plantation—Georgia or no Georgia.

WILLIAM: *(Scornfully)* I hears you.

ROBERT: *You* can do it if you want to, but I'm ashamed of you. I've been away from here six years. *(Boasting)* I've learned something, seen people in Atlanta, and Richmond, and Washington where the football team went—real colored people who don't have to take off their hats to white folks or let 'em go to bed with their sisters—like that young Higgins boy, asking me what night Sallie was comin' to town. A damned cracker! *(To Cora)* 'Scuse me, ma. *(Continuing)* Back here in these woods maybe Sam and Livonia and you and mama and ever'body's got their places fixed for 'em, but not me. *(Seriously)*

Nobody's gonna fix a place for me. I'm old man Norwood's son. Nobody fixed a place for him. *(Playfully again)* Look at me. I'm a 'fay boy. *(Pretends to shake his hair back)* See these grey eyes? I got the right to everything everybody else has. *(Punching his brother in the belly)* Don't talk to me, old slavery-time Uncle Tom.

WILLIAM: *(Resentfully)* I ain't playin', boy. *(Pushes younger brother back with some force)* I ain't playin' a-tall.

CORA: All right, chilluns, stop. Stop! And William, you take Billy and go on home. 'Vonia's got to get supper and she don't like no young'uns under her feet in de kitchen. I wants to talk to Bert in here now 'fore Colonel Tom gets back. *(Exit WILLIAM left. CORA continues to Bert)* Sit down, chile, right here a minute, and listen.

ROBERT: *(Sitting down)* Alright, ma.

CORA: Hard as I's worked and begged and humbled maself to get de Colonel to keep you chilluns in school, you comes home wid yo' head full o' stubbornness and yo' mouth full o' sass for me an' de white folks an' ever'body. You know can't no colored boy here talk like you's been doin' to *no* white folks, let alone to de Colonel and that old devil of a Talbot. They ain't gonna stand fo' yo' sass a-tall. Not only you, but I 'spects we's all gwine to pay fo' it, ever colored soul on this place. I was scared to death today fo' yo' sister Sallie, scared de Colonel warn't gwine let her go back to school, neither, 'count o' yo' doin's, but he did, thank Gawd—and then you come near makin' her miss de train. Did she have time to get her ticket and all?

ROBERT: Sure! Had to drive like sin to get there with her though. I didn't mean to be late getting back here for her, ma, but I had a little run-in about them radio tubes in town.

CORA: What's that? *(Worried)*

ROBERT: The tubes was smashed when I got 'em, and I had already made out my money-order, and so the woman in the Post Office wouldn't give the three dollars back to me. All I did was explain to her that we could send the tubes back—but she got hot because there were two or three white folks waiting behind me to get stamps, I guess. So she yells at me to move on and not give her any of my "educated nigger talk". So I said, I'm going to finish about these tubes before I move on—and then she screamed and called the mail-clerk working in the back, and told him to throw me out. *(Boasting)* He didn't do it by himself, though. Had to call all the white loafers out in the square to get me through that door.

CORA: *(Fearfully)* Lawd have mercy!

ROBERT: Guess if I hadn't-a had the Ford there then, they'd've beat me half-to-death, but when I saw how many crackers there was, I jumped in the car and beat it on away.

CORA: Thank God for that!

ROBERT: Not even a football man *(half boasting)* like me could tackle the whole junction. 'Bout a dozen colored guys standing around, too, and not one of 'em would help me—the dumb jiggaboos! They been telling me ever since I been here, *(Imitating darky talk)* "You can't argue wid whut folks, man. You better stay out o' this Junction. You must ain't got no sense, nigger! You's a fool" . . . . Maybe I am a fool, ma—but I didn't want to come back here nohow.

CORA: I's sorry, too.

ROBERT: Besides you, there ain't nobody in this county but a lot of evil white folks and cowardly niggers. *(Earnestly)* I'm no nigger, anyhow, am I, ma? I'm half-white, and the Colonel's my father— the richest man in the county—and I'm not going to take a lot of stuff from nobody if I do have to stay here, not from the old man either. He thinks I ought to be out there in the sun working, with Talbot standing over me like I belonged in the chain gang. Well, he's got another thought coming! *(Stubbornly)* I'm a Norwood—not a field-hand nigger.

CORA: You means you ain't workin' no mo'?

ROBERT: *(Flaring)* No, I'm not going to work in the field. What did he send me away to school for—just to come back here and be his servant, or work in his hills of cotton?

CORA: He sent you away to de school because I asked him, and begged him, and got down on my knees to him, that's why. *(Quietly)* And now I just wants to make you see some sense, if you can. I knows, honey, you reads in de books and de papers, and you knows a lot more'n I do. But, chile, you's in Georgy—and I don't see how it is you don't know where you's at. This ain't up North—and even up yonder where we hears it's so fine, yo' sister has to pass for white to get along good.

ROBERT: *(Bitterly)* I know it.

CORA: She ain't workin' in no kitchen like de Colonel thinks. She's in a office typewriting. And Sallie's studyin' de typewriter, too, at de school, but yo' pappy don't know it. I knows we ain't 'sposed to study nothin' but cookin' and hard workin' here in Georgy. That's all I ever done, or knowed about. I been workin' on this very place all ma life—even 'fore I come to live in this Big House. When de Colonel's wife died, I come here, and bored you-chilluns. And de Colonel's been real good to me in his way. Let you-all sleep in this house with me when you was little, and sent you-all off to school when you growed up. Ain't no white man in this county done that with his cullud chilluns before, far as I can know. But you—Robert, be awful, awful careful! When de Colonel comes back, in a few minutes, he wants to talk to you. Talk right to him, boy. Talk like you was colored, cause you ain't white.

ROBERT: *(Angrily)* And I'm not black, either. Look at me, mama. *(Rising and throwing up his arms)* Don't I look like my father? Ain't I as light as he is? Ain't my eyes grey like his eyes are? *(The noise of a car is heard outside)* Ain't this our house?

CORA: That's him now. *(Agitated)* Hurry, chile, and let's we get out of this room. Come on through yonder to the kitchen. *(Starts toward the door left)* And I'll tell him you're here.

ROBERT: I don't want to run into the kitchen. Isn't this our house? *(As CORA crosses hurriedly left, ROBERT goes toward the front door)* The Ford is parked out in front, anyway.

CORA: *(At the door left to the rear of the house)* Robert! Robert!
    (As ROBERT nears the front door, COLONEL NORWOOD enters, almost runs into the boy, stops at the threshold and stares unbelievably at his son. CORA backs up against the door left.)

NORWOOD: Get out of here! *(He points toward the door to rear of the house where Cora is standing.)*

ROBERT: *(Half smiling)* Didn't you want to talk to me?

NORWOOD: Get out of here!

ROBERT: Not that way.
    (The COLONEL raises his cane to strike the boy. CORA screams. ROBERT draws himself up to his full height, taller than the old man and looking very much like him, pale and proud. The MAN and the BOY face each other. NORWOOD does not strike. The cane falls to the floor)

NORWOOD: *(In a hoarse whisper)* Get out of here. *(His hand is trembling as he points)*

CORA: *(Opening the door left)* Robert! Come on, come on! Oh, my God, come on!

ROBERT: *(Turning slowly, keeping his eyes on his father, but motioning with one hand toward the door where his mother stands)* Not that way, ma.

(He walks proudly out the front way. CORA exits left. NOR-WOOD, in an impotent rage, crosses the room to a small cabinet right, opens it nervously with a key from his pocket, takes out a pistol, and starts toward the front door. Suddenly he stops, trembling violently, puts the pistol down on the table, and sinks, ashen, into a big chair.)

CURTAIN

Act II, Scene 1

TIME: *After supper. Sunset.*

SETTING: *The same.*

ACTION: *As the curtain rises, the stage is empty. Through the windows the late afternoon sun makes two bright paths toward the footlights. SAM, carrying a tray bearing a whiskey bottle and a bowl of ice, enters left and crosses stage toward the library. He stops at the door right, listens a moment, knocks, then opens the door and goes in. In a moment SAM returns. As he leaves the library he is heard replying to a request of NORWOOD's.*

SAM: Yes, sah, Colonel! Sho' will, sah! Right away, sah! Yes, sah, I'll tell him. *(He closes the door and crosses the stage muttering to himself)* Six o'clock. Most nigh that now. Better tell Cora to get that boy right in here. Can't nobody else do nothin' with that fool Bert but Cora? *(He exits left. Can be heard calling)* Cora! You, Cora. . . .

> *(Again the stage is empty. Off stage, outside, the bark of a dog is heard, the sounds of Negroes singing down the road, the cry of a child. The breeze moves the shadows of leaves and tree limbs across the sunlit paths from the windows. The door left opens and CORA enters.)*

CORA: *(Softly to Robert behind her in the dining room)* It's alright, son. He ain't come out yet, but it's nearly six, and that's when he said he wanted you, but I was afraid maybe you was gonna be late. I sent for you to come up here to de house and eat supper with me in de kitchen. Where'd you eat yo' vittuals at, chile?

ROBERT: Down at Willie's house, ma. After the old man tried to hit me you still want me hang around and eat up here?

CORA: I wanted you to be here on time, honey, that's all. *(She is very nervous)* I kinder likes to have you eat with me sometimes, too, but you ain't et up here more'n once this summer. But this evenin' I just wanted you to be here when de Colonel sent word for you, cause we's done had enough trouble to-day.

ROBERT: He's not here on time himself, is he?

CORA: He's in de library. Sam couldn't get him to eat no supper tonight, and I ain't seen him a-tall.

ROBERT: Maybe he wants to see me in the library, then.

CORA: You knows he don't 'low no colored folks in there 'mongst his books and things 'cept Sam. Some o' his white friends goes in there, but none o' us.

ROBERT: Maybe he wants to see *me* in there, though.

CORA: Can't you never talk sense, Robert? This ain't no time for foolin' and jokin'. Nearly thirty years in this house and I ain't never been in there myself, not once, 'mongst de Colonel's papers. *(The clock strikes six)* Stand over yonder and wait till he comes out. I's gwine on upstairs now, so's he can talk to you. And don't aggravate him no mo' fo' God's sake. 'Gree to whatever he say. I's scared fo' you, chile, de way you been actin', and de fool tricks you done done today, and de trouble about de Post Office besides. Don't aggravate him. Fo' yo' sake, honey, 'cause I loves you, and fo' all de po' colored folks on this place what has such a hard time when his humors get on him—'gree to whatever he say, will you, Bert?

ROBERT: All right, ma. *(Voice rising)* But he better not start to hit me again.

CORA: Sh-s-s. He'll hear you. He's right in here.

ROBERT: *(Sullenly)* This was the day I ought to started back to school—like my sister. I stayed my summer out here, didn't I? Why didn't he keep his promise to me? You said if I came home I could go back to Atlanta again.

CORA: Sh-s-s! He'll be here now. Don't say nothin', chile. I's done all I could.

ROBERT: All right, ma.

CORA: *(Approaching the stairs)* I'll be in ma room, honey, where I can hear you when you goes out. I'll come down to de back door and see you 'fore you goes back to de shack. Don't aggravate him, chile. *(She ascends the stairs.)*

> *(The BOY sits down sullenly, left, and stares at the door opposite from which his father must enter. The clock strikes the quarter after six. The shadows of the window curtains have lengthened on the floor. The sunshine has deepened to a pale orange, and the light paths grow less distinct across the floor. The BOY sits up straight*

in his chair. He looks at the library door. It opens. NORWOOD enters. He is bent and pale. He looks across the room and sees the boy. Suddenly he straightens up. The old commanding looks comes into his face. He strides directly across the room toward his son. The boy, half afraid, half defiant, yet sure of himself, rises. Now that ROBERT is standing, the white man turns, goes back to a chair near the table, right, and seats himself. He takes out a cigar, cuts off the end and lights it, and in a voice of mixed condescension and contempt, he speaks to his son. ROBERT remains standing near the chair.)

NORWOOD: I don't want to have to beat you another time as I did when you were a child. The next time I might not be able to control myself. I might kill you if I touched you again. I been runnin' this plantation for thirty-five years, and I never had to beat a nigra as old as you are. I never had to beat one of Cora's children either—but you. The rest of 'em had sense enough to keep out of my sight, and to speak to me like they should. . . . I don't have any trouble with my colored folks. Never have trouble. They do what I say, or what Mr. Talbot says, and that's all there is to it. I give 'em a chance. If they turn in crops they get paid. If they workin' for wages, they get paid. If they want to spend their money on licker, or buy an old car, or fix up their cabins, they can. Do what they choose long as they know their places and it don't hinder their work. And to Cora's young ones I give all the chances any colored folks ever had in these parts. More'n many a white child's had. I sent you all off to school. Let Bertha go on up North when she got grown and educated. Intend to let Sallie do the same. Gave your brother William that house he's living in when he got married, pay him for his work, help him out if he needs it. None of my darkies suffer. Sent you to school. Would have kept on, would have sent you back today, but I don't intend to pay for no darkie, or white boy either if I had one, that acts the way you've been acting. And certainly for no black fool. Now I want to know what's wrong with you? I don't usually talk about what I'm going to do with anybody on this place. It's my habit to tell people *what to do,* not discuss it with 'em. But I want to know what's the matter with you—whether you're crazy or not. In that case, you'll have to be locked up. And if you aren't, you'll have to change your ways a damn sight or it won't be safe for you here, and you know it—venting your impudence on white women, parking your car in front of my door, driving like mad through the Junction, and doing, everywhere, just as you please. Now, I'm going to let you talk to me, but I want you to talk right.

ROBERT: *(Still standing)* What do you mean, talk right.

NORWOOD: I mean talk like a nigger should to a white man.

ROBERT: Oh! But I'm not a nigger, Mr. Norwood, I'm your son.

NORWOOD: *(Testily)* You're Cora's boy.

ROBERT: Women don't have children by themselves.

NORWOOD: Nigger women don't know the fathers. You're a bastard.
> *(ROBERT clenches his fist. NORWOOD turns toward the drawer where the pistol is, takes it out, and lays it on the table. The wind blows the lace curtains at the windows, and sweeps the shadows of leaves across the paths of sunlight on the floor)*

ROBERT: I've heard that before. I've heard it from Negroes, and I've heard it from white folks, and now I hear it from you. *(Slowly)* You're talking about my mother.

NORWOOD: I'm talking about Cora, yes. Her children are bastards.

ROBERT: *(Quickly)* And you're their father. *(Angrily)* How come I look like you, if you're not my father?

NORWOOD: Don't shout at me, boy, I can hear you. *(Half smiling)* How come your skin is yellow and your elbows rusty? How come they threw you out of the Post Office today for talking to a white woman? How come you're the crazy young nigger that you are?

ROBERT: They had no right to throw me out. I asked for my money back when I saw the broken tubes. Just as you had no right to raise that cane today when I was standing at the door of this house where *you* live, while *I* have to sleep in a shack down the road with the field hands. *(Slowly)* But my mother sleeps with you.

NORWOOD: You don't like it?

ROBERT: No, I don't like it.

NORWOOD: What can you do about it?

ROBERT: *(After a pause)* I'd like to kill all the white men in the world.

NORWOOD: *(Starting)* Niggers like you are hung to trees.

ROBERT: I'm not a nigger.

NORWOOD: You don't like your own race? *(ROBERT is silent)* Yet you don't like white folks either?

ROBERT: *(Defiantly)* You think I ought to?

NORWOOD: You evidently don't like me.

ROBERT: *(Boyishly)* I used to like you, when I first knew you were my father, when I was a little kid, before that time you beat me under the feet of the horses. *(Slowly)* I liked you until then.

NORWOOD: *(A little pleased)* So you did, heh? *(Fingering his pistol)* A pickaninny calling me "papa". I should've broken your young neck for you that first time. I should've broken your head for you today, too—since I didn't then.

ROBERT: *(Laughing scornfully)* You should've broken my head?

NORWOOD: Should've gotten rid of you before this. But you was Cora's child. I tried to help you. *(Aggrieved)* I treated you decent, schooled you. Paid for it. But tonight you'll get the hell off of this place and stay off. Get the hell out of this county. *(Suddenly furious)* Get out of this state. Don't let me lay eyes on you again. Get out of here now. Talbot and the storekeeper are coming up here this evening to talk cotton with me. I'll tell Talbot to *see* that you go. That's all. *(NORWOOD motions toward the door, left)* Tell Sam to come in here when you go out. Tell him to make a light here.

ROBERT: *(Impudently)* Ring for Sam—I'm not going through the kitchen. *(He starts toward the front door)* I'm not your servant. You're not going to tell me what to do. You're not going to have Talbot run me off the place like a field hand you don't want to use any more.

NORWOOD: *(Springing between his son and the front door, pistol in hand)* You black bastard!

(ROBERT goes toward him calmly, grasps his father's arm and twists it until the gun falls to the floor. The older man bends backward in startled fury and pain.)

NORWOOD: Don't you dare put your. . . .

ROBERT: *(Laughing)* Why don't you shoot, papa? *(Louder)* Why don't you shoot?

NORWOOD: *(Gasping)* . . . black . . . hand . . . on me . . . you . . .

ROBERT: *(Hysterically, as he takes his father by the throat)* Why don't you shoot, papa? *(NORWOOD's hands claw the air helplessly. ROBERT chokes the struggling white man until his body grows limp)* Why don't you shoot? *(Laughing)* Why don't you? Huh? Why?

(CORA appears at the top of the stairs, hearing the struggle. She screams)

CORA: Oh my God!

(She rushes down. ROBERT drops the body of his father at her feet in a path of red from the setting sun. CORA stares in horror)

ROBERT: *(Wildly)* Why didn't he shoot, mama? He didn't want *me* to live. Why didn't he shoot? *(Laughing)* He was the boss. Telling me what to do. Why didn't he shoot, then? He was the white man.

CORA: *(Falling on the body)* Colonel Tom! Colonel Tom! Tom! Tom! *(Gazes across the corpse at her son)* He's yo' father, boy.

ROBERT: He's dead. The white man's dead. My father's dead. *(Laughing)* I'm living.

CORA: Tom! Tom! Tom!

ROBERT: Niggers are living. He's dead. *(Picks up the pistol)* This is what he wanted to kill me with, but he's dead. I can use it now. Use it on all the white men in the world, because they'll be coming looking for me now. *(He stuffs the pistol into his shirt)* They'll want me now.

CORA: *(Rising and running toward her boy)* Quick, chile, out that way. *(Pointing toward the front door)* So they won't see you in de kitchen. Make for de swamp, honey. Cross de fields fo' de swamp. Go de crick way. In runnin' water, dogs can't smell no tracks. Hurry, chile!

ROBERT: Yes, mama. I can go out the front way now, easy. But if I see they gonna get me before I can reach the swamp, I'm coming back here, ma, and *(Proudly)* let 'em take me out of my father's house, if they can. *(He pats the gun under his shirt)* They're not going to string me up to some roadside tree for the crackers to laugh at.

CORA: *(Moaning aloud)* Oh-o-o! Hurry! Hurry, chile!

ROBERT: I'm going, ma. *(He opens the door and the sunset streams in like a river of blood)*

CORA: Run, chile!

ROBERT: Not out of my father's house. *(He exits slowly, tall and straight against the sun)*

CORA: Fo' God's sake, hurry, chile! *(Glancing down the road)* Lawd have mercy! There's Talbot and de storekeeper in de drive. They sees ma boy! *(Moaning)* They sees ma boy, *(Relieved)* but thank God, they's passin' him!

> *(CORA backs up against the wall in the vestibule. She stands as if petrified as TALBOT and the STOREKEEPER enter)*

TALBOT: Hello, Cora. What's the matter with you? Where's that damn fool boy o' you'rn goin', coming out the front way like he owned the house? What's the matter with you, woman? Can't you talk? Where's Norwood? *(He enters the room, followed by the STOREKEEPER)* Let's have some light in this dark place. *(He reaches behind the door and turns on the lights. CORA remains backed up against the wall, looking out into the twilight, watching ROBERT as he goes across the field)* Good God, Jim! Look at this!

> *(The two white men stop in horror before the sight of NORWOOD's body on the floor)*

STOREKEEPER: He's blue in the face. *(Bends over the body)* That nigger we saw walking out the door! *(Rising excitedly)* That nigger bastard of Cora's . . . *(Stooping over the body again)* Why, the Colonel's dead!

TALBOT: That nigger! *(He rushes toward the door)* He's running toward the swamps now . . . We'll get him. . . . Telephone town—there, in the library. Telephone the sheriff. Get men, white men, after that nigger. *(STOREKEEPER rushes into the library. He can be heard calling numbers and talking excitedly)* Cora, where's Norwood's car? In the barn? Talk, you black bitch!

> *(TALBOT runs, yelling and talking, out into the yard. A moment later he is followed by the STOREKEEPER who emerges from the library. Sounds of excited shouting outside; the roar of a motor rushing down the drive. In the sky the twilight deepens into early night)*

CORA: *(Still looking into the darkness)* My boy can't get to de swamp now. They's telephoned the white folks down that way. *(She turns and comes back into the room)* He'll come back home now. Maybe he'll turn into de crick and follow de branch back home directly. *(Protectively)* But they shan't get him. I'll make a place for to hide him. I'll make a place upstairs down under de floor, under ma bed. In a minute ma boy'll be runnin' from de white folks with their hounds and their ropes and their guns and everything they uses to kill po' colored folks with. *(Distressed)* My boy'll be out there runnin'. *(Turning to the body on the floor)* Colonel Tom, you hear me? Our boy, out there runnin'. *(Fiercely)* You said he was ma boy— *ma* bastard boy. I heard you . . . but he's yours too—out yonder in de dark runnin'—runnin' from yo' people. *(Pleadingly)* Why don't you get up and stop 'em? He's *your* boy. His eyes is grey—like your eyes. He's tall like you's tall. He's proud like you's proud. And he's runnin'—runnin' from po' white trash what ain't worth de little finger o' nobody what's got your blood in 'em, Tom. *(Demandingly)* Why don't you get up from there and stop 'em, Colonel Tom? What's that you say? He ain't your child? He's ma bastard child? Ma yellow bastard child? *(Proudly)* Yes, he's mine. But don't you call him that. Don't you touch him. Don't you put your white hands on him. You's beat him enough, and cussed him enough. Don't you touch him now. He *is* ma boy, and no white folks gonna touch him now. That's finished. I'm gonna make a place for him. Upstairs under ma bed. *(She backs away from the body and toward the stairs.)*

He's ma chile. Don't you come in ma bedroom while he's up there. Don't you come to ma bed no mo'. I calls you to help me now, and you just lays there. I calls you for to wake up, and you just lays there. Whenever you called me, in de night, I woke up. When you called fo' me to love you, I always reached out ma arms fo' you. I bored you five chilluns and now one of 'em out yonder in de dark runnin' from yo' people. De youngest boy out yonder in de dark runnin'. *(Accusingly)* He's runnin' from you, too. You said he warn't your'n—he's just Cora's po' little yellow bastard. But he is your'n, Colonel Tom, *(Sadly)* and he's runnin' from you. You's out yonder in de dark *(She points toward the door)* runnin' our chile, with de hounds, and de gun in yo' hand, and Talbot's followin' 'hind you with a rope to hang Robert with. *(Confidently)* I been sleepin' with you too long, Colonel Tom, not to know that this ain't you layin' down there with yo' eyes shut on de floor. You can't fool me—you ain't never been so still like this before—you's out yonder runnin' ma boy. *(Scornfully)* Colonel Thomas Norwood, runnin' ma boy through de fields in de dark, runnin' ma poor little helpless Bert, through de fields in de dark to lynch him. . . . Damn you, Colonel Norwood! *(Backing slowly up the stairs, staring at the rigid body below her)* Damn you, Tom Norwood! God damn you!

Act II, Scene 2

TIME: *One hour later. Night.*

SETTING: *The same.*

ACTION: *As the curtain rises the UNDERTAKER is talking to SAM at the outer door. All through this act the approaching cries of the man-hunt are heard.*

UNDERTAKER: Reckon there won't be no orders to bring his body back out here. None of us ain't seen Talbot or Mr. Higgins, but I'm sure they'll be having the funeral in town. The coroner told us to bring it into the Junction. Ain't nothin' but niggers left out here now.

SAM: *(Very frightened)* Yes, sah! Yes, sah! You's right, sah! Yes, sah! Nothin' but us niggers, sah!

UNDERTAKER: The Colonel didn't have no relatives far as you know, did he, Sam?

SAM: No, sah. Ain't had none. No, sah! You's right. No, sah!

UNDERTAKER: Well, you got everything o' his locked up around here, ain't you? Too bad there ain't no white folks about to look after the Colonel's stuff, but every white man that's able to walk's out with the posse. They'll have that young nigger swingin' before ten.

SAM: *(Trembling)* Yes, sah, yes, sah! I 'spects so. Yes, sah!

UNDERTAKER: Say, where's that woman the Colonel's been living— where's that black housekeeper, Cora, that murderin' bastard's mother?

SAM: She here, sah! She's up in her room.

UNDERTAKER: *(Curiously)* I'd like to see how she looks. Get her down here. Say, how about a little drink before we start that ride back to town, for me and my partner out there with the body?

SAM: Cora got de keys to all de licker, sah!

UNDERTAKER: Well, get her down here then, double quick! *(SAM goes up the stairs. The UNDERTAKER leans in the front doorway talking to his partner outside in the wagon)* Bad business, a white man having saucy nigger children on his hands, and his black woman living in his own house.

VOICE OUTSIDE: Damn right, Charlie.

UNDERTAKER: Norwood didn't have a gang o' yellow gals, though, like Higgins and some o' these other big bugs. Just this one bitch far's I know, livin' with him damn near like a wife. Didn't even have much company out here. And they tell me ain't been a white woman stayed here overnight since his wife died when I was a baby. *(SAM's shuffle is heard on the stairs)* Here comes a drink, I reckon, boy. You needn't get down off the ambulance. I'll have Sam bring it out there to you. *(SAM descends followed by CORA, who comes almost down the stairs. She says nothing. Looking up and grinning at Cora)* Well, so you're the Cora that's got these educated nigger children? Hum-m! Well, I guess you'll see one of 'em swinging full of bullet holes when you wake up in the morning. They'll probably hang him up to that tree down here by the Colonel's gate—'cause they tell me he strutted out the front gate past that tree after the murder. Or maybe they'll burn him. How'll you like him swinging there roasted in the morning when you wake up, girlie?

CORA: *(Calmly)* Is that all you wanted to say to me?

UNDERTAKER: Don't get smart now. Maybe you think there's nobody to boss you now. We gonna have a little drink before we go. Get out a bottle of rye.

CORA: I takes ma orders from Colonel Norwood, sir.

UNDERTAKER: Well, you'll take no more orders from him. He's dead out there in my wagon—so get along and get the bottle.

CORA: He's out yonder with de mob, not in your wagon.

UNDERTAKER: I tell you he's in my wagon!

CORA: He's out there with de mob.

UNDERTAKER: God damn! *(To his partner outside)* I believe this black woman's gone crazy in here. *(To Cora)* Get the keys out for that licker, and be quick about it!

> *(CORA does not move. SAM looks from one to the other, frightened)*

VOICE OUTSIDE: Aw, to hell with the licker, Charlie. Come on, let's start back to town. We want to get in on some of that excitement, too. They should've found that nigger by now—and I want to see 'em drag him out here.

UNDERTAKER: All right, Jim. *(To CORA and SAM)* Don't you-all go to bed until you see the bonfire. You niggers are getting besides yourselves around Polk County. We'll burn a few more of you if you don't be careful.

> *(He exits, and the noise of the dead-wagon going down the road is heard)*

SAM: Oh, Lawd hab mercy on me. I Prays, Lawd hab mercy. O, ma Lawd, ma Lawd, ma Lawd! Cora, is you a fool? *Is* you a fool? Why didn't you give de mens de licker, riled as these white folks is? In ma old age is I gonna be burnt by de crackers? Lawd, is I sinned? Lawd, what has I done? *(Suddenly stops moaning and becomes schemingly calm)* I don't have to stay here tonight, does I? I done locked up de Colonel's library, and he can't be wantin' nothin'. No, ma Lawd, he won't want nothin' now. He's with Jesus—or with de devil, one. *(To CORA)* I's gwine on a way from here. Sam's gwine in town to his chillun's house, and I ain't gwine by no road either. I gwine through de holler where I don't have to pass no white folks.

CORA: Yes, Samuel, you go on. De Colonel can get his own drinks when he comes back tonight.

SAM: *(Bucking his eyes in astonishment at CORA)* Lawd God Jesus!

> *(He bolts out of the room as fast as his old legs will carry him.)*
> *(CORA comes down stairs, looks for a long moment out into the dark, then closes the front door, and draws the blinds. She looks down at the spot where the Colonel's body lay)*

CORA: All de niggers runnin' from you tonight. Po' Colonel Tom, you' too old now to be out with de mob. You got no business goin', but you had to go, I reckon. I 'members that time they hung Luke Jordon, you sent yo' dogs out to hunt him. Then next day you killed all de dogs. You were kinder soft-hearted. Said you didn't like that kind o' sport. Told me in bed one night you could hear them dogs howlin' in yo' sleep. But de time they burnt de court house when that po' little cullud boy was locked up in it cause they said he hugged a white girl, you was with 'em agin. Said you had to go help 'em. Now you's out chasin' ma boy. *(A noise at the door, left)* What's that? *(LIVONIA, the cook, enters)* What you want, 'Vonia? You know Colonel Tom don't 'low you in here.

LIVONIA: *(With her hat and cloak on)* What's de matter with you, Cora? De Colonel ain't here, and you sho' don't think now I wants a dead man. . . . I ain't made a practice o' sleepin' with white men no how, like you. I's goin' . . . down to Rev. Martin's shack by de Cross Roads church. I ain't gwine stay in this big old house this night. *(She shudders)* Don't know if you know it or not, but mighty nigh all de field hands is gone from out o' de quarters, tryin' to get in town, if they don't run into de white folks comin' out. And yo' son William's out yonder in de kitchen, wants to know whether he can come in here to see you or not. *(Evilly)* I told him, yes, to come on in here. You high-toned colored folks was sholy usin' de parlor 'fore de Colonel died—and I reckon it *(Sarcastically)* belongs to you now . . . Well, I'm leavin', ma-self. White folks'll never catch me here. *(She exits, muttering.)* Yes, I told William to come on in.

CORA: *(To the shadow of the body on the floor)* There goes yo' other woman, Colonel Tom, runnin' from you too, now. She would've wanted you last night. Been wantin' you again ever since she got old and fat and you stopped layin' with her. Don't think I don't know, Colonel Tom. Don't think I don't remember them nights when you used to sleep in that cabin down by de spring. I knew 'Vonia was there with you. I ain't no fool, Colonel Tom. But she ain't bore you no chilluns. I'm de one what bore 'em. *(Musing)* White mens, and colored womens, and little bastard chilluns—that's de old way of de South—but it's ending now. Three of your yellow brothers yo' father had by Aunt Sallie Deal—what has to come and do your laundry now to make her livin'. Thems de ways o' de South—mixtries, mixtries. *(WILLIAM enters left, silently as his mother talks. She is sitting in a chair now. Without looking up)* Is that you, William?

WILLIAM: Yes, ma, it's me.

CORA: Is you runnin' from him, too?

WILLIAM: Well, ma, you see . . . Don't you think kinder. . . . well, I reckon I ought to take Libby and ma babies on down to de church house with Rev. Martin and them, or else get 'long to town if I can hitch up them mules. They's scared to be out here, Libby and her ma. All de folks done gone from de houses down yonder by de branch, and you can hear de hounds a bayin' off yonder by de swamp, and cars is tearin' up that road, and de white folks is yellin' and hollerin' and carryin' on somethin' terrible over toward de brook. I done told Robert 'bout his foolishness. They's gonna hang him sure. Don't you think you better be comin' with us, ma, that is you want to? 'Course we can go by ourselves, and maybe you wants to stay here and take care o' de big house. I don't want to leave you ma, but I . . . I . . .

CORA: Yo' brother'll be back, son, then I won't be by myself.

WILLIAM: *(Bewildered by his mother's sureness)* I thought Bert went . . . I thought he run . . . I thought. . . .

CORA: No, honey. He went, but they ain't gonna get him out there. I sees him comin' back here now, to be with me first. I's gwine guard him 'til he can get away.

WILLIAM: Then de white folks'll come here, too.

CORA: Yes, de Colonel'll come back here sure. *(The deep baying of the hounds is heard at a distance through the night.)* He'll come after his son.

WILLIAM: My God, ma! Come with us.

CORA: Go on, William, go on! Don't wait for them to come back. You never was much like neither one o' them—neither de Colonel or Bert—you's mo' like de field hands. Too much o' ma blood in you, I guess. You never liked Bert much, neither, and you always was afraid of de Colonel. Go on, son, and hide yo' wife and her ma an' de chilluns. Ain't nothin' gonna hurt you. You never did fight nobody. Neither did I, till tonight. Tried to live right and not hurt a soul, white or colored. *(Addressing space)* I tried to live right, Lord. *(Angrily)* Tried to live right, Lord. *(Throws out her arms resentfully as if to say, "and this is what you give me".)* What's de matter, Lawd, you ain't with me?

(The hounds are heard howling again)

WILLIAM: I'm gone, ma. *(He exits fearfully as his mother talks)*

CORA: *(Bending over the spot on the floor where the Colonel has lain. She calls)* Colonel Tom! Colonel Tom! Colonel Tom! Look! Bertha and Sallie and William and Bert, all your chilluns, runnin' from you, and you layin' on de floor there, dead. *(Pointing)* Out yonder with de mob, dead. And when you come home, upstairs in my bed on top of my body, dead. *(She goes to the window, returns, sits down, and begins to speak as if remembering a far-off dream)* Colonel Thomas Norwood; I'm just poor Cora Lewis, Colonel Norwood. Little black Cora Lewis, Colonel Norwood. I'm just fifteen years old. Thirty years ago, you put your hands on me to feel my breasts, and you say, "you're a pretty little piece of flesh, ain't you? Black and sweet, ain't you?" And I lift up ma face, and you pull me to you, and we laid down under the trees that night, and I wonder if your wife'll know when you go back up the road into the big house. And I wonder if my mama'll know it, when I go back to our cabin. Mama said she nursed you when you was a baby, just like she nursed me. And I loved you in the dark, down there under that tree by de gate, afraid of you and proud of you, feelin' your grey eyes lookin' at me in de dark. Then I cried and cried and told ma mother about it, but she didn't take it hard like I thought she'd take it. She said fine white mens like de young Colonel always took good care o' their colored womens. She said it was better than marryin' some black field hand and workin' all your life in de cotton and cane. Better even than havin' a job like ma had, takin' care o' de white chilluns. Takin' care o' you, Colonel Tom. *(As CORA speaks the sounds of the approaching mob gradually grow louder and louder. Auto horns, the howling of dogs, the far-off shouts of men increase in volume, full of malignant force and power)* And I was happy because I liked you, 'cause you was tall and proud, 'cause you said I was sweet to you and called me purty. And when yo' wife died—de Mrs. Norwood *(Scornfully)* that never bore you any chilluns, the pale Mrs. Thomas Norwood that was like a pine tree in de winter frost . . . I knowed you wanted me. I was full with child by you then—William, it was— our first boy. And ma mammy said, go up there and keep de house for Colonel Tom. Sweep de floors and make de beds, and by and by, you won't have to sweep no floors and make no beds. And what ma mammy said was right. It all come true. Sam and Rufus and 'Vonia and Lucy did de waitin' on you, and me, and de washin' and de cleanin' and de cookin'. And all I did was a little sewin' now and then, and a little preservin' in de summer, and a little makin' of pies and sweet cakes and things you liked to eat on Christmas. And de years went by. And I was always ready for you when you come to me in de night. And we had them chilluns, your chilluns and mine, Tom

Norwood, all of 'em! William, born dark like me, dumb like me; and then Baby John what died; and then Bertha, white and smart like you; and then Bert with your eyes and your ways and your temper, and mighty nigh your color; then Sallie, nearly white too, and smart, and purty. But Bert was yo' chile! He was always yo' chile. Good-looking, and kind, and headstrong, and strange, and stubborn, and proud like you, and de one I could love most 'cause he needed de most lovin'. And he wanted to call you "papa", and I tried to teach him no, but he did it anyhow and *(Sternly)* you beat him, Colonel Thomas Norwood. And he growed up with de beatin' in his heart, and your eyes in his head, and your ways, and your pride. And this summer he was like you that time I first knowed you down by de road under them trees, young and fiery and proud. And there was no touchin' him, just like there was no touchin' you. I could only love him, like I loved you. I could only love him. And I couldn't talk to him because he hated you. He had your ways—and you beat him! After you beat that chile, then you died, Colonel Norwood. You died here in this house, and you been living dead a long time. You lived dead. *(Her voice rises above the nearing sounds of the mob)* And when I said this evenin', "Get up! Why don't you help me?" you'd done been dead a long time—a long time before you laid down on this floor, here, with the breath choked out o' you—and Bert standin' over you living, living, living. That's why you hated him. And you want to kill him. Always, you wanted to kill him. Out there with de hounds and de torches and de cars and de guns, you want to kill ma boy. But you won't kill him! He's comin' home first. He's comin' home to me. He's comin' home. *(Outside the noise is tremendous now, the lights of autos flash on the window curtains, there are shouts and cries. CORA sits, tense, in the middle of the room)* He's coming home!

A MAN'S VOICE: *(Outside)* He's somewhere on this lot.

ANOTHER VOICE: Don't shoot, men. We want to get him alive.

VOICE: We closed in on him. He must be in them bushes by the house.

FIRST VOICE: Porch! Porch! Porch! There he is yonder running to the door.

> *(Suddenly shots are heard just outside the door. The door bursts open and ROBERT enters, firing back into the darkness. The shots are returned by the mob, breaking the windows. Flares, lights, voices, curses, screams, motors, shots, cries)*

VOICES: *(Outside)* Nigger! Nigger! Nigger! Get the Nigger!

(CORA rushes toward the door and bolts it after her son's entrance)

CORA: *(Leaning against the door)* I was waiting for you, Honey. Yo' hiding place is all ready, upstairs, under ma bed, under de floor. I sawed a place there fo' you. They can't find you there. Hurry 'fore yo' father comes.

ROBERT: *(Panting)* No time to hide, ma. They're at the door now. They'll be coming up the back way, too. *(Sounds of knocking and the breaking of glass)* They're coming in the windows. They're coming in everywhere. And only one bullet left, ma. It's for me.

CORA: Yes, it's fo' you, chile. Save it. Go upstairs in mama's room. Lay on ma bed and rest.

ROBERT: *(Going slowly toward the stairs with the pistol in his hand)* Goodnight, ma. I'm awful tired of running, ma. They been chasing me for hours.

CORA: Goodnight, son.

(CORA follows him to the foot of the steps. The door begins to give to the forcing of the mob. As ROBERT disappears above, it bursts open. A great crowd of white men pour into the room with guns, ropes, clubs, flashlights, and knives. CORA turns on the stairs, facing them quietly)

(The LEADER of the mob stops)

LEADER: Keep still, men. He's armed. *(To CORA)* Where is that yellow bastard of yours—upstairs?

CORA: Yes, he's going to sleep. Be quiet, you-all. Wait. *(She bars the way with out-spread arms)*

LEADER: *(Harshly)* Wait, hell! Come on boys, let's go! *(A single shot is heard upstairs.)* What's that?

CORA: *(Calmly)* Ma boy. . . . is gone . . . . . . to sleep!

(As the mob rushes up the stairway, CORA makes a final gesture of love toward the room above. Then, overcome with a great helplessness, she sinks slowly to the floor at the edge of the vindictive flow of human feet. Yelling and shouting, through all the doors and windows, a great crowd pours into the room. The roar of the mob fills the house, the whole night, the whole world.)

CURTAIN

Mule Bone
A Comedy of Negro Life

1930

With Zora Neale Hurston

Finally performed from January 20 to April 14, 1991, at New York's Lincoln Center, *Mule Bone* was written by Langston Hughes and Zora Neale Hurston in 1930. Based on Hurston's short story "A Bone of Contention," itself based on a folk tale, *Mule Bone* was intended to be the first "real Negro folk comedy," grounded in African American vernacular traditions and embodying the "gift of laughter," as Jessie Fauset had called the humor with which African American expression is imbued. In Hurston's story, the quarrel is over a turkey, but in the play it is over a woman, Daisy, with the romantic triangle providing dramatic structure for a story whose resolution turns on humorous biblical exegesis.

Who did what in this literary collaboration is hard to untangle. "I plotted out and typed the play based on her story," Hughes wrote in *The Big Sea*, "while she authenticated and flavored the dialogue and added highly humorous details. We finished a first draft . . . and from this draft I was to work out a final version." Both Hughes's biographer, Arnold Rampersad, and Hurston's biographer, Robert Hemenway, consider Hughes's allocation accurate. It is difficult, however, to identify and attribute with accuracy the various drafts and typescripts in the Langston Hughes Papers. According to Henry Louis Gates Jr., the version reproduced here, dated Cleveland 1931, is the most complete of the drafts.[1] It can be found in the Arthur Spingarn Papers at Howard University's Moorland-Spingarn Research Center and is the version chosen by Gates for publication (New York: HarperPerennial, 1991) to coincide with the play's premiere.[2] This is not, however, the text performed at Lincoln Center.

Characters

Principal Characters

JIM WESTON, guitarist, Methodist, slightly arrogant, aggressive, somewhat self-important, ready with his tongue

DAVE CARTER, dancer, Baptist, soft, happy-go-lucky character, slightly dumb and unable to talk rapidly and wittily

DAISY TAYLOR, Methodist, domestic servant, plump, dark and sexy,
self-conscious of clothes and appeal, fickle

JOE CLARKE, the Mayor, storekeeper and postmaster, arrogant, ignorant and powerful in a self-assertive way, large, fat man, Methodist

ELDER SIMMS, Methodist minister, newcomer in town, ambitious,
small and fly, but not very intelligent

ELDER CHILDERS, big, loose-jointed, slow spoken but not dumb;
long resident in the town, calm and sure of himself

KATIE CARTER, Dave's aunt, little old wisened dried-up lady

MRS. MATTIE CLARKE, the Mayor's wife, fat and flabby mulatto,
high-pitched voice

THE MRS. REV. SIMMS, large and aggressive

THE MRS. REV. CHILDERS, just a wife who thinks of details

LUM BOGER, young town marshall about twenty, tall, gangly, with big
flat feet, liked to show off in public

TEETS MILLER, village vamp who is jealous of DAISY

LIGE MOSELY, a village wag

WALTER THOMAS, another village wag

ADA LEWIS, a promiscuous lover

DELLA LEWIS, Baptist, poor housekeeper, mother of ADA

BOOTSIE PITTS, a local vamp

MRS. DILCIE ANDERSON, village housewife, Methodist

WILLIE NIXON, Methodist, short runt

Minor Characters

HAMBO
GOODWIN
BRAZZLE
CODY
JONES
SAM MOSELY

TAYLOR
MRS. TAYLOR
MRS. JAKE ROBERTS
(VOICE OF MRS. MOSELY)
SENATOR BAILEY (BOY)
LITTLE MATILDA
OLD MAN
FRANK WARRICK
OLD WOMAN
SISTER THOMAS
SISTER JONES
MARY ELLA
SISTER PITTS
SISTER LUCAS
MRS. HAMBO
MRS. NIXON
MRS. BLUNT
(CHILDREN)
(LOUNGERS)

Act I

SETTING: *The raised porch of JOE CLARKE's Store and the street in front. Porch stretches almost completely across the stage, with a plank bench at either end. At the center of the porch three steps leading from street. Rear of porch, center, door to the store. On either side are single windows on which signs, at left, "POST OFFICE", and at right, "GEN-ERAL STORE" are painted. Soap boxes, axe handles, small kegs, etc., on porch on which townspeople sit and lounge during action. Above the roof of the porch the "false front", or imitation second story of the shop, is seen with large sign painted across it "JOE CLARKE'S GENERAL STORE". Large kerosine street lamp on post at right in front of porch.*

   Saturday afternoon and the villagers are gathered around the store. Several men sitting on boxes at edge of porch chewing sugar cane, spitting tobacco juice, arguing, some whittling, others eating peanuts. During the act the women all dressed up in starched dresses parade in and out of store. People buying groceries, kids playing in the street, etc. General noise of conversation, laughter and children shouting. But when the curtain rises there is a momentary lull for cane-chewing. At left of porch four men are playing cards on a soap box, and seated on the edge of the porch at extreme right two children are engaged in a checker game, with the board on the floor between them.

When the curtain goes up the following characters are discovered on the porch: MAYOR JOE CLARKE, the storekeeper; DEACON HAMBO; DEACON GOODWIN; Old Man MATT BRAZZLE; WILL CODY; SYKES JONES; LUM BOGER, the young town marshall; LIGE MOSELY and WALTER THOMAS, two village wags; TOM NIXON and SAM MOSELY, and several others, seated on boxes, kegs, benches and floor of the porch. TONY TAYLOR is sitting on steps of porch with empty basket. MRS. TAYLOR comes out with her arms full of groceries, empties them into basket and goes back in store. All the men are chewing sugar cane earnestly with varying facial expressions. The noise of the breaking and sucking of cane can be clearly heard in the silence. Occasionally the laughter and shouting of children is heard nearby off stage.

HAMBO: *(To BRAZZLE)* Say, Matt, gimme a jint or two of dat green cane—dis ribbon cane is hard.

LIGE: Yeah, and you ain't got de chears in yo' parlor you useter have.

HAMBO: Dat's all right, Lige, but I betcha right now wid dese few teeth I got I kin eat up more cane'n you kin grow.

LIGE: I know you kin and that's de reason I ain't going to tempt you. But youse gettin' old in lots of ways—look at dat bald-head—just as clean as my hand. *(Exposes his palm.)*

HAMBO: Don't keer if it tis—I don't want nothin'—not even hair—between me and God. *(General laughter—LIGE joins in as well. Cane chewing keeps up. Silence for a moment.)*

(Off stage a high shrill voice can be heard calling:)

VOICE: Sister Mosely, Oh, Sister Mosely! *(A pause)* Miz Mosely! *(Very irritated)* Oh, Sister Mattie! You hear me out here—you just won't answer!

VOICE of MRS. MOSELY: Whoo-ee . . . somebody calling me?

VOICE of MRS. ROBERTS: *(Angrily)* Never mind now—you couldn't come when I called you. I don't want yo' lil ole weasley turnip greens. *(Silence)*

MATT BRAZZLE: Sister Roberts is en town agin! If she was mine, I'll be hen-fired if I wouldn't break her down in de lines (loins)—good as dat man is to her!

HAMBO: I wish she was mine jes' one day—de first time she open her mouf to beg *anybody,* I'd lam her wid lightning.

JOE CLARKE: I God, Jake Roberts buys mo' rations out dis store than any man in dis town. I don't see to my Maker whut she do wid it all. . . . Here she come. . . .

> *(Enter MRS. JAKE ROBERTS, a heavy light brown woman with a basket on her arm. A boy about ten walks beside her carrying a small child about a year old straddle of his back. Her skirts are sweeping the ground. She walks up to the step, puts one foot upon the steps and looks forlornly at all the men, then fixes her look on JOE CLARKE.)*

MRS. ROBERTS: Evenin', Brother Mayor.

CLARKE: Howdy do, Mrs. Roberts. How's yo' husband?

MRS. ROBERTS: *(Beginning her professional whine)* He ain't much and I ain't much and my chillun is poly. We ain't got 'nough to eat! Lawd, Mr. Clarke, gimme a lil piece of side meat to cook us a pot of greens.

CLARKE: Aw gwan, Sister Roberts. You got plenty bacon home. Last week Jake bought . . .

MRS. ROBERTS: *(Frantically)* Lawd, Mist' Clarke, how long you think dat lil piece of meat last me an' my chillun? Lawd, me and my chillun is *hongry!* God knows, Jake don't fee-eed me! *(MR. CLARKE sits unmoved. MRS. ROBERTS advances upon him)* Mist' Clarke!

CLARKE: I God, woman, don't keep on after me! Every time I look, youse round here beggin' for everything you see.

LIGE: And whut she don't see she whoops for it just de same.

MRS. ROBERTS: *(In dramatic begging pose)* Mist' Clarke! Ain't you goin' do nuthin' for me? And you see me and my poor chillun is starvin'. . . .

CLARKE: *(Exasperated, rises)* I God, woman, a man can't git no peace wid somebody like you in town. *(He goes angrily into the store followed by MRS. ROBERTS. The boy sits down on the edge of the porch sucking the baby's thumb.)*

VOICE OF MRS. ROBERTS: A piece 'bout dis wide. . . .

VOICE OF CLARKE: I God, naw! Yo' husband done bought you plenty meat, nohow.

VOICE OF MRS. ROBERTS: *(In great anguish)* Ow! Mist' Clarke! Don't you cut dat lil tee-ninchy piece of meat for me and my chillun! *(Sound of running feet inside the store.)* I ain't a going to tetch it!

VOICE OF CLARKE: Well, don't touch it then. That's all you'll git outa me.

VOICE OF MRS. ROBERTS: *(Calmer)* Well, hand it chear den. Lawd, me and my chillun is *so* hongry. . . . Jake don't fee-eed me. *(She re-*

enters by door of store with the slab of meat in her hand and an outraged look on her face. She gazes all about her for sympathy.) Lawd, me and my poor chillun is *so* hungry . . . and some folks has *every*thing and they's so *stingy* and gripin'. . . . Lawd knows, Jake don't fee-eed me! *(She exits right on this line followed by the boy with the baby on his back.)*

    (All the men gaze behind her, then at each other and shake their heads.)

HAMBO: Poor Jake . . . I'm really sorry for dat man. If she was mine I'd beat her till her ears hung down like a Georgy mule.

WALTER THOMAS: I'd beat her till she smell like onions.

LIGE: I'd romp on her till she slack like lime.

NIXON: I'd stomp her till she rope like okra.

VOICE OF MRS. ROBERTS: *(Off stage right)* Lawd, Miz Lewis, you goin' give me dat lil han'ful of greens for me and my chillun. Why dat ain't a eyefull. I ought not to take 'em . . . but me and my chillun is *so* hongry . . . Some folks is so stingy and gripin'! Lawd knows, Jake don't *feed* me!

    (The noise of cane-chewing is heard again. Enter JOE LINDSAY left with a gun over his shoulder and the large leg bone of a mule in the other hand. He approaches the step wearily.)

HAMBO: Well, did you git any partridges, Joe?

JOE: *(Resting his gun and seating himself)* Nope, but I made de feathers fly.

HAMBO: I don't see no birds.

JOE: Oh, the feathers flew off on de birds.

LIGE: I don't see nothin' but dat bone. Look lak you done kilt a cow and et 'im raw out in de woods.

JOE: Don't y'all know dat hock-bone?

WALTER: How you reckon we gointer know every hock-bone in Orange County sight unseen?

JOE: *(Standing the bone up on the floor of the porch)* Dis is a hock-bone of Brazzle's ole yaller mule.

    (General pleased interest. Everybody wants to touch it.)

BRAZZLE: *(Coming forward)* Well, sir! *(Takes bone in both hands and looks up and down the length of it)* If 'tain't my ole mule! This sho was one hell of a mule, too. He'd fight every inch in front of de plow . . . he'd turn over de mowing machine . . . run away wid de wagon . . . and you better not look like you wanter *ride* 'im!

LINDSAY: *(Laughing)* Yeah, I 'member seein' you comin' down de road just so . . . *(he limps wid one hand on his buttocks)* one day.

BRAZZLE: Dis mule was so evil he used to try to bite and kick when I'd go in de stable to feed 'im.

WALTER: He was too mean to git fat. He was so skinny you could do a week's washing on his ribs for a washboard and hang 'em up on his hip-bones to dry.

LIGE: I 'member one day, Brazzle, you sent yo' boy to Winter Park after some groceries wid a basket. So here he went down de road ridin' dis mule wid dis basket on his arm. . . . Whut you reckon dat ole contrary mule done when he got to dat crooked place in de road going round Park Lake? He turnt right round and went through de handle of dat basket . . . wid de boy still up on his back. *(General laughter)*

BRAZZLE: Yeah, he up and died one Sat'day just for spite . . . but he was too contrary to lay down on his side like a mule orter and die decent. Naw, he made out to lay down on his narrer contracted back and die wid his feets sticking straight up in de air just so. *(He gets down on his back and illustrates.)* We drug him out to de swamp wid 'im dat way, didn't we, Hambo?

JOE CLARKE: I God, Brazzle, we all seen it. Didn't we all go to de draggin' out? More folks went to yo' mule's draggin' out than went to last school closing . . . Bet there ain't been a thing right in mule-hell for four years.

HAMBO: Been dat long since he been dead?

CLARKE: I God, yes. He died de week after I started to cuttin' dat new ground. *(The bone is passing from hand to hand. At last a boy about twelve takes it. He has just walked up and is proudly handling the bone when a woman's voice is heard off stage right.)*

VOICE: Senator! Senator!! Oh, you Senator?

BOY: *(Turning, displeased, mutters)* Aw, shux. *(Loudly)* Ma'm?

VOICE: If you don't come here you better!

SENATOR: Yes ma'am. *(He drops bone on ground down stage and trots off frowning.)* Soon as we men git to doing something dese wimmen. . . . *(Exits, right.)*

> *(Enter TEETS and BOOTSIE left, clean and primped in voile dresses just alike. They speak diffidently and enter store. The men admire them casually.)*

LIGE: Them girls done turned out to be right good-looking.

WALTER: Teets ain't as pretty now as she was a few years back. She used to be fat as a butter ball wid legs just like two whiskey-kegs. She's too skinny since she got her growth.

CODY: Ain't none of 'em pretty as dat Miss Daisy. God! She's pretty as a speckled pup.

LIGE: But she was sho nuff ugly when she was little . . . little ole hard black knot. She sho has changed since she been away up North. If she ain't pretty now, there ain't a hound dog in Georgy.

> *(Re-enter SENATOR BAILEY and stops on the steps. He addresses JOE CLARKE.)*

SENATOR: Mist' Clarke. . . .

HAMBO: *(To SENATOR)* Ain't you got no manners? We all didn't sleep wid you last night.

SENATOR: *(Embarrassed)* Good evening, everybody.

ALL THE MEN: Good evening, son, boy, Senator, etc.

SENATOR: Mist' Clarke, mama said is Daisy been here dis evenin'?

JOE CLARKE: Ain't laid my eyes on her. Ain't she working over in Maitland?

SENATOR: Yessuh . . . but she's off today and mama sent her down here to get de groceries.

JOE CLARKE: Well, tell yo' ma I ain't seen her.

SENATOR: Well, she say to tell you when she come, to tell her ma say she better git hime and dat quick.

JOE CLARKE: I will. *(Exit BOY right.)*

LIGE: Bet she's off somewhere wid Dave or Jim.

WALTER: I don't bet it . . . I know it. She's got them two in de go-long.

> *(Re-enter TEETS and BOOTSIE from store. TEETS has a letter and BOOTSIE two or three small parcels. The men look up with interest as they come out on the porch.)*

WALTER: *(Winking)* Whut's dat you got, Teets . . . letter from Dave?

TEETS: *(Flouncing)* Naw indeed! It's a letter from my B-I-T-sweetie! *(Rolls her eyes and hips.)*

WALTER: *(Winking)* Well, ain't Dave yo' B-I-T-sweetie? I thought y'all was 'bout to git married. Everywhere I looked dis summer 'twas you and Dave, Bootsie and Jim. I thought all of y'all would've done jumped over de broomstick by now.

TEETS: *(Flourishing letter)* Don't tell it to me . . . tell it to the ever-loving Mr. Albert Johnson way over in Apopka.

BOOTSIE: *(Rolling her eyes)* Oh, tell 'em 'bout the ever-loving Mr. Jimmy Cox from Altamont. Oh, I can't stand to see my baby lose.

HAMBO: It's lucky y'all girls done got some more fellers, cause look like Daisy done treed both Jim and Dave at once, or they done treed her one.

TEETS: Let her have 'em . . . nobody don't keer. They don't handle de "In God we trust" lak my Johnson. He's head bellman at de hotel.

BOOTSIE: Mr. Cox get money's grandma and old grandpa change. *(The girls exit huffily.)*

LINDSAY: *(To HAMBO, pseudo-seriously)* You oughtn't tease dem gals lak dat.

HAMBO: Oh, I laks to see gals all mad. But dem boys *is* crazy sho nuff. Before Daisy come back here they both had a good-looking gal a piece. Now they 'bout to fall out and fight over half a gal a piece. Neither one won't give over and let de other one have her.

LIGE: And she ain't thinking too much 'bout no one man. *(Looks off left.)* Here she come now. God! She got a mean walk on her!

WALTER: Yeah, man. She handles a lot of traffic! Oh, mama, throw it in de river . . . papa'll come git it!

LINDSAY: Aw, shut up, you married men!

LIGE: Man don't go blind cause he gits married, do he? *(Enter DAISY hurriedly. Stops at step a moment. She is dressed in sheer organdie, white shoes and stockings.)*

DAISY: Good evening, everybody. *(Walks up on the porch.)*

ALL THE MEN: *(Very pleasantly)* Good evening, Miss Daisy.

DAISY: *(To CLARK)* Mama sent me after some meal and flour and some bacon and sausage oil.

CLARKE: Senator been here long time ago hunting you.

DAISY: *(Frightened)* Did he? Oo . . . Mist' Clarke, hurry up and fix it for me. *(She starts on in the store.)*

LINDSAY: *(Giving her his seat)* You better wait here, Daisy. *(WALTER kicks LIGE to call his attention to LINDSAY's attitude)* It's powerful hot in dat store. Lemme run fetch 'em out to you.

LIGE: *(To LINDSAY)* Run! Joe Lindsay, you ain't been able to run since de big bell rung. Look at dat gray beard.

LINDSAY: Thank God, I ain't gray all over. I'm just as good a man right now as any of you young 'uns. *(He hurries on into the store.)*

WALTER: Daisy, where's yo' two body guards? It don't look natural to see you thout nary one of 'em.

DAISY: *(Archly)* I ain't got no body guards. I don't know what you talkin' about.

LIGE: Aw, don' try to come dat over us, Daisy. You know who we talkin' 'bout all right . . . but if you want me to come out flat footed . . . where's Jim and Dave?

DAISY: Ain't they playin' somewhere for de white folks?

LIGE: *(To WALTER)* Will you listen at dis gal, Walter? *(To DAISY)* When I ain't been long seen you and Dave going down to de Lake.

DAISY: *(Frightened)* Don't y'all run tell mama where I been.

WALTER: Well, you tell us which one you laks de best and we'll wipe our mouf *(Gesture)* and say nothin'. Dem boys been de best of friends all they life, till both of 'em took after you . . . then good-bye, Katy bar de door!

DAISY: *(Affected innocence)* Ain't they still playin' and dancin' together?

LIGE: Yeah, but that's 'bout all they do 'gree on these days. That's de way it is wid men, young and old. . . . I don't keer how long they been friends and how thick they been . . . a woman kin come between 'em. David and Jonather never would have been friends so long if Jonather had of been any great hand wid de wimmen. You ain't never seen no two roosters that likes one another.

DAISY: I ain't tried to break 'em up.

WALTER: Course you ain't. You don't have to. All two boys need to do is go git stuck on de same girl and they done broke up . . . *right now!* Wimmen is something can't be divided equal.

> *(Re-enter JOE LINDSAY and CLARKE with the groceries. DAISY jumps up and grabs the packages.)*

LIGE: *(To DAISY)* Want some of us . . . me . . . to go long and tote yo' things for you?

DAISY: *(Nervously)* Naw, mama is riding her high horse today. Long as I been gone it wouldn't do for me to come walking up wid nobody. *(She exits hurriedly right.)*

> *(All the men watch her out of sight in silence.)*

CLARKE: *(Sighing)* I God, know whut Daisy puts me in de mind of?

HAMBO: No, what? *(They all lean together.)*

CLARKE: I God, a great big mango . . . a sweet smell, you know, with a strong flavor, but not something you could mash up like a strawberry. Something with a body to it.

> *(General laughter, but not obscene.)*

HAMBO: *(Admiringly)* Joe Clarke! I didn't know you had it in you! *(MRS. CLARKE enters from store door and they all straighten up guiltily)*

CLARKE: *(Angrily to his wife)* Now whut do you want? I God, the minute I set down, here you come. . . .

MRS. CLARKE: Somebody want a stamp, Jody. You know you don't 'low me to bove wid de post office. *(He rises sullenly and goes inside the store.)*

BRAZZLE: Say, Hambo, I didn't see you at our Sunday School picnic.

HAMBO: *(Slicing some plug-cut tobacco)* Nope, wan't there dis time.

WALTER: Looka here, Hambo. Y'all Baptist carry dis close-communion business too far. If a person ain't half drownded in de lake and half et up by alligators, y'all think he ain't baptized, so you can't take communion wid him. Now I reckon you can't even drink lemonade and eat chicken perlow wid us.

HAMBO: My Lord, boy, youse just *full* of words. Now, in de first place, if this year's picnic was lak de one y'all had last year . . . you ain't had no lemonade for us Baptists to turn down. You had a big ole barrel of rain water wid about a pound of sugar in it and one lemon cut up over de top of it.

LIGE: Man, you sho kin mold 'em!

WALTER: Well, I went to de Baptist picnic wid my mouf all set to eat chicken, when lo and behold y'all had chitlings! Do Jesus!

LINDSAY: Hold on there a minute. There was plenty chicken at dat picnic, which I do know is right.

WALTER: Only chicken I seen was a half a chicken yo' pastor musta tried to swaller whole cause he was choked stiff as a board when I come long . . . wid de whole deacon's board beating him in de back, trying to knock it out his throat.

LIGE: Say, dat puts me in de mind of a Baptist brother that was crazy 'bout de preachers and de preacher was crazy 'bout feeding his face. So his son got tired of trying to beat dese stump-knockers to de grub on the table, so one day he throwed out some slams 'bout dese preachers. Dat made his old man mad, so he tole his son to git out. He boy ast him, "Where must I go, papa?" He says, "Go on to hell I reckon. . . . I don't keer where you go."

So de boy left and was gone seven years. He come back one cold, windy night and rapped on de door. "Who dat?" de old man ast him. "It's me, Jack." De old man opened de door, so glad to see his son agin, and tole Jack to come in. He did and looked all round de place. Seven or eight preachers was sitting round de fire eatin' and drinkin'.

"Where you been all dis time, Jack?" de old man ast him. "I been to hell," Jack tole him.

"Tell us how it is down there, Jack."

"Well," he says, "It's just like it is here . . . you cain't git to de fire for de preachers."

HAMBO: Boy, you kin lie just like de cross-ties from Jacksonville to Key

West. De presidin' elder must come round on his circuit teaching y'all how to tell 'em, cause you couldn't lie dat good just natural.

WALTER: Can't nobody beat Baptist folks lying . . . and I ain't never found out how come you think youse so important.

LINDSAY: Ain't we got de finest and de biggest church? Macedonia Baptist will hold more folks than any two buildings in town.

LIGE: Thass right, y'all got a heap more church than you got members to go in it.

HAMBO: Thass all right . . . y'all ain't got neither de church nor de members. Everything that's had in this town got to be held in our church. *(Re-enter JOE CLARKE.)*

CLARKE: What you-all talkin'?

HAMBO: Come on out, Tush Hawg, lemme beat you some checkers. I'm tired of fending and proving wid dese boys ain't got no hair on they chest yet.

CLARKE: I God, you mean you gointer get beat. You can't handle me. . . . I'm a tush hawg.

HAMBO: Well, I'm going to draw dem tushes right now. *(To two small boys using checker board on edge of porch.)* Here you chilluns, let de Mayor and me have that board. Go on out an' play an' give us grown folks a little peace. *(The children go down stage and call out:)*

SMALL BOY: Hey, Senator. Hey, Marthy. Come on let's play chick-me, chick-me, cranie-crow.

CHILD'S VOICE: *(Off stage)* All right! Come on, Jessie! *(Enter several children, led by SENATOR, and a game begins in front of the store as JOE CLARKE and HAMBO play checkers.)*

JOE CLARKE: I God! Hambo, you can't play no checkers.

HAMBO: *(As they seat themselves at the checker board)* Aw, man, if you wasn't de Mayor I'd beat you all de time.

> *(The children get louder and louder, drowning out the men's voices.)*

SMALL GIRL: I'm gointer be de hen.

BOY: And I'm gointer be de hawk. Lemme git maself a stick to mark wid.

> *(The boy who is the hawk squats center stage with a short twig in his hand. The largest girl lines up the other children behind her.)*

GIRL: *(Mother Hen)* *(Looking back over her flock)* Y'all ketch holt of one 'nother's clothes so de hawk can't git yuz. *(They do.)* You all straight now?

CHILDREN: Yeah. *(The march around the hawk commences.)*

HEN AND CHICKS: Chick mah chick mah craney crow
    Went to de well to wash ma toe
    When I come back ma chick was gone
    What time, ole witch?
HAWK: *(Making a tally on the ground)* One!
HEN AND CHICKS: *(Repeat song and march.)*
HAWK: *(Scoring again)* Two! *(Can be repeated any number of times.)*
HAWK: Four. *(He rises and imitates a hawk flying and trying to catch a chicken. Calling in a high voice:)* Chickee.
HEN: *(Flapping wings to protect her young)* My chickens sleep.
HAWK: Chickee. *(During all this the hawk is feinting and darting in his efforts to catch a chicken, and the chickens are dancing defensively, the hen trying to protect them.)*
HEN: My chicken's sleep.
HAWK: I shall have a chick.
HEN: You shan't have a chick.
HAWK: I'm goin' home. *(Flies off)*
HEN: Dere's de road.
HAWK: My pot's a boilin'.
HEN: Let it boil.
HAWK: My guts a growlin'.
HEN: Let 'em growl.
HAWK: I must have a chick.
HEN: You shan't have n'airn.
HAWK: My mama's sick.
HEN: Let her die.
HAWK: Chickie!
HEN: My chicken's sleep. *(HAWK darts quickly around the hen and grabs a chicken and leads him off and places the captive on his knees at the store porch. After a brief bit of dancing he catches another, then a third, etc.)*
HAMBO: *(At the checker board, his voice rising above the noise of the playing children, slapping his sides jubilantly)* Ha! Ha! I got you now. Go ahead on and move, Joe Clarke . . . jus' go ahead on and move.
LOUNGERS: *(Standing around two checker players)* Ol' Deacon's got you now.
ANOTHER VOICE: Don't see how he can beat the Mayor like that.
ANOTHER VOICE: Got him in the Louisville loop. *(These remarks are drowned by the laughter of the playing children directly in front of the porch. MAYOR JOE CLARKE disturbed in his concentration on the*

checkers and peeved at being beaten suddenly turns toward the children, throwing up his hands.)

CLARKE: Get on 'way from here, you limbs of Satan, making all that racket so a man can't hear his ears. Go on, go on! *(THE MAYOR looks about excitedly for the town marshall. Seeing him playing cards on the other side of porch, he bellows:)* Lum Boger, whyn't you git these kids away from here! What kind of a marshall is you? All this passle of young'uns around here under grown people's feet, creatin' disorder in front of my store. *(LUM BOGER puts his cards down lazily, comes down stage and scatters the children away. One saucy little girl refuses to move.)*

LUM BOGER: Why'nt you go on away from here, Matilda? Didn't you hear me tell you-all to move?

LITTLE MATILDA: *(Defiantly)* I ain't goin' nowhere. You ain't none of my mama. *(Jerking herself free from him as LUM touches her.)* My mama in the store and she told me to wait out here. So take that, ol' Lum.

LUM BOGER: You impudent little huzzy, you! You must smell your-self . . . youse so fresh.

MATILDA: The wind musta changed and you smell your own top lip.

LUM BOGER: Don't make me have to grab you and take you down a buttonhole lower.

MATILDA: *(Switching her little head)* Go ahead on and grab me. You sho can't kill me, and if you kill me, you sho can't eat me. *(She marches into the store.)*

SENATOR: *(Derisively from behind stump)* Ol' dumb Lum! Hey! Hey! *(LITTLE BOY at edge of stage thumbs his nose at the marshall.) (LUM lumbers after the small boy. Both exit.)*

HAMBO: *(To CLARKE who has been thinking all this while what move to make)* You ain't got but one move . . . go ahead on and make it. What's de matter, Mayor?

CLARKE: *(Moving his checker)* Aw, here.

HAMBO: *(Triumphant)* Now! Look at him, boys. I'm gonna laugh in notes. *(Laughing to the scale and jumping a checker each time)* Do, sol, fa, me, lo . . . one! *(Jumping another checker)* La, sol, fa, me, do . . . two! *(Another jump.)* Do, sol, re, me, lo . . . three! *(Jumping a third.)* Lo, sol, fa, me, re . . . four! *(The crowd begins to roar with laughter. LUM BOGER returns, looking on. Children come drifting back again playing chick-me-chick-me-cranie crow.)*

VOICE: Oh, ha! Done got the ol' tush hog.

ANOTHER VOICE: Thought you couldn't be beat, Brother Mayor?

CLARKE: *(Peeved, gets up and goes into the store mumbling)* Oh, I coulda beat you if I didn't have this store on my mind. Saturday afternoon and I got work to do. Lum, ain't I told you to keep them kids from playin' right in front of this store? *(LUM makes a pass at the nearest half-grown boy. The kids dart around him teasingly.)*

ANOTHER VOICE: Eh, heh . . . Hambo done run him in his store . . . done run the ol' coon in his hole.

ANOTHER VOICE: That ain't good politics, Hambo, beatin' the Mayor.

ANOTHER VOICE: Well, Hambo, you done got to be so hard at checkers, come on let's see what you can do with de cards. Lum Boger there got his hands full nursin' the chilluns.

ANOTHER VOICE: *(At the table)* We ain't playin' for money, nohow, Deacon. We just playin' a little Florida Flip.

HAMBO: Ya all can't play no Florida Flip. When I was a sinner there wasn't a man in this state could beat me playin' that game. But I'm a deacon in Macedonia Baptist now and I don't bother with the cards no more.

VOICE AT CARD TABLE: All right, then, come on here Tony *(To man with basket on steps.)* let me catch your jack.

TAYLOR: *(Looking toward door)* I don't reckon I got time. I guess my wife gonna get through buying out that store some time or other and want to go home.

OLD MAN: *(On opposite side of porch from card game)* I bet my wife would know better than expect me to sit around and wait for her with a basket. Whyn't you tell her to tote it on home herself?

TAYLOR: *(Sighing and shaking his head)* Eh, Lawd!

VOICE AT CARD TABLE: Look like we can't get nobody to come into this game. Seem like everybody's scared a us. Come on back here, Lum, and take your hand. *(LUM makes a final futile gesture at the children.)*

LUM: Ain't I tole you little haitians to stay away from here?

> *(CHILDREN scatter teasingly only to return to their play in front of the store later on. LUM comes up on the porch and re-joins the card game. Just as he gets seated, MRS. CLARKE comes to the door of the store and calls him.)*

MRS. CLARKE: *(Drawlingly)* Columbus!

LUM: *(Wearily)* Ma'am?

MRS. CLARKE: De Mayor say for you to go round in de back yard and tie up old lady Jackson's mule what's trampin' sup all de tomatoes in my garden.

LUM: All right. *(Leaving card game.)* Wait till I come back, folkses.

LIGE: Oh, hum! *(Yawning and putting down the deck of cards)* Lum's sho a busy marshall. Say, ain't Dave and Jim been round here yet? I feel kinder like hearin' a little music 'bout now.

BOY: Naw, they ain't been here today. You-all know they ain't so thick nohow as they was since Daisy Bailey come back and they started runnin' after her.

WOMAN: You mean since she started runnin' after them, the young hussy.

MRS. CLARKE: *(In doorway)* She don't mean 'em no good.

WALTER: That's a shame, ain't it now? *(Enter LUM from around back of store. He jumps on the porch and takes his place at the card box.)*

LUM: *(To the waiting players)* All right, boys! Turn it on and let the bad luck happen.

LIGE: My deal. *(He begins shuffling the cards with an elaborate fan-shape movement.)*

VOICE AT TABLE: Look out there, Lige, you shuffling mighty lot. Don't carry the cub to us.

LIGE: Aw, we ain't gonna beat you . . . we gonna beat you. *(He slams down the cards for LUM BOGER to cut.)* Wanta cut 'em?

LUM: No, ain't no need of cutting a rabbit out when you can twist him out. Deal 'em. *(LIGE deals out the cards.)*

CLARKE'S VOICE: *(Inside the store)* You, Mattie! *(MRS. CLARKE, who has been standing in the door, quickly turns and goes inside.)*

LIGE: Y-e-e-e! Spades! *(The game is started.)*

LUM: Didn't snatch that jack, did you?

LIGE: Aw, no, ain't snatched no jack. Play.

WALTER: *(LUM's partner)* Well, here it is, partner. What you want me to play for you?

LUM: Play jus' like I'm in New York, partner. But we gotta try to catch that jack.

LIGE: *(Threateningly)* Stick out your hand and draw back a nub. *(WAL-TER THOMAS plays.)*

WALTER: I'm playin' a diamond for you, partner.

LUM: I done tole you you ain't got no partner.

LIGE: Heh, Heh! Partner, we got 'em. Pull off wid your king. Dey got to play 'em. *(When that trick is turned, triumphantly:)* Didn't I tell you, partner? *(Stands on his feet and slams down with his ace violently)* Now, come up under this ace. Aw, hah, look at ol' low, partner. I knew I was gonna catch 'em. *(When LUM plays)* Ho, ho, there goes the queen . . . Now, the jack's a gentlemen. . . . Now, I'm playin' my knots. *(Everybody plays and the hand is ended.)* Partner, high, low, jack and the game and four.

WALTER: Give me them cards. I believe you-all done give me the cub that time. Look at me . . . this is Booker T. Washington dealing these cards. *(Shuffles cards grandly and gives them to LIGE to cut.)* Wanta cut 'em?

LIGE: Yeah, cut 'em and shoot 'em. I'd cut behind my ma. *(He cuts the cards.)*

WALTER: *(Turning to player at left, FRANK, LIGE's partner)* What you saying, Frank?

FRANK: I'm beggin'. *(LIGE is trying to peep at cards.)*

WALTER: *(Turning to LIGE)* Stop peepin' at them cards, Lige. *(To FRANK)* Did you say you was beggin' or standin'?

FRANK: I'm beggin'.

WALTER: Get up off your knees. Go ahead and tell 'em I sent you.

FRANK: Well, that makes us four.

WALTER: I don't care if you is. *(Pulls a quarter out of his pocket and lays it down on the box.)* Twenty-five cents says I know the best one. Let's go. *(Everybody puts down a quarter.)*

FRANK: What you want me to play for you partner?

LIGE: Play me a club. *(The play goes around to dealer, WALTER, who gets up and takes the card off the top of the deck and slams it down on the table.)*

WALTER: Get up ol' deuce of deamonds and gallop off with your load. *(To LUM)* Partner, how many times you seen the deck?

LUM: Two times.

WALTER: Well, then I'm gonna pull off, partner. Watch this ol' queen. *(Everyone plays)* Ha! Ha! Wash day and no soap. *(Takes the jack of diamonds and sticks him up on his forehead. Stands up on his feet.)* Partner, I'm dumping to you . . . play your king. *(When it comes to his play LUM, too, stands up. The others get up and they, too, excitedly slam their cards down.)* Now, come on in this kitchen and let me splice that cabbage! *(He slams down the ace of diamonds. Pats the jack on his forehead, sings:)* Hey, hey, back up, jenny, get your load. *(Talking)* Dump to that jack, boys, dump to it. High, low, jack and the game and four. One to go. We're four wid you, boys.

LIGE: Yeah, but you-all playin' catch-up.

FRANK: Gimme them cards . . . lemme deal some.

LIGE: Frank, now you really got responsibility on you. They's got one game on us.

FRANK: Aw, man, I'm gonna deal 'em up a mess. This deal's in the White House. *(He shuffles and puts the cards down for WALTER to cut.)* Cut 'em.

WALTER: Nope, I never cut green timber. *(FRANK deals and turns the card up.)*

FRANK: Hearts, boys. *(He turns up an ace.)*

LUM: Aw, you snatched that ace, nigger.

WALTER: Yeah, they done carried the cub to us, partner.

LIGE: Oh, he didn't do no such a thing. That ace was turned fair. We jus' too hard for you . . . we eats our dinner out a the blacksmith shop.

WALTER: Aw, you all cheatin'. You know it wasn't fair.

FRANK: Aw, shut up, you all jus' whoopin' and hollerin' for nothin'. Tryin' to bully the game. *(FRANK and LIGE rise and shake hands grandly.)*

LIGE: Mr. Hoover, you sho is a noble president. We done stuck these niggers full of cobs. They done got scared to play us.

LUM: Scared to play you? Get back down to this table, let me spread my mess.

LOUNGER: Yonder comes Elder Simms. You all better squat that rabbit. They'll be having you all up in the church for playin' cards.

> *(FRANK grabs up the cards and puts them in his pocket quickly. Everybody picks up the money and looks unconcerned as the preacher enters. Enter ELDER SIMMS with his two prim-looking little children by the hand.)*

ELDER SIMMS: How do, children. Right warm for this time in November, ain't it?

VOICE: Yes sir, Reverend, sho is. How's Sister Simms?

SIMMS: She's feelin' kinda po'ly today. *(Goes on in store with his children)*

VOICE: *(Whispering loudly)* Don't see how that great big ole powerful woman could be sick. Look like she could go bear huntin' with her fist.

ANOTHER VOICE: She look jus' as good as you-all's Baptist pastor's wife. Pshaw, you ain't seen no big woman, nohow, man. I seen one once so big she went to whip her little boy and he run up under her belly and hid six months 'fore she could find him.

ANOTHER VOICE: Well, I knowed a woman so little that she had to get up on a soap box to look over a grain of sand.

> *(REV. SIMMS comes out of store, each child behind him sucking a stick of candy.)*

SIMMS: *(To his children)* Run on home to your mother and don't get dirty on the way. *(The two children start primly off down the street but just out of sight one of them utters a loud cry.)*

SIMMS'S CHILD: *(Off stage)* Papa, papa. Nunkie's trying to lick my candy.

SIMMS: I told you to go on and leave them other children alone.

VOICE ON PORCH: *(Kidding)* Lum, whyn't you tend to your business.

> *(TOWN MARSHALL rises and shoos the children off again.)*

LUM: You all varmints leave them nice chillun alone.

LIGE: *(Continuing the lying on porch)* Well, you all done seen so much, but I bet you ain't never seen a snake as big as the one I saw when I was a boy up in middle Georgia. He was so big couldn't hardly move his self. He laid in one spot so long he growed moss on him and everybody thought he was a log, till one day I set down on him and went to sleep, and when I woke up that snake done crawled to Florida. *(Loud laughter.)*

FRANK: *(Seriously)* Layin' all jokes aside though now, you all remember that rattlesnake I killed last year was almost as big as that Georgia snake.

VOICE: How big, you say it was, Frank?

FRANK: Maybe not quite as big as that, but jus' about fourteen feet.

VOICE: *(Derisively)* Gimme that lyin' snake. That snake wasn't but four foot long when you killed him last year and you done growed him ten feet in a year.

ANOTHER VOICE: Well, I don't know about that. Some of the snakes around here is powerful long. I went out in my front yard yesterday right after the rain and killed a great big ol' cottonmouth.

SIMMS: This sho is a snake town. I certainly can't raise no chickens for 'em. They kill my little biddies jus' as fast as they hatch out. And yes . . . if I hadn't cut them weeds out of the street in front of my parsonage, me or some of my folks woulda been snake-bit right at our front door. *(To whole crowd)* Whyn't you all cut down these weeds and clean up these streets?

HAMBO: Well, the Mayor ain't said nothin' 'bout it.

SIMMS: When the folks misbehaves in this town I think they oughta lock 'em up in a jail and make 'em work their fine out on the streets, then these weeds would be cut down.

VOICE: How we gonna do that when we ain't got no jail?

SIMMS: Well, you sho needs a jail . . . you-all needs a whole lot of improvements round this town. I ain't never pastored no town so way-back as this one here.

CLARKE: *(Who has lately emerged from the store, fanning himself, overhears this last remark and bristles up)* What's that you say 'bout this town?

SIMMS: I say we needs some improvements here in this town . . . that's what.

CLARKE: *(In a powerful voice)* And what improvements you figgers we needs?

SIMMS: A whole heap. Now, for one thing we really does need a jail, Mayor. We oughta stop runnin' these people out of town that misbehaves, and lock 'em up. Others towns has jails, everytown I ever pastored had a jail. Don't see how come we can't have one.

CLARKE: *(Towering angrily above the preacher)* Now, wait a minute, Simms. Don't you reckon the man who knows how to start a town knows how to run it? I paid two hundred dollars out of this right hand for this land and walked out here and started this town befo' you was born. I ain't like some of you new niggers, come here when grapes' ripe. I was here to cut new ground, and I been Mayor ever since.

SIMMS: Well, there ain't no sense in no one man stayin' Mayor all the time.

CLARKE: Well, it's my town and I can be mayor jus' as long as I want to. It was me that put this town on the map.

SIMMS: What map you put it on, Joe Clarke? I ain't seen it on no map.

CLARKE: *(Indignant)* I God! Listen here, Elder Simms. If you don't like the way I run this town, just' take your flat feets right on out and git yonder crost the woods. You ain't been here long enough to say nothin' nohow.

HAMBO: *(From a nail keg)* Yeah, you Methodist niggers always telling people how to run things.

TAYLOR: *(Practically unheard by the others)* We do so know how to run things, don't we? Ain't Brother Mayor a Methodist, and ain't the schoolteacher a . . . ? *(His remarks are drowned out by the others.)*

SIMMS: No, we don't like the way you're runnin' things. Now looka here. *(Pointing at the Marshall)* You got that lazy Lum Boger here for marshall and he ain't old enough to be dry behind his ears yet . . . and all these able-bodied mens in this town! You won't 'low nobody else to run a store 'ceptin' you. And looka yonder *(happening to notice the street light)* only street lamp in town, you got in front of your place. *(Indignantly)* We pay the taxes and you got the lamp.

VILLAGER: Don't you-all fuss now. How come you two always yam-yamming at each other?

CLARKE: How come this fly-by-night Methodist preacher over here . . . ain't been here three months . . . tries to stand up on my store porch and tries to tell me how to run my town? *(MATTIE CLARKE, the Mayor's wife, comes timidly to the door, wiping her hands on her apron.)* Ain't no man gonna tell me how to run my town. I God, I 'lected myself in and I'm gonna run it. *(Turns and sees wife standing in door. Commandingly.)* I God, Mattie, git on back in there and wait on that store!

MATTIE: *(Timidly)* Jody, somebody else wantin' stamps.

CLARKE: I God, woman, what good is you? Gwan, git in. Look like between women and preachers a man can't have no peace. *(Exit CLARKE.)*

SIMMS: *(Continuing his argument)* Now, when I pastored in Jacksonville you oughta see what kinda jails they got there . . .

LOUNGER: White folks needs jails. We colored folks don't need no jail.

ANOTHER VILLAGER: Yes, we do, too. Elder Simms is right . . .

(The argument becomes a hubbub of voices.)

TAYLOR: *(Putting down his basket)* Now, I tell you a jail . . .

MRS. TAYLOR: *(Emerging from the store door, arms full of groceries, looking at her husband)* Yeah, and if you don't shut up and git these rations home I'm gonna be worse on you than a jail and six judges. Pickup that basket let's go. *(TONY meekly picks up the basket and he and his wife exit as the sound of an approaching guitar is heard off stage.)*

> *(Two carelessly dressed, happy-go-lucky fellows enter together. One is fingering a guitar without playing any particular tune, and the other has his hat cocked over his eyes in a burlesque, dude-like manner. There are casual greetings.)*

WALTER: Hey, there, bums, how's tricks?

LIGE: What yo' sayin', boys?

HAMBO: Good evenin', sons.

LIGE: How did you-all make out this evening, boys?

JIM: Oh, them white folks at the party shelled out right well. Kept Dave busy pickin' it up. How much did we make today, Dave?

DAVE: *(Striking his pocket)* I don't know, boy, but feels right heavy here. Kept me pickin' up money just like this . . . *(As JIM picks a few dance chords, DAVE gives a dance imitation of how he picked up the coins from the ground as the white folks threw them.)* We count it after while. Woulda divided up with you already if you hadn't left me when you seen Daisy comin' by. Let's sit down on the porch and rest now.

LIGE: She sho is lookin' stylish and pretty since she come back with her white folks from up North. Wearin' the swellest clothes. And that coal-black hair of hers jus' won't quit.

MATTIE CLARKE: *(In doorway)* I don't see what the mens always hanging after Daisy Taylor for.

CLARKE: *(Turning around on the porch)* I God, you back here again. Who's tendin' that store? *(MATTIE disappears inside.)*

DAVE: Well, she always did look like new money to me when she was here before.

JIM: Well, that's all you ever did get was a look.

DAVE: That's all you know! I bet I get more than that now.

JIM: You might git it but I'm the man to use it. I'm a bottom fish.

DAVE: Aw, man. You musta been walking round here fast asleep when Daisy was in this county last. You ain't seen de go I had with her.

JIM: No, I ain't seen it. Bet you didn't have no letter from her while she been away.

DAVE: Bet you didn't neither.

JIM: Well, it's just cause she can't write. If she knew how to scratch with a pencil I'd had a ton of 'em.

DAVE: Shaw, man! I'd had a post office full of 'em.

OLD WOMAN: You-all ought to be shame, carrying on over a brazen heifer like Daisy Taylor. Jus' cause she's been up North and come back, I reckon you cutting de fool sho 'nough now. She ain't studying none of you-all nohow. All she wants is what you got in your pocket.

JIM: I likes her but she won't git nothin' outa me. She never did. I wouldn't give a poor consumpted cripple crab a crutch to cross the River Jurdon.

DAVE: I know I ain't gonna give no woman nothin'. I wouldn't give a dog a doughnut if he treed a terrapin.

LIGE: Youse a cottontail dispute . . . both of you. You'd give her anything you got. You'd give her Georgia with a fence 'round it.

OLD MAN: Yeah, and she'd take it, too.

LINDSAY: Don't distriminate the woman like that. That ain't nothing but hogism. Ain't nothin' the matter with Daisy, she's all right. *(Enter TEETS and BOOTSIE tittering coyly and switching themselves.)*

BOOTSIE: Is you seen my mama?

OLD WOMAN: You know you ain't lookin' for no mama. Jus' come back down here to show your shape and fan around awhile. *(BOOTSIE and TEETS going into the store.)*

BOOTSIE and TEETS: No, we ain't. We'se come to get our mail.

OLD WOMAN: *(After girls enter store)* Why don't you all keep up some attention to these nice girls here, Bootsie and Teets. They wants to marry.

DAVE: Aw, who thinkin' 'bout marryin' now? They better stay home and eat their own pa's rations. I gotta buy myself some shoes.

JIM: The woman I'm gonna marry ain't born yet and her maw is dead. *(GIRLS come out giggling and exit.)* *(JIM begins to strum his guitar lightly at first as the talk goes on.)*

CLARKE: *(To DAVE and JIM)* Two of the finest gals that ever lived and friendly jus' like you-all is. You two boys better take 'em back and stop them shiftless ways.

HAMBO: Yeah, hurry up and do somethin'! I wants to taste a piece yo' weddin' cake.

JIM: *(Embarrassed but trying to be jocular)* Whut you trying to rush me up so fast? . . . Look at Will Cody here *(pointing to little man on porch)* he been promising to bring his already wife down for two months . . . and nair one of us ain't seen her yet.

DAVE: Yeah, how you speck me to haul in a brand new wife when he can't lead a wagon-broke wife eighteen miles? Me, I'm going git one soon's Cody show me his'n. *(General sly laughter at CODY's expense.)*

WALTER: *(Snaps his fingers and pretends to remember something)* Thass right, Cody. I been intending to tell you . . . I know where you kin buy a ready-built house for you and yo' wife. *(Calls into the store.)* Hey, Clarke, come on out here and tell Cody 'bout dat Bradley house. *(To CODY.)* I know you wants to git a place of yo' own so you kin settle down.

HAMBO: He done moved so much since he been here till every time he walk out in his back yeard his chickens lay down and cross they legs.

LINDSAY: Cody, I thought you tole us you was going up to Sanford to bring dat 'oman down here last Sat'day.

LIGE: That ain't de way he tole me 'bout it. Look, fellers, *(Getting up and putting one hand on his hips and one finger of the other hand against his chin coquettishly)* Where you reckon I'll be next Sat'day night? . . . Sittin' up side of Miz Cody. *(Great burst of laughter.)*

SYKES JONES: *(Laughing)* Know what de folks tole me in Sanford? Dat was another man's wife. *(Guffaws.)*

CODY: *(Feebly)* Aw, you don't know whut you talkin' bout.

JONES: Naw, I don't know, but de folks in Sanford does. *(Laughing)* Day tell me when dat lady's husband come home Sat'day night, ole Cody jumped out de window. De man grabbed his old repeater and run out in de yard to head him off. When Cody seen him come round de corner de house *(Gesture)* he flopped his wings and flew up on de fence. De man thowed dat shotgun dead on him. *(Laughs)* Den, man! Cody flopped his wings lak a buzzard *(Gesture)* and sailed on off. De man dropped to his knees lak dis *(Gesture of kneeling on one knee and taking aim)* Die! die! die! *(Supposedly sound of shots as the gun is moved in a circle following the course of Cody's supposed flight)* Cody just flew right on off and lit on a hill two miles off. Then, man! *(Gesture of swift flight)* In ten minutes he was back here in Eatonville and in he bed.

WALTER: I passed there and seen his house shakin', but I didn't know how come.

HAMBO: Aw, leave de boy alone. . . . If you don't look out some of y'all going to have to break his record.

LIGE: I'm prepared to break it now. *(General laughter.)*

JIM: Well, anyhow, I don't want to marry and leave Dave . . . yet awhile. *(Picking a chord.)*

DAVE: And I ain't gonna leave Jim. We been palling around together ever since we hollered titty mama, ain't we, boy?

JIM: Sho is. *(Music of the guitar increases in volume. DAVE shuffles a few steps and the two begin to sing.)*

JIM: Rabbit on the log.
    I ain't got no dog.

How am I gonna git him?

God knows.

DAVE: Rabbit on the log.

Ain't got no dog.

Shoot him with my rifle

Bam! Bam!

(Some of the villagers join in song and others get up and march around the porch in time with the music. BOOTSIE and TEETS re-enter, TEETS sticking her letter down the neck of her blouse. JOE LINDSAY grabs TEETS and WALTER THOMAS grabs BOOTSIE. There is dancing, treating and general jollification. Little children dance the parse-me-la. The music fills the air just as the sun begins to go down. Enter DAISY TAYLOR coming down the road toward the store.)

CLARKE: *(Bawls out from the store porch)* I God, there's Daisy again.

(Most of the dancing stops, the music slows down and then stops completely. DAVE and JIM greet DAISY casually as she approaches the porch.)

JIM: Well, Daisy, we knows you, too.

DAVE: Gal, youse jus' as pretty as a speckled pup.

DAISY: *(Giggling)* I see you two boys always playin' and singin' together. That music sounded right good floating down the road.

JIM: Yeah, child, we'se been playin' for the white folks all week. We'se playin' for the colored now.

DAVE: *(Showing off, twirling his dancing feet)* Yeah, we're standin' on our abstract and livin' on our income.

OLD MAN: Um-ump, but they ain't never workin'. Just round here playing as usual.

JIM: Some folks think you ain't workin' lessen you smellin' a mule. *(He sits back down on box and picks at his guitar.)* Think you gotta be beatin' a man to his barn every mornin'.

VOICE: Glad to be round home with we-all again, ain't you Daisy?

DAISY: Is I glad? I jus' got off special early this evenin' to come over here and see everybody. I was kinda 'fraid sundown would catch me 'fore I got round that lake. Don't know how I'm gonna walk back to my workin' place in the dark by muself.

DAVE: Don't no girl as good-lookin' as you is have to go home by herself tonight.

JIM: No, cause I'm here.

DAVE: *(To DAISY)* Don't you trust yourself round that like wid all them 'gators and moccasins with that nigger there, Daisy *(Pointing at JIM)* He's jus' full of rabbit blood. What you need is a real man . . . with good feet. *(Cutting a dance step.)*

DAISY: I ain't thinking 'bout goin' home yet. I'm goin' in the store.

JIM: What you want in the store?

DAISY: I want some gum.

DAVE: *(Starting toward door)* Girl, you don't have to go in there to git no gum. I'll go in there and buy you a carload of gum. What kind you want?

DAISY: Bubble gum. *(DAVE goes in the store with his hand in his pocket. The sun is setting and the twilight deepens.)*

JIM: *(Pulling package out of his pocket and laughing)* Here your gum, baby. What it takes to please the ladies, I totes it. I don't have to go get it, like Dave. What you gimme for it?

DAISY: A bushel and a peck, and a hug around the neck. *(She embraces JIM playfully. He hands her the gum, patting his shoulder as he sits on box)* Oh, thank you. Youse a ready man.

JIM: Yeah, there's a lot of good parts to me. You can have West Tampa if you want it.

DAISY: You always was a nice quiet boy, Jim.

DAVE: *(Emerging from the store with a package of gum)* Here's your gum, Daisy.

JIM: Oh, youse late. She's done got gum now. Chaw that yourself.

DAVE: *(Slightly peeved and surprised)* Hunh, you mighty fast here now with Daisy but you wasn't that fast gettin' out of that white man's chicken house last week.

JIM: Who you talkin' 'bout?

DAVE: Hoo-oo? *(Facetiously)* You ain't no owl. Your feet don't fit no limb.

JIM: Aw, nigger, hush.

DAVE: Aw, hush, yourself.

> *(He walks away for a minute as DAISY turns to meet some newcomers. DAVE throws his package of gum down on the ground. It breaks and several children scramble for the pieces. An old man, very drunk, carrying an empty jug enters on left and staggers tipsily across stage.) (MAYOR JOE CLARKE emerges from the store and looks about for his marshall.)*

CLARKE: *(Bellowing)* Lum Boger!

LUM BOGER: *(Eating a stalk of cane)* Yessir!

CLARKE: I God, Lum, take your lazy self off that keg and go light that town lamp. All summer long you eatin' up my melon, and all winter long you chawin' up my cane. What you think this town is payin' you for? Laying round here doin' nothin'? Can't you see it's gettin' dark?

> (*LUM ROGER rises lazily and takes the soap box down stage, stands on it to light the lamp, discovers no oil in it and goes in store. In a few moments he comes out of store, fills the lamp and lights it.*)

DAISY: (*Coming back toward JIM*) Ain't you all gonna play and sing a little somethin' for me? I ain't heard your all's music much for so long.

JIM: Play anything you want, Daisy. Don't make no difference what 'tis I can pick it. Where's that old coon, Dave? (*Looking around for his partner.*)

LIGE: (*Calling DAVE, who is leaning against post at opposite end of porch*) Come here, an' get warmed up for Daisy.

DAVE: Aw, ma throat's tired.

JIM: Leave the baby be.

DAISY: Come on, sing a little, Dave.

DAVE: (*Going back toward JIM*) Well, seeing who's asking . . . all right. What song you like, Daisy?

DAISY: Um-m. Lemme think.

VOICE ON PORCH: "Got on the train, didn't have no fare."

DAISY: (*Gaily*) Yes, that one. That's a good one.

> (*JIM begins to tune up. DAVE touches DAISY's hand.*)

VOICE: (*In fun*) Hunh, you all wouldn't play at the hall last week when we asked you.

VOICE OF SPITEFUL OLD WOMAN: Daisy wasn't here then.

ANOTHER VOICE: (*Teasingly*) All you got to do to some men is to shake a skirt tail in their face and they goes off their head.

DAVE: (*To JIM who is still tuning up*) Come if you're comin' boy, let's go if you gwine.

> (*The full melody of the guitar comes out in a lively, old-fashioned tune.*)

VOICE: All right now, boys, do it for Daisy jus' as good as you do for dem white folks over in Maitland.

DAVE and JIM: (*Beginning to sing*)

> Got on the train,
> Didn't have no fare,
> But I rode some,

I rode some.
Got on the train,
Didn't have no fare,
But I rode some,
But I rode some.
Got on the train,
Didn't have no fare,
Conductor asked me what I'm doin' there,
But I rode some!

Grabbed me by the neck
And led me to the door.
But I rode some,
But I rode some.
Grabbed me by the neck
And led me to the door.
But I rode some,
But I rode some.
Grabbed me by the neck,
And led me to the door.
Rapped me cross the head with a forty-four,
But I rode some!

First thing I saw in jail
Was a pot of peas.
But I rode some,
But I rode some.
First thing I saw in jail
Was a pot of peas.
But I rode some,
But I rode some.
The peas was good,
The meat was fat,
Fell in love with the chain gang jus' for that,
But I rode some.
   (DAVE acts out the song in dancing pantomime and when it ends
   there are shouts and general exclamations of approval from the
   crowd.)

VOICES: I don't blame them white folks for goin' crazy 'bout that . . .

OLD MAN: Oh, when I was a young boy I used to swing the gals round
  on that piece.

DAISY: *(To JIM)* Seem like your playin' gits better and better.

DAVE: *(Quickly)* And how 'bout my singin'? *(Everybody laughs.)*

VOICES IN THE CROWD: Ha! Ha! Ol' Dave's gittin' jealous when she speaks o' Jim.

JIM: *(To DAVE, in fun)* Ain't nothin' to it but my playin'. You ain't got no singin' voice. If that's singin', God's a gopher.

DAVE: *(Half-seriously)* My singin' is a whole lot better'n your playin'. You jus' go along and fram. The reason why the white folks gives us money is cause I'm singin'.

JIM: Yeah?

DAVE: And you can't dance.

VOICE IN THE CROWD: You oughta dance. Big as your feet is, Dave.

DAISY: *(Diplomatically)* Both of you all is wonderful and I would like to see Dave dance a little.

DAVE: There now, I told you. What did I tell you. *(To JIM)* Stop woofing and pick a little tune there so that I can show Daisy somethin'.

JIM: Pick a tune? I bet if you fool with me I'll pick your bones jus' like a buzzard did the rabbit. You can't sing and now you wants to dance.

DAVE: Yeah, and I'll lam your head. Come on and play, good-for-nothing.

JIM: All right, then. You say you can dance . . . show these people what you can do. But don't bring that little stuff I been seein' you doin' all these years. *(JIM plays and DAVE dances, various members of the crowd keep time with their hands and feet, DAISY looks on enjoying herself immensely.)*

DAISY: *(As DAVE cuts a very fancy step)* I ain't seen nothin' like this up North. Dave you sho hot.

   (As DAVE cuts a more complicated step the crowd applauds, but just as the show begins to get good, suddenly JIM stops playing.)

DAVE: *(Surprised)* What's the matter, buddy?

JIM: *(Envious of the attention DAVE has been getting from DAISY, disgustedly)* Oh, nigger, I'm tired of seein' you cut the fool. 'Sides that, I been playin' all afternoon for the white folks.

DAISY: But I though you was playin' for me now, Jim.

JIM: Yeah, I'd play all night long for you, but I'm gettin' sick of Dave round here showin' off. Let him git somethin' and play for himself if he can. *(An OLD MAN with a lighted lantern enters.)*

DAISY: *(Coyly)* Well, honey, play some more for me then, and don't mind Dave. I reckon he done danced enough. Play me "Shake That Thing."

OLD MAN WITH LANTERN: Sho, you ain't stopped, is you, boy? Music sound mighty good floatin' down that dark road.

OLD WOMAN: Yeah, Jim, go on play a little more. Don't get to acting so niggerish this evening.

DAVE: Aw, let the ol' darky alone. Nobody don't want to hear him play, nohow. I know I don't.

JIM: Well, I'm gonna play. *(And he begins to pick "Shake That Thing". TEETS and BOOTSIE begin to dance with LIGE MOSELY and FRANK WARRICK. As the tune gets good, DAVE cannot resist the music either.)*

DAVE: Old nigger's evil but he sho can play. *(He begins to do a few steps by himself, then twirls around in front of DAISY and approaches her. DAISY, overcome by the music, begins to step rhythmically toward DAVE and together they dance unobserved by JIM, absorbed in picking his guitar.)*

DAISY: Look here, baby, at this new step I learned up North.

DAVE: You can show me anything, sugar lump.

DAISY: Hold me tight now. *(But just as they begin the new movement JIM notices DAISY and DAVE. He stops playing again and lays his guitar down.)*

VOICES IN THE CROWD: *(Disgustedly)* Aw, come on, Jim . . . You must be jealous . . .

JIM: No, I ain't jealous. I jus' get tired of seein' that ol' nigger clownin' all the time.

DAVE: *(Laughing and pointing to JIM on porch)* Look at that mad baby. Take that lip up off the ground. Got your mouth stuck out jus' because some one is enjoying themselves. *(He comes up and pushes JIM playfully.)*

JIM: You better go head and let me alone. *(To DAISY)* Come here, Daisy!

LIGE: That's just what I say. Niggers can't have no fun without someone getting mad . . . specially over a woman.

JIM: I ain't mad . . . Daisy, 'scuse me, honey, but that fool, Dave . . .

DAVE: I ain't mad neither . . . Jim always tryin' to throw off on me. But you can't joke him.

DAISY: *(Soothingly)* Aw, now, now!

JIM: You ain't jokin'. You means that, nigger. And if you tryin' to get hot, first thing, you can pull off my blue shirt you put on this morning.

DAVE: Youse a got that wrong. I ain't got on no shirt of yours.

JIM: Yes, you is got on my shirt, too. Don't tell me you ain't got on my shirt.

DAVE: Well, even if I is, you can just lift your big plantations out of my shoes. You can just foot it home barefooted.

JIM: You try to take any shoes offa me!

LIGE: *(Pacifying them)* Aw, there ain't no use of all that. What you all want to start this quarreling for over a little jokin'.

JIM: Nobody's quarreling . . . I'm just playin' a little for Daisy and Dave's out there clownin' with her.

CLARKE: *(In doorway)* I ain't gonna have no fussin' round my store, no way. Shut up, you all.

JIM: Well, Mayor Clarke, I ain't mad with him. We'se been friends all our lives. He's slept in my bed and wore my clothes and et my grub. . . .

DAVE: I et your grub? And many time as you done laid down with your belly full of my grandma's collard greens. You done et my meat and bread a whole lot more times than I et your stewed fish-heads.

JIM: I'd rather eat stewed fish-heads than steal out of other folkses houses so much till you went to sleep on the roost and fell down one night and broke up the settin' hen. *(Loud laughter from the crowd)*

DAVE: Youse a liar if you say I stole anybody's chickens. I didn't have to. But you . . . 'fore you started goin' around with me, playin' that little box of yours, you was so hungry you had the white mouth. If it wasn't for these white folks throwin' *me* money for *my* dancin', you would be thin as a whisper right now.

JIM: *(Laughing sarcastically)* Your dancin'! You been leapin' around here like a tailless monkey in a wash pot for a long time and nobody was payin' no 'tention to you, till I come along playing.

LINDSAY: Boys, boys, that ain't no way for friends to carry on.

DAISY: Well, if you all gonna keep up this quarrelin' and carryin' on I'm goin' home. 'Bout time for me to be gittin' back to my white folks anyhow. It's dark now. I'm goin', even if I have to go by myself. I shouldn't a stopped by here nohow.

JIM: *(Stopping his quarrel)* You ain't gonna go home by yourself. I'm goin' with you.

DAVE: *(Singing softly)*
    It may be so,
    I don't know.

But it sounds to me

Like a lie.

WALTER: Dave ain't got as much rabbit blood as folks thought.

DAVE: Tell 'em 'bout me. *(Turns to DAISY)* Won't you choose a treat on me, Miss Daisy, 'fore we go?

DAISY: *(Coyly)* Yessir, thank you. I wants a drink of soda water.

> *(DAVE pulls his hat down over his eyes, whirls around and offers his arm to DAISY. They strut into the store, DAVE gazing contemptuously at JIM as he passes. Crowd roars with laughter, much to the embarrassment of JIM.)*

LIGE: Ol' fast Dave jus' runnin' the hog right over you, Jim.

WALTER: Thought you was such a hot man.

LUM BOGER: Want me to go in there and put Daisy under arrest and bring her to you?

JIM: *(Sitting down on the edge of porch with one foot on the step and lights a cigarette pretending not to be bothered.)* Aw, I'll get her when I want her. Let him treat her, but see who struts around that lake and down the railroad with her by and by.

> *(DAVE and DAISY emerge from the store, each holding a bottle of red soda pop and laughing together. As they start down the steps DAVE accidentally steps on JIM's outstretched foot. JIM jumps up and pushes DAVE back, causing him to spill the red soda all over his white shirt front.)*

JIM: Stay off my foot, you big ox.

DAVE: Well, you don't have to wet me all up, do you, and me in company? Why don't you put your damn foot in your pocket?

DAISY: *(Wiping DAVE's shirt front with her handkerchief)* Aw, ain't that too bad.

JIM: *(To DAVE)* Well, who's shirt did I wet? It's mine, anyhow, ain't it?

DAVE: *(Belligerently)* Well, if it's your shirt, then you come take it off me. I'm tired of your lip.

JIM: Well, I will.

DAVE: Well, put your fist where you lip is. *(Pushing DAISY aside.)*

DAISY: *(Frightened)* I want to go home. Now, don't you-all boys fight.

> *(JIM attempts to come up the steps. DAVE pushes him back and he stumbles and falls in the dust. General excitement as the crowd senses a fight.)*

LITTLE BOY: *(On the edge of crowd)* Fight, fight, you're no kin. Kill one another, won't be no sin. Fight, fight, you're no kin.

(JIM jumps up and rushes for DAVE as the latter starts down the steps. DAVE meets him with his fist squarely in the face and causes him to step backward, confused.)

DAISY: *(Still on porch, half crying)* Aw, my Lawd! I want to go home. *(General hubbub, women's cries of "Don't let 'em fight." "Why don't somebody stop 'em?" "What kind of men is you all, sit there and let them boys fight like that." Men's voices urging the fight: "Aw, let 'em fight." "Go for him, Dave." "Slug him, Jim." JIM makes another rush toward the steps. He staggers DAVE, DAVE knocks JIM sprawling once more. This time JIM grabs the mule bone as he rises, rushes DAVE, strikes DAVE over the head with it and knocks him out. DAVE falls prone on his back. There is great excitement.)*

OLD WOMAN: *(Screams)* Lawdy, is he kilt? *(Several men rush to the fallen man.)*

VOICE: Run down to the pump and get a dipper o' water.

CLARKE: *(To his wife in door)* Mattie, come out of that store with a bottle of witch hazely oil quick as you can. Jim Weston, I'm gonna arrest you for this. You Lum Boger. Where is that marshall? Lum Boger! *(LUM BOGER detaches himself from the crowd.)* Arrest Jim.

LUM: *(Grabs JIM's arm, relieves him of the mule bone and looks helplessly at the Mayor.)* Now I got him arrested, what's I going to do with him?

CLARKE: Lock him up back yonder in my barn till Monday when we'll have the trial in de Baptist Church.

LINDSAY: Yeah, just like all the rest of them Methodists . . . always tryin' to take undercurrents on people.

WALTER: Ain't no worse then some of you Baptists, nohow. You all don't run this town. We got jus' as much to say as you have.

CLARKE: *(Angrily to both men)* Shut up! Done had enough arguing in front of my place. *(To LUM BOGER)* Take that boy on and lock him up in my barn. And save that mule bone for evidence.

(LUM BOGER leads JIM off toward the back of the store. A crowd follows him. Other men and women are busy applying restoratives to DAVE. DAISY stands alone, unnoticed in the center of the stage.)

DAISY: *(Worriedly)* Now, who's gonna take me home?

CURTAIN

Act II, Scene 1

SETTING: *Village street scene; huge oak tree upstage center; a house or two on back drop. When curtain goes up, SISTER LUCY TAYLOR is seen standing under the tree. She is painfully spelling it out. (Enter SISTER THOMAS, a younger woman [In her thirties] at left.)*

SISTER THOMAS: Evenin', Sis Taylor.

SISTER TAYLOR: Evenin'. *(Returns to the notice)*

SISTER THOMAS: What you doin'? Readin' dat notice Joe Clarke put up 'bout de meeting? *(Approaches tree)*

SISTER TAYLOR: Is dat whut it says? I ain't much on readin' since I had my teeth pulled out. You know if you pull out dem eye teeth you ruins yo' eye sight. *(Turns back to notice)* Whut it say?

SISTER THOMAS: *(Reading notice)* "The trial of Jim Weston for assault and battery on Dave Carter wid a dangerous weepon will be held at Macedonia Baptist Church on Monday, November 10, at three o'clock. All are welcome. By order of J. Clarke, Mayor of Eatonville, Florida." *(Turning to SISTER TAYLOR)* Hit's makin' on to three now.

SISTER TAYLOR: You mean it's right *now.* *(Looks up at sun to tell time)* Lemme go git ready to be at de trial 'cause I'm sho goin' to be there an' I ain't goin' to bite my tongue neither.

SISTER THOMAS: I done went an' crapped a mess of collard greens for supper. I better go put 'em on 'cause Lawd knows when we goin' to git outa there an' my husband is one of them dat's gointer eat don't keer whut happen. I bet if judgment day was to happen tomorrow he'd speak I orter fix him a bucket to carry long. *(She moves to exit, right)*

SISTER TAYLOR: All men favors they guts, chile. But what you think of all dis mess they got goin' on round here?

SISTER THOMAS: I just think it's a sin en' a shame befo' de livin' justice de way dese Baptis' niggers is runnin' round here carryin' on.

SISTER TAYLOR: Oh, they been puttin' out the brags ever since Sat'day night 'bout whut they gointer do to Jim. They thinks they runs this town. They tell me Rev. Childers preached a sermon on it yistiddy.

SISTER THOMAS: Lawd help us! He can't preach 'em let lone gittin' up dere tryin' to throw slams at us. Now all Elder Simms done wus to explain to us our rights . . . what you think 'bout Joe Clarke runnin' round here takin' up for these ole Baptist niggers?

SISTER TAYLOR: De puzzle-gut rascal . . . we oughter have him up in conference an' put him out de Methdis' faith. He don't b'long in there—wanter tun dat boy outa town for nothin'.

SISTER THOMAS: But we all know how come he so hot to law Jim outa town—hit's to dig de foundation out from under Elder Simms.

SISTER TAYLOR: Whut he wanta do dat for?

SISTER THOMAS: 'Cause he wants to be a God-know-it-all an' a God-do-it-all an' Simms is de onliest one in this town whut will buck up to him.

(*Enter SISTER JONES, walking leisurely*)

SISTER JONES: Hello, Boyt, hello, Lucy.

SISTER TAYLOR: Goin' to de meetin'?

SISTER JONES: Done got my clothes on de line an' I'm bound to be dere.

SISTER THOMAS: Gointer testify for Jim?

SISTER JONES: Naw, I reckon—don't make such difference to me which way de drop fall . . .'Tain't neither one of 'em much good.

SISTER TAYLOR: I know it. I know it, Ida. But dat ain't de point. De crow we wants to pick is: Is we gointer set still an' let dese Baptist tell us when to plant an' when to pluck up?

SISTER JONES: Dat *is* something to think about when you come to think 'bout it. (*Starts to move on*) Guess I better go ahead—see y'all later an tell you straighter.

(*Enter ELDER SIMMS, right, walking fast, Bible under his arm, almost collides with SISTER JONES as she exits.*)

SIMMS: Oh, 'scuse me, Sister Jones. (*She nods and smiles and exits.*) How you do, Sister Taylor, Sister Thomas.

BOTH: Good evenin', Elder.

SIMMS: Sho is a hot day.

SISTER TAYLOR: Yeah, de bear is walkin' de earth lak a natural man.

SISTER THOMAS: Reverend, look like you headed de wrong way. It's almost time for de trial an' youse all de dependence we got.

SIMMS: I know it. I'm tryin' to find de marshall so we kin go after Jim. I wants a chance to talk wid him a minute before court sets.

SISTER TAYLOR: Y'think he'll come clear?

SIMMS: (*Proudly*) I *know* it! (*Shakes the Bible*) I'm goin' to law 'em from Genesis to Revelation.

SISTER THOMAS: Give it to 'em, Elder. Wear 'em out!

SIMMS: We'se liable to have a new Mayor when all dis dust settle. Well, I better scuffle on down de road. *(Exits, left.)*

SISTER THOMAS: Lord, lemme gwan home an' put dese greens on. *(Looks off stage left)* Here come Mayor Clarke now, wid his belly settin' out in front of him like a cow catcher! His name oughter be Mayor Belly.

SISTER TAYLOR: *(Arms akimbo)* Jus' look at him! Tryin' to look like a jigadier Breneral.
  (Enter CLARKE hot and perspiring. They look at him coldly.)

CLARKE: I God, de bear got me! *(Silence for a moment)* How y'all feelin', ladies?

SISTER TAYLOR: Brother Mayor, I ain't one of these folks dat bite my tongue an' bust my gall—what's inside got to come out! I can't see to my rest why you cloakin' in wid dese Baptist buzzards 'ginst yo' own church.

MAYOR CLARKE: I ain't cloakin' in wid *none*. I'm de Mayor of dis whole town. I stands for de right an' ginst de wrong—I don't keer who it kill or cure.

SISTER THOMAS: You think it's right to be runnin' dat boy off for nothin'?

CLARKE: I God! You call knockin' a man in de head wid a mule bone nothin'? 'Nother thing, I done missed nine of my best-layin' hens. I ain't sayin' Jim got 'em, but different people has tole me he burries a powerful lot of feathers in his back yard. I God, I'm a ruint man! *(He starts towards the right exit, but LUM BOGER enters right.)* I God, Lum, I bean lookin' for you all day. It's almost three o'clock. *(Hands him a key from his ring)* Take dis key an' go fetch Jim Weston on to de church.

LUM: Have you got yo' gavel from de lodge-room?

CLARKE: I God, that's right, Lum. I'll go get it from de lodge room whilst you go git de bone an' de prisoner. Hurry up! You walk like dead lice droppin' off you. *(He exits right while LUM crosses stage towards left.)*

SISTER TAYLOR: Lum, Elder Simms been huntin' you—he's gone on down 'bout de barn. *(She gestures)*

LUM BOGER: I reckon I'll overtake him. *(Exit left.)*

SISTER THOMAS: I better go put dose greens on. My husband will kill me if he don't find no supper ready. Here come Mrs. Blunt. She oughter feel like a penny's worth of have-mercy wid all dis stink behind her daughter.

SISTER TAYLOR: Chile, some Folks don't keer. They don't raise they chillon, they drags 'em up. God knows if dat Daisy wus mine, I'd throw her down an' put a hundred lashes on her back wid a plow-line. Here she come in de store Sat'day night *(Acts coy and coquettish, burlesques DAISY's walk)* a wringing and a twisting!

    (REV. CHILDERS enters left with DAVE and DEACON LIND-SAY and SISTER LEWIS. Very hostile glances from SISTERS THOMAS and TAYLOR towards the others.)

CHILDERS: Good evenin', folks.

    (Sisters THOMAS and TAYLOR just grunt. MRS. THOMAS moves a step or two towards exit. Flirts her skirts and exits.)

LINDSAY: *(Angrily)* What's de matter, y'all? Cat got yo' tongue?

MRS. TAYLOR: More matter than you kin scatter all over Cincinatti.

LINDSAY: Go 'head on, Lucy Taylor. Go 'head on. You know a very little of yo' sugar sweetens my coffee. Go 'head on. Everytime you lift yo' arm you smell like a neet of yellow hammers.

MRS. TAYLOR: Go 'head on yo'self. Yo' head look like it done wore out three bodies. Talkin' 'bout *me* smellin'—you smell lak a nest of grand daddies yo'self.

LINDSAY: Aw rock on down de road, 'oman. Ah don't wantuh change words wid yuh. Youse too ugly.

MRS. TAYLOR: You ain't nobody's pretty baby, yo'self. You so ugly I betcha yo' wife have to spread uh sheet over yo' head tuh let sleep slip up on yuh.

LINDSAY: *(Threatening)* I done tole you I don't wanter break a breath wid you. It's uh whole heap better tuh walk off on yo' own legs than it is to be toted off. I'm tired of yo' achin' round here. You fool wid me now an' I'll knock you into doll rags, Tony or no Tony.

MRS. TAYLOR: *(Jumping up in his face)* Hit me! Hit me! I dare you tuh hit me. If you take dat dare, you'll steal uh hawg an' eat his hair.

LINDSAY: Lemme gunn down to dat church befo' you make me stomp you. *(He exits, right.)*

MRS. TAYLOR: You mean you'll *git* stomped. Ah'm goin' to de trial, too. De nex trial gointer be *me* for kickin' some uh you Baptist niggers around.

    (A great noise is heard off stage left. The angry and jeering voices of children. MRS. TAYLOR looks off left and takes a step or two towards left exit as the noise comes nearer.)

VOICE OF ONE CHILD: Tell her! Tell her! Turn her up and smell her. Yo' mama ain't got nothin' to do wid me.

MRS. TAYLOR: *(Hollering off left)* You lil Baptis' haitians leave them chillun alone. If you don't, you better!
> *(Enter about ten children struggling and wrestling in a bunch. MRS. TAYLOR looks about on the ground for a stick to strike the children with.)*

VOICE OF CHILD: Hey! Hey! He's skeered tuh knock it off. Coward!

MRS. TAYLOR: If y'all don't git on home!

SASSY LITTLE GIRL: *(Standing akimbo)* I know you better not touch me, do my mama will 'tend to you.

MRS. TAYLOR: *(Making as if to strike her)* Shet up you nasty lil heifer, sassin' me! You ain't half raised. *(The little girl shakes herself at MRS. TAYLOR and is joined by two or three others.)*

MRS. TAYLOR: *(Walkin' towards right exit)* I'm goin' on down to de church an' tell yo' mammy. But she ain't been half raised herself. *(She exits right with several children making faces behind her.)*

MARY ELLA: Y'all ole Meth'dis' ain't got no window panes in yo' church down yonder in de swamp.

ANOTHER GIRL: *(Takes center of stand, hands akimbo and shakes her hips)* I don't keer whut y'all say, I'm a Meth'dis' bred an' uh Meth'dis' born an' when I'm dead there'll be uh Meth'dis' gone.

MARY ELLA: *(Snaps fingers under other girl's nose and starts singing. Several join her.)*
> Oh Baptis', Baptis' is my name
> My name's written on high
> I got my lick in de Baptis' church
> Gointer eat up de Meth'dis' pie.
>> *(The Methodist children jeer and make faces. The Baptist camp make faces back; for a full minute there is silence while each camp tries to outdo the other in face making. The Baptist makes the last face.)*

METHODIST BOY: Oo e on, less us don't notice 'em. Less gwan down to de church an' hear de trial.

MARY ELLA: Y'all ain't de onliest ones kin go. We goin', too.

WILLIE: Aw, haw! Copy cats! *(Makes face)* Dat's right. Follow on behind us lak uh puppy dog tail. *(They start walking toward right exit, switching their clothes behind.)*
> *(Baptist children stage a rush and struggle to get in front of the Methodists. They finally succeed in flinging some of the Methodist children to the ground and come behind them and walk towards right exit haughtily switching their clothes.)*

WILLIE: *(Whispers to his crowd)* Less go round by Mosely's lot an' beat 'em there!

OTHERS: All right!

WILLIE: *(Yellin' to Baptists)* We wouldn't walk behind no ole Baptists!
      (The Methodists turn and walk off towards left exit, switching their clothes as the Baptists are doing.)

SLOW CURTAIN

Act II, Scene 2

SETTING: *Interior of Macedonia Baptist Church, a rectangular room. Windows on each side, two Amen Corners. Pulpit with a plush cover with heavy fringe, door in front of church, two oil brackets with reflectors on each side wall, with lamps missing on all but one. One big oil lamp in center.*

ACTION: *At the rise, church is about full. A buzz and hum fills the church. Voices of children angry and jeering heard from the street. The church bell begins to toll for death. Everybody looks shocked.*

SISTER LEWIS: Lawd! Is Dave done died from dat lick?

SISTER THOMAS: *(to her husband)* Walter, go see.
      (He gets up and starts down the aisle to front door. Enter DEACON HAMBO by front door.)

WALTER: Who dead?

HAMBO: *(Laughing)* Nobody. Jus' tollin' de bell for dat Meth'dis' gopher dat's gointer be long, long gone after dis trial. *(Laughter from Baptist side. Enter TONY TAYLOR and his wife. TONY is about to go to front of church but MRS. TAYLOR jerks him down into a seat on the aisle on the Methodist side.)*

WALTER: Y'all sho thinks you runs dis town, dontcher? But Elder Simms'll show you somethin' t'day. If he don't God's up gopher.

HAMBO: He can't show us nothin' cause he don't know nothin' hisself.

WALTER: He got mo' book-learnin' than Rev. Childers³ got.

HAMBO: Childers mought be unletter-learnt, but he kin drive over Simms like a road plow.

METHODIST CHORUS: Aw naw! Dat's a lie!
      (Enter REV. SIMMS by front door with open Bible in hand. A murmur of applause rises on the Methodist side. Grunts on the Baptist side. Immediately behind him, comes LUM BOGER leading JIM WESTON. They parade up to the right Amen Corner and

seat themselves on the same bench. JIM between the Marshall and preacher. A great rooster-crowing and hen-cackling arises on the Baptist side. JIM WESTON jumps angrily to his feet.)

JIM: Wisht tuh God I had dat mule bone agin! Ah'd make some uh you mud turtles cackle out de other side yo' mouf. *(Loud laughter of derision from the Baptists. LUM looks scared.)*

SIMMS: Sit down, son; sit down. Be c'am.

(Enter by front door REV. CHILDERS and DAVE. DAVE's head is bandaged, but he walks firmly and seems not ill at all. They sit in the left Amen Corner. Jeering grunts from the Methodist side.)

SISTER THOMAS: Look at ol' Dave tryin' to make out he's hurt.

METHODIST VOICE: And Childers lookin' like ten cents worth of have-mercy.

BAPTIST VOICE: Yes, but you ought to heard that hell fire sermon he preached yesterday on fightin'.

METHODIST VOICE: Yeah, tryin de case fo' de trial come up.

BAPTIST VOICE: Well, sho is a sin to split a man's head, ain't it?

LIGE: Everybody know uh Baptis' head is harder'n uh rock. Look like they'd be skeered tuh go in swimmin' do, they heads would drown 'em. *(General laughter on Methodist side.)*

SISTER TAYLOR: Some folks is a whole lot more keerful 'bout a louse in de church than dey is in dey house. *(Looks pointedly at Sister Lewis.)*

SISTER LEWIS: *(bristling)* Whut you gazin' at me for? Wid your pop-eyes lookin' like skirt ginny-nuts?

SISTER TAYLOR: I hate to tell you whut yo' mouf looks like. I thinks you an' soap an' water musta had some words. Evertime you lifts yo' arm you smell like a nest of yellow hammers.

SISTER LEWIS: Well, I ain't seen no bath tubs in your house.

SISTER TAYLOR: Mought not have no tub, but tain't no lice on me though.

SISTER LEWIS: Aw, you got just as many bed-bugs and chinces as anybody else. I seen de bed-bugs marchin' out of yo' house in de mornin', keepin' step just like soldiers drillin'.

SISTER TAYLOR: You got that wrong, I—

(Enter BROTHER NIXON with his junper jacket on his arm and climbs over the knees of a bench full of people and finds a seat against the wall directly beneath an empty lamp bracket. He looks around for some place to dispose of his coat. Sees the lamp-bracket and hangs the coat there. Hitches up his pants and sits down.)

SISTER LEWIS: Wait a minute *(rising and glaring at NIXON)* Shank Nixon, you take yo' lousy coat down off these sacred walls. Ain't you Meth'dis' niggers got no gumption in de house of wash-up!

(*NIXON mocks her by standing akimbo and shaking himself like a woman. General laughter. He prepares to resume his seat, but looks over and sees DEACON HAMBO on his feet, and glaring angrily at him. He quickly reaches up and takes the coat down and folds it across his knee.*)

SISTER TAYLOR: *(Looks very pointedly at SISTER LEWIS, then takes a dip of snuff and looks sneering at LEWIS again.)* If I kept de dirty house you keeps ma mouth would be a closed book. *(Loud laughter from the Meth'dis' side.)*

SISTER LEWIS: *(furious, rises arms akimbo.)* Well, my house might not be exactly clean, but there's no fly-specks on my cha*rac*ter! They didn't have to git de sheriff to make Willie marry *me* like they did to make Tony marry *you*.

SISTER TAYLOR: *(jumping up and starting across the aisle. She is pulled back out of the aisle by friends.)* Yeah, they got de sheriff to make Tony marry me, but he married me and made me a good husband too. I sits in my rocking cheer on my porch every Sat'day evenin' an' say: "Here come Tony and them."

SISTER LEWIS: *(scornfully)* Them what?

SISTER TAYLOR: Them dollars, that's what! Now you sho orter go git de sheriff and a shot gun and make some of dese men marry yo' daughter, Ada.

SISTER LEWIS: *(Jumpin' up an' startin' across the aisle. She is restrained, but struggles hard.)* Lemme go, Jim Merchant! Turn me go! I'm goin' to stomp her till she can't sit down.

SISTER TAYLOR: *(also struggling)* Let her come on! If I get my hands on her I'll turn her every way but loose.

SISTER LEWIS: Just come on out dis church, Lucy Taylor. I'll beat you on everything but yo' tongue, and I'll give dat a lick if you stick it out. *(to the men holding her)* Turn me go! I'm goin' to fix her so her own Mammy won't know her.

SISTER TAYLOR: *(trying to free herself.)* Why don't y'all turn dat ole twist mouth 'oman loose? All I wants to do is hit her one lick. I betcha I'll take her 'way from here faster than de word of God.

SISTER LEWIS: *(to men holding Mrs. Taylor)* I don't see how come y'all won't let old Lucy Taylor a loose. Make out she so bad, now. She may be red hot but I kin cool her. I'll ride her just like Jesus rode a jackass.

> *(As they subside into their seats again, but glare at each other, MAYOR CLARKE comes thru the pulpit door. He is annoyed at the clamor going on. He tries to quell the noise with a frown.)*

SISTER TAYLOR: Dat ain't nothin' but talk. You looks lak de Devil before day, but you ain't so bad; not half as bad as you smell.

MAYOR CLARKE: Order, please, court is set.

SISTER LEWIS: You looks like de devil's doll baby, but all I want you to do is put it where I kin git it an' I'll sho use it.

MAYOR CLARKE: *(booming)* Here! Here! *(feeling everywhere for the gavel)* Lum Boger! Where's dat gavel I done told you to put here?

LUM BOGER: *(from beside prisoner)* You said *you* was gonna bring it yo'self.

MAYOR CLARKE: *(going up in the air)* I God, Lum, you gointer stand there like a bump on a log and see I ain't got nothin' to open court wid? Go 'head an 'fetch me dat gavel. Make haste quick before dese wimmen folks tote off dis church house. *(LUM exits by front door.)*

SISTER TAYLOR: *(to LEWIS)* Aw, shut up, you big ole he-looking rascal you! Nobody don't know whether youse a man or a woman.

CLARKE: You wimmen, shut up! Hush! Just hush! *(He wipes his face with a huge handkerchief.)*

SISTER LEWIS: *(To SISTER TAYLOR)* Air Lawd! Dat ain't your trouble. They all knows whut you is eg-zackly.

LINDSAY: Aw? why don't you wimmen cut dat out in de church house? Jus' jawin' an chewin' de rag!

SISTER TAYLOR: Joe Lindsay, if you'd go home an' feed dat rawbony horse of yourn, you wouldn't have so much time to stick yo' bill in business that ain't yourn.

SISTER LEWIS: Joe Lindsay, don't you know better than to strain wid folks ain't got sense enough to tote guts to a bear? If they ain't born wid no sense, you can't learn 'em none.

LINDSAY: You sho done tole whut God love now. *(glaring across the aisle)* Ain't got enough gumption to bell a buzzard.

> *(Enter LUM by front door with gavel in one hand and mule bone in the other. He walks importantly up the aisles and hands CLARKE the gavel and lays the bone atop the pulpit.)*

WALTER: Huh! Marshall had done forgot de bone.

METHODIST SISTER: It's a wonder he ain't forgot hisself.

CLARKE: *(rapping sharply with gavel)* Here! you moufy wimmen shut up. *(to LUM)* Lum you go on back there and shut dem wimmen up or put 'em outa here. They shan't contempt this court. *(He wipes his eye glasses.)*

   (LUM starts walking importantly down the aisle towards SISTER TAYLOR. She almost rises to meet him.)

SISTER TAYLOR: Lum Boger, you fresh little snot you! Don't you dast to come here trying to put me out; many diapers as I done pinned on you! *(fiercely)* Git away from me before I knock every nap off of yo' head, one by one. *(LUM BOGER hurries away from her apologetically. He turns towards MRS. LEWIS.)*

MRS. LEWIS: *(calmly)* Deed God knows you better not lay de weight of yo' hand on me, Lum. Gwan way from here before I kick yo' clothes up round yo' neck like a horse collar. *(All the men laugh. LUM looks worried and finally goes back and takes his seat beside the prisoner.)*

CLARKE: *(glaring ferociously)* This court is set an' I'm bound to have some order or else. *(The talking ceases. Absolute quiet.)*

CLARKE: Now less git down to business. We got folks in dis town dat's just like a snake in de grass.

SISTER PITTS: Brother Mayor! We ain't got no business goin' into no trial for nothin' else 'thout a word of prayer to be sure de right spirit is wid us.

VOICE ON METHODIST SIDE: Thass right, Elder Simms. Give us a word of prayer. *(He rises hurriedly.)*

VOICE ON BAPTIST SIDE: This is a Baptist church an' de paster is sittin' right here. How come he can't pray in his own church?

TAYLOR: Y'all done started all dis mess, how you goin' to git de right spirit here? Go 'head Rev. Simms.

LEWIS: He cain't pray over me. Dis church says: One Lord, one faith, one Baptism, and a man that ain't never been baptised at all ain't got no business prayin' over nobody.

CLARKE: *(rapping with gavel)* Less sing. Somebody raise a tune.

VOICE ON BAPTIST SIDE: *(begins)* "Onward Christian Soldiers" *(and the others join in)*

VOICE ON METHODIST SIDE: *(Begins)* "All hail the power of Jesus name" *(and the Methodists join in. Both shout as loud as they can to the end of the verse. Clarke lifts his hands rapidly as if to bless a table.)*

CLARKE: *(Praying, quickly)* Lowd be with us and bless these few remarks we are about to receive amen. Now this court is open for business. All of us know we come here on serious business. This town is bout to be tore up by backbiting and malice and mouthy women. *(Glaring at the Sisters)* Now everybody that's a witness in this case, stand up. I wants the witness to take the front seat. *(Nearly everybody in the room rises. Clarke tries to count them.)*

HAMBO: *(Frowns across the aisle at MRS. LUCAS, who is standing.)* Whut you doing standing up for a witness? I know you wuzn't there.

SISTER LUCAS: I got just as much right to testify as you is. I don't keer if I wasn't there. Any man that treats they wife bad as you can't tell nobody else they eye is black. You clean round yo' own door before you go sweeping round other folks.

SISTER LINDSAY: *(to NIXON)* Whut you doing up there testifyin'? When you done let yo' hawg root up all my p'tater patch?

NIXON: Aw, shut up woman. You ain't had no taters for no pig to root up.

SISTER LINDSAY: Who ain't had no taters? *(to LIGE)* Look here, Lige, didn't I git a whole crokus sack full of tater slips from yo' brother, Sam?

LIGE: *(Reluctantly)* Yeah.

SISTER LINDSAY: Course I had sweet p'taters! And if you stand up there and tell me I ain't had no p'taters, I'll be all over you just like gravy over rice.

NIXON: AW, shut up. We ain't come here to talk about yo' tater vines. We come—

SISTER LINDSAY: *(to her husband)* Joe! Whut kind of a husband is you! Sit here and let Nixon 'buse me out lak dat.

WALTER THOMAS: How is Joe goin' give anybody a straightenin', when he needs straightenin' hisself?

SISTER HAMBO: Aw, you ain't got no right to talk, Walter. Not low down as you is. If somebody stump their toe in dis town you bolt over to Maitland an' puke yo' guts out to de white folks, and God knows I 'bominates a white folks nigger.

WALTER THOMAS: Aw, you jus' mad 'cause I wouldn't let your old starved-out cow eat up my cow-peas.

CLARKE: *(Pounding)* Hush and lemme count.

SISTER HAMBO: *(triumphantly)* UNhumh! I knowed you was the one knocked my cow's horn off! And you lied like a doodle-bug goin' backwards in his hole an' made out you didn't do it.

WALTER THOMAS: I didn't do no such a thing, woman.

SISTER HAMBO: I say you did, and I belong to Macedonia Baptist Church an' I can't lie.

DEACON HAMBO: Walter Thomas, talk dat biggity talk to me, not to my wife. Maybe you kin whip her, but if you can't whip me, too, don't bring de mess up.

CLARKE: *(rapping)* Y'all men folks shut up before I put you both under arrest. Come to order everybody.

LINDSAY: I just want a say this before we go any further. Nobody bet' not slur my wife in here. Do, I'll strow 'em over de country.

MRS. NIXON: Aw, youse de nastiest threatener in three states, but I ain't seen you do nothin'. De seat of yo' pants is too close to de ground for you to be crowin' so loud. You's so short you smell right earthy.

CLARKE: Shut up! We didn't come here to wash an' iron niggers! We come here for a trial. *(raps)*

MRS. NIXON: *(to CLARKE)* I ain't goin' to shut up nothin' of de kind.

CLARKE: Sister Nixon, shut up!

MRS. NIXON: You can't shut me up, not the way you live. When you quit beatin' Mrs. Mattie an' dominizing her all de time, then you kin tell other folks what to do. You ain't none of my boss, not de way you sells rancid bacon for fresh.

CLARKE: *(to MARSHALL)* Lum Boger, git me a pencil. *(to MRS. NIXON)* Big a bill as you owe ma store, you ain't gonna get nothin' else till you pay.

MRS. NIXON: Huh! I can trade in Maitland—an' see if I pays you now.

NIXON: AW, honey, hush a while, please, and less git started. You don't pay de bills no how. *(The men laugh.)*

JIM: Lawd! Lawd! We done set de whole town fightin'.

DAVE: Boy', we sho is!

CHILDERS: Son, don't talk wid yo' 'sailent. He's a wicked man.

DAVE: How come I can't talk wid him? Known him all ma life.

CHILDERS: Shss. He done tried to kill you.

DAVE: Was our fight, warn't it?

JIM: You niggers just tryin to get us messed up on some kind o' mess. Dave knows I ain't meant to hurt him.

SIMMS: *(to JIM)* Deserved to be hurt.

DAVE: No, he didn't. We's just friendly-fightin'-like.

CHILDERS: He sho tried to kill you!

(CLARKE raps. A momentary quiet falls on the place. MAYOR glowers all over the place.)

CLARKE: Here! Quiet till you's called on. *(Turns to LUM)* Lum, git a piece of paper an take de names of all de witnesses *who was there* while de fight was goin' on.

LUM: *(Pulling a small tablet and pencil out of his coat pocket)* I brought it with me.

CLARKE: Now everybody who was at de fight hold up yo' hands so Lum kin know who you are. *(Several hands go up. SISTER ANDERSON puts up her hand.)*

CLARKE: You wuzn't there, Sister Anderson, not at that time.

SISTER ANDERSON: I hadn't been gone more'n ten minutes.

CLARKE: But you didn't see it.

SISTER ANDERSON: It don't make no difference. My husband heered every word was spoke an' told me, jes' lak it happen. Don't tell me I can't testify.

DEACON HAMBO: Nobody can't testify but them what seen it.

SISTER ANDERSON: Dat's all right, but I know whut they was fightin' 'bout. It was Daisy Taylor.⁴

MRS. BLUNT: Jus' you take my chile's name right out yo' mouf, Dilcie Anderson. She was on her way back to her white folks when all this happen.

SISTER ANDERSON: Well, God knows if dat Daisy was mine, I'd throw her down an' put a hundred lashes on her back wid a plow-line. Here she comes in de store Sat'day night. *(Acts coy and coquettish, burlesques Daisy's walk)* A wringing and a twisting!

MRS. BLUNT: You better hush while you able! You niggers got my Daisy's name all mixed up in dis mess, an' she at work, can't defend herself.

MRS. TAYLOR: You musn't mind, Sister Blunt. People jus' *will* talk. They's talkin' in New York an' they's talkin' in Georgy an' they's talkin' in Italy.

SISTER PITTS: Chile, if you listen at folkses talk, they'll have you in de graveyard or in Chattahoochee—one. You can't pay no 'tention to talk.

MRS. BLUNT: Well, I know one thing. De man or woman, chick or child, grizzly or gray, that tells me to my face anythin' wrong 'bout *my* chile, I'm goin' to take *my* fist *(Rolling up right sleeve and gesturing with right fist)* and knock they teeth down they throat. *(She looks ferocious)* 'Case y'all know I raised my Daisy right round my feet till I let her go up North last year wid them white folks. I'd ruther her to be in de white folks' kitchen than walkin' de streets like some of dese gals round here. If I do say so, I done raised a lady. She can't help it if all dese mens get stuck on her.

MRS. TAYLOR: You'se tellin' de truth, Sister Blunt. That's whut I always say: Don't confidence dese niggers. Do, they'll sho put you in de street.

MRS. THOMAS: Naw indeed, never syndicate wid niggers. Do, they will distriminate you.

MRS. BLUNT: Just as sho as you snore. An' they better leave Daisy's name outa dis, too, an' Daisy better not leave them white folks' house today to come traipsin' over here scornin' her name all up wid dis nigger mess. Do, I'll kill her. No daughter of mine ain't goin' be mixed up in nothin' like this.

MRS. THOMAS: That's right, Sister Blunt. I glory in yo' spunk.

MAYOR CLARKE: Sit down, Sister Blunt an' shet up. Ain't gonna mention Daisy a-tall. Ain't gonna drag no woman's name in dis trial long as I's presidin'.

METHODIST SISTER: Dis ain't no trial. Dis is a mess!

REV. SIMMS: You sho said a mouthful, Sister. Dis sho is a mess. Can't help from bein' uh mess. *(Glares at MAYOR)* Holdin' a trial in de Baptist Church! Some folks ain't got sense enough to do 'em till four o'clock, an' its way after half past three right now.

MAYOR CLARKE: Shet up, dere, Simms! Set down! Who ast yo' pot to boil, nohow? A church trial is de bes' trial they is, anyhow, cause you better have a good experience here an' a strong determination. *(Raps vigorously)* Now lemme tel *y'all* somethin'. When de Mayor sets court, don't keer when I sets it nor where I sets it, you got to git quiet and stay quiet till I ast you tuh talk. Set down! All o' yuh! I God, you sound lak a tree full uh blackbirds! Dis ain't no barbecue, nor neither no camp meetin'. We 'sembled here tuh law uh boy on a serious charge. *(A great buzz rises from the congregation. MAYOR raps hard for order and glares all about him.)* Heah! Heah! All o' us kin sing at de same time, but can't but one o' us talk at a time. I'm doin' de talkin' now, so de res' o' you dry up till I git through. I God, you sound lak uh passel uh dog fights! We ain't here for no form and no fashion and no outside show to de worl'. We'se here to law!

(For a moment, there is silence, then a small boy, peeping in window on the Methodist side says:)

BOY: *(Thru window, right)* Aw, haw! Y'all ole Baptis' ain't got no book-case in yo' church.

SMALL GIRL: *(In window on opposite side, left, with other children)* Y'all ole Meth'dis' ain't got no window panes in yo' church down yonder in de swamp.

CLARKE: *(Booming)* You chillun shut up and get out o' them winders. You, Lum! *(LUM stops taking names to go shoo the children. The old people aid him, and the children on left run off singing:)*

CHILDREN: Oh, Baptis', Baptis' is my name,
My name's written on high.
I got my lick in de Baptis' Church,
Gointer eat up de Meth'dis' pie.

CLARKE: *(Rapping)* You done got all de witnesses straight an' got they names down?

LUM: Yassuh, I got it all straightened out.

CLARKE: Well, read de names out and let de witnesses take de front seats. Who is they?

LUM: *(Reading)* Mrs. Lucy Taylor, Sister Katie Pitts, Sister Doll Nixon, Deacon Hambo, Brother Lige Mosely, Brother Joe Lindsay. . . .

LINDSAY: Brother, my eye!

LUM: *(Continuing the reading of the list)* Mr. Sykes Jones, Sister Laura Carter, Mr. Pat Jenkins. And they was lots mo' there but they say they ain't gonna witness. *(Those whose names were read begin to rise and start forward.)*

JIM: They better not neither.

SIMMS: Shss! De devil can't hurt you, son. An' them what speaks against you is devils.

CLARKE: Won't witness, heh? Huh-um! Well, I see they's some wit-nessin' whut warn't there. Lucy Taylor, you know you left mah store fo' dat fight come off!

SISTER TAYLOR: *(In attitude of defiance)* Well, I'm gonna witness! An' I ain't gonna bit mah tongue neither. You knows you cheat-ed me outa half a pound o' salt pork Sat'day night. I weighed dat piece when I got home, and 'twarn't no bigger'n mah fist here.

SISTER PITTS: Huh! Dat's a common thing, chile.

CLARKE: *(Calmly)* Is dat all?

SISTER TAYLOR: No, that ain't all. You waters yo' cider, an' yo' sells bag meal.

CLARKE: An' yo' been buyin' outa mah store fo' God knows how long.

Yo' owes me Thirty-eight Dollars and Ten Cents, an' can't nobody whuts in mah debt testify in this court. Set down!

SISTER TAYLOR: You'se a lie! You'se a . . . *(But the noise of the gavel drowns her out. In the meantime, the other witnesses are all seated at the front.)*

CLARKE: Now, we'll go on with this trial. We's tryin' Jim Weston fo' 'saultin' Dave Carter wid a dangerous weepon. Did he or did he not done it, that's what we got to fin' out? You, Lum! You was there. You'se de Marshall. You saw it. Now, what went on?

LUM: *(Startled, drawls)* Well . . .

DAVE: You better, "Well . . ." *(Mocking LUM)*

LUM: Daisy come. . . .

SISTER BLUNT: Uhm-uh! Not Daisy.

LUM: I mean *(turning to CLARKE in distress)* Well, you say I should take Jim and lock him up, an' that's whut I done, jus' like you tol' me.

CLARKE: You sho did, but I God, I ast you whut you seed befo' I told you to take Jim and lock him up? *(DAVE, JIM and SISTER TAYLOR eye LUM dangerously)*

LUM: *(Shifting nervously)* Well, I ain't seen much.

CLARKE: *(Rapping impatiently)* Whut did you see?

LUM: Well, ole lady Pitts' mule was tied in yo' back yard a-tearin' up Mis' Mattie's tomato vines, an' Mis' Mattie say, 'Lum, you go 'roun' an' tend to dat mule', an' I went, an' that mule sho drawed back to kick me.

CLARKE: *(To SISTER PITTS)* I God, yo' mule drawed a hoof on de marshall?

SISTER PITTS: Dat's a lie! Mah mule don't kick.

CLARKE: G'wan, Lum!

LUM: An' I was busy wid dat mule.

LIGE: Looks like de marshall warn't at de scene o' action.

SISTER LEWIS: Dat's de kin' o' men de Mayor hires to do de duties o' dis town.

CLARKE: Set down, Lum. Ain't worth de dust it took to make you. *(To HAMBO)* Hambo, you was settin' an' loafin' right on mah front porch all day Sat'day, and night, too. Get up an' tell whut you saw.

HAMBO: *(Rising)* Now, in de first place, Joe Clarke, I warn't loafin'. I'se a deacon in de church an' you knows I don't waste mah time wid dem low niggers whut hangs aroun' yo' store.

LIGE: Do you hear that?

HAMBO: An' furthermo', I don't know if I wuz there or not, now dat you so sure I wuz.

SISTER HAMBO: Make him prove it! Make him prove it!

CLARKE: I God, Hambo, you know you wuz there!

CHILDERS: *(Quickly)* He were there, yo' honery, but he warn't loafin'. *(To HAMBO)* You mah main witness, Brother Hambo. Now tell jus' how dis vileness was done. You sees our lamb all hurted here. *(Pointing to DAVE's head. JIM laughs.)*

DAVE: Hush, fool! You'se in court.

JIM: Boy, yo' head sho is soft.

HAMBO: *(To JIM)* An' you'll soon be gone. *(To the MAYOR)* Clarke, it were like dis. These two boys here started fightin' over Dais . . . *(sees SISTER BLUNT half rise in her seat)* over somethin' or nother o' no importance . . . *(BAPTISTS all murmur in agreement)* an' dat there triflin' rascal, for no cause whatinsoever, hit this boy in de head with a mule bone.

CLARKE: Um-hmmm! Dat's right.

SISTER THOMAS: Hear him, Lord! How he kin lie!

SISTER NIXON: An' then re-lie!

HAMBO: *(To CLARKE)* You 'lows dese 'ruptions in de court?

CLARKE: *(To WOMEN, rapping)* Hush! I say, hush! Hambo, is you through?

HAMBO: *(Sitting down pompously)* I is.

CLARKE: *(To OLD WOMAN)* Sister Pitts, le's hear whut you got to say!

SISTER PITTS: Brother Mayor, I wan't there, but I been knowin' this boy Dave since he was knee-high to a duck an' that boy wouldn't hurt nobody, but that varmint yonder *(Pointing to JIM)* is de crookedist limb of Satan that de Lawd ever made. He is a scoundrel, a rat, a low-down dog, a . . .

SIMMS: *(Jumping up)* I objects! I objects! Nobody's got de right to call my charge no names like dat. *(As CLARKE is silent and SISTER PITTS goes on, "rascal, heathen, etc.")* I objects! *(Dances in front of MAYOR's face)* I objects!

CLARKE: I God, Simms, if you don't set down an' stop spittin' in mah face I'll lam you over de head wid dis mallet.

SIMMS: *(Weakly)* I objects.

CLARKE: Dat'll do! Dat'll do! Dry up, suh! *(Turning to DAVE)* Stand up, Dave. Since youse de one got hurted, you tell me jus' whut went on out dere. *(DAVE rises slowly)*

MRS. TAYLOR: Dat's right, Dave. Git up dere an' lie lak de cross ties from New York to Texas. You greasy rascal, you! You better go wash yo'self befo' you go testifyin' on people.

DAVE: *(Calmly)* I'm jus' as clean as you. *(JIM laughs)*

CHILDERS: *(Jumping to his feet)* Wait a minute! 'Tain't none o' y'all got no call to be throwin' off on dis boy. He come here to git justice, not to be slurred an' low-rated. He ain't 'ssaulted nobody. He ain't stole no chickens. He's a clean boy. He set at mah feet in Sunday School since he was so high *(Measures knee height)* and he come through religion under de sound of mah voice an' I baptized him an' I know he's clean.

MRS. TAYLOR: It'll take more'n uh baptizin' to clean dat nigger.

DAVE: I goes in swimmin' nearly every day. I'm jus' as clean as anybody else.

MRS. TAYLOR: *(MAYOR begins rapping for order. She shouts out)* Swimming! Dat ain't gointer clean de crust offa you. You ain't had a good bath since de devil was a hatchet.

CLARKE: I'm goin' to have order heah or else! G'wan, Dave!

DAVE: It's jus' lak you seen it Sat'day night. You-all was there.

CLARKE: Yeah, but dat wuz at de store. Dis is in court an' it's got to be tole.

SIMMS: Just uh minute, Brother Clarke, before we any further go, I wants to ast de witness uh question dat oughter be answered before he opens his mouf.

CLARKE: Whut *kind* of question is dat?

SIMMS: Dave, tell de truth. Ain't yo' heart full of envy an' malice 'gainst dis chile? *(Gestures towards JIM. DAVE shakes his head and starts to deny the charge, but SIMMS hurries on)* Wait a minute, now! Wait till I git thru. Didn't y'all used to run aroun' everywhere playin' an' singin' an' everythin' till you got so full of envy an' malice an' devilment till y'all broke up? Now, Brother Mayor, make him tell de truth.

DAVE: Yeah, I useter be crazy 'bout Jim, and we was buddies till he tried to back bite me wid my girl.

JIM: Yo' girl! Never *was* yo' girl, nohow! I reckon I ain't none of yo' buddy. I ain't got no buddy, they kilt my buddy tryin' to raise me. But I did useter lak you till you tried to root me out wid Dais. . . .

SISTER BLUNT: Jes' dare!

MAYOR: Aw, table dat business, an' le's open up new business. We ain't here to fin' out whose girl it is an' we ain't gonna mention no woman's name. We wants to know 'bout dis fight, an' who hit de first lick, an' how come. Go 'head on, Dave, an' talk.

CHILDERS: Yes, Dave, talk, son.

DAVE: Well, we was all dancin' an' a singin' in front o' yo' store, an' seem like Jim kinder got mad 'bout somethin' or nother an' so I went in de store an' left de ole nigger. Well, near as I can remember, when I come out seems like I kinder step on his ole big foot whut had no business where it wuz nohow. An' then he up and knocks mah soda all ovah mah clean shirt.

JIM: Who's shirt?

DAVE: De shirt I had on. An' then I hits him. An' fo' I knowed it, he done picked up that bone an' lammed me ovah de head wid it.

CHILDERS: He hit you, didn't he?

DAVE: Yes, sir.

CHILDERS: He assaulted you, didn't he?

DAVE: I reckon he did.

CLARKE: Uh-humm!

> (*DAVE resumes his seat and JIM drops his head for a moment then snatches it up arrogantly and glares at the BAPTISTS. The whole place is very silent for a moment. Then MAYOR CLARKE clears his throat, raps with his gavel and looks sternly at JIM.*)
> Jim Weston, stand up, suh! (*JIM rises sullenly*) You'se charged wid 'ssaultin' Dave Carter wid uh dangerous weepon. You heard de charge. Guilty or not guilty?

JIM: (*Arrogantly*) Yeah, I hit him an' I'll hit him agin if he crowd me. But I ain't guilty of no crime. (*He hitches up his pants and sits down arrogantly.*)

CLARKE: (*Surprised*) Whut's dat you say, Jim? (*Raps sharply*) Git up from there, sir! Whut's dat you say?

JIM: (*Rising*) I say, yeah, I lammed ole Dave wid de mule bone, but I ain't guilty uh nothin'. (*There is a stark silence for a few seconds. Then CLARKE raps nervously.*)

CLARKE: How come you ain't guilty?

SIMMS: (*To JIM*) Set down, Jim, and lemme show dese people dat walks in de darkness wid sinners an' republicans de light.

(JIM sets down amid jubilant smiles of METHODISTS. SIMMS chuckles out loud and wipes his face with his handkerchief. He gets to his feet still laughing.)

CHILDERS: You jus' as well tuh hush up befo' you start then, Simms. You can't show nobody uh light when you ain't got none tuh show.

HAMBO: Ain't dat de gospel?

NIXON: Aw, let de man talk! Y'all soun' lak uh tree full uh blackbirds. Go 'head on, Elder Simms.

WALTER THOMAS: Yeah, you can't teach 'em nothin', but talk on. We know whut you talkin' 'bout.

CLARKE: *(Rapping once or twice)* I God, tell it . . . whutever 'tis you got tuh tell!

SISTER NIXON: Law 'em from Genesis to Revelations, Elder.

SISTER LEWIS: Aw yeah, hurry up an' tell it. I know it ain't goin' tuh be nothin' after you git it tole, but hurry up an' say it so you kin rest easy.

THOMAS: Aw, shet up an' give de man uh chance.

SISTER LEWIS: My shetters ain't workin' good. Sposin' you come whet me up, Walter. Den you'll know it's done right.

LIGE: Aw, whyn't y'all ack lak folks an' leave de man talk!

CLARKE: *(Rapping repeatedly)* Order in dis court, I God, jus' like you wuz in Orlando! *(Silence falls)* Now, Simms, talk yo' chat.

SIMMS: *(Glances down into his open Bible, then looks all around the room with great deliberation. It is evident he enjoys being the center of attraction. He smiles smugly as he turns his face towards the pulpit. He speaks slowly and accents his words so that none will be lost on his audience.)* De Bible says, be sho you're right, then go ahead. *(He looks all around to collect the admiration he feels he has earned.)* Now, we all done gathered an' 'sembled here tuh law dis young lad of uh boy on uh mighty serious charge. Uh whole passel of us is rarin' tuh drive him way from home lak you done drove off his daddy an' his brothers.

HAMBO: We never drove off his pappy. De white folks took an' hung him for killin' dat man in Kissimmee for nothin'.

SIMMS: Dat ain't de point, Brother Hambo.

HAMBO: It's jes' as good uh pint as any. If you gointer talk, tell de truth. An' if you can't tell de truth, set down an' leave Reverend Childers talk.

SIMMS: Brother Mayor, how come you let dese people run they mouf lak uh passel uh cowbells? Ain't I got de floor? I ain't no breath-an'-britches. I was *people* in middle Georgy befo' I ever come to Floridy. Whut kin' of chairman is you, nohow?

CLARKE: *(Angrily)* Heah! Heah! Don't you come tryin' show yo'self round me! I God, I don't keer whut you wuz in Georgy. I kin eat fried chicken when you cain't git rainwater tuh drink. Hurry up an' say what you got in yo' craw an' set down. We needs yo' space more'n we needs yo' comp'ny.

NIXON: Don't let him skeer yo', Elder Simms. You got plenty shoulders tuh back yo' fallin'.

HAMBO: Well, each an' every shoulder kin hit de groun' an' I'll git wid 'em.

THOMAS: Hambo, everybody in Orange county knows you love tuh fight. But dis is uh law hearin', not no wrassle.

HAMBO: Oh, you Meth'dis' niggers wants tuh fight, bad enough, but youse skeered. Youse jus' as hot as Tucker when de mule kicked his mammy. But you know you got plenty coolers.

SISTER TAYLOR: Aw, ain't nobody skeered uh you half-pint Baptists. God knows ah'm ready an' willin'. *(She glares at MRS. LEWIS. SISTER LEWIS jumps to her feet, but is pulled back into her seat. MAYOR CLARKE raps for order and the room gets quiet.)*

CLARKE: Aw right, now, Simms. I God, git through!

SIMMS: *(Pompously)* Now y'all done up an' took dis po' boy an' had him locked up in uh barn ever since Sat'day night an' done got him 'ccused uh 'ssault an' I don't know whut all, an' you ain't got no business wid yo' hands on him a-tall. He ain't done no crime, an' if y'all knowed anythin' 'bout law, I wouldn't have tuh tell you so.

CLARKE: I God, he *is* done uh crime an' he's gointer ketch it, too.

SIMMS: But not by law, Brother Mayor. You tryin' tuh lay uh hearin' on dis boy an' you can't do it 'cause he ain't broke no law. I don't keer whut he done so long as he don't break no law you can't touch him.

CHILDERS: He committed assault, didn't he? Dat sho is breakin' de law!

SIMMS: Naw, he ain't committed no 'ssault. He jus' lammed Dave over de head, dat's all. *(Triumphantly)* Yuh see y'all don't know whut you talkin' 'bout. Now I done set in de court house an' heard de white folks law from mornin' till night. *(He flips his Bible shut.)* I done read dis book from lid tuh lid an' I knows de law. You got tuh have uh weepon tuh commit uh 'ssault. An' tain't in no white folks law an' 'tain't in dis Bible dat no mule bone is no weepon.

CLARKE: *(After a moment of dead silence)* I God, whut's dat you say?

SIMMS: *(Sitting down and crossing his legs and folding his hands upon his Bible.)* You heard me. I say you ain't got no case 'ginst dis boy an' you got tuh turn him loose.

CHILDERS: *(Jumping up)* Brother Chairman!

CLARKE: *(Raps once and nods recognition)* You got de floor.

CHILDERS: I ain't book-learnt an' I ain't rubbed de hair offen my head agin no college wall, but I know when uh 'ssault's been committed. I says Jim Weston did 'ssault Dave. *(He points at Dave's head.)*

SIMMS: *(Arrogantly)* Prove it!

> *(Childers stands silent and puzzled. The METHODIST side breaks into a triumphant shout of "Oh, Mary don't you weep, don't you moan, Pharoah's Army got Drownded." CHILDERS sinks into his seat. When they have shouted out three choruses, SIMMS rises to speak.)*

SIMMS: I move dat we sing doxology an' bring dis meetin' to uh close. We'se all workin' people, Brother Mayor. Dismiss us so we kin g'wan back to our work. De sun is two hours high yet. *(Looks towards the METHODIST side.)* I second de motion.

CHILDERS: *(Arising slowly)* Hol' on there uh minute wid dat motion. Dis ain't no lodge meetin'. Dis is uh court an' bofe sides got uh right tuh talk. *(Motions towards SIMM's Bible)* Youse uh letter-learnt man, but I kin read dat Bible some, too. Lemme take it uh minute.

SIMMS: I ain't uh gointer do it. Any preacher dat amounts to uh hill uh beans would have his own Bible.

CLARKE: I God, Childers, you right here in yo' own church. Come on up an' read out yo' pulpit Bible. I God, don't mind me bein' up here. Come on up. *(A great buzzing breaks out all over the church for order. CHILDERS mounts the pulpit. SIMMS begins to turn the leaves of his Bible.)*

SIMMS: Brother Mayor, you oughter let us outa here. You ain't got no case 'ginst dis boy. Don't waste our time for nothin'. Leave us go home.

CLARKE: Aw, dry up, Simms, you done talked yo' talk. I God, leave Childers talk his. *(To CHILDERS)* Step on out when you ready, Reverend.

CHILDERS: *(Reading)* It says here in Judges 18:18 dat Samson slewed three thousand Philistines wid de jaw-bone of an ass.

SIMMS: *(On his feet)* Yeah, but dis wasn't no ass. Dis was uh mule, Brother Mayor. Dismiss dis meetin' an le's all go home.

CHILDERS: Yeah, but he was half-ass. A ass is uh mule's daddy, and he's bigger'n uh ass, too. *(Emphatic gestures)* Everybody knows dat, even de lil chillun.

SIMMS: *(Standing)* Yeah, but we didn't come here to talk about no asses, neither no half-asses, nor no mule daddies. *(Laughter from METHODISTS)* We come to law uh boy for 'ssault an' larceny.

CHILDERS: *(Very patiently)* We'se comin' to dat pint now. Dat's de second claw uh de sentence we'se expoundin'. I say Jim Weston did have uh weepon in his hand when he 'ssaulted Dave. 'Cause y'all knows if de daddy is dangerous, den de son is dangerous too. An y'all knows dat de further back you gits on uh mule de more dangerous he gits an' if de jaw-bone slewed three thousand people, by de time you gits back tuh his hocks, it's pizen enough tuh kill ten thousand. 'Tain't no knives nor no razors ever kilt no three thousand people. Now, folkses, I ast y'all whut kin be mo' dangerous dan uh mule bone? *(To CLARKE)* Brother Mayor, Jim didn't jes' lam Dave an' walk off . . . *(very emphatic)* he 'ssaulted him with de deadliest weepon there is in de worl' an' left him layin' unconscious. Brother Mayor, he's uh criminal an' oughter be run outa dis peaceful town! *(Great chorus of approval from Baptists. CLARKE begins to rap for order.)*

SIMMS: *(Standing)* Brother Mayor, I objects. I done studied jury and I know whut I'm talkin' 'bout.

CLARKE: Aw, dry up, Simms. You'se entirely out of order. You may be slick, but you kin stand another greasing. Reverend Childers is right. I God, I knows de law when I hear it. Stand up dere, Jim! *(JIM rises very slowly. SIMMS rises also. DAVE looks worried.)*

CLARKE: Set down, Simms! I God, I know where to find you when I want you. *(SIMMS sits.)* Jim, I find you guilty as charged an' I wants you to git outa my town an' stay gone for two years. *(To LUM)* Brother Marshall, you see dat he gits outa town befo' dark. An' you folks dat's so anxious to fight, fit on off dis church grounds befo' you starts. An' don't use no knives an' no guns an' no mule bones. Court's dismissed.

CURTAIN

Act III

SETTING: *A high stretch of railroad track thru a luxurious Florida forest. It is near sundown.*

ACTION: *When the curtain rises there is no one on the stage, but there is a tremendous noise and hubbub off-stage right. There are yells of derision and shouts of anger. Part of the mob is trying to keep JIM in town, and part is driving him off. After a full minute of this, JIM enters with his guitar hanging around his neck and his coat over his shoulder. The sun is dropping low and red thru the forest. He is looking back angrily and shouting at the mob. A missile is thrown after him. JIM drops his coat and guitar and grabs up a piece of brick, and makes threatening gestures of throwing it.*

JIM: *(Running back the way he came and hurling the brick with all his might)* I'll kill some o' you old box-ankled niggers. *(Grabs up another piece of brick)* I'm out o' your old town. Now just let some of you old half-pint Baptists let yo' wooden God and Cornstalk Jesus fool you into hittin' me. *(Threatens to throw again. There are some frightened screams and the mob is heard running back.)* I'm glad I'm out o' yo' ole town anyhow. I ain't never comin' back no mo', neither. You ole ugly-rump niggers done ruint de town anyhow.

> *(There is complete silence off stage. JIM walks a few steps with his coat and guitar, then sits down on the railroad embankment facing the audience. He pulls off one shoe and pours the sand out. He holds the shoe in his hand a moment and looks wistfully back down the railroad track.)*

JIM: Lawd, folks sho is deceitful. *(He puts on the shoe and looks back down the track again.)* I never woulda thought people woulda acted like that. *(Laces up the shoe)* Specially Dave Carter, much as me and him done progue'd round together goin' in swimmin' an' playin' ball an' serenadin' de girls an' de white folks. *(He sits there gloomily silent for awhile, then looks behind him and picks up his guitar and begins to pick a tune. The music is very sad, but he trails off into, "YOU MAY LEAVE AN' GO TO HALIMUHFACKS, BUT MY SLOW DRAG WILL BRING YOU BACK." When he finishes he looks at the sun and picks up his coat.)*

JIM: Reckon I better git on down de road and git somewhere. Lawd knows where. *(Stops suddenly in his tracks and turns back toward the village. Takes a step or two.)* All dat mess and stink for nothin'. Dave know good an' well I didn't mean to hurt him much. *(He takes off his cap and scratches his head thoroughly. Then turns again and starts on down the road left. Enter DAISY, left, walking fast and panting, her head down. They meet.)*

DAISY: Oh, hello, Jim. *(A little surprised and startled)*

JIM: *(Not expecting her)* Hello, Daisy. *(Embarrassed silence.)*

DAISY: I was just coming over town to see how you come out.

JIM: You don't have to go way over there to find dat out . . . you and Dave done got me run outa town for nothin'.

DAISY: *(Putting her hand on his arm)* Dey didn't run you outa town, did dey?

JIM: *(Shaking her hand off)* Whut you reckon I'm countin' Mr. Railroad's ties for . . . just to find out how many ties between here and Orlando?

DAISY: *(Hand on his arm again)* Dey *cain't* run you off like dat!

JIM: Take yo' hands off me, Daisy! How come they cain't run me off wid you and Dave an' . . . *every*body 'ginst me?

DAISY: I ain't opened my mouf 'gainst you, Jim. I ain't said one word . . . I wasn't even at de old trial. My madame wouldn't let me git off. I wuz just comin' to see 'bout you now.

JIM: Aw, go 'head on. You figgered I was gone too long to talk about. You was haulin' it over to town to see Dave . . . dat's whut you was doin' . . . after gittin' *me* all messed up.

DAISY: *(Making as if to cry)* I wasn't studyin' 'bout no Dave.

JIM: *(Hopefully)* Aw, don't tell me. *(Sings)* Ashes to ashes, dust to dust, show me a woman that a man can trust. *(DAISY is crying now.)*

JIM: What you crying for? You know you love Dave. I'm yo' monkey-man. He always could do more wid you that I could.

DAISY: Naw, you ain't no monkey-man neither. I don't want you to leave town. I didn't want y'all to be fightin' over me, nohow.

JIM: Aw, rock on down de road wid dat stuff. A two-timin' cloaker like you don't keer whut come off. Me and Dave been good friends ever since we was born till you had to go flouncing yourself around.

DAISY: What did I do? All I did was to come over town to see you and git a mouf-ful of gum. Next thing I know y'all is fighting and carrying on.

JIM: *(Stands silent for a while)* Did you come over there Sat'day night to see me sho nuff, sugar babe?

DAISY: Everybody could see dat but you.

JIM: Just like I told you, Daisy, before you *ever* left from round here and went up North. I could kiss you every day . . . just as regular as pig-tracks.

DAISY: And I tole you I could stand it too—just as regular as you could.

JIM: *(Catching her by the arm and pulling her down with him onto the rail)* Set down, here, Daisy. Less talk some chat. You want me sho nuff? Hones' to God?

DAISY: *(Coyly)* 'Member whut I told you out on de lake last summer?

JIM: Sho nuff, Daisy? *(DAISY nods smilingly)*

JIM: *(Sadly)* But I got to go 'way. Whut we gointer do 'bout dat?

DAISY: Where you goin', Jim?

JIM: *(Looking sadly down the track)* God knows.
    (Off stage from the same direction from which JIM entered comes the sound of whistling and tramping of feet on the ties.)

JIM: *(Brightening)* Dat's Dave! *(Frowning)* Wonder whut he doin' walkin' dis track? *(Looks accusingly at DAISY)* I bet he's goin' to yo' work-place.

DAISY: Whut for?

JIM: He ain't goin' to see de madame—must be goin' to see you. *(He starts to rise petulantly as DAVE comes upon the scene. DAISY rises also.)*

DAVE: *(Looks accusingly from one to the other)* Whut y'all jumpin' up for? I . . .

JIM: Whut you gut to do wid us business? Tain't none of yo' business if we stand up, set down or fly like a skeeter hawk.

DAVE: Who said I keered? Dis railroad belongs to de *man*—I kin walk it as good as you, cain't I?

JIM: *(Laughs exultantly)* Oh, yeah, Mr. Do-Dirty! You figgered you had done run me on off so you could git Daisy all by yo'self. You was headin' right for her work-place.

DAVE: I wasn't no such a thing.

JIM: You was. Didn't I hear you coming down de track all whistling and everything?

DAVE: Youse a big ole Georgy-something-ain't-so! I done got my belly full of Daisy Sat'day night. She can't snore in my ear no more.

DAISY: *(Indignantly)* Whut you come here low-ratin' me for, Dave Carter? I ain't done nothin' to you but treat you white. Who come rubbed yo' ole head for you yestiddy if it wasn't me?

DAVE: Yeah, you rubbed my head all right, and I lakted dat. But everybody say you done toted a pan to Joe Clarke's barn for Jim before I seen you.

DAISY: Think I was going to let Jim lay there 'thout nothing fitten for a dog to eat?

DAVE: That's all right, Daisy. If you want to pay Jim for knockin' me in de head, all right. But I'm a man in a class . . . in a class to myself and nobody knows my name.

JIM: *(Snatching Daisy around to face him)* Was you over to Dave's house yestiddy rubbing his ole head and cloaking wid him to run me outa town . . . and me looked up in dat barn wid de cows and mules?

DAISY: *(Sobbing)* All both of y'all hollerin' at me an' fussin' me just cause I tries to be nice . . . and neither one of y'all don't keer nothin' bout me.

> *(Both boys glare at each other over DAISY's head and both try to hug her at the same time. She violently wrenches herself away from both and makes as if to move on.)*

DAISY: Leave me go! Take yo' rusty pams offen me. I'm going on back to my work-place. I just got off to see bout y'all and look how y'all treat me.

JIM: Wait a minute, Daisy. I love you like God loves Gabriel . . . and dat's His best angel.

DAVE: Daisy, I love you harder than de thunder can bump a sump . . . if I don't . . . God's a gopher.

DAISY: *(Brightening)* Dat's de first time you ever said so.

DAVE and JIM: Who?

JIM: Whut you hollering "Who" for? Yo' fat don't fit no limb.

DAVE: Speak when you spoken to . . . come when you called, next fall you'll be my coon houn' dog.

JIM: Table dat discussion. *(Turning to DAISY)* You ain't never give me no chance to talk wid you right.

DAVE: You made *me* feel like you was trying to put de Ned book on me all de time. Do you love me sho nuff, Daisy?

DAISY: *(Blooming again into coquetry)* Aw, y'all better stop dat. You know you don't mean it.

DAVE: Who don't mean it? Lemme tell you something, mama, if you was mine I wouldn't have you counting no ties wid *yo'* pretty lil toes. Know whut I'd do?

DAISY: *(Coyly)* Naw, whut would you do?

DAVE: I'd buy you a whole passenger train . . . and hire some mens to run it for you.

DAISY: *(Happily)* Oh-ooh, Dave.

JIM: *(To DAVE)* De wind may blow, de doorway slam
    Dat shut you shootin' ain't worth a dam.
      (To DAISY) I'd buy you a great big ole ship . . . and then, baby,
      I'd buy you a ocean to sail yo' ship on.

DAISY: *(Happily)* Oh-ooh, Jim.

DAVE: *(To JIM)* A long train, a short caboose
    Dat lie whut you shootin', ain't no use.
      (To DAISY) Miss Daisy, know what I'd do for you?

DAISY: Naw, whut?

DAVE: I'd come down de river riding a mud cat and loading a minnow.

DAISY: Lawd, Dave, you sho is propaganda.

JIM: *(Peevishly)* Naw he ain't . . . he's just lying . . . he's a noble liar. Know whut I'd do if you was mine?

DAISY: Naw, Jim.

JIM: I'd make a panther wash yl' dishes and a 'gater chop yo' wood for you.

DAVE: Daisy, how come you let Jim lie lak dat? He's as big as a liar as he is a man. But sho nuff now, laying all sides to jokes, Jim there don't even know how to answer you. If you don't b'lieve it . . . ast him something.

DAISY: *(To JIM)* You like me much, Jim?

JIM: *(Enthusiastically)* Yeah, Daisy I sho do.

DAVE: *(Triumphant)* See dat! I tole you he didn't know how to answer nobody like you. If he was talking to some of them ol' funny looking gals over town he'd be answering 'em just right. But he got to learn how to answer *you*. Now you ast *me* something and see how I answer you.

DAISY: Do you like me, Dave?

DAVE: *(Very properly in a falsetto voice)* Yes ma'am! Dat's de way to answer swell folks like you. Furthermore, less we prove which one of us love you do best right now. *(To JIM)* Jim, how much time would you do on de chain-gang for dis 'oman?

JIM: Twenty years and like it.

DAVE: See dat, Daisy? Dat nigger ain't willin' to do no time for you. I'd *beg* de judge to gimme life. *(Both JIM and DAVE laugh)*

DAISY: Y'all doin' all dis bookooin' out here on de railroad track but I bet y'all crazy 'bout Bootsie and Teets and a whole heap of other gals.

JIM: Cross my feet and hope to die! I'd ruther see all de other wimmen folks in de worl' dead than for you to have de toothache.

DAVE: If I was dead and any other woman come near my coffin de undertaker would have to do his job all over . . .'cause I'd git right up and walk off. Furthermore, Miss Daisy, ma'am, also ma'am, which would *you* ruther be a lark a flying or a dove a settin' . . . ma'am, also ma'am?

DAISY: 'Course I'd ruther be a dove.

JIM: Miss Daisy, ma'am, also ma'am . . . if you marry dis nigger over my head, I'm going to git me a green hickory club and season it over yo' head.

DAVE: Don't you be skeered, baby . . . papa kin take keer a *you*. *(To JIM)* Countin' from de finger *(Suiting the action to the word)* back to de thumb . . . start anything I got you some.

JIM: Aw, I don't want no more fight wid you, Dave.

DAVE: Who said anything about fighting? We just provin' who love Daisy de best. *(To DAISY)* Now, which one of us you think love you de best?

DAISY: Deed I don't know, Dave.

DAVE: Baby, I'd walk de water for you . . . and tote a mountain on my head while I'm walkin'.

JIM: Know what I'd do, honey babe? If you was a thousand miles from home and you didn't have no ready-made money and you had to walk all de way, walkin' till ye' feet start to rolling, just like a wheel, and I was riding way up in de sky, I'd step backwards offa dat aryplane just to walk home wid you.

DAISY: *(Falling on JIM's neck)* Jim, when you talk to me like dat I just can't stand it. Less us git married right now.

JIM: Now you talkin' like a blue-black speller. Less go!

DAVE: *(Sadly)* You gointer leave me lak dis, Daisy?

DAISY: *(Sadly)* I likes you, too, Dave, I sho do. But I can't marry both of y'all at de same time.

JIM: Aw, come on, Daisy . . . sun's getting low. *(He starts off pulling DAISY)*

DAVE: Whut's I'm gointer do? *(Walking after them)*

JIM: Gwan back and dance . . . you make out you don't need me to play none.

DAVE: *(Almost tearfully)* Aw, Jim, shucks! Where y'all going?
    (DAISY comes to an abrupt halt and stops JIM)

DAISY: That's right, honey. Where *is* we goin' sho nuff?

JIM: *(Sadly)* Deed I don't know, baby. They just sentenced me to go . . . they didn't say where and I don't know.

DAISY: How we goin' nohow to go when we don't know where we goin'?

> (*JIM looks at DAVE as if he expects some help but DAVE stands sadly silent. JIM takes a few steps forward as if to go on. DAISY makes a step or two, unwillingly, then looks behind her and stops. DAVE looks as if he will follow them.*)

DAISY: Jim! *(He stops and turns)* Wait a minute! Whut we gointer do when we git there?

JIM: Where?

DAISY: Where we goin'?

JIM: I done tole you I don't know where it is.

DAISY: But how we gointer git something to eat and a place to stay?

JIM: Play and dance . . . just like I been doin'.

DAISY: You can't dance and Dave ain't gointer be ther.

JIM: *(Looks appealingly at DAVE, then away quickly)* Well, I can't help *dat*, can I?

DAISY: *(Brightly)* I tell you whut, Jim! Less us don't go nowhere. They sentenced you to leave Eatonville and youse more than a mile from de city limits already. Youse in Maitland now. Supposin' you come live on de white folks' place wid me after we git married. Eatonville ain't got nothin' to do wid you livin' in Maitland.

JIM: Dat'a a good idea, Daisy.

DAISY: *(Jumping up into his arms)* And listen, honey, you don't have to be beholden to Dave nor nobody else. You can throw dat ole box away if you want to. I know ehre you can get a *swell* job.

JIM: *(Sheepishly)* Doin' whut? *(Looks lovingly at his guitar)*

DAISY: *(Almost dancing)* Yard man. All you have to do is wash windows, and sweep de sidewalk, and scrub off de steps and porch and hoe up de weeds and rake up de leaves and dig a few holes now and then with a spade . . . to plant some trees and things like that. It's a good steady job.

JIM: *(After a long deliberation)* You see, Daisy, de Mayor and corporation told me to go on off and I oughter go.

DAISY: Well, I'm not going trippin' down no railroad track like a Maltese cat. I wasn't brought up knockin' round from here to yonder.

JIM: Well, I wasn't brought up wid no spade in my hand . . . and ain't going to start it now.

DAISY: But sweetheart, we got to live, ain't we? We got to git hold of money before we kin do anything. I don't mean to stay in de white folks' kitchen all my days.

JIM: Yeah, all dat's true, but you couldn't buy a flea a waltzing jacket wid de money *I'm* going to make wid a hoe and spade.

DAISY: *(Getting tearful)* You don't want me. You don't love me.

JIM: Yes, I do, darling, I love you. Youse de one letting a spade come between us. *(He caresses her)* I loves you and you only. You don't see *me* dragging a whole gang of farming tools into us business, do you?

DAISY: *(Stiffly)* Well, I ain't going to marry no man that ain't going to work and take care of me.

JIM: I don't mind working if de job ain't too heavy for me. I ain't going to bother wid nothin' in my hands heavier than dis box . . . and I totes it round my neck 'most of de time.

> *(DAISY makes a despairing gesture as JIM takes a step or two away from her. She turns to DAVE finally.)*

DAISY: Well, I reckon you loves me the best anyhow. You wouldn't talk to me like Jim did, would you, Dave?

DAVE: Naw, I wouldn't say what he said a-tall.

DAISY: *(Cuddling up to him)* Whut would *you* say, honey?

DAVE: I'd say dat box was too heavy for me to fool wid. I wouldn't tote nothing heavier than my hat and I feel like I'm 'busing myself sometime totin' dat.

DAISY: *(Outraged)* Don't you mean to work none?

DAVE: Wouldn't hit a lick at a snake.

DAISY: I don't blame *you*, Dave *(Looks down at his feet)* cause toting dem feet of yourn is enough to break down your constitution.

JIM: *(Airily)* That's all right . . . dem foots done put plenty bread in our moufs.

DAVE: Not by they selves though . . . wid de help of dat box, Jim. When you gits having fits on dat box, boy, my foots has hysterics. Daisy, you marry Jim cause I don't want to come between y'all. He's my buddy.

JIM: Come to think of it, Dave, she was yourn first. You take and handle dat spade for her.

DAVE: You heard her say it is all I can do to lift up dese feets and put 'em down. Where I'm going to git any time to wrassle wid any hoes and shovels? You kin git round better'n me. You done won Daisy . . . I give in. I ain't going to bite no fren' of mine in de back.

DAISY: Both of you niggers can git yo' hat an' yo' heads and git on down de road. Neither one of y'all don't have to have me. I got a good job and plenty men beggin for yo' chance.

JIM: Dat's right, Daisy, you go git you one them mens whut don't mind smelling mules . . . and beating de white folks to de barn every morning. I don't wanta be bothered wid nothin' but dis box.

DAVE: And I can't strain wid nothin' but my feets.

> *(DAISY walks slowly away in the direction from which she came. Both watch her a little wistfully for a minute. The sun is setting.)*

DAVE: Guess I better be gittin' on back . . . it's most dark. Where you goin', Jim?

JIM: I don't know, Dave. Down de road, I reckon.

DAVE: Whyncher come on back to town. 'Taint no use you proguein' up and down de railroad track when you got a home.

JIM: They done lawed me way from it for hittin' you wid dat bone.

DAVE: Dat ain't nothin'. It was my head you hit. An' if I don't keer whut dem old ugly-rump niggers got to do wid it?

JIM: They might not let me come in town.

DAVE: *(Seizing JIM's arm and facing him back toward the town)* They better! Look here, Jim, if they try to keep you out dat town we'll go out to dat swamp and git us a mule bone a piece and come into town and boil dat stew down to a low gravy.

JIM: You mean dat, Dave? *(DAVE nods his head eagerly)* Us wasn't mad wid one 'nother nohow. *(Belligerently)* Come on, less go back to town. Dem mallet-heads better leave me be, too. *(Picks up a heavy stick)* I wish Lum would come tellin' me 'bout de law when I got all dis law in *my* hands. And de rest o' dem gator-faced jigs, if they ain't got a whole sto' o' mule bones and a good determination, they better not bring no mess up. Come on, boy.

> *THEY start back together toward town, JIM picking a dance tune on his guitar, and DAVE cutting steps on the ties beside him, singing, prancing and happily, they exit, right, as*

THE CURTAIN FALLS

Scottsboro, Limited
A One-Act Play

1931

Hughes began his involvement with the Left in the 1920s, when he started to publish in such Leftist journals as *New Masses* and to associate with various radical causes taken up by both black and white writers of the period, most notably that of convicted murderers Nicola Sacco and Bartolomeo Vanzetti. By 1931, Hughes's work was appearing with great frequency in *New Masses*, as well as in other publications connected with the American Communist Party (CPUSA).

The subject of this play is the Scottsboro case, which involved nine black youths in Alabama who, in the spring of 1931, were convicted of rape on flimsy evidence; eight were sentenced to execution and one to life imprisonment. Later a cause célèbre, the Scottsboro case profoundly concerned Hughes from the beginning, and his commitment to the Left deepened when the International Labor Defense, the legal arm of the CPUSA, took up the defense after the NAACP failed to do so. Written during the fall of 1931, *Scottsboro, Limited* is classic agitprop: its concise analysis of its subject, rhythmic language and choreographed movement, audience involvement, and final call for action are all typical of the form.

Scottsboro, Limited was first performed in Los Angeles on May 8, 1932, an earlier production having been prevented by the police. It was also produced in Paris and in Moscow and translated into Russian during Hughes's Moscow visit later that year. The version given here is the one that appeared in *New Masses* in October 1931.

Characters

EIGHT BLACK BOYS
A WHITE MAN
TWO WHITE WOMEN
EIGHT WHITE WORKERS
VOICES IN THE AUDIENCE

SETTING: *One chair on a raised platform. No curtains or other effects needed.*

THE PLAY OPENS: *The eight BLACK BOYS, chained by the right foot, one to the other, walk slowly down the center aisle from the back of the auditorium. As they approach the middle of the house, there is a loud commotion, and the WHITE MAN rises in the audience.*

MAN: *(To BOYS)* What are you doing here? *(The BLACK BOYS continue marching without turning their heads. The MAN shouts louder, and more sternly.)* What are you-all doing in here? *(As the BOYS mount the stage, the MAN rushes up to them threateningly.)* What the hell are you doing in here, I said?

1ST BOY: *(Turning simply)*
> We come in our chains
> To show our pain.

MAN: *(Sneeringly)* Your pain! Stop talking poetry and talk sense.

8TH BOY: *(As they line up on the stage)*
> All right, we will—
> That sense of injustice
> That death can't kill.

MAN: Injustice? What d'yuh mean? Talking about injustice, you coon?

2ND BOY: *(Pointing to his comrades)*
> Look at us then:
> Poor, black, and ignorant,
> Can't read or write—
> But we come here tonight.

MAN: *(Sitting down jauntily on the edge of stage)* Not supposed to read or write. You work better without it.

1ST BOY: *(Shrugging his shoulders)*
> O.K. Chief,
> We won't argue with you.
> Tonight there's
> Too much else to do.

MAN: Now that you got the public eye, you want to show off, heh?

2ND BOY: *(Seriously)* Not show off—die!

5TH BOY: *(Earnestly)*
> So the people can see
> What it means to be
> A poor black workman
> In this land of the free.

2ND BOY: *(Harshly)*
> Where every star in the flag
> Is stained with a lie!

MAN: Do you want to get arrested for treason?

8TH BOY:
> We're already in jail.
> Have you got a darker cell
> Any worse
> Than this-here Southern Hell?

7TH BOY: Can a man die twice?

MAN: You-all ain't dead.

8TH BOY: *(Defiantly)*
> No, but we will be dead
> If we stay quiet here.
> That's why we come tonight
> To lift our troubles high.
> Like a flag against the sky.

2ND BOY:
> To show that we're living—
> Even though we die.

3RD BOY:
> To let the world see
> That even in chains
> We *will* be free!

4TH BOY: Watch this play for our misery:
> *(The chains break away, and the BOYS find themselves on a moving freight train. They sit down in a haphazard line on the stage, as though they were seated on the top of boxcars, rocking back and forth as the train moves.)*

6TH BOY: *(Happily)*
> Man this train sho is speedin'!
> Look a-yonder at de Sunny South.

4TH BOY:
> I wish I had some sugar cane in ma mouth.
> I'se hongry!

7TH BOY:
> Well it's sho too bad
> How when you ain't got no job
> Things get sad.

5TH BOY:

> I ain't got no job.

1ST BOY: Neither is I, but I wish I had.

2ND BOY: Looks like white folks is taking all de work.

5TH BOY: Is niggers got *exclusive* rights on work?

3RD BOY: Shut up, boy!

4TH BOY: He ain't joking, Perk.

2ND BOY:

> All them little town jobs we used to do,
> Looks like white folks is doin' 'em now, too.

1ST BOY: Just goes to prove there ain't no pure nigger work.

6TH BOY: *(In wonder)*

> Look a-yonder you-all, at dem fields
> Burstin' wid de crops they yields.
> Who gets it all?

3RD BOY: White folks.

8TH BOY: You means de rich white folks.

2ND BOY:

> Yes, 'cause de rich ones owns de land.
> And they don't care nothin' 'bout de po' white man.

3RD BOY:

> You's right. Crackers is just like me—
> Po' whites and niggers, ain't neither one free.

8TH BOY: Have to work like a fool to live and then you starve dead.

4TH BOY: Man, this country is sho too bad! *(The train stops and the rocking motion of the BOYS ceases. One or two of them get up and stretch.)*

3RD BOY: Uh-O! This train done stopped. Where is this?

7TH BOY: Well, wherever it is, I'm gonna take a—. *(Turning his back.)*

5TH BOY: No, you ain't. Can't you see this is a town?

MAN: *(As SHERIFF, at foot of stage, with a police star and a club)* Come on, you niggers, and get down.

6TH BOY: Uh-ooooo! Yonder stands the sheriff!

2ND BOY: Ha-ha-ha! Uh!

3RD BOY: Fool, this ain't no time to laugh.

SHERIFF: Come on and get down off that train!

6TH BOY: Yes, sir, Mister Boss Man!

4TH BOY: Soon's we can. *(The BOYS climb down.)*

SHERIFF: *(To BOYS who line up before him)* What you-all doin' on that train?

BOYS:
> Just tryin' to bum our way on through
> To Memphis where maybe there's work to do.

SHERIFF: *(Yelling up the line)* Get everybody off this train, deputy. *(To BOYS)* Stand over there, boys. *(Shouting to deputy)* What you say? Some girls getting off dressed in overalls? White girls? *(To himself)* Whee-oooo! *(To the BOYS)* What you-all doin' on the same train with them white women there?

BOYS: *(In wonder)* Where?

SHERIFF: There!

BOYS: Where?

SHERIFF: *(Fiercely)* You'll see where! Get back and let these white ladies by.

> *(While the succeeding action goes on the BOYS get behind the chair, four on each side in a line—convicts already.)*

MOB VOICES IN AUDIENCE: *(Murmuring and muttering)* Damned niggers . . . white girls and niggers riding together . . . nerve of them niggers . . . had no business in there . . . etc.

SHERIFF: *(As the two white GIRLS enter left, powdered and painted, but dressed in overalls.)* What you doin', girls? Out for a ride?

1ST GIRL: Yes sir.

SHERIFF: Where to?

1ST GIRL: Goin' home, I reckon.

SHERIFF: Where?

2ND GIRL: Huntsville.

SHERIFF: And these niggers on the train with you!

1ST GIRL: Ain't seen 'em before.

SHERIFF: Ain't these black brutes been botherin' you?

GIRLS: No, they ain't been near.

SHERIFF: Is that true? *(Sternly)* Ain't they had their hands on you?

GIRLS: *(Wavering)* Well, they . . . er . . .

SHERIFF: *(Positively)* I knew it! Which one of these black apes touched you?

GIRLS: Why . . . er . . .

SHERIFF: We'll have a trial and burn 'em up. And you'll get paid for testifying, and your pictures in the paper. Which ones?

1ST GIRL: That two there.

SHERIFF: Two? You sho it wasn't more?

2ND GIRL: No, we ain't sure.

1ST GIRL: It might-a been all right.

SHERIFF: All right? A trial's too good for black bastards like that. *(Pompously)* But we owe it to the state.

> *(He parades sternly up to the raised chair. He is the judge now and, as he mounts the legal bench, he puts on a black gown that has been lying there. The GIRLS slip off their overalls, displaying cheap loud dresses underneath, and powder their faces tittering. It is the court room, and the black prisoners come forward before the judge. The trial is conducted in jazz tempo: the white voices staccato, high and shrill; the black voices deep as the rumble of drums.)*

MOB VOICES: *(Murmuring)* Imagine a trial for niggers . . . a trial for niggers . . . a trial for niggers . . . etc.

JUDGE: *(From the chair)* The State of Alabama versus Andy Butler, Willie Johnson, Clarence Bates, Olen Jones, Ozie Jenkins, Roy Perkins, Ted Lucas, and Haywood Lane. *(The GIRLS sit, one on either side of the stage, grinning and pleased)* You raped that girl? *(Pointing at each boy in turn.)*

1ST BOY: No.

JUDGE: You raped that girl? *(Pointing from one girl to the other in rotation.)*

2ND BOY: No.

JUDGE: You raped that girl?

3RD BOY: No.

JUDGE: You raped that girl?

4TH BOY: No.

JUDGE: You raped that girl?

5TH BOY: No.

JUDGE: You raped that girl?

6TH BOY: No.

JUDGE: You raped that girl?

7TH BOY: No.

JUDGE: You raped that girl?

8TH BOY: No.

JUDGE: *(To GIRLS)* How about it girls?

1ST GIRL: They lie!

2ND GIRL: They raped us in a box car underneath the sky.

JUDGE: You niggers lie.

BOYS: We lie . . . White man always says we lie. . . . Makes us work and says we lie . . . Takes our money and says we lie.

JUDGE: Shut up. No talking back in the court. *(Pointing at each one in turn)* You had a gun.

1ST BOY: No.

JUDGE: You had a gun.

2ND BOY: No, sir.

JUDGE: You had a gun.

3RD BOY: *(Shaking head)* Not one.

JUDGE: You had a gun.

4TH BOY: Not nary one.

JUDGE: You had a gun.

5TH BOY: We didn't have none.

JUDGE: You had a gun.

6TH BOY: No gun.

JUDGE: You had a gun!

7TH BOY: No, sir, none.

JUDGE: You had a gun.

8TH BOY: No gun.

JUDGE: How about it, girls?

1ST GIRL: They lie.

2ND GIRL: They all had guns.

JUDGE: *(To BOYS)* You all had guns. *(To GIRLS)* And they raped you, one by one. *(GIRLS nod heads)* How long did it take? How long was it?

1ST GIRL: Why they didn't even let us up to spit!

2ND GIRL: It was rough!

JUDGE: To spit what?

GIRLS: Snuff!

JUDGE: You hear that, Jury? This court is done.

1ST GIRL: Convict these brutes. *(Smiling at audience.)*

2ND GIRL: Every black one. *(Also smiling)*

MOB VOICES: Convict 'em! Ever damn black one!

JUDGE: Don't worry, folks, 'tis done.

MOB VOICES: Kill the niggers! Keep 'em in their places! Make an example of 'm for all the black races . . . etc.

BOYS: *(Rising and circling round and round the chair echoing the angry mob)* Kill the niggers! Keep them in their places! Make an example of 'em for all the black races, for all the black races, for all the black races.

JUDGE: *(Descending from the bench, to audience)* Don't worry folks, the law will take its course. They'll burn, and soon at that.

(He and the GIRLS exit, talking and smiling)

MOB VOICES: *(Applauding and shouting)* Make it soon. Kill the niggers. Let 'em die.

BOYS: *(Echoing the Voices)* Make it soon. Let us die. Make it soon. Soon. Soon.

6TH BOY: *(Breaking away from the dumb circle)* No, no, no! What do they want to kill us for?

3RD BOY: I'll break free!

> *(The BOYS divide up into groups of two's now, in a row across the stage, in the cells of the death house, some of them sitting down, some of them weeping, some of them pushing against the bars with their hands.)*

2ND BOY:

> How you gonna git out o' here
> With these iron bars and this stone wall
> And the guards outside and the
> Guns and all?

8TH BOY:

> There ain't no way for a nigger to break free,
> They got us beaten, and that's how we gonna be
> Unless we learn to understand—
> We gotta fight our way out like a man.

5TH BOY: Not out o' here.

4TH BOY:

> No, not out o' here,
> Unless the ones on the outside
> Fight for us, too,
> We'll die—and then we'll be through.

MOB VOICES:

> You oughta be through—
> Oughta be through.
> In this white man's land
> There's no place for you.

MURMUR OF RED VOICES: *(In audience)*

> We'll fight for you, boys. We'll fight for you.
> The Reds will fight for you.

6TH BOY:

> We'll die, and then we'll all be through—
> Through livin', through lovin', through lookin'

at the sky.
I don't wanta die.

8TH BOY:

Who does want to die?
That's why all the free black men
Have got to fight,
Or else we'll all die in poverty's night.

3RD BOY: You're right.

RED VOICES:

We'll fight! The Communists will fight for you.
Not just black—but black and white.

3RD BOY: Then we'll trust in you.

MAN: (*Become the PRISON KEEPER now, marching across the front of the cell-row with a long stick in his hand.*)

Shut up in there, with your plots and plans.
Don't you niggers know yet this is a white man's land?
And I'm the keeper, understand.

8TH BOY:

We ain't half as low as you!
Paid to kill people, that's what you do.
Not just niggers—but your white brothers too.

RED VOICES: (*Stronger now*)

That's true! True!

PRISON KEEPER: (*Striking boy*) Shut up!

8TH BOY:

I won't shut up.
I've nobody to talk for me,
So I'll talk for myself, see.

RED VOICES: And the red flag, too, will talk for you.

1ST BOY:

Listen, boys! That's true—they've sent a lawyer
to talk for me and you.

6TH BOY: But they told us not to bother with a communist.

8TH BOY: But who else is there will help us out o' this?

3RD BOY:

And not just us, but help all the black South
Hungry for freedom, and bread, and new words in their mouth.

MAN: (*Entering this time as a PREACHER, sanctified, with a Bible in his hand.*)

Ashes to ashes and dust to dust—

If the law don't kill you then the lynchers must.

(Piously) I've come to say a little prayer

Before you go away from here.

3RD BOY: *(Questioning)*

A prayer to a white God in a white sky?

We don't want that kind of prayer to die.

6TH BOY:

I want a prayer!

(The Death Bell rings)

Oh, Lord, I want a prayer.

8TH BOY:

No prayer! No prayer!

Lemme out o' here.

Take me on to the chair

With no God damn prayer.

(To the PREACHER)

May they choke in your mouth,

Every praying white lie!

PREACHER: *(In horror, hurrying out)* Let the niggers die!

MOB VOICES: Let 'em die!

8TH BOY: *(Starting on the march to the chair, walking straight across the stage to the center, then turning, straight back to the Electric Chair where he seats himself, unafraid, slipping his hands into the cords that bind him to the arms of the chair.)*

Because I talked out loud, you kill me first:

Death in the flesh is the fighters curse.

MOB VOICES: Yes, you must die! Let the nigger die! Let all of 'em die!

8TH BOY:

Let all of us die:

That's what the mobs cry.

All I've ever known:

Let the niggers die!

All my life long:

Let the niggers die!

BOYS: *(Helplessly crouching back at the foot of chair.)*

Let us die! Let us die!

MOB VOICES:

Let 'em die!

Beat 'em! Shoot 'em!

Hang 'em with a rope,

Burn 'em in the chair.
Let 'em choke.
BOYS:
Burn us in the chair!
The chair! The Chair!
Burn us in the chair!
8TH BOY:
Burn *me* in the chair?
NO!
(*He breaks his bonds and rises, tall and strong.*)
NO! For me not so!
Let the meek and humble turn the other cheek—
I am not humble!
I am not meek!
From the mouth of the death house
Hear me speak!
RED VOICES: Hear him speak! Hear him speak!
MOB VOICES: Shut up, you God-damn nigger!
RED VOICES: Hear him speak!
BOYS: Hear us speak!
8TH BOY:
All the world, listen!
Beneath the wide sky
In all the black lands
Will echo this cry:
I will not die!
BOYS: We will NOT DIE!
MOB VOICES: (*Snarling*)
Quick! Quick! Death there!
The chair! The electric chair!
8TH BOY:
No chair!
Too long have my hands been idle
Too long have my brains been dumb.
Now out of the darkness
The new Red Negro will come:
That's me!
No death in the chair!
BOYS: (*Rising*) No death in the chair!
RED VOICES: (*Rising in audience*) NO DEATH IN THE CHAIR!

BOYS: NO DEATH IN THE CHAIR! *(They circle platform and lifting the electric chair up, they smash it on the stage.)* NO DEATH IN THE CHAIR!

MOB VOICES: *(Roaring helplessly)* Aw-w-w-w-ooo-aw!

RED VOICES:

> No death in the chair.
> Together, we'll make the world clean and fair.

8TH BOY:

> Too long have we stood
> For the whip and the rope.

RED VOICES: Too long! Too long!

8TH BOY:

> Too long have we labored
> Poor, without hope.

BOYS: Too long!

RED VOICES: Too long!

8TH BOY:

> Too long have we suffered
> Alone.

BOYS: Alone!

8TH BOY: But not now!

RED VOICES: No, not now.

8TH BOY:

> The voice of the red world
> Is our voice, too.

RED VOICES: The voice of the red world *is* you!

8TH BOY:

> The hands of the red world
> Are our hands, too.

RED VOICES: The hands of the red world *are* you!

8TH BOY:

> With all of the workers,
> Black or white,
> We'll go forward
> Out of the night.

BOYS: Out of the night.

8TH BOY

> Breaking down bars,
> Together.

BOYS: Together.

RED VOICES: Together. *(The RED VOICES of the white workers come forward toward the stage.)*

BOYS: *(Breaking their bars and coming forward toward the front of the stage to meet their white comrades)* Seeking the stars!

RED VOICES: Seeking the stars of hope and life.

8TH BOY: Not afraid of the struggle.

BOYS: Not afraid of the strife.

RED VOICES: Not afraid to fight:

8TH BOY: For new life!

BOYS: New life!

RED VOICES: New life!

 (The white workers and black workers meet on the stage)

BOYS: Comrades!

RED VOICES: Comrades!

 (They clasp hands and line up in a row of alternating blacks and whites.)

BOYS: Joining hands to build the right.

RED VOICES: White and black!

BOYS: Black and white!

8TH BOY: To live, not die!

ALL: To fight! To fight!

8TH BOY:

 In the heart of a fighter, death is a lie:
 O, my black people, you need not die!

RED VOICES: All the down trodden—you need not die!

AUDIENCE: We need not die! We need not die!

8TH BOY:

 Black and white together
 Will fight the great fight
 To put greed and pain
 And the color line's blight
 Out of the world
 Into time's old night.

BOYS AND REDS: All hands together will furnish the might.

AUDIENCE: All hands together will furnish the might.

RED VOICES: Rise from the dead, workers, and fight!

BOYS:

 All together, black and white,
 Up from the darkness into the light.

ALL: Rise, workers, and fight!
AUDIENCE: Fight! Fight! Fight! Fight!
  (Here the Internationale *may be sung and the red flag raised above the heads of the black and white workers together.)*
THE END

Harvest

1934
With Ella Winter and Ann Hawkins

In earlier drafts called "Blood on the Field," and "Blood on the Cotton," *Harvest* is a documentary drama depicting events connected to a bitter, but successful, strike by farmworkers in the San Joachim Valley, near Carmel, California. It was in Carmel that Hughes lived with friends on his return from the USSR in 1933. Written with journalist Ella Winter, the wife of writer Lincoln Steffens, the dialogue in *Harvest* is drawn from newspaper accounts or from interviews with farmworkers and others. The fictional Jennie Martin is based on union organizer Carolyn Decker, who became a frequent guest in the Steffens-Winter home, and many other characters in the play are easily identifiable. All the incidents in the play are also recognizable.[1]

Certain aspects of the intended staging of *Harvest* derive from theatrical techniques that Hughes encountered in Moscow; it is also likely that Hughes had seen one or more of the documentary plays on strikes that were performed on the East Coast in the early 1930s.[2] In the fall of 1934, Hughes and Winter submitted the play to the Theater Union. When it was rejected, they enlisted the help of the third collaborator, director and leftist writer Ann Hawkins. The Production Note below is by Hughes; however, the play was never produced.

This text is the most complete version in the Langston Hughes Papers. Ellipses and longer series of dots are given as in the original and do not indicate deletions or illegible passages. Hughes did not include any accents for Spanish names or words, and we have followed that practice.

Production Note

This play should give the effect of a mass play. It is suggested that the audience as well as the stage be used, that runways be employed, and that the old frame of the proscenium be broken . . . . . . Between scenes, a "newspaper" curtain might be used, reproducing actual portions of the reporting of the strike. Bits from the strikers' handbills, or from the

Vigilantes' and growers' advertisements could be flashed on the screen. (Such as the enclosed "Notice to the Citizens of Tulare.")

If possible, one or two Filipinos might be included among the strikers, to add to the melting pot of races that is California's low-paid agricultural reserve.

In the possession of the author is a huge album of pictures, clippings, leaflets, handbills, etc., of the strike. This material is at the disposal of the producer.

Act I, Scene 1

A California road. Night. Sound in distance of a noisy rattle-trap approaching. Sputtering, it slows almost to a stop, its weak headlights pale on the road. A lantern for a tail light. Sound of gears and brakes, and a sputter of curses in Spanish as the old Ford jerks to a dead stop. In the darkness Mexican voices are heard within the stalled car.

JOSE: *Cabron!*

DOMINGO: *(In a weary quaver)* What's the matter?

ROSITA: *(Sleepily) Porque no anda?* Why we stop?

> *(In the darkness a young man gets out, goes round to the back of the car and detaches the lantern hanging there. He approaches the hood and raises it up. Curses in Spanish and tinkers with the engine.)*

JOSE: Car's broken down.

> *(Tall old man climbs over the side of the old car, knocking into the road a big bundle of bedding. DOMINGO stands holding the lantern while JOSE inspects the engine.)*

MILLIE: *(Whimpering)* 'S matter, mama? Why we stop here?

ROSITA: *(Crossly)* We no stop here. Car stop here.

JOSE: *(Bending over car) Jesus,* no gas!

DOMINGO: No gas! *(Comes with lantern)* Jose; look in can.

JOSE: *(Picking up a can tied to running board and shaking it)* Empty.

> *(For a moment there is a dead silence. Then ROSITA begins to mutter in Spanish inside car. Suddenly a baby begins to cry)*

ROSITA: *Ay, Maria!*

> *(She rises and climbs from the car, reaches inside and picks up the baby. As the men talk, she sits down on the running board and suckles the child. Two older children with American names, a boy,*

*ROY, and a little girl, MILLIE, pile out of the car. They stand
shivering in the road. The old man puts down the lantern.)*

DOMINGO: *(To JOSE)* Where's nearest gas station?

JOSE: Bakersfield, I guess.

ROSITA: What for you talk gas? Who got money? Got one quarter
left, buy can beans, buy milk for *ninos*. These child no milk today,
yesterday . . .

DOMINGO: *Tienes razon.* No money. *(Pleadingly to wife)* Rosita, maybe buy one gallon gas?

JOSE: *(Matter of fact)* No get there on one gallon gas. Tilden ranch
thirty, forty miles.

ROSITA: *(Positively)* No buy gallon gas! *(Angrily to JOSE)* Why you no
say ranch so far? *Ay! Que cosa!*

MILLIE: *(Shivering)* Mama, put mattress down for me to sleep.

ROY: Mama, I'm tired.

ROSITA: Sleep, heh? Tomorrow's work day, we lost eighty cents if we
stop here sleep. Then you get no beans, no tortillas. *(Wrapping up
her baby, to the neglect of the other children)*

JOSE: Maybe 'nother car come by. *(He rolls and lights a cigarette from
the lantern flame)*

ROSITA: Why we leave Oxnard? Beets good. We pick beets we live. . . .

DOMINGO: What you mean good? Pay no good. Sixty cents day.
Contractor take some, commissary take some, you take some. What
I got?

JOSE: Yah, better go pick cotton.

DOMINGO: *(Pointing at his children)* Kids can help pick cotton.

ROSITA: *(To ROY)* Come here. *(She pulls the skinny boy to her side on
running board and puts a part of her ragged coat about him)*

MILLIE: *(Envying her brother wrapped in mother's coat)* Me cold, too,
mama.

ROSITA: *(Sharply)* Get back in Ford, go to sleep.

> *(MILLIE begins to cry. The woman rises to push her into car. The
> baby begins to cry too. The old man curses in Spanish. JOSE stands
> forlornly with the lantern, when the sound of a motor is heard. Pale
> headlights flood the road—picking out the broken down Ford and
> the miserable Mexicans standing there. JOSE begins excitedly to
> swing his lantern. ROSITA grabs their bundle from the road and
> throws it in the car)*

DOMINGO: *(Crossing himself)* Audame, Jesus querida, audame.

JOSE: *(Standing squarely in the road swinging the lantern)* Get out way!

(The old Mexican, the woman, and the children scatter to side behind the Ford. Sputtering and rattling, the approaching car is forced to come to a noisy stop)

ADAM: *(The high thin voice of a Southern white in the car)* Don't get funny, greaser,—standing there in the road. What do you mean? What you want?

JOSE: Gas.

ADAM: This ain't no travellin' gas station.

JOSE: We got no gas.

LUTHER: *(Voice in car)* Goddam! . . . . . . Go on . . . . . . What the hell? Stoppin' like that, wakin' everybody up.

DOMINGO: You give us ten cents gas. My boy he suck it out tank.

ADAM: Ain't got enough for myself.

MARTY: *(A woman's voice in car)* Give 'em a little gas, Adam. Look like they mighty nigh po' as we air.

ADAM: Let 'em buy it, like us. Damned Mexicans! That's why a white man ain't got no work here now.

SHORTY: Reckon won't hurt to give 'em enough to get to Bakersfield, pa. *(To JOSE)* Whar you-all goin', boy?

JOSE: Tilden Ranch.

(There is a burst of voices in the white folks' car)

SHORTY: That's where we goin.

MARTY: You-all goin' to pick?

ADAM: *(Climbing out of his car)* What they payin' up there for a-pullin bolls? You heard?

JOSE: Maybe 40¢ hundred.

ADAM: 40¢! A human can't live on that!

MARTY: Give 'em some gas, honey, and let's go on.

LUTHER: *(Gets out of car, morosely)* Why let 'em take the bread out o' our mouths? Greasers.

(JOSE and the old Mexican are already busy getting a hose and can. A short stocky young white fellow, SHORTY, gets out of the second car and glares at LUTHER)

SHORTY: What's that to you? And you payin' no fare? *(To JOSE at gas tank)* Take wot you need, but remember we ain't the Standard Oil.

MARTY: *(To Mexicans)* You-all got children with you, ain't you?

ROSITA: Si, lady.

MARTY: It's hard enough trapsin' over the country lookin' for work yourself, let alone with young ones.

ROSITA: We no can pay, lady.

LUTHER: That's how they all are—steal, but no pay! No honesty in these wops.

MARTY: *(Gently to ROSITA)* I ain't askin' you 'bout payin'.

SHORTY: Aw, Dad, let 'em have it. It won't kill us.

ADAM: They said ten cents worth.

ROSITA: *(Pleading)* No can pay. We got one quarter, no eat all day.

MARTY: *(Calling)* Let 'em have it, Adam. This is my car. I reckon I got some say-so.

LUTHER: Generosity's cheap, Aunt Marty.

ADAM: *(To Mexicans)* Alright, go ahead. *(To woman)* You mighty worried about a car load o' greasers tryin' to beat us to the Tilden Ranch to take the bread out o' our mouths.

> *(JOSE begins to suck out some gas. There is a flood of light on the road and the sound of a popping motor)*

SHORTY: One eyed car coming. We gotta move. *(JOSE picks up gas can. SHORTY calls to the driver)* Pull aside, pa, somethin' comin'.

> *(A motorcycle COP pulls up before the white family can clear the road)*

COP: What the hell are you doin, blocking the highway?

JOSE: No gas, Mister.

COP: Where are you going?

SHORTY: *(Under his breath)* What's that to you, General Perishing?

COP: What's your name? *(Flashes light on license plates)*

DOMINGO: We go pick cotton, Mister.

COP: Where you come from? *(To the whites)* Where's your home?

SHORTY: Home? Ha! Ha!

MARTY: Home's in Arkansas. Little Rock, Arkansas.

COP: *(To Mexicans)* Where'd you come from?

JOSE: Mexico.

COP: I mean now?

DOMINGO: Come from Oxnard now.

COP: *(Suspiciously)* Oxnard, heh? You had trouble down there, didn't you?

DOMINGO: No, senor, no trouble.

COP: You come up here to pick cotton, heh?

JOSE: Yes.

COP: *(To whites)* Where're you going?

> *(His flashlight plays on the white family's car)*

MARTY: *(Sharply)* We goin' where there's a few bolls to pull.

COP: The whole lot of you cotton pickers, heh? Did you pick cotton here last year, any of you?

ADAM: No.

COP: *(To JOSE)* Where was you last year?

JOSE: Pick melons, El Centro.

COP: *(To DOMINGO)* And *you?*

DOMINGO: I pick oranges, Riverside.

SHORTY: I was lappin' up that lousy soup from Pasadena relief.

COP: Lousy, heh? What you do to earn it?

SHORTY: I hope *you* have to drink it once, big boy.

COP: That's enough out of you. *(To both groups)* You can't bum around here. This Valley's overrun with tramps now. Get your gas and keep moving. Keep on going.

JOSE: We pick cotton.

SHORTY: *(To COP)* That's more'n you do!

COP: *(To SHORTY)* I got a good mind to pick you up. *(Angrily)* Where's your driver's license?

 (The Mexicans begin to back away. SHORTY stands his ground)

SHORTY: My old man's drivin, not me.

ADAM: *(To his wife)* Marty, look in the car pocket for my license.

COP: *(Takes the license from ADAM and notes down its number. To the Mexicans)* Let's see your license.

 (DOMINGO searches in his pockets for the license)

COP: Hurry up! I haven't got all night.

DOMINGO: Yes, sir.

COP: *(Glaring around)* Lousy foreigners.

LUTHER: You made a mistake, brother. We ain't foreigners.

COP: Well, I'm keepin' track of you, too. You look to me like one of those goddam trouble-makers.

LUTHER: Oh no. But I can tell you who *is.* *(Looks significantly at SHORTY)*

SHORTY: You sonofabitch! So that's your gratitude fer us bringin' you out. *(Socks him)*

COP: *(Making a grab for SHORTY)* Startin' a riot—afore you even get to the cotton fields!

 (SHORTY dodges)

MARTY: *(Screams)* O-ooo-oo!

SHORTY: And you look out too, you big bully!

COP: *(Lifts his night stick)* I'll get you yet, you. . . . .

(COP looks the two families up and down, his motorcycle sputters and pops, then he drives away)

SHORTY: Bastard!

JOSE: Why he so angry? What we do?

ADAM: *(Mildly)* Nothing! But Shorty's too quick tempered. *(To LU-THER)* And as for you . . . . . .

LUTHER: *(Sulky)* Aw, pipe down. I just wanted to git the cop out o' the road.

MARTY: *(To her family)* If you want to be in them fields tomorrow, let's git goin'. Adam, come on.

MEXICANS: *Vamanos! Andale! Ya nos vamos.*

The whites pile in and drive away. The Mexicans climb into their car, too. Rattle! Bang! Pop, pop, pop, pop! The road is clear as the

CURTAIN FALLS

Act I, Scene 2

A cotton field on the Tilden Ranch. Mid-morning. Blazing sun. Many men, women, and children, whites, Mexicans, and a few Negroes are working in the field, dragging cotton sacks behind them. The men wear overalls with leather knee pads. Some of the women also have on overalls, others ragged dresses. During the action there is a constant slow movement of pickers up and down the rows.

SHORTY: *(To a Negro carrying two full cotton sacks on his back across the field)* Heavy, bo?

BUSTER: *(Drawling)* It ain't light. I'm carryin mine an' ma girl's too.

SHORTY: *(Joking)* Who collects the cash?

BUSTER: I collects—but she takes it away from me.

FRANKIE MAE: *(Straightening up to fix her hair)* She's got the right idea.

SHORTY: How do *you* know, baby?

MARTY: *(Sharply to SHORTY)* Standin there a-jawin, that's why we can't get ahead o' the darkies. Old as I am, I picked more cotton 'n you did yestidday.

BUSTER: How much?

MARTY: *(Proudly)* Nigh 130.

BUSTER: Sho is good.

MARTY: *(Sees ROY going towards stream)* Boy, don't you go a-drinkin that gulley water. *(To the others)* I found a calf's foot in our bucket this mawnin!

FRANKIE MAE: You have to boil it first.

BUSTER: We ain't got nothin to boil it in yit.

MARTY: Why don't you buy something?

BUSTER: Bucket cost 95 cents in that there Ranch commissary.
(JOSE enters with an old bag)

BUSTER: *(To JOSE)* You gwine lose all de cotton you pick, all dem holes in yo' bag. *(He exits with his cotton on his back)* Lemme go weigh this here.

SHORTY: *(Seeing JOSE and recognizing him as the boy on the road)* Well, if it ain't old Pancho Villa himself what held us up for gas. When'd you get here?

JOSE: This mornin.

MARTY: *(To JOSE)* We put in a whole day a-ready.

JOSE: Car break down four times. Had to push it.

SHORTY: *(Stopping to play, mimicking accent)* Strong man, him push-a da car! *(He gives a punch at JOSE across the cotton row)*

ADAM: We gonna be pushing that rattle trap o' ours if we don't make some money here to buy a new set o' plugs.

LUTHER: *(Lazily)* Well, I don't see how you gonna do it. They don't pay but 50¢ a hundred on this damn ranch.

ADAM: If you work, it's alright. You never did care much for work, did you, Luther?

LUTHER: My back is weak.

SHORTY: You sure it ain't your head?

MACK SAUNDERS: We need some solid food, comrades, that's what's the matter. Eating this commissary canned stuff—and not enough o' that.

MARTY: An' they make a lot of profit on it too, don't they?

ROY: *(Barefooted)* I'm tired.

MARTY: Well, set down and rest. Pore as a Mexican chile, havin' to pick.

LUTHER: *(Squatting on the ground rolling a cigarette)* I never seed such shiftlessness.

MACK: We ought to have more for breakfast, that's the truth. We can't eat decent, on this pay.

LUTHER: *(Righteous)* I can eat on it.

ADAM: I sho can't.

FRANKIE MAE: It gives me a rash.

(BUSTER returns dragging his empty sack through the rows)

SHORTY: How much'd you weigh in?

BUSTER: 'Bout enough to pay for the string on this sack.

JOSE: How much sack cost?

SHORTY: *(Mimicking)* Sack him cost-a more you make-a one day.

ADAM: *(Sarcastic)* Stop makin fun o' that greaser, Shorty. They're human, ain't they? First thing you know he'll slice you.

JOSE: I no slice nobody, mister. I wanta know how much new bag cost this year.

BUSTER: Dollar forty cents, pal. That's what they cost.

JOSE: Last year bag cost eighty-seven cents.

MACK: Sure, everything gone up.

BUSTER: Last year they ain't paid but forty cents around here.

MACK: Yes, but eats has gone up a hell of a lot more. Your fifty cents is worth around twenty-five now.

MARTY: Any ranches around here got better water, Mister?

MACK: No, and most got worse toilets.

BUSTER: I wuz wo'kin on the W'ite place afore I cum here and their water was about two miles from camp. Had to carry it in buckets all the way.

MARTY: No better 'n it was down Cal'patria all I kin hear.

MACK: *(Interested)* You bin down there?

MARTY: Sho have.

MACK: Well, I'm afraid there's going to be sickness in all these camps. Ditch water, and holes in the ground for toilets all over this area.

MARTY: That ain't sanitary!

FRANKIE MAE: It's no life for a lady.

SHORTY: Wot you want? Runnin hot and cold pianos in marble-tiled bathrooms?

LUTHER: *(Agreeing)* That's what I say! *(To SHORTY)* Not often we agree, eh, pal?

(As they are picking down the rows they catch up with some Mexicans, including the Rodriguez)

SHORTY: Hi, greasers, yo'all workin hard? Goin to put by yer savin's fer a Rolls Royce? I heard yer Ford's none too good—but I see you a-pickin quite well.

DOMINGO: Before, I never pick cotton.

ADA: *(A Negro girl wearing ten-cent pieces in her ears)* Yo gits pretty expert at it aftah a time. I kin pick two hundred a day when I'm well, can't I, Buster?

BUSTER: Uh-hum.

MARTY: *(Enviously)* Yo' can? *(Aside to ADAM)* Them niggers'll be stealin the bread out uv our children's mouths.

MACK: That's a funny thing to say, Mrs., er—Mrs.—

SHORTY: Dobbs, me lad. Dobbs, rimes wi' sobs and mobs and robs and a hell of a lot other things we might be doin before long.

MARTY: Shut up, Shorty. *(To MACK)* What do you mean—funny?

MACK: I mean the white folks out here, big ranchers, is to blame, Mis' Dobbs, not the Mexicans or the Negroes. When the growers wanted cheap hands for this valley, they sent agents to Washington askin 'em not to limit immigration so they could get plenty Mexicans and Filipino boys to pick cotton and grapes and lettuce. They offered train fare and promised good wages and schools for their children. Then when they got all the help they needed, the growers started payin' the starvation wages we're gettin' now.

MARTY: I ain't blamin them pickers. I'd as soon blame them farmers livin in big houses and eatin the fat o' the land and me out here breakin my back in the sun.

> *(A loud cry is heard and a pretty young Mexican girl comes running by sobbing and screaming followed by PANCHO)*

JUANITA: *Madre mia!* Oh, save me! Don't let him hit me. Help, help!

PANCHO: *(An elderly Mexican)* *Cabron del diablo!* I'll show you! No daughter o' mine, you!

> *(He rushes toward her, brandishing knife. SHORTY and MACK hold him)*

FRANKIE MAE: *(Excitedly)* Help! Aw-oo-o!

MACK: Quiet, quiet, what d' you want, the cops on top of us?

PANCHO: *(Cursing and half sobbing)* Cops, yes, polizia! Let 'em come, take her jail. No daughter o' mine.

> *(Everyone in the field has stopped picking, turning around to listen, putting their hands in the bend of the back where it hurts as they straighten)*

BUSTER: *(To PANCHO)* Keep yo' shirt on, bo. Why, she's on'y a little girl.

PANCHO: Little girl? *Madre de dios!* Yes, little, an' already bad . . . . . . I kill 'er. *(Struggling to get loose)*

JUANITA: *(Crying with fright)* Oh, help me! Help me!

> *(People edge in slowly from all parts of the field to hear the excitement)*

LUTHER: Damn fool Mexicans!

MARTY: *(Stepping up angrily)* Here! Here! When I'm a-pullin boles I don't want no trouble. What's the matter with you?

PANCHO: Senora, she make me disgrace. She—she—gonna have baby!

SHORTY: Is that all?

    (There is a murmur of relief and amusement in the crowd)

MARTY: Well, she ain't the first woman what's had a baby. You put that knife down.

ADA: You gonna kill her fer that?

PANCHO: Si! Si! Baby without *padre.*

    (Smiles and some laughter)

SHORTY: It's gettin' better and better.

PANCHO: *(Furious)* She make me disgrace.

ADA: *(Placidly)* You can't tell. It might be a sweet child. *(To JUANITA)* Who's its father?

SHORTY: *(Singing line from Casey Jones)* She's got a lovin' papa on the Salt Lake Line.

BUSTER: Po' chile.

MARTY: *(To JUANITA)* Hush yore cryin, now. He ain't gonna hurt you.

JUANITA: *(Sobbing)* Yes, he will, he wants to kill me. Night time, he kill me.

LUTHER: You can stay with me, baby, in the night time.

MARTY: *(Sharply)* You Luther! *(To JUANITA)* Come here, child. Where is yore baby's father? *(She puts an arm around the girl)*

JUANITA: Maybe he El Centro, I don't know.

BUSTER: A no-good son of a gun!

JUANITA: *(Defensively)* He good boy. I love him. He want marry me, but we got no money. No can marry, no can love. *(Sobbing)* I want die! I want die!

FRANKIE MAE: *(Dabbing her eyes)* Ain't it sad?

ADA: It's sho a hell of a life, honey. You right about that.

MACK: She's right. This ain't no way to live, the way we have to. *(Passionately)* Never makin enough to settle down, sleepin in tents and shacks, no decent place to lay your head at night. This girl's sure right. It's a hell of a life! And we got to do something about it. *(The workers have gradually gathered around MACK. JUANITA's sobs are less violent. From the crowd there are mostly dumb stares, but some grunts and nods of agreement as MACK continues)* We got to at least make enough to buy food and live like humans in shacks. We ain't fools, are we?

JOSE: *(Listens to MACK intently)* No.

PICKERS:

> Sho ain't.
>
> No, sir!
>
> *Verdad que no.*
>
> I ain't.

MACK: Look at this Ranch. This here cotton. *(Pointing around him)* We pick it, the growers sell it. They get thousands of dollars. We get nothing. They said they would give us cabins, wood, and water! And what happens? Nothing.

LUTHER: *(Spitting tobacco)* Who's he, shootin' his mouth off?

SHORTY: Shut up, and listen.

> *(But LUTHER exits)*

MARTY: These here Mexicans is terrible, workin for nothin.

MACK: Mexicans ain't terrible, Mrs. Dobbs. We ought to get together. You heard about the Gallus Peach Ranch. The pickers there struck for more money—and got it.

DOMINGO: Not always get more in strike, Mister.

MACK: No, but you stay broke if you don't *try*.

ADAM: *(To MACK)* Well, talkin 'bout gettin together, what should we do?

MACK: There's to be a little meetin Saturday in _____? [*sic*] Come down there and talk to the other fellows.

> *(MACK returns to his row. The others slowly begin to scatter. While some are still standing talking, the ranch foreman comes striding into their midst. Behind him straggles LUTHER, who left as MACK was talking)*

FOREMAN: What the hell is this? Who's standin gabbin here? *(To the Mexicans)* You greasers 're on this ranch to pick cotton, not to stand around and jabber. *(To SHORTY, standing defiantly upright)* What are you up to?

SHORTY: *(Sweetly)* Lookin' at the moon.

FOREMAN: Be careful who you're talkin' to. Are you the fellow come in here with that bunch last Monday?

SHORTY: Oh, no, I was born on this ranch. *(He lights a cigarette)*

FOREMAN: *(Hot, sweating, and mad)* Are you trying to start something?

SHORTY: Start what?

FOREMAN: You better weigh in your bag and get on off.

MARTY: He don't mean nothing, mister.

FOREMAN: Who're you?

MARTY: His mother.

FOREMAN: Well, what was goin on here when I come up? What're you talkin so loud about?

LUTHER: Talkin about strikes.

SHORTY: You dirty son of a bitch!

FOREMAN: *(To the informer, LUTHER)* Go call a deputy. I knowed there was agitators in this field.

(LUTHER exits)

FOREMAN: *(To SHORTY, who stares at him belligerently)* Get to work.

SHORTY: I'm gettin paid by the pound, not by the minute.

FOREMAN: You'll get out of here.

ADAM: *(Comes up)* What's the matter?

FOREMAN: I'll tell you what! We don't intend to have no trouble here this summer out of a lot o' agitators, and I'm warning you the Tilden Ranch don't put up with trouble makers.

DEPUTY: *(Entering)* What's the matter here, Bill?

FOREMAN: Half a field had stopped working when I came by. *(To LUTHER)* Who was makin that speech?

LUTHER: *(Frightened at the stares of the workers and the clenched fists)* I-I-I-don't know who . . . . . .

DEPUTY: I thought you *knew.*

SHORTY: He's too short to see over the crowd, that runt.

FOREMAN: *(Pointing to SHORTY)* I don't trust him. He's too smart.

MACK: Nobody has to be smart to see what a sweat shop this ranch is.

FOREMAN: You!

DEPUTY: That's an agitator?

SHORTY: Who's agitatin? You gettin all agitated.

FOREMAN: *(Angrily)* I'll have you locked up so tight it'll be winter when you get out. *(To SAM and BUSTER)* As for you two, one more cackle and I'll pay you off.

DEPUTY: *(Going toward SHORTY)* This the trouble maker?

MARTY: My son ain't done a thing!

SHORTY: They just scared o' me. *(He glares at the DEPUTY)*

MACK: *(Starts to speak to DEPUTY)* Say, this man . . . .

DEPUTY: *(To SHORTY)* Come on.

SHORTY: *(Jocularly)* Have I got to walk?

(As the DEPUTY and the FOREMAN exit left with SHORTY between them, MARTY and MACK stand looking after them)

MARTY: *(Fiercely)* If you put him in jail, I'll call a strike meself.

(There is a low murmur of approval from the field. Someone spots LUTHER, the informer, bending over a row. Dan gives him a quick jerk of the collar and points after the DEPUTY. LUTHER sneaks fearfully away.)

ADAM: We must get Shorty out.

DAN: We'll make a union.

(The field stops to listen)

BUSTER: You gonna let colored in it?

ADAM: *(Hesitates)* Well . . . . . .

MACK: Sure!

BUSTER: *(Slowly)* Then that's a good union.

ADAM: *(To his wife)* Marty, you hear that?

(But MARTY only nods)

MACK: *(To JOSE)* You pass the word around to all the Mexicans. Tonight let's hold a meetin. Right tonight. Everybody come.

JOSE: I tell everybody.

(He begins to pass the word among the Mexicans)

THE CURTAIN FALLS

Act I, Scene 3

Conference room: a table at one end. Rows of men talking to each other, smoking, laughing, some standing. A few in conference. A good deal of the conversation is about superficial matters but there is tension and a sense of strain and uneasiness underneath. Obviously, it is not just one more luncheon meeting. Gradually, groups move toward the front of the room. At the table is a man with a gavel, the ranch owner and bank agent, HARRY TILDEN. Also at the table are BUD PETERSON, ED LOWE, the small-town capitalist, and a woman stenographer taking down the proceedings in short hand.

ED LOWE: *(In a high thin voice)* Higby says the World's Fair's a sight to see. I ought to go to Chicago.

TILDEN: *(Across the table)* I'd like to see that fan dancer.

VOICE: Why don't they get going, boy. I'm anxious for a foursome.

SETH FLOORS: *(Looking out the window)* You sure won't be stopped by rain today.

MARTIN BURTLE: A little rain wouldn't hurt.

FLOORS: Well, you won't get none for a month yet.

BURTLE: No?

FLOORS: No. My crops O.K. I'm glad I put in them extra acres this year. When you going to start pickin?

BURTLE: When the bolls open, when d' you think? I'm at the end of the irrigation line, and that bastard Johnson took all the water for ten days, and I had to wait.

ROY WILLIAMSON: *(A poor farmer)* Paid your water bill yet? I'm having a hell of a time payin mine.

LITTLE: No. I signed a I.O.U.

BURTLE: Yep, the bank's goin to take it.

LITTLE: I thought they had the whole valley already.

WILLIAMSON: I thought under the N.R.A. they give you a two year moratorium so's they couldn't take farms away?

BURTLE: That only applies to houses.

PETERSON: *(Yelling across room)* Who won between Delano and Taft, Tim?

BURTLE: *(Answering from his seat)* I lost my five bucks. Delano beat the hell out of 'em—four touchdowns.

SETH FLOORS: Not like it was when we all-stars ran the team!

BURTLE: Nothing's what it used to be.

LITTLE: That government check I get for not planting wheat, that's how I paid for my seeds this year. Just came in right.

LOWE: *(Who has crossed the room)* Did you sign up not to plant?

BURTLE: I certainly did. That's how I got my seed planted this year.

LOWE: That's how I got my land planted. Wouldn't had a row o' cotton otherwise.

PETERSON: *(A big fat fellow)* That's how Milt got his water assessment paid, only he ain't lettin on. Nothin's ever right for Milt.

BURTLE: I just found out I could sign up a contract not to raise any hogs this year, and I got ninety dollars for it. *(Laughs)* And I wasn't gonna raise hogs!

PETERSON: Pigs will be pigs.

BURTLE: George Caldwell said he wouldn't sign up. The government wasn't gonna tell him how many sows to foal.

LITTLE: It'll cost him five cents a pound to raise and he'll get four.

(The group of poorer farmers have been listening in to the more prosperous ones)

WILLIAMSON: I certainly wish I knew what all this is about—getting money for what you don't do.

LITTLE: I read in the papers that when in history they cut down on crops there's always a famine afterwards.

PETERSON: Well, we haven't got to a drought yet. How many hampers to an acre do you figure, Martin?

BURTLE: Oh, I'll be all right if they don't pull any monkey stuff on us.

PETERSON: *(Aggressively)* What do you mean, strikes? Not a chance. Tilden'll show 'em. He's a smart guy. *(Assuredly)* You can't fool these big fellers. They know just how to do it.

LITTLE: Well, what do you think we gotta pay them pickers?

PETERSON: That's what we come to hear, ain't it?

BURTLE: There ain't gonna be no use in askin me to pay no more than I been payin. *(Positively)* I can shut up shop.

TILDEN: *(Bangs on table)* The meeting will come to order, gentlemen. Well *(hesitating momentarily)* gentlemen, last year we got our cotton picked without any trouble. Because we paid a fair wage. And we intend always to pay a fair wage. But we must keep the return to labor in harmony with a fair return to the grower. *(General nods of assent)* This year, basic prices of commodities have gone up because of the NRA; the things we farmers have to buy have gone up a lot more than what we farmers have to sell; and if we pay labor a wage that won't leave us a fair profit on our investment, you and I can't stay in business. We have to steer a fair and square middle course. *(Emphatically)* We aren't going to get along paying fifty cents. There's been trouble other places in the state; in Pascano they set the same wage as last year, and that gave the agitators their excuse to come in, and the growers lost money and had a lot of trouble. Now I have a report that this Cannery and Agricultural Workers Industrial Union *(laughter)* say they're going to make trouble for us, they say we've got to pay a dollar a hundred. *(Laughter)* Now, we won't want trouble. And prices have been going up, I guess a can of beans costs a Mexican a little more this year than it did last. That's about all a Mexican buys, a can of beans a day and he's fixed; and I guess I ought to know, our company store hardly makes any more profit than it takes to be worth while. Well, we want to be fair to labor, and *(significantly)* we don't want any trouble. So we have decided that the picking rate this fall be raised to sixty cents a hundred.

(This announcement causes general commotion and a murmur of resentment rises.)

VOICES:

Good God! I can't make a damn thing on that!

Why the hell *sixty?*

Never paid that in my life, and I won't.

Say, they must be in league with the agitators!

FLOORS: I'm payin forty. That's enough!

LITTLE: I might as well give up right now. Can't even get to first base at sixty.

WILLIAMSON: Well, the price has gone up this year. It's ten cents a pound.

BURTLE: Cotton ought to be twelve or fourteen cents before a man can make anything on it.

FLOORS: Mexicans can live on forty cents. Why pay more?

BURTLE: And let 'em make a fuss. They ain't got the guts to carry it through.

TILDEN: Gentlemen: let us hear your opinions.

(There is silence and hesitation, but general mumbling)

WILLIAMSON: *(Calling out from his seat)* What good is this holding up cotton planting, and plowing-under, going to do to the price of cotton?

TILDEN: There'll be a better price this year, gentlemen. The Chicago market assures us of that.

LITTLE: *(Turning toward a prosperous group)* You're a fine bunch to be talking about prices. You didn't even buy our cotton at your gins last fall for enough cash for us to get seeds this year.

PETERSON: *(A big gin owner)* Can't you fellows see that all that gin owners can pay is what cotton's worth on the market? They don't make much.

LITTLE: Well, who did make the money then?

(There is a knock at the door)

TILDEN: Come in. *(A BELL-BOY walks in with a note. TILDEN reads it, turns to the others at the table and confers with them in a worried manner. LOWE frowns. TILDEN speaks soothingly, then addresses the crowd)* Friends, a delegation from the pickers. *(To BELL-BOY)* Tell them to. . . . . . .

(LOWE plucks at his sleeve and TILDEN bends to listen)

LOWE: *(In a low voice)* Harry! One's enough.

TILDEN: *(To the BELL-BOY)* Tell *one* to come in. *(To the gathering)* The pickers have sent a delegation: I propose we hear their views.

LOWE: *(Calling BELL-BOY as he turns to leave)* Boy! Bring me the evening paper as soon as it comes out.

BELL-BOY: Yes sir. *(He exits)*

PETERSON: The pickers are damn restless this year, Harry. There's agitators come in here.

LOWE: No wonder, with the White House gone socialistic!

(Enter MACK. There is a stony silence)

TILDEN: What have you to say?

MACK SAUNDERS: *(A little overwhelmed at first. He speaks in a low voice that takes on strength as he talks—as he is made more certain by his words that they are justified)* This meeting has been called to decide on the price to be paid for picking cotton this year, so I understand. I come from the Field Pickers' Union of the San Vincenze Valley with the demands of my union. *(Reading)* "In view of the rise in the cost of living and the considerable unemployment of cotton pickers last year, our union has unanimously decided to demand a wage of one dollar a hundred for picking cotton this year, clean drinking water, and recognition of our union."

FLOORS: *(Snarls)* Well!

TILDEN: *(Interrupting)* Thank you.

MACK: I should like to address your meeting a few minutes. I. . . . . . .

TILDEN: We have heard your demands, thank you. *(Waits)*

MACK: I. . . . . . .

(LOWE whispers impatiently to TILDEN. There is a sullen murmur in the room)

TILDEN: This meeting has heard you. Good afternoon.

(MACK looks uncertainly around at the hostile faced farmers, then goes out)

FARMERS:

Demands! For Christ's sake!

Goin to dictate to us!

Did you hear that?

A dollar a hundred!

They're crazy!

PETERSON: Can you imagine those guys comin' here and *demandin'* from us.

BURTLE: They think they own everything. The brass of the bastards!

FLOORS: That's what you can expect from a union—a gang of agitators!

BURTLE: *(Stands up)* Mr. Chairman, you never should have raised them from 20 to 40 last year. There was plenty of labor at 20 cents. I told you then, Harry, if we gave in, we'd be in for trouble.

LITTLE: Sure, that comes from going soft and giving in to 'em. Here we are, trying to make a living—and they asking for a dollar a hundred.

WILLIAMSON: What the hell are we going to do, if we have a strike here?

PETERSON: Well, you fellows will have to get together and be deputies again this year. I'm ready.

BURTLE: All you have to do is to stick together and knock the hell out of those rats. There are plenty of people who want work.

FLOORS: *(Darkly)* They oughta be lynched, them reds.

PETERSON: If the sheriff can't take care of them, we can.

WILLIAMSON: *(To MILT LITTLE)* Doan' know as I particularly relish going around knocking pickers on the head.

LITTLE: Say, you got too much sympathy. Don't you know where they get their money—what's that furrin town in Russia?

FLOORS: If we have a real sheriff here we'll have no trouble about 40 cents.

LOWE: *(Rising)* What business has that Red coming here today talking for Mexicans and niggers. I've always got along with my labor. I never had trouble and don't need outsiders telling me my business.

PETERSON: That's right. Who the hell told Mexicans about *running water*?

FLOORS: And their rights!

> *(General laughter)*

BURTLE: They want a privy and there's ten thousand acres of land!

LITTLE: If we did put in a tap the Mexicans'd let it run all day.

BURTLE: They're all communists.

FLOORS: I hear we got a fine new order o' tear gas that oughta fix 'em up. You oughts to seen 'em run in Lodi.

PETERSON: Yeah, I was there then. You'd have laughed yer head off if ye'd seen 'em coughing and spitting and running like scared hens.

LOWE: *(To the bunch of prosperous farmers)* Why don't you boys get a Legion Post started?

BURTLE: Bet a fiery cross'd work wonders.

FLOORS: *(Darkly)* Yes, they walked out on me once just when I had my hops ready to pick. After that, no more quarter for any striking bastards. I joined the Klan.

TILDEN: *(Who has been whispering to LOWE)* Gentlemen: I do not think we have to fear anything from a strike in this valley, especially since we're proposing to pay them more than last year. Sixty cents a hundred will net some of these pickers over two dollars a day. Mexican labor is completely satisfied. We might have to deal with a few alien agitators, but our police know how to meet them quite adequately. We are aware that many of us could not earn fair profits at a higher rate. We therefore propose that sixty cents be the basic wage for this year's crop. Any dissension? *(There is no sound)* Then the meeting is closed. We will hold our next meeting . . . . . . *(A BELL-BOY enters and lays the afternoon papers on the conference table. LOWE bends over to glance at the headlines. His eyes bulge, his hands grip the table, he is obviously agitated)* At that meeting we will take up. . . . . . .

LOWE: *(Shouting)* A strike has been called. It says here . . . . . .
> *(The men at the conference table rise excitedly, reach for the papers, and lean over LOWE's shoulder to read the news)*

VOICES:
> What?
> What are you talking about?
> Strike?

LOWE: Where at? *(Holding up paper and reading)* Five thousand cotton pickers have voted to walk out next Monday unless . . . . . .
> *(But by now the room is in an uproar as men rise, gesticulate. Suddenly the gavel sounds on the table)*

TILDEN: *(Rising, the center of tense attention as he speaks slowly and with sinister determination)* There will be no strike, gentlemen.
> *Murmurs of approval as the*

CURTAIN FALLS

Act I, Scene 4

A meeting of the Central Strike Committee in an empty barn. The members of the Committee sit on boxes on the floor.

BUSTER: What if we lose the strike, Miss?

JENNIE: We don't lose strikes, comrade. If we don't win all our demands, we win some. And we will have shown our strength to the bosses, and we'll have taught organization to many thousands. That's the big lesson they have to learn.

FRANK: The men are kind of scared, Miss, specially the Yankees. One guy come to me and says "My boss is a pretty good guy, he give me a bottle of wine one day . . . . . ."

JOHN VIZA: Many say, their bosses not so bad.

JENNIE: Yes, there are guys who'll hand out a piece of wood or an extra blanket once in a while. Or likker. But we aren't asking for charity, to let them square themselves with their conscience. We're asking for our rights.

BUSTER: But farmers *do* get mad. I dowanna get my curls ironed out.

JOHN VIZA: They put out extry tear gas and riot bombs in our county. The Council voted for 'em last week.

BUSTER: Dat tear gas burn your eyes, fo' sure. And s'pose they stop relief, Miss, and we don't get any food at all? Guys ask, what they'll live on during the strike?

JENNIE: Of course. Relief is the backbone of a strike. We should get relief trucks out collecting food at once. Who'll volunteer?

VOICES: We will.

JENNIE: Good. Who else?

> *(Silence)*

JENNIE: What about the new comrade from the Tilden Ranch?

JOSE: I will do for you what you say, senorita.

JENNIE: *(Not noticing his warm voice, business like)* That's good, comrade. Mack here will show you the ropes. Go to the small farmers and shopkeepers and ask them to contribute to strikers' relief. If the pickers make higher wages, it will be good for *them*.

JASPER: How do we explain that, ma'am?

JENNIE: Because the extra wages the pickers earn are spent here. Our pickers don't go to Monte Carlo like Mr. Tilden.

> *(Loud knock on the door. They all huddle together)*

SHORTY: *(In a loud whisper at the door)* Mack Saunders here? It's alright, you guys. It's me, Shorty—Shorty Dobbs. I jest escaped from the lousy jail.

> *(Someone strikes a match)*

MACK: Shorty? *(Letting him into the barn)*

SHORTY: Yeh. I jes' escaped. They're after me, but I threw 'em off. I went by Tilden's, and ma told me you was meetin here.

MACK: Did anyone see you?

SHORTY: No, I gave 'em the slip. The cops in Purtley they had a load o' greasers they was razzin' and in the mixup I skipped out the open door.

MACK: They'll be after you!

SHORTY: Un-un. I got out afore they got me fingerprinted and mugged.

BUSTER: What's a jail look like?

JASPER: You should not have fled, brother. The Lord'll comfort those who in His infinite wisdom he hath run into jail.

SHORTY: Oh yeah. *(SHORTY sits down in the meeting)*

JENNIE: Report from Buttonwillow?

FRANK: *(Reeling it off as if he'd learned it by heart, or had said it several times at meetings already)* We don't have no fresh water. A pair of overalls that was eighty-six cents is one ninety-three now. We niver gets firewood. No 'lectric lights. Kids go barefoot. We know we.... *(The CURTAIN SLOWLY DROPS during this speech. When the CURTAIN RISES AGAIN there are faint streaks of dawn. Men are yawning, their faces are whiter, their shirts open. Smoke lies heavy over everything. One man is asleep. Their hair is rumpled, beards grown heavier overnight. Their fingers are stained with tobacco. They yawn, stretch, cross and uncross their legs. Dark rings under their eyes. Two candles are guttering)*

JENNIE: Does anyone want to ask any questions?

MASCARO: What if they deport us to Mexico?

JENNIE: Comrades, you must all get in your heads that we have to stick together, be solid, fight side by side like members of one big family in spite of all.

BUSTER: Couldn't we leave dat fighting to dem greasers?

JOHN VIZA: *(Angry)* Greasers!

MACK: Buster! Leave that word to the bosses.

JENNIE: Comrades! Is it clear to you all now? Can you go back to your locals and get the men all out?

SHORTY: Greasers never understand anything but women and craps.

JENNIE: *(To SHORTY, reprovingly)* Many of the workers don't understand. We are trying to help them learn. They have been sold out and betrayed by corrupt unions so often.

JASPER: All unions are rotten as Sodom and Gomorrah.

JENNIE: *(Losing patience)* Comrade Waters: your job is to show them that our union is different.

JASPER: I remember the time the Wobblies.......

MACK: Wobblies!

JASPER: *(Hurt)* You said one big union!

MACK: Yes, one big union ...... but we ain't annarkists an' we don't believe in violence. No weapons, no force used unless you are attacked.

MASCARO ESTRADA: Isn't 60 cents enough? My wife, she say we can live on tortillas.

JENNIE: *(Losing her temper)* Really, comrades, here we are trying to make a Rev...... *(Corrects herself)* call a strike to better conditions for you, and after four and one half hours of planning you still ask......

JOSE: *(Gently)* Senorita, Mexicans have big *families*. Worry, worry all the time,

JENNIE: *(Quickly contrite)* You're right. *(JOSE glows, gratified, looks at her for some personal recognition, but JENNIE goes on)* We musn't be impatient. But this strike must be fought uncompromisingly, to show the bosses we won't stand for slavery. The picket line is what wins a strike. *(Her fire mounts)* They'll come to us with arbitration and sell out proposals, they'll hire thugs and gangsters and try terror and intimidation—but our answer is the picket line. Who'll undertake to captain picket trucks?

SHORTY: You bet me! I'm spoilin' to get at the throat of some o' them goddam cops.

WORKERS:
> And me.
> Me too.
> You bet yer.
> Si.

BUSTER: Sure, boy, we'll get the bastards out o' them scab fields.

JENNIE: The strike is on. Tomorrow, why no . . . *(Seeing the gray dawn creeping up) this* morning, picket trucks will leave to pull out the ranches that are still at work. Every cotton field must be emptied. From today on there musn't be an ounce of cotton picked until we have won our strike.
> *(Meeting breaks up. Workers get up, shuffle, stretch, yawn, put on shoes, straighten shirts, collect in groups, begin to go to door)*

MACK: Let's go, Jose. We got a long walk. Shorty, you goin' back to Tilden's to sleep?

SHORTY: Sure. I ain't scared.

JOSE: *(Goes up to Jennie shyly)* I like you say goodnight to me, Senorita!
> *He gazes at her as the*

CURTAIN FALLS

Act I, Scene 6[3]

The cabins of the cotton pickers on the Tilden Ranch. Sunrise. Several frail and dilapidated huts built like sheds, of plain boards, some with only wooden flaps for window openings, shingles coming off, doors hanging on one hinge, steps broken down. No porches, no paint, no beauty. A dusty yard-way in which may be seen a broken down car or two, one

with a canvas flap sheltering a man and wife. Back of the huts a small
tent or two may be seen, and a make-shift hovel of sacking and boards,
from which a sleeping man's feet protrude. Beyond are the cotton fields,
with the bolls bursting white in the morning sun. The stage is empty,
but from one of the cabins, CHARLIE's Negro voice is heard singing.

BUSTER: *(In slow syncopation)*
    I'm writin you this letter, babe,
    Three days sence I et.
    The stamp on de envalope's
    Gwine to put me in debt.

    I was just about to swallow
    A good meal yestiday
    When de garbage man come and
    Took de can away.

ADA: *(Cross and sleepy, within cabin.)* Buster whut you doin makin all
    that racket so early this mornin and you know I'm sick?

BUSTER: Woman, I'm hongry. *(He opens the door and stands stretching*
    in the rising sunlight.)

ADA: You know we ain't got nary scrap in de pot.

BUSTER: *(joking)* Damn? That ain't no way for a Christian woman to
    talk. Wasn't you prayin last night fo' the Lawd to send some manna
    down?

ADA: Don't you make fun o' me, man! De Lawd *will* send somethin
    down if he intend for us to win this strike. Uh, I sho' feels bad.

    (Buster picks up a cook pot and starts off left. He stops before the
    next cabin door and knocks on it with the cook pot.)

SHORTY: *(From within cabin.)* What the hell you want?

BUSTER: *(Cracking open the door and peeping in.)* Looky yonder! All
    you single-men's-bachelors ain't up yet? Shorty, throw me out a
    cigarette.

SHORTY: *(Throwing a cigarette through the door.)* Here, mug.

MACK: *(Voice inside the cabin.)* What time is it, Shorty?

BUSTER: Time you was workin, if you wasn't strikin. How was de
    meetin last night?

MACK: Swell, it lasted all night.

BUSTER: Um-m-huh! *(He starts off left, lighting the cigarette with his*
    head down. He bumps into FRANKIE MAE, who enters carrying a
    blanket.) 'Cuse me!

FRANKIE MAE: *(Slightly embarrassed)* O, goodmornin, Mis' Dobbs.

MARTY: *(Chewing on her snuff stick.)* Sleepin out?

FRANKIE MAE: I just can't stand them crowded cabins, Mis' Dobbs.

MARTY: *(sarcastically)* So you picks up your bed and walks.

FRANKIE MAE: *(Coyly)* I'm a outdoor girl, Mis' Dobbs.

> *(SAM comes in, left, after FRANKIE MAE, and starts to enter the cabin occupied by MACK and SHORTY. He sees MARTY and looks guilty.)*

MARTY: I reckon Sam's a outdoor boy, too.

> *(She splits, and passes on. Exit FRANKIE MAE as SAM goes into the cabin. By now several doors have opened and people are stirring in the dusty yard. A man passes with an armful of brush wood. Another goes toward the field with a piece of newspaper. The feet under the hovel of sacking and boards stir. Somewhere a baby cries. A boy whistles. Inside the curtained Ford, DAN and ELLA begin to take down the canvas that has sheltered them for the night.)*

MARTY: *(Continuing her walk, speaks to ADA who is standing in the door-way pulling a comb through her hair.)* Howdy.

ADA: Right po'ly, Mis' Dobbs. How're you?

MARTY: I would feel better if I knowed how this strike was gonna turn out.

ADA: So would I. You reckon de Lawd ever meant for po' folks to go around kickin up trouble sich as this, Mis' Dobbs? I declare to Jesus, I don't believe He did.

MARTY: Now, talkin 'bout the Lord, I ain't bringin Him into this a-tall, 'cause I don't believe He's got nothin to do with raisin wages and buildin out-houses. That's man's business.

ADA: Well, He's carried me through to where I am today, bless Gawd!

MARTY: *(calmly)* But where is you? *(She passes on.)*

ROSITA: *(Waddling in from the left with her MILLIE and ROY across the stage. At right another Mexican worker, MANUEL, enters.)* Buenos Dias, senor.

> *(Meanwhile MARTY has approached the cabin occupied by MACK, SHORTY, and SAM.)*

MARTY: You Mack, when you gonna start the picket line. Why don't you-all get up from there and put on yo' pants. Shorty, too.

MACK: Yes, Mrs. Dobbs. Comin' out. We just got an hour's sleep.

> *(CHARLIE returns with the water and enters his cabin.)*

MARTY: *(Mounting the steps of MACK's cabin.)* You know you the head o' this here ranch local. And if I'm gonna follow you, I want you to act like you the head and get things started to goin. *(She stands in the door of cabin. With sudden belligerence she addresses her nephew within.)* You, Sam, look at me, sir! Layin out all night with hussies! You a grown man with a half-grown child. You ought to be shame o' yoreself. *(She stares at him fiercely.)* Don't say nary a word to me. Shorty and Mack, you-all come and get yo' breakfast. I reckon I can feed you both today, cause I don't want no hongry organisers.

SAM: *(meekly)* I'm comin', too. Aunt Marty.

MARTY: *(Leaving the cabin.)* You can go eat with Frankie Mae. *(muttering)* If she's got any victuals.

    (BUD returns carrying an empty water bucket. He calls to his Aunt who is still talking with JUANITA.)

BUD: Aunt Marty! Hey, Aunt Marty!

MARTY: Stop that yellin at me way cross the yard.

BUD: They wouldn't let me have no water at the pump. The foreman says when we go back to work, we get pump water. When we don't work, to hell with us.

    (MACK and SHORTY have emerged from their cabin. SHORTY is tucking his shirt tail in.)

MARTY: Lord-a-mercy me!

MACK: So they're pullin that on us, heh?

SHORTY: Damn 'em, I'll go up there and take the pump.

    (Several others gather around to hear about the denial of the water.)

BUD: Not a drap. They was lots o' men up yonder round the pump, and more of 'em on up by the ranch house. Looked like cops to me. And I was scared, too.

SHORTY: *(Kidding Bud.)* Could they chew nails?

MARTY: *(Shortly)* No, and neither can you drink plain coffee beans. You and Bud go and git a bucket full o' that ditch water then, and hurry up so's the mud can settle, cause I ain't fitten to fight cops nor nobody else till I get some coffee in me this mornin.

FRANKIE MAE: You sure are right, Mis' Dobbs. A body don't feel good in the mornings till they had their java.

MARTY: *(sharply)* You was up so early, you should-a had yours.

    (SAM has emerged from cabin and sits drooping on the steps. FRANKIE MAE strolls over to him. ROSITA and her children return carrying twigs and bits of fire wood they have gathered. The little girl looks ill and is holding her stomach.)

ROSITA: *(In friendly fashion to everybody.)* Buenos Dias, Buenos Dias.

MACK: Say, Mrs. Rodriguez, where's Jose?

ROSITA: He be here soon. I send him commissary buy ten cents corn meal. Make plenty all-day tortillas.

MACK: You tell him and Domingo, by and by me go out picket line.

ROSITA: Pick 'em time? What time?

MACK: No, pick-et line. You know, keep scabs out of fields. You tell him, PICKET LINE. He understands.

ROY: I know, mama.

ROSITA: Pickum lime. O.K. I tell him.

ROY: *(Correcting his mother.)* Picket line. *(In good English)*

> *(ROSITA, ROY and MILLIE exit. SHORTY and BUD come back with the bucket of muddy water and cross the stage.)*

SHORTY: Come and get it, Mack.

BUD: Chow time.

> *(SHORTY and BUD exit. MACK stands talking with a small group for a moment.)*

MACK: *(To one of the men standing near him.)* Say, Shag, you go around and see how many's got gas, and how many they can carry in their cars out to the picket line, will you?

MACK: We gotta circle all the ranches in this region. Ten, fifteen miles, maybe. And if they ain't walked out over at Peterson's or Wardman's, we gotta pull 'em out. We gotta persuade 'em.

SAM: *(Rising and leaving FRANKIE MAE.)* I'm gonna try.

> *(MILLIE is seen running through the cabins toward the fields whimpering with a piece of newspaper in her hand.)*

FRANKIE MAE: That child's got the "trots".

MACK: Dysentery?

FRANKIE MAE: Something like that. Cholera, or something.

MACK: There's four or five kids sick here. Can't help but be, drinkin muddy water and using open privies and eatin with the flies for company.

FRANKIE MAE: Quit your kidding, Shag! Mack, honey, can I ride in the Buick?

MACK: *(Absently minded)* I guess so. Come on, Sam, let's eat. *(Exits.)*

FRANKIE MAE: *(Following MACK and SAM as they exit right.)* I wonder should I wear my red and white dress on the picket. . . . . . . *(Exits.)*

ADA: *(Looking after FRANKIE MAE.)* She sho is a red hot mama, but Mis' Dobbs got her water on.

BUSTER: That Mack's a right nice guy, though, ain't he?

ADA: I don't know. I ain't never seed no white folks I thought was right nice. All they wants you in de union for is to strike and git yo' haid broke, and then they'll put you out.

BUSTER: Aw, Ada, you don't know . . . .

> *(A loud burst of Mexican voices at right behind the cabins. CHAR-LIE and ADA rush out.)*

VOICES: *Que tu dices, hombre? Yo no voy ninguna parte. Donde esta mi machete? Ay, dios! Que cabronazo!*

> *(Followed by men, women, and children, JOSE enters, right, from behind the cabins and goes toward the hut in which MACK and SHORTY slept.)*

JOSE: *(calling)* Mack! Hey, Mack!

BUSTER: What's the matter now?

> *(From tents and cars the men and women tumble out.)*

JOSE: *(Excitedly)* Mr. Tilden gonna put everybody off ranch right now.

BUSTER: Huh?

JOSE: *(Seeing the door open and the cabin empty.)* WHERE's Mack?

MACK: *(Voice some distance away, right.)* Yal?

WOMAN: I told you they would put us out o' their damn cabins.

MAN: Well, they can't put me out 'cause I'm sleepin on the ground as it is.

CHARLIE: They can sho move you off the ground though.

JOSE: Plenty deputies, plenty foremen all around cross-roads.

> *(MACK and SHORTY enter on the run, followed later by SAM, MARTY, FRANKIE MAE, ADAM, and BUD. There is general confusion and talking.)*

MACK: What's up, kid?

JOSE: *(Breathless)* I go down commissary. Commissary closed up. Cops all around. One man say to me, work. I say, no, strike. He say, shut up your mouth or I take you off to jail. He give me one push with gun and say, get your traps out o' them cabins. I say, where am I gonna sleep? He say, I'm coming up there and clear everybody out in a minute.

JUANITA: *(crying)* Ay, Jesus mio!

SHORTY: So that's their game!

MANUEL: I got one good gun.

PANCHO: I got a plenty sharp corn knife.

MACK: Shut up and listen. Our strike committee's made plans for an emergency like this. What we gonna do is go into a camp of our own. But I gotta find out where. Jennie and Joe Richards suggested trying to get that big strip of empty land near Culver that belongs to Roy Williamson. I'll find out today if we got it.

MARTY: Somebody find out now.

MACK: I mean now, right away. I'll go. Jose, you help get the picket line off. *(To the crowd.)* Now, listen, you know the orders. No weapons. Understand? We don't want nobody locked up. Sure, the ranchers got guns. But that's different. They'll be looking for chances to arrest us, don't give 'em that chance. I'll be back. Come on, Manuel. *(He and the young Mexican exit through the crowd.)*

ADAM: I heard they gonna bring scabs in from Texas.

SHORTY: We ought to keep scabs out.

JOSE: You right, Shorty.

ROSITA: *(Sitting on the ground holding MILLIE and the baby.)* This child so sick.

ADA: Me, too.

MARTY: Maybe you both needs a good dose o' castor oil.

ROSITA: Yes, ma'm.

MARTY: *(Garrulously)* But now you take little Bud, he's a right delicate child. His pa don't take no care o' him. Sam's too damn lazy to take care o' his self.

BUSTER: Do he belong to our union, Mis' Dobbs?

MARTY: No, Sam don't belong to nothin but the Sons o' Rest.

BUD: *(Running into MARTY and ADAM.)* Aunt Mart, the men's done come and start to throwin your bed clothes out o' the house.

ADAM: Well, goddamn!

ADA: *(Coming out in the middle of yard with her poker and pointing toward the disturbance off stage.)* Buster, you see that? *(Standing staunchly with the poker.)* Lawd, and me sick!

> *(By now a number of persons have come into center of yard and are looking toward the racket off stage that is becoming louder and louder. The voices of the deputies commanding the cotton pickets to vacate can be clearly heard.)*

VOICES: *(Deputies, off stage)*

> Orders 're orders.
>
> Move on, and move quick.
>
> Work or get out.
>
> You dumb greasers.
>
> Three days notice? Ha, ha, ha, haw!
>
> Take that tent.

ADA: Lawd! Lawd! Lawd!
> *(Entering right, a RANCHER-DEPUTY walks towards the cab-ins.)*

DEPUTY: You pickers get out. Come on, get a move on.

BUSTER: What's the big idea?
> *(Those evicted farther down begin to move across the stage toward the roadway. Several deputies and the RANCH FOREMAN now come onto the scene. MARTY, ADAM, SHORTY, and BUD carrying various belongings move into sight.)*

FOREMAN: Orders are everybody clear out. *(As nobody says anything.)* Clear out! Understand?

MEXICAN: *(Stolidly.)* But we on strike.

FOREMAN: *(As the deputies laugh.)* Strike! You can't strike. You can quit, but you can't strike.

SHORTY: *(Putting down his bundle of bedding.)* Is that so?

MARTY: *(Standing beside her bundles, to BUD.)* Where is Sam, that good for nothing pappy o' your'n?

BUD: *(Half-crying.)* I don't know.

DEPUTY: Folks, get a move on. *Vamanos.* Scat. *(He begins to move among the crowd with a club which he carries.)*

FOREMAN: And you who go, don't need to come back to this ranch any more.

BUSTER: Who gonna pick yo' cotton?

FOREMAN: Don't you worry. You just take your black bottom on down the road.
> *(Some folks have begun to pack up and move. A pregnant woman wanders about calling MANUEL. From now on until the end of the scene, there is a constant stream of people leaving the grounds, crossing the stage right to left with their few belongings, some with babies in arms, some with a lean dog or a kitten, a child with a baseball bat, a Mexican with a guitar, etc. Through all this, ROSITA sits calmly on the ground holding MILLIE and the baby, and ROY leans at her side.)*

FRANKIE MAE: *(Strolling by in a red dress and a wide floppy white hat, and carrying a worn beauty case.)* Who's got room in their car for a lady?

JOSE: *(Entering, left, out of breath, calling.)* Mama, *mamacita!* Where is mama? *(He sees her sitting in the dust with the children.)*

ROSITA: *Aqui estamos.*

JOSE: *(Running to his mother and embracing her. Helping her to rise, speaking in a flood of Spanish.)* Mama, *tenemos que ir. Donde esta* papa?

ROSITA: *(Calmly)* You make pickum line?

(MILLIE begins to cry.)

JOSE: You go to car, mama. I find papacito. *(He exits right asking everyone.)* Where is Domingo? *Domingo esta Domingo?*

(ROSITA and the children exit left, MILLIE clinging to her mother and sobbing.)

DEPUTY: Come on, what's holding you? Pick up. Gwan.

FOREMAN: *(To a Mexican who is arguing heatedly with him.)* Now you boys don't start trouble.

SHAG: The law says three days notice.

DEPUTY: *(Approaching belligerently with gun bared.)* Get on!

(SHORTY enters left. Calls to MARTY.)

SHORTY: Come on, ma.

(He is helping her with their bundles when there is a great commotion in the doorway of CHARLIE's cabin. A DEPUTY is attempting to put them out. ADA and the DEPUTY struggle through the door and down the steps, ADA fighting like a fiend. Suddenly she breaks away and stands in the center of the stage holding her poker aloft.)

ADA: *(To the sweating deputy.)* Don't you tech me, white man! Don't you lay your hands on me!

DEPUTY: *(Making a lunge for the enraged woman.)* I told you to get out. *(The DEPUTY attempts to grab ADA and receives a sound whack on the head with the poker.)* Aw-ooo! *(He bellows with pain.)*

ADA: *(Holding her own.)* I told you not to fool with me!

FOREMAN: *(Coming to the aid of the deputy.)* I'll attend to you.

(He grabs ADA from behind, but SHORTY comes to the rescue even before CHARLIE.)

SHORTY: *(Flinging back the FOREMAN.)* You keep your hands off.

ADA: *(Spitting like a cat.)* You————! You————! You————!

(There is a protective murmur from the crowd as the DEPUTY and the FOREMAN withdraw thwarted.)

MARTY: You Shorty! Come on here. I'll pick you up dead yet, stopping to fight over niggers.

SHORTY: They belong to the union, ma.

BUSTER: *(To ADA.)* You see, I tole you, Ada, some white folks's alright. *(ADA still glares about her with her poker raised.)* Now you put that poker up and come on let's leave here.

(BUSTER picks up their suit case from the cabin door and they start out right. As she exits, ADA flings back a last word at the DEPUTY. The DEPUTY glares after them as they exit. In the doorway of one cabin several Mexicans laugh loudly at the scene. The DEPUTY and the FOREMAN turn on them from the house.)

DEPUTY: You greasers make yourselves scarce quick. Gwan. Git.

FOREMAN: If you want these lousy clothes *(throwing a bundle into the yard)* pick 'em up and beat it.

DEPUTY: You black Indian-looking bastards. Get out. Get.

(He pushes them and their belongings from the yard. They struggle. Someone throws a heavy tin can. General pandemonium breaks out. There is cursing and struggling all over the stage. General cries.)

VOICES:

Get the hell out.

Help! Help!

Swat him one, Ken!

Move, you bastards.

Don't hit that woman.

O-ooo-oo-oo-o!

Hit him, Bill.

Stop! Stop!

(PANCHO, under arrest, enters right with two deputies, his head bloody. He has apparently been fighting with them, refusing to be evicted. JUANITA rushes at the deputies, crying. She is flung back hard against the wall of a cabin, and stands there faint, her hands over her pregnant belly.)

JUANITA: *(As the deputies continue across stage with her father.)* O, my baby! *(She falls to the ground, weeping hysterically, but in a few moments, rises and rushes after her father and the deputies who exit left, crying.)* Adone va con mi papa? *(Exits.)*

(At right, MR. TILDEN, the ranch owner, enters in a business suit and a wide Stetson hat.)

TILDEN: Say! Say! *(In a loud voice.)* What's the matter here? Can't you men handle things any better than this? All this commotion to evict a few strikers?

(There is a silence. The remaining persons exit or step aside revealing to MR. TILDEN the old Ford in which DAN and his wife live, and before which they are standing now, in an attitude of defiance.)

FOREMAN: Mr. Tilden, this man won't move this car off your property.
TILDEN: *(Without ceremony.)* Turn the car over boys, if they don't want
  to move it.
FOREMAN: That got 'em, Mr. Tilden.
TILDEN: I've dealt with 'em before in the I.W.W. days. They ain't
  got nothing. Just a lot of goddamn tramps, that's all. Day after
  tomorrow, they'll be back here, or a hundred more just like 'em,
  ready and willing to work for what I want to pay.
    *(He mops his brow and looks about. The whole place is cleared of
    people, save one man, LUTHER, sitting barefooted in front of his
    lean-to of boards and sacking.)*
TILDEN: *(To deputies.)* Who's that?
FOREMAN: He's alright. He'll work.
LUTHER: *(Rising meekly)* You know me, Mr. Tilden.
TILDEN: *(Recognizing an old scab.)* Oh! *(Turns his back on LUTHER
  and walks away, but stops suddenly and calls to him.)* Say, come here.
  (LUTHER approaches.) Listen! You go on strike, too, see? Get with
  the rest of them ———. Hang around that union office of theirs in
  Purtley, go to the meetings, and come back here every night and tell
  me what's going on. I'll pay you as usual.
LUTHER: *(Grinning obsequiously.)* Yes, sir, Mr. Tilden. I sure will. *(He
  returns to his lean-to and puts on his shoes, sitting on the ground.)*
FOREMAN: We threw 'em out on their cans, alright. *(As they walk
  toward the right, he picks up a baby's cap that has been lost in the exodus.
  He stops and looks around.)* Well, here's plenty of empty cabins now,
  a lot o' cotton—and one goddamn scab! *(He handles the baby cap,
  holding it up appraisingly.)* Say, maybe my kid could wear this.
    They exit right as the
CURTAIN FALLS

ACT II[4]

*Camp Culver. Late afternoon. This scene has the most elaborate setting.
A barbed wire fence runs across the front, at the proscenium line.
Tents, lean-to-shelters, etc. on lower and upper levels. Camp kitchen R,
long table (two-by-fours resting on a clothes horse and some boxes) with
bench above it and upended boxes below it, to sit on. A typewriter and
some papers at the upper end. COOK, JOHN VIZA, SHORTY, and*

JASPER at lower end, idling. MARTY and MISS PRATHER visible in DOMINGO's tent, L, with the sick ROSITA.

COOK: You fellers don't need to come here lookin for no breakfast tomorrow cause there ain't gonna be none—less they bring some relief or other in here soon.

JASPER: Just you keep the fires burning, Cook. The Lord will provide for his lambs.

> *(Cut the COOK's next line, as JASPER's gets a laugh, and the COOK's is not strong enough to force a second laugh.)*
> *(MARTY comes out of the tent, crosses to the table.)*

MARTY: Can I have some hot water, Cookie? *(He gets it.)* It's a shame we got no permit yit to get Rosita in a hospital.

SHORTY: Just cause she's a striker! How is she, Marty?

MARTY: Worse. *(Takes water, returns to tent.)*

> *(Enter ROLLINS—reporter—R.)*

JASPER: *(Primping up.)* You come to take our pictures?

COOK: What's goin on down yonder at the gate? Who're they keepin out now?

ROLLINS: The guys standing guard say they got orders from Jennie to let in the arbitrators. And the health officials have just started around inspecting.

SHORTY: *(Grinning)* You better clean up this joint, Cookie.

COOK: I ain't got nothin to clean up. These pots been licked clean long ago.

SHORTY: Inspectors never come around inspectin any growers' camps I ever worked in.

> *(JOHN VIZA grunts assent, picking up paper.)*

SHORTY: They want to close us up, that's all.

ROLLINS: Tilden's got 25 scabs pickin on his ranch. Got them off the bread line in Los Angeles.

COOK: Hell, city stiffs can't pick cotton. Get all the bread lines and put them in the fields, if they ain't used to pickin cotton they can't pick it.

> *(Enter Health Officer 'MEYERS' and KING, R., with MACK.)*

MEYERS: There have been many complaints that your sewage system is unsatisfactory. The piping is insufficient, and the dirty water is spilled out on the ground.

MACK: No, there isn't much piping. We've been doing just about like the pickers are used to in the growers' camps.

MEYERS: We are here to determine whether the camp constitutes a public nuisance.

> *(MEYERS speaks to the cook, inspects the kitchen arrangements meticulously, tut-tutting at the makeshifts. Enter JENNIE and PROFESSOR BANKLEY, L.)*

MACK: *(To KING, whom he otherwise almost ignores; jerking his head.)* Union secretary. You wanted to see her? *(Remains near table, watching MEYERS.)*

KING: *(Crossing to JENNIE.)* Well, well, and so this is the little lady I have been hearing so much about? I am so very glad to meet you in person, my dear little Miss Martin! My name is King; I have flown out from Washington to act as Arbitrator in—

JENNIE: Good afternoon. *(She refuses to shake hands.)* I am sorry. We know your record in the East.

MACK: *(Under his breath.)* Strikebreaker!

JENNIE: We should like you to know, Mr. King, before you start your investigating, that our men are sore. Police and thugs are persecuting us at every turn. They have arrested hundreds of strikers. And now the health department is looking for a chance to break up our camp—and we have nowhere else to go.

KING: That does sound like a list of calamities, doesn't it? We shall have to look into them all. I should like to have a little talk with the men in this camp. I want you to know that we are here to help you, to listen to you. It is to all our interest to settle the difficulty in this valley. We will give both sides a fair hearing—there is right and wrong on both sides. This strike will end in peace.

BANKLEY: How do you do, Mr. King? I am Professor Bankley, of State University. I have been trying to tell this fiery little lady myself that there are two sides to every question.

KING: Glad to meet you, Professor.

JENNIE: Isn't your first suggestion going to be for the men to go back to work, pending arbitration? To break the strike first, and then arbitrate in the growers' favor?

> *(KING says something superior and pacific, insists upon going through the camp without a striker guide, and joins the health officer, who is ready to go on.)*

SHORTY: Just a minute, Doctor. You see this fellow's head here? He couldn't get treated at Purtley Hospital. Nor that woman in there *(indicates tent)* couldn't. They won't take strikers.

MEYERS: Why the hospital's pretty well taxed, I believe. It's small—it's run for the benefit of residents of the country. Outsiders pay.
> *(This line is given to a cop, as written; but a cop would not be admitted to the camp, surely?)*[5]

JOHN VIZA: They told me if I went back to work, they fix me up.

MEYERS: Then you'd be able to pay, wouldn't you?
> *(Exeunt MEYERS, KING, L. SHORTY spits contemptuously.)*

MACK: Shorty, how come you aren't out hustlin some relief food from the farmers?

SHORTY: Out o' gas.
> *(MACK leans against the table, depressed. He rarely sits down.)*

BANKLEY: *(LC with JENNIE.)* But I did want to ask you this, Miss Martin. Do you think—was this exactly a wise time to strike? Can the farmers pay higher wages? They have so many costs to meet, which are constantly going up—and they have rent, mortgages—so many costs to meet, which are constantly going up—

JENNIE: Then they must strike too, against the banks and the power companies. A lot of farmers are organizing. We're helping all the small farmers in this valley to form a union too.
> *(ROLLINS strolls across to them.)*

ROLLINS: 'Morning Jennie. What's the latest on the strike front?

JENNIE: Oh, what's the use of giving you anything? You don't put it in the paper as we give it to you. Last Thursday in that story of the evictions you wrote it as if the strikers started the rioting.
> *(BANKLEY occupies himself with a child who is curious.)*

ROLLINS: I give you my word, Miss Jennie, I wrote it as Mack told me. But the city desk changed it. They always do. Standing orders.

JENNIE: Then why don't you give up working for a lousy sheet like the *Herald?* You ought to be ashamed of yourself.

ROLLINS: Would you give me a job here at twenty a week? I'd work for you, kid.

JENNIE: You'd want your twenty bucks. No one here has had a cent in wages since the strike began. We can't collect enough for the picket lines. Five picket trucks didn't go out this morning—they can't go out because they haven't got any gas and oil. Why don't you go down and hustle us some?

ROLLINS: O.K., kid. Will you have supper with me tonight?

JENNIE: If you'll drive me to Buttonwillow afterward. I have a meeting there tonight.

(He asks her about posing some pictures; children for choice, and the office wants more of her because of her looks; disgusted, she expresses herself briefly on the subject of singling out individuals. ROLLINS retires to the background. He does not exit. All the opponent forces gradually collect from this point on.)

(Enter JOSE in a hurry.)

JOSE: Mack—they take my truck!

JENNIE: What—?

MACK: The relief truck?

STRIKERS: Jesus Maria! What a dirty trick! How we gonna eat now?

JOSE: *(Ashamed.)* I tell the cops they cannot take food, it is relief for our companeros. I stay in my truck. . . . *(Pauses. JENNIE and BANK-LEY cross to the table.)* They pull me out my seat. *(To JENNIE)* Companera, they say we use the truck for picketing. They pull me out.

JENNIE: And the food?

JOSE: They throw it all in road. Spill sacks of flour and sugar all over.
(He adds news of arrests, which ROLLINS supplements by bail figures.)

BANKLEY: I am convinced, Miss Martin, from what I have seen here, that the ranchers are adding gunpowder to the situation. And the police seem to encourage them. I understand now what you mean by your phrase, "lawless law". The official brutality against your pickets is outrageous, for picketing is not a crime. I shall try to make that clear to my students.

JENNIE: You will send a protest to the governor?

BANKLEY: My connections with the state university—it's a little difficult—

MACK: Well, will you help us raise bail?

BANKLEY: I wish I could do something. Think of putting a little Mexican boy under ten thousand dollars bail. It's outrageous. I will impress upon my students how our courts abuse the rights of citizens.

MACK: Of workers, Mr. Bankley. This is a class war.

BANKLEY: I would hardly say that. Can't we all solve it together? We should work toward cooperation, don't you think? It must not be a war, must it?

JENNIE: They make it a war, not we. We aren't armed.
(Enter MISS PRATHER, L.)

MISS PRATHER: Oh, good morning, Miss Martin. What good luck to find you. I want to speak to you about the relief situation. I am giving relief to families now, but we have some trouble.

JENNIE: Yes? Our people haven't been getting much government relief.

MISS PRATHER: That's just it. We have to have certain information, and your families seem suspicious of giving it. But there is nothing to it at all. We always ask for the license numbers of automobiles, and we have to have the nationality of the recipient, of course, *(rapidly)* just as we have to have their birth and marriage certificates, name of their father and mother's father and last address.

JENNIE: We gave orders that the strikers should not give their license numbers or nationality.

MISS PRATHER: But why? We are here to help you, we are here to bring government relief to your families.

JENNIE: We know just how the information you get is used. The car numbers are a black-list. If the owners are Mexicans you deport them.

MISS PRATHER: But we take no part in political questions, no sides—

JENNIE: If the state authorities ask for your lists you give them to them.

MISS PRATHER: Would you have us hinder the Administration?

JENNIE: I'm afraid I'm very busy this afternoon. I'd appreciate it if you'd take this up with one of the boys.

MISS PRATHER: Really! When all one wants to do is to help—

MACK: Well, Miss, our people haven't been getting relief.

MISS PRATHER: Do you expect us to get around quicker than we do in this heat? I am worked off my feet as it is—but one can't expect gratitude.

ROLLINS: How many relief workers are there?

MISS PRATHER: Two, and we work all day.

MACK: Two relief workers for fourteen thousand strikers and their families—on a strike front of two hundred miles! And your paper says Federal relief is being distributed to all the strikers—and kicks about it.

> *(Re-enter MEYERS and KING, trailed by a group of curious strikers, including FRANKIE MAE.)*

MEYERS: Miss Martin, we have completed our tour, and I can certify this camp is not at present a danger to health. Of course, at any moment matters may come to a head—that is, conditions may alter. *(Earnestly)* I do advise you to tell these women not to empty their dish water on the ground.

MISS PRATHER: Oh, how do you do, Mr. King? May I have a few words with you? I have a most regrettable situation to discuss. I must tell you about the relief situation—

KING: Isn't that Mr. Hopkinson's province?

MISS PRATHER: These people simply will not take our milk—we have hundreds of gallons here spoiling—good milk from the United States government and they won't take it! You know how misled and ignorant these people are . . . . . . Well, they are afraid if they take government milk they will have to go back to work. They are quite misinformed—

KING: Who told them that?

MISS PRATHER: Oh, I assure you, Mr. King, no one, they are just naturally suspicious, they don't understand the laws of this country. I've explained to them so patiently—

KING: Have you explained to Miss Martin?

MISS PRATHER: We were told to keep government relief quite separate from the relief being collected by these people—there's quite a good deal of complaint from the farmers that we're feeding them at all—and then of course, as you know, we do not mix in controversial questions—

MACK: No milk at all at Delano. Babies drinkin coffee and tea.

MISS PRATHER: Oh, oh, I don't mean they didn't want the milk. It was a sight, those poor babies standing around with crying babies, and this beautiful rich milk provided by the Government of the United States specially—

SHORTY: Specially laid by Uncle Sam's cows.

MISS PRATHER: They have some ideas—some misconception—

MACK: The government relief workers demand that we sign a paper to go back pending arbitration, if we are to have the milk. That's why we don't take it.

(*MACK walks away. Enters SHERIFF, WILLIAMSON, and MEXICAN CONSUL, R.*)

JENNIE: Hello, Mr. Williamson.

WILLIAMSON: Miss, could I speak to you a moment?

JENNIE: Why, yes. (*To MEXICAN CONSUL*) You were refused entrance. How did you get in?

CONSUL: With the sheriff. I come to speak to my fellow Mexicans, why not?

JENNIE: You have been trying to separate the white and the Mexican comrades. You urge the Mexicans to go back to work and break the strike.

CONSUL: I do only what my government demands me to. I tell the Mexicans . . .

SHERIFF: *(To MACK)* You-all have to leave here. *(Hands him paper.)*

MACK: *(Reading aloud slowly)* It says this camp is a menace to the health of the community and must be evacuated by nightfall tomorrow. Signed, Board of Supervisors, Culver County.

JENNIE: The Health Officer has just pronounced the camp healthy.

WILLIAMSON: But that paper says I am personally responsible for maintaining a public nuisance. It's addressed to me as owner of the land. I don't want you to leave, but—

JENNIE: Well, Mr. Health Officer?

MEYERS: I was merely expressing my private opinion. Sanitary arrangements are in a very bad condition. The sewage system is inadequate. Yes, it will be a public safeguard to have the camp evacuated.
(General stir.)

BANKLEY: But, Dr. Meyers, you just said—

SHORTY: The dirty sons!

JENNIE: Comrades: we must get into action. Protest delegation to the Board of supervisors—a mass delegation. Redouble picketing.
(The crowd is growing. The light is dimming—it is after sunset.)

SHERIFF: Anybody starts a riot'll be run in. Get back! Move on, now, move on.
(LUTHER is visible on the outskirts of the crowd, DC. He runs off R.—throwing a brick just as he disappears. The SHERIFF blows his whistle. Two policemen rush in.)

SHERIFF: *(Pointing at SHORTY)* I know you too—jailbreaker! Arrest that man.

SHORTY: Hey, comrades, don't let them arrest us.

MACK: Defense squad, forward!
(The strikers make a wall around SHORTY; he disappears in their midst. The visitors back downstage and stand against the barbed wire, back to audience.)

SHERIFF: Well—I guess we scared 'em. Come on, boys.
(SHERIFF offers protection to the visitors, who leave with him. FRANKIE MAE has been making up to the CONSUL, and makes a date with him; he is thus the last to go.)

MACK: *(Mutters)* Diseased offshoots of capitalism. . . . . . . tolerance—
(to F.M.) but there are limits. That consul's a class enemy.

FRANKIE MAE: Boring from within, comrade! *(She goes upstage.)* That means five bucks worth of gas for the picket trucks.
(MACK, JENNIE, SHORTY, JOSE, JOHN VIZA, MARTY gather at the table to plan the strikers' resistance to eviction.)

FRANKIE MAE: *(reads paper)* "What has she got that I ain't got?"

MACK: We ain't goin. We can't go, we got nowhere to go to. So we've gotta figure how we can stay here.

> *(They plan a mass meeting in Purtley; they set guards. JOSE begins to patrol the barbed wire fence. JENNIE has a fit of tears, from exhaustion; the rest hearten her roughly, and the comfort of having them there dries her eyes. On the way out she asks after ROSITA. MARTY goes into the tent. The others go. The COOK lies down in an improvised bunk.)*

BUSTER: *(In tent at edge of upper level.)* Baby, take them dimes out o' your ears and buy some beans.

ADA: I sho' won't. My first husband give me these dimes and I'm gonna wear 'em.

BUSTER: Aw, hell, I'm hongry.

ADA: Stop cussin' or you'll be burnin in hell, and I'll be settin on the front tiers of unclouded glory!

BUSTER: You'll be settin in de po' house, if we don't win dis strike.

> *(ROY, MILLIE, and BUD wander in at left.)*

JOSE: Go home, kids. Go to sleep. *Andale.*

MILLIE: Where's mama?

JOSE: She sick. You go my tent and sleep.

> *(He leads ROY and MILLIE off; enter SAM, and BUD runs to him.)*

BUD: Pop, where you goin?

SAM: Purtley. *(He reaches into his pocket for a dime.)* Here, buy yourself some bananas.

BUD: Thanks, pop. I'm gonna give it to Aunt Marty.

SAM: Naw you don't, I ain't helpin to take care of Shorty and Mack and all these guys. Let em feed themselves.

BUD: Where'd you get so much money, pop?

SAM: That's all right where I got it.

> *(Re-enter JOSE, patrolling. SAM starts back between the tents for a moment.)*

BUD: *(Low voice.)* Pop. You ain't against the strike, are you, pop?

SAM: Where'd you get that idea?

BUD: I heard Mack askin about you. And he said if you was against the strike, you was just goin against yourself.

SAM: Strikes ain't doin me no good, boy.

BUD: You ain't against the strike, are you, pop?

SAM: *(Savagely)* Shut, up, you little bastard. *(He strikes BUD. The boy begins to cry.)*

BUD: Pop, you ain't against the strike?

> *(Exit SAM past JOSE. The child disappears in the shadows upstage. A moment's silence, in which ROSITA is heard moaning. JOSE hears it and shakes his head. SHORTY comes in, L., and lights his cigarette at the stove. He sits down at the cook table.)*

SHORTY: How's your ma?

JOSE: She going to die.

SHORTY: Too bad.

JOSE: She think the strike kill her. She was sick before the strike—it's work-time, not strike-time, kill her.

SHORTY: Your kid brother's in jail. . . . . . and Shag . . . . . . and Steve. I hope they don't get Jennie or Mack.

JOSE: What for they lock up Jennie? They mustn't.

SHORTY: They'd like to lock us all up.

> *(JOSE paces the length of the wire. SHORTY stretches himself on the table.)*

SHORTY: Pretty old moon, isn't it?

JOSE: Like Mexican moon.

SHORTY: Mexico? What's it like down there?

JOSE: Pretty, kind o' like California. All over mountains and deserts, and moon like this. But plenty poor people, they don't get along so good. We make plenty revolution once. My papa fight with Zapata, try to get land and work. But the generals win—and they kill us. Always, they kill us poor peoples.

SHORTY: It's hell, ain't it?

> *(A low scream is heard from the tent.)*

JOSE: Plenty poor people sleep on ground in Mexico, go hungry, starve. Like here. They fight. They always get beat down.

SHORTY: Hell, ain't it?

JOSE: But someday, maybe we no beat down. Someday, maybe we win.

SHORTY: Yeah. *(Pause)* It's sure tough about your mom.

JOSE: *Si.* But just as good to die striking as starving.

SHORTY: Yeah. Just as good to die fighting as starving.

CURTAIN

Act III, Scene 1

A lodge room in Purtley. Same night. The Farmers' Protective Association is
meeting. There is a raised platform with a rostrum behind which, on the
wall, hangs a flag and on either side of it portraits of George Washing-
ton and Abraham Lincoln. Benches and cuspidors. In the chairman's
chair sits ED LOWE, a tight-lipped, dried-up little man, cruel and
powerful in a subtle provocative way. HARRY TILDEN is also on the
platform with a notebook. Several of the growers we have seen before. In
the back, a silent observer, sits SPRAGUE, the district attorney. Near
him are TOM ROLLINS and CLEM HOGAN taking notes for their
papers. During the meeting a petition circulates among the crowd. Most
of the men sign it readily.

As the curtain rises, the grower, BUD PETERSON, usurps the platform
in the midst of a fiery and demagogic speech. He lifts his arms, bellows.
His fat paunch with its gold chain and lodge emblem bounces up and
down. His jowls jiggle.

PETERSON: . . . . and in all the years I lived in this state,
men, I ain't never seen the time before when a dirty bunch of
Mexicans would rare up on their hind legs and defy a white man.
(Wiping the sweat from his face and continuing loudly and hoarsely.)
That's what they're doing today in the richest cotton county of
this state, gathered out yonder *(pointing)* in their Culver Camp,
four thousand strong, in league with alien agitators, plotting and
planning to tear down our government and that flag up there, *(points*
behind him) to ruin our crop, and reduce the good farmers and
honest business men of this state to nothing! That's their game!
They talk about wanting higher wages! Why, everybody knows a
Mexican can live on a dime's worth of beans a day. They talk about
wanting their union recognized—*(scornfully)* union—gather in all
the greasers and niggers and shiftless bums the alien agitators can
collect a nickel from and calling it a union. Recognize, hell! Men,
what are we going to do about it? Are we Americans—or not?

VOICES:
> Yes! Hell, yes.
> Nobody'll dictate to us.
> Down with foreign interference.
> Deport the lot of 'em.
> Run 'em out.

PETERSON: They talk about suffering. We're the ones that suffer. Look at our cotton busting open, standing unpicked, and who knows when rain will come? Can't get it picked, can't get it ginned. Why? Because a lot of foreign agitators have come down to this valley and got our pickers stirred up. I say, fellow Americans, any self-respecting man would run 'em out of here. (*Again he stops to wipe his brow and catch his breath.*)

LOWE: (*Rising*) I think you have well-expressed the sentiment of this meeting, Mr. Peterson. (*PETERSON, very pleased with himself, steps down from the platform and stands at the edge of the crowd.*) And don't forget, fellow citizens, we've already voluntarily raised their wages fifty per-cent over last year! We can't give those people enough, it seems. You see how they abuse any concessions you make. Sixty cents a hundred now. The more rope you give them, the more they take. *Wages* isn't what they want.

BURTLE: (*Interrupting*) Castor oil's what they need. Something to start 'em running.

PETERSON: (*Showing his gun*) This'll start 'em.

FLOORS: What're we waiting for? Why don't we run 'em out of town.

TILDEN: What's the matter with the sheriff?

LOWE: The sheriff has been unable to keep the trucks off the road.

FLOORS: Three of my picking gangs walked off yesterday, scared.

PETERSON: What are we paying taxes for, if that bunch in politics can't even protect our property and keep law and order?

BURTLE: I'm a red blooded American citizen! My gall rises at the thought of Americans knuckling under to a gang of aliens who should never have come into this country.

CLEM HOGAN: Why don't you guys give 'em the bum's rush?

LOWE: Why doesn't the sheriff put them in a bull pen?

LITTLE: Tar and feather's that's better. Why don't we call out the troops?

BURTLE: Hell, we don't need no troops. Ain't we got guns?

FLOORS: Seems to me we left things to *officials* too long.

WARDMAN: (*Rising on the platform.*) Look at this sheet I picked up to-day. (*Showing a leaflet and reading therefrom.*) It says, "Comrades, force the bosses to give you a living wage. Smash the ginning companies' reign of terror. Defend your rights!"

PETERSON: Who owns this country, yellow livered greasers or us red-blooded Americans?

TILDEN: The agitators don't want higher wages. They're *communists*. I know it. I went to one of their meetings at Buttonwillow last night, and I heard that Mack Saunders say, "We workers have got to fight our battle united on the whole world front until everything belongs to us."

FLOORS: Lynch the bastards!

PETERSON: Lynching's too good for them. Com-*mun*ists!

LITTLE: Who gives 'em their money?

PETERSON: Moscow!

ED LOWE: *(Using the gavel.)* If they win this strike, it means we will have to pay out. Can you afford it? How many of you are behind on your loans now?

LITTLE: I thought we was goin to get lower interest rates this year.

TILDEN: *(Suavely)* Certainly, men, the banks could have granted them if there hadn't been this strike.

FLOORS: Them goddam agitators.

TILDEN: Why should the bankers make all the sacrifice? Has Germany paid us back?

LITTLE: After we fought their war!

BURTLE: Aliens are all the same, fattening off the American farmers. We're just suckers.

FLOORS: *(threatening)* Not I!

OTHERS: NOR I. Me neither! Not me.

PETERSON: *(At edge of platform.)* All right fellows. How're we goin to get this viper out of here? Democracy is our watch-word. I say we take off our hats to the *flag* for a change, and not stand here and pay tribute to traitors who'd step on that flag and tear it limb for limb. How's for our gettin up fer once and saluting our flag, and telling it: Our Country, we are here! And to the racketeers who stir up strikes and destroy the principles of Liberty and Justice on which our country was founded, let's say to them: You shall not pass.
    (wild applause)

SIMMONS: Why, I'd let my cotton rot in the ground before I'd bow down to them striking bastards.

TILDEN: *(insinuatingly)* Do we want drastic action?

PETERSON: A ten million dollar crop going to waste!

FLOORS: Break that damn strike!

BURTLE: Why don't we stop the picket lines from going out?

FLOORS: We should clean out their hall.

ED LOWE: *(using the gavel)* And our Government pampering them with tons of food. They're living better than you or me. Have you gentlemen seen the truck-loads of delicacies that come to them and that Jennie Martin, she sweethearts with the whole bunch, greasers and all. That's how she gets her hold on them! Our daughters have to live in the same town with that————. It's time we got our country cleaned up.

BURTLE: That little————!

ED LOWE: Gentlemen, is the petition fully signed? If so, pass it up front.

LITTLE: *(Rising slowly holding the petition.)* It says here, "eliminate the leaders". Ain't that word kinder strong?

PETERSON: *(snorting)* Huh!

FLOORS: What do you want? Take 'em out on velvet carpets?

ED LOWE: We mean to get rid of them, Milt.

LITTLE: But couldn't they be locked up? Bloodshed never gits you nowhere.

BURTLE: *(pointing at TURNER)* Put that bastard out if he don't want to act like an American!

LITTLE: I'm as American as any here, gentlemen. Our Government wasn't founded on force and bloodshed, and violence don't get you nowhere.

> *(He is howled down. ED LOWE pounds with gavel. WARDMAN rises.)*

TILDEN: You needn't sign it, Milt.

FARMER: Maybe there's something to what Milt says.

> *(Again howls of protest.)*

PETERSON: *(booming)* Let's have that petition! Who else here wants to side with agitators? *(Silence.)* Nobody? Well, then. . . . . *(He hands the petition to ED LOWE.)* We'll handle this uprising from now on.

VOICES: Yes, sir! You tell 'em, Bud!

> *(The SHERIFF enters followed by LUTHER who remains at the back of the room.)*

BURTLE: Well, look who's here!

TILDEN: Come up front, Sheriff and tell how you're handling things.

SHERIFF: I haven't got a one of them ring-leaders yet. Can't get my hands on 'em.

FLOORS: You should of had 'em long ago.

SHERIFF: But I've asked the City Council for two hundred more riot guns.

BURTLE: Asked for 'em! Why ain't you got 'em?

SHERIFF: The Supervisors have ordered the camp closed by Monday.

FLOORS: Who's gonna close it?

PETERSON: We'll run 'em out, boys.

SHERIFF: I'd rather you'd let the police handle it.
      (General mocking laughter.)

BURTLE: You haven't done it.

PETERSON: Suppose we took on the job, Sheriff? *(Sees SPRAGUE)* There's the District Attorney back there. How about it, Sprague?

SPRAGUE: *(A good politician)* Well—we wouldn't have to see you.

VOICES: That's the spirit! Smart man! It's O.K. now.

SHERIFF: I'd like to say, if you gentlemen will let me, I think it's better to do it legally.

SEVERAL:
      Ah you! You let em get away with murder!
      You never arrested a mouse yet!
      You can't get yer cops to pinch a cow!

SHERIFF: I arrested every man that broke the law! The jail is full!

BURTLE: They need more'n arresting.

PETERSON: What's the law for? To protect us and our property, or any alien radical that chooses to come in here?

TILDEN: Why don't you arrest that tin madonna Jennie Martin?

SEVERAL:
      Vote him out!
      Get rid of him!
      You'll never get re-elected.

FLOORS: We're running our own business from now on.

SHERIFF: *(Very pale)* All right, gentlemen. You do it your way. I'll say nothing. You are all citizens and voters. Certainly, that's what I'm here for—to do what you want done—if I can.

SPRAGUE: Most of you men are deputized. Those responsible ranchers who are not, see me tomorrow and I'll swear you in.

PETERSON: That's the spirit, boys!
      (Loud approval from the assembly.)

ED LOWE: *(Using gavel)* Let us bring matters to a close. The statement has been signed by all here but one or two. They don't matter. *(Reading)* "We agree, we farmers met here tonight in the duly organized Farmers' Protective Association, to take the law into our own hands and eliminate the agitators from our fields and from the entire San Vincenze Valley." *(Puts paper down.)*

BURTLE: Deputized or not, we're going to uphold the law, and put a little patriotism and loyalty into this community.
> *(Loud applause)*

ACT III, Scene 2

Street and sidewalk of the Union Headquarters at Purtley. Saturday afternoon. On the windows of the old store front that serves as JENNIE's office are several strike notices and placards. On the door a dirty piece of cardboard: STRIKE HEADQUARTERS (with the S back to front) and below the same in Spanish: OFFICINA DE LA HUELGA. Over the door there is an American flag. The office is in the middle of the block, and on either side may be seen the windows of a cheap hot dog stand and a grain and feed store.

During the action a few passers-by, typical small-town types, youths, children, old ladies, ranchers, pass on the sidewalk. As the curtain rises JENNIE and PROF. BANKLEY are emerging from the headquarters.

PROF. BANKLEY: I am convinced, Miss Martin, from what I have seen here, that the ranchers are adding gunpowder to the situation. And the police seem inclined to wink at their violations! The brutality against your pickets is outrageous. I shall try to make that clear to my students.

JENNIE: *(Brushing the inessentials out of the way to get to the heart of what she needs.)* Will you yourself send a protest to the governor?

PROF. BANKLEY: *(Embarrassed)* Er—my connections with the university would-er-er . . . .

JENNIE: Well, will you help us raise bail? We have to get a hundred thousand dollars property-bail to release our jailed comrades.

PROF. BANKLEY: I-I-er, I really wish I could do something. Our courts do abuse the rights of citizens!

JENNIE: Workers, Mr. Bankley. This is a class-war.

PROF. BANKLEY: Well, now——Miss Martin. Can't we all solve it together?

WILLIS: How?

PROF. BANKLEY: We should work toward cooperation!

JENNIE: *(Short)* They make it a war, not we. We aren't armed.

PROF. BANKLEY: *(Waving his hands.)* Tch-tch-tch-t!
> *(Two housewives pass with their marketing.)*

1ST HOUSEWIFE: Those Reds, at it again.

2ND HOUSEWIFE: *(Looking back)* But he don't look like no red.

1ST HOUSEWIFE: He's in disguise.

PROF. BANKLEY: Well, I must get on, Miss Martin. I have to be in Berkeley tonight. *(Holds out his hand.)* Goodbye.

JENNIE: Goodbye. Do what you can for us.

PROF. BANKLEY: *(As he exits.)* I will.

JENNIE: *(Calling, as she picks up some scraps of paper from front of sidewalk.)* Juanita, bring out the broom and sweep up the front of this place.

JUANITA: *(Voice within)* Si, senorita.

> *(Exit JENNIE into headquarters. JUANITA emerges and begins to sweep off the sidewalk.)*

ADA: *(Entering slowly)* Lawd, chile, I's so sick!

JUANITA: *Buenas tardes.*

ADA: Wonder is Jennie got any aspirins here. I sho feels bad.

JUANITA: What senora?

ADA: You don't understand American, does you? Un-huh! I's so sick!

JENNIE: *(Coming to door)* Anybody around could mail a letter for me? Oh, hello, Mrs. Walker.

ADA: Goodmornin, Mis' Jen. *(Brightly)* Is you seen Buster?

JENNIE: Not this morning. Guess he's on the picket line. You know we're massing everyone today.

COLLINS: Have you noticed anything funny this afternoon?

JENNIE: No.

COLLINS: Well, I've noticed that the cops are scarce. You don't see 'em about town, do you?

JENNIE: They're probably somewhere drinking.

COLLINS: Well, id [*sic*], up at the hall they're saying that the police left town purposely, so the vigilantes can clean up.

JENNIE: *(A little pale)* The cops have never helped us, have they? Don't worry, if anything happens, they'll be right here to throw their tear gas.

> *(As she speaks, several strikers enter and go into the headquarters.)*

COLLINS: I'm not so sure. A lot of kids and drug-store cowboys walking around today with arms.

A MOTHER: *(Entering with a switch, driving a barefoot boy before her.)* I told you not to stay away all day. All them reds in town this afternoon. You stay home.

BOY: *(Whimpering)* Aw, ma, all the other kids is out.

MOTHER: *(Switching his legs.)* You listen to me, young man!. . . . . . .
       (They exit, the BOY crying. Off stage, the sound of a guitar is heard.)

ADA: *(Coming to the door and moving her hips to the distant music.)* They comin, Jennie. But, Lawd, I wish they'd let Buster play that guitar! *(Pausing.)* Say, they gettin out o' the trucks way up the street. Why for?

JENNIE: *(within)* Police orders—no trucks in this block, Ada.

ADA: Um-m! Listen to that music.
       (The sound of the guitar and of many voices grows louder. As the Mexicans enter, left, laughing and singing, the stool-pigeon, LUTHER, shaven and in Sunday clothes, enters at right and stands before the hot-dog stand, a half-amused look on his face, later he goes down a runway into audience, and leans against the left wall. The Mexicans stand speaking in Spanish, others go inside the headquarter.)

MEXICANS:
       Viva la Secretaria!
       Buenos tardas, companero!
       Viva la huelga!

PANCHO: *(To Ada)* You seen my girl?

ADA: She's around. Where's Buster?

PANCHO: *(Going in)* He come.
       (Enter JASPER WATERS, ADAM, MARTY, SHORTY, BUSTER, ROSITA, the children and others. BUSTER carries a placard on a pole reading Black and White Unite to Fight.)

ADA: Hy, you-all.

MARTY: Tired out. I picketed thirty miles today.

BUSTER: *(Picking up one foot after another and holding it.)* The truck did, you mean.
       (Enter MANUEL)

VOICES:
       Hello, Manuel!
       Hollo, papa.
       How's the proud father today.

ADA: Manuel, your wife sho bored you a sweet chile.

MANUEL: Fine baby, heh? I go inside, tell Jennie about him. *(Exits within)*
       (Enter ELLA, the COOK, and "DOC" LEE.)

COOK: All set? Gee, we hurried! Busted my last tire.

PAT: Say, did you hear them Vigilantes was planning to come after us?

BUSTER: What's vigilantes, Ku Klux?

PAT: Same thing.

STEVE: I heard all the Legioneers was gettin deppetized.

PAT: Jim Morales said he met two new ones with guns.

A STRIKER: What if we do get killed? It's a dog's life, anyway.

SHORTY: Aw, they're all too yellow-bellied to *do* anything, the cowards.

JASPER: You all is somewhat wrong. My boy, Ezekiel, he met Mrs. Jason's hired girl in the drugstore and she heard Mart Burtle say they were going to *end* this strike today!

SHORTY: *(laughs)* Or they'd know the reason why, eh? They always add that!

COOK: No, they'd teach us a lesson.

JASPER: Maybe some of us'll have to learn things we don't know yet. Dark things are being said hereabouts and I'm prayin.

    (MANUEL emerges with a box which he sets on the sidewalk in front of the right window.)

SHORTY: Say, pal, that box ain't big enough! Go get a big one, *(spreads his hands apart)* so we can put a chair on it.

    (He and MANUEL exit within. Enter JOHN VIZA.)

JOHN VIZA: *(Goes up to JACK)* Comrade, there was a drunken spree at that hotel last night after the farmers' meetin, and Lupe tell me they said they would bust up this meeting here today. Better tell Jennie.

COOK: *(seriously)* Who was there?

VIZA: Lupe said the highway police and Cop Tod Barker and that bunch of growers that hang out round the poolroom here. I hate to worry Jennie, but. . . . .

SHORTY: Let's get the Defense Corps ready.

VIZA: *(seriously)* Those men have guns.

DOC. LEE: Don't frighten people, Comrade.

    (More and more the stage is filling with picketers carrying banners and placards. They examine each others' posters and comment on them. Among them are DAN, FRANKIE MAE, DOMINGO, JOSE, and others. The banners read: DON'T SCAB, SOLIDARITY WINS, NOT AN OUNCE OF COTTON FOR LESS THAN A DOLLAR A HUNDRED, UNITE AND FIGHT, ONE BIG UNION.)

BUSTER: *(shouting)* Ada, I thought you was sick?

ADA: You ain't thought I was gonna miss this meetin, did you? Gimme a flag. *(From someone she gets a placard.)*

(SHORTY and MANUEL emerge carrying the box and a chair which they put in place. Others come out with leaflets and begin distributing them. Strikers keep arriving. JASPER WATER mounts the soapbox and stands beside the chair.)

JASPER: Now, folks, we're about to start. If you are not all here, you should-a-been. Time nor tide————.

COOK: There he goes! Talking again.

JASPER: Now, Miss Jennie'll be out here directly. Meantime, I'll keep yo' spirits movin. Now, this strike has done something for all of us, folks. It's brought us together. And like Daniel was delivered from the lion's den of entiquity, so this strike's due to deliver us from the sinful wiles of them gin-owners, cause by the help of God and mass-picket lines, we'll win. But, brothers, and sisters . . . .

(Just then JENNIE emerges from Headquarters. A cheer goes up from the crowd which prevents JASPER saying any more. He dismounts. JOSE helps her up on the chair. JASPER tries to get to her to whisper something but too many Mexicans get in between and he is pushed off the box. The strikers are shouting and cheering.)

STRIKERS:

Viva la Secretaria!
Viva la Huelga!
Hurah! Hurah!
Viva la Companero!
(Clapping and shouts. JENNIE holds up her hand.)

JENNIE: Comrades, and fellow workers . . . .

(Suddenly a brick comes whizzing through the air, thrown by LUTHER from the audience where the vigilantes are crouched in the aisles. Everybody turns, shouts, curses, and screams. It is the beginning of panic.)

SHORTY: *(Shouting across the footlights.)* The bastards!

(Another missile follows. The defenseless workers make a dash down the streets in all directions, some into headquarters—others look around for missiles. Someone pulls JENNIE down. DAN grabs the chair to use as a weapon. Others begin to rip the box apart and throw the pieces in the direction from which the rocks come. There is short exchange of missiles, and DAN advances toward the approaching vigilantes with the chair upraised. Suddenly there is a shot. DAN grabs his arm. The chair falls. Another shot, and DAN

drops mortally wounded. Women scream. Confusion and panic. Satiric laughter from the wings. Gun-fire. The strikers draw together in a surging mass, but now from every direction the guns of the vigilantes bark. The workers try to crowd into union headquarters. Some tumble from the steps. The windows shatter. ADA grabs her shoulder where a bullet has penetrated. MAX, holding a piece of box in one hand and leaflets in another, falls scattering the leaflets over the sidewalk. Blood flows.)

ADA: *(Shreaking)* Buster, Buster! *(She collapses.)*
  (Several strikers fall wounded, their banners falling with them. Some attempt to crawl to the door. By now the street is pretty well cleared. A hysterical child runs through the melee. BUSTER tumbles into the dust holding a placard, the blood streaming down his face and remains motionless. He is dead. JOSE runs across the stage.)

JOSE: *(yelling)* Jennie, Jennie!
  (He sees her standing against the brick wall between the headquarters and the shop, a perfect target. He flings himself in front of her. Again shots ring out and JOSE falls. JENNIE shrieks, falls to her knees, and spreads out her arms in front of JOSE. In one second everyone has vanished. Shouts and firing have stopped.)

JENNIE: Jose! Jose! *(She lifts his head.)*

JOSE: *(Dying)* You here, senorita? Listen, listen to me. You hear me? I want tell you—I love you. I love you, Comrade Jennie—like I love the revolution. You understan?

JENNIE: Jose! *(She is crying.)* You one of—our best—our best comrade!—Jose! You hear me?

JOSE: *(Pleading)* I love you, senorita——and —

JENNIE: We were comrades, Jose. *Companeros.* That is the greatest love.

JOSE: *(Holding her hand very tightly, suffering death.)* Yes! Comrades! You. . . . . loved . . . . .me. . . . a little.
  (JENNIE with great gentleness takes the dying boy's head in her arms. He loses consciousness. A police whistle is heard far down the street. SHORTY rushes in with a bruised and bloody face, and torn clothes.)

SHORTY: The bulls are coming, Jennie.
  (JENNIE shakes her head, motioning him to be quiet. Tears are streaming down her face.)

SHORTY: *(In horror and grief.)* Oh! Christ Jose?

JENNIE nods, unable to shake. SHORTY looks down, his face contorted. He picks up banner. BLACK AND WHITE UNITE TO FIGHT. The shrill sound of police whistles and the approaching patrol-wagon are heard as the

CURTAIN FALLS

Angelo Herndon Jones

1935

Hughes won first place in a contest sponsored by the leftist *New Theatre* magazine for this play invoking the history of the African American
Communist organizer Angelo Herndon. In 1932, Herndon had been
sentenced to twenty years on a Georgia chain gang for leading a protest
over conditions for blacks. He was released on appeal in 1934. The Herndon case, along with Scottsboro, was often cited as an egregious example
of racism in the American courts. Offered to the Gilpin Players, *Angelo
Herndon Jones* was rejected because the actresses refused to play prostitutes. There is no known production.

Characters

BUDDY JONES, a young Negro worker
LANK, his pal
MA JENKINS, an old washerwoman
VIOLA, her daughter
SADIE MAE, streetwalker
LOTTIE, streetwalker
A WORKMAN
A NEGRO COP
A WHITE COP
A LANDLORD
DEPUTIES
DETECTIVES
PASSERS-BY
WORKERS
POLICE
VOICES

SETTING: *The stage is divided into two parts by a portion of a wall, three
feet wide, in the very center of the stage. On the wall there is a poster
announcing a Herndon Meeting. The Poster reproduces a large picture
of Angelo Herndon, the young working class leader.*

On the left side of the wall there is an inner room, a poor room containing a cot and a kitchen stove. Here MA JENKINS lives, and her twenty year old daughter, VIOLA.

On the right side of the wall there is another inner room in another house (the rooms may be miles away, since the wall is only a symbolic barrier) in which there is a cheap iron bed, a table, a stand for books. In this room, BUDDY JONES lives, and his pal, LANK.

Sometimes the light shines in both rooms at once. Sometimes only in one room. Sometimes only on the poster announcing the Herndon meeting.

As the Curtain Rises one sees only the poster. Out of the darkness, two girls enter. They are obviously prostitutes.

SADIE MAE: Gimme a drag, will yuh? Mine's all run out.

LOTTIE: Draggin's mighty poor this evenin'. *(Handing her a nub of a cigarette.)*

SADIE MAE: So is hustlin'. I ain't made a dime tonight.

LOTTIE: Look at this hot papa's picture on the wall, Sadie Mae. I wish I had a nice young brown like that for a boy friend.

SADIE MAE: I reckon I'll keep Slug. He do get me out of jail when the need arises.

LOTTIE: I wonder who that guy is—Angelo Herndon?

SADIE MAE: I dunno. What do it say? You can read.

LOTTIE: *(Reading slowly)* It say: Mass Meeting Friday. Great Speaker on Negro Rights. Clark Hall.

SADIE MAE: Is they gonna dance? *(She cuts a few steps)*

LOTTIE: It don't seem to mention it. We couldn't go nohow.

SADIE MAE: Slug'd let me go if he thought I could make a dollar.

LOTTIE: Well, I got to hug this corner.

SADIE MAE: Yonder comes a pickup, Lottie! Look!

LOTTIE: *(Peering. Then disappointedly)* Yal, the cop.

> *(Both girls lean back against the wall, one on either side of the poster, as a Negro policeman enters)*

SADIE MAE and LOTTIE: *(To COP)* Hello, Sugar! Hy, Big Shot!

NEGRO COP: You sugarin' me tonight, heh? I can't use no sugar—I'm out of cigarettes.

SADIE MAE: So is we.

NEGRO COP: *(Pointedly)* I smoke Camels. Two for a quarter.

LOTTIE: Alright, here. *(She hands him a quarter)* Now, don't forget, here's mine for the night, so leave me be.

NEGRO COP: Sweet Papa Big Billy never forgets. *(He punches her playfully in the belly with his night stick and walks on)*

SADIE MAE: A graftin' bastard! You make a quarter and they take it from you. We ain't even got smokes ourselves.

LOTTIE: You ought to be a police woman, Sadie, darlin', then you'd rake in, too, instead of givin' out. Between the cops and the pimps, we don't never have nothin'. *(She turns back to the poster)* I wish I had a nice fella like this for my man.

SADIE MAE: I'm gonna keep Slug. He knows the racket. You see, it wasn't *me* that cop shook down for a quarter, cause Slug's got me all fixed up with headquarters.

LOTTIE: Oh, yeah? Well, be careful they don't haul you and Slug both in sometime . . . Hey, here comes a trick. *(Glances off right as footsteps approach. A colored workman in overalls passes)* Hello, baby!

SADIE MAE: What's your hurry, boy-friend?

WORKMAN: *(Going on, to exit left)* I'm C.C.C.ing on S.E.R.A. time, sweetie, and my check don't come for thirty days—then I spends it all on sales-tax.

SADIE MAE: *(Suggestively)* There ain't no sales-tax on what we got.

WORKMAN: I'll have to tell Roosevelt. He must've overlooked you.
(Exits, as a young man enters, left, in cap and sweater)

BUDDY: *(To girls)* Hello!

LOTTIE: Out walkin', Jonesy?

BUDDY: No, ridin', Lottie. *(Peering at poster)* So that guy's coming! I want to hear him.

SADIE MAE: *(Smiling)* How about hearin' me, Lovie?

BUDDY: *(Reading poster)* Friday night, tomorrow. Say, he's a great guy, that Herndon. You know what he did?

LOTTIE: No, what's he do, Buddy?

BUDDY: He done got white folks and colored folks together right in the middle of the South, Lottie, and that ain't no lie.

SADIE MAE: Huh! I does that up North.

LOTTIE: Shut up, fool.

BUDDY: I mean lots of 'em, white and colored, for a good purpose—to get themselves something to eat.

LOTTIE: To eat?

BUDDY: Yes, organized people what was starvin', black and white, and got 'em together.

LOTTIE: Then what did they do?

BUDDY: Went to the City Hall to demand something to eat.

LOTTIE: Lawd, I should a-been there!

SADIE MAE: Me, too.

LOTTIE: *(Pointing to poster)* I told you that boy on that picture was somebody, Sadie Mae.

SADIE MAE: Yeah, but I'll keep Slug.

BUDDY: Slug Martin?

SADIE MAE: Yal. Know him?

BUDDY: Sure, I know that bozo. Has he ever had a job since his nightclub closed?

SADIE MAE: No, I'm his meal ticket. He eats, alright.

> *(Just then two men pass off stage left in a car. They honk the horn and call to the girls)*

LOTTIE: Two white guys, Sadie Mae! Come on, honey, here's dough!

SADIE MAE: *(Waving)* Hello, dear! Sure I want a ride.

LOTTIE: Coming, pretty papa.

> *(The two girls rush off left and the sound of a car is heard departing)*

BUDDY: *(Staring after them)* Ain't that a hell of a way to make a living. *(He calls up the street)* Hurry up, Lank.

LANK: *(Entering)* Man, I'm too tired to hurry.

BUDDY: I thought you was gonna be all night buying them two cigs.

LANK: The man didn't want to bust a package. Wants three cents for two Piedmonts.

BUDDY: They high in this neighborhood.

LANK: You *would* have a gal what lives in a hincty neighborhood.

BUDDY: Quit your kiddin'. There ain't no hincty slums.

LANK: How is she, Buddy?

BUDDY: Man, I'm worried. She's gonna have that baby, Viola is, sure's you born.

LANK: She is? Why didn't you buy the stuff in time?

BUDDY: I didn't have the dollar, Lank.

LANK: Then why don't you get married?

BUDDY: I ain't got the money for no license.

LANK: Then why don't you live together?

BUDDY: We ain't got no room.

LANK: You can have ours, fella. I'll move out.

BUDDY: Then where'll you stay—with my mother-in-law to be?

LANK: I could try it. Ma Jenkins ain't so bad for her age, I reckon.

BUDDY: Come on home, man. We got to get some sleep to turn out at five o'clock in the morning and walk them six miles—cause we ain't got no carfare. If we get out yonder to that foundry on time, we might accidentally get on.

LANK: *Accidentally* is right these days and times. You know damn well, Buddy Jones, they ain't gonna hire no jigs around here nohow. They just gonna let us starve to death to get rid of us. (*They continue talking as they exit, right*)

BUDDY: Herndon's coming tomorrow . . .

    (*Their voices die in the distance. For a second the stage is empty. Then the NEGRO COP enters, approaches the Herndon poster, looks at it scornfully a minute, and punches its face, tearing the paper. He goes on to exit right as the light dies out on the wall*)

***

DARKNESS

***

    (*Violent ringing of an alarm clock in the room at right. Sounds of a bed creaking and someone jumping up suddenly. A match flares weakly, an oil lamp is lighted. LANK stands in his underwear and calls to BUDDY who is still sleeping.*)

LANK: Hey, Jones, get on out o' that bed. It's five o'clock.

BUDDY: (*Sleepily*) Alright.

LANK: If I don't get me a job today, I really is gonna raise hell with somebody. (*Pulling on overalls as he talks*)

BUDDY: (*sitting up*) Yal, me, too, man, cause I'm gonna have that baby to feed in no time.

    (*While BUDDY and LANK dress the light dies in their room, as gradually the dawn enters the window of the other room at the left of the stage where an old woman and her daughter are sleeping near the stove*)

MA JENKINS: (*Turning over*) Ay, Lawd! Lemme get up from here and start that white woman's clothes to boilin'. I ain't had but one washin' in two weeks. Lawd knows I needs this seventy-five cents. (*She gets slowly out of bed and begins to dress in the half-dark, muttering to herself*) Hard times, Lawdy! Lawd!

    (*As she puts on her clothes, she hears her daughter, VIOLA, sobbing softly with her face to the audience wall*)

VIOLA: (*Smothering her sobs with a pillow*) Oh! Oh! Oh!

MA JENKINS: Honey, what's de matter with you?

VIOLA: Nothing, ma.

MA JENKINS: (*Bending over the bed*) Yes, they is, too. Your pillow is all wet, just like as if you been cryin' all night. (*Commandingly*) You tell me what's wrong, now, Viola!

VIOLA: I don't what to do, ma.

MA JENKINS: Don't know what to do about what?

VIOLA: I'm gonna have a baby.

MA JENKINS: *(Loudly)* What that you say?

VIOLA: Me and Buddy's gonna have a baby.

MA JENKINS: You and starvation's gonna have a baby, you better say. Buddy Jones ain't a-bearin' nothin'. And he ain't likely to be a-feedin' nothin' neither, a young rascal! So that's why you's cryin'? I told you-all to be careful! And you ain't married, neither.

VIOLA: *(Bitterly)* That's all you ever tell anybody—is to be careful. Why can't you tell us how we can get married, how we can get jobs, how we can live, or something useful?

MA JENKINS: De Lawd'll tell you that, daughter—if you ain't too mixed up with de devil. *(She begins to make a coal fire)*

VIOLA: *(Getting out of bed)* Well, I wish the Lord would pay our rent then.

MA JENKINS: He will, don't worry.

VIOLA: He ain't, not for four months. And the man's coming back to collect again today.

MA JENKINS: Shut up doubtin' de Lawd, Viola, and get up from there and help me wash out these clothes, or go look for a job, one. I ain't been sendin' you to school all your life to lay up in bed and do nothin' but fool with Buddy and doubt de Lawd.

VIOLA: You know I can't get no job. I been tryin' all summer. *(Pulling on her stockings)* I wish I'd gone in that nightclub of Slug Martin's when it was runnin'.

MA JENKINS: Yes, and you'd a-been on de streets by now, a street-walker.

VIOLA: I wouldn't a-been starvin'—me and this child I got inside me.

MA JENKINS: You wouldn't a-had no child.

VIOLA: Maybe I wouldn't a wanted one! Goddamn it!

MA JENKINS: Hush up! Speakin' against God!

VIOLA: *(Almost hysterical)* There ain't no God! There ain't no God! If there was one . . .

MA JENKINS: Shut up, I say! . . . Shut up!

> *(The light fades out, comes on again where the torn poster hangs against the wall in the pale grey dawn. The two prostitutes stagger on left, emerging from a car that drives off noisily.)*

VOICES: *(Ribald shouts of men offstage in car)* So long, sweetheart! . . . So long, kid! . . . See you in the funny paper, baby!

SADIE MAE: So long, you cheapskates, you.

LOTTIE: *(Drunkenly)* Shut up, them's white folks. *(Pretending plea-sure)* They paid you a quarter more'n jigs would. *(Waving to them)* Thank you, darlings.

SADIE MAE: *(Pathetically)* I want to get home to Slug.

LOTTIE: *(Staring at the torn poster)* I wish I had a man like that. I wish I had a baby would grow up nice like Herndon. *(Wetting the torn paper and pasting it back on the wall)* Honey, who punched your face and tore it all up that a-way?

SADIE MAE: *(Looking at the money in her hand)* A lousy seventy-five cents!

> *(They stagger off left. People start passing. The sun rises full and red. Noises of trucks in the street. An ice man yelling. Dirty children on their way to school. Two deputies and a man with papers in his hand come by. Light in the room where MA JENKINS is alone, washing. A knock at the door)*

MA JENKINS: Come in.

> *(Enter the LANDLORD and DEPUTIES)*

LANDLORD: Er-Mrs. Jenkins, you've had your notice according to the law, and plenty of time to move. If you can pay, pay. If you can't settle with me for your back rent, then pack up, because we're putting you out.

MA JENKINS: How'm I gonna pay, when I ain't got not even two cents in de house?

LANDLORD: Alright, boys, start setting the heavy pieces on the side-walk.

> *(The deputies start rolling up the mattress and taking down the bed)*

MA JENKINS: Here! Here! What you-all doin? I got washin' to get out today.

LANDLORD: Washing for who?

MA JENKINS: Miss Pettiford.

LANDLORD: Well, you gonna get paid for that, ain't you? Take the money and get another flat.

MA JENKINS: *(To the men who are taking out her bed)* You ain't gonna throw me out in de cold, is you, at my age? *(They keep right on moving out the furniture)* Oh, my Lawd! Help me! Wait till my daughter comes home, please. Maybe she's got work. Maybe she done found a job today. Wait, I asks you, for de Lawd's sake, wait!

LANDLORD: I been waitin'. Looks like neither you, nor the Lord, nor your daughter pays their rent.

MA JENKINS: *(Holding the last piece of the bedstead desperately)* I tell you to put my things down.

LANDLORD: *(Grabbing her arm as men wrench the bedstead from her)* None of that now, you black wench! It's lucky I ain't had you sent to jail.

MA JENKINS: *(Wailing)* Take your hands off of me! . . . Lawd! Oh, Lawd! Oh, Lawd!

> *(Lights fade out in the room, but shine on the torn poster announcing Angelo Herndon and on the crowd passing on the sidewalk as the furniture sets beside the wall. An old black woman presently takes her place in the rocker, the tears streaming down her face. The late afternoon sun shines on the kids coming home from school, on the workers coming home with their dinner pails, on the tawdry prostitutes emerging as dusk falls. Enter SADIE MAE and LOTTIE who speak to MA JENKINS as she rocks beside her meagre furniture in the street)*

LOTTIE: Ain't this Mis' Jenkins? . . . Lawd, yes! . . . Ma Jenkins, ain't it kinder late to have all your things settin' out here airin'?

MA JENKINS: They ain't airin', honey. I's been put out o' my place.

SADIE MAE and LOTTIE: Put out?

MA JENKINS: *(Weeping)* In my old age, with no place to go. And I don't know where is Viola.

LOTTIE: Where is she? . . . I know Viola ain't left you? . . . Where is she?

MA JENKINS: Went out this mornin' to look for work and she ain't come home yet, and here's me settin' in de street. Her mama! De child'll find me settin' in de street.

SADIE MAE: Somebody else done took your room?

MA JENKINS: No, it's empty.

SADIE MAE: Empty?

MA JENKINS: Yes, empty.

LOTTIE: Well, you ought to move back in then. That landlord's got more money than you. He can wait for his rent.

MA JENKINS: He say he won't wait no longer. *(Looks up)* But thank God, here comes Viola. *(Her daughter enters)*

VIOLA: Mama, what's this? What you doin' out here?

> *(The old woman weeps)*

LOTTIE: They put her out.

SADIE MAE: They ain't let her stay in.

VIOLA: You mean we're evicted?

MA JENKINS: I been waitin' for you, honey, to see what we can do, cause we ain't got no place to stay. Is you found any kind o' work or anything to earn a dime today?

VIOLA: No, ma, not a thing. *(Angrily)* But they're not gonna make us stay in the street. No, they won't make us do that.

SADIE MAE: Don't say what they won't do honey. White folks don't care nothin' about you.

VIOLA: *(To LOTTIE)* One of you-all stay with ma, and I'm goin' and get Buddy. He's gone to the Herndon meeting, I reckon. I'm gonna find him. *(She exits right)*

MA JENKINS: And I'm gonna pray. *(She kneels down beside the furniture)*

SADIE MAE: And I'm gonna try and make a dollar tonight to give to this old woman so she can get herself a room.

LOTTIE: *(Looking at poster)* I wish I could go to that Herndon meeting, too.

SADIE MAE: Watch out, girl! Here come the cops, two of 'em tonight. *(A NEGRO COP and a WHITE COP enter and walk slowly and importantly across the stage. It is almost dark now)*

WHITE COP: *(To MA JENKINS)* You'll have to get that stuff off the sidewalk tonight or we'll run you in.

MA JENKINS: *(Helplessly)* Where'm I gonna take it?

NEGRO COP: To the junk heap, if nowhere's else.

WHITE COP: Just get it away from here, that's all we care.

NEGRO COP: *(Walking away)* And don't be here when we come back. *(They exit swinging their clubs)*

LOTTIE: *(Calling)* Don't you need some cigarettes tonight, *(Under her breath)* you bastard?

SADIE MAE: *(Laughing)* Ma Jenkins don't know nothin' about payin' off the cops, does she? If she'd give them flatfeet a buck a day, she could rent the sidewalk for a speakeasy. I'll have to get Slug to fix her up at headquarters.

LOTTIE: *(To the old woman)* Don't cry. Buddy can help you. Wait till he gets back from that meeting. You seen them cops, didn't you, Ma Jenkins? Black and white cops teamed up against us! Well, if black and white can team up to keep *us down*—looks like we poor folks could team up, too, against them. If Herndon can bring black and white together down South, it sure can be done up North here, too, where we're just as hungry. And I tell you, Sadie Mae . . .

(The lights go out, but in the darkness, growing louder and louder, there is the sound of applause, and Herndon's voice is heard speaking)

VOICE: . . . I tell you let them imprison me. Let them send me to the chain gang, but a thousand Angelo Herndons will arise to take my place. A million Angelo Herndons. All over the country in every city and town! I am the working class. *(applause)* Black and white unite to fight.

(The strains of the INTERNATIONALE are heard. Then VIOLA's voice speaking to BUDDY)

VIOLA: And all our things are out in the street, Buddy. On the sidewalk in the night, in the cold.

BUDDY: You hear that, comrades, what Viola says? She and her mother's been thrown out of their room by the landlord.

VOICES:

We'll put 'em back.

They won't stay out.

They won't stay out.

We'll go right there, from this meeting, *now.*

BUDDY: Come on, Viola! Come on, honey! Now you have comrades!

(The strains of the INTERNATIONALE grow louder as the light comes on again and the Negro and White workers are seen filling the stage as they carry the furniture back into the room, left, that had been emptied by the landlord and his deputies. A throng of workers fill the night. Then a cop's whistle is heard, then another. Sirens, police gongs, as patrols and squad cars arrive. Faces of black and white cops. Black and white workers. Struggle! But the furniture goes back . . . As the noise fades away, and the light dies in the Jenkins' room, loud voices are heard in the other room at the right, and LANK is revealed surrounded by detectives who are searching his and Buddy's place)

DETECTIVES: *(Looking under mattress, as his fellow-dicks search in drawers, etc.)* Where'd you find out about that meeting? What were you doing there? Where's this Buddy Jones who lives with you? What books do you read? Who gives you incendiary literature?

LANK: What you talkin' about, man? I don't need to read no books to know I'm hungry. I don't need to read books to know I ain't got no job, to know I'm black, to know they ain't no chance for me in America long as people like you runs things.

DETECTIVE: Shut up! Where's Buddy Jones?

LANK: How I know where Buddy Jones is? I ain't his mammy.

DETECTIVE: Aw-right! Aw-right! We'll run you in if you get too fly. You just stay away from them Herndon meetings, and everything like 'em, you hear? The red quad ain't gonna stand for that, niggers and white folks meeting together—to take up for niggers.

LANK: And how about me being hungry? You gonna stand for that?

DETECTIVE: *(Glaring)* You know what I mean? *(To the others)* Did you find anything, boys? If not, let's go. We got some more nigger houses to search tonight. *(They exit)*

LANK: *(Laughing to himself)* They sure don't know how to look for nothing. *(He pulls down the window shade and out tumble several copies of various magazines, and a pamphlet life of Herndon)* I got my life of Herndon right here!

> *(Lights die out, come on flooding the Herndon poster on the wall. Then in the room at the left, by the dim flicker of an oil lamp, MA JENKINS is seen snoring in her bed, as BUDDY and VIOLA talk in a corner)*

BUDDY: . . . and he's right, Viola, Herndon is. I ain't never heard no-body so right before. Black and white workers *can* get together and rule the whole world. That boy, Angelo Herndon, knows what he's talking about. You seen how they came and put your furniture right back in the house tonight, colored and white helping us. They didn't draw no color line, did they? No, sir-ree! And I'm gonna join up with them kind o' people.

VIOLA: Me, too, honey.

BUDDY: And maybe by the time our baby grows up, this country won't be like it is today—folks hungry, folks Jim-crowed, folks put out o' their houses.

VIOLA: I hope it won't be like it is now.

BUDDY: *(Positively)* Well, it won't be! We gonna change all that.

MA JENKINS: *(Waking up and turning over)* You Buddy Jones! Why don't you go on home to yo' bed?

BUDDY: Yes, ma'am. *(To VIOLA)* I better go. Gee, it must be late.

VIOLA: I'll walk as far as the corner with you, honey. I need air, after so much excitement.

BUDDY: Alright, as far as the corner.

> *(They blow out the light and exit. The Herndon poster is bright under the street lights as the two lovers stop beneath it)*

VIOLA: Goodnight. *(As they stand close to each other)*

BUDDY: I hate to leave you, baby, but soon's I can, we'll get a room together.

VIOLA: Alright, Buddy. We ain't got much, but we got our love.

BUDDY: Love and struggle, honey, and a baby coming! But we'll get there, don't worry. We got leaders like him, *(Points to the Herndon poster)* that are gonna show us how to make a new world. He's a great young guy, that Herndon, ain't he, sweet?

VIOLA: He sure is. *(She snuggles close to Buddy)* And so are you, Buddy. *(Suddenly)* Say, listen, honey! You know what I'm gonna name our child?

BUDDY: No, what you gonna name him?

VIOLA: *(Looking at the poster, then straight at Buddy)* Angelo Herndon Jones!

BUDDY: *(slowly)* Angelo . . . Herndon . . . Jones.

> *They kiss as the*

CURTAIN FALLS

Little Ham

1935

Little Ham premiered at the Karamu Theatre in Cleveland, Ohio, on March 24, 1935, to warm reviews and was revived there several times. There was even talk of it going to Broadway. A program note for the play's first run observes that *Little Ham* reveals "certain aspects of Harlem life centered around the numbers. It is a play without serious reason for being. It is just to laugh and in laughing to be happy." Yet the play's satiric elements are clear. Harlem, here depicted in the loving manner of a folk comedy, may seem to belong to black folk, but "whites run it"; in fact, white gangsters take over the numbers business in Act I. This original text places *Little Ham* in the midst of depression Harlem. An occasional "hit" is the only economic opportunity for the Harlem residents who parade through Paradise Shining Parlor and Tiny's Beauty Shop, each portrayed comically and together presenting a fond portrait of a community Hughes would draw upon his whole life.

Although probably not the original performance text, this version of *Little Ham* is close to it. It is set in the 1930s, black vernacular is more pronounced than in later versions, and certain expressions reflect the era. While working with Webster Smalley on what would become *Five Plays by Langston Hughes*,[1] Hughes decided to make *Little Ham* a play of the twenties; however, he changed only a few of the references and made a few others generic; for example, "truckin'," a dance of the thirties, became the charleston, the Ubangi Club became the Cotton Club, and Masculine Lady was stripped of her link to the famous entertainer Gladys Bentley, who, in the early 1930s, reigned in the Ubangi Club, backed by a chorus of men in drag. However, he did not change references to boxer Joe Louis, whose rise to fame began in 1934; to Father Divine, whose movement was at its height in the 1930s; and to Haile Selassie, who became emperor at the beginning of that decade. Hughes did change Little Ham's middle name from Hambone to Hitchcock, moving him out of the realm of the folk to that of one of the geniuses of modern cinema.[2]

Characters

MADAM LUCILLE BELL, proprietress of the Paradise Shining Parlor
SHINGLE, a lazy shine boy
CUSTOMER, on the shine stand
JANITOR, a numbers addict
SUGAR LOU BIRD, a Harlem chorus girl
LITTLE HAM, a sporty young shoe shiner
MATTIE BEA, a married woman
OLD LADY
SHABBY MAN
BOSS LEROY, a Harlem racketeer
MAN IN BOOTS
TINY LEE, a hair dresser
LITTLE BOY
1ST DETECTIVE
2ND DETECTIVE
YOUTH
JASPER, night shine boy
WEST INDIAN
DEACONESS
TALL GUY
HOT STUFF MAN
PRETTY WOMAN
MASCULINE LADY
NEWSBOY
BUTCH, gangster
DUTCH, gangster
JIGGERS, gang leader
OPAL, manicurist
DARK CUSTOMER
LULU, a hairdresser
MAMA, a customer
SNOOKS, her child
STAID LADY, a customer
MISSOURI, her little girl
LODGE LADY
DIVINITE
DELIVERY BOY
A COP

JACK, Lulu's boy-friend
GILBERT, Tiny's used-to-be
MASTER OF CEREMONIES, at the Hello Club Ball
BERIBBONED COMMITTEE MEMBERS
DANCERS
ORCHESTRA

ACT I

*The interior of the Paradise Shining Parlor, three chairs mounted on a dais,
a rack of weekly Negro newspapers and Dream Books, at opposite side of
stage from door a cigar counter and cash register behind which a stately
middle-aged yellow woman called MADAM BELL presides, a telephone
booth, a closet, a gas stove, a few stools, a radio, a poster announcing
the Hello Club's Social Trucking Contest and Ball.*

*When the curtain rises the radio is blaring a Cab Calloway recording.
MADAM BELL sits behind the register taking down a number from a
client, the JANITOR of the building, who wishes to play.*

MADAM BELL: *(To one of the shine boys)* Turn that radio down, Shingle,
   so I can take this number. That noise gets on my nerves.

SHINGLE: *(Leaving customer whose shoes he is shining)* Yes, ma'am.

JANITOR: *(At cigar stand)* 702, in a box. I dreamt it sure as I'm
   standing here, last night.

MADAM: How much—a dime?

JANITOR: No'm, a nickel a piece.

MADAM: Thirty cents. *(Opening drawer in stand)* Haven't you got any
   change?

JANITOR: Only this here half-dollar.

MADAM: I wish you-all'd bring change for these numbers. Shingle, can
   you change this? I don't want to ring this register and get my store
   account all mixed up with the number money.

SHINGLE: *(Leaving customer again)* All I got is 15 cents. *(Drawling)*
   Tips ain't amounted to nothing today.

MADAM: All right, All right. *(Ringing register and taking change out)*
   I'll have to give you some pennies.

JANITOR: Well, I tell you—put ten cents on a run down, 702 to 712,
   'cause I know 7 something is coming today.

MADAM: Now you're talkin'. That's the way to win. Why don't you
   put that other dime on bolito, nickel on the first and last?

JANITOR: I believe I will, 7-0 and 0-2.

MADAM: *(Putting the numbers down and making him out a slip)* Them's good numbers, Janitor, I might play 'em myself.

JANITOR: I believes they lucky.

MADAM: Yes, indeed! Well, now, you don't get no change.

JANITOR: That's the last cent I got till pay day, so you know I believes in them numbers. I dreamt 702 just as plain last night.

SHINGLE: I hope you warn't in your lickers.

JANITOR: I never drinks 'cept on pay day. Don't have nothing to drink on.

CUSTOMER: *(On stand)* Well, I drinks—and don't play. I never plays numbers. I'd rather have mine in my belly than in somebody's else's pocket.

JANITOR: That's you. But if I ever hit, I'm gonna live on de fat o' the land. *(Exits)*

SHINGLE: *(Pointedly, as CUSTOMER descends from stand)* Well, I never plays neither. I takes my tips home to my wife and children.

CUSTOMER: *(Handing him two dimes)* You're a good man. Here's a dime for yourself.

SHINGLE: *(As CUSTOMER exits)* Thank you, sir! Thank you! *(As soon as CUSTOMER is gone, SHINGLE goes to the MADAM, who rings up a dime for the shine)* Here, Madam Bell, here's yo' dime, and put my ten cents on 942, will you, straight? That's the number of my new girl friend's house, where she just moved in, and I know it's lucky, 'cause I went by there last night and helped her put up the bed, and she say, "Baby, I feels like something good's gonna happen in this house!"

MADAM: *(Putting down numbers)* Wife and babies! Shingle, you's an awful liar!

MATTIE BEA: *(Sticking head in door)* S'cuse me, you-all! Ain't Little Ham got here yet?

SHINGLE: No'm he ain't showed up as yet, lady.

MATTIE BEA: Well, tell him I were here and'll be back directly.

SHINGLE: Yes'm.

    (Exit MATTIE BEA)

MADAM: *(Handing him paper)* Here's your slip. That makes about five numbers you done played already today, ain't it?

SHINGLE: Yes'm. I sho better hold on to my next tip 'cause it's almost lunch time, and I's hongry.

MADAM: It's about time for Ham to show up, too. He relieves you today, don't he?

SHINGLE: Yes'm. I wish I was as lucky as little ole Ham. He sure do have plenty good womens, and he's always hittin' de numbers. For such a little man, he musts done got a charm or something 'nother.

MADAM: Well, if you just work hard, Shingle, you'll have something some day, too, son.

SHINGLE: What kind o' son you mean, Madam Bell?

MADAM: Son of Ethiopia, my boy, waiting to stretch forth your hand. *(Putting scarf about her shoulders)* Shingle, turn up that gas a little. It's getting cold. Looks like snow. And see if you can't get something good on the radio. I hate classics.

SHINGLE: Sho is cold. What month is we at now?

MADAM: October.

SHINGLE: *(Going to radio and monkeying with dials)* Next month's Christmas, ain't it?

MADAM: No, Thanksgiving.

SHINGLE: Um-uh! I hope I hits 942, by then, so's I can buy my girl friend a turkey.

MADAM: Just keep on playing it. 942's bound to come out some time.

SHINGLE: If I don't run out first.

(Enter good-looking chorus girl, SUGAR LOU BIRD)

SUGAR LOU: Quick shine, please. I got a rehearsal today.

SHINGLE: Yes, Ma'am. Just mount the chair, Miss Bird, I'll be through with this radio in a minute!

(All sorts of fantastic and discordant sounds come out of the radio as the two women try to top it with their conversation)

SUGAR LOU: *(Shouting)* How you been, Madam Bell?

MADAM: Not bad, not bad, Sugar Lou.

SUGAR LOU: What's been running lately?

MADAM: The fours and sevens. 467 and 347've both come out this week.

SUGAR LOU: Well, put me a quarter straight on 744. That ought to hit it in the bread basket.

MADAM: What'd you say? *(To SHINGLE)* You, Shingle, tone it down!

SUGAR LOU: 7 - 4 - 4.

MADAM: That's a good number, girlie.

SHINGLE: *(Drawling as he dials back to the record program and approaches shine stand)* If I just had a dime, I'd play that number, too.

SUGAR LOU: Put a dime on it for Shingle, too. (*To him*) And that'll be your tip.

SHINGLE: Thank you! THANK YOU! I'm gonna shine 'em till you can see your pretty face in de toes.

SUGAR LOU: Well, hurry then. These are hand-made shoes from abroad, boy. They take a good shine.

SHINGLE: You been all over Europe, ain't you, Miss Bird? That's what you get for dancin' with the show.

SUGAR LOU: Yep, I been most everywhere. How about you?

SHINGLE: I been to Paris.

SUGAR LOU: Paris, Kentucky?

SHINGLE: No'm. Paris, London. And I took a train and went from there to Chicago. Then I come by zeppline here.

(*The phone rings loudly! SHINGLE goes to answer it*)

MADAM: (*Making out slips and calling SHINGLE to get them*) Here, hand that to Miss Bird. (*To the GIRL*) How's your show doing, Sugar Lou?

SUGAR LOU: Shaping up right well. Opens next week. Looks like we might go to London after a run here. You know I was over there all last year with the Dixie Vamps, toured the Continent everywhere.

MADAM: How'd you like it?

SUGAR LOU: How'd they like me, you mean? Honey, they musta thought I was chocolate. They nearly ate me up. Looked like I'd never get out of France. (*To SHINGLE as he turns from phone*) Hurry up, boy. I got to get down to the theatre.

MADAM: Who was that for?

SHINGLE: Little Ham.

MADAM: Some woman, I suppose.

SHINGLE: Naturally.

SUGAR LOU: Shingle, please hurry. I've got a rehearsal.

SHINGLE: Yes'm.

MADAM: It must be nearly noon, ain't it?

SUGAR LOU: (*Raising her sleeve and displaying eight or ten wrist watches*) You mean here in New York, I presume?

MADAM: Yes, darling.

SUGAR LOU: Well, it is 11:30 here.

SHINGLE: (*Noticing her many watches*) Um-uh!

MADAM: Why so many watches, darling? I ain't never seen the like.

SUGAR LOU: I got one for each European capital, honey. I collected 'em while I was over there, and I wear 'em all just to tell the time o'

day in each place. They came from Paris, Berlin, Monaco. Now, for
instance, an Indian Prince, Naboo, gave me this little platinum thing
in Paris, and I told him I'd never let it run down, nor change the
hour until we met in Paris again. *(Sighing)* It's 6:30 in the evening
in Paris right now.

SHINGLE: Well, I'll be a Abyssinian! Miss Bird, what time is it in
Ethiopia?

SUGAR LOU: I'm sorry, but I never met Haile Selassie.

SHINGLE: *(As he finishes her shoes)* I knows it's lunch time in Harlem,
and I ain't got nary dime to get myself a pig's foot.

SUGAR LOU: You broke?

SHINGLE: Always broke. Look like I just can't hit de numbers.

MADAM: Shingle! *(To GIRL)* Don't pay him no mind, Sugar Plum.
That boy's always got his hand out. I'm gonna fire him if he don't
watch out—asking for tips.

SUGAR LOU: That's alright! Here, Shingle, pay for my numbers and
yours, and keep the change. *(Hands him fifty cents.)*

SHINGLE: Yes, ma'am. Thank you! Thank YOU!

SUGAR LOU: Be seeing you, Madam Bell.

> *(As she exits, she bumps into LITTLE HAM, who enters in a
> hurry—late, as usual. He steps back with a flourish, tips his hat
> and bows)*

HAM: Howdy do, Miss Sugar Lou.

SUGAR LOU: Hello, Little Ham! How're you?

HAM: I'm your man! If you ain't busy after the show, lemme know.

SUGAR LOU: I might, at that, Little Ham. You got any new trucking
steps you can teach me?

HAM: Sho have. Look here!

> *(He trucks across the room toward the MADAM to the music of the
> radio. Laughs aloud and turns and waves at SUGAR LOU)*

SUGAR LOU: *(Smiling)* Goodbye, boy! That sends me! *(Exits)*

HAM: *(Still trucking)* I sho likes to dance, Lucille. When I'm dancing,
feels like I'm loving a million women all at once!

MADAM: *(Peeved)* You better get here, Ham. You devil! You know you
'spose to come at eleven. Shingle, turn down that radio!

SHINGLE: *(As he turns dial)* That joker can't keep time. Ham can't do
nothin' but truck and love.

HAM: *(In surprise)* What time is it?

SHINGLE: Six o'clock in Paris.

HAM: How you know?

SHINGLE: Sugar Lou Bird just told me.

HAM: You keep your mind off Sugar Lou, boy. She's got her eye on me.

SHINGLE: She don't know you livin', less'n she see you.

HAM: Didn't you glimpse her just givin' me that "truck on up and see me some time" look as she went out the door?

MADAM: You come on in here and truck them shoe brushes! It's high noon and Shingle's got to go and get his lunch, and some o' you boys clean up that shine stand, too, before Boss Leroy comes. It's filthy.

SHINGLE: Yes'm, I sho will, but just lemme play a dime on 645 first.

MADAM: *(Making out a slip)* 645 straight?

SHINGLE: Um-huh. And put this other dime on bolito, back and front.

MADAM: Bolito, each way.

SHINGLE: Ham, you lend me a dime to eat some trotters on, please, beings I ain't kicked about you being late, and tips is poor.

HAM: *(Tossing him a dime)* Money's nothing to me. Here, boy. Lemme see you go! Has Mattie Bea been here asking for me?

SHINGLE: Some woman or 'nother stuck her head in here about half a hour ago, and say she'd be back.

HAM: What she look like? *(Beginning to unbutton his street clothes)*

SHINGLE: Like a coal scuttle blonde with purple powder on.

HAM: That's Mattie Bea. She promised to bring me a muffler today. My neck is cold.

SHINGLE: Why don't you buy one yourself?

HAM: I likes to give the women pleasure. They loves to present me with things.

SHINGLE: How come they never presents *me* with nothing, I wonder?

HAM: You just not the type, Shingle, you not the type.

SHINGLE: Some woman named Laura called up here, too.

HAM: I ain't interested in that.

SHINGLE: How come?

HAM: She's just a used blade, and I got a new razor.

MADAM: Shingle, go on and get your lunch.

> *(Meanwhile HAM has been taking off his sporty overcoat with the extra broad shoulders and removing his coat and vest, while SHINGLE takes his old coat out of the closet and puts it on, sporty, too, but very well worn. HAM dons a snappy white jacket and begins to straighten up the shoe shine stand)*

SHINGLE: *(Moving toward door)* Don't you go grabbing off all the women customers this afternoon after I gets back. I wants to look at some legs, too.

HAM: Aw, go on and eat your pig's feet. Lemme miss you! You know you ain't no Clark Gable like I is.

> *(SHINGLE exits)*

MADAM: Ham, you's a mess!

HAM: *(Coming toward her)* That's why the womens like me, Lucille. You still likes me a little bit your ownself, don't you?

MADAM: I lets you stay around here even if you is late all the time.

HAM: But you done got yourself all tied up with that numbers Baron, now, and can't go for nobody else.

MADAM: We makin' money though, Ham. You know yourself, I didn't hardly make my rent out o' this place before I met Leroy, and he set me up as one of his agents for takin' bets. And, you must admit Leroy's way up yonder with the big shots when I comes to writing numbers. Why Manny Hudgins, the biggest gangster in New York's behind Leroy's outfit. He made Leroy chief o' this section o' Harlem himself. 'Fore long you'll see me wearing more diamond wristwatches than Sugar Lou Bird brought back from the Old Country with the Dixie Chorus.

HAM: Well, I hope you'll gimme just one to put on my big old black arm so I can tell de time.

MADAM: I sure will, Ham, for old time's sake.

> *(They hold hands. She sighs)*

HAM: Lucille, is they anything I can do for you?

MADAM: *(Coming to herself)* You might give me a shine. *(Leaves cash register and mounts the shine stand)*

HAM: *(Suddenly busy)* You know I'll do that.

MADAM: *(Looking down at LITTLE HAM)* Ham, honey, sometimes I worries about you. Honest I do, even if we did bust up. You fools around with too many women. And you don't take none of 'em serious. Someday, someone of 'em's gonna get mad and cut you from here to yonder.

HAM: Not me, baby! Oh, no! When it comes to cuttin' and shootin', that's when I'm gone. Me and weapons don't mix.

MADAM: That's why I couldn't let myself like you any more than I did. I'd a-been in the electric chair by now and you'd a-been in your grave.

HAM: Aw, baby, don't talk so mean.

MADAM: But, I'm glad I didn't hurt you.

HAM: Why?

MADAM: You too cute, Ham, to get all cut up.

HAM: You tellin' me?

> *(Enter MATTIE BEA)*

MATTIE BEA: Oh, here you is. I been by here three or four times tryin' to catch you. *(Noticing MADAM BELL glaring at her)* Ham, I wants to talk to you—when you gets through.

HAM: Just sit down. I'll be with you in a minute, baby.

> *(MATTIE BEA sits down as an OLD LADY enters, poorly dressed)*

OLD LADY: Is I too late to play my numbers back today?

MADAM: Plenty of time, plenty of time. They ain't collected yet.

OLD LADY: I just got a few pennies my daughter give me. I wants to play 403, 862, and 919, and put. . . . . . .

> *(She and MADAM BELL talk at the cigar counter as HAM and MATTIE BEA get together)*

HAM: Girl, you oughtn't to bother me during my working hours. Don't you know I don't 'low no women to mix in with my profession?

MATTIE: Well, honey, I just had to see you. *(Pulling out a package from beneath her coat)* Didn't you tell me your neck was cold? I done brought you this nice warm red muffler. *(Unwraps and offers him the muffler. HAM tries it on)*

HAM: *(Looking in glass)* I reckon it'll do. It's mighty red, though. Liable to burn me up!

MATTIE BEA: Don't you like red, honey?

HAM: I reckon so, since you brought it to me.

MATTIE BEA: Is you coming by the Silver Dollar tonight?

HAM: Well, er - er, now my business. . . .

MATTIE BEA: *(Impatiently)* Now, you know you ain't got no business. . . .

HAM: Shss - s - s! How you know what I got?

MATTIE BEA: *(Loudly)* I know—you just getting tired o 'me, that's all, or else you actin' like you is. You must think I enjoy staying home with my husband.

HAM: No, baby. I don't. But can't you see this ain't no place to talk like that. *(Enter a shabby but neatly dressed MAN who mounts the shine stand)* I got a customer.

MATTIE BEA: Well, I'll be back by and by. I wants you to go with me to the Hello Club Social tomorrow night, anyhow. They havin' a truckin' contest.

HAM: Baby, you know you can't truck. *(Beginning to shine the SHABBY MAN's shoes)*

MATTIE BEA: I know I can't, but we can sit there and look.

HAM: Well, I wants to dance, not look, when I goes to a party.

MATTIE BEA: I can two-step.

HAM: You can't do that good.

MATTIE BEA: Well, you goin' with me, whether you want to or not.

HAM: Shss-ss-s! Here comes de boss, anyhow

MATTIE BEA: I'll be coming back. *(Starts toward door)*

HAM: O.K.

MATTIE BEA: You go hang your muffler up, Ham, so you won't get it dirty.

> *(Exits, as BOSS LEROY enters and looks around importantly.)*

OLD LADY: *(At cigar counter)* And if I don't catch today, don't know how I'm gonna play tomorrow, but the Lawd will provide, I reckon. Fact is, I know he will.

MADAM: He always do, don't he?

OLD LADY: Yes, he do!

LEROY: *(To HAM)* Get them papers and cigar butts off that shine stand. It looks like a pig pen in here.

HAM: *(Insolently)* O.K., big boy!

LEROY: What'd you mean—big boy?

HAM: You de big boss, ain't you?

LEROY: *(Satisfied)* Well, alright then. *(Approaches register and greets MADAM BELL)* Hello, dear. Got the slips ready for me to check up on? We ain't got much time. *(Puts his arm around her as they check over the numbers. The OLD LADY exits)*

MADAM: Hello, babe! I ain't seen you all day, LeRoy, Honey.

LEROY: Been busy as hell, darling. Didn't get a chance to run by. One of our best writers is in jail, too. The damn fool sold a slip to a plain-clothes man. I've got to try to replace him, if I can. *(Looking over the slips)* Now, let's see. . . .

> *(They check up and converse as HAM shines the SHABBY MAN's shoes)*

HAM: Gettin' kinder cold, ain't it?

SHABBY MAN: Yes, it is, for certain. But I had some good luck today. First time in two years.

HAM: What'd you do, hit the numbers?

SHABBY MAN: No, I got a job! At least, I think I did. That's why I'm getting a shine. They told me to come back at three this afternoon, dressed up. It's waiting table.

HAM: Kinder hard to shine shoes as old as these is.

SHABBY MAN: I know it, but they all I got. I ain't hardly got a nickel to get down town after I pay for this shine, either.

HAM: Then, that's alright, buddy. You don't have to pay, I been broke, too. You just keep it.

(Enter SHINGLE)

SHABBY MAN: *(Getting down)* Thank you! Thank you! *(Bowing as he exits)* Thank you!

SHINGLE: Ham, you must-a-done give the man a tip.

HAM: I ain't give him nothin' but a shine. *(Loudly)* But as long as you stayed out, you must-a-done et up a whole hog, not just the feet.

(BOSS LEROY and MADAM both look at SHINGLE)

LEROY: I think I'll have to get a time clock in here. *(Lowering his voice)* And I want you to get rid of that fresh Little Ham.

SHINGLE: *(Turning up the radio)* I had to drop by on Pauline a minute.

HAM: I lets the women drop by on me.

SHINGLE: They gonna gang up on you some day, and then you'll be sorry they knows where you at.

HAM: Don't worry 'bout me, big boy.

SHINGLE: *(Pointing at HAM's neck and the red muffler)* What's the matter, forest fire burnin' you up?

HAM: *(Taking off muffler)* This here's my present from Mattie Bea, so don't touch it.

SHINGLE: Don't worry. I wouldn't put my neck in nothin' that red. They liable to take me for a Rooshian.

MADAM: *(Loudly)* Turn down that radio so I can hear my ears.

SHINGLE: *(As he takes off his overcoat)* Yes'm. *(Looking at contest poster)* Ham, what do that mean—Social Trucking Contest?

HAM: Social—meanin' don't nobody get mad. Don't draw no guns nor knives.

SHINGLE: Oh! Then I might go.

HAM: Ugly as you is, though, you liable to make 'em get mad anyhow.

(Phone rings)

SHINGLE: *(To HAM)* Go on! I know it's for you.

(HAM enters phone booth)

LEROY: *(Putting money into a chamois bag which he secretes in an inner pocket)* Not bad, darling. But we gonna run our intake up to a hundred bucks a day, you wait and see! Now, I'll just take these duplicate tickets and run on. Also the cash. I've got to report to Manny's secretary. *(Whispering)* There's a little shake-up going on in the racket today, but I reckon it'll come out alright. I'm just sitting tight. *(Looking at watch)* You can let 'em play until two, then close up till the papers come out.

> *(A MAN in muddy riding boots enters and mounts the shine stand, but SHINGLE avoids him, lazily continuing to clean the shine stand)*

SHINGLE: *(Singing to himself) In my solitude . . . . . .*

LEROY: *(To MADAM)* See you later, babe. I'll drop back by and pick up the other entries in half an hour or so. *(Suddenly)* Did you play today, Lucille?

MADAM: My usual 6 - 7 - 8, in a box.

LEROY: For how much?

MADAM: Quarter a piece.

HAM: *(In the phone booth, speaking loudly in a feminine voice)* I tell you Ham don't work here no more. . . . No, indeed! There ain't nobody here by the name o' Ham. *(Hangs up the receiver with a bang and emerges from the booth. To SHINGLE)* That warn't nobody but Laura, tryin' to find out is Ham here. *(Mimicking her voice)* And come talkin' 'bout a winter coat somebody by the name 'o Little Ham done promised to buy her a month ago, and ain't sent it to her yet.

SHINGLE: *(Dryly)* Here's a customer for you. *(Indicating the MAN IN BOOTS)*

HAM: *(Noting size and dirtiness of the boots)* Go on boy, it's your turn.

SHINGLE: I ain't got my cleanin' done yet.

HAM: Well, I got to go to de washroom myself.

LEROY: *(Barking)* Give that customer service!

HAM and SHINGLE: Yes, suh!

> *(As soon as BOSS LEROY's back is turned, HAM eases toward the door, so SHINGLE is forced to take the hard job. Begins to wipe off the boots)*

SHINGLE: *(Mumbling to HAM)* All you wants to do is wait on de womens.

HAM: You sho is right.

SHINGLE: Well, I gets tired. . . .

> *(Just then a large fat brownskin WOMAN enters)*

HAM: Step right up, lady. (*Helps her on stand, holding her hand until she is well seated*) You desires a shine?

TINY: I don't want no *shampoo*!

HAM: Well, I am at your service. (*As he shines*) I ain't seen you in these parts before.

TINY: I just moved up this way. My business is down on 128th Street.

HAM: You's a business woman?

TINY: (*Placidly chewing gum*) I'm a hairdresser. And I owns my own beauty parlor.

HAM: Now that is what I like in a woman. That she be her own boss.

TINY: That I is.

HAM: You don't need nobody private-like to boss you, does you?

TINY: You mean a man?

HAM: That's just what I mean.

TINY: I don't see nary one I could use.

HAM: You must not be lookin' down then, is you?

TINY: Oh, you mean yourself? I ain't acquainted with you.

HAM: That's no difficulty. I'm Ham, just Little Hambone Jefferson Jones.

TINY: And I'm Tiny Lee, that's all.

HAM: Baby, you could be a Christmas doll to me.

TINY: I hope you don't mean a rag doll.

HAM: Woman, I mean a sugar doll. (*Confidentially*) I could eat you up, plump as you is.

    (*Noise of people running down the street and shouting*)

SHINGLE: What's goin' on out there?

    (*A LITTLE BOY cracks the door and sticks his head in*)

LITTLE BOY: Joe Louis is goin' by down at the corner.

SHINGLE: (*Dropping his brushes*) Well, black my soul: Joe Louis! (*Exits*)

MAN IN BOOTS: I got to see him! (*Exits also*)

LEROY: I'm ready to go anyhow. See you later, Lucille. (*Exits*)

MADAM: I'd like to see that boy, too, world's greatest prize fighter. Ham, you watch the cash register. (*Takes coat from closet and exits also*)

HAM: Ain't nothin' in the cash register—now that LeRoy's been here.

TINY: I done seen Joe Louis. I was at his last fight.

HAM: You was? Who took you, high as them seats were?

TINY: I took myself. I makes money.

HAM: Don't you need somebody to escort you places?

TINY: Where'd you get that idea?

HAM: A sweet little woman like you's got no business at a fight all alone by her little she-self.

TINY: Now you know I ain't little. *(Coyly)* Don't nobody like me 'cause I'm fat.

HAM: Well, don't nobody like me 'cause I'm so young and small.

TINY: You's a cute little man. You mean don't nobody like you?

HAM: *(Woefully)* Nobody that amounts to nothin'.

TINY: *(Impulsively)* Well, from now on Tiny likes you.

HAM: *(Holding his shine-rag)* You really gonna like me, baby?

TINY: Sho I'm gonna like you, and they better not nobody else dare look at you neither.

HAM: Who would want to look at me? I know I sho won't look at nobody myself. But, I'm gonna be the boss, ain't I, Tiny?

TINY: Sho you kin be de boss—long as I boss you! But first, I got to know something about you. Ham, is this yo' place?

HAM: Yes'm. *(Shining shoes)*

TINY: Is you tellin' the truth?

HAM: No'm.

TINY: Then this ain't your place?

HAM: Yes'm.

TINY: What you mean?

HAM: I mean it ain't my place.

TINY: That's what I thought! Where you from?

HAM: Alabam.

TINY: Alabam?

HAM: Yes, but I don't give a damn about it.

TINY: Is you got any relatives?

HAM: None a-tall.

TINY: Neither is I. I's all alone.

HAM: You all alone?

TINY: All alone.

HAM: Well, from now on you ain't! Not with Ham around.

TINY: Neither is you, long as Tiny's here.

HAM: *(Looking up soulfully)* Darling!

TINY: Honey! Come on up here and kiss me, 'cause I'm too big and fat to get down to you.

> *(HAM climbs up on the stand and TINY takes him in her arms. Just then the door opens and SHINGLE and MADAM return)*

SHINGLE: Dog take my soul!

MADAM: *(Acidly)* After all, Ham, you ain't John Barrymore.

TINY: No, but I'm a black Jean Harlow, folks, and nobody yet has took a man from me.

SHINGLE: Ham has met his match.

HAM: *(Getting down)* What you mean, match?

SHINGLE: I mean a woman that can hold you down now.

HAM: *(Embarrassed)* I ain't had no womens before, long as you knowed me.

SHINGLE: Then I was born tomorrow.

TINY: Well, what he has had, and what he will have, is two different things! He belongs to Tiny now, don't you, Ham, honey?

HAM: I sho do. *(Mannishly)* That is, you belong to me. You my little Tiny.

TINY: And you're Tiny's little Ham.

   (Enter JANITOR to play numbers again)

JANITOR: Did you all see Joe Louis passing?

SHINGLE: Sho, we saw him.

MADAM: I not only say him, I touched him! What a man!

JANITOR: Madam, I got a penny here. Believe I'll put it on 8-8-8. Tribles. There's jest 8 letters in Joe Louis' name.

MADAM: *(Beginning to write out slip)* Tribles is always good. I used to play 3–3-3 and 7–7-7 all the time.

HAM: Babe, I sho feels lucky, findin' you. I feels so lucky I believes I sees a number in the toe of your shoe.

EVERYBODY: What number?

HAM: *(Staring)* 1 - 1 - 6, yes sir! 116!

SHINGLE: Damn if I ain't gonna play it. Is I got time, Madam?

MADAM: Two minutes. I believe I'll play it myself. Ham might really be lucky.

TINY: *(Opening her pocketbook)* Course he's lucky. Put me a dollar on it for me, straight.

JANITOR: *(Woefully)* I wish somebody'd lend me a dime. I come in here to get a pack o' cigarettes on credit until Sat'day, but I jest got to play this one mo' number if Ham say it's good.

HAM: *(Tossing him a dime)* Here, buddy, try yo' luck. *(To MADAM)* And Madam, put this quarter on it for me.

TINY: *(Looking down)* Ain't you got no mo'n a quarter, Ham?

HAM: I really ain't.

TINY: *(Hands him a dollar)* Here, take this buck.

HAM: And right on 116 it goes. We gonna be rich tomorrow.

MADAM: We gonna bust the bank.

SHINGLE: I'm gonna buy my gal a hot-stuff dress right straight from Fifth Avenue—by way o' some fire escape.

TINY: Help me down, 'cause I got to go now. My customers is waiting to get they hair ironed out. Don't you forget, Little Ham, you is mine! Here, honey, is my card, shop number, house number, telephone number, and everything, written down, printed so you can't go wrong.

HAM: I couldn't never go wrong on you, sweet chile.

TINY: *(Pinching his cheek)* You is a cute little man! You keep my slip, and if the number come out, we share and share alike.

HAM: Okeydoky! Sweetheart, I'll see you tonight.

TINY: I'll see you tonight. I mean *tonight. (Exit)*

SHINGLE: *(To MADAM)* You see that Ham! He's just got a way with women, that's all!

MADAM: A taking way, I'd say. If this number does hit, she'll never see Ham nor the money either.

(*She hands out the slips. JANITOR exits*)

HAM: Now you-all just hush. *(Musingly)* You know, I believes I really does like that big old fat gal.

SHINGLE: For what?

HAM: To boss around. The bigger the woman, the bigger boss I be's.

SHINGLE: You mean the more bossed you will be, 'cause you really got something on your hands now.

MADAM: *(Acidly)* He's got an elephant.

HAM: *(Hurt)* Now, Lucille, don't say that.

MADAM: Well, I will say it! You got an elephant. But even at that, she looks like a better woman than that corn-colored hussy that brought you that muffler.

SHINGLE: That one's married, ain't she?

HAM: You-all mean Mattie Bea? Yah, she's married—but she's broad-minded.

MADAM: *(Acidly)* Her mind's so broad you could lay on it!

SHINGLE: Ham ain't studyin' 'bout her mind.

HAM: Naw, I'm studyin' 'bout Tiny now. You know, I believes I loves her.

SHINGLE: You always loves the last one you just meets.

HAM: Well, she's de last.

SHINGLE: You don't know what love is nohow.

HAM: Sho I know what love is.

SHINGLE: What is love?

HAM: Love is takin' till you can't give no mo'.

SHINGLE: And what does you ever give?

HAM: Myself.

SHINGLE: What does you take?

HAM: Now, Shingle!

MADAM: He takes the soul-case out of you, that's what he takes. He drives me mad.

HAM: Now, Lucille, you. . . .

(Enter TWO WHITE MEN before he can finish his sentence)

SHINGLE: *(Under his breath)* Uh-oh! I know these two don't want no shines.

(MADAM begins to secrete the file of number slips hurriedly in her bosom. HAM is very busy with the blacking cans, hiding his slips therein. SHINGLE looks as if he is paralyzed. They all know the MEN are detectives)

1ST DETECTIVE: I judge you give shines in here?

HAM: Yes, sir! Oh, yes, sir! Black or tan shoes, grey, yellow, or white.

2ND DETECTIVE: You say you shine white shoes, too?

HAM: If you wants 'em shined. I'm a shiner, that's what I is.

1ST DETECTIVE: Is that all you are?

HAM: Most nigh all.

2ND DETECTIVE: *(Savagely)* What do you mean, most nigh?

HAM: *(Nonchalantly)* Don't you understand the English language? Who is you?

SHINGLE: *(Frightened—To HAM)* Here, here, now! Ham, hush!

2ND DETECTIVE: I guess you don't know who I am?

HAM: I sho don't.

2ND DETECTIVE: Well, looky here! *(Pulls back coat and reveals badge)*

SHINGLE: I knowed it all de time.

2ND DETECTIVE: Well, come here then you, if you know so much.

(SHINGLE approaches like molasses in the winter time, slower than slow. Meanwhile, the other DETECTIVE examines the cigar stand, the cash register, etc., looking for number slips, but MADAM has hidden them all in her bosom)

MADAM: A poor woman can't run a decent business without being suspicioned. I never wrote a number in my life, nor played one either.

HAM: Numbers? What is that? I can't even count.

2ND DETECTIVE: Never went to school, did you?

HAM: I skipped that and went to barber college.

MADAM: You just must look in my cash register?

1ST DETECTIVE: We just must, lady. *(Opens register, finds nothing)*

2ND DETECTIVE: *(Suddenly shaking SHINGLE while two or three dozen number slips fall out of his pockets)* Ah, here's the evidence!

SHINGLE: And all of 'em due to win today!

2ND DETECTIVE: Where'd you get 'em?

SHINGLE: *(Stuttering)* God knows.

1ST DETECTIVE: The judge'll find out then—and not from God!

SHINGLE: I-I-I was movin' and I just packed up some old papers. . . .

2ND DETECTIVE: Did you play 'em here in this shine parlor?

HAM: He sho didn't.

MADAM: I should say not!

SHINGLE: Naw, sir.

1ST DETECTIVE: Where'd you get 'em from?

SHINGLE: Well, I can't tell you de name o' the place, but I can take you to the street, and see maybe can I find it.

1ST DETECTIVE: You can?

SHINGLE: I reckon I can.

MADAM: *(Clamping her hand over her mouth as she stares at window)* LEROY! *(Nearly faints then looks relieved as he evidently goes on)*

2ND DETECTIVE: Well, Biggs, we didn't find nothing here, so let's take this fellow and let him lead us on. And he better lead us right, or else he'll get a year in jail for every slip he's got on his person.

SHINGLE: I ain't got no slips now, you-all got 'em all.

HAM: *(To SHINGLE)* Then they'll give the years to you and the money to them, if any one of 'em hit.

2ND DETECTIVE: You shut up!

SHINGLE: This ain't no laughin' matter. Send somebody to come and bail me out.

MADAM: I will, Shingle. Don't worry.

1ST DETECTIVE: *(To the MADAM)* Don't hire boys that play the numbers, sister. It ain't wise. It's a bad habit. They're liable to steal your money to play with.

MADAM: Thank you for the good advice. You all certainly gave me a shock coming in here like this. My nerves are all jittering.

2ND DETECTIVE: Next time we'll give you a warning.

MADAM: *(Taking them seriously)* Please do. Won't you have a cigar before you go? *(Offers box)*

1ST DETECTIVE: Don't mind if I do. *(Takes one. To his pal)* Go ahead, Bill.

2ND DETECTIVE: Thank you, lady.

HAM: *(As they start out)* Have a shine, too?

DETECTIVES: No, thanks. *(Nodding at SHINGLE)* We got one shine, that's enough. *(They exit with SHINGLE)*

MADAM: *(Nearly hysterical)* Lord! Oh, my Father, oh! Oh! Oh! I near had heart failure! Did you see LeRoy come right there to the door and notice 'em just in time not to come in? If he'd a come in here then, the game would've been up. They'd a found all them slips and money and everything on him.

HAM: But, Lucille, now it'll be too late to put in my 116. All them last slips we made out, Boss LeRoy done passed on by on account o' the dicks, and didn't collect 'em. Now it's past time, ain't it? Suppose my number do come out?

MADAM: *(Distressed)* They had to come around just before the number comes out!

HAM: Just before our number got in, you mean. *(Then remembering)* But this here's a depot. They oughta pay off here, anyhow. You done wrote it down.

MADAM: Ham, that's got me scared. They must-a suspicioned this place, or they never would-a-come here. And you know I don't want to go to jail! Oh, I don't care if we are makin' a lot o' money. I wish I'd never met that LeRoy. My nerves can't stand it. He's the first racketeer I ever loved.

HAM: If this had just stayed a nice little shine shop like it was when I first met you and you took me for your little Ham.

MADAM: Yes, till you got wild and went runnin' off with other women! Oh, Lord, life's nothin' but troubles, nothin' but troubles! *(Weeping)* And oh! poor Shingle! They'll get him down to that police station maybe and beat him, and just make him tell where he played those numbers.

HAM: They ain't gonna make Shingle tell nothing. He's more afraid o' Boss LeRoy and the white gangsters what runs the numbers, than he is of any cops.

MADAM: I'm just so distressful!

HAM: I feels right blue myself.

> *(Enter EFFEMINATE YOUTH)*

YOUTH: Can I get a polish?

HAM: You mean your nails?

YOUTH: I mean my slippers. *(Mounting the stand)*

HAM: Well - er, are you - er, what nationality is you?

YOUTH: I'm a Creole by birth, but I never draw the color line.

HAM: I know you don't. Is you married?

YOUTH: Oh, no, I'm in vaudeville.

HAM: I knowed you was in something. What do you do?

YOUTH: I began in a horse-act, a comic horse-act.

HAM: A who?

YOUTH: A horse-act. I played the hind legs.

HAM: In other words, you was de horse's hips.

YOUTH: I used to be. But I got out of that. I've advanced.

HAM: To what?

YOUTH: I give impersonations.

HAM: Is that what they call it now?

YOUTH: I impersonate Mae West.

HAM: Lemme see.

YOUTH: Of course.
> *(Begins to talk like Mae West, giving an amusing impersonation of that famous screen star)*

HAM: You a regular moving picture!

YOUTH: Indeed I am.
> *(Enter JASPER, the third shine boy)*

JASPER: Hello!

YOUTH: Who is that?

HAM: That's the night shine boy.

JASPER: *(Who is very dark)* None o' your cracks now, Hambone, first thing soons I gets here. I know I'm a dark black.

HAM: Who's crackin'? I'm tellin' de truth, ain't I, Jasper? You does work at night.

JASPER: Yes, and I work in the day time too, from two o'clock on. Is de number out yet?

MADAM: *(Jumping)* Shs-s-s! Don't mention numbers here.

JASPER: How come, don't mention numbers here?

HAM: Shs-ssh! De man has been here, him and his brother.

JASPER: Who?

YOUTH: What man?

HAM: Two dicks lookin' for numbers.

YOUTH: Oh, those kind o' men!

JASPER: *(Frightened)* They have? If they come here again, you gonna miss me!

MADAM: They arrested poor Shingle.

JASPER: For what? He don't write no numbers.

HAM: No, but he plays 'em.

YOUTH: Can you play here?

HAM: Not after 2 o'clock.

MADAM: Not a-tall! Not a-tall! Not now!

>   *(Enter WEST INDIAN)*

JASPER: *(Motioning to chair)* Right up here, sir.

WEST INDIAN: I wahnt a parfick shine!

JASPER: Is you got perfect shoes?

WEST INDIAN: Naw sawh, but whan I pay me maney, I wahnt a parfick shine.

JASPER: You ain't pay your money yet.

MADAM: Shine the gentleman's shoes, Jasper, and don't talk so much, please. And turn down the radio, it's ruining my nerves.

WEST INDIAN: Yes, 'cause I dadn't come in here to hear no tunes nor to play no number.

YOUTH: *(Ecstatically)* I just love that dialect.

WEST INDIAN: *(Glares at him)* Air you tawlkin' 'bout me?

YOUTH: Oh, no! I realize you're giving an impersonation. I give impersonations, too, that's why I'm interested in your art!

>   *(Enter a DEACONESS in her church bonnet and carrying a hymn-book)*

DEACONESS: Gawd bless you all!

HAM: Gawd bless you, too, sister.

DEACONESS: I would like to have a shine for the glory of Gawd.

HAM: Well, get right up here and your toes'll twinkle like de mornin' star when I get through wid you.

DEACONESS: *(Taking chair between YOUTH and WEST INDIAN)* That's a precious lamb. *(As HAM helps her up)* We got to help one another now—because in 397 years this world will end.

>   *(As he, JASPER and the YOUTH all draw out pencils and take that number down)*

HAM: I'm gonna play that number tomorrow, 397.

MADAM: *(With a start, clasping her breast where the slips are hidden)* Don't mention numbers!

WEST INDIAN: They air an abawnanation, de numbers!

DEACONESS: That's right! Are you a Christian?

WEST INDIAN: I'm a Church of Englander, lady. Firm and true.

DEACONESS: Well, I'm a Wash Foot Baptist. Touch my foot and you'll find it clean. My soul's the same way! How about you, son?

>   *(YOUTH pays her no mind)*

HAM: Call him daughter and see will he answer.

YOUTH: Oh, you're speaking to me? I'm New Thought—and we don't bother with such common things as washing feet.

DEACONESS: Well, you better, 'cause God ain't gonna let nobody in heaven 'thout their feet is clean. How about you, son?

HAM: I was baptized and reverted when I were 10 years old, and I ain't had a dirty foot since. Amen!

JASPER: Amen, hell!

DEACONESS: Hallelujah! how about that other young man, so industrious here?

HAM: Who? Old Jasper? He smokes reefers!

JASPER: That's a damn lie.

YOUTH: *(Gasps)* Oh!

HAM: Don't tell me you don't. 'Cause I seen you smokin'.

JASPER: But I don't run with married womens.

YOUTH: Neither do I.

WEST INDIAN: Sister, I think you have come to a nest o' devils.

HAM: That Jasper just ain't got no business o' his own to mind, that's all.

DEACONESS: You all is sweet boys, and I'm gonna save you souls. Now you-all listen fluently.

HAM and JASPER: Yes'm.

> *(They listen and shine, tapping their cloths on the toes of the shoes in rhythm)*

DEACONESS: I'm gonna recite you-all a little verse, that I made up myself.

> Don't you drink no licker,
> Don't you shoot no dice.
> Don't you do nothing
> You think ain't nice.
> Don't you dance on Sunday.
> Don't forget to pray,
> And you'll go to Heaven
> On judgement Day!

WEST INDIAN: Amen!

HAM: Hallelujah! I'm heaven bound.

JASPER: The green pastures is sho gonna see one black lamb.

YOUTH: Well, we believe in mind over matter, spirit over flesh.

WEST INDIAN: And I believe in the Bri-tish faith.

DEACONESS: And I believe in washin' feet.

JASPER: And I believes in shining shoes, 'cause I got the shoe-shine blues.

HAM: Let's go, boy. (*HAM and JASPER begin to pop their rags as they shine in syncopated time, each shining three shoes at once, so that they finish with the three people on the stand at the same time. Meanwhile another customer, a TALL GUY, comes in, and shortly after him, the HOT STUFF MAN, who goes across to MADAM and begins to show her some silk stockings he pulls from a travelling bag.*) (*As he and JASPER finish shining*) Yes, sir! Yes, Ma'am!

    (*They help the DEACONESS and the YOUTH down, and collect for their work. The WEST INDIAN sits there critically inspecting his shine a moment. The TALL GUY approaches the stand just as the WEST INDIAN steps down. He steps on the TALL GUY's toes*)

TALL GUY: I beg your pardon.

WEST INDIAN: Why dawn't you gimme chance to beg yours? I stepped on your toes.

TALL GUY: I'm just tryin' to be a gentleman. But if you want to get tough about it, then step on my corns again and see what I'll do.

DEACONESS: My! My! My! He's gonna start some stuff!

WEST INDIAN: What'll you do?

TALL GUY: Knock you half way into next week, that's what I'll do.

WEST INDIAN: (*Raising his cane like a sword*) Yes, and you'll have a duel on your hands.

TALL GUY: (*Raising his fists*) I don't duel, I dukes, and I'll choose you out.

WEST INDIAN: (*Contemptuously*) Aw, mawn, hush! I'll take you outside and wrop you round de downside o' that manhole where de sewer run.

DEACONESS: Do, Jesus!

YOUTH: My dear!

TALL GUY: Who you gonna wrap around the downside of a manhole?

WEST INDIAN: (*Pointedly*) Somebody blacker'n me.

TALL GUY: I'm a light brownskin compared with you. You blacker'n a new made buggy. Looks like you just got your face shined instead o' your shoes.

DEACONESS: God don't love ugly! You boys behave!

WEST INDIAN: Don't play with my complexion. I got that from my mother, and I don't 'low nobody to talk about my mother.

TALL GUY: I ain't mentioned your mother.

WEST INDIAN: You did! You just said the word, mother.

TALL GUY: Well, alright, then, I did. What you gonna do about it?

WEST INDIAN: Go to the butcher shop and buy a bone for you to throw your mama when you get home.

TALL GUY: Who's mother?

WEST INDIAN: Yours!

> *(They go into a clinch. The WOMEN and the YOUTH scream and wring their hands. The HOT STUFF MAN puts his suitcase down, still open. HAM lifts a velvet evening coat out of it)*

MADAM: *(Coming between them)* Stop that! Just stop! I don't allow no fighting here.

WEST INDIAN: I kill you so quick you won't know de death you died, 'cause mawn, I'm a fightin' cock and my spurs is out.

TALL GUY: *(His hand going toward his back pocket)* Yes, and if I draw my gun and start burnin' powder, you'll be so full o' holes your wife can use you for a tea strainer.

> *(At the mention of a gun the YOUTH and DEACONESS huddle near the door)*

WEST INDIAN: *(Hand going to back pocket also)* And if I pull mine, I'll blow you from here back into prohibition days, and then some.

MADAM: Jasper, call the cops! *(Clutching her breast and remembering the numbers)* No, don't. . . . Oh, my nerves!

HAM: *(With the evening coat on his arm)* You all stop that foolishness now. Here's the Hot Stuff Man and I wants to pick out a present for my woman, if he got anything big enough. *(Raising up the belligerent's coat tails)* Ain't neither one of you all got a gun, no-how.

WEST INDIAN: I know it.

TALL GUY: You know what?

WEST INDIAN: You ain't got no gun.

TALL GUY: You'd be surprised. *(He pulls out a pistol)* Now get out!

WEST INDIAN: *(Still belligerent, but moving)* Don't tell me what to do! I don't have to do but four things—eat, sleep, stay black, and die.

TALL GUY: Well, you sho will die if you fool with me.

> *(Raises gun and snaps it once. MADAM dives behind the cash register, JASPER behind the cigar stand, the YOUTH and the DEACONESS out the door, and the WEST INDIAN starts to bolt, but HAM grabs him by his coat tail)*

HAM: Pay me for that shine first.

WEST INDIAN: *(Running his hand in his pocket and producing a coin)* Here, mawn, here! Lemme go!
> *(He bolts out the door, as the TALL GUY again cocks his gun which fails to go off)*

HAM: *(Looking at coin)* He gimme a Canadian dime!

JASPER: *(Peeping over cigar stand)* It's better'n a Canadian nickel.

TALL GUY: What's the matter with this gun? It's loaded.

HAM: Whatever's the matter with it, put it down, or up, one, or leave here!

MADAM: *(Coming out angrily)* Put that thing away! You're ruining my nerves!

JASPER: *(Scornfully)* Huh! I thought it would shoot!

TALL GUY: *(Puzzled)* I just bought it. It ought to. *(Inspecting it)* Aw, no wonder! *(He begins to fire, with the result that everybody goes back into hiding, and HAM out the door)* I had the safety on.
> *(He ceases firing and sits calmly down on the stand to await a shine. HAM pokes his head back in the door)*

HAM: Is you through yet?

TALL GUY: Of course, of course! I knew that gun would shoot.
> *(The others come out of hiding, MADAM, the HOT STUFF MAN, and JASPER. The YOUTH has fainted on the footboard of the shine-stand)*

HAM: Get some water and throw on Mae West there.

MADAM: Somebody attend to me! I can't stand it! Jasper, go get me a bucket of beer! I'm about gone.

JASPER: Yes'm. *(Exit Jasper)*

HAM: *(To HOT STUFF MAN)* How much is this here coat? With another piece o' goods in it, 'bout two feet wide, it'd fit Tiny.

HOT STUFF MAN: That's one of the finest things I've got a-hold of this season. A man that worked right in a Fifth Avenue store got me this. An inside job. Brand new, right off the counter. I'll let you have it cheap. For a little o' nothing 'cause it's too hot for me to hold. How about ten dollars spot cash?

HAM: I'll give you nine.
> *(The YOUTH begins to come to, smoothing his hair and preparing to rise)*

TALL GUY: I want a shine.

HAM: Jasper'll be back in a minute. I only shine white shoes. *(Going on with his deal)* Is that there coat velvet?

RADIO: *(Suddenly loud)* Ladies, use the Venus lipstick to achieve that ravishing virginal look. *(Continuing until MADAM turns it down)* No other lipstick on the market gives the same demure yet fascinating tint to the lips. And it costs less than any other, etc. etc.

HOT STUFF MAN: Pure gelatine velvet with a frigidaire collar, this coat is!

YOUTH: *(Listening to radio)* Shss-ss! You all be quiet so I can hear the beauty news.

HAM: *(Feeling the coat again)* I might take it. Fact is, I think I will. Nine?

HOT STUFF MAN: No, Ten.

(Enter MATTIE BEA)

MATTIE BEA: Hello, there, little Ham. I tole you I'd be back. *(Sniffing)* Smells like smoke in here.

HAM: That's you—one smoke too many.

MATTIE BEA: Is you buyin' me a present, baby? I could go for that coat.

HAM: I wouldn't want you to wear no hot stuff, honey. You might get arrested. These is stolen goods.

MATTIE BEA: Everything I got is hot, stoled and re-stoled. Lemme try on that coat.

(HOT STUFF MAN gives her the coat. She admires herself)

YOUTH: *(Hovering around)* Oh, ain't that a sweet garment!

MATTIE BEA: Ham, I just got to have this.

TALL GUY: *(Yelling)* I want a shine!

HAM: Jasper be right back. *(Offers him a DREAM BOOK)* Here, take this here Dream Book and pick out your numbers for tomorrow while you're waiting.

TALL GUY: I don't believe in dreams. Gimme a *Baltimore Afro-American*.

(HAM hands him the Negro paper, for which he pays ten cents)

MATTIE BEA: Buy this coat for me, honey.

HOT STUFF MAN: *(To HAM)* You said you liked it.

HAM: I like it, and I'm gonna take it. But by and by, by and by. Just hold it for me.

MATTIE BEA: *(Returning the coat)* Ah, Ham, you're just too sweet. I'll wear it to the Hello Club Social tomorrow.

HAM: Um-hum.

MATTIE BEA: That's why I stopped by, to leave you a couple o' tickets for the Ball. One for you and one for me. I thought I'd better buy

'em in advance. Here, you keep 'em, daddy. *(Reading tickets)* Hello
Club Social Trucking Contest. Saturday. Tomorrow night.

HAM: Alright! Now you run on home, Mattie Bea, and I'll see you by
and by. In the Chop Suey Joint.

MATTIE BEA: You gonna bring the coat?

HAM: Sho, I'll have de coat when I come.

MATTIE BEA: *(As she exits)* Goodbye, Sweetheart.

HAM: So long. *(After door closes)* If I ever come! That woman's got a
husband anyhow.

TALL GUY: *(Shouting angrily)* I'll shoot you all if I don't get a shine.

YOUTH: *(Nearly fainting again)* Aw-ooo!

HAM: *(To HOT STUFF MAN)* Leave me that coat. But it's not for her.
(Indicating the departed MATTIE BEA) Here's ten bucks! *(Gives
him the money)* And help this Creole honeysuckle *(Pointing to the
YOUTH)* out of here when you go—before he faints again. We play
too rough for him.

YOUTH: *(Leaving on the arm of the HOT STUFF MAN)* Goodbye,
Little Ham.

HAM: *(To TALL GUY)* Lend me your gun. *(Begins to shine his shoes as
JASPER returns with the beer)*

JASPER: Refreshments is served.

MADAM: Jasper, if LeRoy don't come in a few minutes, you better call
him up. I want to get rid of these slips. I can't keep 'em in my bosom
all day. I wonder why don't he phone, or come. He seen I was in
trouble, them dicks in here. *(She drinks her beer)* And he's got to go
down to the station and bail out Shingle besides.

JASPER: Poor Shingle! He in jail, ain't he? I tell him 'bout playing them
numbers so much.

MADAM: If somebody didn't play, how would we live?

JASPER: Go on relief, I reckon.

HAM: They ought to make the numbers one of the P.W.A. industries,
then everybody could bet, and work.

JASPER: You mean like bringing licker back? Everybody drinks, but
nobody works. *(Woefully)* And where is the money?

HAM: Just around the corner.

    (JANITOR enters)

JASPER: Ain't the number out yet? I ain't got a cent to buy a paper to
see.

HAM: T'ain't out yet. 'Bout time though.

JANITOR: I think I'm due to catch today on some one o' them numbers.

HAM: I know we gonna catch! Ain't I done seen the number in the toe o' my baby's shoe,—1-1-6, and ain't I done brought her a coat on the strength o' what I know is coming?

JANITOR: What's coming?

JASPER: Christmas.

(Phone rings, HAM starts, but MADAM answers it)

MADAM: No, the number's not out yet. Paper's due here any minute.

(A PRETTY WOMAN enters limping slightly)

PRETTY WOMAN: I've got a tack in my shoe.

HAM: *(Forgetting the TALL GUY whose shoes he is shining)* Lemme see!

PRETTY WOMAN: *(Mounting the shine stand)* Please do. It hurts.

HAM: I certainly am sorry. *(Leaving TALL GUY entirely)* Jasper, you finish this man's shoes, here. A lady is in trouble. *(Begins to remove her shoe, fondling her feet tenderly)* Is you married?

PRETTY WOMAN: Yes, but my husband is taking a rest-cure.

HAM: A who?

PRETTY WOMAN: A rest-cure.

HAM: Rest from what?

PRETTY WOMAN: He over-exerted himself.

HAM: Over which?

PRETTY WOMAN: Exerted, over-worked, tired himself out.

HAM: One blip I bets he never gets rested long as he's got you. *(Begins to hammer loudly on the tack in her shoe)*

JASPER: I bet two blips, if you was him, you'd be dead!

JANITOR: *(To MADAM)* You know, lady, if I ever hit that number, I'm gonna take me a vacation. I been a janitor o' this building for four years, ain't had me a week off yet.

MADAM: 'Bout the only vacation you get is coming in here to play, ain't it?

JANITOR: Sho is.

(Enter SUGAR LOU BIRD)

SUGAR LOU: Rehearsal's off until eight o'clock. Thought I'd drop by and wait for the number to come out.

MADAM: Just sit down, honey. We'll know in no time. I'm bettin' on 1–1–6 today, myself, so I'm anxious, too.

(Enter OLD LADY)

OLD LADY: Hit ain't out yet, is hit?

JASPER: Not yet, but soon.

OLD LADY: *(Tottering up to cigar stand)* You can't sell a body a little snuff on credit, can you?

MADAM: Sorry, but we don't have snuff, Mis' Dobson.

JANITOR: Why, that's out o' style now, ma.

OLD LADY: Style or no style. Snuff is snuff, and I likes it.

    (TALL GUY leaves stand and pays JASPER for his shine)

JASPER: Thank you, sir.

TALL GUY: I might as well wait around and see what the number is so I'll know how to play tomorrow.

JASPER: Sure, make yourself at home.

    (TALL GUY goes to cigar stand and buys a pack of cigarettes. Lights one and sits down on a stool with his paper. A big MASCU-LINE WOMAN, looking exactly like Gladys Bentley, walks in and straight across to the cigar stand)

MASCULINE LADY: *(In bass voice)* Gimme a five cent cigar. *(MADAM offers her the box and accepts payment as everybody in the shop stares)* Is the number out yet?

MADAM: Not yet.

MASCULINE LADY: Then I'll pick it up later. *(Turns and strides out)*

HAM: Whew! What's the world coming to?

JANITOR: I don't care what it comes to, just so I hits the numbers.

MADAM: Numbers! Numbers! Numbers!

SUGAR LOU: That's one thing I sure miss in Europe, the numbers. They don't seem to know how to play 'em over there.

HAM: They started in Harlem, didn't they?

MADAM: And they'll be the end of Harlem, too. They've just about whipped my nerves to a frazzle.

PRETTY WOMAN: *(Her shoe fixed, leaves stand, opens her purse)* Thank you! How much?

HAM: Nothing a-tall! No charge—to you.

PRETTY WOMAN: That's awfully nice of you.

HAM: I hopes to see you again.

PRETTY WOMAN: That's very possible.

HAM: Then come again.

PRETTY WOMAN: Maybe I will. Goodbye. *(She exits)*

HAM: Goodbye.

SUGAR LOU: Untrue to me already, huh, Little Ham?

LITTLE HAM: Untrue as I can be—at the shine stand.

JANITOR: *(Hearing newsboy's cry)* Listen! There they come!

    (Sound of NEWSBOY crying offstage. He enters)

NEWSBOY: Racing edition of the evening paper. Get the number.

EVERYBODY:

>Gimme one. . . .

>What's the number, boy?

>Here, you got change?

>Let's have a copy.

HAM: *(Opening paper to sporting page. Shouting)* Dog-gone my soul! I won!

JANITOR: Thank God-a-mighty, I won too, then.

MADAM: Ham, your number hit!

SUGAR LOU: What was it?

HAM: 1-1-6, folks, 116! I mean good ole 1-1-6 has done come out—that I seen in the toe o' my baby's shoe. Hot damn! Lemme call her up and tell her. Where is that card she gimme? *(Searches in his pocket for card, finds it, and goes to phone)* Done hit the number!

JASPER: You lucky rascal! You must carry a black cat's bone.

SUGAR LOU: Well, it's luck for you all. Ham wins, but I lose!

OLD LADY: I lose too! Lawd, I lose!

SUGAR LOU: But, maybe I'll hit tomorrow. If I don't, I'll pawn a wrist watch till that show opens.

MADAM: Which watch, darling?

SUGAR LOU: Oh, I think the one a duke gave me in Buda-pest. Nobody cares what time it is in Budapest.

JASPER: Where's that, Miss Bird?

SUGAR LOU: Somewhere in - er - Norway, I believe.

OLD LADY: *(Weeping)* I can't never hit. My last penny, and I can't never hit. My daughter give me that money to get some matches with to light the gas.

MADAM: Here, grandma, I'll give you a box of matches. *(Hands her matches)*

OLD LADY: But ain't you got no snuff?

MADAM: No snuff! No snuff!

>*(Exit OLD LADY)*

HAM: *(At telephone)* Hello! Hello! Tiny's Hairdressing Parlor?. . . . Well, is Tiny there?. . . . Yes. Is this Tiny?. . . . Well, this is Little Ham! Baby, we done hit the numbers! Yes!!! That number I saw in the toe o' your shoe. . . . You's a lucky old big old sweet something, you is! Come on up here and get your money! I wants to see you anyhow. I got a present for you . . . Yes, I is . . . And two tickets to the Hello Club Ball . . . O-key-do-ky!

JASPER: Some woman, as usual, on the phone.

MADAM: Ham, call LeRoy, see is he coming back here. We want to collect what we won.

HAM: What's his number—Edgecombe 4–1909?

MADAM: That's it.

> (*HAM dials and listens*)

HAM: Hello—er - er. . . . (*Hangs up suddenly, looks scared*)

MADAM: What's the matter?

HAM: I don't get nothing but a funny voice. Then somebody answers sounds like cops or gangsters, one! The toughest voice I ever heard.

MADAM: (*Clutching her breast*) Oh, my God!

> (*Suddenly the door opens, and in comes LEROY, wild and disheveled. The afternoon begins to darken*)

LEROY: (*Hurrying across to cash register*) Lucille, baby, I got to talk to you.

HAM: Man, I done hit the numbers. Stop right here!

JANITOR: Me, too!

LEROY: Just a minute! Just a minute! I ain't payin' off no numbers today. Harlem's all torn up now. The Danny Jiggers gang's trying to muscle in against Manny Hudgins, and there's hell to pay. I just saw two big New Jersey cars outside my apartment, so I didn't go in.

MADAM: (*As SUGAR LOU and TALL GUY leave*) Oh, my nerves! My nerves!

JANITOR: Well, what about my number that come out 1-1-6?

LEROY: It never went in. Didn't no numbers from my route go in today. I tell you, Harlem's on the spot. Who's gonna report numbers with the Jiggers gang in town?

HAM: I just knowed something'd go wrong.

JANITOR: De Lawd never intended a poor man to win money! My last fifty cents gone, and pay day two weeks off yet! I tell you I want to be paid off on that number. (*Hysterical*) I hit it: 1-1-6!

LEROY: (*Hand to pocket*) Hush, and get out of here! Or I'll blow you to bits. The gang's on my trail now, more'n likely, and you talkin' 'bout payin' off on a lousy ten cent number.

JANITOR: It's a racket! That's what it is! A racket!

LEROY: Sure, we know it.

JANITOR: Everyday, all my money gone on the numbers.

LEROY: You have something to look forward to, don't you? Some day you might win.

JANITOR: Not from lousy cheaters like you!

LEROY: Get out of here!

    (JANITOR exits)

MADAM: Put that gun away! If another shot's fired this afternoon, I'll die! I'll die! Here *(Reaching into her bosom)*—take these slips. I just want to get 'em out of my hands. Why did I ever go into this number's game? Why? Oh, why?

LEROY: Quiet, Lucille, quiet! Everything'll be alright. I got three thousand dollars here, which ever way the gang war goes. That's yours and mine, darling. Understand?

    (Just as he is about to hand it over to her, three strange WHITE MEN enter. They are obviously gangsters. Each has one hand in his pocket)

BUTCH: So here's where little Boss LeRoy holds forth after the numbers come out?

DUTCH: No wonder his apartment's empty.

JIGGERS: Hand us over today's collection, you. We told that punk of a Hudgins we were taking over this field way last week. But he just kept right on, and you helpin' him. Well, now he's where the daisies'll tickle his nose when they come up in the spring. *(Savagely)* And that's where you'll be if you don't act right.

MADAM: *(Loudly)* My heart! My nerves! My heart! *(She glares at the gangsters)*

JIGGERS: Just hold tight, sister. It'll be over in a minute. *(Referring to JASPER and HAM)* Who're these two there?

MADAM: They're my shine boys.

DUTCH: They look like men to me. *(To JASPER)* Who're you?

JASPER: John Jasper Armstrong Smith.

DUTCH: What do you do?

JASPER: Shine shoes, that's all.

BUTCH: *(To HAM)* How about you?

HAM: Oh, I'm just here. Part of the decorations. Take the place, you take me. I just hit this afternoon for a dollar with 1-1-6.

JIGGERS: One of these lucky birds, heh? Well, you're the kind of a guy we need to write for us, don't we, Butch. Fly and lucky. Folks like to play with personality lads like you. Come over here. *(HAM approaches)* What's your name?

HAM: Little Hambone Jefferson Jones.

JIGGERS: Your age?

HAM: Indiscriminate.

JIGGERS: Well, if you're old enough to play numbers, you're old enough to write 'em. Ever do it?

HAM: No, indeedy!

LEROY: *(Interrupting)* I always choose my own writers in this district.

JIGGERS: You'll be lucky to choose yourself from now on. We're running this racket in Harlem now.

DUTCH: You're going for a ride, more'n likely.

JIGGERS: *(To HAM)* Report tomorrow to our headquarters over on Lenox. *(To MADAM BELL)* Are you with us, lady? I guess you are if you want to stay in business. Keep this here Shine Parlor as your base and keep on writing numbers. Only we'll send *our* men to collect.

MADAM: I'm with you—if my nerves'll stand it.

JIGGERS: Listen, both of you. *(To HAM and MADAM)* If you ever get in any trouble, just give my fixer's name to the cop, the judge, the jailor, anybody, and they'll turn you loose. We're payin' heavy protection. Just say—Schnabel.

HAM: Schnabel, Schnabel, Schnabel. I sho will try to remember that.

JIGGERS: That's it, Schnabel. He's the pay-off from now on.

DUTCH: *(To the MADAM)* How about you?

MADAM: I'll recall it.

JIGGERS: *(To LEROY)* As for you, didn't you get word yesterday to lay off writing for Manny?

LEROY: I didn't get nothing.

JIGGERS: Well, come with us now, and we'll talk it over. There might be some hope for you then. But we can't use you no more, no-how. You were too thick with the old crowd.

(Enter TINY, puffing and blowing)

TINY: Bless God, we won! Little Ham, I come for you and our money.

HAM: You sho come at a busy time, baby.

TINY: Didn't you phone for me?

HAM: Yes, but that was before the crisis.

TINY: What do you mean? Thay ain't payin' off?

JIGGERS: Of course, we're paying off. Our outfit always pays off. Did you hit today, lady? Where's your slips?

TINY: *(To HAM)* Ain't you give 'em the slips, baby?

HAM: I ain't had time. *(Fumbling in his pockets)* Here they is, one for me and one for you, 1-1-6. *(Hands them to JIGGERS)*

JIGGERS: Perfectly good. *(To LEROY)* Pay 'em off, you. They hit for a dollar apiece. We're not going to start our business with no dissatisfied clients. *(As LeRoy hesitates)* Pay 'em off!

LEROY: We're short on cash. I done turned mine in.

JIGGERS: *(To DUTCH and BUTCH)* Search him, boys! If I find a dollar on him, I'll blow his brains out.

MADAM: *(Screams)* Don't shoot no gun in here.

LEROY: Wait, wait, wait! Here, lemme see. I might have a few bills. *(He produces a wad of several thousand dollars)*

JIGGERS: Two or three grand, that's all. Pay 'em off, and give me the rest.

LEROY: *(Hesitantly, to HAM)* You hit for a dollar, heh?

HAM: Dollar and a quarter.

LEROY: Then you gets 675 dollars.

HAM: I sho do.

> *(LEROY begins to count out the money)*

TINY: You is both lucky and cute!

HAM: You tellin' me?

JIGGERS: That's real money. That's just how my bank'll pay off from now on.

LEROY: *(To TINY)* And you hit for a dollar?

TINY: That sho is right.

LEROY: Five Hundred and forty then.

TINY: Five Hundred and forty gets it.

DUTCH: If I wasn't toting a gun, I'd play these fool numbers myself.

MADAM: *(To LEROY)* I had a quarter on that too, LeRoy. Here's my slip.

LEROY: One Hundred thirty-five to you then, baby.

MADAM: That small change is right.

LEROY: *(Sadly)* I won't have a thing left.

JIGGERS: Only about two thousand bucks. Give it here! We'll use it to buy cigarettes. *(LEROY hands over the money angrily)* And come on!

> *(They start toward the door)*

LEROY: *(Looking back)* Lucille! Lucille!

MADAM: My nerves won't stand it! Go on! I can't help you! *(Savagely)* Go on!

> *(They exit)*

JASPER: I sho wish I'd a-played that number—1-1-6.

TINY: Baby, who's them white men?

HAM: They the new bosses o' this shop.

TINY: I thought it belonged to colored folks.

HAM: It do, but whites run it. How about it, Madam?

MADAM: Little bit more, and they can have it! My nerves won't stand this number racket. *(As HAM begins to put on his coat)* Ham, is you going off and leave me, too?

HAM: I'm off at five, ain't I? Jasper's de night man. *(Begins to don his street clothes)*

MADAM: Come back and talk to me later. I need comfort.

TINY: Not this evening, no sir. Comfort is with me . . . Come on here, boy! From now on you's Tiny's Little Ham. *(As he hands her the velvet coat)* Um-hum! Is that my present? Ain't you sweet. It looks kinder small, but I'll have me a nice gold brocaded back put in it in the morning, and wear it to the Hello Club's Big Apple Ball tomorrow night. You got tickets, ain't you, Sugar?

HAM: Sho I got tickets. They havin' a trucking contest. And just like we hit that number today, we gonna win that contest tomorrow. Girl, can you truck?

TINY: Sho, I can truck. Where you s'pose I been all my life?

HAM: Well, come on then. Let's truck on away from here!

> *(JASPER turns up the radio and TINY and HAM dance on out the door)*

CURTAIN

Act II

Saturday afternoon.

Interior of TINY's Beauty Shop. Street door center. At immediate left of door, manicurist's table. At right an overstuffed chair and floor lamp. Two operators' booths, one on either side of door. TINY presides over the booth at the left. LULU over the booth at right. At extreme right, just outside LULU's booth, a radio beside a door marked "Ladies Room." At extreme left, next to TINY's booth, a kind of little open store room, sink, and closet where coats, street clothes, etc., are hung.

As the curtain rises, both TINY and LULU are busily engaged straightening heads. SUGAR LOU is in TINY's chair. The manicurist, OPAL, is occupied applying red tinting to the nails of a dark customer. A little girl is waiting for her mama in the big chair. All the women are chattering full blast, the radio going, smoke rising from oily heads, noise of traffic outside.

TINY: *(Yelling to manicurist)* Opal, is you seen Bradford today?

OPAL: No, Tiny, there ain't been a number writer in here today. They must be all scared out by the gang war I read about in the *Mirror*.

DARK CUSTOMER: *(At table)* I hear they just a-switchin' and a-changin' all them writers up here in Harlem. Looks like a new lot of downtown chisslers done took over things. I hear they put out LeRoy.

TINY: Well, my new fella's writin' for the new outfit. They the ones what paid off my hit yesterday, and they give him a job, right then and there. We sure knocked 1-1-6 for a row.

OPAL: Did you box it?

TINY: Naw, I didn't box it. Didn't need to this time.

OPAL: Always box your numbers, girl. If they don't come straight they might come some other way. You lucky you caught it right straight out like you did.

TINY: You sure is right, I'm lucky. I'm gonna play that same number right back today, and this time I'll box it and bolito it, too. 116's a good number! And sometimes them pari-mutuel's repeats they figures, you know!

LULU: No, they don't either, sister. I ain't never seen a number repeat hand-running no two times.

SUGAR LOU: Me neither.

OPAL: Well, I have, girl! 417 come out twice hand-running not more'n two or three months ago.

LULU: Well, I must-a been in Jalapy, cause I ain't seen it, and I plays every day in the year, and ain't left New York in ten years.

OPAL: I don't believe you ever leaves Harlem even much, do you, Lulu?

LULU: Not hardly. What business I got downtown with them white folks? I can get everything I wants right here in Harlem, even to Fifth Avenue dresses so hot that they just stole 'em fresh the night before.

TINY: Girl, my man bought me the prettiest velveteen evening coat you ever seen yesterday from a hot selling huckster up in 145th Street.

SUGAR LOU: *(In TINY's chair)* He did?

TINY: Naturally the coat wasn't made to fit my size, exactly, but I took it early this morning to a seamster and am having a gold brocaded back put in it so I can shine like the sun at that there Hello Club Ball tonight.

OPAL: Say, what time do that Truckin' Contest come off?

TINY: I don't know, but whatever time it comes off, me and my little short papa's gonna be there rarin' to go.

SUGAR LOU: Comes off at midnight, they tell me. I'm gonna try and make it if rehearsal's over.

LULU: We gonna close up early, sis?

TINY: You-all can stay here if you wants, but I'm gonna be gone. Stay if you need to make that extra commission. If you don't, leave early— just like me. I don't care. After I been fryin' heads all day and all week, I needs myself a little recreation on Saturday nights. And Lulu, you know we goin' to that dance.

OPAL: Me, too.

SUGAR LOU: I sure am glad I got my appointment this afternoon. You-all gets so busy late on Saturdays.

TINY: Busy all day Saturdays, no matter what time you come. That's that day we really take in the money. But I just hit for five hundred and forty bucks yesterday, so you know I'm gonna have myself one really good time tonight.

MAMA: *(In LULU's chair)* So am I, kid. I'm goin to that Ball.

SNOOKS: *(The CHILD in the big chair)* Mama, hurry up!

MAMA: How kin I hurry up, and one half o' my head's still looking like a gooseberry bush in August?

SNOOKS: Well, I'm tired.

MAMA: Well, get yourself a funny paper and see can't you find me a good number. Look in Popeye, or else in Skippy.

LULU: Child, sometimes I gets the best numbers out of Little Orphan Annie.

MAMA: I don't never win nothing on them Annie numbers.

LULU: Maybe you don't play them the right day.

MAMA: Something's wrong, something's wrong. To tell the truth, the only thing I ever catches on is funeral wreaths. Everytime I see a crepe on the door, anywhere, I'm right there to take down the house number. Them kind o' numbers is always my best bet.

OPAL: *(Calling)* How about the numbers of the hymns in Church?

TINY: Them ain't no good. They gives out too many of 'em. Seven or eight hymns every service.

MAMA: Yes, and some o' them ministers is such devils. They ain't got Christ in 'em. Naturally their numbers ain't no good.

OPAL: 'Bout the best way is to pick some number that's hit good once, like Tiny's 1-1-6, and play it everyday for two or three months. It's bound to come back sometime.

LULU: No, 'tain't, neither. I don't believe in them repeats, I tell you. You gotta wait too long.

TINY: Sometimes you waits that long anyhow. Turn down that radio, Lulu, so I can hear my ears.

LULU: Alright, sis! *(LULU turns down radio)*

DARK CUSTOMER: *(At OPAL's table)* Well, I'm telling you, if 'twarn't for the numbers, I don't know how I'd get along. I plays six or eight dollars a week, and I always wins three or four dollars, every week.

OPAL: Do you?

DARK CUSTOMER: Why, everything I own 'cept my husband I bought with my winnings, I don't never play them back, I just plays with my salary.

OPAL: I see.

DARK CUSTOMER: But I dreamt a dream last night that I sho don't know how to play. I got to look it up. Is you-all got a Dream Book around here?

TINY: I might have one back yonder by the sink. I'll look in a minute.

LULU: What were the dream?

DARK CUSTOMER: I dreamt about a yellow woman washing a green dress in a white lady's back yard. Now what do that mean?

MAMA: Lemme think.

DARK CUSTOMER: What number should I play? Any o' you-all know?

MAMA: Well, er - *green* is 448, if I remembers rightly.

TINY: Yes, 'tis, that's right. In Rajah Simm's Book it's 448.

LULU: Yes, but she say a *yellow* woman washing a *green* dress in a *white* lady's back yard. That's more colors than one.

SUGAR LOU: Certainly is!

DARK CUSTOMER: Yes, and the dress faded, too.

MAMA: Do, Jesus!

DARK CUSTOMER: When she got through washing it, it weren't no color a-tall.

LULU: There now! Then you wouldn't look up *green.*

MAMA: No, you wouldn't.

TINY: I think you'd look up *dress.*

SUGAR LOU: I think you add 'em all together, subtract the difference and play that.

LULU: What kind o' dress were it?

DARK CUSTOMER: Seem like to me it were a calico dress.

OPAL: Then look up *calico.* Who knows what that would be?

TINY: I'll go see can I find that book right now.

(She leaves her booth and goes back where the sink and shelves are. Searches until she finds the book. Meanwhile a STAID LOOKING WOMAN enters with a LITTLE GIRL of ten or twelve)

STAID LADY: I want a hot oil treatment, and I want you-all to see if you can do anything with my child's hair, too, to try and bring out the white blood that's in her. Light as she is, her head sure went back on her.

OPAL: Just have a seat. One of the operators'll take you in a minute now.

STAID LADY: *(To SNOOKS)* Get up, child, and let me sit down. You children can sit on the arms of the chair.

SNOOKS: Why don't *you* sit on the arms of the chair yourself and let us sit here?

STAID LADY: Because I'm grown, that's why, and you and Missouri are nothing but tots.

SNOOKS: Her name's Missouri?

STAID LADY: That's it.

SNOOKS: That's a state, ain't it?

MISSOURI: Yes, but it's a name, too. What's your name?

SNOOKS: Samantha. But they calls me Snooks for short.

MISSOURI: That sounds like a funny paper name to me.

SNOOKS: Well, your name sounds like mud to me.

MAMA: *(Yelling from LULU's booth)* You Snooks! Just hush. I'm ashamed o' you.

STAID LADY: *(To her offspring)* Sit over here and keep still. I told you not to speak to every stranger you meet.

TINY: *(Returning to front with the Dream Book)* Here's the Dream Book. Now, I'd advise you to look up wash, cause that's what you was doin' in the dream, washing a dress. Lemme see what it is. *(Searches in book)*

OPAL: Yes, but she was washing a *green* dress, girl.

TINY: Well, if it was me, I'd play the number for wash and let the colors and dress and white lady and all go. Here it is—wash—964. That's it. *(Hands book to OPAL's customer)* Howdy-do! *(To the new arrival in chair)*

STAID LADY: Howdy do! I'm in need of a hot oil treatment. And a pull for this child.

TINY: Yes'm. Just a few minutes now, and I'll be with you.

(*TINY returns to SUGAR LOU and takes the apparatus out of her hair. SUGAR LOU has a beautiful croquinolle. Looks at herself in the mirror*)

SUGAR LOU: Honey, that's wonderful. I'll knock 'em dead at the Hello Club tonight.

TINY: You sho' will. Who you goin' with, Sugar Lou?

SUGAR LOU: A new hot papa I just met down at the theatre—that is, if I can sneak away from my butter and egg man.

TINY: What's his name?

SUGAR LOU: Which one, the young one or the old one?

TINY: I mean the one what pays your bills here, darling.

SUGAR LOU: You ought to know him. He's the biggest undertaker in Harlem. Has three funeral parlors, and ten to twenty funerals a day.

TINY: You ain't talkin' 'bout old man Willis, is you?

SUGAR LOU: That's him. He's my board and upkeep at the moment.

TINY: Why he is so old his features all run together!

SUGAR LOU: He's generous, though, honey. He says he's gonna gim-me a half dozen more watches for this arm.

TINY: No, he ain't!

SUGAR LOU: Yes, he is, too.

TINY: Well, keep him chile, keep him, even if he is ninety! You ain't met my sweet papa, though, has you? I mean, my real one.

SUGAR LOU: Who is he?

TINY: (*Proudly*) His name is Little Ham.

SUGAR LOU: Not little sporty Ham that shines shoes in the Paradise?

TINY: That's him! And believe me, he ain't shining shoes no mo'. Not after last night. He's gone into business.

SUGAR LOU: He has? What kind o' business?

TINY: He's gone into numbers. Them new racketeers what took over the field in Harlem's working him right in with them. They say he's got per-son-ality and winning ways.

SUGAR LOU: He has that, allright. Smoothest little sawed-off dark joker this side of Abyssinia! He's got a way with the lady-folks, too.

TINY: That might-a been. He might-a had a way—but he belongs to Tiny now.

SUGAR LOU: Congratulations.

TINY: Thank you.

SUGAR LOU: But, say, where's Gilbert?

TINY: I done put that lounge-lizard out o' my life. Gilbert warn't no good for nothing but what my white actress lady where I used to work calls "horizontal refreshment."

SUGAR LOU: Gilbert always dresses nice.

TINY: Yes, but on my money. I want a man what gives *me* things, like Little Ham. Besides Gilbert's a married man.

MAMA: Speaking about men, you-all heard about the run-in Geraldine had over her little old used-to-be, ain't you?

TINY: Geraldine who?

MAMA: Geraldine Richards.

OPAL: Not that little old scrawny mud-colored girl what comes in here every Thursday afternoon from the Bronx?

MAMA: That's her. She don't get off but once a week, but when she do have that day off, she wants to find her man ready and waiting just for her.

OPAL: I know she do.

MAMA: But this time she come in from her white folks house and the man was nowhere to be found.

TINY: What you say?

MAMA: Nowhere to be found. She went to his rooming house, and she went to the pool hall where he usually hang out, and no George.

LULU: There now!

MAMA: Then she met Gussie. You know, Gussie Mae Lewis?

TINY: Gussie's a trouble-maker. Always talking.

OPAL: She is for sure.

LULU: Yes, she's too broadcast.

MAMA: And Gussie say she has just seen George, 'bout two hours before going down the street with Luella Johnson.

TINY: No, he wasn't!

MAMA: Yes, he was! Gussie seen him. So what did Geraldine do but take her little scrawny self right straight to the pawn shop and buy herself a gun!

LULU: My! Lawd! I know she was burnt!

MAMA: And went just as straight as she know how, up to where Lucille rooms, and caught 'em redhanded in the bed.

TINY: Naw!

MAMA: Yes, sir!

OPAL: Huh!

SNOOKS: Mama, hurry up. I wanna go out o' here.

MAMA: Shut up, and wait for me. Play with that other little girl. (*STAID LADY gathers her CHILD to her protectively, motioning SNOOKS away)* Yes, ma'am, Geraldine caught that buck right in the mood for love.

TINY: And what did she do to him?

MAMA: She wore his hips out with bullets, that's what she did.

LULU: There now!

MAMA: But seem like in her excitement, she couldn't shoot very straight, so ain't none o' the bullets proved fatal. But George is in the hospital this week-end, and they say he can't sit down.

LULU: Why? Did he run?

MAMA: Run? He streamlined! But Luella's gun were faster'n he was. Them bullets caught him.

OPAL: And now about that hussy of a Johnson girl?

MAMA: They say Geraldine scared her so bad she jumped out the window. It was just the second floor, so I reckon it didn't hurt the hellion. And ain't nobody seen her since.

TINY: *(As SUGAR LOU leaves the chair)* Well, I'm a decent woman! I don't believe in no shootin' and cuttin'. When I gets mad, I just use my fists, that's all. And they's enough!

LULU: Believe me, they are! I seen Tiny knock a heifer out here one night, come startin' some stuff about she wasn't gonna pay no dollar-seventy-five—after she done had mighty nigh every treatment, shampoo, and process they is in the shop. She say back where she came from in North Carolina, she get all that for six-bits.

TINY: Yes, chile, and I say, well, in Harlem, New York, it cost just one dollar more. And she say, it do, huh? Well, I ain't gwine pay it! And I say, you'll pay it or else. And she say, I'll else then! And lift her dress in my face, and that is where I hit her.

LULU: She was glad to pay to get out!

SUGAR LOU: Let me sign for my bill.

TINY: O.K., honey.

(Produces pad, and SUGAR LOU signs, and exits)

SUGAR LOU: Goodbye, you all. See you tonight at the Ball.

EVERYBODY: Goodbye!

TINY: *(To the STAID LADY)* Now, I'll take you.

STAID LADY: *(To her CHILD)* You sit right here until they ready for you, too.

MISSOURI: Yes'm.

(Her MOTHER goes into TINY's booth)

SNOOKS: *(To the other CHILD)* My mama don't make me sit down.

(For the moment MISSOURI ignores her)

STAID LADY: *(To TINY)* I wish there wasn't so much gossip and scandal and talk about numbers in these hair-dressing parlors. It hurts my child's morals.

TINY: Your child's who?

STAID LADY: Her morals, to hear such stuff. She gets her mind full of sin.

TINY: Is that where her morals is, in her mind?

STAID LADY: I'm speaking of her soul. It's awful here in Harlem to raise a child.

TINY: I were raised here, myself.

STAID LADY: Yes, that's what I mean.

TINY: What *does* you mean?

STAID LADY: I'm sure you understand what I mean. Let's not discuss it further. And don't burn my head.

TINY: I hope not.

STAID LADY: Some of these hair shops is just terrible. One of 'em gave a dark friend of mine a bleaching treatment and just ruined her. She was brown skin—but when they got through with her, she looked like she were on her last round-up. Just took all the pigment out of her skin.

TINY: The pig-meat?

STAID LADY: Pigment! Color! Made her a deathly white, all chalky. Her husband like to have whipped her when he saw her, he was so mad.

TINY: Some of them operators is terrible! They just dissects the hair from your scalp, their combs is so hot.

STAID LADY: And they're so careless. And so immoral. Why they raided a shop near me and confiscated all the hair tonic.

TINY: I reckon it was licker.

STAID LADY: It probably was. That little she-woman that run it was always drunk.

TINY: You don't say!

LULU: A girl was in here this morning say she know where you can buy the number.

OPAL: Where at?

LULU: She says she know a man, what know a man, that is a friend of the man that works at the track and can get the number a hour or more before it comes out in Harlem. And for Fifty Dollars he'll phone it to anybody that wants it, in time for them to play it before the books close.

STAID LADY: A racket, that's what it is.

TINY: I spects it is, cause can't nobody be sure about that number till it come out.

MAMA: Don't nobody know how them racing machines gonna add up.

LULU: I'm just tellin' you what the girl told me. But Lawd knows I ain't gonna try it, cause I ain't got no Fifty Dollars.

DARK CUSTOMER: *(Rising)* Thank you. *(Yelling)* And thank you, Tiny, for the Dream Book. I'll see you-all sometime next week.

TINY: Thank you, and come back. I hopes you hit on that *wash* number.

DARK CUSTOMER: I'm gonna play *dress* and *wash*, too.

TINY: You doin' right. Good luck. Burn a black candle.

OPAL: Be sure and box 'em.

LULU: And use luck incense, child.

DARK CUSTOMER: Goodbye, you-all. *(Exits)*

EVERYBODY: Goodbye.

OPAL: Thank God for a minute to breathe. *(She goes to Ladies Room)*

MISSOURI: *(Fidgeting in chair, to SNOOKS)* Do you know any bad words?

SNOOKS: I know two.

MISSOURI: Tell me one of 'em.

SNOOKS: Damn!

MISSOURI: Aw, I know a better one than that.

SNOOKS: What?

MISSOURI: *(Whispering)* . . . . . . And I dare you to say it.

SNOOKS: I dare you to say this one. *(Whispers to MISSOURI)*
    (MAMA gets out of chair and pays her bill)

MISSOURI: 'Tain't as bad as mine.

SNOOKS: Your word ain't as bad as mine, either.

MISSOURI: Yes, it is. Mine's badder.

SNOOKS: I'll be damned if it is!

STAID LADY: *(Shouting)* Missouri, come here!

SNOOKS: I ain't gonna let her. *(Blocks other child's path)*

MISSOURI: Lemme by.
    (Pushes SNOOKS and SNOOKS grabs her by her bushy hair. MIS-SOURI begins to cry. MAMA emerges from booth and shakes SNOOKS)

MAMA: I told you to behave yourself. I won't take you to the Apollo if you don't act right.

SNOOKS: Well, she started it.

STAID LADY: *(As MISSOURI comes sniffing into TINY's booth)* Just
hush now. I tell you about fooling with strangers.

MAMA: Come on, Snooks. Goodbye all. *(Exits)*

EVERYBODY: Goodbye.

*(OPAL returns to her table. LULU rearranges her tools. MATTIE
BEA enters. TINY talks with the STAID LADY)*

MATTIE BEA: Howdy.

OPAL: Howdy do!

MATTIE BEA: I had an appointment with Miss Lulu for two o'clock.
I'm just a little late.

OPAL: That's alright. She's ready for you now. Just step right in.

(MATTIE BEA enters LULU's booth)

MATTIE BEA: Hello, there!

LULU: Just waitin' for you. I said to myself, now I know she's gonna
be late.

MATTIE BEA: Yes, I had to stop by the Paradise Shine Parlor to look
up a friend o' mine, but he wasn't there. He's s'posed to pick me up
for the dance tonight.

LULU: Hello Club Ball?

MATTIE BEA: Un-hum!

LULU: Everybody's goin' there, ain't they? That Truckin' Contest'll
sho be hot. Does you truck?

MATTIE BEA: Well, I ain't learned it yet, but I'm gonna try! I never
was much of a dancer. You see, I was raised up in the Baptist Church
and didn't get away from it till I growed up. My pa was a deacon.

LULU: Mine was too, child, but I didn't let that hold me back.

MATTIE BEA: I don't play cards till yet.

LULU: You don't?

MATTIE BEA: Naw, child. I was taught that every card in the deck is a
devil, and the aces—they is Satan's claws.

LULU: Now, ain't that something? Does you play the numbers?

MATTIE BEA: Oh, yes! I wasn't taught nothing about them when I
was little.

LULU: They didn't have 'em then.

*(Enter a large BUXOM LADY of commanding presence, a lodge
ribbon across her breast)*

LODGE LADY: Kin I get a 'pointment for this afternoon? I got to
have something done to this hair o' mine before tomorrow. The
grand Lodge's havin' a turn out, and I'm the High Grand Daughter
Ruler.

OPAL: Certainly, we can find a place for you today. *(Looking at her appointment sheet)* How about four o'clock?

LODGE LADY: Which operator's that?

OPAL: Miss Tiny.

LODGE LADY: All right then! I likes Tiny cause she never yet has burnt a strand o' my hair. I'll be here at four.

OPAL: *(Writing in book)* I'm putting you down.

LODGE LADY: *(Exiting)* Thank you kindly.

MATTIE BEA: And they had a new shine boy there, that's what worried me. Madam Bell say my fella's gone to writing numbers. Ain't shining shoes no more.

LULU: There's been a new pay-off down at city hall, and they say they changing lots o' writers up there. The new gang o' gangsters don't want the old crew no more. They almost all got bad reputations, them old writers. People would hit, and then never see the runner no more. He'd collect the money, and keep it hisself. It were awful!

MATTIE BEA: Yes, it were. And everybody in Harlem on relief, too. Don't hardly get enough money to play one number a day. Let alone eat.

(They continue to talk among themselves.)

(OPAL is busy polishing her own fingernails. TINY is working on the STAID LADY's head)

TINY: I been in this business for ten years now. And when I straighten a head, it's really straight. Wait till you see what I does to your daughter's head when I get round to it. I sends anybody out o' here ready to put a man in the mood for love!

STAID LADY: I don't want no love for my daughter. I'm preparing her to be baptized tomorrow.

TINY: Then why straighten her hair out? I'll frizzle right up again. Ain't' no kind o' treatment that's water proof.

STAID LADY: I want her to look her best when Reverend Hinds pushes her down into that water to receive the spirit of the Lord.

MISSOURI: Is I got to go all the way down in the water, mama?

STAID LADY: Every inch of you's got to get wet, daughter, or you ain't baptized right. And I want you *right*. This Harlem's a place o' sin, child, and I want you protected.

TINY: Religion's protected me, I know. I been a Baptist for years, and ain't sinned since I was seventeen.

STAID LADY: What did you do then?

TINY: Told a half-lie. I told a man Lulu was my sister and 'twarn't so. She's my half-sister.

STAID LADY: Well, I ain't sinned since I were ten.

TINY: What did you do then?

STAID LADY: I smoked a cigarette out in the barn with my brother, but the next month I was converted to Christ, and I ain't smoked since.

TINY: Hallelujah!

STAID LADY: Amen!

TINY: Religion is a wonderful thing!

STAID LADY: Yes, indeed it is! Bless God!

   (A verse of "Old Time Religion" may be sung or hummed)

TINY: *(Half shouting)* Oh, my! My! My! Praise the Lawd!

LULU: Amen! Amen!

   (Enter LITTLE HAM. He is very sportily dressed and wears the red muffler MATTIE BEA gave him)

OPAL: Howdy do!

HAM: How are you?

OPAL: Right well, I thank you. Did you wish to see someone?

HAM: Is this the shop o' Miss Tiny Lee?

OPAL: You ain't missed it.

HAM: And who is in charge?

OPAL: I make appointments.

HAM: Well, put me down for one.

OPAL: With me, or Miss Tiny?

HAM: *(Looking around)* Where is Tiny at?

OPAL: Right there. *(Indicating booth at right)*

HAM: Oh, then put me down for Tiny. And tell her I needs to see her bad.

OPAL: Shall I interrupt her work?

HAM: Sure, tell her Little Ham is here!

OPAL: O.K. *(Rises and goes to TINY's booth)* Here is Mr. Ham!

TINY: He is? Well, bless my soul! *(Leaves the hot comb in STAID LADY's hair and comes out)* Hello, there, darling! Sugar lump sweetness! This is the first time you been in my shop, ain't it? Well, it's full o' old ladies now! Come on back here where we can talk a minute. *(Takes him back to the sink and storage corner)* You little old Ham you! *(Kissing)*

HAM: How's tricks?

TINY: O.K., baby! I sent my new coat over to the seamster this morning to be extended, and she say she'll have it all ready and bring it back to me this afternoon, so I can wear it to the dance tonight. It ought to be here most any time now. How's things by you?

HAM: I done wrote up most Fifty Dollars worth o' numbers today.

TINY: Naw you ain't!

HAM: Yes, I did, too! Folks just seem to take to me for a natural born number writer.

TINY: *(Worried)* Honey, don't get pinched now.

HAM: Babe, I done been to headquarters! Them gangsters got a office over yonder in East Harlem bigger'n ten Shine Parlors put together, and seven hair-dressing shops thrown in. And I seen the head man, the big shot, the one the G-men even much never seen. I seen him! And he told me everything's all fixed with them that's in politics, and if by accident a detective or a policeman should happen to nab me by mistake, not knowin' I's one o' their men, all I got to do is say that name his first lieutenant told me last night—and the turn key, or judge, or whoever got me locked up'll let me right out. He say just say. . . . What were it darling?

TINY: Snizzle, or Snopple or something like that, weren't it? You told me.

HAM: Supple, I believe.

TINY: It were something like that.

HAM: But anyhow, I ain't gonna get locked up. I'm a fool-proof number writer, anyhow. They can't ketch me in no trap. I'm just gonna write for my friends and my friends' friends, and I got a million friends in Harlem.

TINY: *(Coyly)* And who is your best friend?

HAM: You is, Tiny!

(They embrace fervently)

TINY: Then make me know it!

STAID LADY: *(Yelling)* Aw-ooo-o! My haid is burning up! *(Her hair is smoking)*

MISSOURI: Aw-ooo-o! Mama's burning up!

TINY: I loves you, Ham.

HAM: And me you, too.

TINY: Is you ever gonna leave me?

HAM: Never.

TINY: And is you takin' me to the Ball?

HAM: Understood.

TINY: We's gonna strut our stuff!

HAM: Gonna truck on down!

STAID LADY: *(Loudly)* Yow-ooow!

TINY: Oh, my lands! That woman's haid! *(Rushes to her booth)* Darling, is you burnt?

STAID LADY: *(Angrily)* Lemme out of here! Just lemme out of here!

HAM: *(Appearing in the door of the booth)* Don't you want to play a number today, lady? I can still get it in for you.

STAID LADY: Just lemme out of this place! It's possessed of the devil. *(Putting her hat on angrily over her uncombed hair)*

MISSOURI: Let us out of this damn place!

TINY: Well, go on then! A little thing like a burnt haid might happen any time, specially when it's tight and nappy as yours is!

STAID LADY: I thought you had religion! But I'll get back at you, Tiny Lee, don't worry! An eye for an eye and a tooth for a tooth.

TINY: Yes, and a nap for a nap.

(Enter a FEMALE MEMBER of FATHER DIVINE's cult)

DIVINITE: Peace, angel!

OPAL: Peace!

DIVINITE: All o' Father's beauty parlors is full to overflowin' this afternoon, so I comes to you.

OPAL: We'll take you on, sister.

DIVINITE: I wants my hair straightened.

OPAL: Just have a seat. One o' our operators'll take you directly.

(DIVINITE sits down)

DIVINITE: It's truly wonderful!

STAID LADY: *(Going toward door)* It's full of devils. That's what I say about Harlem. Why my head feels like I been in hell, it's so burnt up. *(Exits)*

DIVINITE: Peace!

TINY: That's what I say—peace!

HAM: Peace, sister! I'm selling the numbers! Who wants it?

DIVINITE: I don't need no numbers. I got Father and he's truly wonderful! Peace! Little Ham!

HAM: *(Surprised as he recognizes DIVINITE)* Peace! Why, if it ain't Gertrude! Is you done got righteous?

DIVINITE: Indeed I have, you devil you! And my name ain't Gertrude no mo'. I done took a new name in the Kingdom.

HAM: What is it?

DIVINITE: Sweet Delight! That's what they calls me now. Sweet Delight!

(She follows TINY into booth)

HAM: *(To OPAL)* I'm taking 'em down, girl, any number you want to play.

OPAL: Well, put me down for—wait a minute. *(Looks in DREAM-BOOK)* What's the number for *green*? Also *dress*? I wants to play 'em, boxed.

HAM: I drempt you was handlin' money last night.

OPAL: Drempt *I* was handlin' money? Why, you didn't even know me last night!

HAM: No, but I drempt I knowed you last night.

OPAL: Well, I want to play 448 for *green* and 006 for *dress*. Put me down, papa.

HAM: I sho, will, sweet.

TINY: *(Calling)* Opal, how many more appointments is I got before supper time?

OPAL: *(Looking at book)* Four.

TINY: Oh, pshaw! I thought I might get a chance to run out and have a drink or two with Little Ham. Say, Ham, what about that boy, Shingle, that you told me got arrested yesterday?

HAM: Aw, he's out. Five Dollar fine, that was all, for carrying concealed slips.

TINY: And how about Boss LeRoy?

HAM: Don't know for sure, but I hear he's been put out o' the racket. Madam's still in, though. The Shine Parlor's writing numbers today, even if Madam do say her nerves can't go it.

TINY: She's just puttin' on—that old hard-fisted woman! Baby, don't you want a glass o' beer? I wish I could go out with you.

(MATTIE BEA in other booth pricks up her ears)

HAM: I wish you could, too, darling. But I know you got to work. *(To OPAL)* How much you puttin' on these numbers?

OPAL: Box 'em, and put a nickel on each. That makes sixty cents, don't it?

HAM: You are perzactly correct.

OPAL: *(Paying him)* Come around every day.

HAM: As sho as the sun rises and sets and Roosevelt's a white man.

OPAL: I ain't never heard o' no black Roosevelt.

HAM: Neither is I. *(Going toward LULU's booth)* Lemme see, is there any business over here? *(Looks in and sees MATTIE BEA, and is terribly embarrassed)* Howdy do!

MATTIE BEA: *(Dryly)* So you's a number writer now.

HAM: I is. Just started today!

MATTIE BEA: No wonder I couldn't find you up at the Paradise! I been there three times lookin' for you today. I want to know what time you coming by to get me to go to the dance tonight.

HAM: That's pro-bli-ma-ti-cal.

MATTIE BEA: And what do that mean?

HAM: I mean—that's a problem.

MATTIE BEA: What kind o' problem? You see me sittin' up here gettin' my hair all straight and ready to go. Now, you don't mean to say you ain't gonna take me, does you?

HAM: I mean to say that since I got to be a number writer, I works nights, too. I got to count up all these numbers, and divide up all this change.

MATTIE BEA: You mean you ain't goin' to the Ball?

HAM: Honey, I don't see how I can.

MATTIE BEA: *(Leaning forward)* And me done spent my good money for tickets, too. And done give 'em to you yesterday.

LULU: Keep still, please. You'll make me burn you.

MATTIE BEA: You ain't gonna pull no stuff on me!

(TINY comes out of her booth to listen)

HAM: Shss! I ain't tryin' to pull no stuff on you. I'll take you, baby, but it can't be till late.

MATTIE BEA: *(Delighted)* I knowed you'd take me, honey! You just wanted to tease me a little, didn't you.

HAM: That's all, darling.

MATTIE BEA: You little sweet ole devil you. Come here and hold my hand. I knowed you'd take me.

TINY: *(Approaching)* Take *who* where?

MATTIE BEA: Take *me* to the Hello Club Ball and Truckin' Contest.

TINY: Naw he don't! He's *my* man. He ain't takin' you no where. What put that in your head? And who is you?

MATTIE BEA: Who is *you*, Jumbo?

TINY: *(Hands on hips)* I'm a real good mama that can shake your peaches down!

MATTIE BEA: Sister, my tree's too tall for you! You'd have to climb and climb again.

TINY: *(Loudly)* I hear you cluckin', but your nest must be far away. Don't try to lay no eggs in here. *(Putting her arms around HAM)* This rooster belongs to me, don't you, Little Ham?

MATTIE BEA: *(Rising)* Take your hands off that man, you heifer, before I stomp your head!

LULU: Lawd have mercy!

TINY: Heifer ain't my name—but I'll take it in my left hand. If you give it to me in my right, it's your hips!

MATTIE BEA: *(Removing towel from neck)* Yes, you's a heifer! No other she-varmint'd try to take a woman's man away from her right under her very nose. And you'll never take Ham from me. Come on, Ham. Let's get out of here.

HAM: Now don't act that way, Mattie Bea, you know I ain't nothin' to you.

TINY: *(To HAM)* So you knows the wench's name, does you? Well, I want you to forget it!

HAM: Alright, darling.

DIVINITE: *(In TINY's booth)* Peace, Father!

MATTIE BEA: This place's too small to whip a cat in, without getting fur in your mouth, but I'm sho gonna whip you, Tiny Lee.

LULU: Now here, don't start no ruckus in my booth, knocking over my oils and things. If you want to fight—you, Tiny, or anybody, back on out of here.

> *(The belligerents back on toward the entrance. OPAL gathers up her manicure tools and backs toward the sink. The DIVINITE comes out, her hair bushy, to intercede)*

TINY: I'll whip you less you fly to Jesus!

DIVINITE: *(Touching TINY's sleeve)* Peace, daughter!

TINY: Peace, nothing! She says she's gonna take my Ham.

DIVINITE: *(Gently)* You can buy mo' Ham in the butcher shop.

TINY: But not this sweet black kind! Stand back you-all.

MATTIE BEA: Little Ham, get out o' the way! Don't you get hurt.

> *(Just as they prepare to fight, in comes a DELIVERY BOY with a package)*

DELIVERY BOY: Coat for Miss Tiny Lee.

TINY: Lemme see if it's fixed right. Gimme it here.

> *(She opens the box. MATTIE BEA recognizes it as same coat HAM promised to buy for her the day before from the HOT STUFF MAN)*

MATTIE BEA: That's my coat, ain't it, Ham?

HAM: *(Disclaiming responsibility)* It ain't none o' mine, I know that much.

TINY: *(Lifting out coat)* It belong to me. Ham bought it, and it belongs to me. I paid my own money to have this solid gold extension back put in it for the Hello Club Ball tonight. *(To HAM)* And we gonna go too, ain't we, papa? But first lemme attend to this here she-dog! *(Putting down coat)*

MATTIE BEA: Oh! Ham, get out of the way!

(MATTIE BEA ups with her purse and hits TINY on the head)

TINY: That's a dying lick. I'll limb you, woman!

(TINY reaches for MATTIE BEA's jaw. The DIVINITE runs screaming "Peace" through the door, and the DELIVERY BOY exits as the manicure table falls. MATTIE BEA grabs for and secures TINY's hair. Just then the LODGE LADY enters, sees the turmoil, and rushes out calling, Police!)

LODGE LADY'S VOICE: Police! Police! Murder! Police!

LULU: Fight her to a finish, Tiny, before the cops come. Do it to her, sister! You and me had the same mama, if not the same papa!

TINY: Yes, indeedy! Just get back and gimme room.

OPAL: You-all better stop!

HAM: Do it, Tiny, cause I know you can! I'm backing you up!

MATTIE BEA: Ham, you turn against me?

HAM: Sister, you small potatoes and few in the pot to me.

MATTIE BEA: After all I did for you? Take off my muffler!

(She reaches out and grabs the muffler from HAM's throat, then resumes her struggle with TINY)

TINY: Leave him, and everything he owns alone.

MATTIE BEA: The little tramp don't own nothing. You, Ham, take off that overcoat I bought you last year.

HAM: What you mean, woman?

MATTIE BEA: I show you what I mean, if I ever get loose here.

(She grabs the collar of HAM's coat, and as she and TINY push and shove, HAM is almost choked. He has to struggle to get loose. TINY releases her grip to puff and blow a moment. And just as a COP comes in, HAM is pushing MATTIE BEA roughly away. It looks as if he has been beating her, so the COP grabs him)

COP: You dirty little woman-beater, you, come with me! You know it's against the law to hit a lady.

HAM: She hit me.

COP: That's no difference. Come on, now.

TINY: But, officer. . . .

COP: That's alright, Miss Lee. I know you keep a decent place. I'll take this little ruffian out of here.

TINY: But I don't want you to take him.

MATTIE BEA: Neither does I. He ain't done a thing.

HAM: I sho ain't.

TINY: He sho ain't.

COP: I know you women's got good hearts. *(Loudly)* But I ain't got no heart for a brute that would hit a lady. *(Jerks him roughly)* Come on!

HAM: *(Rapidly)* Shovel, Shrivel, Chapel! What's that word?

COP: Is he crazy?

HAM: *(Frantically)* Tiny, what's the word? What's the word?

TINY: Sappy, soopy, sippy. . . . Oh, my God, I can't remember!

COP: Well, all you all must be fools. I'm gonna call the wagon. *(Roughly)* Stand up! *(Drags HAM by the coat collar out into the street. The wails of the WOMEN follow him. At the door he turns and pushes the WOMEN back inside)* Don't bring that noise out here in the street, if you do, I'll arrest you-all, too.

MATTIE BEA: He ain't done nothing! Not a thing!

TINY: Naw, he ain't. He's the sweetest little man in the world.

MATTIE BEA: And he belongs to me.

TINY: If he do, then go take him back from that cop.

MATTIE BEA: I'll take some of your hide first.

TINY: I'll give your collar-bone a permanent wave!

MATTIE BEA: You mean you'll try. Well, come on to me.
　　(She reaches down in her stocking and produces a knife)

TINY: Uck-oh! Lulu, hand me your hot comb.
　　(LULU hands TINY a red-hot straightening comb)

LULU: *(To MATTIE BEA)* Don't you cut my sister!

TINY: I'll brand her like I would a bull.

MATTIE BEA: And I'll cut you like a dog.
　　(MATTIE BEA ups with the knife, but TINY sears her across the back of the hand, and the knife falls to the floor. MATTIE BEA stoops to get it and TINY brands her on the cheek while LULU pokes her with a curling iron. MATTIE BEA shrieks and rises to run toward the door. TINY jabs the hot comb at her back as she escapes into the street)

LULU: Now, maybe we can have some peace in here.

TINY: I hope we can. Is there anybody else wants some o' this comb? *(Looks pointedly at OPAL)* I heard you talkin' to Ham. Don't think I didn't. *(Mocking her)* "Come back again." Playin' numbers with my Little Ham.

OPAL: *(Pleading)* That's all I was doin', Miss Tiny.

TINY: And that's all you'll ever do, too! Take it out of here now! Get! And take your tools. You don't work for me no more.

OPAL: *(Rushing into her coat)* Yes, Ma'am.

TINY: Anybody wants any of my Ham, they'll pay for it. Cause I'll put my brand on 'em.

OPAL: I'm goin' now, Miss Tiny. You won't have no trouble out o' me.

TINY: *(Swiping at her from a distance with the hot iron)* Go!

OPAL: Ow-ooo-o! *(Exits)*

TINY: There ain't no woman faithful to you where a man is concerned.

LULU: Nobody but you sister.

TINY: *(Bursting into tears)* Now Ham is gone, locked up, and I couldn't think o' that word for him to tell the judge! Snibble, Snozzle, Snoozle! Lulu, lock the door! I can't work no more today. And turn down the radio, sister, so I can cry out loud! *(Bawling)* Little Ham is gone! *(She buries her face in the velvet coat with the gold brocaded back and weeps aloud)*

CURTAIN

Act III, Scene 1

Tiny's apartment in Harlem.

TIME: *That night.*

> *Her boudoir, very silken and sleek; soft lights and gay colors. Large shiny photos of Harlem theatrical celebrities all around. Big box of chocolates on the table. Radio going. Telephone by bed.*

AT RISE: *As the curtain rises, TINY, en deshabille, and an illegitimate part-Pekinese, named NELSON, are running wildly about the room, TINY evidently in great distress.*

TINY: *(To the dog)* Nelson, why don't you lay down, gettin' right under my feet all the time. Can't you see, worried as I is, I'm liable to step on you and mash your gizzard out? Get from under my feet! *(She goes to the telephone)* Edgecombe 4–9676. Lawd, I'm so nervous I can't hardly work this dial . . . . . . Hello! Hello! That you, Lulu!. . . . Honey, I wish you'd come right on over here!. . . . Naw, Ham ain't out yet. Leastwise, he ain't here. . . . Naw . . . . . . Yes, I been callin' and a-callin' up de jail. And he been a-callin' me from the police station. We been tryin' to remember that name. That name the white gangster told him to say last night, and they'd let him right out. I heard it, too, but I disremembers myself. Seem like it were

Snopple . . . . . . Heh? You say maybe it was Snozzel! Naw, he's in "Jumbo" . . . . . . It's a gangster's name. The name that works like magic down at City Hall . . . . . . Aw, Lawd, I don't know what I'm gonna do, sister. Here 'tis long past time to go to the Hello Club affair, and my Ham's in jail. . . . Naw, I can't get nobody on the phone now, since seven o'clock. They got him up in police court, I reckon. And if he could just tell the judge that name, I know they'd let him out . . . . . . Sure, I called Boss LeRoy. But he ain't Boss no more in Harlem. This new gang's got a new boss up here. Some Detroit Jigaboo they imported . . . . . . Yes . . . . . . Please do, Lulu, Come right over. . . . I'm liable to faint before you gets here. This thing's got me so worried it's gimme nervous prostitution . . . . . . The first and only man I ever really loved, and he done gone and got locked up protecting me. Honey, wasn't it marvelous the way he lit into that other woman? Ham is a man, I'm tellin' you. . . . yes, he is. . . . Honey, bring me a pint o' gin when you come. I don't know if I can keep my senses or not till you get here . . . . . . The dance? . . . . . . Naw, I ain't goin' to no dance by myself . . . Yes, I got my clothes all laid out, red gown and velvet coat and all, but I ain't goin' nowhere without Ham. . . . Gilbert? Naw I ain't studyin' lettin' Gilbert take me. . . . Should you bring him along? Gilbert? Well, bring him if you want to, but you and I know and he knows that he ain't my man no mo'. He ought to stay home with his wife. I called him up and told him so last night after Ham left here. I told him he were a good old wagon, but he done broke down—far as I'm concerned. He didn't care nothing about me no how. . . . What you say? He say he gonna shoot Ham? He'll have me to kill if he do!. . . . Um-hum! You mean take Gilbert back just for tonight, so we can go to this Truckin' Contest?. . . . I tell you I can't truck, worried as I is about my little, short, sweet, brand new papa. . . . Well, yes, tell Gilbert he can come up here, but to behave himself, if he do. You say you bringing your boy friend, too?. . . . Well, hurry up, some o' you-all and come on, 'cause I'm just about to die o' worryment. And I can't stand being alone. Nelson ain't no company. And my *heart* is in jail. . . . Take a taxi. . . . Goodbye. *(She rises and goes to mirror and begins to comb her hair. Takes a chocolate from box. To dog)* Nelson, I reckon if you was a human, you'd be grey-headed by now, old as you is, and as much worryment as they is in this world! But you ain't never been in love with no man in jail, has you? . . . . . . Huh?. . . . I wonder did you care much about that police dog you tried to reach up

to last month on the floor below? She were too tall for you, wern't she? Po' boy! I must take you out where some small dogs is, in the spring! Yes, sir! . . . . . . Lawd, if I could only think of that name, to 'phone Ham! Snapple, snipple, snopple, skipple, bipple! Aw, hell! The devil! Shupple, maybe that were it! Naw, more like Scrapple! Scrapple! That's right, I think. Lemme see can I get the police station on the phone . . . . *(Dialing)* Plaza 3–9600 . . . . . . Hello! De Captain? . . . . . . Yes, you-all tell Hambone Jones, Scrapple is the name. . . . What? . . . . . . Yes, I'm the same woman done called six times, and I'll call six more times if I wanta. . . . I pays taxes for you-all bulls to live on, and I votes for Aldermen, and I knows every ward-boss they is in Harlem, and knows 'em well. Was married to one of 'em—in name only—once. And I'll tell him to take your job, if you gimme any rough talk . . . . . . Sure, I'd be just as brave if I was down there as I am on the 'phone. . . . You tell my Little Ham Scrapple was the name. . . . My Name? . . . . . . Naw! *The* name. . . . Huh? You say you ain't got no Ham nor no Scrapple neither there?. . . . Then where is Ham? You-all discharge him? . . . . . . What? You don't know? I have to call the night court? And they ain't got no 'phone? Oh, Lawd! *(Hangs up receiver)* Oh, Lawd! Nelson, Ham is up before the Judge! *(Praying)* Oh, Lawd, give that Judge a kind heart. Ham weren't doin' a thing but defending me. I hope he et up all them policy slips on him before they got him down to the station! *(To the dog, as the door bell rings)* Nelson, get out of my way!
   (Goes to door and admits LULU and her boy friend, JACK, and also GILBERT, her own former flame)
LULU: Girl, I'm sorry you feelin' so bad. Maybe this gin'll cheer you up a bit. We brought lemons and ice, too. Where's your shaker?
TINY: Nothin' could cheer me up tonight. Hello, Jack. *(Coldly)* Hello, Gilbert.
GILBERT: Don't bass at me, woman. I ain't bit you.
TINY: Now, don't start no stuff, Gilbert.
LULU: *(to JACK)* Come on, Jack, lets go out in the kitchen and mix up a cocktail. We going on to Ball, soon's we drink it, too. Let the other two of 'em stay here if they want to.
GILBERT: Naw, we ain't gonna stay neither. Tiny's goin' to that dance *with me.*
TINY: You got that wrong!
LULU: Come on, Jack. Let's go mix the drinks.
   (They exit into kitchen)

TINY: I ain't steppin' out with you *no more*. I done told you that by 'phone last night.

GILBERT: I know you weigh two tons more'n a switch engine, but you can't sidetrack me like that, I'm sweet papa Gilbert from Texas where even the rabbits are tough. And I don't let no woman quit me. I quit them, but they don't quit me.

TINY: Now, Gilbert, you know you ain't been a-near me for three days.

GILBERT: I come up here last night and wouldn't nobody open the door. Don't think I didn't see the light. I went out in the alley and looked. Not only saw the light, but I saw shadows, too—two shadows on that back window shade—and big as you is, you can't cast but one.

TINY: Is you insinuating?

GILBERT: Then why didn't you answer the door bell? Or at least answer the 'phone? Naw, you waited till one o'clock in the morning and then called me up to tell me you didn't want me in your life no more.

TINY: And I sure don't.

GILBERT: But don't think I don't know who you done took up with. A dumb little shoe-shiner named Hambone Jones.

TINY: He ain't no shoe-shiner. He's a business man.

GILBERT: *(Scornfully)* What kind o' business man?

TINY: He deals in figures.

GILBERT: So do I. I plays numbers, too.

TINY: *(Triumphantly)* Well, he writes them!

GILBERT: No wonder he's in jail then.

TINY: He's in jail for defending me from attack.

GILBERT: Who'd attack you, you hippopotamus!

TINY: Don't you call me out o' my name!

GILBERT: Then get your clothes on and come on let's go to this dance. We liable to win that cup, good as you and I can truck.

TINY: I'll never truck with you no more. Last time I went to a dance with you, you danced all night with some meriney hussy looked like a faded out jack-o-lantern.

GILBERT: *(Chicking her under the chin)* Aw, come on, baby, be sociable. I'll dance with you tonight.

TINY: After all I gived you, you come tellin' me I'm too dark to offer any competition. You wants a yaller woman.

GILBERT: Aw, sweetness, I was just kidding.

TINY: And said my size was underslung.

GILBERT: You never forgets, do you? You just like an elephant.

TINY: Naw, I don't forget! But I done forgot you. Get out o' my life! I'm goin' and see about them cocktails. *(Starts into kitchen, but backs back suddenly)* Oh, excuse me! I didn't know you-all was engaged.

GILBERT: *(Harshly)* Tiny, I guess you realize I really don't give a damn about you. But I'm a man! And ain't no woman gonna quit me. When I get ready to leave you, then I leaves. But you ain't gonna tell me *you* is through. No, indeed! You gonna see plenty more of Gilbert, till I get good and ready to lay off.

TINY: There won't be no more of *you* to see if you fools with me!

GILBERT: You must forget that I carries a gun.

TINY: *(As LULU and JACK enter with the cocktail shaker and glasses)* I ain't forgot nothing.

LULU: Have somethin' coolin' and refreshin'.

TINY: *(Pointedly, to her sister)* You all need something coolin'. That's what I say about love. Last week right on Lenox Avenue, I had to throw water on Nelson here, that dog were so excited.

JACK: Did you-all decide to go to the Truckin' Contest?

TINY: You-all truck on down and take Gilbert with you. I'm stayin' here.

GILBERT: We takin' Tiny, too.

LULU: *(Pouring cocktails)* I wish she'd come.

TINY: Just wish right on, 'cause I ain't.

(A loud knock at the door combined with the ringing of the bell)

LULU: What a racket!

TINY: *(Shouting)* Who's there?

HAM: *(Voice without)* Little Ham, that's who!

LULU: Oh!

GILBERT: *(Sinisterly)* Aw!

JACK: Who?

TINY: *(Jubilantly)* Thank God A—Mighty! Nelson, your daddy's come home. *(Rushes toward the door, then turns suddenly, recalling GILBERT. Whispering:)* Gilbert, he might have a gun, baby. *(Sweetly to her old lover)* Just step in this closet a minute till I finds out.

(Sulkily GILBERT steps into the closet. TINY closes the door, locks it, and takes the key with her, as she goes to let HAM in)

HAM: *(Sulking)* You took long enough! I just got out of jail, and looks like you don't want me in here. Ain't you glad to see me?

TINY: *(Ecstatically)* Baby, I certainly is! *(Takes him in her arms)* Lawd knows I is!

LULU: So glad you're out, Ham.

JACK: What'd they fine you?

HAM: Not a tack.

TINY: Baby, did you ever think o' the magic name?

HAM: Never did.

LULU: Is you out on bail?

HAM: Naw, I'm freed, released, don't have to go back no more.

TINY: Ain't that wonderful! Tell us about it.

HAM: Well, as luck would have it, it were a woman judge.

LULU: A woman judge?

HAM: Yes, a woman judge! *(Conceitedly)* So I just conversationed her.

JACK: Boy, ain't you something.

HAM: I just told her any man would defend a woman, and I was a man!
    She say, that's right! And I say, it sure is.

TINY: And they ain't found no numbers on you?

HAM: Sure they found some few little slips, but I just said, now, that
    one there, that's my mother's telephone number what just moved to
    San Juan Hill. And that other one, why, that's my initiation number
    in the Elks. They just initiated me last night, so I had to write it
    down to remember it. And them other slips there, the last four they
    found, why, that's my Horoscope. I paid a astrologer ten dollars
    to figger that out for me and he wrote it in four pieces, what time
    my star comes due—at 1:16 the third month of the 47th year plus
    One thousand, minus 2–92. And the lady judge say, did I ever read
    Evangeline Adams, who knew all about the heavens? And I say no,
    but that I follows Father Divine who knows more about heaven
    than anybody. And the Judge says, Peace, Father! And I said, Peace,
    Angel. And she lemme out.

TINY: It's truly wonderful!

LULU: Amen!

JACK: Well, now that you're here, let's go to the Ball.

HAM: Let's go. I'm ready! Honey, put on your clothes.

TINY: Give Ham a drink first. You-all just turn your backs while I dress.
    *(HAM, LULU and JACK gather round the cocktail shaker while
    TINY slips off her negligee and puts on a red lace evening gown,
    red slippers, and a rhinestone tiara)*

LULU: *(While TINY dresses)* Well, that woman what dreamed about a
    colored lady washing a green dress in a white lady's back yard was
    right. One of her numbers come out this afternoon.

JACK: What number?

HAM: o-o-6. That's dress! It sho' come out.

LULU: If she really played it, she sho' caught, too.

TINY: That's a lucky lady. She catch all the time. *(Pulls open drawer to get her jewels and six or eight men's pictures fall out. Looks around anxiously to see if HAM notices. Relieved, she picks them up quickly)*

LULU: I wish it'd been me that hit today.

TINY: *(Still dressing)* I knowed a 6 was coming out somewhere. o-o-6 came mighty near being our 1-1-6 again didn't it, Ham?

HAM: It sho' did. But we can't catch every day, baby.

TINY: Sho' can't. It's enough I caught you—and five hundred and forty dollars both—inside o' two days. *(Coming toward them dressed)*

HAM: And I got you! Baby, how pretty you look!

TINY: It's all for you, sugar!

JACK: Tons and tons of it!

LULU: Drink up and let's go.

> *(They lift their glasses and drink)*

HAM: *(Looking at his wrist watch)* Hurry up, and we'll be just in time for the Truckin' Contest. It starts at midnight. Maybe I'll stop by my flat and put on my razor edge suit. This one ain't been pressed today. 'T'won't take but a minute.

TINY: Sho', if you want to. I want my papa lookin' hot. *(Takes her new coat and gives it to HAM to hold)* Jack, you see this pretty coat Ham bought me yesterday. I didn't have to do a thing to it to make it fit, but put a new back in it, and believe me, it's solid gold.

JACK: You look like a Queen o' Sheba.

LULU: You certainly look sweet, sis.

TINY: Let's go! *(To dog)* Nelson, you stay here.

HAM: Come on.

LULU: Everybody truck on down! *(Opens exit door)*

GILBERT: *(Thumping in closet, in loud voice)* Lemme out o' here!

HAM: *(Stopping dead still)* Who's that?

TINY: Aw, come on, honey! That's some old wild man in the next apartment who's always making a lot of noise.

HAM: *(Doubling up his fists)* Well, if he just must get out, I'll take him on.

TINY: Is you got a gun with you, darling?

HAM: I ain't got no gun, but I'm a man.

GILBERT: I'm a man, too, and I'll take you on.

HAM: Sounds like he's talkin' to me.

TINY: Oh, no he ain't, darlin'. Come on.

LULU: Yes, for God's sake, come on.

JACK: I'm going myself. *(Pulls LULU by the arm, but she does not move from doorway)*

GILBERT: Hambone Jones, I say lemme out.

HAM: Well, hot-damn! Now, I know that's me! *(Approaching closet)* Which dark horse is you?

GILBERT: Unlock this door and you'll see! Tiny, come here and open this door! You know you got me locked up in here.

TINY: You'll stay there, too, far as I'm concerned.

HAM: Don't think I'm afraid, whoever you is. You might be bigger'n I am, but I'm ever' inch a man.

GILBERT: I got more feet than you got inches, runt. And if you-all don't lemme out o' here, you'll know it.

HAM: Who you callin' runt?

GILBERT: You, you stunted cockroach!

HAM: *(To TINY)* Lemme at him, whoever he is!

TINY: *(Pleading)* Come on to the Ball, baby. We'll attend to him by and by. I don't want to get my clothes all mussed up.

GILBERT: *(Angrily)* You all, none of you, didn't have no mammy!

LULU: Aw-ooo!

HAM: *(Stepping toward door)* Well, you'n must-a ben a mole, what bore you in a coal mine, 'cause even your voice sounds black.

GILBERT: *(Shooting his pistol through the door)* Take that, you so-and-so-and-so. *(He fires five shots, one after another, making five holes in the door. TINY, LULU, JACK, and HAM press back against the wall)* Take that! *(Bang!)* And that! *(Bang!)*

TINY: *(Calmly, after the shooting is over)* Well, now that's over! His kind o' gun don't carry but five bullets—and he ain't hit a thing but the other wall. Come on, you-all, let's go! I don't let no Abyssinian spoil my evening. Come, Ham, let's win that truckin' cup, like we done said we would!

HAM: I'll give you a taste o' my forty-four when I come back, creeper. Just stay there and breathe through them holes.

GILBERT: *(In closet)* Please lemme out! Tiny, please lemme out 'fore you go.

TINY: *(Yelling back from the doorway)* I wants to spare your life, Gilbert. For your wife's sake. I can't have no murder here, no how, 'cause Little Ham would tear you to pieces, wouldn't you, Ham?

HAM: I'd limb him limb from limb! *(Taking empty gin bottle from tray and poking its neck through one of the bullet holes in the closet door)*

Here, smell this till I get back with my pistol. You might need
something stronger than gin to help you, by and by.

GILBERT: *(Moaning)* Tiny, help me, baby!

TINY: Help you, hell! Me and Ham's going to the Hello Club Ball.
(Turns out the light) Goodbye, Nelson.

> *(All exit except the dog. NELSON remains to bark loudly in the
> dark as GILBERT yells and pounds on the locked door)*

GILBERT: Lemme out! Lemme out! Lemme out!

CURTAIN

Act III, Scene 2

Ballroom in Harlem.

TIME: *Midnight.*

AT RISE: *The orchestra may be in sight or hidden (as producer chooses)
but the front of the platform should be seen. The MASTER OF CERE-
MONIES stands thereon, the Grand Silver Truckin' Trophy in hand,
to be awarded to the winning couple of the contest about to take place. A
brilliant crowd of Harlem's suavest and sportiest set, boxers, numbers
writers, theatrical folks, hairdressers, maids, sweetmen, sports, and their
ladies. Women in evening gowns, men in extravagantly cut suits from
tuxedos to pleated backs, hair lacquered, diamonds flashing. MADAM
BELL and LEROY are there together; SUGAR LOU and her new
boyfriend, SHINGLE, out of jail, and his company; JASPER and a
fair YOUNG LADY; the WEST INDIAN and a BAHAMA DAN-
CER—but not yet TINY and HAM, nor JACK and LULU.*

> *As the curtain rises, the orchestra is just coming to the end of a
> blues number to which everybody is dancing. As the piece cools off,
> the M.C. signals for a loud chord to indicate that silence is desired.
> EVERYBODY stops dancing.*

M.C.: Ladies and gentlemen, Lad-dees and gentel-mun! And gigolos! I
have in my hand the Grand Silver Truckin' Trophy engraved with
the name of Harlem's most prominent, high-toned society institu-
tion, the Hello Club. *(Applause)* This club has been ruling supreme
amongst the Harlem Four Thousand for many years, and is known
from Central Park North to the Yankee Stadium, and from the
Harlem River to Sugar Hill, from the Ubangi Club to the Silver
Dollar.

VOICE: And from the police station to the Harlem Hospital.

M.C.: Also! We are known everywhere! The Hello Club leads where others follow.

VOICES:

>Yeah, man!. . . .

>Yes, indeedy!. . . .

>True! True!

M.C.: And when we give a ball, we gives a ball!

VOICE: Yes, sir!

(Enter LULU and JACK, TINY and HAM)

M.C.: And tonight we are presenting the Hello Club's First Annual Social Truckin' Contest, and Big Apple Ball. This here cup I got in my hand is to be awarded to the couple that, in the opinion of the audience, and of the applauses they receives, has done the best job of real righteous Oh-my-soul-truckin' on the floor. Everybody starts at once, and the judges will go around and eliminate them that ain't got the right movements in they feet, nor truckin' in their souls. Now listen, when the man taps you on the shoulder, that means go off the floor and *be* audience. And I don't want nobody to get bull-headed and not withdraw.—'cause that would spoil the social part. *(Gaily)* Everybody, now, let your spirits go to your feet, let the rhythm go to your heads, let the music move your souls, and truck on down! *(Lifting his baton)* Orchestra, give it to me!

>*(The Orchestra begins a truckin' piece, and everybody starts to truck, couples prancing, rocking and swaying in a carnival of joy. Two or three gentlemen, committee members, with ribbons across their chests, the colors of the Hello Club, are tapping those couples on the back who are dancing with the least originality and abandon. They withdraw to the sidelines. As the music goes on, finally all but four couples are eliminated. Those remaining include two unknown couples, MADAM and LEROY, and LITTLE HAM and TINY. The M.C. stops the music)*

M.C.: Ladies and gentlemen! and truckers! The Contest is now reaching its final and most important stage! That of who shall win! Somebody's gotta win. Now it's up to you to show, by your applause, just who deserves the cup. We'll take these last four couples in rotation, for the crowing feature of the Hello Club Ball! Couples, line up over yonder! As I give the signal, truck on out across the floor. . . . First couple let's go! *(The first couple come out and do their truck. They have probably been practicing nightly for the last three weeks at the Savoy. But it is obvious that they are trying too hard, although the crowd gives them a good hand as they finish on the opposite side of the floor)* Second couple, bring it to me! Let's go, band! *(The second couple come truckin' out across the floor, bowing and tapping, parting and swaying, circling around one another like a rooster and hen. They get a good hand, as they finish on the left in front of the M.C.)*

VOICES:

> Pretty good, Joe!. . . .
>
> Too tight!. . . .
>
> Young stuff!. . . .
>
> Oh, my!. . . .

M.C.: All right now, Madam Bell of the Paradise Shining Parlors and her partner, Big Boss LeRoy! Let's go! *(LEROY and the MADAM truck on out to the center of the floor and break)* Aw, Break!. . . . Do it, Madam Lucille Bell!

MADAM: Let's go to town!

LEROY: How we gonna get there?

MADAM: Truckin' on down.

VOICES: *(And laughter)*

> Do, it, old folks!. . . .
>
> Lawd, look at Madam Bell!. . . .
>
> Aw, strut it, Boss. . . .
>
> Oh, my, my, my, my!. . . .

LEROY: Let's break!

MADAM: Hey! Hey!

> *(They finish up to great applause just in front of the M.C.)*

M.C.: And now for the last round up! Come on, Little Ham!

> *(LITTLE HAM and TINY take the floor)*

VOICES:

> Lawd! Lawd! Lawd!. . . .
>
> Boy, haul that load!. . . .

HAM: All the way to town!

TINY: *(Trucking)* I'm coming, baby!

M.C.: Rock, church, rock!

> *(TINY and LITTLE HAM do the most exciting, original and jazzy truck of the whole evening, breaking, clutching, parting, and dancing on a dime until the entire crowd rocks with laughter, cheers, and applause)*

VOICES:

> That's the best!. . . .
>
> Two tons o' rhythm!. . . .

Look at that little boy go . . .
My! My! My! My!
(They finish, sweating and out of breath)
HAM: Yes, Tiny!
TINY: Yeah, man!
M.C.: That sends me! *(Holding up the cup)* Now, all four couples truck
around the hall, one at a time, and the applause will tell who gets
the trophy. *(To the band)* Come on, boys, let's go, trucksters!
*(The band strikes up again, and in turn the four couples dance
around the hall. LITTLE HAM and TINY get the most applause,
much to the chagrin of BOSS LEROY)*
VOICES:
Give it to Ham!
Yeah, man!
Ham and Tiny!. . . .
M.C.: You-all must mean Tiny and Ham! Is that right? *(To TINY and
HAM)* Step out here in the middle of the floor. *(As they do so)* Is this
who the crowd wants?
VOICES: *(And applause)*
Yes!. . . .
They get it!. . . .
Sure!. . . .
Little Ham's won!. . . .
You're right!. . . .
Give Tiny that cup!
M.C.: They surely deserve it. My compliments! Quiet, please. *(Signals
the orchestra for a chord)* Ladies and trucksters! On behalf of the
Hello Club's social committee and the entire membership of our
estimable organization, I am delighted and exuberated to present
this here Grand Solid Silver Truckin' Trophy to the winners of our
contest tonight, Mr. Hambone Jones, and Miss Tiny Lee!
VOICES:
'Ray!. . . .
Good!. . . .
Yes!. . . .
That's right!. . . .
*(TINY and HAM receive the cup amid much applause, LULU
and JACK rush forward to shake their hands, also JASPER and
SHINGLE. LEROY stands in a corner moping with MADAM)*

LEROY: Here I done lost my job with the numbers and can't even win a dancing cup! When a man is down, he's down.

MADAM: Baby, you can have Little Ham's job, shining shoes. He's out in the field now.

LEROY: *(Incensed, raises his arm to hit MADAM)* Woman, don't tell me. . . .

> *(A COMMITTEE MEMBER grabs him)*

COMMITTEE MEMBER: This here's a social, Brother.

LEROY: Oh, all right! Then I won't fight. *(Mumbling)* Come offering me a job shining shoes. *(To MADAM)* Come on, Lucille, let's go!

MADAM: Yes, darling, let's go. *(They start toward door, but MADAM BELL suddenly pauses as MATTIE BEA enters. Excitedly)* Look, LeRoy, there's Ham's other woman!

LEROY: Who? Where? Which one?

MADAM: *(Pointing)* Mattie Bea!

LEROY: Uh-oh!

MADAM: *(In anticipation)* The fur'll fly now.

> *(MATTIE BEA pauses, looks around, clenches her fists and advances toward the bandstand with venom in her eyes. HAM and TINY do not see her. Suddenly, however, the door is flung open and GILBERT stalks in)*

GILBERT: *(Loudly)* Everybody stand back. I'm here! *(Everybody turns toward the door. TINY and MATTIE BEA both scream)* I done broke down one door tonight, and I'll turn this place out!

TINY: Oh! The lion is loose!

HAM: Who? Where? What lion?

MATTIE BEA: *(Yells in astonishment)* My husband!

HAM: *(Sees her for the first time and looks worried)* Mattie Bea! *(He hides behind TINY)*

GILBERT: *(Mollified)* My wife! Mattie Bea, what you doin' here?

MATTIE BEA: How about you, Gilbert? I thought you said you had to work tonight?

GILBERT: I did. I just got off, honey.

MATTIE BEA: Then who you lookin' for here?

GILBERT: You, baby. *(HAM and TINY both seem much relieved)* I thought you might be at this dance.

MATTIE BEA: Well, all right, then! I hates to be at a dance all by myself. But what made you come in so loud, honey?

GILBERT: I just want everybody to know we's here, that's all, me and you. We ain't been to a dance together for so long, it's a shame!

MATTIE BEA: Sho is! *(Sweetly)* But now we's here, Gilbert, and you looks so nice tonight, I believes I'm in love with you all over again. Take off your coat, and let's dance.

> *(The Orchestra begins to play the "St. Louis Blues")*

GILBERT: I always was in love with you, sweetheart, even since we been married.

MATTIE BEA: Let's rest our wraps. This here's another honeymoon.

> *(They disappear, pulling off their wraps as the door fills with dancers)*

MADAM BELL: *(To LEROY)* Sugar, let's dance one more time.

LEROY: Why not?

M.C.: All right now, everybody rock!

> *(Entire crowd begins to dance. TINY places the cup in front of platform and embraces HAM)*

HAM: *(While dancing)* Tiny, is you happy, baby?

TINY: Ham, I ain't nothin' else but!

HAM: You's a truckin' thing!

TINY: And so is you, darling!

HAM: What we gonna do with this cup?

TINY: Take it to my house, and keep it there—'cause I'm gonna keep you there, too.

HAM: What about the man in the closet?

TINY: Who? Oh, you mean Gilbert? Honey, yonder he is dancing with that there Mattie Bea. He's her husband, I reckon.

HAM: So that's her husband!

TINY: He never was no headache of mine, baby.

MATTIE BEA: *(Dancing with GILBERT at the other end of the stage)* De old love is always best, ain't it, honey?

GILBERT: Does you mean to say I'm old, darling?

MATTIE BEA: Just old enough to be sweet, that's all. Kiss me, sugar-pie.

> *(As they dance, they kiss. Meanwhile, the spotlight picks out the various couples dancing in the arms of love: MADAM BELL and LEROY; SUGAR LOU and her BOY-FRIEND; SHINGLE and his LADY; JASPER and his HARLEM BLONDE; the WEST INDIAN and a BAHAMA GIRL; JACK and LULU; and at the end, TINY and HAM)*

TINY: *(Shyly, as they dance in the spotlight)* You ain't mad about Gilbert, is you, Ham?

HAM: Naw, honey! I know things like that can happen. *(Pauses)* You ain't mad about nothin' I ever did, is you?

TINY: Naw, darling. The past is past, ain't it?

HAM: Long gone!

TINY: And I don't care nothing about nobody, no how, but you. I don't want to have no more trouble today, no ways. We ain't had nothing but trouble since we got engaged yesterday.

HAM: Trouble and luck put together! Money from the numbers, and a cup from truckin'.

TINY: That's what life is, ain't it, baby? Trouble and luck, put together.

HAM: I reckon it is, but it's more *luck* than trouble when a man's got the woman he loves.

TINY: Ain't it the truth! That's the way I feel about you!

   (The orchestra plays increasingly loud the sad-gay-doleful strains of the "St. Louis Blues." SHINGLE and his lady-friend dance near TINY and HAM as the lights go dim and soft colors begin to play over the dance floor)

SHINGLE: *(Yelling)* Hello, boy! You lucky dog!

HAM: You see I got my arms full, don't you, Shingle? And boy, we're dancing right on through life—happy—just like this!

   Music and rose-colored darkness as the

CURTAIN FALLS

Soul Gone Home

1936

A poignant and disturbing play that Rowena Jelliffe, director of the Gilpin Players, admired but never produced, *Soul Gone Home* most certainly expressed Langston Hughes's difficult relationship with his own mother. Hughes wrote to composer Ulysses Kay, with whom he was discussing an operatic version of the play:

> [I]t is NOT a heavy tragic sentimental play. It is a TRAGI-COMEDY, with the accent on the comic elements in the boy's role, who is haunting his mother as much for fun as for spite. The SON is a slyly humorous, evil, badly raised little teen-ager who, if he had lived, would have been a street-corner jitterbug, a be-bop boy, a mambo dancer, a pool room sharpie—but who blames his mother, more or less justly, for his defects, particularly for neglecting and starving him to death, and who is getting a kick out of coming back from the dead to remind her of it. There should be as many laughs as possible in the way the SON's part is written and played—otherwise the tragi-comedy will not come through, and it will be merely an over sentimental and unpleasantly grim piece. The MOTHER is half-acting, mostly feigning her grief—for show—anyway. And both of them are hard-boiled marginal people, slum-shocked products of the rip tides of life.[1]

This text was first published in *One Act Play* magazine in July 1937.

Characters

THE MOTHER
HER SON
TWO MEN

SETTING: *Night. A tenement room, bare, ugly, dirty. An unshaded electric-light bulb. In the middle of the room a cot on which the body of a Negro youth is lying. His hands are folded across his chest. There are pennies on his eyes. He is a soul gone home.*

AS THE CURTAIN RISES, *his MOTHER, a large, middle-aged woman in a red sweater, kneels weeping beside the cot.*

MOTHER: *(Loudly)* Oh, Gawd! Oh, Lawd! Why did you take my son from me? Oh, Gawd, why did you do it? He was all I had! Oh, Lawd, what am I gonna do? *(Looking at the dead boy and stroking his head.)* Oh, son! Oh, Rannie! Oh, my boy, speak to me! Rannie, say something to me! Son, why don't you talk to your mother? Can't you see she's bowed down in sorrow? Son, speak to me, just a word! Come back from the spirit-world and speak to me! Rannie, come back from the dead and speak to your mother!

SON: *(Lying there dead as a doornail. Speaking loudly.)* I wish I wasn't dead, so I *could* speak to you. You been a hell of a mama!

MOTHER: *(Falling back from the cot in astonishment, but still on her knees.)* Rannie! Rannie! What's that you say? What you sayin' to your mother? *(Wild-eyed.)* Is you done opened your mouth and spoke to me? What you said?

SON: I said you a hell of a mama!

MOTHER: *(Rising suddenly and backing away, screaming loudly.)* Awo-ooo-o! Rannie, that ain't you talkin'!

SON: Yes, it is me talkin', too! I say you been a no-good mama.

MOTHER: What for you talkin' to me like that, Rannie? You ain't never said nothin' like that to me before.

SON: I know it, but I'm dead now—and I can say what I want to say. *(Stirring.)* You done called on me to talk, ain't you? Lemme take these pennies off my eyes so I can see. *(He takes the coins off his eyes, throws them across the room, and sits up in bed. He is a very dark boy in a torn white shirt. He looks hard at his mother.)* Mama, you know you ain't done me right.

MOTHER: What you mean, I ain't done you right? *(She is rooted in horror.)* What you mean, huh?

SON: You know what I mean.

MOTHER: No, I don't neither. *(Trembling violently.)* What you mean comin' back to hant your poor old mother? Rannie, what does you mean?

SON: *(Leaning forward.)* I'll tell you just what I mean! You been a bad mother to me.

MOTHER: Shame! Shame! Shame, talkin' to your mama that away. Damn it! Shame! I'll slap your face. *(She starts toward him, but he rolls his big white eyes at her, and she backs away.)* Me, what bored you! Me, what suffered the pains o' death to bring you into this world! Me, what raised you up, what washed your dirty didies. *(Sorrowfully.)* And now I'm left here mighty nigh prostrate 'cause you gone from me! Rannie, what you mean talkin' to *me* like that—what brought you into this world?

SON: You never did feed me good, that's what I mean! Who wants to come into the world hongry, and go out the same way?

MOTHER: What you mean hongry? When I had money, ain't I fed you?

SON: *(Sullenly.)* Most of the time you ain't had no money.

MOTHER: 'Twarn't my fault then.

SON: 'Twarn't *my* fault neither.

MOTHER: *(Defensively.)* You always was so weak and sickly, you couldn't earn nothin' sellin' papers.

SON: I know it.

MOTHER: You never was no use to me.

SON: So you just lemme grow up in the street, and I ain't had no manners nor morals, neither.

MOTHER: Manners and morals? Rannie, where'd you learn all them big words?

SON: I learnt 'em just now in the spirit-world.

MOTHER: *(Coming nearer.)* But you ain't been dead no more'n an hour.

SON: That's long enough to learn a lot.

MOTHER: Well, what else did you find out?

SON: I found out you was a hell of a mama puttin' me out in the cold to sell papers soon as I could even walk.

MOTHER: What? You little liar!

SON: If I'm lyin', I'm dyin'! An lettin' me grow up all bowlegged and stunted from undernourishment.

MOTHER: Under-nurse-mint?

SON: Undernourishment. You heard what the doctor said last week?

MOTHER: Naw, what'd he say?

SON: He said I was dyin' o' undernourishment, that's what he said. He said I had T.B. 'cause I didn't have enough to eat never when I were a child. And he said I couldn't get well, nohow, eating nothin' but beans ever since I been sick. Said I needed milk and eggs. And you said you ain't got no money for milk and eggs, which I know you ain't. *(Gently.)* We never had no money, mama, not even since you took to hustlin' on the streets.

MOTHER: Son, money ain't everything.

SON: Naw, but when you got T.B. you have to have milk and eggs.

MOTHER *(Advancing sentimentally.)* Anyhow, I love you, Rannie!

SON: *(Rudely.)* Sure you love me—but here I am dead.

MOTHER: *(Angrily.)* Well, damn your hide, you ain't even decent dead. If you was, you wouldn't be sittin' there jawin' at your mother when she's sheddin' ever tear she's got for you tonight.

SON: First time you ever did cry for me, far as I know.

MOTHER: Tain't! You's a lie! I cried when I bored you—you was such a big child—ten pounds.

SON: Then *I* did the cryin' after that, I reckon.

MOTHER: *(Proudly.)* Sure, I could of let you die, but I didn't. Naw, I kept you with me—off and on. And I lost the chance to marry many a good man, too—if it weren't for you. No man wants to take care o' nobody else's child. *(Self-pityingly.)* You been a burden to me, Randolph.

SON: *(Angrily.)* What did you have me for then, in the first place?

MOTHER: How could I help havin' you, you little bastard? Your father ruint me—and you's the result. And I been worried with you for sixteen years. *(Disgustedly.)* Now, just when you get big enough to work and do me some good, you have to go and die.

SON: I sure am dead!

MOTHER: But you ain't decent dead! Here you come back to hant your poor old mama, and spoil her cryin' spell, and spoil the mournin'. *(There is the noise of an ambulance gong outside. The MOTHER goes to the window and looks down into the street. Turns to SON.)* Rannie, lay down quick! Here comes the city's ambulance to take you to the undertaker's. Don't let them white men see you dead, sitting up here quarrelin' with your mother. Lay down and fold your hands back like I had 'em.

SON: *(Passing his hand across his head.)* All right, but gimme that comb yonder and my stocking cap. I don't want to go out of here with my hair standin' straight up in front, even if I is dead.

> *(The MOTHER hands him a comb and his stocking cap. The SON combs his hair and puts the cap on. Noise of men coming up the stairs.)*

MOTHER: Hurry up, Rannie, they'll be here in no time.

SON: Aw, they got another flight to come yet. Don't rush me, ma!

MOTHER: Yes, but I got to put these pennies back on your eyes, boy! *(She searches in a corner for the coins as her SON lies down and folds his hands, stiff in death. She finds the coins and puts them nervously on his eyes, watching the door meanwhile. A knock.)* Come in.

(Enter TWO MEN in the white coats of city Health employees.)

MAN: Somebody sent for us to get the body of Rannie Bailey? Third floor, apartment five.

MOTHER: Yes, sir, here he is! *(Weeping loudly.)* He's my boy! Oh, Lawd, he's done left me! Oh, Lawdy, he's done gone home! His soul's gone home! Oh, what am I gonna do? Mister! Mister! Mister! The Lawd's done took him home! *(As the MEN unfold the stretchers, she continues to weep hysterically. They place the boy's thin body on the stretchers and cover it with a rubber cloth. Each man takes his end of the stretchers. Silently, they walk out the door as the MOTHER wails.)* Oh, my son! Oh, my boy! Come back, come back, come back! Rannie, come back! *(One loud scream as the door closes.)* Awo-ooo-o!

(As the footsteps of the men die down on the stairs, the MOTHER becomes suddenly quiet. She goes to a broken mirror and begins to rouge and power her face. In the street the ambulance gong sounds fainter and fainter in the distance. The MOTHER takes down an old fur coat from a nail and puts it on. Before she leaves, she smooths back the quilts on the cot from which the dead boy has been removed. She looks in the mirror again, and once more whitens her face with power. She dons a red hat. From a handbag she takes a cigarette, lights it, and walks slowly out the door. At the door she switches off the light. The hallway is dimly illuminated. She turns before closing the door, looks back into the room, and says)

MOTHER: Tomorrow, Rannie, I'll buy you some flowers—if I can pick up a dollar tonight. You was a hell of a no-good son, I swear!

CURTAIN

Mother and Child
A Theatre Vignette

1936

Mother and Child is based on a short story that was first published in *New Masses* and included in Hughes's collection *The Ways of White Folks* (1934). He so liked his defiant and transgressive little piece that he turned it into a play. The version published here is from a typescript, undated but certainly 1936, in the Langston Hughes Papers.

Characters

SISTER WIGGINS
MATTIS CRANE
CORA PERKINS
LOTTIE MUMFORD
LUCY DOVES
MRS. SAM JONES
SISTER HOLT
SISTER JENKINS
SISTER PRIME
MADAM PRESIDENT

SETTING: *The parlor of a small farm house in southern Ohio crowded with old-time furniture. Springtime. Bright sunlight through the lace curtains at the windows.*

AS THE CURTAIN RISES: *the monthly meeting of the Salvation Rock Missionary Society, a religious organization of rural colored ladies, is being held. The members are beginning to gather. SISTER WIGGINS, MATTIS CRANE, CORA PERKINS, and SISTER HOLT are already present. They are gossiping as usual, but today the gossip centers persistently around a single tense and fearful topic—a certain newborn child that has come to Boyd's Center. As the curtain rises, the hostess, LOTTIE MUMFORD, her apron still on, is answering the door. Enter LUCY DOVES and MRS. SAM JONES.*

LOTTIE MUMFORD: *(At the door)* Howdy, you-all! Howdy! 'Scuse my apron, Sister Jones, I'm makin' some rolls for the afterpart. *(She laughs)*

OTHER SISTERS: Howdy! Howdy-do!

LOTTIE MUMFORD: Lucy Doves, all I wants to know is, what news you got? Is you seen that chile?

MATTIS CRANE: Yes, is you seen it? You lives right over there by 'em.

LUCY DOVES: *(bursting to talk)* Ain't nobody seen it. Ain't nobody seen it, but the midwife and the doctor. And her husband, I reckon. They say she won't let a soul come in the room.

LOTTIE MUMFORD: Ain't it awful?

LUCY DOVES: But it's still livin' cause Mollie Ransom heard it cryin. And the woman from Downsville what attended the delivery says it's as healthy a child as she ever seed, indeed she did.

SISTER WIGGINS: *(From a rocking chair)* Well, it's a shame it's here.

MATTIS CRANE: Sho is!

SISTER WIGGINS: I been livin in Boyd's Center for twenty-two years, at peace with these white folks, ain't had no trouble yet, till this child was born—now look at 'em. Just look what's goin on! People actin like a pack o' wolves.

CORA PERKINS: It's ter'ble, ter'ble.

MRS. SAM JONES: *(Taking off her hat)* Poor little brat! He ain't been in the world a week yet, and done caused more trouble than all the rest of us in a life-time. I was born here, and I ain't never seen the white folks up in arms like they are today. But they don't need to think they can walk over Sam and me . . .

SISTER HOLT: Nor me!

MRS. SAM JONES: *(Continuing)* For we own our land, it's bought and paid for, and we sends our children to school. Thank God, this is Ohio. It ain't Mississippi.

CORA PERKINS: Thank God!

LUCY DOVES: White folks is white folks, honey, South or North, North or South. I's lived both places and I know.

SISTER WIGGINS: Yes, but in Mississippi they'd lynched Douglass by now.

MATTIS CRANE: Where is Douglass? You all know I don't know much about this mess. Way back yonder on that farm where I lives, you don't get nothin straight. Where is Douglass?

LUCY DOVES: Douglass is here! Saw him just now out in de field doin his spring plowin when I drive down de road, as stubborn and bold-faced as he can be. We told him he ought to leave here.

SISTER HOLT: Huh! He's a *man*, ain't he?

SISTER WIGGINS: Well, I wish he'd go on and get out, if that would help any. His brother's got more sense than he has, even if he is a seventeen-year-old child. Clarence left here yesterday and went to Cincinnati. But their ma, poor Sister Carter, she's still tryin to battle it out.

LOTTIE MUMFORD: She told me last night, though, she thinks she have to leave. They won't let her have no more provisions at de general store. And they ain't got their spring seed yet. And they can't pay cash for 'em.

CORA PERKINS: Po' souls.

MRS. SAM JONES: Don't need to tell me! Old man Hartman's got evil as de rest of de white folks. Didn't he tell ma husband Saturday night he'd have to pay up every cent of his back bill, or he couldn't take nothin out of that store? And we been tradin there for years!

LUCY DOVES: That's their way o' strikin back at us colored folks.

MRS. SAM JONES: Yes, but Lord knows my husband ain't de father o' that child.

LUCY DOVES: Nor mine.

MRS. SAM JONES: Sam's got too much pride to go foolin round any old loose white woman.

SISTER WIGGINS: Child, you can't tell about men.

MATTIS CRANE: I knowed a case once in Detroit where a colored man lived ten years with a white woman and her husband didn't know it. He was their chauffeur.

SISTER WIGGINS: That's all right in the city, but please don't come bringin it out here to Boyd's Center where they ain't but a handful o' us colored—and we has a hard enough time as it is.

LOTTIE MUMFORD: You right! This sure has brought de hammer down on our heads. *(Jumps)* Oh, lemme go see about my rolls! *(Exits into kitchen)*

SISTER WIGGINS: Lawd knows we's law-abidin people, ain't harmed a soul, yet some o' these white folks talkin 'bout tryin to run all de colored folks out o' de county on account o' Douglass.

SISTER HOLT: They'll never run me out!

MRS. SAM JONES: Nor me!

LUCY DOVES: Don't say what they won't do, cause they might. *(A*

knock and the door opens. SISTER JENKINS enters) Howdy, Sister
Jenkins:

OTHERS: Howdy!

SISTER JENKINS: Good evenin! Is you bout to start?

MRS. SAM JONES: Yes, de meetin due to start directly.

MATTIS CRANE: Soon as Madam President arrives. Reckon she's havin
trouble gettin over that road from High Creek.

SISTER WIGGINS: Sit down and tell us what you's heard, Sister Jenkins.

SISTER JENKINS: About Douglass?

SISTER HOLT: Course 'bout Douglass. What else is anybody talking
'bout nowadays?

SISTER JENKINS: Well, my daughter told me Douglass' sister say they
was in love.

MATTIS CRANE: Him and that white woman?

SISTER JENKINS: Yes. Douglass' sister say it's been goin on 'fore de
woman got married.

MRS. SAM JONES: Un-huh! Then why didn't he stop foolin with her
after she got married? Bad enough, colored boy foolin 'round a
unmarried white woman, let alone a married one.

SISTER JENKINS: Douglass' sister say they was in love.

SISTER WIGGINS: Well, why did she marry the *white* man, then?

MATTIS CRANE: She's white, ain't she? And who wouldn't marry a
rich white man? Got his own farm, money and all, even if he were a
widower with grown children gone to town. He give her everything
she wanted, didn't he?

SISTER HOLT: Everything but the right thing.

MRS. SAM JONES: Well, she must not o' loved him, sneakin 'round
meetin Douglass in de woods.

CORA PERKINS: True, true!

MATTIS CRANE: But what you reckon she went on and had a colored
baby for?

SISTER WIGGINS: She must a thought it was the old man's baby.

LUCY DOVES: She don't think so now! Mattis say when the doctor left
and they brought the child in to show her, she like to went blind. It
were near black as me.

MATTIS CRANE: Do tell!

CORA PERKINS: And what did her husband say?

LUCY DOVES: Don't know. Don't know.

SISTER HOLT: He must a fainted.

(Re-enter LOTTIE MUMFORD, Pulling off her apron)

LUCY DOVES: That old white woman lives across the crick from us said he's gonna put her out soon's she's able to walk.

MRS. SAM JONES: Ought to put her out!

SISTER JENKINS: Maybe that's what Douglass waitin for.

MATTIS CRANE: I heard he wants to take her away.

SISTER WIGGINS: He better take his fool self away, 'fore these white get madder. Ain't nobody heard it was a black baby till day before yesterday. Then it leaked out. And now de white folks are rarin to kill Douglass.

CORA PERKINS: I sure am scared.

LOTTIE MUMFORD: And how come they all said right away it were Douglass?

LUCY DOVES: Honey, don't you know? Colored folks knowed Douglass been eyein that woman since God knows when, and she been eyein back at him. You ought to seed 'em when they meet in de store. Course, they didn't speak no more 'n Howdy, but their eyes followed one another round just like dogs.

SISTER JENKINS: They was in love, I tell you. Been in love.

MRS. SAM JONES: Mighty funny kind o' love. Everybody knows can't no good come out o' white and colored love. Everybody knows that. And Douglass ain't no child. He's twenty-six years old, ain't he? And Sister Carter sure did try to raise her three chillun right. You can't blame her.

SISTER WIGGINS: Blame that fool boy, that's who, and that woman. Plenty colored girls in Camden he could of courted ten miles up de road. One or two right here in Boyd's Center. I got a daughter myself.

MRS. SAM JONES: No, he had to go foolin round with a white woman.

LOTTIE MUMFORD: Yes, a white woman.

MATTIS CRANE: They say he loved her, though.

LOTTIE MUMFORD: What do Douglass say, since it happened?

LUCY DOVES: He don't say nothin. Just goes on with his plowin.

SISTER HOLT: He's a *man*, ain't he?

MRS. SAM JONES: What could he say?

SISTER WIGGINS: Well, he needn't think he's gonna keep his young mouth shut and let de white folks take it out on us. Down yonder at de school today my Dorabelle says they talkin 'bout separatin de colored from de white and makin all de colored children go in a nigger room next term.

MRS. SAM JONES: Ain't nothin like that ever happened in Boyd's Center long as I been here—these twenty-two years.

LUCY DOVES: White folks is mad now, child, mad clean through.

LOTTIE MUMFORD: Wonder they ain't grabbed Douglass and lynched him.

CORA PERKINS: It's a wonder!

LUCY DOVES: And him calmly out yonder plowin de field this afternoon.

MATTIS CRANE: He sure is brave.

SISTER HOLT: Douglass is a *man*.

SISTER WIGGINS: Woman's husband liable to kill him.

MRS. SAM JONES: Her brother's done said he's gunnin for him.

CORA PERKINS: They liable to burn us Negroes' houses down.

SISTER WIGGINS: Anything's liable to happen, Lawd, I'm nervous as I can be.

LUCY DOVES: You can't tell about white folks.

LOTTIE MUMFORD: I ain't nervous. I'm *scared*.

SISTER HOLT: Huh! Ain't you-all got no weapons?

CORA PERKINS: Don't say a word! It's ter'ble!

MATTIS CRANE: Why don't Sister Carter make him leave here.

MRS. SAM JONES: I wish I knew.

LOTTIE MUMFORD: She told me she were nearly crazy.

SISTER WIGGINS: And she can't get Douglass to say nothin, one way or another—if he go, or if he stay. *(A knock and the door opens. Enter MADAM PRESIDENT and SISTER PRIME)* Howdy, Madam President.

OTHERS: Good evenin, Madam President.

> *(The gossip does not halt. MADAM PRESIDENT goes to a little table and takes a small bell from her purse.)*

SISTER JENKINS: I done told you Douglass loves her.

MATTIS CRANE: He wants to see that white woman, once more again, that's what he wants.

MRS. SAM JONES: A white hussy!

SISTER WIGGINS: He's foolin with fire.

LOTTIE MUMFORD: Poor Mis' Carter. I'm sorry for his mother.

CORA PERKINS: Poor Mis' Carter.

SISTER JENKINS: Why don't you say poor Douglass? Poor white woman? Poor child?

> *(The PRESIDENT taps importantly on her bell, but the women continue in an undertone.)*

MATTIS CRANE: Madam President's startin de meetin.

SISTER PRIME: Is it a boy or a girl?

LUCY DOVES: Sh-s-s! There's de bell.

SISTER WIGGINS: I hear it's a boy.

SISTER PRIME: Thank God, ain't a girl then.

MATTIS CRANE: I hope it looks like Douglass, cause Douglass' a fine-lookin nigger.

SISTER HOLT: And he's a *man*!

SISTER WIGGINS: He's too bold, too bold.

MRS. SAM JONES: Shame he's got us all in this mess.

CORA PERKINS: Shame, shame, shame!

SISTER PRIME: Sh-ss-ss!

LOTTIE MUMFORD: Yes, indeedy!

SISTER HOLT: Mess or no mess, I got ma Winchester.

MRS. SAM JONES: They'll never run Sam and me out, neither!

MATTIS CRANE: Amen!

MADAM PRESIDENT: Sisters, can't you hear this bell?

LUCY DOVES: Sh-ss!

MADAM PRESIDENT: Madam Secretary, take your chair.

> *(MRS. SAM JONES comes forward.)*

CORA PERKINS: Ter'ble, ter'ble! *(Again the bell taps)* Sh-ss-s!

MADAM PRESIDENT: The March meetin of the Salvation Rock Ladies' Missionary Society for the Rescue o' the African Heathen is hereby called to order. Sister Holt, raise a hymn. *(As the talking continues—)* Will you ladies *please* be quiet? What are you talkin 'bout back ther, anyhow?

LUCY DOVES: Heathens, daughter, heathens.

SISTER WIGGINS: They ain't in Africa, neither!

SISTER HOLT: *(singing from her chair in a deep alto voice as the others join in.)*

> I shall not be,
> I shall not be moved.
> Oh, I shall not be,
> I shall not be moved.
> Like a tree that's
> Planted by the waters,
> I shall not be moved.

CURTAIN

Emperor of Haiti
(Troubled Island)

1936

Langston Hughes had a deep and abiding connection to Haiti and began planning a play about the Haitian revolution as early as 1928. Premiered at Karamu Theatre on November 18, 1936, under the title *Troubled Island, Emperor of Haiti* is an ambitious rendering of the most successful slave revolt in the African Diaspora. This signal moment in Haitian history—and what followed in the period from 1791 to 1806—is dramatically compressed and attributed to the leadership of Toussaint L'Ouverture's successor Dessalines, who declared himself Emperor of Haiti in 1804 and was assassinated two years later.

Hughes departs from the historical record in order to provide a single hero. The Dessalines of Act I is clearly based on the slave leader Boukman, and aspects of the portrayal of Dessalines in Act II, particularly the thoughtfulness of his discussions with the character Martel, seem more appropriate to the historical Toussaint L'Ouverture, who was noted for his acumen, administrative skill, and vision. However, it was Dessalines who proclaimed Haitian independence in 1803 and who decreed the return of Saint-Domingue to its aboriginal name of Haiti. A great general, Dessalines was legendary for his savagery, although the brutal slaughter that perpetuated the Haitian revolution is little in evidence in this play. Yet Hughes has attended quite carefully to the historical record; for example, almost all the names in the play are of historical persons, as are the various titles accorded to members of the Emperor's court. Dessalines's assassination also reflects historical details, including the presence of an old peasant woman who tended to the Emperor's stripped and mutilated body.

More generally, during the period depicted in the play, tensions among the French colonizers, the mulatto class created by their sexual liaisons, and the large black population, consisting mostly of African-born slaves, created a shifting set of betrayals and alliances, as strategies and goals changed. These are collapsed into a simpler, but deep, mistrust between blacks and mulattoes—a tension not unfamiliar to African American audiences—and the immense difficulties confronting a newly free, unlettered, agricultural population trying to construct a politically and economically stable and independent state.

Hughes originally conceived of *Emperor of Haiti* as a "singing play" and imagined Paul Robeson as the lead. Even before the premiere of the stage play, Hughes had begun work on a libretto, and African American composer William Grant Still agreed to collaborate on an opera. This work, called *Troubled Island,* was finally performed by the New York City Opera Company in 1949.[1]

This text is probably not the stage version as it was premiered, but it likely is close to it. The typescript contains some changes by Hughes, as well as musical cues in another hand. It also incorporates some changes made in an earlier draft by the director, Rowena Jelliffe. However, its list of characters differs slightly from that in the Karamu program. It is virtually the same as the versions published by Darwin Turner in *Black Drama in America: An Anthology* (1971) and by Errol Hill in *Black Heroes: Seven Plays* (1989). Hughes did not use the diacritics for French names, nor have earlier editors. We have followed that practice.

Characters

(In order of Appearance)

JOSEF, a young slave, later Grand Marshal
AZELIA, wife of Dessalines
MARTEL, an elderly slave, later Chief Counsellor
DESSALINES, slave leader, later Emperor
CONGO, a slave, later a Baron
XAVIER, a slave
ANTOINE, a slave, later a Baron
MARS, a one-armed slave, later a Duke
POPO, a slave, later Chief Attendant
CELESTE, a slave, later a Lady
LULU, a slave, later a Lady
DEMBU, a slave, later a Major
PIERRE, a child, later Chief Bugler
PAPALOI, Voodoo Priest
MAMALOI, Voodoo Priestess
VUVAL ⎫
BEYARD ⎬ Free Mulattoes, later Counts
STENIO ⎭

FIRST OLD WOMAN }
SECOND OLD WOMAN } Servants at the Court
CLAIRE HEUREUSE, Consort of the Emperor
LORD BOBO, Grand Treasurer
MANGO VENDOR }
PEPPER VENDOR }
COCONUT VENDOR }
MELON VENDOR } Market Women on the Quay
THREAD VENDOR }
YAM VENDOR }
TALL FISHERMAN
SHORT FISHERMAN
RAGMUFFINS
SOLDIERS
Slaves, Dukes, Duchesses, Courtiers, Servants, Butlers, Pages, Ladies-
    of-the-Presence, Lady-in-Waiting, A Ragged Boy, a Flower Girl,
    dancing girls, a male dancer, two children

Act I

TIME: *The year 1791.*
PLACE: *An abandoned sugar-mill in the French colony of Haiti, then
    officially known as St. Domingue. It is night. Through the broad open
    door the moon shines. Without, tall cocoanut palms stand against the
    stars, and hills rise in the distance.*
AT RISE: *JOSEF, a young black man, stands in the doorway, the curve of
    a cane-knife in his hand. Carefully he inspects the knife. At the noise
    of footsteps and the breaking of underbrush, his body becomes tense. He
    listens, then cries in a loud whisper.*
JOSEF: *(Softly, but with great sternness)* Halt! Who's there?
AZELIA: *(A woman's voice in the darkness)* Once . . .
JOSEF: *(To complete a password)* . . . a slave . . .
AZELIA: *(Continuing the formula)* . . . but soon no more!
JOSEF: Free?
AZELIA: Free! It's me, Azelia, from the Riviere Plantation.
JOSEF: Come on, then. You gave the password.
AZELIA: *(Entering, a load of bananas in a flat wicker tray on her head)*
    Jean Jacques's coming, too, so I run ahead to see if all's safe here.
JOSEF: *(Astonished)* Did Jean Jacques send you?

AZELIA: Course not! Jean Jacques fears nothing in Haiti, or anywhere. But he stopped to speak with a guard at the bridge, so I come on. *(Putting her burden down on a corner of the cane-grinder)* Look, Josef, under these bananas all the arms I could find. *(Laughing)* I put this fruit on top to hide what I was carrying, weapons for tonight.

JOSEF: Did you pass any Frenchmen?

AZELIA: Only one old planter on horseback, and he didn't stop us. We kept to the woods mostly. Look! Lift up these bananas.

JOSEF: *(Helping her move the fruit)* Um-umh!

AZELIA: Three machetes! See! Two pistols, stolen from the overseer, the butt end of an ax. *(They inspect the weapons)* Jean Jacques brings a Spanish rifle and a dozen flails.

JOSEF: We'll need 'em all, I reckon. Do the whites on your plantation smell a rat yet?

AZELIA: Don't think so. But the air's full of evil. The overseers drove us like dogs today in the fields.

JOSEF: On our place, as well.

AZELIA: And I'm tired, so tired I can't hardly drag. This "fruit" was heavy.

JOSEF: I'm tired as hell, too. But this is one night we've got to stay awake. *(Turning)* Say, didn't I hear there was a whipping on your place this morning?

AZELIA: Yes.

JOSEF: Who?

AZELIA: Jean Jacques was whipped.

JOSEF: You mean you . . . ?

AZELIA: My man.

JOSEF: Good Lord! For what?

AZELIA: Being off the place at night without permission. They caught him coming back this morning.

JOSEF: What'd he tell them?

AZELIA: That he'd been to a voodoo meeting.

JOSEF: Then . . . ?

AZELIA: Then they hit him across the mouth.

JOSEF: And after that?

AZELIA: They called all the slaves together to watch him beaten. The foreman gave him fifty lashes, hard. And master and his sons stood around and laughed to see a slave with such a fine name take a lashing.

JOSEF: What about his name?

AZELIA: They said Jean Jacques Dessalines was too much name for a slave to have. Let slaves have just one name, that's what they said.

JOSEF: Well, after tonight nobody'll give orders to a slave. I cut my last acre of cane today—if I live or die.

AZELIA: And Jean Jacques's took his last beating—if we succeed.

JOSEF: We'll succeed, or else stay in the hills like the run-away maroons until we're free. *(A noise is heard outside)* Be quiet! *(They stop to listen. JOSEF goes to the door)* Halt! Who's that?

MARTEL: *(An old man's voice)* Once . . .

JOSEF: A slave . . .

MARTEL: . . . But soon no more.

JOSEF: Free?

MARTEL: Free?

JOSEF: Come in, Martel. We need you wise old man.

MARTEL: *(Entering)* Good evening, Josef, son! Azelia, good evening! Where's Dessalines?

AZELIA: Jean Jacques's nearby, Father Martel. I'll tell him you're here.

MARTEL: Thank you, daughter. But keep to the shadows, the moon is bright. *(AZELIA exits) (To the young man)* Josef, yon moon in sky, mark you how it stares at us?

JOSEF: Yes, Father Martel.

MARTEL: A long time that moon's looked down upon Haiti. And tears of dew have fallen from its face in pity upon our troubled island where men are slaves.

JOSEF: True, Father Martel.

MARTEL: Even now yon moon looks out across the silver ocean, watching the slave ships sail toward the western world with their woeful burdens. The cries of black men and women, and the clank of chains in the night, rise up against the face of the moon.

JOSEF: My mother came that way, Martel, in a slave ship. She still remembers Africa.

MARTEL: Africa! So long, so far away! But tonight the moon weeps tears of joy, son, for Africa. And when in its next passage across the sea, it shines on our sweet motherland, it'll smile and say, "Thy black children in Haiti have thrown off the yoke of bondage, and are men again!" Josef, my children grew up slaves. My grandchildren, too . . . but yours will be free!

JOSEF: I wait for the beat of the drums to tell me when to lift this knife. *(He raises his machete)*

MARTEL: For seventy years I've waited. Now is our time come. When

the slave Boukman lays his fingers on the great drum hidden in the
cane-brake tonight, he'll beat out a signal that'll roll from hill to hill,
slave hut to slave hut, across the cane-fields, across the mountains,
across the bays from island to island, until every drum in Haiti throbs
with the call to rise and seek freedom. Then the moon will smile, son.

JOSEF: And I'll smile, too, Martel.

MARTEL: But come! I've orders for you, Josef. Time is passing.

JOSEF: Yes, sir, I'm listening.

MARTEL: *(Motioning to Josef to make a light)* Let us light a lantern. It's
safe since sentries now are posted around this mill like the spokes of
a wheel. I've just helped Yayou place twenty men who accompanied
us from Dondon. So we can have a light. And you need no longer
call for the password at the door.

JOSEF: Then what, sir?

MARTEL: Go station yourself by the spring and see that no man poisons
our water, should there be traitors among us.

JOSEF: Yes, Father Martel.

MARTEL: When the drums sound, then come here for instructions from
Dessalines.

JOSEF: From Jean Jacques Dessalines?

MARTEL: Jean Jacques. Tonight in the name of the slaves the Council
chose him for our leader.

JOSEF: I'm glad, for he's strong.

MARTEL: And to be trusted.

JOSEF: No one hates the French more than he does.

MARTEL: And no one's worked harder preparing for this night. Jean
Jacques has not slept for weeks. Twice he's been caught coming in at
dawn and beaten for it by the overseers. But be about your business,
son.

JOSEF: I'm going now. *(He goes to the door, but pauses there)* Someone
is coming. It's Jean Jacques— *(As he salutes)* Dessalines!

DESSALINES: *(Entering. A powerful black man in ragged clothing, followed by AZELIA)* Hello, Josef. You salute me like a French soldier!

JOSEF: You're our leader now, Jean Jacques.

DESSALINES: *(Pleased)* I'm your leader, Josef.
        (He returns the salute. JOSEF exits)

MARTEL: Good evening son! I'm glad you're early.

DESSALINES: I'm glad to find you already here. *(They shake hands
and immediately busy themselves with plans)* You can tell me where
the rations are hidden in the hills, can't you, Martel? Twenty miles

from the foot of Timber Mountain on the road to Le Trou our first supplies are buried? And the sign is three curved marks on a tree? Is that right?

MARTEL: Yes, Jean Jacques.

DESSALINES: Then forty paces in from the road we'll find a scattering of seashells? And there, dig?

MARTEL: Yes, that's how 'twas planned. Food's hidden there in the earth, and arms.

DESSALINES: *(To Azelia)* Have the women been told to bring cook-pots?

AZELIA: We looked out for that. Those little things . . .

DESSALINES: Nothing's a little thing now, Zelia.

AZELIA: *(Jokingly)* How about your pipe, Jean Jacques? *(Producing it from her hair)* It's a little thing you're crazy about, but you forgot to bring it.

DESSALINES: *(Impatiently)* Don't trifle, Azelia. There's too much to do.

AZELIA: Forgive me. *(She puts her arm about his shoulder and offers him the pipe)* Go on with your plans.

DESSALINES: *(Loudly)* Don't touch me! God! My shoulder's raw as meat!

AZELIA: Oh, I'm sorry, Jean Jacques.

DESSALINES: *(Sarcastically)* We have a kind master, Martel.

MARTEL: He'll be master no more when the sun rises.

DESSALINES: He'll be less than nothing. He'll be dead. Our gentle master will burn in his bed this evening, roasted between his silken sheets.

AZELIA: Poor man!

DESSALINES: *(Turning on her)* Strange you should say *"Poor man,"* Azelia! What's he to you? *(Fiercely)* Have you ever been one of his mistresses? Every black woman he's wanted he's had.

AZELIA: Not me! No, no! Not me!

DESSALINES: Then why cry pity on him? I know you must hate him. But when you say, *"Poor man,"* you make me laugh. The whites never have pity on us. We're just slaves, dogs to them.

AZELIA: You're right, Jean Jacques!

DESSALINES: They burned Mackandal[2] for trying to be free, didn't they? They had no mercy on him. We'll show no mercy on them now.

MARTEL: I remember well the burning of Mackandal. Thirty years gone by, 'tis. They made the slaves for miles around witness it, as an example of what happens to any Negro who wants to be free. Burning is a horrible thing, Jean Jacques! I hate to think that we must do it, too.

DESSALINES: You're over kind, Martel. I do not love my master.

MARTEL: I'd let them live, if they'd leave us free.

DESSALINES: They won't, so there's no *if* about it. We have no choice but to kill . . . wipe out the whites in all this island . . . for if the French are left alive to force us back to slavery, we'll never get a chance to rise again. And for us, you and me—Boukman, Christophe, Toussaint, and all our leaders—there'd be only the rack, the wheel, or burning at the stake like Mackandal. Mackandal! *(Turning and appealing to the night)* Great Mackandal! Dead leader of rebellious slaves, fight with us now.

MARTEL: Mackandal is with us, son. His spirit walks the Haitian hills crying the name of freedom.

DESSALINES: But the only way to be free is to fight! Or else to die.

MARTEL: Tonight we fight to live, Jean Jacques.

DESSALINES: To live! Men free, alive! Alive! Go, Martel, and tell that to the men on guard without, for some are even yet afraid. I saw it in their eyes. Tell them tonight we strike with all our force, and none must be afraid. There are two ways of being free . . . alive or dead. We'll live! This time, the French will die.

MARTEL: I'll go, Jean Jacques. *(He exits)*

AZELIA: *(Drawing near her husband)* But you and I, Jean Jacques, we must live. *(Fiercely)* I will not have you dead.

DESSALINES: Why must *we* live any more than the others, Azelia?

AZELIA: Because we have loved so little, Jean Jacques, been happy too little. Never a night is mine alone—never just you and me—

DESSALINES: That's true, Azelia, but—

AZELIA: Every night there's been something to keep you from me. Ever since we've had a hut together, you've been stealing out to crawl through the forest, in the dark, to some secret meeting of the slaves, planning this break for freedom—and I'm left alone. Tonight has taken all our nights, Jean Jacques, the cane-field all our days.

DESSALINES: But what I've planned—it is good, Azelia?

AZELIA: Good, Jean Jacques. But for a woman, love, too, is good.

DESSALINES: Yes, yes, I know, but at a time like this, it's foolish. *(He busies himself inspecting a pistol)*

AZELIA: Foolish, I know, but I love you, Jean. *(Fearfully)* Listen to me! If we fail, the French will kill you. They'll tear your body on the rack or break you on the wheel.

DESSALINES: We will not fail, Azelia. Don't worry.

AZELIA: But if we did, I'd share death, too. We've shared so much together. When we were children running wild in the slave quarters, we ate from the same trough where our master fed the dogs. Together we learned to pick the cotton clean. Then in the green cane-fields, I watched you swing your knife, big and strong in the sunlight. My man! My Jean Jacques! We tied the cane into bundles, and in the long night learned to stir the bubbling syrup in its copper kettles. But there came a dawn when the kettles boiled, forgotten. That night we knew that love was sweeter than the syrup. Then our little hut together, and I your wife.

DESSALINES: Wife? *(Laughing)* A word the whites use. We never had a priest, nor papers, either.

AZELIA: We had ourselves. You, me! I, you!

DESSALINES: *(Bitterly)* And neither of us freedom.

AZELIA: You always talk of freedom, Jean Jacques! I want to be free too, but—

DESSALINES: But what?

AZELIA: I'm afraid . . . .

DESSALINES: Afraid? Afraid of what? Don't rile me, Azelia.

AZELIA: *(Slowly)* Afraid freedom'll take you away from me.

DESSALINES: Don't be a fool! Why, when we're free, we can go anywhere and do anything we want to, you and me together.

AZELIA: I just want to be together, always with you.

DESSALINES: Then don't worry, I'm not going to leave you. I'll even get a paper and marry you like the white folks do, if that's what you want—except that we couldn't read what's on the paper.

AZELIA: Are we too old to learn to read now?

DESSALINES: I expect we are, Azelia. But not too old to be free. *(Rising)* Come on, Azelia, let's look about the mill and see if there're any spies hiding in the rafters, or in that vat yonder, waiting to run back to the white folks with word of our meeting place. *(As AZELIA puts out her hands to detain him, he flinches with pain)* Take care, woman.

AZELIA: Forgive me, Jean Jacques, and kiss me just once, for all the years that love has been our chain.

DESSALINES: And slavery our master.

AZELIA: And freedom your hope.

DESSALINES: You're fighting with me, Azelia?

AZELIA: Until the end, Jean Jacques.

DESSALINES: *(As he kisses her)* Azelia! Azelia! *(Turning away)* The crowd'll be here in no time, now. Let's look in this bin here and see if it's empty. *(He tries to lift the wooden lid)* By God, it's heavy! Help me, Zelia.

CONGO: *(A deep voice inside the bin)* Hands off, less'n you want a shot through the belly.

DESSALINES: *(Brandishing his cane-knife)* Who's there?

CONGO: *(Calmly, from within)* Who's out there?

DESSALINES: Jean Jacques!

CONGO: *(Drawling)* Jean Jacques, who?

DESSALINES: Jean Jacques Dessalines.

CONGO: *(Lifting up lid of box and emerging)* Well, tell me something, pal! *(With a half-lazy salute)* Hello, Jean Jacques! Hello, Azelia!

DESSALINES: What're you doing, Congo?

CONGO: I'm on guard.

DESSALINES: On guard?

CONGO: On guard—locked in the box, so nobody can bother me—nor the guns, neither, we got stacked in there.

DESSALINES: What did you open up for, then, you careless fool?

CONGO: Who wouldn't know your voice, boy, as many times as I heard you talking to us slaves around the fire at night—when the white folks thought we was just having a little voodoo dance? You gets around a-plenty, Jean Jacques.

DESSALINES: You knowed me by my voice?

CONGO: Every black man in North Haiti knows you. We're waiting for you to lead us, if them old slaves in the council ever make up their minds who they gonna pick out.

DESSALINES: Then close the box and lock it until I give the word, Congo, for *I am* leader now. *(Proudly)* Tonight the Council picked me.

CONGO: That's good, boy! I'm glad!

DESSALINES: Are there two hundred rifles in there, as there should be?

CONGO: Two hundred, Jean Jacques.

DESSALINES: Then remain on guard! But not inside.

CONGO: I got you, chief.

DESSALINES: *(Laughing)* Chief?

CONGO: Like in Africa, Jean Jacques—Chief.

DESSALINES: Can you remember Africa, Congo?

CONGO: Sure. I was a big boy when that English ship got hold of me. That's why I can do our dances so well. I learnt 'em in Africa.

DESSALINES: Well, tomorrow, boy, we'll dance a-plenty. If I can loosen up my back.

CONGO: Not whipped again?

DESSALINES: Yes, whipped.

CONGO: You sure got a mean old master. What kind of whip he use?

DESSALINES: A cat-o'-nine tail 'cross my shoulders.

CONGO: *(Laughing)* Huh! That's nothing! My master uses a tree limb on my head.

DESSALINES: *(Angrily)* And you laugh and like it?

CONGO: *(Suddenly sober)* I don't like it, that's why I'm guarding these guns.

AZELIA: *(In the doorway)* Listen! I hear a horse down the road, coming fast.

CONGO: *(Listening)* I hear it, too. There ain't no slaves got horses.

DESSALINES: Some free mulatto, perhaps. One of our allies! It's time for everybody to be here, and so far they've only come from Dondon. Where's everyone else? Where's the crowd from Milot, and from Limbe? This is no time to be late!

AZELIA: You know how careful everybody's got to be tonight. You warned them yourself not to hurry in case the white folks get to looking out the corners of their eyes.

CONGO: Folks what's been working all day's just naturally slow, anyhow. I know I am.

DESSALINES: Not when their life depends on it. *(As the horses hoofs approach)* Let me go see who's coming there. *(He goes to the door)*

CONGO: It *must* be a mulatto. No Negro's got a horse to ride on. *(Muttering)* And I don't trust them mulattoes, myself.

AZELIA: Black mother, white father, free.

CONGO: Free or not, their white fathers treat 'em almost as bad as us slaves.

AZELIA: But they sometimes leaves them land and money.

CONGO: Then the mulattoes think they're white for sure!

AZELIA: And look down on us for being black.

CONGO: And for being slaves.

DESSALINES: Keep quiet, you. The mulattoes who've joined us hate the whites.

CONGO: A little hate ain't enough. If they'd ever been driven to the fields like us, they'd know how to hate a-plenty; I tell you, I don't trust 'em.

DESSALINES: Well, they're smart. They've been to school and got an education. We need their heads.

CONGO: I'd like too cut their heads off and play nine-pins with 'em.

DESSALINES: Not those that are with us, Congo. *(Going outside the door)* But that's no mulatto on that horse. Even the moon don't brighten up his face. *(Calling)* Who's there?

XAVIER: *(Voice out of breath)* Me, Jean Jacques!

AZELIA: It looks like Xavier from Breda Plantation.

DESSALINES: It is Xavier. *(As a man comes running toward him)* What's up? A message?

XAVIER: *(Entering, panting)* Yes, Jean Jacques! A message! Bad news! Some of the white folks done found out.

DESSALINES: What? Where?

CONGO: How?

AZELIA: *(In terror)* Oh!

XAVIER: That mulatto, Gautier, we thought was with us, he got cold feet and sent his family into the Cape for safety. The whites on the next plantation, related to him, asked what's up, and he told them they'd better leave for the Cape, too. Then the white man grabbed him by the throat and made him confess there's trouble in the air.

DESSALINES: A yellow dog! What then?

XAVIER: The house slaves knew something must be wrong, and old Bajean came out and told me. I gave orders to set fire to the house as soon as I got started on this horse I stole from the stables.

DESSALINES: And did they fire the house?

XAVIER: I didn't see it burning as I looked back.

DESSALINES: It's wise they didn't. T'would alarm the plain for miles about. Everyone had orders not to fire until the drums are beaten. Our plans are to let the whites think they've escaped. Then shoot them down on the road. And the false mulattoes, too! Damn their chicken-hearted souls! Are there many people on the way, Xavier?

XAVIER: The roads were empty as I came, but all along in the woods, slaves creep towards here. Soon there'll be a crowd. And all are wondering who is chief?

DESSALINES: I am, Xavier.

XAVIER: *(Stepping forward and shaking hands)* We trust you, Jean Jacques.

DESSALINES: Thank you, friend. Now back to your plantation and see if your master's escaped. And if the mulatto who squealed is still living, kill him ere the drums beat.

XAVIER: I will, chief.

> *(He leaves. Horse's hoofs. Sounds of movement and voices without)*

CONGO: You see, I tell you about mulattoes! They're dangerous.

DESSALINES: They're not all alike, Congo. Some we can trust. Vuval is one. Stenio's another. These mulattoes are with us. *(Looking out)* But say, here come the men we're waiting for. *(Calling)* It's time you got here.

> *(Several enter, including the slaves, ANTOINE, MARS, POPO, and the women, CELESTE and LULU, with her child, PIERRE, a boy of six or seven. Greetings are exchanged)*

ANTOINE: Greetings, Jean Jacques! We're glad you're leader.

> *(They shake hands)*

LULU: Hello, Azelia! Ain't you proud of your man now?

AZELIA: I am that, Lulu. He's chief.

POPO: Hello, Jean Jacques.

DESSALINES: Hello, Popo. Congratulate me, boy!

POPO: I knew they'd pick you, Jean Jacques! It couldn't be nobody else. We're sticking with you, partner.

LULU: Well, it looks like Negroes is getting together at last.

CELESTE: It sho do, Lulu!

DESSALINES: *(To CELESTE)* How about a dance tomorrow night, Celeste, to celebrate our freedom?

CELESTE: *(Laughing)* Not with Azelia's say-so! I'm scared of you, Jean Jacques. You're a lady-killer.

DESSALINES: Not much! Too busy now. *(Turning to MARS)* Hello, Mars! Is Dembu, the powder-maker, with you?

MARS: He was right behind me.

DEMBU: *(Entering)* Here I am, Jean Jacques.

DESSALINES: Come aside a moment. I want to talk with you.

> *(They withdraw into the shadows)*

CONGO: *(To the child, PIERRE, who has climbed up on the box of guns)* Boy, you better get down off that box, you'll burn your feet.

PIERRE: Why, what's in here? *(As he hugs Congo around the neck)*

CONGO: You'll see by and by. Stop hugging me! I ain't your pappy.

LULU: *(To her child)* Pierre, behave yourself. Get down, now, hear?

> *(The CHILD gets down)*

ANTOINE: *(To POPO, who is bare from the waist up)* Popo, where's your shirt?

CELESTE: Maybe he ain't got none.

POPO: Yes, I got one, but I hid it soaked in oil in my master's store-house. My girl's to fire it, when the signal's given.

CELESTE: *(Peering at Popo's breast)* You've sure had a lot of masters, ain't you, Popo? All them brands they done burnt on your breast.

POPO: I been sold four times, but one master was kind, and didn't put his mark on me. Old man Thibault, he said he liked the way I played the drums.

CELESTE: You was lucky. When Thibault owned me, he branded me twice. Sure wished I'd learned to play the drums.

MARS: *(A man with one arm)* Talk about drums, we got the biggest drum on the North Plain hidden on our place. Old Lucumi's ready waiting down in the banana grove. He's gonna beat out the freedom signal so's the slaves across the mountains can hear it.

LULU: Them big old goat drums sure can rock the stars.

PIERRE: How far can they sound, mama?

LULU: Forty kilometres, I reckon, son, or more. Can't they, Mars?

MARS: Farther than that on a clear night.

PIERRE: I'd rather have a bugle, that's what I want.

CELESTE: For what?

PIERRE: A bugle blows pretty. All the white children have 'em.

CELESTE: The white children's free.

MARS: Anyhow, a drum can sound twenty times as far as any bugle ever blowed. Bugles don't belong to black folks.

PIERRE: That's how come I want one.

LULU: You can have one, honey, when we's free.

PIERRE: Tomorrow?

LULU: I 'spects tomorrow.

CELESTE: Drums is what our gods like, though. Drums is for Legba and Dambala, Nannan and M'bo.

CONGO: African gods been knowin' drums a long time. Them tinny bugles just cain't reach they ears.

ANTOINE: Goat's blood, cock's blood, and drums.

MARS: The drum's a black man's heart a-beatin'. Tonight that beatin's goin' to set the Frenchmen's hair on end.

CONGO: This is our night tonight.

CELESTE: A mighty night it'll be, too. Bless Legba!

MARS: My one good arm is ready. *(He lifts his single arm)*

PIERRE: Where's your other arm, Monsieur Mars?

MARS: *(Bitterly)* The Black Code, son. The French've got it all writ' down that if a slave raise his hand against a white man, they can cut it off. They cut off mine.

CONGO: We'll remember that tonight.

ANTOINE: Let the French dwell a thousand years in hell, they'll never forget this night.

POPO: If there is a hell, I hope I meet no Frenchmen there.

LULU: Hell's a place for Christians, ain't it? Not for us.

ANTOINE: That's all. Voodoo gods ain't mixin' with the white gods.

CELESTE: Legba's better.

POPO: White folks must have a special hell, anyhow, for themselves, reserved. They wouldn't go where us black folks goes, would they?

CONGO: They'll find out what hell they're headed for mighty soon.

(Sounds of chanting and rattles without. People clear the doorway as a PAPALOI, in anklets of bone and a high feathered headdress enters, followed by a MAMALOI of powerful physique, carrying a live cock. The man has a rattle in one hand and an African drum under his arm)

LULU: There's the mamaloi from Lembe.

CELESTE: And she carries a live cock to sacrifice on the mountain.

PIERRE: The papaloi's got a drum. Lemme go see!

(The WOMEN and the CHILD join a crowd that now clusters, chanting, about the high priest and priestess of voodoo, who chatter in an African tongue, calling on the gods)

PAPALOI: Uglumbagola ta! Damballa! Solomini! Keetai!

MAMALOI: Legba! Legba! Legba!

(The WOMEN cry and shout)

DESSALINES: *(Who is in council with a group)* Not so loud, there, women. We've plans to make. Call the gods a little softer. Please!

(The GROUP about the priests becomes less noisy.

(Three mulattoes enter, VUVAL, BEYARD, and STENIO. They are better dressed than the slaves, and much more polished. They seem out of place)

ANTOINE: Who're those mulattoes? Why do they come here?

MARS: Vuval and his friends. They're on our side. They're all right.

ANTOINE: The smart half-breeds!

CONGO: Better we didn't have them with us. They've never been slaves.

MARS: But Vuval's a poor mulatto.

POPO: His French father didn't leave him a thing but books.

ANTOINE: And half-freedom.

CONGO: They're half-men, not black, not white either. Bah!

MARS: *(As the mulattoes approach)* Hello, Stenio. Evening, Vuval.

STENIO: Gentlemen, good evening.

VUVAL: Good evening, comrades. *(Indicating Beyard)* My cousin, Beyard.

BEYARD: *(Rather pompously)* Greetings in the name of liberty.

POPO: *(Shortly)* Howdy!

    (The mill has gradually begun to fill with slaves standing in groups talking in low voices)

VUVAL: Is it true, the slave council has chosen Dessalines as leader?

MARS: It's true, and good, ain't it?

BEYARD: I doubt it's being good. He's ignorant and head-strong.

VUVAL: A brave fellow. But he's been nowhere, and he knows nothing.

CONGO: He knows the whip well enough to hate it.

ANTOINE: And he's not afraid.

POPO: He's the finest man in the North Plain. I grew up with him, and worked beside him. He's my friend.

BEYARD: Friendship has no judgment, Popo.

VUVAL: I thought they might have chosen Stenio, or some one of us as leader who can read and write, as well as speak.

CONGO: Speaking's not what we need now, Vuval.

ANTOINE: We know what the words are—the same as the French use in Paris! Liberty, Equality, Fraternity.

MARS: But Frenchmen keep us slaves in Haiti.

POPO: We want those words in action, here, now, for blacks as well as whites.

VUVAL: There are many ways of recreating words, Popo.

STENIO: Oh, don't be literary, Vuval. Slaves can't appreciate it. This is not the poetry club we once had in Cap Francais, before the French accused us of being Jacobins.

BEYARD: And closed our meetings.

POPO: You mean before you decided to join with us slaves.

VUVAL: Yes, we mulattoes didn't always realize you blacks were our natural allies, by force of circumstance.

POPO: And you didn't always think we needed to be free, did you?

VUVAL: Perhaps not.

CONGO: You were free already, so you didn't give a damn about us, did you, until you needed our help yourselves?

POPO: *(Bitterly)* White fathers, yellow skins. You bastards!

VUVAL: I don't like that word, *bastard*.

POPO: I don't like you, Vuval.

VUVAL: *(Stepping forward to strike the Negro)* You dirty slave!

BEYARD: *(Grabbing Vuval's arm)* Stop!

POPO: Let me at him! The yellow dog!

  (But ANTOINE holds him back)

DESSALINES: *(His voice booming out of the darkness)* Who's starting trouble there? Whoever it is, I'll bust his brains out with my fist!

ANTOINE: A couple of hot-heads, Jean Jacques! Lost their tempers, nothing more.

VUVAL: Somebody lost his tongue.

DESSALINES: What's wrong, Popo?

POPO: I'm all right, but this yellow dog's been turning his tongue against you.

DESSALINES: *(Laughing)* What did he say that could hurt Jean Jacques?

POPO: He said he's fit to lead himself.

DESSALINES: That might be true. I'll let him lead with me—what would you think of that, Vuval? I know our need of you.

VUVAL: But I don't relish being called a bastard, Jean Jacques.

DESSALINES: *(Laughing)* Is that all? Why let a word upset you? Only the French have priests and wedding rings. *(To Popo)* Popo, have a little care what names you call our allies.

AZELIA: *(As she approaches)* Jean Jacques, the councillors have come. They're ready to begin. Martel's waiting for you.

  (DESSALINES and AZELIA disappear in the crowd about the sugar grinder. The mulattoes withdraw to one side as several old men and women enter. They are the council of slaves. MARTEL is among them)

MARS: It must be mighty near midnight!

ANTOINE: Soon, brother!

POPO: I'm ready!

CONGO: There's all the elders.

ANTOINE: And the old man from Limbe.

MARS: Wise old Martel!

POPO: Sss, you! They're beginning.

  (MARTEL is standing on a box that lifts him slightly above the throng. Around him are several very old slaves, both men and women. The crowd gradually becomes silent as someone knocks three times. MARTEL begins to speak)

MARTEL: Children of slavery, the time is come! For months, in secret and in danger, we've laid our plans. Now we gather here for the final hour. You are the tried and faithful. We old men and women born in slavery and weary with unpaid labor, have chosen a leader for you. Not one of ourselves, for our backs are bending. We have chosen a man who's young and strong, wise and brave, to lead the slaves of the north to victory in union with all the blacks of Haiti who answer the call of the drums tonight. Your leader is Dessalines.

VOICES: *(In cheers)*

> Dessalines!

> Jean Jacques!

> Dessalines!

> *(DESSALINES' face glows in the lantern light as the old man puts his hand on his head in a gesture of blessing. Then MARTEL steps down and gives him the box)*

DESSALINES: *(In a hoarse voice, stirred by emotion)* I don't need to talk, for we're ready.

VOICES:

> Yes, indeed!

> Ready! Ready!

DESSALINES: But I must tell you how full my heart is tonight, and how I keep remembering back to when I was a little naked slave among the slaves. Every day an old man came to dump a pot of yams into a trough where we ate, and the pigs and the dogs, they ate, too. And we got down alongside 'em, on all fours, and ate—us and the dogs. I thought I, too, was a beast. I didn't know I'd ever grow to be a man. I thought only white folks grew up to be men. The Frenchman drove his sheep to market—just so they drove our parents to the fields when the sun came up. They owned them, too. Overseers with their dogs, whip in hand, always driving Negroes to the fields. And when the white man saw me growing tall, big enough to work, he drove me, too. Slowly I moved, too slow. The overseer lifted high his whip and cut me 'cross the back. And when I turned, he lashed me in the face. I cried out, he struck again. Then I lifted up my head and looked him in the eyes, and I knew I was a man, not a dog! I wanted to be free!

VOICES:

> Free! Free!

> Want to be free!

> Free!

DESSALINES: Not I alone—thousands of slaves like me wanted to be free! All over Haiti! Now, we're ready. We will not fail! Our time has come!

VOICES:

> Come! Come!
>
> It's come!
>
> *(Cries of "Legba! Legba! Legba!" from the women, and the chanting of the MAMALOI and PAPALOI grow ever louder as DESSALINES continues)*

DESSALINES: Our masters on this island are fifty thousand whites to *five hundred thousand* Negro slaves. Count on your fingers, black to white—ten to one! Ten Negroes to one white, and yet we're slaves! Shall we go on slaves?

VOICES: No! No! No! No!

DESSALINES: In France, white men—free men have risen against the king and torn the Bastille down. How much more reason have we, we who are slaves, to rise against our masters! How much more reason to strike back at those who buy and sell us, who beat us with their whips and track us down with their dogs! Why, even the mulattoes are turning against their white fathers and are ready to take our side, too. The poem-writer, Vuval, and his cousins are with us tonight.

VOICES: *(Murmuring)*

> Don't want 'em.
>
> Can't trust 'em.
>
> Put 'em out.
>
> Don't need 'em.

DESSALINES: We do need them, my friends. We need their help. Make no mistake of that. They can read and write. I've chosen Vuval as my aide. *(To the mulatto)* Come forward, Vuval, show yourself and march with us. *(VUVAL takes his place beside DESSALINES)* And now for our plans! Soon the drums of freedom will begin to sound. We'll start for the hills, burning and killing on the way, setting fire to all that's French, their mansions, their barns, their store-houses, their cane-fields. Everything from here to Gonaives, Le Mole to Acul, will go up in smoke tonight—tomorrow not a Frenchman must live to tell the tale. In the hills, we'll meet our fellow-slaves from the coast, the slaves from the west and all the leaders. Boukman will be there, Christophe, and Toussaint. Food and arms are buried. There on the mountain top we'll sacrifice a goat to Legba. We'll dance obeah. We'll make powder and bullets, and gather strength until the time is ripe for us to come down to the coast to seize the ports, and claim all Haiti as our own. Then we'll be free!

VOICES: *(With a great shout)*
>Free! Free!
>Great God-A-Mighty! Free!

DESSALINES: Our hills await us. Our hills—where freedom lives, our hills—where the French, with their cannons, can never climb. The French! Bah! How my tongue burns when I say that word! Masters of all this sun-warmed land! Cruel monsters of terror! The French, who broke the bones of Oge on the rack! The French—who tortured Chevannes until his life blood ran down, drop by drop—dead for freedom! The French, who cut their scars upon my back—too deep to ever fade away! Look! *(He rips his shirt wide open, exposing his back covered with great red welts)* Look what they've done to me! Look at my scars! For these the whites must pay!

VOICES:
>The whites must pay!
>Make 'em pay!
>Make 'em pay!
>Oh, make 'em pay!
>*(Women begin to sob and moan)*

DESSALINES: The sacks of sweet white sugar the French ship off to Paris goes stained with our blood!

VOICES: Blood! Blood! Blood!

DESSALINES: The soft white cotton the French weave into garments is red with my blood!

VOICES:
>Blood! Blood!
>Blood! Blood!

DESSALINES: The coffee our masters sup in the cool of evening on their wide verandas is thick with blood!

VOICES: Blood! Blood!

DESSALINES: Our masters live on blood!

VOICES:
>Black blood!
>Black blood!
>Black blood!

DESSALINES: Oh, make them pay! *(Pausing)* Make . . . them . . . pay!
>*(Afar off, a drum begins to beat.*
>*(The VOICES rise to a frenzy at its sound)*

VOICES:
>Pay! Pay! Pay!

Make 'em pay!

(Instantly, the distant drum-beat multiplies and spreads from plantation to plantation, carrying its signal across the night, until the whole island is throbbing with drum-beats. In the crowded sugar-mill there are moans and shouts, hysterical sobs, curses, cries, a crush and swirl of movement.

(CONGO opens the box and begins to distribute guns. Above the tumult, the voice of DESSALINES rises in command:)

DESSALINES: Revolt! Arise! For Freedom!

VOICES: *(Echoing his words)* Freedom! Freedom!

DESSALINES: Revenge! Revenge! To the hills!

VOICES:

To the hills!

To the hills!

DESSALINES: Free! Kill to be free!

VOICES:

Free! Free!

To be free!

DESSALINES: Fire the cane-fields! Poison the springs!

VOICES: To be free! Free!

DESSALINES: Choke the rivers! Ambush the roads!

VOICES: Free! Free!

DESSALINES: *(Raising his cane-knife like a sword)* Kill the whites! Kill to be free!

VOICES: *(In a mighty shout)*

Kill!

Kill!

Kill!

CELESTE: *(A woman's voice, high and clear)* To be free!

(With cane-knives and rifles held high, the SLAVES pour forth into the night.

(Outside, flames are visible as the canefields burn. The drums beat louder, ever spreading. Shots are heard. In the distance, harrowing cries, the march of feet.

(DESSALINES stands with his arms uplifted, his back bare. In the lantern light, great red scars gleam like welts of terror across his shoulders.

(The MAMALOI whirls through the crowd, lifting high the sacred cock. The PAPALOI chants above his drum, his hands flying, his eyes wild, his feathered headdress waving. VUVAL stands, deathly pale,

with his back to the cane-grinder, as if in mortal terror. Above the tumult, CELESTE's voice is heard crying in a high, musical cry:)

CELESTE: I want to be free! Let me be free! Free!

AZELIA: *(Lifting her rifle in both hands and calling:)* Jean Jacques! Jean Jacques! Jean Jacques!

(He does not hear her. AZELIA disappears in the crowd that pours through the door. Voices and drum-beats fill the night)

THE CURTAIN FALLS

Act II, Scene 1

Dessalines' Palace, near Petite Riviere.

TIME: *Several years later.*

The Council Chamber; a table against red velvet curtains. A coat-of-arms. A chair, empire style, of plush and gilt with a high back. Two smaller chairs.

AT RISE: *The Emperor, DESSALINES, is seated behind the table, many papers before him. He is obviously tired and worried.*

VUVAL sits at one end of the table, reading a letter.

VUVAL: *(Reading)* " . . . forty acres of sugar-cane, two hundred plantain trees, an estimated three thousand coffee bushes, seventy pepper trees. Beyond that, I have nothing more to report to the Emperor. Signed: Beyard, Count of Acul."

DESSALINES: Is that all?

VUVAL: That's all. Every acre of land on his plantation is productive.

DESSALINES: And yet he says he cannot pay his tax, and so demands another tribute from the peasants?

VUVAL: We have very few markets, sire.

DESSALINES: Why doesn't he plant pineapples? There's always a market for them in the States.

VUVAL: It takes time.

DESSALINES: Time? Time! Always excuses on account of time. We've been free long enough to flourish here. And you mulattoes were always free! Yet Beyard can't make his own plantation pay its tax.

VUVAL: He knows how well enough. He can get your money easily by taxation.

DESSALINES: I don't want it by taxation. By work I want it. We must produce.

VUVAL: *(Shrugging)* Perhaps!

DESSALINES: If I permit this draining of the peasants, they'll turn on me. Yet if the Empire goes without taxes, how shall we build roads, hire teachers, or run this court? *(Commandingly)* Write the Count of Acul I must have from him at once the twenty thousand francs he owes the Treasury.

VUVAL: But I thought, perhaps, since Beyard is my cousin . . . .

DESSALINES: I have granted you too many favors now, Vuval. I'll give him no reduction, and no further time. *(Leaning back)* Read the next communication.

VUVAL: It is from General Gedeon's headquarters, signed by Major Longchamps. He wants, post haste, ten burro loads of powder, to be used at the fall manoeuvres, and three hundred new winter uniforms for his men, preferably salmon pink with orange trimmings. He writes that he wants his regiment to look as good as Major Loguet's. He also requests a purple plume for his helmet.

DESSALINES: *(Roaring)* Tell him . . . tell him! *(Impatiently)* Damn it, I wish I could write! Tell him to go to hell!

VUVAL: Very well, sir; but . . . .

DESSALINES: But nothing!

VUVAL: He's an important officer.

DESSALINES: Well, send the powder. But as for the uniforms, tell him, no! Everybody in Haiti wants to dress like me—and I'm the Emperor.

VUVAL: True!

DESSALINES: We'd need ten thousand spinning mills to turn out cloth enough to clothe them as they wish.

VUVAL: And a million dyers to dye it, if we had sufficient colors.

DESSALINES: What next?

VUVAL: *(With a gesture of fatigue)* But you haven't forgotten there's a State Banquet tonight, have you, Emperor? It's already dusk.

DESSALINES: The next letter, Vuval. We must get done with this. *(He wipes his brow)*

VUVAL: *(Reading)* "Most High and Mighty King of Haiti, Emperor Jean Jacques Dessalines, Chief General of the army and leader of the Blacks, your humble servant begs of you this favor. The peasants of Gros Morne have made bricks and built ourselves a school. We are six hundred grown-ups and sixty-seven children. We want to learn to read and write, so will you please send to us a teacher? We have already wrote three times to the Duke of Marmalade, Chief Grand Commissioner of Education, but we never got no answer. We are anxious to learn from books and put our school to a good use. Please, Emperor to the Blacks, if you have time, answer this letter yourself. We send you our humble regards. The love of the liberated people of Gros Morne goes to you. Respectfully yours, Henri Bajean, Blacksmith."

DESSALINES: *(Sadly, after painful silence)* I can't read myself. And we have no teachers. *(Louder)* Vuval, why did so many mulattoes run away to Paris? We black people need you—you were educated. Now we have no teachers to send to Gros Morne.

VUVAL: *(Carelessly)* That little village couldn't afford to pay a teacher, anyhow.

DESSALINES: Pay? Pay! Pay! Always pay! Does no one know that need fulfilled is pay enough? *(Angrily)* Does no one, loving Haiti, find his pay in doing for her? But it's money we need, is it? Then change that letter I ordered you to write—tell Beyard I ask forty thousand francs instead of twenty.

VUVAL: *(Controlling his anger)* You have given me too many letters today, sire. I cannot write them all.

DESSALINES: Write that one now to Beyard and bring it here to me.

(VUVAL begins to gather up his papers, as POPO enters)

POPO: The Counsellor Martel's to see you, sire. And I've done laid out your robes of state for the banquet. I put the ruby crown out, too, and polished up the scepter. It shine like a lightning rod.

DESSALINES: Let Martel in, Popo. I'll come to dress directly. *(POPO exits.)* *(To Vuval)* Write that letter now, and bring it back and leave it. It must be signed tonight.

VUVAL: *(With a note of contempt)* All right, I will.

(MARTEL enters, very bent and old, but impressive in his simple robes of Court)

MARTEL: Jean Jacques, you must be tired. You've been at this all day.

DESSALINES: *(As VUVAL exits)* If only we had people who would help, Martel. It seems nobody cares. Nobody wants to work.

MARTEL: That's our problem, son. *(Gently)* But do you think it's all the people's fault? When we was slaves, lots of us thought if we was free, we'd never have to work again. And now it seems there's need of harder work than ever. The peasants wonder why.

DESSALINES: You and me work night and day, work hard. But what comes of it? It's every arm in Haiti we need. *(Wistfully)* I have a dream for Haiti, Martel. I mean to see it true. That's why I made a law that all of us must work all day, and those who own land pay a tax that Haiti may have roads, and docks and harbors fine as any country in the world. The peasants do not understand. They think I'd make them slaves again. And those to whom *I* gave the land, they call me tyrant now. *(Puzzled)* How would they have me build, how dam the rivers, how make factories—

MARTEL: Some have no vision, son.

DESSALINES: No use to talk, I've talked till I'm hoarse, talked every-where. I've told them of this Haiti I would make—where every black man lifts his head in pride, where there'll be schools and palaces, big armies and a fleet of boats, forts strong enough to keep the French forever from our shores. *(Confidently)* But I'm their Liberator. The peasants know that. They know 'twas Dessalines alone that drove the whites away.

MARTEL: But there are still whites in the world, Jean Jacques. And we have need of them, as they once needed us. You've often heard me say, it's time to stop turning our guns against them now.

DESSALINES: Why?

MARTEL: We're free. Let's act like free men, ready to meet others as equals—and no longer speak of *all* white men as enemies. *(Sitting down)* Our ports are open now, to English traders. In time, we'll open to the French. The world will drink our coffee. From them we'll buy things in return. We'll need the French.

DESSALINES: The French? The French! I never want to hear that word again, Martel. *(Slowly)* Even now, although I'm Emperor, my back still aches from the blows they've laid upon it.

MARTEL: I know. All my years, before our freedom, I, too, never saw the sun rise but to curse it, but now free men can dream a bigger dream than mere revenge.

DESSALINES: What dream, Martel?

MARTEL: A dream of an island where not only blacks are free, but every man who comes to Haitian shores. Jean Jacques, I'm an old man. But in my old age, I dream of a world where no man hurts another. Where *all* know freedom, and black and white alike will share this earth in peace. Of such, I dream, Jean Jacques.

DESSALINES: Too big a dream, Martel. If I could make Haiti a land where *black* men live in peace, I'd be content.

(A light knock at the door and a woman's silvery voice calling:)

CLAIRE: *(Outside)* Jean Jacques, may I come in?

(Without waiting for an answer, CLAIRE HEUREUSE, consort of the Emperor, enters, arrayed in white, ready for the banquet.

She is a lovely mulatto with long black hair. DESSALINES rises, smiling)

DESSALINES: Claire Heureuse! Come in!

(She runs to him and kisses him lightly)

CLAIRE: Don't you ever get through work, you two? It's time to play. Hurry, Jean Jacques, get dressed to receive your guests. Father Martel, it's a gorgeous evening. You ought to be in the garden. The sunset is like gold. *(Glancing at the table full of papers)* It's hot and musty in here. I'm going to run out, Jean Jacques, and get a flower for my hair. On the way, I'll stop by the banquet terrace and see if our stupid servants overlooked anything. Hurry, darling, and put on your crown.

(She pats him on the cheek as if he were a child, then turns and exits, laughing)

DESSALINES: Claire, my dear, take care you don't catch cold!

CLAIRE: *(Calling back)* Oh, how funny! As hot as it is tonight.

MARTEL: *(As the door closes)* The Empress is very beautiful, Jean Jacques.

DESSALINES: Beautiful, yes. More beautiful than any woman I have ever had.

MARTEL: The others were slave women. *(Coughing)* They told you, I suppose, in the Lord Treasurer's Office, that Azelia would not accept the pension you bestowed upon her?

DESSALINES: *(As if remembering)* Azelia? Oh, yes! My first wife. They told me so, Martel. Poor, stupid woman! She was good . . . . but . . . well, you know! That was before I was an Emperor. *(Defensively)* How could I have an empress that can't read or write?

MARTEL: The Emperor himself . . . .

DESSALINES: *(Good humoredly)* Can at least sign his name! Vuval has taught me that. But where is Azelia? I loved her—once. *(Musingly)* And I remember how she stood by me in those years of battle— nursed my wounds and washed my clothes! Where is she?

MARTEL: They say she's a vendor of fruit in a village on the coast . . . .

DESSALINES: She could have had a job here at Court. At least a servant . . . .

MARTEL: My son!

DESSALINES: Or maybe, Mistress of the Linens. I wonder why she wouldn't take the pension?

MARTEL: They say she makes her own living—although a poor one— and that she looks much older than she really is.

DESSALINES: Well . . . . . *(Then hesitating, as if loath to say more)* Come Martel, let's go. The day's been long and hard. I'm tired.

MARTEL: *(Rising)* Tomorrow, son, you must take up that matter of the officers wanting a raise in pay.

DESSALINES: Yes, yes—

MARTEL: And you know there's been no word from General Gerin of late, nor Yayou, either?

DESSALINES: Angry, perhaps? I refused to grant them money from the government to go upon a journey.

MARTEL: Gerin's a dangerous man, Jean Jacques. He'll bear watching. He's been known to talk against you.

DESSALINES: I have no fear, Martel. I can take my Palace Guard and wipe up the earth with Gerin. More business for tomorrow?

MARTEL: Nothing pressing. *(Smiling)* Except that Congo has petitioned several times to be raised from the title of Baron to that of Count.

DESSALINES: *(As they walk toward the exit)* Damn Congo! He's had all the titles in the book already.

MARTEL: Yes, but he's about to marry Lady Celeste, and he wants to make her a Countess.

DESSALINES: Oh, well, let's make them both Princes and be done with it. Titles are easier to get than money, anyhow.

MARTEL: They're easy enough, but taxing on the brain to think them up.

DESSALINES: The French Napoleon gave himself the name of Emperor. I, too, am Emperor by my own hand. *(He snaps his fingers)* We might as well get a little glory out of life.

MARTEL: It's not wise to want too much.

DESSALINES: Well, I've got what I want. I built this palace and I've bought myself a crown or two. I am the Emperor, and no one can make me a slave again. What was that Toussaint said about *liberty*, before he left us? How was that, now, Martel?

MARTEL: Toussaint said, "You can lay low the tree of liberty, but it'll shoot forth again from the roots."

DESSALINES: And he was right! Napoleon thought if he imprisoned one of our leaders, there'd be no other. But when Toussaint went down as Governor-General of Haiti, I came up. *(Proudly)* I've created the first black Empire in the world, so why shouldn't I glory in it, Martel? I'm a king! I'm on top! I'm the glory of Haiti!

MARTEL: The glory of Haiti lies in no one man, Jean Jacques.

DESSALINES: Where does it lie?

MARTEL: In the people's love for freedom.

DESSALINES: Too much freedom—if they no longer obey me, their liberator. I'm their freedom—and this Court's their glory.

MARTEL: Glory is a passing thing, Jean Jacques! Take care!

DESSALINES: *(Laughing)* This sword takes care of me, Martel. I still can use it!

MARTEL: Swords won't solve all problems, my son.

DESSALINES: No, but they solve a-plenty. Come on, let's dress for the banquet. *(He takes the old man's arm as they exit.*

(VUVAL enters, followed by STENIO, approaching the table with a sheaf of papers. VUVAL addresses his friend)

VUVAL: If the Emperor could read, he'd never sign most of the letters I write for him.

STENIO: *(Laughing)* A dumb clown! He thinks by letting Claire Heureuse read them over for him, he's safe, not knowing she was on our side before she ever met "His Majesty."

VUVAL: A true mulatto, Claire.

STENIO: That's why we brought her back from Paris. I knew he'd fall for her. A mulatto Empress in a black Empire! That's enough to make him the laughing stock of the peasantry.

VUVAL: The fool!

STENIO: His Majesty's head is rather thick.

VUVAL: But not too thick to be broken. If he knew six garrisons in the South revolted against him this morning, he wouldn't sit so pompously beneath his crown tonight.

STENIO: You've had word from Gerin?

VUVAL: Yes, and from General Yayou, too, Port-au-Prince has gone over to the rebels. The mulattoes are in full charge.

STENIO: An end of this black rule at last! Maybe now I can get off to Paris again.

VUVAL: Paris! *La Ville Lumiere!* Oh, how I long to see that city of lights, Stenio. It's so damn dark here.

STENIO: In more ways than one, Vuval.

VUVAL: But it won't be long now until I'm out of Haiti. Tonight, we'll flee the Court, while His Majesty wears his crown and stuffs himself with food.

STENIO: Good! As for me, that's not soon enough. What are your plans for Claire?

VUVAL: She's coming by carriage tomorrow. Her jewels are packed except for a few cheap baubles she'll wear tonight. But it's a ten-hour ride to the coast after dark. You'd better order your men ready to start at once, Stenio. And you, too, go ahead. I'll catch you. I've a splendid horse.

STENIO: Do you suppose the Black Napoleon will miss me from his banquet table? If not, I'll order the Guard away shortly.

VUVAL: I'll say you're ill of fever, if he asks.

STENIO: Yes, the fever of being bored.

> (*POPO enters. The mulattoes look startled. The negro stops near the door on seeing them*)

POPO: The Emperor sent me for his letters.

VUVAL: (*Pushing them across the table*) There they are. I wish the Emperor would learn to write.

POPO: (*Seriously*) He will, some day.

VUVAL: (*Sarcastically*) Perhaps you, too, "Count" Popo.

STENIO: (*Lightly*) Don't be absurd, Vuval. Such poetic fancies on your part! My! My! Come, let's drink a bit of champagne in the garden.

> (*VUVAL and STENIO exit, leaving POPO with the letters in his hands. Slowly and bitterly, POPO begins to tear the letters into bits as his eyes follow the two mulattoes*)

CURTAIN

Act II, Scene 2

A terrace.

TIME: *Immediately following Scene 1.*

> *A covered terrace, consisting of two levels, whose arched portals are open to the sky. It is early evening. The air is still rosy with sunset. On the upper level, a raised banquet table stretches across the width of the entire terrace, its white linen cloths falling to the floor. At either side, steps to the table. The terrace is not yet lighted, but on the table in silhouette against the evening sky may be seen tall silver candle sticks and great bowls of fruit, pineapples, mangoes, grapes, cocoanuts, bananas, pomegranates, plums. There are goblets for wine; and china, crystal, and silver.*

AT RISE: *SERVANTS move about arranging the table, and two OLD WOMEN in front of the table on the floor level are preparing flowers, putting the fruit into bowls, polishing silver.*

FIRST OLD WOMAN: It's getting mighty dark here. How come we can't have no light to work by?

SECOND OLD WOMAN: You know the Emperor don't believe in wasting candles. He don't believe in wasting nothing.

FIRST OLD WOMAN: Tight-fisted, if you ask me! If I had all the money he's got, I'd fling gold to winds every time I kicked up my heels.

SECOND OLD WOMAN: At your age, still talking about kicking up your heels!

FIRST OLD WOMAN: Huh! I might be old, but my heart ain't got no wrinkles.

SECOND OLD WOMAN: Well, I hope the day'll come when we all can have a good time, and nothing else. Look like I work as hard now that I'm free as I did before.

FIRST OLD WOMAN: Well, the Emperor says he want to make Haiti rich—and just as grand as when it belonged to the white folks.

SECOND OLD WOMAN: Huh! Only thing grand I see around here is that hussy of a new wife he's got and all them diamonds she's a-wearing.

FIRST OLD WOMAN: Shsss! you better stop talking that a-way about the Empress. Lady Celeste'll hear you and out you'll go.

SECOND OLD WOMAN: Lady my eye! Housekeeper, that's what Celeste is!

FIRST OLD WOMAN: Anyhow, Baron Congo's crazy about her. They about to get married.

SECOND OLD WOMAN: Congo's a baron, and she's a Lady. If he marry her, what title do that give 'em both?

FIRST OLD WOMAN: What you mean, 'em both? Celeste gonna run him just like she do everything else, and he'll be a Mr. Lady Baron, that's what! *(Getting to work)* Hush, here she comes!
   (Enter CELESTE)

CELESTE: Hurry up, you servants, and put the flowers on the table. We've got to clear things up now. The guests'll soon be arriving.

FIRST OLD WOMAN: We's hurrying.

SECOND OLD WOMAN: We sure are.

CELESTE: *(Calling)* Lady Lulu! Oh, Lady Lulu! *(To the Servants)* Have any of you-all seen the High Grand Keeper of the Linens? There's no napkins on this table yet.

SERVANT: *(Behind table)* Here she comes, now.
   (Enter LULU, well-gowned, carrying a pile of napkins)

LULU: I'll have you know, Lady Celeste, that you don't need to yell for me like as if I were a dog.

CELESTE: Why, Lady Lulu, I weren't yelling, were I?

LULU: *(Still peeved)* Well, even if you is engaged to a Baron, I don't have to stand it. My son's a Grand Alimony, hisself.

CELESTE: What's that, Lulu? I didn't know Pierre were anything but the Chief Bugle-Blower. I remember, he always wanted a bugle when he were a little slave.

LULU: *(Placing the napkins)* Don't bring up them distasteful epochs, Celeste.

CELESTE: Well, we was slaves, once, wasn't we, Lulu?

LULU: And still half-is! I'm gonna give that Jean Jacques a piece of my mind soon, tired as I is o' working in this palace. I want to take myself a trip to Port-au-Prince and look up a new husband!

CELESTE: A husband?

LULU: Yes, a new husband! These men around here's too banana-bellied to suit my taste.

CELESTE: I bet you're sorry you ain't got a man like Congo. He's all right.

LULU: Huh! I could've had Congo long ago, if I'd a-wanted him.

CELESTE: *(Angered)* Lulu, I'll turn that table over getting to you if you don't hush. You know Congo's never even looked at you!

LULU: *(Starting around the table)* Just hold your horses, *Lady* Celeste, till I get down to your level.

FIRST OLD WOMAN: *(Warningly)* You better shsss! Here comes the Empress.

CELESTE: *(Flustered)* Oh! If you're through your work, you-all just gather up your things and get out of the way. The Empress wants to inspect the table, I guess.

> *(CLAIRE enters, accompanied by VUVAL. The servants exit gradually, scowling. LULU follows them)*

CLAIRE: This really is a charming terrace, isn't it, Vuval? Such a lush background? Those palm trees and the early evening stars! *(Looking around)* But why must these serving women be forever getting things ready? Lady Celeste, you! *(CELESTE jumps)* Can't you manage to prepare a banquet table in less than a week?

CELESTE: I - I - I - started this morning, Empress.

CLAIRE: *(Sighing)* Oh, well! I suppose I must remember I'm not in Paris where service is an art. *(Dismissing her)* Go on, Celeste, I'll look about alone.

(Exit CELESTE)

VUVAL: I can hardly wait to see Paris with you, Claire. You've been there so often and know it so well. You can show me everything—the Louvre, the Bois, the Odeon—all the places the great writers write about.

CLAIRE: Of course.

VUVAL: Do you suppose I'll ever be a great writer, Claire?

CLAIRE: *(Lightly)* If you write enough letters for the Emperor, you might perhaps develop.

VUVAL: Don't joke about it, Claire. It's too near my heart. *(Passionately)* Darling, there're just two things I want—you, and to write poems as beautiful as Andre Chenier's.

CLAIRE: You have me, dear. Only don't put your hands on my white gown. They may have ink on them. And I have to look nice tonight—for this—am I safe in saying—the last supper at this stupid Palace.

VUVAL: No doubt our last, Claire—for the mulattoes have taken over Port-au-Prince, and Gerin the forts to the North! And listen! Should a messenger arrive with news of the uprising for the Emperor, I have given orders to intercept it. Let Dessalines eat, drink and be merry once without being bothered. In the meantime, Stenio can reach the coast.

CLAIRE: Has he gone?

VUVAL: Yes, he's well-started. And while you entertain your royal husband at the table, I'll slip away from the banquet early and get off, too. On the way, I'll persuade the garrison commanders to side with us. That ought to be easy, for I've been writing the officers vulgar letters lately, calling them all sorts of names, as you know, and the Emperor in his ignorance has signed them—thinking they're what he's dictated.

CLAIRE: Clever, Vuval.

VUVAL: Now the generals think Dessalines has turned against them. No wonder they're revolting.

CLAIRE: No wonder!

VUVAL: Whereas, on the other hand, the peasants are sure they are going to starve if they don't get a change of government. *(Pleased)* You see, darling, everything's all set. And early tomorrow, you'll come on to the coast with your attendants. We'll have a boat waiting. It's perfectly planned.

CLAIRE: Most cleverly arranged, Vuval. I didn't know you were such a strategist.

VUVAL: Will you be glad to get away from Haiti, darling?

CLAIRE: Will I be glad? I hate these ignorant people and their drums. I can't stand those drums every night, beating, beating, back there in the hills.

VUVAL: And Jean Jacques?

CLAIRE: That fool, my husband? Vuval, darling, often I can't bear to look at him. He's so common and so—so boorish! And his back! *(With a little cry)* I cannot bear to touch his back! It's all covered with welts! Ugh! Marks of a rebellious slave! And yet he thinks I love him! Bah!

VUVAL: You've played your part well, Claire.

CLAIRE: I had to. My people were ruined, as were yours. We had to get back our land, and our money. Now, my brother's put away a half-million francs in a Bordeaux bank.

VUVAL: As have my cousin, Beyard, and I.

CLAIRE: We'll be safe now, you and I—married in Paris. So you see why I've played my part well! *(Laughing)* I've always wanted to be an actress, anyway. Perhaps to be Juliet.

VUVAL: And I your Romeo! Sweet Claire! *(Remembering something)* But, say, darling, look! With all I've had to do today, I still found time to compose a poem for you.

CLAIRE: Oh, read it to me.

VUVAL: *(Taking a manuscript from his pocket)* Here it is! Listen! *(Reading:)*

TO THE VENUS OF THE ANTILLES, CLAIRE HEUREUSE

    Your eyes are twin stars
    In a snow-white face,
    Your lips are two rubies
    Loveliness has traced,
    Your body a flower
    Of marble grace—
    Oh, Venus strayed
    Into a savage place!
    Do you like it, Claire?

CLAIRE: *(Laughing)* I like that part about the "savage place." But it's so short! Is that all you could think to say about me, Vuval?

VUVAL: Claire, darling! No pen could write all the lovely things I think of you.

CLAIRE: Dear boy! Give me the poem to keep.

VUVAL: Of course! *(Handing her the manuscript)* And my heart as well!

CLAIRE: Someone's coming! *(Voices are heard approaching)* Let us go into the garden a moment, where we can be alone. I've still to get a flower for my hair, my sweet.

> *(Exit CLAIRE and VUVAL, as MARTEL and POPO enter from the other side)*

MARTEL: In times like these, if Toussaint l'Ouverture were only here to guide us, Popo! Napoleon's heart must be like stone to trick so great a leader away from his people.

POPO: I wish Toussaint was here. It looks like Jean Jacques don't know how to run things very well. I wish I could help him.

MARTEL: Jean Jacques is a mighty soldier, Popo, and a brave man. He's not a statesman. But he's our friend, and we love him—so we must help him.

POPO: We must, Father Martel.

MARTEL: As you protect his body, I'll try to guard his mind. *(Despairingly)* But sometimes I don't know, Popo, I don't know. *(Looking upward through the open portals)* Haiti, land that should be so happy, grown instead so sad! Land of golden moonlight and silver rain, bright birds, and brighter sun, perfumed breezes and a sea so green, hills of great woods and valleys of sweet earth. Why can't it be a happy land? So many years of struggle, and still vile intrigue binds our wings like spider webs. Oh, most unhappy Haiti! When the drums beat in the hills at night, mournful and heart-breaking, I can feel your sorrow. No wonder the Empress hates your drums! Where is their power now to make the gods smile upon this troubled island?

POPO: Don't you think, Father Martel, Jean Jacques ought to let the Papaloi come back into Court?

MARTEL: Jean Jacques doesn't believe in voodoo, son. You know that.

POPO: I know, but our people do—and we can't change them overnight. Now, the voodoo doctors are mumbling against the Emperor and stirring up the peasants.

MARTEL: And the mulattoes are angry because he has designated Haiti officially as the *Black* Empire. They don't like the word *Black*.

POPO: Their mothers were black.

MARTEL: Yes, it's true! Still, they stand apart and claim their white blood makes them better. But what troubles me most, Popo, is why there's been no news from the coast of late. Two days ago,

I sent Xavier to see what's happening. He's due back, but he hasn't come.

POPO: Do you think something's happened to Xavier?

MARTEL: I don't know. Be alert, son. All's not well, though it would seem so here at the Palace. *(In a lighter tone)* But come now! Let's look carefully at the table to see if it's properly set. The Emperor is most particular about these occasions of state. And this one must be perfect—for tomorrow I shall warn him that with the treasury in this present state, the Court cannot often afford such lavishness.

POPO: Even if we go back to eating dried fish and yams, I'll stick by him. Jean Jacques has been a friend of mine ever since we were slaves together.

> *(Enter CELESTE and CONGO. CONGO is carrying a huge pot of flowers)*

CELESTE: Put it down right there in the center, so's the air'll smell sweet.

CONGO: *(Grunting as he stoops)* Huh!

CELESTE: And stop grunting! What'd you come up here mooning at me for, anyhow, in my busiest hours?

CONGO: *(Standing up, resplendent in a nile-green uniform with golden tassels on the shoulders)* I come to show you my new suit, Celeste. This here makes twelve brand new uniforms I bought. How do you like it?

CELESTE: *(Critically)* I'd like it better if it had more gold on it. *(Approaching Martel and Popo)* Good evening, Father Martel. How are you tonight?

MARTEL: Only fair, daughter, only fair.

CELESTE: I hope you got over that little spell of indigestion yesterday so's you can eat this evening well. This is gonna *be* a banquet. And no fooling! We got a dozen roast sheep out there in the ovens, sweet as butter. I wish you could smell 'em.

CONGO: *(Loosening a buckle)* Um-hum! Lemme loosen up this belt.

> *(MARTEL and POPO laugh as they exit)*

CELESTE: Lemme go get dressed, as befits a Lady. All them Duchesses are gonna be here tonight, so I wants to look grand, too. Come on, Baron.

CONGO: Gimme a little kiss first.

CELESTE: Can't you wait till we get married?

CONGO: Not for just a kiss.

CELESTE: *(Kissing him)* Here!

CONGO: It tastes sweeter'n a honey bee.

CELESTE: *(As she starts off)* Wait till you feel the stinger!

CONGO: *(Running after her)* Um-huh! Gimme another one.

CELESTE: Come on, man! The guests are arriving. And the orchestra's playing in the throne room. I want to see the excitement. Besides, I'm saving up one for you tonight—if you're around to get it.

> *(CELESTE exits as the TWO OLD WOMEN and other servants enter)*

CONGO: Aw, come back here and gimme a double kiss now.

CELESTE: *(Calling off-stage)* By and by, baby, by and by.

> *(CONGO exits)*

FIRST OLD WOMAN: The Throne Room's just full o' high falutin' hens and prancin' cocks a-cacklin' and crowin' all over the place.

SECOND OLD WOMAN: *(As she lights candles)* Some of 'em's gonna crow their last in a little while, too. Folks is gettin' tired o' seeing some people have everything and the rest of us workin' like dogs. I don't know what the Emperor's thinking about. Why ain't he gived me no velvet dress? I'm human!

FIRST OLD WOMAN: I reckon we can't all be Duchesses, and such.

SECOND OLD WOMAN: Well, if we can't be Duchesses, we at least ought to be let alone to dance obeah if we wants to, and have our voodoo here in the Court. Legba's gonna curse Dessalines yet, you watch.

FIRST OLD WOMAN: That hussy of a Claire Heureuse went and brought a Catholic priest over from France for herself—and a French one at that.

SECOND OLD WOMAN: Voodoo was good enough for her mamma. It ought to do for her.

> *(Softly, in the distance, the music of an orchestra playing European airs is heard)*

FIRST OLD WOMAN: Lawsy! We better hurry up. They done opened the big doors! I reckon the procession's forming to march to the tables. *(To a ragged boy)* Boy, scramble up there and light that big oil lamp, over His Majesty's head. He likes plenty light.

> *(The BOY lights the hanging lantern, and the terrace is flooded with golden light. Noise and music afar—then a bugle call in the distance. The OLD WOMEN leave, as THREE BUTLERS, in livery, enter and take places, one at each end of the table near the head of the steps, the other behind the tall chair reserved for the Emperor. On the lower terrace, a FLOWER GIRL enters scattering*

rose leaves. There is a roll of drums; PIERRE, a big boy now, and Chief Bugler, enters, crosses the stage, turns with military precision and blows a blast on his horn. The orchestra begins a march.

(JOSEF, the Grand Marshal of the Palace, takes his place at the far end of the table. With a long parchment list in hand, he announces, in a loud voice:)

JOSEF: Hear ye! Hear ye! Hear ye! The Guests of the Emperor bidden to a Banquet of State in honor of His Majesty. *(The band continues, and GRAND MARSHAL reads from his list, and in the order named, the guests enter from the lower terrace, strutting grandly across it to stand in front of the table, waiting there before mounting the steps until the EMPEROR himself arrives. Their costumes are gorgeously grotesque copies of various European Court styles and periods, but giving in the ensemble an effect of gay and savage splendor. Some of the guests are enjoying themselves immensely, but others are obviously uncomfortable in their regal clothes, while many are gnarled old peasants, too bent by slavery to ever appear at ease in Parisian finery. JOSEF reads, and in the order called, marching gaily to the music, the Royalty of Haiti enter)*

The Duke and Duchess of Dondon.

Count and Countess Claudel de Zouba.

General Abelard and Madame La Pompeuse.

Lord and Lady Tountemonde.

Baron Antoine and the Baroness Antoine.

The Duke of Marmelade and Countess Louise Camille Chaucune Nereide.

The Chevalier of Gonaives and the Chevalieress.

The Governor of Milot, Sir Emil Tuce with Madame the Duchess of Limonade.

Major General Joli-Bois and Lady Fify Beauregard.

The Most High Grand Keeper of Records and Seals, Count Vuval.

Major General Dembu and Lady Lulu Minette.

The Duke de Savanne-a-Roches and Duchess Coloma Lutetia Floreal.

Grand Duke Mars and Princess Dianne.

Baron Congo with Lady Celeste.

The Grand Chief Treasurer of the Realm, His Highness Lord Bobo Levy.

Duchess Suzanne Roseide and her husband.

(As the last couple enter the terrace and line up before the table, the music ceases.

(There is a moment of silence, giggling, and whispering. Several late arrivals sneak in, unannounced)

LORD BOBO: *(Sneezing)* A-choo!

LULU: Your Highness, Lord Bobo, why don't you use better snuff?

BOBO: It ain't my snuff, Lady Lulu. It's that loud perfume some of you-all ladies uses, done got in my nostrils.

DUKE MARMELADE: This collar's mighty near choking me to death!

COUNTESS NEREIDE: But it looks gorgeous, Duke.

DUCHESS OF LIMONADE: Lawd! *(Picking up her feet in pain)* I'm sure gonna take off these shoes soon as I get myself back home. They ain't my size.

COUNT CLAUDEL: I'm tired of this business, coming here all dressed up every time I turn around.

CELESTE: Shsss! Stop all that giggling and talking! You know the Emperor likes silence when he enters.

LORD BOBO: *(After a moment of stillness)* A-choo!

(Loud giggling from the women)

BARON ANTOINE: That were sure good wine they just passed out in the throne room, huh, Baroness?

BARONESS ANTOINE: It were champagne—but I wants to *eat,* now.

GRAND DUKE MARS: That'll be some time off yet, Baroness. The Emperor serves in courses.

PRINCESS DIANNE: A little bit at a time.

CELESTE: First course is always just tid-bits to give you an appetite.

DUCHESS SUZANNE: I got a appetite already!

CONGO: I wants to taste that roast goat.

LADY FIFI: Me, too, Baron.

(The LADY IN WAITING to the Empress enters on the upper terrace and proceeds to arrange Her Majesty's seat.

(The BUGLE BOY blows a mighty blast as the drums roll)

JOSEF: The Court arrives! *(Another roll of the drums)* His Majesty, the Emperor, First Liberator of the Blacks and Chief Ruler of Haiti, Jean Jacques Dessalines.

(Preceded by TWO PAGES, DESSALINES enters on the upper terrace and strides to his chair. He is followed by MARTEL in his robes of state, and by POPO carrying the royal scepter. Immediately behind comes the EMPRESS CLAIRE HEUREUSE, accompanied

*by the LADIES OF THE PRESENCE. All the guests turn and bow
low as they enter. The EMPEROR and EMPRESS take their seats.
An ATTENDANT offers the EMPEROR his crown on a silken
cushion; POPO presents the royal scepter. A great cheer arises)*

VOICES:

Hail the Emperor!

Hail Dessalines!

Hail! Hail! Hail!

*(The cymbals clash and the drums roll. The band strikes up a lively
march. The guests file around both ends of the table to their respective seats. At a trumpet blast from PIERRE, they sit down simul-
taneously, a glittering row of velvet busts and dark, genial faces
behind the banquet table with its crystal and silver)*

LULU: *(Proudly, to Congo)* That's my son blowing that bugle! You hear
him?

CELESTE: Honey, your son ought to learn a new tune! That one hurts
my ears.

*(As the BUTLERS pass, filling the glasses, the orchestra begins to
play a syncopated melody, and a dozen DANCING GIRLS whirl
across the lower terrace into the empty space before the table. They
are wearing anklets of beaten gold; their bushy hair is adorned with
precious stones. As they dance before the Court, a weird drum beat
becomes audible in the music, gradually louder and more insistent,
until finally it drowns out all the other instruments. To the African
rhythm of drums alone, a MALE DANCER enters, feathered and
painted like a voodoo god. The GIRLS sink to the floor as the tall,
god-like one does his dance of the jungle, fierce, provocative, and
terrible.*

*(Suddenly, the EMPRESS turns her head, and covers her ears with
her hands. She calls to Dessalines:)*

CLAIRE: *(Appealingly)* Jean Jacques! Jean Jacques!

(DESSALINES rises, raising his hand in command)

DESSALINES: *(Loudly)* Stop it! Stop! The Empress don't like drums!
Stop it, I say! *(The music ceases—but no sooner than the drums on the
terrace are silent than another drum, far off in the hills, carries on
their beat. DESSALINES cries frantically)* Stop them drums, I say.
Stop them!

POPO: They are stopped, sire. That drum we hear now's away off in the
hills someplace.

DESSALINES: I don't care where it is! Order it stopped! My Empress don't like drums! Vuval!

VUVAL: *(Rising)* I will send someone to see can it be located.
> *(He leaves the table and confers with one of the ATTENDANTS. The ATTENDANT exits. But the drum is never silent during the rest of the scene. Its monotonous beat continues, as if calling for one knows not what)*

DESSALINES: *(Who has remained standing, begins to berate his guests)* Drums in the Court! The idea! Suppose we had guests from abroad, what would they think of us? They'd think we were all savages, that's what. Savages! Here I am, trying to build a civilization in Haiti good as any the whites have in their lands. Trying to set up a Court equal to any Court in Europe. And what do I find—voodoo drums in the banquet hall! Who gave orders for that? *(Ominously)* Whoever did, will suffer. I'll find out tomorrow. We ought to be done with voodoo drums—all of us! But listen! *(He pauses as the distant drum continues its throbbing beat)* The peasants, up all night playing drums! And the fields only half productive. But not only the peasants are to blame. You Lords and Ladies, Dukes and Counts are to blame, too. I give you land, and you neglect to work it. Then when crops are scanty, you try to bully your taxes out of the people, taking back their hard earned money to pay me what the Treasury demands. But that's not what I want. And you're not helping Haiti. The land must produce its own riches. Our peasants must work the land, and make it fertile. Being free frees no man from working. We *do* have to work. And I'm tired of telling you! I'm tired of sending out orders! I've made up my mind to tell my soldiers to *make* you work from now on!

VOICES:
> What?
>
> Do you hear that!
>
> Huh! I'm no slave!

DESSALINES: *(Thunderously. Drum stops)* Silence! Listen to me! We've fought to make Haiti free! I'm going to keep you free—the French'll never return. I'm going to make a great country, trading with all the world—wealthy, and full of plenty to eat. You're going to help me. *(Pausing)* Long ago I dreamed a dream that I want to carry through. If you won't help me willingly—then I'll make you. I'm the Emperor! Your Liberator! Jean Jacques Dessalines, who came up from a slave hut to a Palace, to a crown on my head and an ermine cape covering my scars, to this jeweled scepter in my hand. I did it by fighting. The whites called me The Tiger! *(Fiercely)* If I have to be a tiger to you, too—I will be! *(Pausing—then lifting his glass)* Drink to your Emperor! *(Bellowing an imperious command)* Drink!

(The frightened guests leap to their feet, raising their glasses in trembling hands)

VOICES: *(As they drink)* To the Emperor!

DESSALINES: *(Calmly)* Now, let there be music and dancing—violins, not drums! *(The orchestra plays a minuet as DESSALINES resumes his seat. The guests come down from the table and begin to dance with knees still shaking. They are awkward at the minuet, some pitifully grotesque in their attempts at European graces. Some few of the older folks remain in their places at the table. VUVAL disappears. Gradually the DANCERS dance off-stage out of sight at either end of the terrace as the EMPEROR talks with the EMPRESS)* Claire, darling, don't you like the wine? And this caviar? I ordered it all the way from Russia especially for you.

CLAIRE: I like you better than wine, Jean Jacques! You're so strong, so wonderful and wise.

DESSALINES: Maybe not so wise. *(Boastfully)* But nobody'll get the best of me fighting.

CLAIRE: I'm sure they won't, dear.

DESSALINES: Why, Napoleon ordered me shot once—all the way from France—but I'm not dead yet! *(He laughs)*

CLAIRE: Not at all, darling.

DESSALINES: But plenty of Napoleon's soldiers are buried right here on Haitian soil, defeated by my troops. Bonaparte rules France—but I rule Haiti!

CLAIRE: And nobly!

DESSALINES: Oh, I know I'm nothing much but a fighter, Claire. *(Determinedly)* But if fighting's the only way to get things done— then I'll get 'em done!

CLAIRE: You've accomplished such a lot already, dear! And with what ignorant people! Every jewel in that crown's a testimony to your greatness. Why, your scepter holds a realm of power. *(She rubs her fingers over the scepter, purposely touching his hand)* What beautiful rings you have on your fingers tonight, darling. Some of them I've never seen before. That emerald! *(Lifting his hand)* Oh, how lovely! Why, it's green as the sea at dawn! Please, let me try it on.

DESSALINES: *(Taking off his huge emerald and slipping it on her finger)* It's too big for you, dear.

CLAIRE: Not much. Let me keep it tonight, darling. I won't let it slip off. It's too lovely!

DESSALINES: Women always want to play. *(Rising and offering his arm)* Shall we dance?

CLAIRE: Jean Jacques, you know you haven't learned the minuet. You'll step on my slippers.

DESSALINES: You're right, darling. *(Sitting down again)* I'm clumsy as an ox. Let's just sit here and drink our wine. *(A clatter of horses' hoofs is heard outside)* What's that? Who could that be riding into the courtyard at this time of night? Popo, go see!

> *(POPO exits. MARTEL rises and looks over the edge of the terrace. The distant drum is ever louder in the darkness.*
> *(CLAIRE toys nervously with the emerald on her finger)*

CLAIRE: Perhaps it's some distant guest arriving tardily.

DESSALINES: I hope it's nobody bringing a message. I've had enough to worry my head today. Now, I just want to enjoy you tonight, and this wine, and the cool breeze. I'm tired, honey.

CLAIRE: *(As loud VOICES are heard without)* Don't worry with anything more this evening, darling, please. Refuse to receive whatever it is.

DESSALINES: I hope I can, but it may be something pressing. *(As POPO enters hurriedly)* What is it, Popo? What? *(POPO, his eyes bulging, whispers to the Emperor. DESSALINES leaps up so quickly he overturns his wine, it runs like blood across the banquet cloth)* Order my horse! Bring him to the terrace. Tell Stenio to report to me at once with my garrison ready to march. *(POPO exits, as DESSALINES addresses the Treasurer, LORD BOBO, who sits nearby)* Lord Bobo, are your vaults locked?

LORD BOBO: Of course, Your Majesty!

DESSALINES: Then give me the keys to the gold.

LORD BOBO: *(Rising, trembling)* Of course, Your Majesty. But, but, but— *(He gives Dessalines a huge key fastened to his belt)*

DESSALINES: Martel, remain here! Continue the banquet. I'm going to the coast.

MARTEL: But what is it, Jean Jacques? What's happened?

DESSALINES: Word from Archaie that the peasants have revolted. They're burning the crops, and Yayou's soldiers have joined them. That mulatto Gerin's at the bottom of this. But I'll stop it. Every man will return to his post, or I'll wipe them off the face of the earth!

MARTEL: Take care, son, take care!

> *(The remaining guests quickly leave the table and exit hurriedly. Sounds of departing carriages without. The servants, too, have disappeared. Only PIERRE, the bugler, remains)*

POPO: *(Returning)* Your horse is ready, sire, and mine.

PIERRE: *(Approaching)* Emperor, I ride with you, too.

DESSALINES: You'll have to ride fast, Pierre. *(To POPO)* Here, take the scepter, and my crown. Bring me my sword. Is the guard forming?

POPO: General Stenio is missing, sire! And the guards are gone.

DESSALINES: *(Roaring)* What?

POPO: Stenio left word that he precedes you to the Port. Vuval's gone, too.

DESSALINES: The insubordinate rascals! Who gave orders for them to leave? I'll bring them back in chains! Quick! My sword! *(POPO exits. DESSALINES hangs his ermine cape on the back of a chair. CLAIRE takes it. He addresses MARTEL)* Martel, the Tiger rides again.

MARTEL: Would it not be wise, Jean Jacques, to send some trusted friend ahead to see what conditions are? And would it not be best to pick your soldiers carefully for such a trip?

DESSALINES: No soldier can ride as fast as me, Martel. Besides, I'm commander of all the troops in Haiti, and if any have been misled by their rascally commanders, they've but to hear my voice to call me Chief again. I'm going directly to the headquarters of Gerin and take charge. Then I'll subdue the peasants enough. *(To his wife)* Claire, go to your rooms. I'll be back within a day, no doubt. Or certainly by the second dawn.

CLAIRE: *(With a peculiar intonation)* Good luck, Your Majesty. And goodbye.

DESSALINES: Not goodbye, darling. Merely goodnight. *(He kisses her. She draws back slightly. As she exits, she wipes his kiss away. DESSALINES address MARTEL:)* An Emperor has his troubles, too, same as a slave.

MARTEL: It's not wise to ever be a master, Jean Jacques.

DESSALINES: What do you mean, Martel? A master?

MARTEL: It is not wise.

POPO: *(Entering)* Here, sire, is you hat! Your sword!

DESSALINES: *(Putting on a plumed helmet and fastening his sword at his belt)* Somebody's got to govern, Martel. The peasants can't rule themselves.

MARTEL: Some day they can, son.

DESSALINES: Until that day comes, them, I'll be their ruler. The French used a whip! *(Brandishing his sabre)* I use a sword!

(Exit DESSALINES, POPO and PIERRE)

MARTEL: *(Looking after them)* Take care! Take care, Jean Jacques! *(He peers over the terrace as the clatter of horses' hoofs dies down the road)* Oh, son, beware! Beware! *(The far-off beating of a voodoo drum fills the silence.*

(The old man stands alone, facing the stars. Behind him is the cluttered banquet table where wine has spilled like blood. Slowly, MARTEL turns and begins to blow out the tapers) We might as well save candles, I reckon.

CURTAIN

Act III

SCENE: *The quay in a little fishing village on the coast.*

TIME: *The following day. Early afternoon.*

> *At Left, the side of a grey stucco building with a sign hanging from the corner: HEADQUARTERS, ROYAL HAITIAN ARMY, Division of the South. On the wall, below, a tattered poster advertising rhum. Rear, the low stone wall of an embankment with steps, center, leading up to a sea-wall, and down on the other side to the beach. Beyond the wall may be seen the tops of sails belonging to fishing boats in the harbor. Hanging from a palm tree, a large fishing net is drying in the sun. At the foot to the wall on the ground, bare-foot MARKET WOMEN have spread their wares in the shade of the embankment; mangoes, melons, yams, oranges, limes, sugarcane, cocoanuts, little piles of red peppers. One VENDOR has thread, thimbles and other trinkets. The WOMEN in bright headcloths, sit with their backs to the wall.*

AT RISE: *The MARKET WOMEN are laughing and chattering among themselves. Some dip snuff. One smokes a pipe.*

MANGO VENDOR: It sho' is a fine day.

PEPPER VENDOR: Yes, indeedy!

COCOANUT VENDOR: I likes weather like this myself.

MELON VENDOR: You can smell the sea when the breeze blow. Don't it smell good?

THREAD VENDOR: Sho' do!

> *(TWO FISHERMEN enter)*

TALL FISHERMAN: Hello, ladies dressed so fine! Who's got a good man on her mind?

MANGO VENDOR: Where's the good man at?

TALL FISHERMAN: Right here! Ain't you got a mango for me?

SHORT FISHERMAN: *(To the WOMEN)* Ask him what he's got for you?

MANGO VENDOR: *(Laughing)* My mangoes are too sweet for men I don't love. *(Holding up a pretty one)* But I'll sell you one for a sou.

TALL FISHERMAN: You'll want one of my fish some of these days. *(Mounting the sea-wall)* My brother's boat's on the horizon now, just loaded down with nice sweet fish.

COCOANUT VENDOR: *(Tossing her head)* You men always think we womens want something you got. We does very well by ourselves.

SHORT FISHERMAN: Until night comes.

THREAD VENDOR: Huh! If it wasn't for us womens, half the time you mens wouldn't eat. Storm comes, you don't catch nary fish, and we have to feed you.

TALL FISHERMAN: We supposed to eat! Ain't we worth our board and keep?

THREAD VENDOR: I gets tired feeding you-all myself. Every time I turn around, looks my husband's asking me for ten sous. Ten sous for this, or for that—tobacco, rum, snuff, always something he wants.

MANGO VENDOR: Wouldn't be a man if he didn't.

THREAD VENDOR: Yes, but I gets tired. It looks like all an apron does is work for pants.

SHORT FISHERMAN: Suppose you didn't have us men to work for, then what'd you do?

THREAD VENDOR: Do without.

SHORT FISHERMAN: *(Strutting)* My woman says she can't do without me.

COCOANUT VENDOR: She must be weak.

MANGO VENDOR: Don't pay no attention to them mens. They's always lying. Here, have a fruit. *(She tosses them each a mango)* And go on, stop pestering us.

TALL FISHERMAN: I'll see you later, sweetheart, when my ship comes in.

MANGO VENDOR: I hope it ain't no row-boat!

SHORT FISHERMAN: If I got any nice sea-crabs clawing around in the bottom of the boat, I'll give 'em to you when I come back.

THREAD VENDOR: I don't like crabs myself. Rather have squibs.

MANGO VENDOR: I'll take the crabs and don't pass me by, neither. I'll be sitting here till sundown.

(The FISHERMEN exit over the sea-wall toward the water)

MELON VENDOR: Sweet mens! I love 'em! Say, who's still got the same husband they had when they was freed?

YAM VENDOR: Lord, chile, I done had me six husbands since then!

MANGO VENDOR: What's the use of being free if you can't change husbands?

PEPPER VENDOR: *(A very old woman)* Well, I's still got the man I always had.

THREAD VENDOR: Aw, Mama Sallie, you know you too old to change.

PEPPER VENDOR: *(Snappily)* I warn't but seventy when the freedom broke out. What's the matter with you?

(Enter TWO CHILDREN, who make a purchase of some sticks of sugar-cane, then exit, sucking the cane)

MANGO VENDOR: A man is like a palm-leaf fan to me. When I feels the need, I picks one up, and when I cools off, I put him down.

YAM VENDOR: And me, too.

COCOANUT VENDOR: Well, it ain't moral, the priest says.

MANGO VENDOR: That's right, Zoune, you belongs to them white folks' church, don't you? How long you been in there?

COCOANUT VENDOR: *(Righteously)* Since before the freedom. My master made all his slaves join the Catholic Church. He said if we didn't, he'd beat the stuffings out of us. I been going to mass mighty near as long as I been colored.

YAM VENDOR: That's been a long time!

THREAD VENDOR: Then how come I seed you at the last voodoo dance, just a-calling on Legba?

COCOANUT VENDOR: Oh, I believes in voodoo, too. Who says I didn't? Might as well believe in all kinds of gods, then if one fails you, you got another one to kinder help out.

MELON VENDOR: Right!

(Enter an OLD WOMAN, bearing a tray of bananas on her head. As she turns around, one recognizes AZELIA)

AZELIA: Bananas! Bananas! Who wants to buy bananas?

THREAD VENDOR: *(As AZELIA stoops wearily and is about to sit down)* Here! You don't pay no taxes for a public stall. Move on!

YAM VENDOR: Yes, sister, move on! We pays to have our market by this wall. General Gerin sends an officer out here to collect every morning of the world.

AZELIA: All right, I'll move on. Maybe I can sell something to the soldiers in the barracks yonder.

COCOANUT VENDOR: Ain't no soldiers. They been gone since sun-up.

YAM VENDOR: Well, go on, anyhow.

(AZELIA tries to lift her basket and fails)

COCOANUT VENDOR: What's the matter? You weak?

AZELIA: Tired, awful tired! This basket's mighty heavy. *(Brightening)* You-all know, I got weapons in here. It's full of weapons!

YAM VENDOR: Huh? What you mean?

MANGO VENDOR: Shsss! Don't pay her no mind.

AZELIA: Don't you see? *(Raising up bananas but disclosing nothing beneath)* See there! *(Her eyes gleaming)* Machetes! Three machetes, two pistols, the butt end of an axe to fight our way to freedom. And whips! Oh, yes, two whips!

THREAD VENDOR: *(Rising)* Get on! Get on! That's enough of your chatter.

MELON VENDOR: Do, Jesus! She's mad as a loon!

AZELIA: *(Lifting her basket and going on)* That's why I'm tired! So tired! *(As she exits)* This here's a heavy load. Freedom's heavy load.

MANGO VENDOR: Poor thing! She's crazy.

YAM VENDOR: Oh, so that's it?

THREAD VENDOR: Yes, she's been around here a long time. We know her. Cracked in the head. Always talking about when the slaves rose up against the French.

MANGO VENDOR: Yes, and even claiming she used to be Dessalines's wife before he got to where he is.

(Everybody laughs)

YAM VENDOR: What Dessalines? Not the Emperor?

MANGO VENDOR: That's the one.

COCOANUT VENDOR: *(Still giggling)* Such lies! Such lies!

YAM VENDOR: I know she's crazy. What's her name?

THREAD VENDOR: Azelia, but the soldiers nick-named her Defilee.

YAM VENDOR: Why?

THREAD VENDOR: I reckon 'cause she runs after them so much. I don't know. She's always following the troops, selling bananas.

MANGO VENDOR: If she was younger, her basket might not be so heavy. Machetes and pistols! Huh! Don't that take the cake? *(She rises and mounts the steps)* I'm going up on the wall and see what I can see. Whee! That sun is strong.

THREAD VENDOR: You just want to see what old long tall fisherman's doing, I reckon.

MANGO VENDOR: I ain't studyin' him.

> *(A band of RAGMUFFINS enters, three or four, pushing and playing with each other, laughing loudly and jabbering in a strange dialect)*

PEPPER VENDOR: *(To the RAGMUFFINS)* Get away, you-all! Get away!

> *(They run to an opposite corner of the stage, laughing)*

YAM VENDOR: Old bad boys, just running wild. No manners nor nothing.

MELON VENDOR: Ragmuffins right out of the back country, that's what they is! Can't even talk so's you can understand them.

THREAD VENDOR: They got a dialect all they own, them peoples back yonder in the woods.

PEPPER VENDOR: They're hungry back there, that's why they come to town.

COCOANUT VENDOR: They're just too lazy to work the farms, that's all. The Emperor give 'em land, but they won't work it. They're too free now.

THREAD VENDOR: Then if somebody makes 'em work, they yell about, "We ain't slaves no more!" That's the way with men! Men is lazy.

MELON VENDOR: Lazy, lazy, lazy! If it wasn't fun out riding in a boat on the sea, I don't 'spect they'd even fish.

YAM VENDOR: Well, anyhow, to tell the truth, the farmers ain't got no plows to work with. Looks like since we drove the French out, don't no more ships come here bringing tools nor nothing.

THREAD VENDOR: Things is kinder at a stand-still. Haiti's even mighty nigh out o' thread and thimbles.

MANGO VENDOR: *(On the embankment)* Say, look, you-all! I see a strange ship coming. A new one. It's got big red sails!

(The WOMEN all rise and peer over the wall, or mount the steps)

MELON VENDOR: It ain't no fishing boat, either, is it?

THREAD VENDOR: It's a passenger boat, I believe.

MANGO VENDOR: I seed it once before, at Saint Marc. It belongs to some of the Emperor's officers. Some rich mulatto or 'nother, I reckon.

THREAD VENDOR: It's sure a big one, all right, 'cause it's anchoring way out in deep water.

(As the WOMEN look at the ship, the RAGMUFFINS steal up to the fruit on the ground. One slyly grabs a melon, another a handful of yams, another a mango)

MANGO VENDOR: *(Turning and seeing them. Screaming:)* You rascals! Get away from here! Scat!

(The BOYS scatter)

YAM VENDOR: Curse your rotten hides! Beat it!

MELON VENDOR: *(Pursuing them)* Put down my melon, you thieves! Gimme back my melon.

(The RAGMUFFINS exit with their fruit, yelling and laughing)

THREAD VENDOR: Can't take your eyes off things these days. Thieves is getting awful. Young thieves, too.

MELON VENDOR: *(Panting)* I wish I could get my hands on them hooligans.

COCOANUT VENDOR: We ought to have polices, that's what we needs. Soldiers ain't no good. They steals themselves.

MANGO VENDOR: They ain't even a soldier around today, nohow.

YAM VENDOR: *(Going back to the steps and looking toward the shore)* Wonder what that boat's here for?

COCOANUT VENDOR: I reckon they getting ready for one of their yachting parties. The spend-thrift devils!

PEPPER VENDOR: And Haiti gone to rack and ruin.

MELON VENDOR: 'Way back there in the country where I goes to fetch my melons, the farmers done refused to pay taxes.

YAM VENDOR: Yes, and General Gerin took his soldiers away from the barracks today. They say he's put 'em all in that fort ten kilometres down the coast.

THREAD VENDOR: I hear General Yayou's marching, too.

MELON VENDOR: Looks like they getting ready for some more fighting. Look like we'll never be done fighting here in Haiti.

PEPPER VENDOR: Something's wrong! Something's wrong! And poor Jean Jacques, he don't know what to do.

THREAD VENDOR: Huh! All the Emperor knows is fight! He's done killed off all the white folks. Now he's looking for somebody else to chop up.

MANGO VENDOR: He's a brave man, though! You can't say he ain't. And 'cause of him, I'm free.

PEPPER VENDOR: True, thank God!

YAM VENDOR: Well, he ought to chop off some o' these taxes we got to pay every time I turn around. That's why I never has a sou to my name.

MANGO VENDOR: You got more'n you ever had when you was a slave.

PEPPER VENDOR: Right! Some of you-all's even got shoes.

MELON VENDOR: *(Whispering)* But the papaloi says there's gonna be a change soon.

COCOANUT VENDOR: That's what the priest said, too.

THREAD VENDOR: Then you-all's Gods all agree. I 'spect the devil's in it, myself.

MELON VENDOR: Somebody's coming! They look like soldiers to me. *(Beginning to cry her wares)* Melons! Nice, cool melons!

YAM VENDOR: They is soldiers. Yams! Yams! Yams! Mulatto officers, too! Yams! Must be a high class brigade. Yams! Yams!

MANGO VENDOR: There ain't but a handful, though. We won't sell much to them. Melons! Melons!

THREAD VENDOR: Every little bit helps. Needles! Thimbles! Thread!

> *(Enter a squad of SOLDIERS, led by STENIO. VUVAL follows. The MARKET WOMEN hold out their fruits, calling and beckoning)*

STENIO: Squad halt! *(The SOLDIERS halt)* Left face! *(The SOLDIERS obey)* Men, we'll remain here. Clear the square. Get all these old women out. *(Commanding)* Break ranks and go ahead.

> *(Loud chatter and protestation among the WOMEN)*

MELON VENDOR: What's this?

COCOANUT VENDOR: You gonna clear us out?

THREAD VENDOR: What officer is he?

MANGO VENDOR: He don't belong around here.

YAM VENDOR: Don't he know we pay for this space?

STENIO: You women'll have to clear out at once! Military orders! So move and move quickly! And shut up! Or else my soldiers will handle you.

> *(The WOMEN begin to gather up their wares in clothes and bas-*

kets. Meanwhile, VUVAL has mounted the sea-wall. Hurriedly the WOMEN exit, left and right, pushed by the SOLDIERS. One SOLDIER grabs a mango and starts to eat it)

SOLDIERS:

> Move on!
>
> Get!
>
> Step on it!

STENIO: *(To the one who has the mango)* Put that mango down! This is no time to eat. *(To VUVAL)* Is the beach clear?

VUVAL: Yes, only a few fisherman, and they're several hundred yards down the shore. Our boat's approaching, Stenio. Just arrived, apparently, and has anchored in the bay. *(He waves)* They're waving at me now. Yes, look, they're beginning to lower the skiff.

STENIO: Good! Claire won't have to wait when she arrives. She ought to be here before long.

VUVAL: What did the look-out say about Jean Jacques?

STENIO: The look-out that climbed the palm tree? Oh, he said he could see him clearly crossing the valley without field glasses. He'd passed the Red Bridge, so the Emperor ought to be dashing into the village any moment now.

VUVAL: You'd better place the men, then.

STENIO: It's good he can't ride his horse onto the quay here. He'll have to come up those steps on foot. *(To the SOLDIERS)* Squad, attention! *(As they form before him)* Listen carefully, men! A great honor's befallen us, and at the same time a grave patriotic duty! We're chosen by destiny to be the liberators of Haiti! We're to free our country from a power-loving tax-hungry tyrant. It's our privilege and our honor, men, to put an end to the career of a black monster who cares not at all for us, or for Haiti, or for our people, but only for himself. Now his day of reckoning has come. I did not tell you last night why I picked you out so carefully. But I chose you as men loyal to myself and to freedom. Now, we are to strike the blow that will break the shackles of submission forever. We are to put an end to that presumptuous Negro who dares call himself, "His Majesty."

A SOLDIER: What?

SECOND SOLDIER: You don't mean . . . ?

THIRD SOLDIER: Not the Emperor?

STENIO: I mean Dessalines!

SOLDIER: But what'll happen to us?

SECOND SOLDIER: Why, that's treason!

THIRD SOLDIER: I don't want to do that.

FOURTH SOLDIER: We'll be done for!

STENIO: You'll be promoted in rank and made commanders. You need have no fear, men. There'll be a Republic and a President. Perhaps myself as President, General Gerin and General Yayou have already begun to take over the forts for the new government. There'll be an end of Emperors, and of tyranny! And we'll be heroes in the eyes of the people! Heroes, men! Heroes!

SOLDIER: But bullets can't kill Jean Jacques?

SECOND SOLDIER: He's got some kind o' magic about him, I heard.

THIRD SOLDIER: Yes, he has.

STENIO: Aw, don't be foolish. He's got nothing but arrogance!

VUVAL: He's only a man, just like the rest of you.

STENIO: Of course! But he's kept you bluffed too long. We should have done this years ago. But enough talk. That nearby dust cloud makes me think he must be almost here. Men, take the places I'll assign you. At my command, come forth and take them prisoners. *(Pointing out hiding places)* You two, there in the doorway of the Army Headquarters. One man behind the embankment wall, near the steps. And the rest of you take the other side. *(The SOLDIERS hide as ordered)* Vuval, you and I will take our hiding places here where we can see when he dismounts, and be ready to give the command as he approaches. This is a moment I've long awaited, friend.

VUVAL: I shall write a poem about this, Stenio. How two young men, believers in liberty, brought down the voracious Tiger, whose jaws devoured the people of Haiti.

STENIO: Write it tomorrow, Vuval. Let's hide now. His horses approach.

> *(Noise of horses' hooves, then pawing and champing as they are tied nearby. A trumpet blast. DESSALINES enters, striding like an angry giant, followed by POPO and PIERRE)*

DESSALINES: *(Looking around)* It's mighty quiet here, and no one comes to greet me. Can't they hear your bugles, Pierre? That villain Gerin must've gone to the hills and taken the whole garrison with him! But where're all the fishermen and the market women?

POPO: Sire, I don't like the feel of things here.

PIERRE: Nor do I, my Emperor.

DESSALINES: Let's go further.

(As the men advance toward Army Headquarters, STENIO emerges from his hiding place and gives the traitorous orders)

STENIO: Seize the prisoners!

(The SOLDIERS leap up and seize POPO and PIERRE, who struggle with them—but no one dares touch Dessalines. TWO SOLDIERS approach him, but back away in awe and terror)

DESSALINES: Who dares put their hands upon a King? *(The SOLDIERS quail. He turns toward those holding his companions)* Release those men! *(He draws his sword)*

STENIO: *(Also drawing a sword)* You'll give no orders to Stenio's troops, Jean Jacques.

DESSALINES: *(Turning and seeing Stenio for the first time)* You traitorous dog! Your head'll roll at my feet for this! And now!

(He starts toward him with his sword. STENIO backs away, but VUVAL lifts his pistol and fires like a coward from behind. The royal sword clatters to earth. The EMPEROR staggers, turns, looks at Vuval, and tumbles to the ground, dead)

STENIO: *(Laughing)* Dog! Ha! Ha! Dog, am I? *(He kicks the body of the Emperor)* Well, you're less than a dog, now. Food for worms, you! *(He turns and barks at the men holding POPO and PIERRE)* Take those prisoners to the barracks. Lock them up without water. We'll court-martial them shortly. *(They exit)* *(To VUVAL, who stands now as if in a daze)* What's the matter with you, man? You've done well. Don't look so woe-begone, Vuval. Laugh, poet, laugh! It's not *your* heart that's punctured. You're more than a poet now! Why, you're the new Liberator of Haiti. Your name will go down in history, boy. Put your gun away and come, let's see if we can find a glass of wine. Then you'd better go meet the skiff and prepare for Claire's arrival. Meanwhile, I'll ride south to seek Gerin. Tomorrow we'll set up a Provisional Government at Port-au-Prince in which, no doubt, we'll both have more important posts. *(Glancing at the body as they move toward the barracks)* Come on! Leave that for the buzzards. *(VUVAL, still silent, accompanies his friend toward the Headquarters. In passing, STENIO picks up the EMPEROR's sword)* I might keep this trinket as a souvenir.

(THEY exit.

(The fallen ruler lies alone, in the dust, on his back. From either side of the square come the same RAGMUFFINS who earlier plagued the market women. They steal in awe around the body, then silently creep up and touch it. When they see that the corpse does not move,

they cry aloud in their unintelligible dialect, jabbering in wonder at the tassels of gold on his shoulders, the heavy golden cords at his cuffs, his shiny boots. One of the RAGMUFFINS picks up the EMPEROR's hat with the purple plume and puts it on his head)

RAGMUFFIN: *(With the hat)* Ha! Ha! Ha! Ha!

(Two of the BOYS begin to turn the body over as they unbutton his coat and take it off. While they squabble over the coat, a third removes his silken shirt, the color of wine, and rubs it against his face, groaning voluptuously at the sleekness of the cloth)

RAGMUFFIN: *(With the shirt)* Oh! Ah! Th-ssss!

(The body of the EMPEROR now lies on its face, back bare to the sun. The old welts of his slave days stand out like cords across his shoulders.

(AZELIA enters with the tray of bananas on her head. Fiercely, she turns on the RAGMUFFINS, chasing them away)

AZELIA: Get away! Get away! Away! That man's sick! Or dead, maybe! And you young fools dancing and laughing, and robbing him out of his clothes. Get away!

(The three RAGMUFFINS exit, running.

(AZELIA puts her tray on the wall and goes toward the body, unaware of its identity. She kneels to lift his dusty head in her hands. Suddenly her face is frozen with the horror and pain of recognition. Sobbing, she falls across the body)

Jean Jacques! Jean Jacques! *(For a moment her arms cover the heavy scars on his back. Then she rises slowly to her knees and looks down at the man who was once her husband)* Oh, my Jean! My dear! *(Remembering)* So long together! So much we shared! The cane-fields, the slave-hut! Freedom! *(Bitterly)* Our freedom, Jean Jacques! That took you away from me—to a palace with a throne of gold, and silken pillows for your head, and women fairer than flowers who made you forget how much we'd shared together. Once we slept in a slave corral, together, you and I. But when you slept in a palace, you didn't need Azelia. *(Tenderly)* My sweetheart! Oh, my dear! You offered me money, then, too much money for one who loved you. *(Caressingly, she rubs her hand across his body)* But I still love you, Jean Jacques! I still love you!

(The sound of voices approaching.

(TWO SERVANTS cross the steps, carrying a heavy chest, as VU-VAL appears on the sea-wall, pale as a ghost)

VUVAL: *(Directing the men)* Down the beach, to the skiff.

(The SERVANTS exit toward the beach. The OTHERS enter with a similar chest and follow the first pair.

(Then CLAIRE HEUREUSE comes swiftly across the square, accompanied by her MAID. As she passes, in spite of herself she pauses to glance at the body of the fallen man. Quickly she puts her hands across her eyes and shudders with a memory she can never lose)

CLAIRE: *(In a whisper)* Those scars!

(As she mounts the steps, VUVAL takes her in his arms and they disappear toward the beach.

(Moaning in crazy monotones, AZELIA rocks above her dead.

(TWO FISHERMEN appear on the sea-wall, carrying strings of silver fish. They pause to look at the strange pair)

TALL FISHERMAN: Who's that laying over there with that crazy old woman?

SHORT FISHERMAN: *(Coming closer to the body)* He musta been a slave once—from the looks of his back.

AZELIA: *(Without turning her head)* He was a slave, once . . . . . . *(She gently spreads her shawl over his shoulders)* . . . . . . Then a King!

The FISHERMEN remove their hats, as

THE CURTAIN FALLS

When the Jack Hollers
or
Careless Love
A Negro-Folk Comedy in Three Acts

1936
With Arna Bontemps

The rural setting of *When the Jack Hollers* is the imaginative territory of Hughes's dear friend and collaborator Arna Bontemps, whose fiction typically is set in the South. Premiered at Karamu Theatre on April 28, 1936, *When the Jack Hollers,* titled "Careless Love" in early drafts, garnered lukewarm reviews. Yet the play's satiric and comic presentation of such grave topics as rural poverty, sexual exploitation, racism, and even the Ku Klux Klan ventured into areas that had not previously been addressed on stage in a comic vein. Its loving portrait of rural black folk, and gentle representation of their equally poor white neighbors, neither condescends to the characters nor diminishes the pain and sorrow that inflect their lives. Its love theme turns on the belief that the braying of a jack—an ass used to breed mules—makes a woman's love come down.

None of the complete and coherent manuscripts in the Langston Hughes Papers is clearly a performance text. The version included here, copyrighted 1936, but otherwise undated, incorporates changes that were intended, as indicated by a note in Hughes's hand on one of the drafts, to rid the play of certain egregious forms of dialect, specifically "de, dem and ma." As well, *sho'* becomes *sure* in this version. There is also a coherent but undated typescript in the files that does not include these changes.

Characters

VINEY, a young woman
MOUSE, her husband
BOGATOR, brother to Mouse

ROSE, Viney's niece
JERICO, Viney's nephew
AUNT BILLIE BOXER, Mouse's foster-mother
QUEEN ESTHER, Viney's sister from Memphis
ARCIE, her youngest son
LITTLE BITS, a given-child
RONDIE, a skinny old lady
PINE, a young widower
REV. BUDDY LOVELADY, a jackleg preacher
SID LOWERY, a white share-cropper
CAROLINE JENKINS, Pine's girl-friend
GRANDPA BAILEY, a very old Negro
GRANDMA BAILEY, Grandpa's wife
A FAT KLANSMAN, white cropper
TIPPET's voice off-stage
KLANSMEN and others
NOTE: All the characters are extremely poor share-croppers on a plantation in the Mississippi Delta Region. The TIME is Spring; the present.

Act I

Late afternoon.
Interior of a share-cropper's cabin, a dirt floor, a wide barn-like door in the Center. On either side of door there is a window without glass, the kind that can be closed only by a wooden flap. Mud-brick fireplace with cook pot. A rocking chair, home-made cane bottom chairs, boxes, unpainted table, a safe for dishes, a meal-barrel, a cot, a wooden bed with bright patch-work quilts, a shelf at right containing the materials of conjure— boxes of Love Dust, John The Conqueror Roots, Load Stone, Black Cats' Bones, Devil's Shoestrings, Go-And-Stay Bags and bottles of Holy-water from Jerusalem. The house is papered with newspapers, mostly the comic and rotogravure sections. Through the open door can be seen row after row of cotton plants in the late afternoon sun. As the curtain rises, VINEY is busy building a fire and talking to ROSE.
VINEY: *(Singing)* "I wouldn't mind dying, but I hate to go by myself."
    (Rising) Look how that hem of your dress is turned up, chile. Kiss it right quick. You might get a new dress if you do. It's a sign.
ROSE: *(Obeying)* I hope it's the truth.

VINEY: *(Raising the lid off the pot)* Sure were nice of Aunt Billie to put these greens on to bile before she left here this morning.

ROSE: Sure was!

VINEY: *(Kneeling at the fireplace)* Cause I certainly am tired. 'Twere a caution for sure out yonder in the field today. I mighty nigh dropped.

ROSE: We chopped plenty cotton, all right.

VINEY: *That* we did. I believes we womans out-chopped them mens, too.

ROSE: Men—humph! They stops to pant and smoke too much. *(Imitates men dragging lazily around)* But you know what—Aunt Billie the bestest chopper of all, old as she is!

VINEY: Aunt Billie a world-beating champion! Too bad we didn't have her with us today. Aunt Billie the onliest black face around here can get off and go when she wants to.

ROSE: Sure is.

VINEY: I believes the white folks is scared of Aunt Billie, just like most the colored ones is. She got them bluffed—or conjured, one.

ROSE: I know can't you nor me nor Mouse, nor even any the white croppers, never get to town week days, but Aunt Billie go any time she's a mind to. All she have to say is she going go buy some colic-tea.

VINEY: That's a right smart name for corn-licker.

ROSE: I wanted to go and buy myself one of them sixty-nine cents dresses Levine's is selling for the spring sale—but Tippet say naw, I can't go, here in the middle of chopping time. He a mean old white man, that over-seer we got.

VINEY: Close as you is to him, look like he might would let *you* go.

ROSE: I ain't close to him, Viney! You know I ain't—not less I have to be.

VINEY: Except when he call you, that's all. And he call too often—for a married man. Aunt Billie done marked it.

ROSE: I know she is.

VINEY: She don't like it, neither.

ROSE: Then why don't she brew a spell to make him let me alone? She knows so much about conjure.

VINEY: I ain't never seen no spell yet what had much effect on white folks.

ROSE: But Aunt Billie got plenty white customers for her roots and herbs.

VINEY: That she has, but them charms of her'n ain't took none of the evil out of no white folks yet. Not nary one. *(Noise of children outside. VINEY yells)* You, Jerico! You, Little Bits! You all better get up to this house. Playing all up and down the road. *(As JERICO and LITTLE BITS enter laughing)* Don't see how you got the strength to play nohow, hard as we-all done worked today. Lawdy, I'm tired. *(To the boy)* Jerico, run and fetch me a pail of water from the spring. Two pails—all them mens is got to wash directly. And, Little Bits, go see is there any more onions left in that green patch for us to season these greens with. Hurry up! Scat! *(The children exit)* Rose see can you get that fire to burn up, so's I can have some nice ashes for this hoe-cake. *(ROSE begins to attend to the fire. VINEY dips a pot into the meal-barrel)* Lawd-a-mercy. This meal-barrel's scrapping bottom, and the month ain't nowhere near up.

ROSE: Trouble with this fire is they ain't enough wood.

VINEY: Look like tonight there ain't enough of nothing. Except greens—and they without nary piece of fat meat. And hard as times is, you talking about wanting to go traipsing off to town to break your one and only dollar your mama sent you from Memphis.

ROSE: I ain't got nothing to dress up in, neither for church nor for the fishing party.

VINEY: I expects the fishing party's worrying you more'n the church is.

ROSE: Well, the Young and Sanctified Club's giving it.

VINEY: Humph! That collection of sinners don't even know how to shout yet!

ROSE: Aw, Viney!

> *(Noise of old Ford passing in road outside, slows down, a whistle, and then a package comes whizzing through the door)*

VINEY: *(Sticking her head out)* Who's there? *(As she hears the whistle and sees the car)* Oh! *(Comes back in)*

ROSE: *(Going to door)* Oh! *(Smiles a forced smile)*

VOICE: *(From the road)* Here, I brought you that dress, gal. You said you wanted one. It's a red one. Mind you don't wear it in the field.

> *(Ford starts up and drives on)*

ROSE: Thank you, Mister Tippet. *(VINEY stares at the bundle)* I'll take it in the room, Viney. *(Goes into the room at Right)*

VINEY: I don't care where you go with it myself. *(Muttering)* A bundle of sin. *(She goes on with her cooking, singing as she works)* "This time next year I may be dead and gone Oh, Lawdy! This time next year I . . . ." *(Glances out window and calls to Rose)* Younder comes Bogator now. It's a good thing he missed seeing Tippet fling that bundle in here. Lawd! Lawd! Trouble is brewing in this house for sure.

    (Enter BOGATOR, a boy of 17, big for his age)

BOGATOR: I don't smell no victuals hungry as I am! *(Looks at empty water bench)* Where's the water?

VINEY: Ain't no water. I ain't got but two hands. Neither is Rose. And we been out in the field all day just same as you, long side of you. *(Hesitating)* Where's Pine?

BOGATOR: Pine went on down the road a piece to the Jenkins'. Say he'll be back directly, in time for supper. You know he want to spark with Caroline.

VINEY: That hussy!

BOGATOR: *(Teasing)* Pine like her.

VINEY: And his wife ain't been dead three months yet! No wonder Pine wants to come and room and board with us, right by the Jenkins.

BOGATOR: Pine's a friend of Mouse's, ain't he?

VINEY: Well, he go to Caroline's mighty often since that ain't his home.

BOGATOR: What you care? You married.

VINEY: I doesn't care. But he ought to respect them that's dead and buried—his poor wife. I don't know why Mouse brought Pine here, nohow. Old long tall sapper!

BOGATOR: He got a nice singing voice.

VINEY: That's all he got. He don't belong to no church. He ain't neither Holy nor Sanctified nor Methodist nor Primitive Baptist.

BOGATOR: You must like Pine,—worried as you is about him.

VINEY: You hush, now! Just hush.

BOGATOR: Yes'm, done hushed a'ready. *(A pause)* Where's Rose?

VINEY: She in the room.

BOGATOR: *(Calling)* Rose! Oh, Miss Roselee Prettylee Johnson!

ROSE: Wait a minute.

    (Enter JERICO with the water)

VINEY: Time you was getting here, Jerico.

    (He exits into room at Left as ROSE opens her door. She has on the new red dress. It is too large for her)

BOGATOR: *(Astonished)* Where'd you get the dress?

VINEY: Don't ask so many questions.

BOGATOR: I know you ain't been to town.

VINEY: Rose got the dress, so that's all.

BOGATOR: *(As ROSE comes out)* Lemme see! Lemme touch you!

ROSE: Go 'way! Go 'way! *(She backs off)* I'm gonna see why don't Little Bits bring the onions. *(She rushes out the door)*

BOGATOR: Gee, she act funny! *(Drinks from dipper)* Viney, Tippet ain't brung Rose that dress, is he?

VINEY: Yes.

BOGATOR: Oh, I see.

VINEY: Now that you knows, keep your mouth shut, Bogator. Rose ain't no relation of your'n. Neither is she married to you. *(Yelling)* Say, go and fetch me some more wood here. Can't you see this fire is almost out?

BOGATOR: Aw, heck! I'm tired as a plow horse, and hongry, too. I done my day's work in that bucra's cotton. I wants to eat now.

VINEY: You the sittingest-downest young boy I ever did see! How you gonna eat if they ain't no fire to warm the victuals over? I'm gwine tell Aunt Billie when she gets here. *(Calling)* Jerico! Jerico!

JERICO: *(Voice in room at Left)* M'am?

VINEY: Fetch me some wood, and don't drag your feet neither. *(Calling again as JERICO crosses room and exits)* Little Bits! Oh, Little Bits!

LITTLE BITS: *(Outside)* M'am?

VINEY: *(Still at the top of her voice)* You get yourself in here and set this table. You done had time to get all the onions this side of Arkansas. Come in here.

LITTLE BITS: *(Entering with onions)* Yes'm, Aunt Viney!

VINEY: Where is Rose?

LITTLE BITS: She gone on down toward the meadowfield, say she gonna pick some flowers, maybe her mama come tonight.

VINEY: That's right, Queen Esther did write she coming this week, but she been coming for the last four-five years, and ain't got here yet.

BOGATOR: I suspects times in Memphis is so hard she can't buy no ticket to get here with. Train tickets is high.

VINEY: What you know about a train—and you ain't never been on one?

BOGATOR: I saw one once.

LITTLE BITS: You did? Where?

BOGATOR: When I drive Tippet's wagon full of cotton bales to the Junction last fall-time.

VINEY: *(To LITTLE BITS who is standing motionless)* Bogator's lying and you standing there listening to him lie. I never saw the beat! *(Angrily)* Little Bits, stir around here and do something, or else not a spoonful will I put before you-all this evening.

BOGATOR: Black cat musta done crossed your path, Viney. *(Stretching)* Oh-hum! Reckon I got to go sit outside, even if the skeeters do bite my feet. *(Gets up and goes slowly to the wall where he reaches for a battered old guitar)*

VINEY: If you'd move them feet a little, skeeters wouldn't work on them so.

BOGATOR: That's just why I'm taking down this guitar, so I'll have something to pat them to.

VINEY: Well, take care you don't pat them on a snake.

BOGATOR: Me and Mouse done killed two big ones this morning.

VINEY: Um-hummm! I never saw a year when they's been more sarpints round.

BOGATOR: Where is Mouse, anyhow, Viney?

VINEY: Your no-good brother's gone to get my money back from old man Biggs, that's where he is. I'm tired of having nothing to eat in this house. I done told Mouse if he don't go and collect that ten dollars Biggs been owing us nigh on to a year, and collect it right today, that I would. I weren't born and raised up in a sawmill camp for nothing, and I'll slice old Biggs up like a Irish potato, if he don't pay back my money! I warn't broke when we lent it to him, but we sure Lawd's broke now, and we needs it.

BOGATOR: We sure do.

VINEY: Whilst Tippet's off to town, I told Mouse to go get that money, because when the white man's here, he won't let us go nowhere.

BOGATOR: Well, we don't have to wait for Mouse to eat, do we?

VINEY: Now, we don't have to wait, but we *gonna* wait. I ain't no more'n got the corn bread mixed up yet. And Aunt Billie's due back here by sun-down. I know she birthed that baby by now.

BOGATOR: Where she go?

VINEY: Way over younder by Baxter Creek. You ought to know where she go. You was fooling round that gal yourself last summer.

BOGATOR: *(Hastily)* Don't put that washing out. It ain't no chile of mine.

VINEY: Soon's Aunt Billie come back here, we find out who it look like.

BOGATOR: Little old new-born baby don't look like nothing—but sin, that's all.

VINEY: How you know so much about new-borned babies? You ain't married.

BOGATOR: I'm old enough to be. I'm seventeen.

VINEY: That ain't no age to crow about. Gwan, git out of my mouth, anyhow. Is you fed the pigs?

BOGATOR: Yeah, I fed the pig. Now, I'm just gwine cool my heels. *(Takes chair and goes outside, visible against the window, picking on his guitar and singing, as JERICO comes back with wood and begins to fix the fire)*

> "I love you, baby,
> I'll tell the world I do—
> And maybe someday
> You'll learn to love me, too."

VINEY: Ain't nobody gonna learn to love you, if you don't wash your feet when you come in out of the fields.

BOGATOR: Aw, she don't care nothing about me, nohow. Rose done got a dress from the white man.

VINEY: Shut up talking about Rose in front of these chillun. She can't help who take a fancy to her.

BOGATOR: She don't need to act like she's skeered of me, then.

VINEY: She skeered of all the mens and good reason too. Reckon she can't see that you ain't like the rest of them, son.

BOGATOR: *(Grimly)* I gwine fix that cracker's wagon someday.

VINEY: Sh-sh! Don't talk like that, boy. That's dangerous.

BOGATOR: I ain't just talking.

VINEY: *(Frightened)* Shut up, Bogator.

BOGATOR: *(Singing)*

> "I wonder where that evening sun done gone?
> Wonder where that evening sun done gone?
> My mind's been troubled since the early morn.
> Mind been troubled, my fist been doubled tight.
> Mind's been troubled, fist been doubled tight.
> People in this world don't treat a black man right."

VINEY: Bogator, I tell you, you hush.

BOGATOR:

> "Singing blues, Lawd, blue, blue, blue, blue blues.
> Singing blues, Oh, weary, weary blues.
> Everywhere I go there's nothing but bad news.
>   *(LITTLE BITS begins to dance)*

VINEY: Little Bits, stop that dancing! Ain't got enough to eat here now, without you dancing up more appetite.

AUNT BILLIE: *(Hollering down the road)* Yoo-hoo!

VINEY: Lawd, have mercy! Now, listen at that! Them white folks done told Aunt Billie about making all that noise on the big road.

BOGATOR: We gonna eat now, I know.

LITTLE BITS: *(Rushing to door)* Maybe Aunt Billie brunged us something good.

JERICO: I hope she got some licorice candy.

AUNT BILLIE: *(Hollering near the house)* Viney, here I come!

VINEY: Lawd! Lawd! Lawd!

BOGATOR: *(Playing a lively tune)* Hot dog, step it, Aunt Billie!

AUNT BILLIE: Step it, I do! *(Walking to the music, AUNT BILLIE BOXER arrives in the doorway carrying a bundle and a jug of licker) (The children rush to meet her)* Get away! Get away! Ain't got a thing for nary one of you, cept Jerico. *(She fumbles in a pocket and produces a mouth organ)* Here, son. Granny Lou sent you this. I done birthed a child for Maggie.

VINEY: Boy, or girl?

AUNT BILLIE: Boy, and it's black, too, thank Gawd! So black they'll have to cover it up in the mawning to let the day break.

VINEY: Is they paid you anything?

AUNT BILLIE: How they gonna pay me anything when they ain't got penny one, nor nickel none, like the most of us?

VINEY: What they give you?

AUNT BILLIE: That there mouth organ and a jug of corn licker.

VINEY: Now, ain't that damnation?

AUNT BILLIE: Viney, I thought you was a Christian woman?

VINEY: *(Angrily)* I is, but I say, ain't that damnation, when we ain't got a cent.

AUNT BILLIE: Don't worry, Viney! I got a feeling something gonna happen round here, don't know if it's good or bad yet.

VINEY: You always got a feeling of some kind. You gets them out of that jug I reckon.

AUNT BILLIE: I gets them from the bones I crosses and the prayers I prays.

VINEY: Gawd and conjure both, huh?

AUNT BILLIE: And myself throwed in. *(Looking at pot over fireplace)* How's my dandelions doing? Wish we had a square of fat back for to season them with.

VINEY: So do I. I'm gwine tell Mouse to tell that store-keeper something, cutting down on our rations.

AUNT BILLIE: Tain't the store-keeper, honey. It's them white folks what lives in town and goes to the the-ater in stove-pipe hats (*indicating their heights with a hand above her head*) and all such like, what owns the store and what owns this plantation and what owns everything. But, say, Viney, where's everybody? Where's Mouse?

VINEY: Gone to get my money from Biggs. Look like he don't intend to pay it.

AUNT BILLIE: You know, I think Mouse gonna bring something here tonight. I feels it.

VINEY: He better. But I wish Pine and them'd come on here and get they supper.

LITTLE BITS: (*Leaning out window*) Here comes Rose all dressed up in her new dress.

VINEY: (*To Aunt Billie*) Tippet brung Rose a dress from town today and throwed it in the door.

AUNT BILLIE: I knowed that.

VINEY: How you knowed it?

AUNT BILLIE: I knowed it due to happen, that's all.

VINEY: Don't you care?

AUNT BILLIE: Do the tree care when the lightening strikes?

VINEY: What do you mean?

AUNT BILLIE: I say do the tree care?

(*ROSE enters, her arms full of dogwood blossoms*)

ROSE: Hello, Aunt Billie! You back?

AUNT BILLIE: Hello, chile. What you gwine do with the flowers?

ROSE: I thought maybe mama might come tonight. The week's mighty near up. I know she don't see no flowers in Memphis.

AUNT BILLIE: Somebody's coming tonight—two, three folkses—I feels it in my bones.

(*By now the sun is gone. Gradually, during the scenes that follow, twilight comes to the fields outside like a drift of blue smoke. It deepens steadily into night*)

ROSE: I hope it's mama. (*Puts flowers in a lard bucket and places the crude bouquet in a corner*)

AUNT BILLIE: Mighty long time since Queen Esther been here, ain't it, Viney?

VINEY: Sure is. She nothing but trouble when she is here, neither. I got to say it, even if she is my sister. We got plenty trouble without her.

AUNT BILLIE: Little Bit more won't hurt none. That's what I say when that there chile's mammy (*Pointing to Little Bits*) died and gived her to me. Her mammy say, "I'm afraid she be trouble to you, Aunt Billie." And I say, "little bit more won't hurt none." That's why I named her Little Bits.

VINEY: *(Muttering)* Jest wait till I lay eyes on Mouse. Going off staying here, and supper's ready.

AUNT BILLIE: Viney, you just too quarrelsome, these days. I gwine stop your mouth.

VINEY: Mouse should-a been back. Bogator, you go call Pine—less'n he eating down to that Jenkins house.

> *(BOGATOR hangs his guitar inside door, and goes off. Later he can be heard down the road calling Pine. The children come in and look hungrily at the table)*

AUNT BILLIE: Yes, Sir, I gwine give you something to stop your everlasting mouth.

VINEY: *(Suspiciously)* Don't you put no spell on me.

AUNT BILLIE: Ain't gwine be no spell. It gwine be Holy Water.

VINEY: What I want with Holy Water? I done been baptized.

AUNT BILLIE: You wait and see. Soon's I hear Mouse coming. I'm gwine stop your quarreling for this evening. *(Lifts jug)*

VINEY: You take many more sucks out of that jug and you won't know nothing about it.

AUNT BILLIE: *(Paying Viney no mind)* Rose, your dress right pretty.

ROSE: *(Ashamed)* It ain't the kind I wanted.

AUNT BILLIE: Neither is this world the kind I wants, chile. I been thinking about ordering myself up a new one.

LITTLE BITS: *(At window)* Here comes Pine.

VINEY: *(Excited)* Jerico, you Jerico! Fill the wash basin out yonder on the bench so's Pine can wash up.

JERICO: Yes'm. *(Goes outside and is heard filling basin)*

VINEY: Rose! Little Bits! Is that there table all set?

LITTLE BITS: Yes'm.

ROSE: Shall I dish up the greens?

VINEY: Go ahead. When a man come in he want to eat.

ROSE: We ain't gonna wait for Uncle Mouse then?

VINEY: Mouse knows when the eating time is. If he ain't here, that's just his hard luck.

> *(Voices of BOGATOR and PINE talking as they approach the house)*

PINE: *(Nearing window)* Um-hum! Smell greens and dumplings way down the road. Didn't smell nothing like that at Caroline's house.

BOGATOR: What they have down there?

PINE: *(Going to wash bench just outside left window)* I ain't seed nothing but cornbread and molasses.

BOGATOR: Hard times got them for sure. *(Between handfuls of water to his face)* Things getting tougher and tougher, boy!

VINEY: *(Playfully)* I'm gonna toughen *you* if you don't get on in here and eat.

BOGATOR: We coming.

VINEY: Jerico! You chillun, get your pans, and let Aunt Billie dish up your grub.

AUNT BILLIE: *(To children as she dishes up food)* Listen! Did you all catch me any spiders today—you know, like I asked you?

JERICO: I caught you one, a great big black one, and put him in the jar on the shelf.

AUNT BILLIE: Did you screw the top back down?

JERICO: Sure did. You got seven in there now.

AUNT BILLIE: I want me a scorpion, too, and three lizards.

JERICO: Yes'm.

AUNT BILLIE: Also a snake's head.

JERICO: Yes'm.

AUNT BILLIE: Make haste and see that I gets them.

JERICO and LITTLE BITS: Yes'm. We sure will.

PINE: *(Entering. A sort of ball-bearing jointed fellow, uncommonly tall)* How you-all? Good evening, Aunt Billie, Ma'm!

AUNT BILLIE: Evening, Son! Set down and let's we ask the blessing.
> *(PINE and AUNT BILLIE, ROSE and BOGATOR sit at the table. VINEY bows her head nearby)*

AUNT BILLIE: *(Blessing the table)*
> "High and Mighty!
> Omnipotent and whole,
> We thanks you for this food,
> For body and soul.
> Amen!"

BOGATOR, ROSE, PINE: Amen! Amen!

JERICO and LITTLE BITS: *(Standing around)* Amen!

VINEY: You chillun set down somewhere on the bed or anywhere. *(She busies herself with the food and then brings her own plate to the table)*

LITTLE BITS: *(Sitting on the edge of bed)* Feel like something moving in this bed.

JERICO: Aw, you teched in the head, can't nothing move inside a feather tick.

LITTLE BITS: I know I ain't gonna set there. *(Takes her pan of food and sits in doorway)*

PINE: *(Eating heartily)* Somebody sure cooked a mean mess of greens!

BOGATOR: Aunt Billie cooked them.

VINEY: She put them on, but I seasoned them.

PINE: They what you calls eat-more!

VINEY: Another helping waiting for you in the pot, Pine. Is Old Lady Jenkins still ailing?

PINE: I reckon she is.

AUNT BILLIE: Old Lady Jenkins don't do what I tell her, that's why she's ailing.

VINEY: What you tell her to do?

AUNT BILLIE: I told her to wear a brown grasshopper's nest around her neck, shave under her arms, and drink that tea I brewed for her.

BOGATOR: And what didn't she do?

AUNT BILLIE: She ain't been drinking the tea. She say it's too bitter.

VINEY: Um-hum!

AUNT BILLIE: And when I gives out charms, I gives them most frequency in three, and if you don't obey all three my magics, don't nary one of them work. That why old Lady Jenkins ailing—she really need her system cleaned out.

VINEY: I thought the grasshopper's nest do that.

AUNT BILLIE: It do, but with the aid of the tea, chile, the aid of the tea.

VINEY: Well, I know one thing, if that no-good pair of pants named Mouse don't bring me some money back here, I'm gonna run him out of this house. *(Sweetly)* Lemme fill your plate, Pine. *(Rises and refills PINE's plate at fireplace)*

AUNT BILLIE: *(To JERICO)* Son, if you's through eating, reach up yonder on my shelf and hand me that bottle of Jerusalem Water from the Sanctified Well. I needs it for Viney.

VINEY: You don't need to sprinkle no water on me, Aunt Billie, I don't want it.

AUNT BILLIE: *(Glaring)* Soon's you get through eating, you do as I say. I'm tired of you quarreling with Mouse.

BOGATOR: If you stops them two from wrangling, then you is a conjure-woman for sure.

AUNT BILLIE: I been a conjure-woman before you was borned, son. I just don't use it much in my own house, that's all.

PINE: I wish you'd use some to make white folks more generous-like, and times better.

BOGATOR: Now you talking.

AUNT BILLIE: Maybe I will, boy. Maybe I will. I been studying lately. And some of these days I'm gonna make a Black-Cat's-Never-Fail-Bag and put it where it'll do the most good.

BOGATOR: I'll tell you where to put it, too.

AUNT BILLIE: Tell me later, son. Never loose your secrets in the air.

BOGATOR: Yes'm.

VOICE: *(Calling from roadway)* Is you all home? Here I come.

AUNT BILLIE: *(Elated)* Come on in, Rondie, we's here.

RONDIE: *(Entering. She is a wizened, bird-like old woman whose shaggy feathers are her ragged clothes)* How you-all? How you, Billie?

AUNT BILLIE: Sober.

OTHERS:

    Howdy, Miss Rondie!

    Good-evening.

    Howdy-do!

RONDIE: Look like you making out right well.

PINE: I'm feeding my face.

AUNT BILLIE: Get yourself a plate and dish up some greens.

RONDIE: Naw, I thank you.

AUNT BILLIE: You better go there and get something out of that pot like I ask you.

RONDIE: Believe I will take a taste. Jest lemme spit out this snuff first. *(Goes to door and spits, then to pot, picking up plate and filling it)*

PINE: *(To children)* Hand me a drink, some of y'all chilluns.

BOGATOR: Me, too. Greens make you thirsty.

    (LITTLE BITS hands them water bucket and dipper. Both drink)

RONDIE: Ain't you got nothing better than water for to drink, Billie?

AUNT BILLIE: Swig from that jug when you gets through eating. It come from over Baxter Creek way, and it sure got fire mixed in with it. Granny Lou gived it to me. I done birthed her a great-grand-chile.

RONDIE: What kind of looking chile Maggie have?

AUNT BILLIE: Great big baby, look like Jack Johnson.

ROSE: *(In doorway)* Mouse is coming, Aunt Viney.

VINEY: He better get here, mad as I am.
> *(Children toss their empty pans into dish pan and run down the road to meet MOUSE)*

AUNT BILLIE: *(Reaching for bottle)* Here, Viney, take a mouthful of this Holy Water and hold it in your mouth till Mouse done set down and ate his supper. *(She rises and forces bottle to VINEY's mouth, then sprinkles powder in doorway)* Don't you swallow this water!

ROSE: Look like he leading some kind of beast down the road, too.
> *(PINE, RONDIE, AUNT BILLIE and BOGATOR go to door and windows to see. It is now almost dark outside)*

RONDIE: Look like he got a little old mule.

AUNT BILLIE: That ain't no mule, that's a jack.

RONDIE: Oh, Lawd!

LITTLE BITS: What's a jack?

MOUSE: *(Voice outside)* Here, Jerico, tie him to the tree. Whoa! *(Arriving in doorway)* Evening! How you, Rondie?

RONDIE: Tol'able, I thanks you. What you been dragging there?

MOUSE: A jack.

AUNT BILLIE: Where you get a jack at?

MOUSE: *(As VINEY comes to door)* I done collect the debt.

AUNT BILLIE: What you mean?

MOUSE: Deacon Biggs ain't had no money, so this here is the collection.

VINEY: *(Yelling and emitting a stream of water from her mouth)* I don't want no jack, plague take your time. I wants ten dollars.

MOUSE: Now, Viney.

VINEY: Take that varmint away from here and get my money!

MOUSE: Viney, honey . . .

VINEY: *(Still at top of her voice)* Honey, nothing! Aunt Billie, you see what he done brought here?

MOUSE: Now, listen . . .

VINEY: Some little old he-male donkey no good for plowing nor nothing except to breed mules. And what we got to breed him with?

MOUSE: Jenny.

VINEY: Old mare Jenny so old she can't hardly plow, let alone stand up to a half-crazy jack. Take him away from here, I say.

MOUSE: But, maybe . . .

VINEY: Maybe nothing! We got enough varmints and humans round here to feed now, let alone another one.

AUNT BILLIE: *(Placing her bottle back on shelf)* I tell you conjure don't never work in your own house. *(To VINEY and MOUSE)* Quarrel on! Quarrel on! Quarrel on!

RONDIE: That jack don't mean nobody no good.

AUNT BILLIE: Aw, shaw! Ain't nothing wrong to a jack.

RONDIE: Yes, they is, too. Ain't you heard? *(Whispers to AUNT BIL-LIE)* Hee! Hee! Hee!

AUNT BILLIE: Don't take no jack to start them feeling that-away. *(Whispers back to RONDIE)*

VINEY: You say Biggs ain't got no money? Where all his hawgs?

MOUSE: He done eat up his hawgs.

VINEY: Well, you could a-brung back a few laying hens.

MOUSE: His chickens long gone in the pot.

VINEY: Well, ain't he got no potaters stored up you could-a took?

MOUSE: Nary one!

VINEY: *(Positively)* Well, I can't use no jack.

MOUSE: Well, you done told me to collect, ain't you? And Biggs ain't got ten dollars. So he say, "Here, take my jack. Maybe you can make a little something breeding him for stud, and if you can't, jest keep him anyhow.

RONDIE: If you don't breed a jack, they sure do raise hell, too. You got to breed them.

VINEY: I can't use no jack! Sides, they ain't right to have round the house with young growing chillun. They ain't proper.

MOUSE: He a nice little jack.

VINEY: Ain't no nice jacks. I told you not to lend Biggs that money in the first place.

MOUSE: Now, honey, that were more'n a year ago. Don't start that again. *(Appealing to his friend)* Pine, you see how a woman is?

VINEY: Don't look at Pine. He ain't nothing like you is, careless and no-good and don't take care your family. When his wife were living he looked out good for her. *(Weeping)* And here I send you to collect money to buy something to eat with and you come back lugging a little old jack.

MOUSE: All right, Viney! Have it your way. *(To JERICO)* Hey, boy, take the jack and put him in the shed.

VINEY: *(Flaring up)* Naw, you don't. Not in there with my mare. He liable to kick Jenny to death. That mare is mine, my father left her to me when he passed on to glory, and I don't want her bothered in her old age by no nasty little old jack. Don't put him in that shed.

MOUSE: Aw, all right, leave him tied outside the barn, then. Give him a drink first.

JERICO: Yes, sir, Uncle Mouse.

> *(He goes off with the jack. The other children start to follow)*

VINEY: LITTLE BITS, ROSE! You girls stay here. A jack is ruination. *(To her husband)* Mouse, you want to eat?

MOUSE: What you think I am? A dawg what only eat once a day? Sure I wants to eat.

VINEY: Don't give me none of your lip; do, I might fix you so you can't eat.

MOUSE: Don't you go putting no kind of conjure in my food, woman.

> *(Noise down at barn of a horse neighing loudly)*

VINEY: You hear Jenny. She done smelled that jack already.

AUNT BILLIE: That mare's mighty old.

RONDIE: She ain't so old as me. Hee! Hee! And the sap ain't all dreened out of me yet.

MOUSE: That jack won't bother Jenny, brokedown and sway-backed as she is.

VINEY: He better not.

RONDIE: Jenny's liable to bother *him*.

> *(VINEY is stirring pot of greens)*

MOUSE: *(Suspiciously)* Woman, what you doing to that pot? Don't you be stirring evil in my victuals.

VINEY: *(Dishing up)* Here, eat 'em or not, as you's a-mind to.

MOUSE: *(Settling down to the table)* I got a mind not. *(Lights lamp and peers at his plate)* No telling what you put in them. *(Pushes plate away)*

AUNT BILLIE: Aw, son, eat! Viney don't know nothing about no kind of conjure that kin hurt nobody.

MOUSE: Well, if you say they's all right, I'll eat them. *(Eats)*

VOICE: *(Woman in the road, faintly calling)* Hoo-oo-hoo-oo!

PINE: I'll see you-all later. Seem like I hear somebody calling me. *(Looks out door)* Sure enough, it is. *(Calls)* Hello, Caroline.

CAROLINE: *(Voice somewhat nearer)* Ain't you coming out, Pine?

PINE: Sure.

> *(He exits)*
> *(Just then the jack brays, a terrific ear-splitting bray. Everybody jumps. VINEY rushes to door and looks after PINE. ROSE and BOGATOR sway toward each other. LITTLE BITS and JERICO huddle together)*

RONDIE: There now! I told you!

LITTLE BITS: Aunt Viney! Aunt Viney!

VINEY: I sure feels funny, myself.

AUNT BILLIE: *(Offering jug)* Here, Rondie, have a drink.

RONDIE: *(Drinking deeply)* Don't know if this will satisfy me or not.

MOUSE: You-all womens is crazy. Acting like you scared of a jack.

RONDIE: Tain't 'zackly that, Mouse. You don't know like we do.

VINEY: Mouse ain't got no sense.

MOUSE: Now, baby!

BOGATOR: *(To ROSE)* Want to hear a little music, Rose?

ROSE: That would be right nice, Bogator.

BOGATOR: Come on, Jerico, bring your mouth organ.

> *(JERICO produces mouth organ and begins to blow)*

RONDIE: Play something lively, son, 'cause I needs it.

BOGATOR: *(Warming to the rhythm)* Listen to this.

> *(HE plays a dancing tune. All begin to pat their feet and sway in time—except VINEY, who is cleaning up the dishes)*

MOUSE: *(Still eating)* Come on, Rose, let's see you step out there.

ROSE: Can't do much barefooted. *(She begins to dance)*

AUNT BILLIE: That's it, chile.

RONDIE: Go on, Gal!

JERICO: Hey! Hey!

> *(All clap hands as ROSE dances, then JERICO and LITTLE BITS dance. Then old RONDIE raises her dress, showing skinny bird-like legs as she cuts a few steps. Then ROSE begins to dance again. As ROSE is turning rapidly to the music, a shrill whistle sounds outside)*

VINEY: *(In a whisper)* That's Tippet.

> *(The music dies suddenly. ROSE stops dancing. She listens a minute, and as the whistle is repeated, turns and goes slowly out the door)*

BOGATOR: God damn that white man! *(Throws his instrument down and stands with clenched fists)*

AUNT BILLIE: Just wait, son, just wait.

MOUSE: He the boss. When he call, you got to go.

AUNT BILLIE: *(Mumbling to BOGATOR)* I'm gwine to fix him. You see if I don't.

RONDIE: Gimme a swig, Billie.

AUNT BILLIE: Here, take the jug. Mouse, you want some?

VINEY: Not Mouse! I don't like you-all *(looking at RONDIE)* none of

you-all a-drinking round this house nohow. I'm a Christian woman,
I is. Dog if I ain't.

AUNT BILLIE: *(Rises)* Come on, Rondie, let's take our jug and go on
down the road a piece where it's cool. Too many light bugs round
here with the lamp lit anyhow!

> *(The two old women go outside into the soft darkness. Lightning
> bugs glimmer. Crickets call and frogs croak)*

VINEY: *(Shouting)* Little Bits, get them dishes cleared up.

MOUSE: Viney, you sure is evil this evening, hollering at these chilluns.

VINEY: That's neither here nor there, Mouse Wilson. You ought to be
shot for bringing home a devilish jack.

MOUSE: Aw, woman, hush.

VINEY: Hush, nothing! My mouth was made to talk with and I sure
will talk. I just tired of you, anyhow. You don't do nothing right.
(To JERICO as he rakes in fire and gathers a plate full of live coals)
Jerico, get out of that fire. What you doing?

JERICO: I jest gonna feed some live coals to the hopping toads.

VINEY: Well, get out of my face.

> *(He goes and sits in doorway, tossing live coals out into the darkness.
> LITTLE BITS is busy in corner with the dishes)*

MOUSE: Look like to me a jack is better'n nothing since Biggs ain't had
no money to pay us.

VINEY: You the *no*-goodest man I ever did see. Can't make no money!
Can't collect none! Ever since I been married to you we been so
poor I ain't had one nickel to rub against the other.

MOUSE: You was poorer'n that 'fore you married me.

VINEY: I wasn't. My papa owned his own piece of land.

MOUSE: He let the white folks beat him out of it for debt.

VINEY: Hunh! You let them beat *you* out of yourself. You done got so
far in debt sharecropping on this place till you don't even own your
own hide no more. We can't leave this plantation. We jest like slaves.
Every time the cotton's bailed, we owes out more'n we did the year
before, and ain't eat nothing neither but corn meal and fat back,
corn meal and fat back. It's a mystery to me how that commissary
bill get so big.

MOUSE: Ain't no mystery to me. Tippet jest out-figgers us, that's all.

VINEY: Why'nt you say something, then?

MOUSE: *(Disgusted)* Yeah, say something and go to the chain gang.

VINEY: I'd ruther see you there. Least you'd be a man.

MOUSE: Be a man? With a ball and chain on working the roads for nothing. At least, I'm making board and keep here.

VINEY: Board and keep! Humph! And Tippet calling Rose out to pleasure him anytime he want to.

MOUSE: Yes, that's bad.

VINEY: I'm glad you think somethin's bad.

MOUSE: Viney, honey . . .

VINEY: Don't you *honey* me . . . And me without a decent dress to my name.

VINEY: Aw, Viney.

VINEY: Little Bits, throw that dish water out and don't jest thrown it anywhere. Take and pour it on de bait-bed. We needs plenty worms for next week's fishing party. *(She puts dishes away)*

LITTLE BITS: Yes'm, jest lemme put a little this skim on my hair to make it soft. *(She skims off top of greasy dish water and applies it to her hair)*

VINEY: Ain't nothing gwine make that head of your'n soft. *(To JERICO in the doorway)* You chillun go to bed! Gwan! Git! And stop burning up them toad's bellies.

JERICO: We got to wash our feet first.

VINEY: Well, wash 'em then, and make haste about it.

LITTLE BITS: *(Taking dish pan)* Come on, Jerico.
(They disappear outside to empty dish water and wash their feet)

JERICO: *(Yelling from yard)* Aunt Viney, Uncle Mouse, I hears a buggy coming.

LITTLE BITS: *(Running past door)* Somebody's coming.

VINEY: Mouse, go see. I expects it's Queen Esther done come at last.
(MOUSE exits toward road. Voices and greetings. VINEY goes to door)
Lawd! It's my sister!
(Enter QUEEN ESTHER, a gaudily dressed, painted city woman with a young boy, ARCIE, of thirteen or fourteen out-fitted like a man in long pants and sporty tight coat)

QUEEN ESTHER: Sister! Sister! Lawd, I's glad to see you.
(They hug and kiss. Then ESTHER hugs MOUSE and kisses all the children again)

VINEY: I thought it were a lie, you wasn't coming. You done said so many times you were gonna be here, then disappointed us.

QUEEN ESTHER: Had to come now, chile. Times is hard in Memphis! Times is just too tight. *(Calling ARCIE)* Here, this is my other son. You-all ain't never seed him. I didn't bring him last time I were down here five years ago. *(To ARCIE)* Meet your relations, boy. Uncle Mouse . . . Aunt Viney . . . Your brother, Jerico . . . and your foster sister, Little Bits.

VINEY: Bless my soul, I didn't know he were that big!

MOUSE: Queen Esther, you mighty nigh brought home a man here.

ARCIE: I am a man.

QUEEN ESTHER: He ain't but two years younger'n Jerico. I bored him right after I left here and got married the third time.

JERICO: He my brother?

QUEEN ESTHER: Yes, chile. Don't he favor you?

JERICO: No'm, he got straight hair.

QUEEN ESTHER: *(Laughing)* That's just Rise-No-More-Pomade.

JERICO: I wants some, too, to put on my head.

LITTLE BITS: So does I.

ARCIE: I got a whole box in the suitcase. *(Grabbing LITTLE BITS)* I'll give you half of it.

QUEEN ESTHER: Where's my other chile? Rose? My onliest girl?

VINEY: *(Hesitantly)* She'll be back in a minute.

MOUSE: She went down the road a piece.

QUEEN ESTHER: Where Aunt Billie?

VINEY: She's off somewhere with her jug.

QUEEN ESTHER: I wish she'd come back with it.

VINEY: I hope you-all ain't hongry.

QUEEN ESTHER: No, not jest now, I thank you. A porter I met on the train paid for us some sandwiches. He treated us right nice, but later on he kinda made a proposal—you know—but I told him, no, sir! I'm a lady at *all* times.

ARCIE: Mama, I want some more ice cream and gin.

QUEEN ESTHER: Where you think at? This ain't no city, boy! They don't have no ice cream factories out here. *(To others)* This the first time Arcie ever been on a plantation.

ARCIE: I hope it'll be the last time, too, dark as it is out here. Ain't you got no movies nor nothing to go to? What you do at night?

JERICO: We feeds live coals to the hopping toads.

LITTLE BITS: Then we washes our feets and goes to bed.

ARCIE: You go barefooted here? I never seen the beat. *(As others are silent)* Come on, lemme see you feed live coals to the frogs.

VINEY: *(To children)* Naw, you ain't tonight. Time all you-all young-uns was in bed.

QUEEN ESTHER: Yes, won't hurt you none, Arcie, to get your rest. We left Memphis early this morning.

LITTLE BITS: I didn't finish washing my feet yet.

VINEY: Hurry up then and get through.

(LITTLE BITS exits outdoors, followed by ARCIE)

JERICO: *(To QUEEN ESTHER)* I sure am glad you come home, mama. I ain't seen you in such a long time, I most nigh forgot you.

QUEEN ESTHER: Mama's been had a hard time, honey. A hard time. That's why I ain't brung you no presents this time.

JERICO: I don't care about no presents. I'm jest glad to see you.

VINEY: So glad! So glad! To tell the truth, I been had my hands full taking care of these chilluns—and ain't nary one of them my own.

QUEEN ESTHER: Don't Aunt Billie help none?

VINEY: Aunt Billie too busy with her conjure and birthing babies—else she's drunk. You liable to hear her hollering by and by.

MOUSE: Sure good to see you, Queen Esther.

QUEEN ESTHER: I'm here by the hardest. *(Sadly)* You know I ain't had no husband in three years.

MOUSE: He died?

QUEEN ESTHER: Naw, he ain't died. Just quit.

VINEY: *(Going to door and yelling)* You, Little Bits! Oh, Bits!

LITTLE BITS: *(Voice far off)* Ma'm!

VINEY: Get here this minute. What you doing off there in the dark all this time?

LITTLE BITS: *(Closer)* We just playing. Arcie want to catch lightning bugs.

QUEEN ESTHER: I expects Arcie never seen lightning bugs before.

VINEY: Well, you-all get in here.

· *(The two children enter. LITTLE BITS runs to left room)*

LITTLE BITS: *(Quickly)* Good-night! *(Exits into bedroom)*

ARCIE: She's a dumb kid.

JERICO: How come?

VINEY: You boys go to bed now. Arcie, you sleep in yonder with Jerico and Pine and them.

JERICO: Yes'm, I show him. *(Motioning to ARCIE)*

VINEY: And don't forget to say your prayers.

JERICO: Yes'm.

(They exit)

VINEY: The chillun is a trial to me.

QUEEN ESTHER: How come you and Mouse ain't never had none?

MOUSE: Ask Viney.

VINEY: Ask me nothing! Ask Mouse.

QUEEN ESTHER: Well, I sure ain't troubled that away. I don't know what 'tis about me. Fact is, I feels funny now. *(Just then the jack brays at the top of his lungs down by the shed and everybody jumps)* What's that? Aunt Billie?

VINEY: Naw, that's a little old jack Mouse brought here.

QUEEN ESTHER: Well, he's sure raising hell—I mean sand!
       (Noise of horse whinnying)

MOUSE: That the old mare, Jenny. Now *she's* started.

QUEEN ESTHER: Jenny still living?

VINEY: Yes, and she too old to be worried with a jack.

QUEEN ESTHER: They tell me when a jack holler, that makes a wo-man's love come down. Ain't you never heard that, Viney?

VINEY: That's a old saying, but I never did believe it were true.

QUEEN ESTHER: Yes, it is true, too. If a jack jest holler once a day, it's enough to drive a woman mad.

VINEY: No wonder I been feeling so queer tonight.

MOUSE: How you feeling?

VINEY: Mouse, I wants you to take that jack away from here.

MOUSE: I will, then, next week. I'll carry him on back. *(Hesitating)* Though if he gonna affect you like how Queen Esther say, I think I'll keep him around. You been mighty cold-like towards me.

VINEY: Keep him nothing! You takes him back tomorrow—hear? We's got young girls in this house. Little Bits ain't even a woman yet, hardly, and that jack a-hollering and a setting fire to every petticoat! It just won't do!

MOUSE: I can't take him tomorrow. Old Man Biggs gone to town and won't be back till next week. He gone in to communion Sunday.

VINEY: *(Raising her voice again)* You mean we got to have that thing here over Sunday?

MOUSE: I reckon we is. And, oh, yes, I forgot to tell you, the preacher is coming here for dinner Sunday, too.

VINEY: Rev. Lovelady?

MOUSE: Yes, him. Sister Bentley's sick and say she can't take care of our pastor this week. And you know when he come way out here to preach, all the way from Newton, he got to eat.

VINEY: Well, you'll have to rustle round and get something for him to eat then. You know we ain't got nothing fitten for ourselves, even much, let alone company.

QUEEN ESTHER: He can always eat a chicken.

VINEY: You'll never kill neither one of my setting hens.

MOUSE: What we gonna do then?

VINEY: How I know? Maybe Aunt Billie might let us kill one of her frizzly chickens.

MOUSE: Aunt Billie don't care a heap about preachers, nohow, and them frizzly chickens is her good-luck pieces.

QUEEN ESTHER: Is he a nice preacher?

MOUSE: He got a way with the ladies.

VINEY: Sure he is a nice preacher. He's holy and sanctified, too.

QUEEN ESTHER: Amen! I wants to see him . . . But, say, it's getting late here. Where's Rose? I wants to see my daughter before I goes to bed.

MOUSE: *(Going to door)* I reckon I'll wash my feet, too. *(Exits)*

VINEY: She'll be here directly. Sister, *(Pauses . . . then)* I hates to tell you, but Rose *(Another halt, then slowly)* done took up with a white man.

QUEEN ESTHER: My chile? *What* white man? Who?

VINEY: With the over-seer.

QUEEN ESTHER: On this plantation?

VINEY: Yes.

QUEEN ESTHER: Do he make her presents? Money or anything?

VINEY: So far as I can see, he ain't gived her nothing but one dress. He come and throwed it in the door today.

QUEEN ESTHER: *(Disappointed)* That's bad. He sounds like a cheap skate, too.

VINEY: But the chile can't help it. He make her come. You know how they do with any poor colored gal they wants out here in the country.

QUEEN ESTHER: Don't I know? I ain't forgot how Rose herself come in this world.

MOUSE: *(Entering)* I went down to the shed just now, and old Jenny done mighty nigh busted her halter when she yelled.

VINEY: That jack's enough to make her bust her brains out, the way he holler.

MOUSE: *(Proudly)* That's a powerful little old jack, you know it. I believes I'll keep him.

VINEY: If you can't sell that jack and get my ten dollars, then you take it right on back to Biggs.

MOUSE: All right, Viney! I ain't gonna argue no more tonight—we got company. How we gonna sleep?

VINEY: *(Thinking a moment)* I reckon you better make yourself a pallet on the floor over there by the fireplace, and let sister sleep in the bed with me.

MOUSE: All right. Gimme the coverings.

VINEY: *(Loudly)* You big and ugly as I is. Git the coverings down your own self—from the shed room yonder. *(MOUSE goes for covers. He spreads them on floor, then turns his back, takes off his overalls and gets in the pallet clad in his blue field shirt and dirt-colored underwear) (To her sister)* Queen Esther, we all might as well lay down. Aunt Billie, no telling what time she'll be here. And when she do, you'll hear her a-hollering in her lickers. The white folks been threatening to lock her up in the calaboos.

QUEEN ESTHER: They done got a court and jail out here now?

VINEY: Naw, they ain't got nothing like that. This jest Tippet's little private jail he built for this here plantation. It ain't as big as this room.

MOUSE: Hope the skeeters don't bite too much tonight.

VINEY: *(Going toward bed)* I'm gonna turn back the kivvers here sister, and start getting in the bed. *(Emitting a loud yell of terror as she pulls back the covers)* Oh-ooo-ooo-ooo! Aw!

QUEEN ESTHER: *(Springing up)* What on earth?

MOUSE: *(Sitting up in his pallet)* What the . . . ?

VINEY: *(Quickly replacing covers)* They's a snake in this bed!

MOUSE: Is?

VINEY: Yes. A great big old black snake all stretched out. *(Pointing)* Look a-yonder! See him wiggling under the covers!

MOUSE: Sure do. *(Standing up)*

QUEEN ESTHER: Now I knows I'm in the country. Ain't seen a snake in the bed since I were a chile.

VINEY: They's awful out here this year. Sometimes they crawls up in the eves and draps down on the table.

MOUSE: How we gonna kill him?

QUEEN ESTHER: Mash him.

VINEY: Naw! Grab him up in the sheet, Mouse, then hit him with the axe in the yard yonder. That's the best way to kill a snake.

MOUSE: *(Hesitating)* Oh, you wants *me* to grab him up, do you?

VINEY: Mouse, don't you aggravate me! Do, and I'll snatch that snake and throw him on you.

MOUSE: I's jest fooling. You-all get back.

   (QUEEN ESTHER backs away, as MOUSE catches up the sheet—

which is made of flour bags—and with the snake, therein, holds it far from him, then exits to yard and returns with the dead snake in one hand and the sheet in other)

VINEY: He'll never get in no more beds.

MOUSE: You done wriggled your last wiggle and snaked your last hip.

QUEEN ESTHER: I sure glad Arcie didn't see that. He'd be scared to death of the country if he had of.

MOUSE: Well, anyway, Aunt Billie's got a good snake head for her conjure.

VINEY: Don't bother about cutting it off tonight.

MOUSE: Naw, I won't. *(Lifting snake up by his tail)* Looky here. A long varmint, too. *(Throwing it just outside the door)* Leave it in the yard till morning, so the kids can see it.

VINEY: I hope its mate ain't nowhere around.

QUEEN ESTHER: I doubt if I'll sleep a wink tonight. Viney, look in that bed good to see that they ain't no more snakes.

VINEY: I never did find more'n one snake in a bed at once, and that don't happen often.

QUEEN ESTHER: I don't care. Let's we look good.

(The two women take off the quilts and turn over the mattress as MOUSE goes back to bed)

MOUSE: Now, I reckon maybe I can sleep.

QUEEN ESTHER: Jest so we ain't sleeping on no snake.

VINEY: Tired as I is, I could sleep on anything. I wish all them other monkeys would come on home here. Aunt Billie out, Rose out, Pine out.

QUEEN ESTHER: Who's Pine?

VINEY: He ain't really named Pine. They calls him that cause he's *tall* as a Georgia pine.

QUEEN ESTHER: Tall, hunh?

VINEY: Pine's a young man what just recently lost his wife.

QUEEN ESTHER: Now ain't that too bad! How come he staying here? You all took pity on him?

VINEY: He's a friend of Mouse's and we took him here to board.

QUEEN ESTHER: He's company for Mouse, ain't he?

VINEY: Ain't company for nobody much. Spends all his time down the road at that ugly Jenkins gal's.

QUEEN ESTHER: *(Half-joking)* Well, I'm got to see about that.

VINEY: You old enough to be his mammy, near about.

QUEEN ESTHER: Oh, he's pig-meat?

VINEY: I don't know what you mean by that, but he's a young boy about twenty-two, and you jest let him alone.

QUEEN ESTHER: That's what pig-meat means in the city, young and sweet.

VINEY: This bed is ready. Come and get in any time you choose.

QUEEN ESTHER: *(Playfully)* I think I'll wait up for Pine.

VINEY: *(Angrily)* Queen Esther, come on get in this bed like you got some decent sense.

QUEEN ESTHER: Oh, I meant, I'll wait up for Rose.

VINEY: Yes, that's right. I knows you wants to see her. *(Unhooking her dress)* Well, I'm gonna lay down.

> *(QUEEN ESTHER opens her suitcase and takes out a comb. Begins to comb her hair for the night. VINEY kneels down and prays silently. Away down the road a reverberating yell is heard. Yee-hoo!)*

QUEEN ESTHER: Sounds like somebody's snakebit.

VINEY: *(Rising from her knees)* Ain't nobody but Aunt Billie and Rondie drunk. If Rondie ain't already fell by the wayside.

QUEEN ESTHER: Some folks has a little fun down here in the sticks after all.

VINEY: If you calls that fun. *(She gets in bed)*

QUEEN ESTHER: You always was kinder stuck up, Viney.

VINEY: Aw, hush, and lemme go to sleep.

QUEEN ESTHER: Sure. *(Comes over and kisses her)* Good-night, sister. I'll be climbing in there with you by and by. *(QUEEN ESTHER unpacks—cheap pink lingerie, a sleazy red silk gown, a kimono. She hangs the clothes up, slips off her dress and puts the kimono on. Outside it is quiet save for an occasional yell in the distance from AUNT BILLIE. Fireflies glow everywhere. QUEEN ESTHER sits down in her kimono and again combs her hair. A soft gay whistle approaches in the dark. PINE enters)* Oh, good-evening.

PINE: *(Surprised)* Good-evening, Ma'am.

> *(He starts across room to door Right, but QUEEN ESTHER rises)*

QUEEN ESTHER: I'm Queen Esther.

PINE: I'm Pine.

QUEEN ESTHER: Oh, howdy do! I heard about you.

PINE: You heard about me?

QUEEN ESTHER: Yes, about your affliction.

PINE: Oh, you mean my wife dying?

QUEEN ESTHER: I'm surely sorry.

PINE: Oh, that's all right—leastwise, I mean, that's been more'n three months—I means that happens to most everybody.

QUEEN ESTHER: Yes, I know it do. But I never could console myself whenever I lost any of my husbands.

PINE: Yes'm I'm sorry, too.

QUEEN ESTHER: *(Touching his arm—which wears a mourning band—comforting him)* You got my sympathy.

PINE: *(Starting into bedroom again)* Thank you, Ma'm. Goodnight.

QUEEN ESTHER: *(Calling after him)* We found a snake in the bed tonight. My sister Viney was pulling back the covers and there he was.

PINE: Can you beat that!

QUEEN ESTHER: *(Talking fast, trying to delay PINE as long as possible)* And I screamed. You know I been in the city so long, I done most forgot about snakes. I don't know how I'm gonna get along down here again, less'n somebody goes out with me when I take a walk. I mean some menfolks or other what can protect me. I'm scared to death of snakes.

PINE: *(Taking a step toward her)* I'll do that myself if you . . .

VINEY: *(Suddenly turning over)* Queen Esther growed up in the country jest like me. Don't pay her no mind, Pine, cause she's stepped on many a snake. She don't need no pertection. She's just putting on now. Whyn't you-all go to bed anyhow, and let a body sleep?

PINE: Yes'm, Miss Viney. *(He opens door)*

VINEY: Good night, Pine.

PINE: Good-night. *(Exits)*

VINEY: *(To her sister)* Don't think you's in Memphis, can keep people up all times of night. It must be after eight o'clock.

QUEEN ESTHER: Well, I was just getting acquainted with the young man. Besides, since that jack hollered, I need to get acquainted with somebody.

VINEY: You were making mighty good time. You coulda waited till morning. Pine's tired out.

QUEEN ESTHER: He don't look it.

VINEY: *(Sulkily)* Well, if you gonna stay up, turn the light down. It draw too many candle flies. I'm gonna sleep—if I can. That devilish jack! Soften that light.

QUEEN ESTHER: All right. *(Goes to lamp and turns it down. She walks back and closes her suitcase and sits it against the wall. Goes to door and looks out. Comes back and sits down by the table. MOUSE is snoring.*

The boys are snoring in the other room. Finally VINEY begins to snore, too. Frogs croak, night noises rustle, locusts chirp. It begins to get on QUEEN ESTHER's *nerves)* My Gawd! The country! *(Rises and walks about. She turns to face ROSE in the doorway)* Rose! My baby! Honey, chile!

ROSE: *(Disheveled. She does not recognize her mother at once)* Hello!

QUEEN ESTHER: *(Going to caress her)* Don't you remember your mama?

ROSE: *(Drunkenly)* Hello! Hello! I don't care! *(Goes past QUEEN ESTHER to take towel from nail)* I just wanna go to bed. Wash and go to bed. That's all. *(ROSE takes towel and reels toward door Right)*

QUEEN ESTHER: *(Calling)* Rose, honey! Wait a minute!

(ROSE stops. QUEEN ESTHER takes her in her arms)

ROSE: I want to go to sleep, mama, that's all. .

QUEEN ESTHER: *(Gently)* All right, honey, come on. Mama understands.

(Leads ROSE into room Right and closes door. Just then the jack hollers, splitting the very night. VINEY turns, sits up suddenly, looks around. Her eyes stop at door where PINE is sleeping)

VINEY: *(Softly)* Pine! Oh, Pine! *(As the jack brays a second time, VINEY turns her head and calls her husband loudly)* You Mouse! *(MOUSE sits up suddenly)* Come here and get in this bed.

MOUSE rises sleepily and crosses the room as the

CURTAIN FALLS

Act II

SCENE: *The front yard of Mouse's cabin.*

TIME: *Sunday afternoon.*

Merely a cleared space in the cotton, a large flame tree gives shade, a jasmine vine tumbling over the doorway of the house, a washbench at right of door, wash pan on nail, a rocking chair under the tree, chickens, a lean dog running about. Close against the house on the ground, a newspaper in the sun, on it spiders, poisonous insects and a reptile's head drying.

AT RISE: *When the curtain rises, AUNT BILLIE is sitting in the rocking chair, smoking her pipe. QUEEN ESTHER, wearing open-work-sandals, is seated on a box near the door, polishing her fingernails. JERICO is chopping wood. ROSE is picking a chicken and ARCIE is just lolling around.*

AUNT BILLIE: Queen Esther, you should-a gone to church today and heard the sermon, even if your left ear do let out what your right ear catch.

QUEEN ESTHER: Aunt Billie, you know I ain't much on churches and never has been.

AUNT BILLIE: Me neither, but you ought to gone. You'd seen all your old friends there.

QUEEN ESTHER: Hunh! I seen enough of them countrified jigaboos yesterday down at the cross roads store. Come making admiration at my red nails and my clothes, and eyeing the rouge on my face, like it were a sin to try and look pretty. Some of the women didn't even much speak.

AUNT BILLIE: What the mens say?

QUEEN ESTHER: The mens say they ain't seen nothing look as good as me since the last time I were here.

AUNT BILLIE: That's why the womens didn't speak.

QUEEN ESTHER: They eyed me like I were a circus show.

AUNT BILLIE: You does look like one.

QUEEN ESTHER: Aw, Aunt Billie. (*JERICO enters house with wood*) I'm a lady at *all* times. (*Eyeing her nails*)

AUNT BILLIE: Well, I don't know what you doing all that primping out here in the country for, if you ain't going nowhere.

QUEEN ESTHER: The minister's coming for dinner today, ain't he?

AUNT BILLIE: He ain't no more'n me.

QUEEN ESTHER: But he's a man, ain't he?

AUNT BILLIE: Since that jack commenced hollering around here, y'all womens is done got most mighty interested in mens.

QUEEN ESTHER: Jack or no jack, I always did kinda care for mens myself.

AUNT BILLIE: Too well! Too well!

QUEEN ESTHER: Aw, Aunt Billie!

(*Enter LITTLE BITS, her hair slicked down like Josephine Baker's*)

LITTLE BITS: (*Calling*) Aunt Viney, they weren't no eggs nowheres that I could find.

VINEY: (*Sticking her head out a window*) Then Rev'm. Lovelady just have to eat his corn-bread without a egg in it. I ain't gonna use none of my setting eggs for nobody.

AUNT BILLIE: Plain corn pone just as good. I eats it.

QUEEN ESTHER: But he's the minister.

AUNT BILLIE: Shucks!

VINEY: *(To LITTLE BITS)* We's got to have something for the afterpart, so, Little Bits, go out yonder in the woods and see can't you uncover no kind of wild berries somewheres, enough for the preacher to eat for his dessert.

LITTLE BITS: *(To ARCIE)* Yes'm. Arcie, you wants to go with me?

ARCIE: Sure, baby!

AUNT BILLIE: You ought to take off them city clothes you got on, then, boy. You get them all torn off in the brambles. And, Little Bits, be careful a fly don't light on your head. He'll slip and fall off.

LITTLE BITS: *(Passing her hand over her straightened hair)* This here's from the pomade Arcie give me this morning. Don't it look nice?

QUEEN ESTHER: Arcie, maybe you had better take off your good suit. Borrow some overalls from Jerico.

ARCIE: Aw, I don't wanta wear no overalls. Don't people dress up down here on Sunday?

VINEY: When chilluns washes their feet and combs their head, they's dressed up here.

ARCIE: Well, I ain't like that. *(To LITTLE BITS)* Come on, Little Bits, let's go.

> *(LITTLE BITS and ARCIE exit)*

VINEY: Rose, ain't you got that chicken picked yet?

ROSE: Yes, Aunt Viney, I'm coming right in with it.

VINEY: Church be out directly, and the preacher be coming.

AUNT BILLIE: His belly hongrier for chicken than his soul is for Gawd.

VINEY: You oughtn't to talk that way about the preacher.

> *(She vanishes from window. ROSE takes chicken and exits into house)*

AUNT BILLIE: One of my best frizzly chickens gone by way of Sandusky.

QUEEN ESTHER: I'm gonna freshen up my face before the minister comes.

AUNT BILLIE: All right, go on. *(QUEEN ESTHER exits. AUNT BILLIE rises and goes over to newspaper and squats down, picking up dried bits of spiders, other poisonous insects, and the snake head. Mumbles to herself)* Hunh! This here look like it's ready. I must get myself a rock. *(Calling)* Jerico! Where's Jerico?

VINEY: *(Voice in house)* He gone down to pasture Jenny. I don't want her kicking that barn down, slat by slat, every time that jack hollers.

AUNT BILLIE: *(Going to corner of house and calling loudly)* Jerico!

JERICO: *(Voice in distance)* Ma'am!

AUNT BILLIE: Come here. Make haste and bring me a rock, a big flat rock that got some weight to it.

JERICO: *(Off stage)* Yes'm.

ROSE: *(Coming out of house)* What you gonna make, Aunt Billie?

AUNT BILLIE: Don't ask too many questions, Rose! *(Whispering)* Tippet been bothering you, ain't he?

ROSE: He say he want to see me tonight, and I's scared he beat me, if I don't go, or maybe he put Viney and Mouse and you-all off this place.

AUNT BILLIE: He ain't gonna put *me* off of nowhere. But I gwine fix him so he leave you alone, too. Mark my words. *(Slowly)* He gwine fall in the field in the sun. He gwine sink down shouting and a-cussing like he always do at us poor folks out there in the field. Then he ain't gonna cuss no more not right directly, nohow. *(Putting her arm on ROSE's shoulder)* You us stuck on Bogator, ain't you Rose?

ROSE: *(Shyly)* Reckon I is. *(A little embarrassed laugh)* I wish him and me could get married up.

AUNT BILLIE: I gonna sprinkle Love-Dust all over both y'all, chile.

ROSE: Please, Aunt Billie.

    (MAN'S VOICE, high-pitched and nasal, the hill-billy type, is heard calling from the road)

SID LOWERY: Berries! Berries! Nice fresh strawberries!

    (A middle-aged, scrawny poor white enters in overalls, carrying a basket of strawberries)

AUNT BILLIE: Rose, you run on in the house, now.

    (Exit ROSE into house)

SID LOWERY: I got some mighty nice berries my wife and kids picked this morning. You-all in need of some?

AUNT BILLIE: *(Calling)* Viney, you be needing some berries, ain't you?

VINEY: *(Coming to window, leaning head out)* What I got to buy them with? I'm needing more'n berries, but I can't buy it.

SID LOWERY: I'm offering them mighty cheap.

VINEY: Don't keer how cheap you offers them, penny a basket and I couldn't even take one berry. *(Withdraws head)*

SID LOWERY: Times is hard everywhere, ain't they?

AUNT BILLIE: Hard! Hard! Hard!

SID LOWERY: Say, Aunt Billie, I been wanting to see you anyhow, lately. *(Looks around carefully)* I wants to talk to you.

AUNT BILLIE: *(Sitting down with professional dignity)* We is got peace and silence here.

SID LOWERY: I's got something on my mind, Aunt Billie, maybe you can help me with it.

AUNT BILLIE: Be's it a case of body sickness, or is somebody crossed your soul?

SID LOWERY: They crossed my soul, that's what.

AUNT BILLIE: That's a serious thing, Sid Lowery. *(Holding out her cupped hand)* But the conjure don't work without it see a little something in advance. Is you got some money with you?

SID LOWERY: I been trying to sell these berries all day long. Look like ain't nobody got no cash in they pockets, neither in they house.

AUNT BILLIE: *(Unimpressed)* Hunh! That's too bad.

SID LOWERY: *(Eagerly)* But I tell you what I'll do, Aunt Billie. I'll give you this here whole basket of berries—it's worth more'n fifty cents, ain't it?—if you'll jest tell me what to do, or fix me up some kind of charm or nother to see can't I get rid of what's done nearly got me down.

AUNT BILLIE: What is it, Son?

SID LOWERY: It's my wife, Aunt Billie. Seem like she don't love me no more.

AUNT BILLIE: What seem to be the trouble?

SID LOWERY: I don't know. Seem like she jest ain't herself no more. Since we had to cut out going to town so often, 'cause the old Ford done wore out and we ain't got no money to get it fixed, and since she ain't seen no movies nor nothing for a long time, and since our last chile come, seem like she's just mad and complaining every day. Soon as I get in from the field, she start a-jawing and a-jawing.

AUNT BILLIE: She don't work in the field herself, do she?

SID LOWERY: Not no more. She got three babies she have to stay home and tend now.

AUNT BILLIE: That's right, she a white woman! Were she a colored cropper's wife she'd be out there in them fields, babies and all.

SID LOWERY: Expects she would, Aunt Billie. But to tell the truth, we ain't no better off'n you-all is. She don't go to the field, but she tends the chickens and cow, and she picks berries.

AUNT BILLIE: Yes, I know she a right smart little woman. But you say she's quarrelsome. *(Pointedly)* She can't quarrel by herself, can she?

SID LOWERY: I has to answer her back sometimes, she makes me so mad.

AUNT BILLIE: There, now! I got to work on you some, too, then. What do you-all quarrel about?

SID LOWERY: Everything and nothing.

AUNT BILLIE: Most of the quarreling start in the evening, don't it?

SID LOWERY: It sure does, soon's I get in the house and start to eat.

AUNT BILLIE: Well, I got something wonderful for that. I'm gonna go in and get it. Excuse me, just a minute.

> *(AUNT BILLIE goes into the house. SID LOWERY sits on box to await her. JERICO enters with a large stone that he puts down near the rocker)*

JERICO: Howdy-do, suh, Mister Lowery.

SID LOWERY: Howdy, Jerry! How's things with you?

JERICO: Pretty good, suh! We got a jack down yonder at the barn. You ain't got no mare needs breeding, has you? Make a fine mule colt.

SID LOWERY: I ain't got nothing but a cow, and I don't know about crossing a cow wid a jack.

JERICO: You'd sure get something you *couldn't* milk.

AUNT BILLIE: *(Emerging from house with bottles and boxes)* Hey, son!

JERICO: There's your rock, Aunt Billie.

AUNT BILLIE: *(Peering)* It a big flat one?

JERICO: Yes'm.

AUNT BILLIE: Thank you!

> *(JERICO goes into house. AUNT BILLIE sits down and spreads her bottles and materials at her feet. SID LOWERY draws his box near)*

SID LOWERY: You know more about conjure'n anybody in this county, Aunt Billie.

AUNT BILLIE: *(Matter-of-factly)* I sure do!

SID LOWERY: There ain't no white person know near much as you do.

AUNT BILLIE: Sure ain't.

SID LOWERY: I jest wish I could afford to come to see you more often. I think things would be better.

AUNT BILLIE: Sure would! *(She opens boxes and takes out an empty Bull Durham sack, then a pinch of powder here, a dry leaf there, a root from another box)* Now, listen fluently to me, Sid Lowery. You listen—and do jest what I say.

SID LOWERY: Yes, Ma'am!

AUNT BILLIE: *(Concentrating on grinding powder with her thumb in the palm of one hand)*
> Lawd help! Paul, too!
> Moses come! I calls on you!
> John de Conqueror!
> Witches wild!
> Devil, scat! Holy Chile!
> Power be, power is!
> Evil go, wherever you is!
> Amen! Amen!
> *(Commanding)* Say, *Amen,* Sid Lowery.

SID LOWERY: Amen!

AUNT BILLIE: Now you take this bag *(Puts powder in Bull Durham sack)*—and put it underneaf of your pillow at night. Wake up every so often and see is it there, and every time you wakes up, turn over and kiss your wife. Kiss her right hard.

SID LOWERY: *(Pleased)* To tell the truth, I ain't courted her much since I married her.

AUNT BILLIE: I know you ain't. *(Handing him the powder)* Now, this here is Love-Come-Back powder. Can't nobody make it but me. And *don't* give it to nobody.

SID LOWERY: I won't.

AUNT BILLIE: I know you ain't. *(Handing him the powder)* Don't let nobody else see it. Do, and it will lose its strength and 'fluence, and I'll have to go to work and restore its power back—for fifty cents, 'cause them there herbs is hard to find.

SID LOWERY: Yes'm.

AUNT BILLIE: *(Taking a small bottle and pouring water from a larger one)* Now, here is one more charm. You got to work it jest like I tells you. Every time your wife start to quarreling with you, you reach in your pocket and get out this bottle, unbeknowings to her, and you take a mouth full of this. Hold it in your mouth, though. Don't swaller it. Hold it in your mouth till your wife gets tired of talking, till she done talked out, till she ain't got and can't think of no more to say—then you go outside and spit it out and come back and kiss her square in the mouth, and say, "Honey, let's us crawl in the hay." And I'll be bound they won't be another evil word passed in your house that night.

SID LOWERY: I'm sure gonna try it, Aunt Billie. Thank you! *(Rising)* You sho is a smart old colored woman. How much do I owe you?

AUNT BILLIE: That basket of berries, like you said. Conjure don't work for nothing.

SID LOWERY: Here. *(Giving her the basket of berries)* Sorry it can't be in cash money, but you know how times is—and Tippet's a mighty tight overseer. He ain't gived none of us nothing these last two years—nothing.

AUNT BILLIE: That are true.

SID LOWERY: But please, I wish you'd gimme the basket back. That belongs to my wife, and I don't want to have to start using my conjure water soon's I get in the door.

AUNT BILLIE: Naw, 'cause that there water is Holy Water from Jerusalem.

SID LOWERY: How you get it?

AUNT BILLIE: That I cannot tell. *(Calling)* Rose! Rose! Come here and empty out this basket of berries.

ROSE: Coming, Aunt Billie. *(She emerges with a pan and empties the berries into it)* What a nice lot of strawberries!

AUNT BILLIE: Nice as they can be. *(To SID LOWERY)* Here's your basket. Now you do jest as I say, with all what I told you. And if you do as I say, t'won't be no more trouble in your house. But you got to *believe* while you doing it.

SID LOWERY: I ain't disbelieving. I'm jest gonna use this and pray.

AUNT BILLIE: Pray if you wants to, *but have that bag renewed when it runs out.*

SID LOWERY: That I will. And soon's I get home from meeting tonight, I'm gonna try it out.

AUNT BILLIE: *(Interested)* You belong to the lodge?

SID LOWERY: Well, tain't 'zactly no lodge.

AUNT BILLIE: A meeting of mens?

SID LOWERY: Yes.

AUNT BILLIE: Um-hum! Then I know what 'tis.

SID LOWERY: You do? How you know?

AUNT BILLIE: I knows all what's happening around here. You belongs to the Klan, that's what—the Ku Klux Klan!

SID LOWERY: You knows too much, Aunt Billie. Ain't nobody got no business knowing that.

AUNT BILLIE: How I gonna help from knowing it when every tree tells me things, the roads I walks on, too, and the air I breathes?

SID LOWERY: But our burning cross and snow white robes, it tells no secrets.

AUNT BILLIE: The black cat's bone and the joo-joo powder, it find out all. *(Scolding)* How you expects my conjure to do you any good, if you keeps back secrets from me, Sid Lowery? Can't nobody keep nothing back from Aunt Billie Boxer, nohow. That's why I'm Aunt Billie.

SID LOWERY: You're powerful smart, for a old black woman.

AUNT BILLIE: This old woman been here a long time, son, a long time.

SID LOWERY: Well, I reckon I'll be getting along now.

AUNT BILLIE: *(Inquisitively)* You-all getting ready for a parade, ain't you? A night parade?

SID LOWERY: How you know?

AUNT BILLIE: You ain't had none for a long time, that's how I know. I thought maybe your sheets and hoods done near 'bout wore out from not using 'em.

SID LOWERY: *(Disgustedly)* Hard times done got everybody, that's what! Working all day and not hardly getting enough to eat, the Kleagle nor anybody don't feel much like getting out and riding at night.

AUNT BILLIE: You mean walking, don't you? Cause I ain't never seen you-all Klansmen riding round here. Ain't none of you-all got no horses to ride on.

SID LOWERY: *(Proudly)* When the Klan walk, it rides—just the same.

AUNT BILLIE: *Well,* jest so you don't come around here scaring my chilluns next time you parades.

SID LOWERY: *(Putting on* his *act)* Only God knows where the Klan appears and disappears, or when or why!

AUNT BILLIE: Um-hum! Yes—only Gawd, and maybe Aunt Billie.

SID LOWERY: Then you keep your mouth shut.

AUNT BILLIE: Tighter than the tomb. I's a secret-keeper, Sid Lowery. *(With a gesture of farewell)* When that Love-Come-Back powder gives out, come and see me again.

SID LOWERY: Don't worry about that, Aunt Billie. You'll see me again. So long. *(Exits)*

AUNT BILLIE: My compliments to the Grand Goslin, suh. Gawd go with you. *(Turns and goes, muttering to herself, toward her spread of dried spiders)* White skin ain't smarted him up a bit. The Ku Klux Klan! Hunh! Ain't nobody skeered of them no more—hongry and sorry as they looks. *(She starts picking up spiders one by one until she has a handful, then she calls:)* Jerico! Jerico!

JERICO: *(Voice in the house)* Ma'am?

AUNT BILLIE: Bring me a hammer. *(She goes and gets the flattened stone)*

JERICO: Yes'm.

AUNT BILLIE: A hammer and a piece of clean white cloth. Ask Viney for it.

VINEY: *(Yelling from the house)* Where I gonna get any piece of clean white cloth?

ROSE: *(Coming to the window)* I'll find you a piece, Aunt Billie.

AUNT BILLIE: All right, chile, and make haste about it.

   (BOGATOR enters, carrying an axe)

BOGATOR: Hy, Aunt Billie.

AUNT BILLIE: Hello, chile.

BOGATOR: I done chopped down a tree make 'nough wood for a month of Sundays. All cut up, too. *(Calling)* Viney, you hear what I saying?

VINEY: *(Coming to the window)* I hears you. That's the first good thing you done in a long time.

BOGATOR: I know you gonna gimme a piece of chicken now.

VINEY: This here chicken I'm cookin's for the company—for Rev'm Lovelady and Queen Esther. It ain't gonna stretch around to all we-all—jest one chicken.

BOGATOR: Hongry as I is, you ain't even much gonna give me a wing?

VINEY: Now don't start that, Bogator. You know I got to keep a piece for the boarder.

BOGATOR: You means Pine? He ain't no *paying* boarder.

VINEY: He a friend of Mouse's, and he a poor boy what jest lost his wife.

BOGATOR: He done forgot he got crepes on his arm. I bet he setting up right now in the choir beside of Caroline—can't sing *Come to Jesus* for eye-balling at her.

VINEY: If he got any sense, he ain't eyeing Caroline. She don't mean him no good.

AUNT BILLIE: *(Calling)* You, Jerico! Where that hammer?

JERICO: *(In house)* Here it is! I jest found it. *(He emerges with the hammer)*

AUNT BILLIE: And the cloth? You-all slower'n molasses in January!

ROSE: *(Entering from the house)* Here it is, Aunt Billie, a piece of clean white cloth.

AUNT BILLIE: Yes, it got to be white so I can see what color this charm makes on it. *(She takes the cloth and places it on the flat rock well spread out. She puts the hammer down beside it. Then she motions the young people away)* Shoo! Get, you-all! You know I don't allow nobody to see me make my potions. Skat, every living one of you.

(Exit ROSE into the house)

BOGATOR: *(Putting the axe down)* Come on, Jerico, let's we go down and see about the little old jack. Maybe he want some water. His throat must be dry.

JERICO: He ain't yelled today.

(JERICO and BOGATOR exit)

AUNT BILLIE: *(Muttering to herself as she places the dry spiders on the cloth atop the stone)* One-two-three-four-five-six-seven. Seven dried-out spiders . . . One snake head . . . De brains of two scorpions . . . and the liver of a he-male lizard . . . Here 'tis. *(She folds the cloth bag-like, holds the ends and begins to hammer the contents on the stone)* Hunh! . . . Hunh! . . . Hunh! . . .

VINEY: *(Calling from the house)* Aunt Billie, you don't see nothing of Mouse, does you? It's about time he were showing up here from church.

AUNT BILLIE: Keep quiet and let me consumstrate! *(She continues to pound on the rock. Then she lifts the cloth and smells it, draws back suddenly, and begins to pound again. After a while, she opens the cloth, looks at it—all red—and is apparently satisfied. Then she calls:)* Rose! Oh, Rose!! Honey, come here.

ROSE: *(Coming from the house)* Yes, Aunt Billie.

AUNT BILLIE: Listen to me, now. Take back them boxes and bottles and all what you see over yonder by that rocker, and put them on my shelf. Then look 'way back in the corner of the shelf and you'll find a little red tin box. It's all tied up to keep anything or anybody from getting in it. You bring that box here.

ROSE: *(Going to collect the things near the chair)* Yes'm.

AUNT BILLIE: And bring me out a empty vaseline jar, too, one of them clean ones I always keeps ready for things like this.

ROSE: Yes'm, Aunt Billie. *(She goes into the house)*

AUNT BILLIE: *(Putting both hands over the cloth on the stone)*
   "Witch, devil
   Bitch and sow,
   Gather wind for
   Fighting now!
   (Yelling) Zan-gar-ree!!"

ROSE: *(Coming out of the house, startled)* Oh!

AUNT BILLIE: *(Very seriously)* Come here.

ROSE: *(Approaching)* Here's the jar and the box.

AUNT BILLIE: Shsss! *(Takes the articles)* Sit down and keep quiet. *(ROSE sits on the ground beside the stone. AUNT BILLIE opens the box and takes several pinches of the powder therein and puts it into the vaseline jar. Shakes it until the inside of the jar is red. Then she catches both sides of the cloth, puts one end into the jar and pours the contents in, mumbling incantations all the while)* Rose, this got a world of good in it for you. A world of bad in it for anybody else—so be careful. Use it like I say! It's a potion and a charm, a savior and a hell, a joy and a torment, all in one. *(Whispering)* This here one of the strongest charms known to conjure. This here a charm Marie Laveau got out of the book from the black art of the Kings of Egypt and brung to New Orleans and gived to my old grandma to hand down the line to her chilluns' chilluns. This ain't no eve'day charm. This a dark charm. This charm make the stars turn red and the sun stop shining in the sky. You can't fool with this charm, gal, so listen to me and make no mistake. Take this jar. *(ROSE takes the jar)* Put it in the bosom of your dress. *(ROSE puts it there)* And never say a word. Not to me nor nobody that you ever got this charm from anywhere. You ain't seed it, you ain't touched it. It's a silent secret charm. Keep it till Tippet call you. Keep it till he whistle. Then go and be sweet to the white man, sweet as you know how. And Tippet gonna say, "Here, here have a drink," and offer you the licker bottle. Take it, and in the dark you pour this charm into the bottle. Every dusty grain! That's all. Then you don't drink no more from the bottle that night. It's all for him. If he say to you, "Here, have a drink," another time you put the bottle to your lips, but don't let nary drop pass through. Let him drink it all—if he want to. And you a-saying, "Ain't it good, Mister Tippet?"

ROSE: *(Her eyes big)* Yes, Aunt Billie.

AUNT BILLIE: Shsss! Not a word! Not a word from you! This ain't none of your charm. You don't even know you got it. You hears me, you don't know it. You and the charm is silent, silent, silent . . . He gonna be silent, too, when the charm get through. That mean old overseer's gonna be silent, too.

ROSE: *(About to scream, putting her hand to her mouth in horror)* Aw. . . . . . . !

AUNT BILLIE: Naw, not what you think. Not dead! He'll be living—

but jest silent, that's all, and he won't bother you no more . . . And I'm gonna sprinkle Love Dust all around this house and say *BOGATOR* ten times with my big toe crossed, till that boy beg you to get married and be his wife. *(Rising)* Somebody's coming. Here, you take this hammer in the house. *(In fake surprise as she rises)* What is I doing sitting on the ground all this time? Lawdy me! *(Brushing off the back of her dress)* I'm right dusty. Where's my pipe? *(Goes to rocker and begins to smoke as ROSE enters the house)*
> *(RONDIE arrives, carrying a small jug)*

RONDIE: *(Already slightly drunk and hilarious)* Whee! Billie, I feels like I done been to church and got full of religion, and I ain't been nowhere's but outdoors setting under my fig tree all morning.

AUNT BILLIE: You and who else?

RONDIE: Me and my old man Applejack! And believe me, this applejack sure do warm my soul. Here, *(Offering the jug to AUNT BILLIE)* I done brung you a nip. *(Taking snuff and sitting down)* But I ain't come here to drink, myself. I comed to see the preacher. He due this afternoon, ain't he?

AUNT BILLIE: *(Drinking)* Sure as they's a chicken in the pot.

RONDIE: Well, that's who I wants to see. He a cute little old preacher.
> *(Just then, down at the barn, the jack lets out a terrific high-pitched braying thunder. RONDIE leaps into the air, whirling around twice)*

QUEEN ESTHER: *(Desperately coming out of the house)* I wonder where is Pine, the minister, or somebody!

VINEY: *(Sticking her head out of the window)* Is that you, Mouse?

ROSE: *(Coming to the door)* I thought I heard Bogator call me.

AUNT BILLIE: You ain't heard nothing but that jack. Rondie, let's you and me walk down by the shed and see what's going on. That little varmint hollers too terrific to be a Christian.

VINEY: I wish he would hush. *(Withdraws her head into the house)*

RONDIE: I ain't got no business going near that Jack, but I sure would like to see what he look like in broad daylight.

QUEEN ESTHER: Call me as soon as the minister come.
> *(She goes into the house. AUNT BILLIE and RONDIE start toward the barn and run into BOGATOR, who enters the scene)*

AUNT BILLIE: Bogator, Rose say she thought she hear you call her name.

BOGATOR: *(Shortly)* She musta thought it. *(He carries a long, slender limb, suitable for a fishing pole)*

AUNT BILLIE: Come on, Rondie, let's we go see that jack. I wants to show you my herb bed, too.

> (*RONDIE and AUNT BILLIE exit. BOGATOR doesn't even look at ROSE, but sits down on a box and starts whittling one end of the limb*)

ROSE: (*Softly*) Bogator! (*He does not answer*) Bogator!

BOGATOR: Hunh?

ROSE: Listen, Bogator. (*Coming toward him*) Honey, please don't look so mean at me, all the time. I ain't gonna be with that old white man much more.

BOGATOR: (*Looking up*) That must be because I'm gonna kill him, then, first chance I gets.

ROSE: (*Horrified*) No, no, no! You'd get lynched, sure! Jest wait, jest wait a little while.

BOGATOR: Wait for what?

ROSE: Everything'll be all right! He'll be—he won't bother me—no more.

BOGATOR: How you know? What he gonna do?

ROSE: I know.

BOGATOR: How you know?

ROSE: I know, I know.

BOGATOR: (*Jumping up and twisting her arm*) How do you know? Don't you tell me no lie.

ROSE: (*Coming close to him and lifting her face*) Oh, Bogator, don't!

BOGATOR: (*Looking at her a moment, then kissing her hard*) Rose, baby, honey! It's cause I loves you a heap—that's all!

ROSE: I loves you more'n a fly loves sugar.

BOGATOR: I loves you—(*Thinking*)—like a fish de water. (*Between kisses*) Like a chicken loves corn! Like a dog love his sweet ole wallering place!

> (*They pause as LITTLE BITS is heard approaching, crying at the top of her voice*)

LITTLE BITS: (*Enters, running, with her clothes all muddy and wet, and her hair disheveled*) Oh! Aw! Aw! Aw!

ROSE: Honey, what's the matter?

VINEY: (*Coming to the door*) What on earth, now?

LITTLE BITS: (*Going straight to Viney and sobbing in her arms*) Oh! Aw! Aunt Viney! Oh! Aw! Aw!

BOGATOR: Bee must-a stung her!

VINEY: Tell me what it is?

>   (*LITTLE BITS sobs violently in Viney's ear as ARCIE comes in and stands behind the flame tree. AUNT BILLIE and RONDIE enter*)

LITTLE BITS: Arcie pushed me in the creek.

VINEY: What!

LITTLE BITS: He mighty near drowned me.

AUNT BILLIE: Is that chile hurt, or what?

VINEY: (*Dramatically*) Arcie done tried to drown her! Queen Esther, Queen Esther! Your wicked little Memphis brat done tried to drown Little Bits.

QUEEN ESTHER: (*Emerging from the house*) What?

VINEY: He done almost kilt this gal! Look at her!

ROSE: Poor little thing.

RONDIE: That jack sure has a powerful effect on chilluns!

QUEEN ESTHER: (*As ARCIE comes strutting defiantly from behind the tree*) Boy, what you did to that chile? (*She slaps his face*) What you done did?

>   (*She slaps the other cheek, then she grabs him by the back of the neck. Meanwhile, VINEY has taken LITTLE BITS into the house where she can be heard crying. ROSE follows VINEY inside*)

ARCIE: (*Holding his ground*) She made me do it. When she heard that jack holler, she grabbed me by the neck and liked to choke me to death.

QUEEN ESTHER: I'm gonna wear you out, anyhow. No need to push her in the water. Bogator, go get me a switch.

BOGATOR: (*Offering the limb*) You can have this fishing pole, if you want it.

QUEEN ESTHER: I ain't fooling. I wants a sapling switch, and I'll get one myself. Fact is, I'll take you down in da woods where they's plenty switches and whip you till you can't sit down. (*SHE exits toward woods, dragging ARCIE off*)

RONDIE: This world and the next one! Full of worriment! That's why I dips snuff.

AUNT BILLIE: And drinks licker!

RONDIE: But when a jack holler, a grown woman can't hardly stand it, let alone a young chile that's jest beginning to bloom out.

>   (*PINE enters, wiping the sweat from his brow*)

PINE: Whee! Sure is hot and dusty down that road.

AUNT BILLIE: Church out a-ready?

RONDIE: Where the minister?

AUNT BILLIE: And Mouse?

PINE: They'll be along directly, I reckon. I left the Reverend there still a-shaking hands with the sisters. This here collar was choking my neck. I had to get home here and take it off.

BOGATOR: You been bending your old long tall neck down too much, pecking at Caroline all along the road.

PINE: I don't kiss no girl in the public road. What's the matter with you, boy?

BOGATOR: You mean, not in the daytime.

PINE: Well, at night, I don't have no collar on.

AUNT BILLIE: *(Offering the jug)* Here, Pine, you want a little nip before dinner?

PINE: Sure! Yes'm. *(Takes the jug and drinks deeply)*

RONDIE: *(Alarmed)* Here! Here! Here, boy, leave some for me.

PINE: I'm jest trying to take the poison off.

BOGATOR: *(In warning)* Hey, you-all here comes Rev. Lovelady!

> *(Enter REV. LOVELADY and MOUSE as RONDIE and AUNT BILLIE try unsuccessfully to hide the jug. PINE enters the house)*

REV. LOVELADY: *(Pompously)* Good evening, sisters!

AUNT BILLIE: Good evening, Rev'm.

RONDIE: Evening. Rev'm! Gawd bless you, how you been?

REV. LOVELADY: Tolerable, I thanks you, jest tolerable! And you, Sister Rondie?

RONDIE: By the grace of Gawd, I's here. But I has my troubles.

REV. LOVELADY: What they be, sister?

RONDIE: I'm all crippled up with rheumatics. *(Hobbles around to demonstrate, by exaggeration, her infirmity)*

REV. LOVELADY: Does you take it to the Lawd?

RONDIE: Yes, indeedy, that's how come I'm still here—through prayer. Prayer has saved me and brung me through! Amen! Hallelujah!

REV. LOVELADY: Hallelujah! Bless Gawd, sister!

RONDIE: *(Enjoying a brief shout)* Holy is His Name!

REV. LOVELADY: Amen! Amen! *(Suddenly)* Why doesn't you come to church, Sister?

RONDIE: Hunh? Oh! *(Excusing herself)* Well, this morning, don't you know, my cow got loose, and I couldn't catch her for the life of me. She were jest a-galloping way over yonder in Tippet's pasture, and I were scared if I didn't fetch her in, she would jest gorge herself on wild onions and spile the taste of her milk.

REV. LOVELADY: The devil were in that cow, sister.

RONDIE: He were for sure.

REV. LOVELADY: But I certainly missed your bright and shining face from the services this morning.

RONDIE: *(Coyly)* Did you miss me, Rev'm?

REV. LOVELADY: *(Turning suddenly on AUNT BILLIE)* Aunt Billie, that jug!

AUNT BILLIE: *(Unembarrassed)* Here, have a drink.

REV. LOVELADY: Er - er - well - er - a - what is it?

AUNT BILLIE: Jest plain old licker, preacher, but I know your throat must be dry, all the preaching and a-hollering you did this morning.

REV. LOVELADY: Well - er, it is, for sure.

AUNT BILLIE: Mouse, get the Rev'm a cup. A man in his position can't drink out of no jug.

(MOUSE goes into the house and gets a cup)

RONDIE: Rev'm Lovelady always preaches a lovely sermon, too.

AUNT BILLIE: *(Taking cup from Mouse)* He deserves a little refreshment. *(She pours from the jug and hands the drink to the minister)*

REV. LOVELADY: Thank you, sister. *(Then, with a guilty look on his face as he recalls that wine is a mocker, etc., he finds in his mind the words he wants, quoting briefly)* For thy stomach's sake.

(It is uttered like a toast. As he drinks, QUEEN ESTHER enters. Sees the minister and smoothes her hair and dress down and throws away the switch she has carried)

AUNT BILLIE: Good, ain't it?

REV. LOVELADY: *(Smacking his lips)* Pretty good, sister, pretty good. *(Sees Queen Esther)*

AUNT BILLIE: Rev'm, this here is Queen Esther Jones, Viney's sister from Memphis. She's Rose and Jerico's mother.

REV. LOVELADY: *(Elegantly)* Oh, how do you do, Sister Jones. My complimentaries to you, to be sure.

QUEEN ESTHER: In-lighted to meet you! Your worthiness wasn't here when I were commuting in this vicinity a few years pasted, were you?

REV. LOVELADY: Reckon I were still in the seminary in New Orleans.

QUEEN ESTHER: That must be a viracious town. I's heard so much about the Mardi Grass.

REV. LOVELADY: Ah, indeed, sister. It is indeed.

(VINEY and ROSE emerge, sweating, from the house, wiping their hands on their aprons)

VINEY: *(Coming forward)* Rev'm, you is welcome, for sure.

ROSE: Howdy do, Rev. Lovelady.

REV. LOVELADY: God bless you, Sister Viney. Bless my little Rose! How you been? How you-all?

VINEY: Living in Gawd, I thank you!

REV. LOVELADY: That's right! That's right! He'll bring you through.

MOUSE: He sure will!

AUNT BILLIE: *(To Rondie as the others talk together)* Rondie, let's we take this jug and go where I can nip in peace. Too many folks around here. I can't holler.

RONDIE: All right, come on. We can come back later and commune with the Rev'm.

AUNT BILLIE: I don't know about me.

(The old women exit, carrying the licker jug)

REV. LOVELADY: Gawd blessed us with a wonderful service this morning. Your chillun got religion and seven joined the church.

VINEY: Praise the Lawd!

MOUSE: And Old Lady Moseby got happy and shouted so hard, she broke down two benches.

REV. LOVELADY: Ah, the spirit were there today! We took up a tolerable collection, too, things and times being like how they is.

VINEY: I guess you is hongry, Rev'm! Lemme go in and finish getting the table straight. Bogator, go see can you find Jerico. Maybe he set his eyes on a mess of honey and need help to get it out.

BOGATOR: All right. *(He exits)*

VINEY: Come on, you-all, help me get the dinner ready.

(VINEY, ROSE and MOUSE enter the house)

QUEEN ESTHER: *(To the minister)* Have a seat out here where it's cool, Rev'm.

REV. LOVELADY: *(Pointing to the washbench against the house)* Let's set over there in the shade of the house. *(Goes to washbench)* Two can set here more comfortable-like.

QUEEN ESTHER: Okey-dokey.

(SHE and REV. LOVELADY sit side by side on the bench)

REV. LOVELADY: I calculate you's saved?

QUEEN ESTHER: Oh, yes, I were converted at the tender age of ten, but since then I has backslid a few times.

REV. LOVELADY: Ah, sister, but you must come to the fold again.

QUEEN ESTHER: If I were around here long with you, I'd join your church.

REV. LOVELADY: I'd like to labor with you, sister, and bring you back to Gawd.

QUEEN ESTHER: I wish you would, Rev'm. Lovelady. I feels come-backish.

REV. LOVELADY: I will, er - er, Sister—what's your name now?

QUEEN ESTHER: My name's Queen Esther.

REV. LOVELADY: Queen Esther, hunh! That's a fitten name for a nice brownskin lady like you.

QUEEN ESTHER: You likes it?

REV. LOVELADY: I sure do.

QUEEN ESTHER: And what might be your full name?

REV. LOVELADY: Jest plain old Buddy Lovelady, that's me.

QUEEN ESTHER: Buddy, hunh? Buddy Lovelady! And does your last name have a meaning?

REV. LOVELADY: *(Feeling his oats)* You wouldn't believe me if I told you. I'd have to demonstrate, sister. I'd have to demonstrate.

QUEEN ESTHER: You ain't got no ball-and-chain on you, Rev'm. Lovelady. Why don't you show me, then?

REV. LOVELADY: *(Taking her in his arms and kissing her lips with smack)* There!

VINEY: *(Emerging from the house and looking toward the tree)* Dinner's ready. Where is you-all?

> *(QUEEN ESTHER and REV. LOVELADY part before VINEY sees them)*

QUEEN ESTHER: We's sitting here by the house in the shade.

REV. LOVELADY: *(Piously)* Yes, bless Gawd, in the blessed shade!

VINEY: Well, come on in now, and put your feet under the table. *(As she goes in the house)*

QUEEN ESTHER: *(As she and REV. LOVELADY rise)* Buddy, you's got a speck of rouge on the corner of your mouth. *(She takes her handkerchief and wipes his mouth before they go into the cabin*

> *(PINE, BOGATOR, JERICO and ARCIE enter the scene. JERICO is playing on his mouth organ)*

BOGATOR: There they go, gonna pick that chicken clean.

PINE: Play on, Jerico, you's gonna make a right smart musicianeer.

ARCIE: *(Contemptuously)* That ain't nothing, jest playing that little old thing. They's a man in Memphis got hisself a one-man jug-band, and plays a mouth organ, the violin, and the drums all the same time.

BOGATOR: Come on, boy! Tell us some more about Memphis.

ARCIE: You-all ain't never been in a city, is you? I mean a real city with street cars and everything?

PINE: We sure ain't.

JERICO: I ain't never even seen a train.

BOGATOR: I is, though.

PINE: Me, too.

ARCIE: Hunh! Trains—them ain't nothing! You ought to see the street jest full of trains in Memphis, street cars a-running every which a-where, and movie shows on every corner, and cabarets down in every basement. My mama used to be a waitress in a cabaret.

JERICO: Mama did?

ARCIE: Sure she did. And sometimes I used to go and hang around down there until two and three o'clock in the morning.

BOGATOR: Um-hum-m!

ARCIE: In Memphis one whole half the town's colored. And Beale Street, boy! Is you ever heard about Beale Street?

BOGATOR: Naw, tell us about it.

ARCIE: Beale Street's a street about ten miles long, and jest full of pretty womens from one end to the other. Man, I got seven gals on Beale Street myself.

JERICO: You has?

ARCIE: Sure has! And they hair ain't nappy like the gals down here, neither. They got educations, and they wears clothes!

JERICO: You got a education, too, ain't you, Arcie?

ARCIE: Sure, man! I can read reading and read writing, both. I can even much talk in Latin.

BOGATOR: Pig-Latin?

ARCIE: Naw, school-book Latin. I done been in the first year junior high.

BOGATOR: You is?

ARCIE: Sure, I is. I done studied all about Julius Caesar and everybody back in ancient times what talked Latin. They ain't understood American.

BOGATOR: Who's Julia Seize-Her?

ARCIE: He were a big ole King in the days of Moses and he ruled all over Greece.

PINE: What kind of grease?

ARCIE: GREECE! I mean a country, man, by the name of Greece. And one day he were out sporting with a woman by the name of Cleo Patra.

BOGATOR: How she look? Were she yaller?

ARCIE: She were a keen high-brown with long black hair down to her waist.

PINE: My! My! My!

ARCIE: And Julius Caesar had a friend what was jealous of Cleo, 'cause he were in love with her, too.

BOGATOR: Who were he?

ARCIE: He were a general named Brutus. And one day Julius Caesar caught old Brutus with his women, and was he mad! He didn't think his friend would do him that-away. And old Caesar holler in Latin, *Et tu, Brute?* And Brutus say, *Yeah, man!*

PINE: He were a dirty son of a gun!

ARCIE: And Cleo Patra took a rattlesnake and put in her bosom and bit herself to death!

JERICO: What she do that for?

ARCIE: Because both the mens went off and left her.

BOGATOR: Lawd! Lawd! So who's running things over yonder now?

ARCIE: Haile Selassie.

    (A terrific noise breaks out down by the barn. It is the little jack braying again. This time longer and louder than ever. ARCIE jumps)

BOGATOR: Ain't nothing but that little ole jack. Go on. Tell us some more.

    (The jack continues to bray, then his braying seems to get farther and farther away)

PINE: I believe that little old jack done got loose.

MOUSE: *(Comes out the door, yelling)* Some of you-all go see about that jack, seem like to me he running wild.

BOGATOR: *(Looking toward the barn)* He done bust loose his rope for sure.

JERICO: *(Shouting)* Look at him jest a-galloping across that field.

    (BOGATOR, PINE and JERICO exit, running toward the barn, as VINEY comes to the door)

MOUSE: Go get him before he trample that cotton all down.

VINEY: *(In the doorway)* I knowed you'd let something happen to spoil the Rev'm's dinner.

MOUSE: *(Under his breath)* Much chicken as he done eat, it can't be spoiled by now.

VINEY: Mouse, come on back in here and get your strawberries.

MOUSE: I don't want no berries. I didn't get no chicken! What I wants with berries?

VINEY: *(Lowering her voice)* Well, you know the minister and Queen Esther had to be served first. They weren't nothing on that little ole frizzly chicken nohow, but bones.

> *(REV. LOVELADY and QUEEN ESTHER come to the door. QUEEN ESTHER is holding his arm very close)*

QUEEN ESTHER: *(Purring)* That devilish racket got me all upset.

MOUSE: I hope it don't start them chicken wings a-flying around inside of you.

QUEEN ESTHER: Aw, Mouse! I think it jest awful the way that jack do holler.

REV. LOVELADY: Where is the blessed little animal? I'd like to see it.

MOUSE: Yonder it go across the field now. Come on wid me, and I expects you can have it, if the boys ever ketch it.

REV. LOVELADY: You wants to get rid of it?

MOUSE: I sure do.

REV. LOVELADY: Then I might consider his acquisition. *(To QUEEN ESTHER)* Release me for the time being, while I goes with Brother Wilson here, to look at the jack.

QUEEN ESTHER: Oh, be careful! Don't let him kick you.

REV. LOVELADY: God's chillun is well protected, sister.

> *(REV. LOVELADY and MOUSE exit together)*

QUEEN ESTHER: Ain't the Rev'm. handsome?

VINEY: Seem like you think so, the way you keeps yourself stuck up in his face.

QUEEN ESTHER: *(Piously)* I feels myself coming back to the church, Viney. I needs a pillar to lean on.

VINEY: Ump-hum-m!

> *(CAROLINE's voice can be heard calling Pine from the road)*

CAROLINE: Pine, oh, Pine!

VINEY: *(Calling)* He ain't here! He gone down to the field. You can come in and wait for him, if you's a mind to.

CAROLINE: *(Entering)* I thought I heard Pine a-calling me awhile back.

QUEEN ESTHER: *(Rudely)* I reckon you jest felt the jack a-hollering, that's all.

CAROLINE: I knows Pine's voice when I hears it.

VINEY: *(Introducing them)* Caroline, that's my sister, Queen Esther. I don't reckon you knowed her when she were around here before.

CAROLINE: Howdy do.

QUEEN ESTHER: Right well, I thanks you.

CAROLINE: *(Staring at her clothes and painted nails)* I knows you sure ain't from around here.

QUEEN ESTHER: I'm a Memphis girl. I don't be in the country often.

CAROLINE: I heard Pine a-talking about you this morning.

QUEEN ESTHER: *(Eagerly)* Did you? What did he say?

CAROLINE: He say you scared of snakes.

QUEEN ESTHER: He told that right! I sure am! If it wasn't for Pine I don't know how I'd get along around here. He keeps the snakes away from me.

CAROLINE: I'd ruther the snakes kept you away from him. *(Loud neighing down in the field)* My, that old mare's started!

QUEEN ESTHER: What does you mean by that other remark?

CAROLINE: I mean Pine's a nice boy, even if he has been married once. And I don't want him fooling around with no city womans.

QUEEN ESTHER: Fooling around? What do you mean, fooling around? *(Righteously)* I don't allow no mens to fool with me.

CAROLINE: Well, I come to fetch Pine, that's what, and tell him he can move on down to my house, even if my mama's got to make him a pallet on the floor. He ain't safe up here since you came.

QUEEN ESTHER: *(Thoughtfully)* You sounds like a hussy to me.

CAROLINE: I jest don't want no bobbed-headed woman like you messing with him, that's all.

QUEEN ESTHER: *(Putting her hands on her hips and drawing back her head)* Now, here, sister! I'm a lady at *all* times, but if I have to get tough, I'm the toughest bitch ever spit in a boot!

CAROLINE: *(Rising in fear and backing away)* Oh!

    (Just then, MOUSE and REV. LOVELADY enter)

MOUSE: *(In great excitement)* Viney! Oh, Viney! I say, Viney!

VINEY: *(Rushing from the house)* What? What do you want, Mouse?

MOUSE: That darned little old jack done—done. . . .

VINEY: What?

MOUSE: Before the boys could catch him, he done got to that old mare, and—and—and gived her a colt!

VINEY: Oh, Lawd!

QUEEN ESTHER: I told you a mare's never too old to mate.

VINEY: *(Weeping)* But she's too old to have a colt.

REV. LOVELADY: Well, it's happened now, sister. It's the will of Gawd.
    (Enter PINE, BOGATOR, JERICO and ARCIE)

VINEY: *(Half crying)* Damn it, Mouse! 'Scuse me, Rev'm. I told you to take that jack away.

QUEEN ESTHER: *(Indicating Caroline)* This young lady's the one somebody better take away before I—*(calming in front of REV. LOVELADY)*—treat her in a unChristian way.

CAROLINE: *(Calling weakly)* Pine!

PINE: What's the matter, Caroline?

CAROLINE: *(Sobbing)* Pine! Pine! She, she— *(Looking at QUEEN ESTHER but afraid to speak, as QUEEN ESTHER threatens her)* She—oh, Pine, come on down to my house!

PINE: Certainly, darling, don't cry! *(He puts his arms around her and leads her off)* Don't cry, Pine's here, honey!
    (PINE and CAROLINE exit together, she crying against his shoulder)

VINEY: Bogator, Jerico, you boys go on in the house and eat your dinner. Tell Rose to give you all the bread and gravy you wants.

JERICO: Yes'm. *(He enters the house. BOGATOR follows)*

ARCIE: Hunh! Nothing to eat but bread and gravy. This here's a poor place!

VINEY: You ought to be thankful to get that.

QUEEN ESTHER: I guess I'll go in and freshen up myself some. That lady visitor got on my nerves, I reckon. *(Exits into the house, followed by ARCIE)*

REV. LOVELADY: Now, Brother, Wilson, as I were saying, that's a right fine little old jack. I might would consider taking him off your hands.

VINEY: I wish you would. If he stays here another night, I'll go crazy.

REV. LOVELADY: Well, let's talk. *(He sits down on the box)* Now, I'm thinking of going into a little business on the side. That will mean I has to do a right smart amount of traveling. Can you ride that jack?

MOUSE: Sure you can ride a jack, if you breaks him in.

REV. LOVELADY: Un-hum! Well, if I didn't ride him, I could possibly walk myself and tie my pack on his back, because I means to carry considerable. I means to visit all the towns and villages here abouts in a radium of forty-five miles, carrying the word of Gawd and at the same time carrying on my business.

VINEY: What business might it be you going into, Rev'm? I know you always did sell Bibles.

REV. LOVELADY: Well, now, besides the Bibles—Gawd's work coming first—I'm adding a new and catchy sideline that I think for the time being might outsell the Book, 'cause most peoples around here that can read a-tall and them that can't, has got a Bible by now, long as I been peddling them. But I've added something that I know for sure will interest one and all, man, woman, and chile, every black person what's got a speck of race pride in him. *(Rising now and going to a roll which he has left on the washbench)* Pictures, my friends. *(Unrolling the package)* Pictures of that great cullud fighter and bear-cat of the world, Joe Louis! Joe Louis! The sweetest bruiser that ever throwed a rock at Goliath. And, believe me, every knuckle in his fists is a rock!

> *(MOUSE and VINEY, then ROSE and the children come out from cabin, crowding around to look. Loud murmurs and exclamations of joy)*

MOUSE: Looky yonder! Jest looky yonder at them hams!

BOGATOR: I bet he could knock anybody living into the middle of next week.

ROSE: *(Feeling Bogator's muscles)* I bet he ain't as strong as you, Bogator.

JERICO: Yes, he is, too. Joe Louis a hell-lion!

VINEY: You, Jerico, don't you use no such language! *(Smiling)* But that Joe Louis is sure something. Yes, indeedy!

REV. LOVELADY: And I'm selling these pictures of *him* for only twenty-five cents.

BOGATOR: I sure wish I had two-bits. I'd buy me one.

ARCIE: Aw, you can get them for a dime in Memphis.

REV. LOVELADY: Young man, this is not Memphis! These here pictures are a bargain anywhere at this price. Only twenty-five cents.

VINEY: Mouse and me ain't got no money.

REV. LOVELADY: Oh don't mistake me! I wasn't meaning to sell you-all none. I was aiming to *give* you one. You my friends. I reckon one will do for everybody, being's as you all live together. Here you are! Now that's for you, Brother Wilson, Sister Viney, too, Bogator and Jerico. *(Rolls up his package)*

ROSE: Oh, thank you, Rev'm Lovelady!

VINEY: Thank you, indeed!

MOUSE: That surely are a fine thing!

REV. LOVELADY: It's gonna sell like hot cakes. That's why I needs the jack to place my burden on, because I'm gonna carry a roll of two or three hundred. Twenty-five cents! Now, Brother, let's talk business.

MOUSE: I'm willing.

VINEY: You-all chilluns go back in the house to your dinner now.

YOUNG FOLKS: Yes'm.

> (*They all exit, leaving MOUSE, VINEY and REV. LOVELADY to their conversation*)

VINEY: Have the rocker, Rev'm.

REV. LOVELADY: Thank you, thank you, this box'll do. (*He motions Viney to the rocker, and sits down himself on the box. MOUSE squats on the ground*)

> (*A far-off yell of "Yee-hoo!" is heard*)

MOUSE: That Aunt Billie!

REV. LOVELADY: Tut! Tut! Tut! On the Sabbath Day!

VINEY: She oughtn't drink like that on an empty stomach.

REV. LOVELADY: She oughtn't, but as I were saying, I can use that jack. How much he worth to you-all?

VINEY: He ain't worth nothing to me, because I wouldn't have him as a gift.

MOUSE: Now, honey, he is worth something to you, too. I done went and collected him for a ten dollar debt.

VINEY: That was you, not me.

MOUSE: I know it, baby, but I took him, so's we might as well get something out of him if you can.

REV. LOVELADY: Hum-hum! So he worth ten dollars, is he? Well, that ain't such a steep price.

MOUSE: To be sure, it 'tain't.

REV. LOVELADY: No, 'tain't. (*Studying*) Now, I notices you all ain't been to church much the last two or three months.

VINEY: I declare to the Lawd, Rev'm. Lovelady, I wants to come, but when I gets through a week out yonder in them cotton fields, I jest can't walk two or three miles down yonder to the church. It's jest too far.

REV. LOVELADY: I understands that, sister, but you might send your dues.

MOUSE: Trouble about that is, we ain't had no money.

REV. LOVELADY: But the church can't run without money. The gospel is free—free as air—but you is obliged to pay the postage. Now, I were looking over the books last week and you-all're behind on your dues, every last one of you, your whole family and relations here in this house. That's a doggone shame—and the Lawd knows what I means.

VINEY: Indeed it is, Rev'm Lovelady.

MOUSE: We jest ain't had it.

REV. LOVELADY: I believe I counted up where you-all is seven or eight months behind, and being's there so many of you, not to say nothing about Aunt Billie, who never did pay regular nohow, you-all owes me—I means the church—mighty nigh onto twenty or thirty dollars.

VINEY: I expects we does, Rev'm.

MOUSE: I knows we really owes the Lawd a heap.

REV. LOVELADY: Now, that being the case, you know what we could do that would meet with favor in the Master's sight? I could take that little old jack right off your hands and apply the value on the animal to your dues—what's been owing the church so long.

MOUSE: *(Looking at Viney)* You means you take that ten dollars what the jack is worth and apply it to the *whole* dues?

REV. LOVELADY: That is jest what I means, Brother Wilson. That's a right fair proposition, ain't it? What do you think about it, Sister Viney?

MOUSE: *(As VINEY hesitates)* 'Course, I knows we owes you and we wants to get rid of the jack and all like that, but, Rev'm. Lovelady, we ain't got nothing to eat.

REV. LOVELADY: *(Jovially)* Nothing to eat! Why, ha-ha-ha-ha! You call a chicken in the pot nothing to eat? Why, daughter, I thank Gawd for the splendid meal I has eat today. The Lawd will provide! Don't fear about that.

VINEY: Yes, he will provide!

MOUSE: *(Looking at Rev. Lovelady)* He provides for you all right.

REV. LOVELADY: You know it ain't easy to get rid of a jack nowadays.

VINEY: True! If it were, Biggs would-a had this one sold, poor as he is.

REV. LOVELADY: And you knows you owes the church, now don't you?

VINEY: We sure do!

REV. LOVELADY: Now, don't you think that would be a good way to cut down on your debt to the Lawd?

VINEY: Yes, it would! Rev'm, take the jack!

REV. LOVELADY: Gawd bless you, sister. You done gived that jack to the Lawd!

VINEY: Anyhow, I got him off *my* mind.

(MOUSE shakes his head. The shadows deepen on the stage. The sun begins to set)

REV. LOVELADY: *(Rising)* I won't forget to mark it down on the church books. *(To Mouse)* Brother, does you want to bring the jack up here to the road? *(Loudly)* I's about to take off now. Time I walks over to the church and stops to greet my many lambs on the way, it'll be about the hour for evening services.

VINEY: It is getting along toward dusk-dark, ain't it? Mouse, go bring that jack. I wants that little old heathen varmint off my place before sunset. Rev'm., you has took a weight off my mind.

(Exit MOUSE)

REV. LOVELADY: I might be able to add a little to the funds of the church, too, bless Gawd! A-mating other mares on my way about the country if I comes across anybody with a lady-hoss to breed.

VINEY: I likes to see the church prosper.

REV. LOVELADY: I know you does, daughter!

(QUEEN ESTHER emerges from the house, her face freshly powdered and her hat on at a neat angle. She carries gloves)

QUEEN ESTHER: Viney, I thought I might be going to church to-night.

REV. LOVELADY: It would be a pleasure to have you come along with me. 'Course it's a little early, but you might have no objections to strolling calmfully down the road without hurrying, taking in the beauties of the spring.

QUEEN ESTHER: That I wouldn't, Rev'm. Lovelady. It's been so long since I been in the country.

VINEY: *(Loudly)* Well, take that hellion of a Arcie with you. I got enough young 'uns around here to worry me.

QUEEN ESTHER: Oh, Arcie won't be no trouble. He like to go to church, set up, and look at the girls. *(Calling)* Arcie! Come on with mama, honey.

ARCIE: *(Coming from the house, wiping his mouth)* What?

QUEEN ESTHER: Start on down the road, baby. We going to church with Rev'm. Lovelady.

ARCIE: Well, I hope you'll buy me a hot dog on the way, I'm still hongry.

QUEEN ESTHER: Go on, chile. Maybe Rev'm.'ll buy you one. *(ARCIE exits toward the road, whistling a popular tune from Memphis)* Watch out for snakes.

ARCIE: *(Off stage)* To hell with the snakes!

QUEEN ESTHER: Rev'm., that boy needs to be saved.

REV. LOVELADY: When you hear me preach and pray tonight, I'll save you both.

QUEEN ESTHER: I know I can be a real good woman, if I tries.

VINEY: I hope so!

> *(MOUSE arrives off stage, leading the little old jack for the minister. BOGATOR, ROSE, and JERICO come from the house. LITTLE BITS leans out of the window)*

MOUSE: *(Enters)* Rev'm., here the jack!

REV. LOVELADY: That's fine. Now, jest tie my bundle on his back, Jerico.

QUEEN ESTHER: You know, I'd kinder like to follow that jack. He have a vigorating effect on a human. *(Gesture of showing her muscle, as a man might do)*

REV. LOVELADY: Follow me, sister, and you follows the jack.

QUEEN ESTHER: You and your Bibles.

REV. LOVELADY: And Joe Louis.

QUEEN ESTHER: And the jack. All you put together is a knockout.

REV. LOVELADY: *(Prepares to depart)* Thank you, Brother Wilson! Thank you, sister Viney! Gawd bless you for the pleasant afternoon passed in your company! Sister, that were a scrumptious dinner! Gawd prosper all you-all! Come on Sister Esther, let's we go along in the service of the King.

> *(Exit REV. LOVELADY and QUEEN ESTHER in a golden glow of sunset)*

VINEY: Goodbye. Goodbye.

MOUSE: Goodbye!

JERICO: Goodbye, Rev'm. Lovelady.

BOGATOR: So long!

ROSE: Gawd bless you, Rev'm. Goodbye, mama!

QUEEN ESTHER: See you later, Rose darling. Goodbye, Jerico!

VINEY: *(Turning to go in)* Now, I guess I'll straighten up that house.

ROSE: I straightened it up, Aunt Viney. All the dishes is washed.

VINEY: Did you throw the dishwater on the bait bed? And the coffee grounds, too?

ROSE: Yes, Ma'am.

VINEY: *(To LITTLE BITS, in the window)* You better get back in that bed! You done got yourself into enough trouble for one day.

(LITTLE BITS disappears out of the window. VINEY enters the house. JERICO pulls out a handful of the marbles and begins to count them)

MOUSE: *(To himself)* When the jack holler, a woman's love mes¹ down.

JERICO: *(Calling)* Come on, 'Gator, I'll play you a game of marbles.

BOGATOR: *(Coming to the house)* You can't play no marbles, man. Gimme a taw.

(They place marbles in the ring and start a game)

VINEY: *(Emerging from the house)* Rose, honey, sure was nice of you to straighten up everything so pretty.

ROSE: *(In the house)* That's all right, Aunt Viney. But I'm gonna take off this apron now and comb my hair.

VINEY: *(Going toward MOUSE, who is sitting on the washbench)* Then come on out and set down in the cool bye and bye.

ROSE: Yes, Aunt Viney.

VINEY: It's nice out here, now the sun done got kinder low in the sky. *(She sits down beside Mouse)* I sure is glad we got rid of that jack.

MOUSE: *(Slyly)* He kinder sweetened you up, honey.

VINEY: Mouse, you hush! You know I always were sweet to you—you dog you!

MOUSE: *(Putting his arm around her waist)* But you get mad mighty often.

VINEY: Baby, now you know I don't! You know I jest haves to talk, that's all.

MOUSE: Yes, honey.

JERICO: *(In the marble game)* Knuckies! That's mine! My shot!

BOGATOR: Dog-gone my soul, if I don't believe you's beating me!

JERICO: Yeah, man! You ain't no trouble. *(As the music of a guitar floats up from a distance)* Listen at old Pine and them singing down at Caroline's house. *(Shooting)* By! Look at me hit you, two at once!

BOGATOR: Shucks, that ain't nothin'. Watch me here! *(He knuckles one)* One! *(Shooting again)* Two! *(Again)* Three!

(From the road comes a low, insinuating whistle. MOUSE and VINEY sit stone still, their conversation ceases, the boys stop playing marbles. The whistle is repeated. It is the white man, TIPPET.

(BOGATOR rises, as ROSE, in her red dress, comes quickly from the house. She puts the conjure jar in her bosom and holds it there. Looking straight ahead, without noticing the others, she goes across the yard, hesitates a moment, puts her other hand to her breast,

*drops it, and, as the whistle is repeated, she goes toward the road.
(BOGATOR clenches his fists as:*
THE CURTAIN FALLS

Act III

SCENE: *A river bank. Cleared space just behind a rise of ground beneath which the water flows. Weeping willows and other trees on either side of the river. In the foreground a big bonfire from which embers are taken to light other smaller fires all along the bank. At right a large thorn tree, branches extend over stage. During the action the moon rises. Stars sparkle in the sky, frogs croak, locusts chir-rup, and night-birds call in a symphony of evening sounds. As the curtain rises, BOGA-TOR and JERICO are gathering limbs and branches to keep the fire going.*

TIME: *Night. The following week.*

JERICO: Ain't you gonna run no foxes with the men tonight, Bogator? They done gone with the dogs.

BOGATOR: Aw, I don't care nothing about running foxes. That same little old fox that live in these woods done been runned so much, he take it like a game. When he gets tired he just set down, cause him and them dogs is old friends. He know they ain't gonna hurt him. He ain't scared a bit. I'm gonna stay here and wait for the women folks to come out, myself.

JERICO: They ought to be here by now. It's too bad Aunt Billie can't come, ain't it. But Viney, she already got her fishing pole and can of bait and done gone on down the creek apiece, and Rose and Caroline'll be coming here directly to the fire with the coffee pot, I reckon.

BOGATOR: I hopes so. I wants some coffee.

JERICO: You means you wants to see Rose!

BOGATOR: Shut up, short horn! I knows my business.

JERICO: I'm sure glad what happened to Tippet, ain't you? He were a mean old white man.

BOGATOR: Worse plantation foreman we ever had.

JERICO: Well, he won't bother us no more, not soon. Pine say that he heard the doctor say that Tippet can't never work in the sun no more. His head is weak.

BOGATOR: Mouse seen him when he fell off his horse over yonder in the West Bottom Field. Mouse say it look like the sun jest hit him, BAM! in the head with a rock, and he fell right down.

JERICO: Funny don't no colored folks never have no sunstroke, ain't it, 'Gator?

BOGATOR: Man, that's a luxury for white folks to enjoy.

JERICO: Well, one thing certain, ain't it, 'Gator? Tippet won't never bother Rose no more. He done whistled for her his last time.

BOGATOR: Which saves me from having to kill him.

JERICO: I knows you would, too, 'Gator. Now you and Rose gonna get married ain't you?

BOGATOR: *(Hitting at Jerico with a stick of wood)* Keep out of my business, boy! You broadcasts too much!

JERICO: *(Running away)* I bet you is! I bet you is!

BOGATOR: *(Throwing a piece of wood after JERICO)* You little bugger, you!

JERICO: If I was your size, I'd play the dozens with you.

BOGATOR: Stop fooling around, boy! And come out from under that thorn tree before you run a thorn in your eye. You ain't never been worried about nothing, is you?

JERICO: I don't see no use worrying. If some of the womens get their hair caught up in that thorn tree tonight I know I'd sure laugh.

BOGATOR: Yes, jest laugh! Life sure is funny to you, ain't it? Now, here I am in love with a gal that don't even keep her promise to meet me out here by the fire like she say she would, before everybody else start gathering.

JERICO: *(Looking off)* I think Aunt Billie's coming.

BOGATOR: *(Looking around listening)* Where? I neither sees her nor hears her. You know she's in the plantation jail, anyhow, for getting drunk and hollering too loud last night in the white folks yard. You sure must smell her away off, cause Aunt Billie ain't nowhere near here!

AUNT BILLIE: *(Voice off stage)* Yes, I is here, too, son! *(She enters as BOGATOR backs back in astonishment)* Don't you know I learned years ago to come through the woods without making nary sound. Jerico, he were borned with a veil over his face, that's how he know I were coming.

BOGATOR: Aunt Billie, I thought you were in jail!

AUNT BILLIE: I was, but I got tired of that little ole privy-sized jail, so I jest turned it over and come out!

BOGATOR: You turned the jail over!

AUNT BILLIE: Turned it right smack over! It warn't built to hold nobody big as me nohow! And I got tired of being in there without nothing to eat. Since Tippet been sick I reckon they jest forgot about me. Day before yesterday since they handed me ary² plate of cow peas.

BOGATOR: *(Still unbelieving)* And you turned the calaboose over?

AUNT BILLIE: Sure, I turned it over! You act like you don't believe me. Go down yonder and see, and you'll see it laying on its side. I done been out two or three hours, and been by Rondie's house and eat and past our house, too.

(JERICO wanders slowly off toward the river, exits)

BOGATOR: You seen Rose, Aunt Billie.

AUNT BILLIE: Yes, I seen Rose! She combing her hair and primping up mighty much jest to come out here and stare at you, much as she's seen you all her life.

BOGATOR: She's jest now waking up to me, that's why!

AUNT BILLIE: Um-hum! Maybe it is! I don't understand all that fixing and all. When I were a girl you jest braided your hair right tight and washed your feet and said, "Honey, I loves you!" and went on and had the baby.

BOGATOR: *(Laughing embarrassedly)* Rose and me, we don't want to have no baby till we gets married. We gonna do things right.

AUNT BILLIE: A baby is a baby, whether or not the preacher done read out the book beforehand and the white folks collected Three Dollars for a piece of license paper. All babies look the same to me, married or not, and I birthed many a one these seventy-two years I been on this Delta. I reckon I birthed two or three thousand, done lost track and forgot their names. I know I birthed you, boy! And you the one that killed your mother in the birthing of you—that's how come I adopted you and Mouse and your sister what died when she were two years old.

BOGATOR: Yes, Aunt Billie, and you raised us up mighty good, too. You been a mother to us, Aunt Billie. *(Slowly poking in the fire)* But Rose and me, we don't want to have no babies till we gets a house and a little farm and something to feed them with. We don't want them growing up half-hongry.

AUNT BILLIE: That there's a problem, ain't it, Son? Seems like times is getting worser and worser. Last year they plowed under the cotton and killed all the little hogs. And this year they ain't planted but half the acreage. I don't know what the matter with the white folks.

BOGATOR: *(Joking)* You have to brew a spell, Aunt Billie, against the white folks.

AUNT BILLIE: I can brew a spell for one, but I can't for all. They can't all get the sunstroke. Besides that, most of them jest as poor as we is, like Sid Lowery, and jest as bad off. For all they little old played-out Ku Klux Klan they don't amount to a thing. The time done passed when we running jest cause we sees a white sheet in the dark.

BOGATOR: You right, Aunt Billie. We ought to be together. Cullud and white, anyhow, 'stead of scared of one another all the time.

AUNT BILLIE: When we gets more sense than the beasts of the fields, then we will be together.

BOGATOR: *(Slowly)* When we gets more sense than the beasts of the fields.

AUNT BILLIE: But I'm scared I'll never live to see it.

BOGATOR: *(Half joking)* Why'n you sprinkle some conjure all over this plantation, Aunt Billie, maybe it might help some?

AUNT BILLIE: Go on boy! You know you fooling. You young folks don't believe in conjure like we old folks did. I know you don't, you can't fool me. *(Lowering her voice)* To tell you the truth, boy, and I ain't never told nobody else this before—I don't believe in it, neither. Naw, sir! Nary bit of it! And long as you been around me, you ought to notice that ever time I tells the mother of a sick child to dip her finger in blueing and draw a ring around its navel I tells her to give it castor oil, too. And the castor oil is what works! *(BOGATOR draws near to listen)* Sure, I sells black cat's bones, and I brews mare's tea, and I makes charms out of horse-hair—and I sells them to fools like you and Sid Lowery so's I can get a few pennies together to drink my licker and holler. But I don't believe in it! No, sir!

BOGATOR: Don't you really, Aunt Billie?

AUNT BILLIE: I certainly don't—jest like lots of ministers don't believe in what they preach. Now you take Lovelady, for inster. Ain't a bigger devil on wheels!

BOGATOR: But he preach good.

AUNT BILLIE: Sure, he preach good. That's how he gets away with it. I talks good too, when I'm selling Love Lucky Lode Stones.

BOGATOR: I knows where you gets your Holy Water from Jerusalem.

AUNT BILLIE: Sure you know, many times as I've sent you to get it. It come right out of the same spring the rest of the water come out of. I just puts a little soda and salt in it, that's all—and sells it for a quarter.

BOGATOR: But then you holies and consecrates it yourself.

AUNT BILLIE: I sure do. Sometimes I spits in it.

BOGATOR: Aunt Billie, what does you believe in?

AUNT BILLIE: I don't believe in nothing but life and death, son, that's all. I brings people into this world, brews a few spells for them while they's here, then, something bigger'n me takes them out. *(Darkly)* But I can take them out, too, if I wants to. I can sicken and kill.

BOGATOR: They'd lock you up for that, wouldn't they Aunt Billie?

AUNT BILLIE: Why'n they lock me up for birthing folks then? Peers like to me, hard as this life is, it's more a sin helping people to get in the world than it is helping them get out. Sometimes I feels mighty sorry for the little critters I pulls out of black womens guts down here in this Delta, son, mighty sorry.

BOGATOR: *(Wistfully)* If they was only a charm . . .

AUNT BILLIE: *(Impatiently)* But I tells you there ain't no charm! If they were anything a-tall to all this here voo-doo hoo-doo root and conjure business we's always talking about, we'd a-done used it long ago way back in slavery-time to free ourselves with and every since to keep the white folks off our hides, and to get money to send you and Rose off to town where you all could've learned to read and write. Don't you think I would-a?

BOGATOR: Yes, Aunt Billie! *(Slyly)* And to make that jack hush hollering, too.

AUNT BILLIE: The jack! The jack! Shaw! Everybody blaming everything around here on the jack. It's jest spring time and sap-rising that's all. I'm gwine have plenty work birthing babies before another spring roll round. *(Sadly)* Son, I done helped birth too many black chillun for these cotton fields. That's why I drinks licker, so I can holler out loud. *(Yelling)* Yee-hoo! Ye-hee-hee-who!

VOICE: *(In distance)* Yee-hee-ooo-oo-o!

AUNT BILLIE: Hush! What's that!

BOGATOR: Must be an echo.

VOICE: *(Nearer)* Yee-hoo!

AUNT BILLIE: Naw, 'tain't! Ain't nobody but Rondie trying to find her way over here through the dark of that home-made moonshine. *(Rising and calling)* Rondie!

RONDIE: *(In distance)* Billie, I'm a-coming!

AUNT BILLIE: Well, come on then. It's about time we was catching some fish. *(To BOGATOR)* Bogator, you's gonna marry Rose, ain't you.

BOGATOR: I ain't gonna miss it.

AUNT BILLIE: Then I wants to give you some advice. Now, a woman is like a flower garden, son, you got to hoe them and tend them, train them and bend them. But you got to go about it gentle-like—if you don't the stalk's liable to snap and the flower just fade out. You got to treat Rose right, boy, but at the same time, make her know that you's a man!

BOGATOR: Yes'm, Aunt Billie, I'll pay attention to what you say.

AUNT BILLIE: You mind me, chile, and when you needs me, come to me.

BOGATOR: Yes'm.

RONDIE: *(Nearby)* Billie, it's me! *(Entering)* Here I is. Wonder a moccasin ain't bit me, too. This rheumatism's got me so's I can't hardly pick my feet up offen the ground. *(She carries a jug and two home-made fishing poles)*

AUNT BILLIE: Tie a cord string around your neck and drink some licker.

RONDIE: I don't know about the cord string, but I sure will drink the licker! Bogator, is you got some bait?

BOGATOR: No'm, but Viney, she brought a whole can full. She's down the bank yonder somewhere with her line out.

RONDIE: Um-hum! Well, Billie, come on. Let's you and me go on down the stream a ways and find ourselves a quiet place where we can fish in peace. And don't you holler none tonight, do and you'll scare the fish away.

AUNT BILLIE: Don't worry about me. Look out for your ownself!

RONDIE: Besides, I don't want you getting in jail no more.

AUNT BILLIE: Shaw! They'll have to build that jail up again before they puts me in it.

RONDIE: Tippet right low sick anyhow, ain't he?

AUNT BILLIE: Sure he still got sun-stroke, and look like it's gone down in his hips.

RONDIE: They say he ain't gonna die though.

AUNT BILLIE: Naw, but it be's a long time before he'll amount to anything again. That sun were powerful strong Monday morning.

RONDIE: Yes, it were for a fact. Come on here, let's we go fish.

AUNT BILLIE: All right! I hears the young folks coming along anyhow.

        (The two old women exit as laughter and talking is heard nearby)

BOGATOR: *(Calling after them)* I be long after awhile and pick myself out a fish for frying. Catch me a good one, now!

AUNT BILLIE: *(Calling back from off stage)* You better come and catch your own. I done helped you catch a wife. I ain't bothered about no fish.

> *(Enter PINE, CAROLINE, ARCIE, and ROSE. They carry fishing lines and some have bait cans and frying pans. ROSE has a coffee pot)*

PINE: My, there, folks! You looks mighty lonesome out here by yourself.

CAROLINE: We brung you company.

ROSE: I got the coffeepot, 'Gator, and the coffee. Somebody got to go to the spring and get the water.

BOGATOR: Send Arcie.

ARCIE: No, sir, ree-bob! You'll never send me down to that spring by myself in the dark. I'm going on down under the willows anyhow where the girls is fishing at.

> *(ARCIE goes on down the bank of the creek. As the two girls talk and giggle together, PINE addresses Bogator)*

PINE: Boy, me and Caroline's gonna get married soon's I take this mourning band off.

BOGATOR: When's that gonna be?

PINE: Well, the preacher say you supposed to mourn for six months.

BOGATOR: Huh! That's a long time! Me and Rose gonna get married soon's cotton shopping time is over.

PINE: Aw, you lucky dog! *(To his girl)* Come on, Caroline, let's us go get that water for the coffee. We'll send it back by some of the young-uns. You want us to fill up this pot, Rose?

ROSE: Mighty nigh full, Pine, cause they'll be a heap of people wanting coffee by and by.

PINE: What you selling it for?

ROSE: Penny a cup to help the church.

BOGATOR: You means Rev. Lovelady!

CAROLINE: Well, he the church, ain't he!

PINE: Come on, girl. *(He and CAROLINE exit with the big pot)*

BOGATOR: Rose, you sure took your time getting here!

ROSE: I hurried fast as I could. I was sort of waiting thinking maybe mama'd be back from town. She went in with Rev. Lovelady to help him sell Joe Louis pictures.

BOGATOR: Since Queen Esther done joined the church Sunday night, she certainly stick close to that preacher's side.

ROSE: Seem like she all worked up over the Lawd. She even been teaching Arcie to sing spirituals lately. She say they gonna travel with

Rev. Lovelady, and put on revivals in every town they go to. She say they gonna save souls.

BOGATOR: I imagine Queen Esther would be good at that. Your mama got a good Bible name. Queen Esther were in the Bible, wasn't she?

ROSE: I reckon she were, jest like the Queen of Sheba that they called the Rose of Sharon.

BOGATOR: You's the Rose of Sharon to me, honey!

ROSE: *(Sinking back into BOGATOR's arms)* Is I, dear?

BOGATOR: *(Kissing her)* That's what you is to me! *(Softly)* You gonna be mine now, all the time, ain't you, baby?

ROSE: All the time, Bogator, honey, all the time! *(Shyly)* I burnt up the red dress.

> *(Behind the trees the moon begins to rise)*

BOGATOR: Sugar plum!

ROSE: Lump o' 'lasses!

BOGATOR: Strawberry short cake!

ROSE: Honey in the comb!

BOGATOR: Lawdy! Lawd! Kiss me!

> *(They embrace again. Sounds of voices approaching, loud laughter, and joking, and JERICO playing the mouth organ)*

ROSE: Here comes somebody!

BOGATOR: Sure sounds like it. *(He begins to fix the fire)*

VINEY: *(Entering)* Chile, I done caught seven fish myself and ain't half tried. *(She holds up a string of fish)*

LITTLE BITS: *(Entering)* I caught a great big ole bull fish.

GRANDPA BAILEY: *(Entering)* This here's the best night fishing ground I ever seen.

GRANDMA BAILEY: This here are a fine creek for sure, better'n Baxter Creek.

VINEY: Ain't you-all got no coffee ready yet?

ROSE: We jest sent after the water. It'll be here in a minute. Be careful of that thorn tree Vine, don't get your head caught in it.

VINEY: *(Ducking under tree)* Well, gimme a stick of fire to fry my fish. I done hid my pan here. *(Reaches up in fork of tree and takes down a frying pan)*

BOGATOR: *(Taking out a lighted ember)* Where you want it?

VINEY: *(Indicating a spot back in the trees)* Yonder.

BOGATOR: *(Placing it where she wishes)* Here you be, sis.

VINEY: Grandma Bailey, come on and help me fry these fish. I wish somebody'd bring me a little brush wood.

GRANDPA BAILEY: I'll collect an armful myself.

BOGATOR: Naw, I'll do it. (*He exits into woods*)

GRANDPA BAILEY: (*Following him*) I ain't too old to do it. I tell you, even if I is ninety, I still can stoop. (*Exits*)

GRANDMA BAILEY: Grandpa Bailey don't 'low for nobody to make him out old. I'm seventy myself, and last week you'd a thought he was as young as me when that jack hollered.

(*Sounds of persons approaching from the woods*)

BOGATOR: (*Calling*) Rose, here comes your mama.

VINEY: Queen Esther! And I bet she all dressed up to come to a country fish fry jest as if it were a city wedding.

(*From the river side PINE enters with the coffee pot full of water, followed by CAROLINE*)

PINE: Here's your water.

ROSE: Thank you, Pine.

(*Enter REV. LOVELADY leading the jack with QUEEN ESTHER mounted thereon*)

REV. LOVELADY: Good evening, my friends! Gawd's blessings on you all.

GRANDMA BAILEY: Gawd bless you, Reverend.

VINEY: Gawd bless you.

ROSE: Good evening.

QUEEN ESTHER: (*Piously from the back of the jackass*) Gawd bless you all!

VINEY: Well, Amen! Hush my mouth wide open!

ROSE: Mama, I didn't know you could ride!

QUEEN ESTHER: I'm a riding saint, chile, I mean a riding saint!

REV. LOVELADY: Sister Esther is one of the pillars of the Kingdom. Ain't that a Biblical picture, folks.—Queen Esther, seated on the symbolical Beast! Lemme help you down, Esther. We are intending to start on a travelling evangelistical mission to save souls. Ain't we, sister?

(*Enter BOGATOR and GRANDPA BAILEY with wood*)

QUEEN ESTHER: That we is! You gonna preach, I'm gonna testify, and Arcie and all three of us gonna sing. Where's Arcie now?

BOGATOR: Arcie's down the stream there. Want me to call him?

QUEEN ESTHER: (*Dismounting*) Please. We wants to sing you-all a little song we learned to use at our revival meetings this coming summer with the Reverend.

BOGATOR: *(Yelling)* Arcie! Aw, Arcie! Come here! Your mama wants you!

ARCIE: *(From afar)* O.K. I'm coming!

REV. LOVELADY: Sister Esther and me's gonna make one of the best Gospel teams in the South. We gonna enter a town of sin and clean it up!

QUEEN ESTHER: We means body and soul.

REV. LOVELADY: Yes, body and soul!

(Enter AUNT BILLIE and RONDIE slightly tipsy)

AUNT BILLIE: Howdy to you all. If you's happy as me, then you don't need to worry.

RONDIE: Bless Gawd, Reverend, my rheumatis is gone!

REV. LOVELADY: Good evening, sisters! Sister Esther's about to sing a gospel song. We's glad you come in time to hear it.

AUNT BILLIE: What is it, the Saint Louis Blues?

QUEEN ESTHER: No, it's a song about something mighty serious, the Judgement Day.

AUNT BILLIE: *(Laughing loudly)* You must be getting old, Esther!

QUEEN ESTHER: Just getting more and more sanctified, that's all.

AUNT BILLIE: You got a new name for it, daughter, since you started riding a jackass.

VINEY: I wish you-all'd take that animule far far away from here. I thought when I sold it to you I'd done seen the last of his hide.

REV. LOVELADY: We'll be gone on our mission soon enough, Sister Viney.

QUEEN ESTHER: And you'll miss us when we gone. *(To ARCIE who enters)* Come on, son, let's us sing our revival song for the folkses.

ARCIE: Aw, mama, is that all you wanted me for? I thought we was gonna eat.

VINEY: We gonna eat by and by, chile. I'm frying my fish now.

ROSE: And I'm making the coffee.

REV. LOVELADY: Sing, Sister Esther. Bogator, get your guitar and chime in when you catches the tune.

BOGATOR: *(Reaching up in tree for his guitar)* All right!

QUEEN ESTHER: We made this song up ourselves, tune and all, listen! *(She and ARCIE take the center of the scene)* Go ahead, Arcie.

ARCIE: *(Singing)*
>   *What do you want, dear mother?*
>   *What do you want today?*

QUEEN ESTHER:
>   *I want you to go to heaven, son,*
>   *Cause I am on my way.*

ARCIE: *(As BOGATOR chimes in on the guitar and JERICO comes in with his mouth organ)*
>   *What do you want now, mother?*
>   *What do you want now?*

QUEEN ESTHER:
>   *I want you to go to heaven, son,*
>   *And I will tell you how.*

ARCIE:
>   *What must I do, dear mother,*
>   *Tell me, what must I do?*

QUEEN ESTHER:
>   *Keep your mind on the Gospel Plow and*
>   *Don't let the devil trip you*

ARCIE:
>   *I will do that, mother,*
>   *Do just what you say.*

QUEEN ESTHER:
>   *Then Glory! Hallelujah, son!*
>   *We'll meet on the Judgement Day!*

ALL: *(On Chorus)*
>   *Hal-lelujah!*
>   *Halle—halle—low!*
>   *Hal—lalujah!*
>   *You will sure come through!*
>   *Hal—luijah!*
>   *Glory to his name!*
>   *When they call the Saints o' Gawd*
>   *We'll be there jest the same!*
>   *(PINE and CAROLINE have entered attracted by the music, all sway to the rhythm except AUNT BILLIE and BOGATOR)*

REV. LOVELADY: Amen! Amen! Amen!

GRANDMA BAILEY: Glory! Glory! Glory!

VINEY: *(Throwing her arms around her sister)* Bless God, now I know you's saved!

AUNT BILLIE: *(Beside the frying pan)* Viney, you burning up your fish.

ARCIE: I want to eat.

PINE: That fish sure smell good.

ROSE: The coffee's boiling.
    (MOUSE and several other MEN enter, with dogs and sticks)

MOUSE: Womens, we hongry! We done runned and tramped all over these woods. Fish and cornbread is what we craves.

VINEY: You-all mens gather round here and take your fish, it's ready. Get it while it's hot.
    (MEN gather around VINEY, take the hot fish, and eat it atop hunks of cold cornbread. Exclamations of pleasure and enjoyment)

VOICES: Man, this fish is jest too scrumptious! So sweet I could chaw bones and all! These women sure cooks up a mess! Who caught these sugar-fish anyhow? Boy, oh, boy, oh, boy!

BOGATOR: *(At the big fire)* You all better come here and pull out some of these red hot sweet 'taters. Two cents a piece, benefit of the church!
    (From time to time, people come and purchase potatoes that BOGA-TOR rakes out of the ashes. While they are laughing and talking and eating, a strange hooded shadow rises over the bank from the stream, then another, and another, standing silently)

LITTLE BITS: Ain't this fish good, Jerico?

JERICO: Yeah, man!

REV. LOVELADY: The Lawd has indeed blessed us this evening!

QUEEN ESTHER: *(Eating)* He sure has! I loves right fresh fish just out of the water this way.

ARCIE: Don't you wish you had a bottle of beer, mama?

QUEEN ESTHER: *(Sternly)* Arcie, I has put such sinful drinks from me.

REV. LOVELADY: Amen!

RONDIE: *(Noticing the strange shadows on the skyline)* Billie! Billie! Look a-yonder! Mouse what is that?

CAROLINE: *(As another shadow rises)* Lawdy mercy!

PINE: Now here!
    (Everybody backs back on one side of the stage)

QUEEN ESTHER: *(Screaming)* Aw-ooo!

AUNT BILLIE: *(Rising)* Who goes there? *(As there is no answer)* Black cat and rabbit's paw, eagle's tail and bantum's craw, who's there? I say, who's there?

KLANSMEN: *(Stepping forth in white robes and hoods covering entire head and face)* The Klan!

ALL: *(Screaming and backing away)* The Klan! The Ku Kluxers! The Night Raiders! Lawd have mercy!

KLANSMAN: *(Whose voice sounds suspiciously like SID LOWERY's)* The Ku Klux Klan is riding this evening!

AUNT BILLIE: What you riding on?

SID LOWERY: *(In Klansman robe)* On your feet! Everybody salute the Klan! *(Everybody but AUNT BILLIE and BOGATOR lift trembling hands in salute but somewhere a snicker is heard)* Who's that laughing at the Kleagle?

> *(Other KLANSMEN come menacingly forward)*

MOUSE: Some child that ain't got no sense.

GRANDMA BAILEY: Ain't nobody else laughing, sir!

PINE: Naw, Sir!

SID LOWERY: What you-all doing here this time of night?

GRANDPA BAILEY: Jest having a little fish fry benefit of the church, sir!

SID LOWERY: Fish Fry, heh? Well, we heard you yelling way over cross the highway. You making a powerful lot of noise, and the Klan's got keen ears.

AUNT BILLIE: *(Sharply)* I 'spects you got keener noses. I 'spects you smelt this fish?

SID LOWERY: We pay no mind to fish. The Klan keeps order in the South, that's what.

AUNT BILLIE: And when you gets through keeping order, then what you do?

SID LOWERY: We withdraws!

AUNT BILLIE: Then you sees they's order here, ain't they? We ain't doing nothing wrong. Jest frying a little fish.

SID LOWERY: Seeing that that is the true case, and that you got your Reverend here with you, then *(Reluctantly)* I reckon we withdraws.

REV. LOVELADY: May the good Lawd bless you.

SID LOWERY: We works in the Lord's name and burns a holy cross of flame!

AUNT BILLIE: *(To her crowd)* Chilluns, let's we go on and eat.
> *(They begin to talk and eat again, but the KLANSMEN do not move very far. They murmur among themselves)*

SID LOWERY: *(To his followers)* Shall we ask them? *(Loud murmurs)* Or shall we take it?

VOICES: *(Of Klansmen)* Take it! Take it! Take it!

SID LOWERY: *(Stepping forward valiantly and lifting his hand)* In the name of the Klan, I command you-all to give us ten rations of fish and some . . . *(Just then his hood catches on a branch of the thorn tree. The limb pulls the hood from his head—and reveals SID LOWERY. Loud gasps of recognition from the crowd)* Damn that thorn tree!

AUNT BILLIE: I knowed it was Sid Lowery, all the time. Much as I worked out in the field long side him and his family.

BOGATOR: Well, dog-gone my soul!

REV. LOVELADY: Scandalize my name!

LITTLE BITS: Hello, Mister Lowery!

SID LOWERY: *(Very much embarrassed)* Gimme back my hood!

AUNT BILLIE: Calm yourself, we ain't gonna hurt you!

SID LOWERY: *(Trying to regain his dignity)* Well, in the name of the Klan, I—I—I wish you-all'd give us some fish.

AUNT BILLIE: *(Understandingly)* Aw, so that's it. You-all jest hongry, ain't you? I knowed you smelt this fish. And it sure smells good. Do, I reckon! *(To the Negroes)* Folks, we's got company! The white croppers and tenants done come to join us. Let's make them welcome! We chops cotton together, ain't no reason why we can't eat together. *(To the Whites)* But you-all got take off them hoods. Course the robot'll serve you for bibs and napkins, but you can't eat through a hood. Viney, fry some more fish!

SID LOWERY: But—but—this here's a secret order!

(The Whites all look longingly at the fish)

A FAT KLANSMAN: That fish sure smells good!

AUNT BILLIE: Secret nothing! We all knows every one of you. Don't we, folks?

NEGRO VOICES: Sure we knows them. Works with them every day. They belongs to this plantation.

PINE: *(Pointing to a fat Klansman)* That there's Alf Henderson! Fat as he is.

FAT KLANSMAN: I ain't fat, I'm jest sagging. *(Taking off hood)* Gimme a piece of fish.

(Other KLANSMEN follow suit and begin to remove their head-masks)

SID LOWERY: They knows us, boys. Come on, let's eat.

VINEY: Jest make yourselves welcome. Little Bits, pass the basket of corn pone.

RONDIE: 'Gator, dig out a few potatoes for the gentlemen.

AUNT BILLIE: *(As BOGATOR digs potatoes)* "Gentlemens" a mighty high-sounding word. You-all ain't no more'n us, is you, Sid Lowery? Working in the boss man's fields raising cotton and trying to get along.

FAT KLANSMAN: And getting along like hell, too, if you ask me.

PINE: Next year we ought to plant more something to eat and less cotton.

SID LOWERY: You darned right, Pine.

MOUSE: We don't get nothing for our work and the plantation owner say he don't get nothing for the cotton—so why not plant potatoes.

SID LOWERY: Say, lets you colored folks and us white folks what works out here go tell the boss man that. Tell him we tired of planting cotton and starving. What you say?

BOGATOR: *(As everybody murmurs approval)* I say let's do it.

JERICO: And is we colored folks gonna wear masks, too?

SID LOWERY: Don't none of us need masks to open our mouths and say we's hongry.

PINE: Sure don't.

AUNT BILLIE: Nor to fill your faces with fish! This creek sure has kept many a soul from starving. This creek and these woods. By rights, they ought to belong to us what lives on them, and not to some man what lives way off yonder in New Orleans and jest collects the money when the over-seer sells something! Viney, pass out that fish!

SID LOWERY: Aunt Billie you's sure right.

VINEY: Here a fine piece of hot fish!

SID LOWERY: Thank you kindly. *(All take fish and eat)* Bogator, why don't you strike up a tune?

AUNT BILLIE: Yes, play some music, boy! Let's eat, drink and be merry! The Klan and the colored folks done got together. That's sure something to celebrate!

MOUSE: Yes, indeedy!

BOGATOR: What you want to hear, Sid Lowery!

SID LOWERY: How about *Careless Love?*

BOGATOR: Sure, that's a right pretty tune, even if it don't tell the truth. *(To ROSE)* Come here, Rose, and look into my eyes while I plays.

ROSE: Yes, 'Gator.

QUEEN ESTHER: Daughter, obey your man.

ROSE: Yes, mama.

(BOGATOR and JERICO strike up the music. Just then the jack, back in the shadows, lifts his head and hollers ecstatically. All the

couples get closely and affectionately together. CAROLINE crosses to PINE's welcoming arms. LITTLE BITS runs to snuggle close to ARCIE. GRANDMA BAILEY seeks her husband's side)

VINEY: *(Yelling loudly)* Mouse! You, Mouse! Come here!
      (MOUSE comes)

AUNT BILLIE: *(Raising the jug)* I'm gonna see if I can't out-holler that jack yet. *(Rising)* Yee-ee-hoooo!
      (Everybody sings)

ALL: *Love, oh, love, oh, careless love!*
      You go to my head like wine!
      You've broken the heart of many a poor boy
      But you'll never break this heart of mine! Etc.

AUNT BILLIE: *(As the music goes on and SHE dances with her jug)* Yee-hooooooooooooo!

General gaiety and foot-patting. SID LOWERY, the KLANS-MEN, dance too. Again the jack hollers. As the play ends, a wild and playful yelling contest between AUNT BILLIE and the jack rises above the music and continues a moment after

THE CURTAIN FALLS
END

Joy to My Soul
A Farce Comedy in Three Acts

1937

Hughes wrote *Joy to My Soul* to follow on the success of *Little Ham*. Premiered by the Gilpin Players at Karamu Theatre on April 1, 1937, it received mixed reviews, although Hughes and the reviewer for the *Cleveland Plain Dealer* both noted that black members of the audience found it hilarious. Two years later, its revival at Karamu was termed "wonderfully droll and mad" and "an American classic."[1] Subtitling it a farce, Hughes indicated in production notes that all the characters should be played "in the exaggerated manner of Negro minstrelsy, loud, gay, colorful and overdone."

The comedy here assumes a darker edge than that in *Little Ham*. The freaks and ne'er-do-wells surrounding Buster and Wilmetta prey on them and on each other, and the treatment of Suzy Bailey is quite cruel. Yet Buster Whitehead is not only a country bumpkin, he is a wealthy Texas oilman's son, reversing stereotypes of rural poverty and urban opportunity. Moreover, what in *Little Ham* was a loving portrayal of types in *Joy to My Soul* becomes a display that eludes stereotype through exaggeration and caricature.

The version of the play performed by the Gilpin Players in their sixteenth season, and revived in their eighteenth, was set in Cleveland and was topical, as well as local, in its references. The text included in this volume is set in Harlem (although a few references to Cleveland remain) and was certainly written at least after 1954, when Count Basie's version of "April in Paris," mentioned in the last moments of the play, became a hit. The later text was chosen because no coherent version of the Cleveland-based *Joy to My Soul* is available; Hughes used the only complete Cleveland text in his papers—probably the 1937 performance version—to begin his revisions. In the later, undated typescript, in keeping with the "April in Paris" theme, Suzy vows to find herself a Black Frenchman. In the 1937 version, it is a Black Hawaiian she seeks, as Bing Crosby's 1936 recording "Song of the Islands" wafts out of the bar. The Hawaiian theme also plays on the popularity of the 1937 film

Waikki Wedding, which starred Bing Crosby. As for the marching bands that sashay in and out of the action, and whose presence adds to the play's general mayhem, what so delighted Hughes is suggested by his comments in *The Big Sea:*

> Harlem likes spectacles of one kind or another—but then so does all the world. On Sunday afternoons in the spring when the lodges have their turnouts, it is good to stand on the curb and hear the bands play and see the women pass in their white regalia with swinging purple capes, preceded by the brothers in uniform, with long swords at their sides and feathered helmets, or else in high hats, spats, and cutaway coats. Once I saw such a lodge parade with an all-string band. . . . It was thrilling and the music was grand.[2]

Characters
(In order of speaking)

ROTATION SLIM, a pool shark
DESK CLERK, by name Adolphus
MISS KING, a roomer
TOO-TIGHT, the elevator boy
JULIUS, Madam's chauffeur
HEAVY, Coco's trainer
STEP FATHER BROWN, Wilmetta's step-father
WILMETTA, a cigarette girl
SHEBA LANE, a fan dancer
BIG DOG, a gambler
PRINCE ALI ALI, Bootoo's manager
PRINCESS BOOTOO, a midget
COCO KID, a boxer
BUSTER WHITEHEAD, a young man from Texas
MADAM KLINKSCALE, a medium
STEP FATHER BROWN, Wilmetta's other step-father
SUZY BAILEY, a Lonely Heart
MANAGER, by name Mr. Lighthouse
HIGH GRANDWORTHY, leader of Drill Corps
POLICE SERGEANT
CHAUFFEUR
HUSBAND

WIFE

OLD MAID

(Ladies' Drill Corps, Scrub Woman, Cop, Gamblers, Dancers, Knights and Ladies, and others)

Act I

TIME: *The Present.*

PLACE: *The Grand Harlem Hotel, New York.*

SETTING: *Lobby of the Grand Harlem Hotel in the late afternoon.*
Center, double door leading up short flight of stairs from the street. On one side, the registration desk. Nearby, the elevator, and stairs. Opposite is the tobacco stand, and the entrance to the bar and restaurant. At one side, forward, a tiny curtained alcove containing a settee, a table, and a chair.

AT RISE: *A long tall fellow by name ROTATION SLIM is leaning over the desk talking to ADOLPHUS, the desk CLERK, a young Negro with very slick shiny hair. HEAVY, prizefight trainer, sits in a big chair smoking. On the settee in the alcove, a stout middle-aged woman, MISS KING, is unwrapping a parcel. She takes out an old pair of large shoes, pulls off the stylish slippers she is wearing and puts the big shoes on. At the tobacco stand, STEP-FATHER BROWN is talking to WILMETTA, the cigarette girl, evidently begging her for something. During the action other guests and employees of the hotel stroll in and out.*

ROTATION: Yeah man! I beat that joker so quick I made his breath come short. Took me about fifty seconds to win Ten Dollars and pick him clean as a whistle. First crack out of the box, soon's I bust the stack, I made three big balls.

CLERK: No, you ain't. *(Turns head in annoyance as switchboard buzzes)*

ROTATION: Then I hits the one ball so it knocks the 14 square in the pocket. While the cue ball bounces off and sends the 10 dead in the side. The one falls off, and I got my 61 in two shots. And I say Gimme Ten.

(Insistent buzzing of switchboard)

CLERK: You sure can shoot pool, boy! I'm tellin' you!

ROTATION: Who me? Did I ever tell you about the time I ran black ball on a fool in Detroit in three shots?

CLERK: Naw.

ROTATION: Well, listen.

    (Switchboard buzzes again)

CLERK: Aw, hell! Wait a minute. Somebody's always calling up here soon's I gets busy.

MISS KING: *(To the ELEVATOR BOY as he opens the car door and two KNIGHTS of the ROYAL SPHINX in full uniform leave the elevator, cross the lobby, and exit)* Here, Too-Tight, take these dress-shoes of mine and put 'em on back upstairs in Room 317. Doggone if I can make it to the street car with these high heels this evening. My dogs is killing me. I done served 200 people today at lunch.

TOO-TIGHT: *(Taking the shoes)* Goin' back on the job, huh? Most time to serve dinner.

MISS KING: I better go. *(Rising)* Ain't nobody payin' my rent but me. I gived you my numbers to put in as I come down, ain't I?

    (JULIUS, chauffeur, enters door and goes to elevator)

TOO-TIGHT: Yes'm. Four in Goldfield and two in B. & M.

MISS KING: Rick. And if I hit, call me up. You know where I works at that Tea Shoppe. If 36–42 come out for Fifty Cents, I'll stop dead in my tracks and take a vacation.

TOO-TIGHT: Yes, Mis' King.

MISS KING: O.K., Too-Tight, I'm gone. *(She exits out street door)*

TOO-TIGHT: *(Calling across the lobby)* Old Rotation Slim himself! What you sayin', boy?

ROTATION: Take it easy, kid! Want to roll me one, this evenin'?

TOO-TIGHT: I ain't no chump. I know you don't play sociable.

    (CHAUFFEUR walks out of elevator and looks restless)

ROTATION: Dime a game, I don't call that nothin' but sociable.

TOO-TIGHT: I plays policy with my dimes, and my dollars I puts on the horses.

ROTATION: You can't see 'em run.

TOO-TIGHT: No, but I knows when they pay off.

JULIUS: *(To the ELEVATOR BOY)* Say, buddy, ain't you ever goin' up?

TOO-TIGHT: Only way I can go is up. We don't run to the basement.

JULIUS: Well, come on then. I'm in a hurry.

TOO-TIGHT: Just hold your horses, big boy, hold your horses!

HEAVY: *(Calling across the lobby)* Hey, Too-Tight, tell Kid Coco to hurry on down here, we got fifty miles to drive over in Jersey for that fight tonight.

TOO-TIGHT: O.K., I'll give him a holler. *(Exits into elevator and carries CHAUFFEUR up)*

ROTATION: Funny how important some folks gets when they got on a uniform, ain't it, Adolphus?

CLERK: You mean that Stud just went yonder? He's Madam Klinkscale's personal chauffeur.

ROTATION: Madam Klinkscale? Who's she?

CLERK: New guest come in this morning. Mind-reader and medium. They say she's a solid sender.

ROTATION: I needs to meet her. Boy, my future's all mixed up. Wonder could she straighten me out?

CLERK: They say she can straighten out anybody. She knows what's in your mind and everybody else's too.

HEAVY: Do she give out numbers?

CLERK: Sure, she gives out numbers, clearing house and policy.

HEAVY: Well, I'm gonna see her tomorrow.

ROTATION: What time do she receive customers?

CLERK: She ain't working yet. The boss says he don't know if he'll let her use her room or not for mediumology. Seem like it's illegal or something.

ROTATION: Illegal? Huh! Illegal! So's gambling, but you-all runs two games right upstairs, and a horse-racing joint besides.

CLERK: We pays the police for that, so it's legitimate. We got no arrangements to pay off for mediums.

ROTATION: You mean the boss wants to shake Madam down—and she's holding out, huh?

CLERK: Anyhow, she ain't started functioning yet.

ROTATION: When she do, let me know. If she's got bucks, I'm liable to make her. Maybe she needs a real good husband.

HEAVY: Then she better take me.

CLERK: I'll bet she can read your minds from A to Z.

ROTATION: Not Rotation Slim's. I'm a slick hustler, pal, I is.
　　(Switchboard buzzer sounds)

CLERK: Doggone that buzzer. I can't get my work done for them phones. *(Turns to switchboard)* Hello! Hello!

HEAVY: Throw me your nail file, Rotation, so's I can clean my nails whilst I's waiting on Coco Kid.

ROTATION: *(Tossing him a file)* Don't bother me, boy, I'm gonna study this racing form.
　　(Picks up a racing journal from desk and studies it. At the tobacco

*counter, old STEP-FATHER BROWN suddenly begins to whine
to WILMETTA)*

BROWN: You gived *him* Fifty Cents cause I just now met him across
the street putting it on the numbers! And when I wants some small
change to eat with, you won't give me nothing.

WILMETTA: But, Daddy. . . .

BROWN: That shows how little you care about your poor old step-
father. And here you making plenty money.

WILMETTA: Daddy, you know I don't make but eighteen dollars a
week, and between you and Step-Father Johnson, I don't have a
thing left. *(Sternly)* You don't want to eat anyhow, you want to
drink.

BROWN: Wilmetta, I swear I ain't had a mouthful o' food in my stomach today, not even bread.

WILMETTA: Well, then, here! Take this quarter and buy yourself something. I guess I can't see you starve.

BROWN: No, cause I were your mama's favorite husband! *(Muttering)*
Even if she did quit me before she died to marry that old hound
Johnson.

WILMETTA: Now, Daddy, don't talk about step-father Johnson like
that. I like you both. Only I wish you could find a job.

BROWN: I been on the city's snow shovelling emergency list, but somehow it just don't seem to snow no more. Thank you for this quarter.
I'll see you later, daughter darling.

*(He exits. Elevator door opens and TOO-TIGHT emerges, followed
by SHEBA LANE who crosses toward the door to the bar, and BIG
DOG, a gambler, who goes toward the desk)*

SHEBA: Br-rr-r! It's cold in this old hotel! Why don't you-all have some
heat? It ain't summer yet.

HEAVY: That's 'cause you ain't had your pre-breakfast nip, darling.

SHEBA: Child, I was swinging out last night! We had more fun down
here in the bar! A couple of old Knights from Dayton was busting
their vests. Why didn't you come down, Heavy?

HEAVY: We got a fight in Jersey tonight. Coco's got to train some time.
I had to put him to bed.

SHEBA: Well, tell him to stop past the bar and get something under
his belt before you leave so if he gets knocked out, he won't feel it.
(SHEBA exits into bar)

HEAVY: All you-all gamblers better put your money on my boy 'cause
he's gonna win. You hear me Big Dog?

BIG DOG: Win what, the professional Never-Win title?

ROTATION: Time Big Rocky gets through with Coco you gonna bring him home in pieces.

HEAVY: I'll bet you both on that!

ROTATION: I'll take you up.

HEAVY: Lemme see your money.

ROTATION: Lemme see your'n.

HEAVY: Aw, man . . . . . .

TOO-TIGHT: *(Near the street door)* You-all-broke-arched jokers, hush up. Here comes a guest with a carload of baggage.

CLERK: *(Banging on the bell)* Front! Front!

TOO-TIGHT: Cut out all that bell ringing. Don't you see me in front? *(He goes out the door and returns pushing a large black box on rollers, with several bags under his arms as well. Preceding him comes a large dark gentleman in a frock coat and a light green turban, by name ALI ALI. He approaches the registration desk and addresses the CLERK in a booming voice)*

ALI: I'm Prince Ali Ali, young man, direct from the famous city of Cairo, Egypt, Arabia. I bring the world's greatest attraction, known from coast to coast and from Paris, France, to Paris, Kentucky. None other, folks than the original pure Arabian Midget, Princess Bootoo! *(Whereupon one side of the box falls forward revealing seated therein, in a sedan chair, the Midget BOOTOO. All crowd around to see her as ALI ALI takes her up in his arms and places her on the desk)* Give us a suit of rooms.

CLERK: Well, suits is kinder scarce but—

ALI: Suits scarce? How come?

CLERK: The Grand Lodge of Knights and Ladies of the Sphinx meets here tomorrow for their conclave and they just about taken up everything.

ALI: That's how come I'm here because they're meeting. The Knights can't percolate without me. I'm the only one among 'em ever saw the Sphinx, me and the Princess here, ain't we, Princess?

BOOTOO: Um-huh!

ALI: And we must have a suit.

CLERK: Well, sir, I . . . . . .

ALI: I don't care what it costs. We're here to make money and to spend it. The Princess is a special attraction brought at great cost for the Knights' and Ladies' Annual Circus. If you ain't got a suit, vacate one. I mean your best one, too.

CLERK: Madam Klinkscale's got the best one, sir.

ALI: And who might Madam Klinkscale be, if you please? A hootchie-cootchie dancer?

CLERK: No, sir. She's a Spiritual and Mental Socio-psy-copath.

ALI: She's nothing to me. Move her out and give us the rooms.

CLERK: I can't do that, sir, but I might can give you-all two rooms with a bath between you.

ALI: *(Sighing)* If we must, then we'll take it without the bath. And arrange for meals on the bill. My little Princess here can take half-rate board. The tiny doll eats like a child.

BOOTOO: That's a lie.

ALI: Why, Princess!

BOOTOO: *(Loudly)* I eat as much as you, J.C. And don't you go getting no cut-rate board for me, with half an egg for breakfast like you did in Memphis.

ALI: Why, my dear Bootoo, I—

BOOTOO: I, nothing. Lemme down from here, too. I ain't on exhibit, yet.

ALI: Bootoo, darling, you'll rile your nerves.

BOOTOO: Wonder I got any nerves left, fooling around with you. You take me for a dog! *(To the CLERK)* Gimme the key. I wants to go to my room. *(Stamping her foot)* And give it to me damn quick!

ROTATION: *(Aside)* She don't sound like no Arabian to me.

HEAVY: Original Georgia Midget, that's what she is.

CLERK: *(Handing keys to TOO-TIGHT)* Show the Prince and Princess up to 207 and 8, boy.

TOO-TIGHT: *(Picking up the bags)* Princess, take your cage and follow me.

> *(COCO KID enters down the stairs carrying boxing gloves and a bundle. He stares in amazement at the entourage, then begins to berate TOO-TIGHT)*

COCO: I been ringing that elevator bell twenty minutes, damn your hide, Too-Tight.

TOO-TIGHT: *(Loftily)* I has no time for boxers. I'm engaged in royalties. Get out the way, Coco, and let us pass.

> *(TOO-TIGHT, ALI and BOOTOO enter the elevator and exit)*

COCO: *(To HEAVY)* Come on boy, let's go. Have you got the car 'round in front?

HEAVY: How'm I gonna get the car in front and ain't nary a drop of gasoline in it?

COCO: Why didn't you get some then?

HEAVY: With what?

COCO: Ain't you got no money?

HEAVY: Don't talk foolish, Coco. Is you punch drunk?

COCO: Well, ain't this a blipty! Done booked a fight fifty miles off for eight o'clock tonight, and ain't got no money to get there with.

HEAVY: I thought you had some.

COCO: You thought! With what did you thought? You ain't got no head to thought with.

HEAVY: Aw, pal, don't talk that-a way.

COCO: *(Appealingly)* Rotation, lend me a couple of bucks.

ROTATION: I ain't won a dime today, neither on black jack, horses, numbers, nor pool.

COCO: I ain't talkin' about what you won. I'm talking about what you got. *(To the other gambler)* How about you, Big Dog? Lend me a ball or two. I'll pay you back after I win that fight tonight.

BIG DOG: Boy, I wish I could, but I'm flatter'n Frisco after the earthquake.

COCO: That's what I say about friends, never got nothing when you need it, but always ready to take it what *I* got it. *(Looking at the Desk CLERK)* I know Adolphus ain't puttin' out nothing. And Wilmetta's too busy feeding her two step-fathers. Scuffling's rough this evening.

WILMETTA: I wish I could lend you something, Coco.

HEAVY: Maybe Sheba'll lend us gas money.

COCO: Where's Sheba at?

HEAVY: In the bar.

COCO: Come on, let's go see.

> *(As they approach the bar, an over-grown young man enters dressed in western clothes and carrying two carpet-bags. His name is BUSTER WHITEHEAD)*

BUSTER: 'Scuse me, gentlemens, but is this here the Grand Harlem Hotel?

COCO: Ain't nothing different.

BUSTER: Then this is the place I want.

COCO: What you want it for?

BUSTER: I'm looking for my fi-an-cee.

COCO: Your which?

BUSTER: My fi-an-cee.

COCO: Dog, animal, or man?

BUSTER: She's a woman, least-wise, a young girl.

COCO: Right here in the bar then, come on in.

BUSTER: You mean my fi-an-cee's in yonder?

COCO: I don't know about no fi-an-cees, but take a look at Sheba.

BUSTER: I got to find my fi-an-cee first.

COCO: Then go ahead. We're offering you the prettiest woman we know, but if you don't want her, go ahead.

> (*COCO and BUSTER get in each other's way several times as each tries to pass. Finally COCO stops belligerently and BUSTER circles around him toward the tobacco stand. COCO and HEAVY exit into the bar*)

BUSTER: (*Staring, speaks shyly to WILMETTA*) They must've been talking about you.

WILMETTA: Not. me. They talking about Miss Sheba Lane there in the bar. She's a show girl.

BUSTER: Is she prettier'n you is?

WILMETTA: Well, she's different.

BUSTER: But you's pretty. I reckon you's near as pretty as my fi-an-cee.

WILMETTA: Who's your fiancee?

BUSTER: Miss Suzanne Dorine de Bailey. Don't you know her?

WILMETTA: I'm sorry, but I don't.

BUSTER: Gee, you ought to know her.

WILMETTA: I'd like to.

BUSTER: I'll introduce you. I wonder where abouts she's at? She's due to be here somewhere.

WILMETTA: Maybe she belongs to the Royal Sphinx. They ain't all arrived yet.

BUSTER: She don't have to arrive. She's here—in the rendez-vous. Where's that?

WILMETTA: I don't know. You better ask Adolphus at the desk, over there.

BUSTER: (*Approaching the CLERK*) I want to get in touch with Miss Suzanne Dorine de Bailey in your ren-dez-vous. She's my fi-an-cee.

CLERK: I beg your pardon?

BUSTER: Miss Suzanne de Bailey.

CLERK: There ain't no Suzanne de Bailey here.

BUSTER: Well, is you got any ren-dez-vous around?

CLERK: What?

BUSTER: Ren-dez-VOUS! She told me she rents the ren-dez-vous here.

ROTATION: Rendezvous. No doubt he means *rendezvous,* a French word they used in the war. *Rendezvous.*

CLERK: Well, we ain't got none here.

BUSTER: I got to find one—I mean Miss de Bailey's, 'cause I come a long ways to find this one.

ROTATION: From where did you come, may I ask?

BUSTER: Shadow Gut.

ROTATION: Shadow Gut, where?

BUSTER: Shadow Gut, Texas.

CLERK: Whee! That's solid far!

BIG DOG: Too far!

ROTATION: What kind o' place is that?

BUSTER: A right smart place. It's got four or five hundred humans, and twenty head o' cattle. Mostly Indians and Mexicans—and us.

ROTATION: Who's us?

BUSTER: Me and Pa.

ROTATION: And who're you?

BUSTER: Old man Whitehead's boy, Buster. *(Offering his hand all around)* I'm pleased to meet you. Howdy-do! How you been?
(They all shake hands)

BIG DOG: Can you play poker?

BUSTER: Naw, sir.

ROTATION: Can you shoot pool?

BUSTER: Not much.

ROTATION: By and by, I'll show you how to play pool.

CLERK: Just now, don't you want a room?

BUSTER: I don't know how long I'm gonna stay.

CLERK: Didn't you come for the Conclave?

BUSTER: Naw, I come to get married.

CLERK: Married?

ROTATION: Married?

BUSTER: Sure! I turned 21 this past gone July. Now I got a fi-an-cee.

CLERK: Then you want the honeymoon suite?

BUSTER: Course, it's gonna be sweet!

CLERK: But where is *she?*

BUSTER: Here in the Grand Hotel.

CLERK: *(In surprise)* No, she ain't!

BUSTER: Yes, she is, too. She told me to meet her here in her natural ren-dez-vous.

BIG DOG: Well, I'm a green-eyed dog!

CLERK: She's got a French name. Her grandma was a French Canadian Indian, of the Blackfoot Tribe.

CLERK: Ain't nary Indian here.

ROTATION: No, but there's plenty o' Black Feet.

BUSTER: Suzanne Dorine de Bailey's here, ain't she?

CLERK: I beg your pardon, but she ain't here.

BUSTER: But she writ and told me she were here.

CLERK: *(In exasperation)* What room did she say she's in?

BUSTER: Lemme see. *(He searches in his pocket for a letter. Reads:)* Room 4-0-6. That's it! See—406.

CLERK: Oh! You mean old Suzy Bailey?

BIG DOG: It can't be, 'cause she ain't marriageable!

ROTATION: And a long ways from being Indian.

BUSTER: Then I reckon it's her daughter.

CLERK: I ain't never laid eyes on no daughter.

BUSTER: I guess you just don't know her then.

CLERK: I guess not. You say that's a letter from her?

BUSTER: Sure, I got lots of letters from her. This here is just the last one.

CLERK: What do she say?

BUSTER: You all want to hear it? It's mighty sweet. It's liable to make you jealous.

ROTATION: Aw, go on and read it.

BUSTER: All right, listen. It says, *(Reading the letter)* Dear Buster, Sweet Baby Mine, I can hardly wait until you gets here for I know you are my ideal at last, the kind of a man I been waiting for forever. If you did not live so far off in Shadow Gut, Texas, I would come to you, but as it is and things is now, you must come to me. You said your father would let you have the money, so come on and I will be waiting with opened arms. Send me a wire by telegram when you get here and I will fly to greet you fastern a robin to a worm. All these months we been changing kisses by mail has been joy to my soul. When we meets, our joy will be unbounded in the sight of God. I awaits thee, Buster baby of my sweetening dreams. From your loving Heart, Suzanne Dorine de Bailey 45 Oxford Road, the Bronx, where is my suburban home so write me there. But the Grand Harlem Hotel is my natural rendezvous.

ROTATION: *(Correcting his pronunciation)* Rendezvous.

BUSTER: *(Unheeding)* In my natural ren-dez-vous, I awaits you. 406. Suzanne. Now you see what she says. She awaits me.

CLERK: *(At the switchboard)* Well, she must be waiting on Oxford Road, 'cause I'm ringing 406 and there ain't nobody home.

ROTATION: When did you send her the wire you was coming?

BUSTER: Just now, from the station downtown. She said send it when I got here.

CLERK: Oh, no wonder! She ain't had time to get down here from the Bronx where she works.

BUSTER: What kind of work do she do?

CLERK: Kitchen mechanic. Don't you know her?

BUSTER: No, you see, I—

ROTATION: Ain't you never met her?

BUSTER: Well, not in person.

ROTATION: Not in person?

BUSTER: Naw, just by mail.

ROTATION: Well, dog bit my onions!

BUSTER: We's corresponding sweethearts.

ROTATION: What?

CLERK: Who introduced you?

BUSTER: The Lonely Hearts. I met her through that colored newspaper what runs a column for lonesome hearts.

BIG DOG: And is you one of them lonesomes?

BUSTER: I'm Lonely Heart No. 72. That is I was till I met Suzanne. You see, they ain't no colored girls in Shadow Gut.

ROTATION: So you wrote these here Lonely Hearts and picked out a long distance chick by mail?

BUSTER: That's right.

ROTATION: Somebody you ain't never seen?

BUSTER: Yea. But they good girls, 'cause ain't nobody else sees 'em neither.

ROTATION: That's what you think.

BUSTER: That's what I know. You have to get engaged to meet a Lonely Heart in person. They is real strick about that.

BIG DOG: Like in poker, you have to pay to see the cards.

ROTATION: The trouble is, how do you know if you getting a heart or a spade.

CLERK: Looks like *he* drew a joker.
     (General laughter)

BUSTER: You all acts kinder like you's making fun of me or something.

ROTATION: Not-a-tall, friend, not-a-tall.

BUSTER: There ain't nothin' wrong about Miss de Bailey, is there?

BIG DOG: Nothing a-tall!

BUSTER: Shaw, then I bet you fellers is just jealous 'cause a out-of-town man like me's done come along and got the bacon. *(To the CLERK)* How long you think it'll take her to get down here?

CLERK: Well, if she comes right off, about half an hour. Why don't you register now?

BUSTER: Register for what? I don't want to vote.

CLERK: Your room. You see, the Knights and Ladies of the Royal Sphinx convenes tomorrow. Rooms is going fast.

BUSTER: Maybe I won't want no room. I'll just sit down and wait for my fi-an-cee.

ROTATION: *(To BIG DOG as they move away)* That jigaboo's just broke, that's all.

BIG DOG: I can see he ain't no meat for us. Let's go.

ROTATION: No, let's sit around and see what happens when she gets here.

BIG DOG: That might be an idea—cause somebody's gonna blow up when they meet.

CLERK: *(Banging on bell)* Too-Tight, take the gentleman's bags and set 'em out of the way. He's gonna set around awhile.

TOO-TIGHT: Well, tell him not to set too long, 'cause we's busy in this hotel.

CLERK: Pay that no mind, Mr. Whitehead. Sit down and tell us some more about Shadow Gut.

BUSTER: *(Taking a seat near the tobacco stand, pleased)* You-all really want to hear some more about Shadow Gut?

(As he talks, the others lounge around, read papers, etc. They appear only half interested, except for WILMETTA who listens politely)

BUSTER: Course, ain't nobody heard of it much, cause it ain't on no railroad. It sits way back over yonder by Big Sandy, about ten miles past Tarnation Switch. Course, it's familiar to me cause I were borned there. My Pa, he went out there from Florida one day in 1898 when the government were giving away land. He staked his self out a piece, squatted on it, and has been there ever since. I were borned in 1916, then Ma got tired of lookin' at me and Pa both when I was two years old, so she up and left—and ain't nary one of us seed her since. Pa been a widow a long time, and I been a half-orphan.

WILMETTA: I'm a half-orphan, too. My mama's dead.

BUSTER: Ain't that a shame.

WILMETTA: But I got two step-fathers.

BUSTER: I ain't got nary a step-mama. A Indian squaw raised me.

ROTATION: No wonder you look so funny!

BUSTER: I didn't speak nothing but Indian till I were ten years old.

CLERK: Go ahead, and speak some Indian now. Let's hear it. *(Switchboard buzzes)* Doggone this switchboard. Everytime I get busy. . . . Yes! Yes! What you want?. . . . O.K. *(Calling to TOO-TIGHT)* Too-Tight, Princess Bootoo says bring her up a fried chicken, two sweet potatoes, some bristle sprouts, a dish of navy beans, and some cold slaw, to Room 207 quick. *(Phone rings again)* Yes'm. . . . and a slice of apple pie.

TOO-TIGHT: *(Carelessly)* O.K. Just a minute, soon's I hear this Indian talk. Phone the order to the restaurant. Go ahead, boy, talk some Indian.

BUSTER: *(Staring at TOO-TIGHT)* Ug-lum, kiyum ko!

TOO-TIGHT: *(Jumping back)* What'd you call me, fool?

BUSTER: That's a Indian saying. It means, if you got work to do, go on and do it, that's all.

TOO-TIGHT: Huh! That's the last thing I do, work. *(Pointing to RO-TATION)* Go ahead, call old Rotation a dirty name for me, will you?

BUSTER: *(Staring at ROTATION)* Google lum giggle lum gang!

ROTATION: *(Drawing a knife)* I don't play that!

(Exit TOO-TIGHT in bar, laughing)

BUSTER: I ain't said nothing but *Goodmorning, friend,* that's all.

ROTATION: Well, don't talk no Indian around me, you hear! Might get yourself cut up.

BIG DOG: Yes, cause these jigaboos'll think you calling 'em out of their name. Here folks just sits around and thinks up evil. What do you-all do down in Shadow Gut?

BUSTER: We has horse-races and cock fights and eats razorbacked hogs.

CLERK: Don't you work none?

BUSTER: Not much. Once in a while.

CLERK: What do you use for money?

BUSTER: Silver dollars.

ROTATION: And where do you get 'em?

BUSTER: Oh, out o' the bank.

TOO-TIGHT: *(Returning with Midget's dinner on a tray)* Listen at this joker lie! *(He pauses to listen)*

ROTATION: And how do them dollars get in the bank, I asks?

BUSTER: From oil.

EVERYBODY: Oil? What oil?

BUSTER: Most everybody in Shadow Gut's got an oil well in they back yard. Now we got ten or eleven, I disremembers which, and when I left my old man was sinking another one.

> *(General excitement)*

ROTATION: Lord bless my soul!

TOO-TIGHT: Lemme get rid of this dinner. *(He rushes off with the tray)*

CLERK: Well, now, er-er, Mr. Buster, really don't you need some rest? We can give you a fine front suit overlooking Seventh Avenue for $5 a day.

ROTATION: Boy, you spoke of horses. Did you know we got horse races right here?

BUSTER: Where? Is I got time to see 'em run?

ROTATION: You got plenty of time. But you won't see 'em run. You just hears their names called over the phone.

BUSTER: Is that all?

ROTATION: But you can imagine you sees 'em runnin', and the more money you bets on 'em, the better you sees 'em. Come on with me, pal.

BIG DOG: Don't take that young man to no bookie joint. He's seed enough horses, ain't you, son? Come on upstairs where we're running a nice little poker game, deuces wild. Now that's where you can have your sport. How much loose change you got with you?

BUSTER: *(Pulling out a roll of bills)* Oh, I don't know. I reckon about two hundred dollars.

> *(Great excitement and exclamations)*

BIG DOG: My! My! My!

ROTATION: Friend, stick with me!

TOO-TIGHT: *(Returning out of breath)* Lemme git back in here and hustle some, too. That Midget says she wants some ice cream. But damn if I'm gonna bring it.

> *(Enter a KNIGHT and LADY in full regalia, carrying baggage and approaching the desk. The CLERK bangs on the bell)*

CLERK: Front! Front!

TOO-TIGHT: Damn the front! *(To BUSTER)* Say, Mr. Buster, does you shoot dice?

BIG DOG: No, he don't shoot dice. He plays poker.

BUSTER: I's heard tell of dice, but I never done no playin'.

TOO-TIGHT: Well, you sure can learn. And here's your teacher. Come on down in the basement where nobody'll bother us.

(At this moment SHEBA breezes in from the bar, followed by COCO and HEAVY)

SHEBA: Do I smell money? Who is this handsome stranger over here? Baby, I'm Sheba Lane. What's your name?

BUSTER: *(Rising)* Buster Whitehead.

(The two LODGE MEMBERS still carrying their own bags, stand ringing the elevator bell)

TOO-TIGHT: Doggone that bell! Everytime I get busy!

CLERK: *(Banging his bell, also)* Bell-boy, bell-boy! Service, *please.*

TOO-TIGHT: Oh, all right! *(He exits into the elevator followed by the TWO GUESTS)*

SHEBA: Say, Mr. Whitehead, did you know I'm from Texas, too?

BUSTER: Are you sure enough? Where abouts?

SHEBA: Houston, right from Smith Street.

BUSTER: Had I a-knowed they was anything like you in Houston, I might-a stopped there.

SHEBA: There ain't nothing like me there no more—since I left. It's sad and sorry now. But I'm so glad to see you, Mr. Whitehead. Come on, let's sit down in that little alcove and talk awhile.

ROTATION: Oh, no you don't, Sheba. This boy belongs to me.

BIG DOG: I still think he wants to learn how to play deuces wild.

COCO: What! A fine young man like that! He's interested in manly sports, ain't you, Mr. Whitehead? Wouldn't you like to be in on a prize-fight?

BUSTER: What prize-fight?

COCO: Me! I'm gonna fight a chump tonight in Jersey. Sure to win, ain't I, Heavy?

HEAVY: Yes, certainly, sure.

COCO: Now all you got to do is gimme Ten Dollars to put up on myself, and I'll double it for you.

BUSTER: Will you really?

COCO: Of course! The Coco Kid's never been known to fail.

ROTATION: No, just fall.

COCO: You's a prevaricator! *(To BUSTER)* Pal, when I cold-cock 'em, if they don't tumble I look behind 'em to see what's holding him up!

HEAVY: That's no jive neither.

COCO: Gimme Ten, and I'll bring you back Twenty, long about midnight.

BUSTER: *(Taking out the money)* Well, here! I don't mind. I wish I could see you fight, but I got to wait for my fi-an-cee.

COCO: *(As he and HEAVY exit toward the street)* Thank you, Mr. Whitehead. You're what I call a real sport. Thank you.

ROTATION: Well, break me down!

BIG DOG: Now, while you're waiting, Mr. Whitehead, why don't you all, Miss Lane, Rotation, and everybody just come on up to my room. The boys are there, and we can order a bottle of White Horse. That's the horse for me.

BUSTER: My Pa's got a white horse named Cecil.

SHEBA: This one is Scotch, darling. It makes you fly, not ride.

BIG DOG: Come on, boys. *(Taking BUSTER by the arm)*

BUSTER: I reckon I ought to wait for Suzanne.

BIG DOG: Don't worry! Don't worry a-tall. We'll just leave word with Adolphus here at the desk that you're with me in 311 and he can phone us if she comes.

ROTATION: *(ROTATION takes BUSTER's other arm)* But he won't be in 311, Clerk. He'll be in the bookie joint with me.

SHEBA: *(Coming between BUSTER and ROTATION)* Not a-tall! We're going to take a little walk, aren't we, Buster? He wants to see Harlem.

WILMETTA: I think Mr. Whitehead just wants to set here.

(EVERYBODY turns and glares at WILMETTA)

SHEBA: You stay out of this, Prissy.

BIG DOG: Come on, Mr.Whitehead.

BUSTER: To tell the truth, I believe I'd rather hear them horses run. I wants to know how you has races over the telephone.

ROTATION: Sure you do, pal. And I'll pick you some sure winners. Facts is, we can both pick. Now, you gimme half of your money to bet *my* way, and you keep the other half to bet *your* way and . . . . . .

SHEBA: But, Mr. Whitehead, don't we need a little drink first? Come on in the bar with me. Let's play the slot machines and shake up a cocktail.

BUSTER: What kind o' tail is that?

ROTATION: *(Angrily)* Sheba, you're gumming up the works. The fourth race is on by now, and I want to put a Ten on Dog Face at Latonia. Come on, Mr. Whitehead and let that dizzy frail alone.

SHEBA: *(Glaring)* All right, Rotation Slim. Wait till I tell Shag about this.

ROTATION: Shag me eye. I'll knock Shag's back teeth out with my little fingers. Shag can't fight.

BUSTER: Who's Shag?

SHEBA: My grandfather, dear, my Creole grandfather.

BUSTER: Wouldn't nobody hit an old man like your grandfather.

SHEBA: Honey, these men would hit their mammy.

ROTATION: *(Pulling on BUSTER's arm)* Come on afore I get mad. Let's go get a horse.

TOO-TIGHT: Will you play one for me, Mister Buster?

CLERK: *(As buzzer rings)* Princess Bootoo wants her ice cream.

TOO-TIGHT: Can't you see I'm busy?

> *(As the others exit crowding into the elevator, MADAM KLINK-SCALE enters down the stairs out of breath)*

MADAM: I've been ringing that bell for an hour. What's the matter here, a guest can't get no service? I ever saw the beat. I'll have you know I'm Madam Klinkscale!

CLERK: Lady, we had Madam Goldscale here and she couldn't make that elevator run. It just gets stuck sometimes.

MADAM: Well, I'll move if I have to walk down those steps again.

CLERK: There ain't nary another good hotel to move to, far as I know.

MADAM: *(Grandly)* I'll create one. I can create anything I choose. Don't you know I'm a medium? Everything is all mind, anyhow. *(Waving her hand about)* This is mind, all mind.

CLERK: I wish it was all mine. It belongs to Mr. Steinbaum.

MADAM: I thought this was a colored hotel.

CLERK: It is, but colored folks don't own it.

> *(An attractive young GIRL, in a short dress strolls through the lobby. The CLERK's eyes follow her footsteps)*

MADAM: Well, they think they do, so it's all the same, mind! Mind! How powerful is mind! *(Suddenly)* I can tell *you* what's on *your* mind right now.

CLERK: *(Jumping)* Lady, please don't do it.

MADAM: Don't worry. I'd get $5 for doing that. But *you* listen to me, young man, and listen fluently. I want to rent that alcove.

CLERK: You mean right there? A part of the lobby.

MADAM: I mean right there. We can pull the curtains, can't we? I want to be accessible to my public. I don't want them to have to come way up stairs to Room 542 every time they want to consult me as to what they got on their own mind. I want to be right here where I can serve the people.

CLERK: Well, I'll have to ask the manager.

MADAM: Where is the manager? Send for him. Tell him Madam Klink-scale wants him. Get him down here.

CLERK: I'll try. *(He buzzes the switchboard)* But I expect he's still asleep. He handles the night shift, and he's liable to get mad if I wake him up.

MADAM: Then I'll wake him up myself. I'll concentrate on him. *(She screws up her face and concentrates through the ceiling)*

CLERK: *(Over the wire)* Yes, Mr. Lighthouse! No sir, I didn't ring but once, Mr. Lighthouse. You say something seemed to explode inside your head? Well, it wasn't none of me, Mr. Lighthouse.

MADAM: Tell him it was me! Tell him I concentrook on him.

CLERK: It were Madam Klinkscale, sir. She says she concentrook on you. Huh?. . . . *(Turning to the MADAM)* The boss say please unconcentrook on him, cause his head's about to bust wide open . . . . . . Yes, sir, Mr. Lighthouse, I told her.

MADAM: Tell him I want to do business with him.

CLERK: She say she wants to do business with you . . . . . . She wants to rent the alcove—part of the lobby. . . . Yes, sir. . . . you say, let her have it for $10 a day plus $2 protection. . . . Yes, sir. . . . O.K., sir! All right Mr. Lighthouse, I'll tell her . . . . . . Goodbye.

MADAM: What were his decision?

CLERK: His decision were, you can have the alcove for $10 a day and $2 protection.

MADAM: Um-hum! Well, with my professional discount, that'll be seven fifty. And when I gets through concentrating on him it'll be less. As for protection, I don't need to pay no hush money. I'm a legitimate ordained spiritual medium!

CLERK: But, Madam. . . .

MADAM: *(Staring)* Now, young man . . . .

CLERK: Don't concentrate on me, please.

MADAM: I was going to ask you to ring for my chauffeur, but I'll show you that the very thought of him brings him here. Julius!

(CHAUFFEUR appears on the stairs)

JULIUS: Ma'am?

MADAM: Where you been?

JULIUS: That elevator! Madam, I been ringing for five minutes.

MADAM: Julius, arrange the alcove. Then get thee hence and learn everything. *(Whispering)* Find out the name of every guest in this hotel, his business, his wherefores, and his why. And remember! Madam is concentrating!

JULIUS: Yes, Madam!

MADAM: *(To the CLERK)* Is they anybody worth knowing stopping here? Is any of the High Grand Worthy Dignitaries come in yet?

CLERK: No'm, not yet. Some of the members is in, but not the officers. They'll be here tonight or tomorrow.

MADAM: Well, who is here?

CLERK: We got one more distinguished guest besides you, fact is, got two of 'em.

MADAM: I know 'em both before you speak, Clerk. But go on, tell me just the same for your own pleasure.

CLERK: One is Princess Bootoo.

MADAM: Who? That midget?

CLERK: That's right.

MADAM: Well, she'll want to see me the minute she knows I'm here. She's one of my old customers. Ring and tell her I'm in the lobby.

CLERK: *(Ringing)* And the other is Mr. Buster Whitehead from Texas.

MADAM: Wait a minute! I'll tell you his name before you say it. White-head! Buster! Texas!

CLERK: That sure is right. Madam, you's a wonder. *(As she stares at him)* But please don't concentrate on me.

MADAM: I won't. My energy's too precious to waste. Now this White-head.

CLERK: He's a rich oil man.

MADAM: And he came here to . . . . . . *(Gazing at the CLERK)*

CLERK: To get married.

MADAM: To Miss . . . . . . *(Concentrating on the CLERK)*

CLERK: To Miss Bailey.

> *(As CHAUFFEUR stands ringing the elevator bell)*

JULIUS: Doggone this elevator.

MADAM: Where is that elevator boy?

CLERK: *(Banging on the bell)* Front! Front! Front!

MADAM: Never mind, Clerk, I see him in the 5th race at Meadowbrook, but I'll bring him back. *(She concentrates)* Too-Tight! Too-Tight! Bring that elevator down so my handy man can go up. You hear me?

> *(The elevator starts to hum. The CLERK is astounded. The elevator door opens and TOO-TIGHT bounds out and is about to say*

something when he sees MADAM's eyes upon him. He cringes back into the car, and takes the CHAUFFEUR up)

CLERK: Madam, you sure is wonderful.

WILMETTA: I mean she is wonderful.

MADAM: Wonderful! Wonderful! I shall retire to the alcove. Send me Princess Bootoo when she comes down.

CLERK: Yes, Madam Klinkscale.

MADAM: *(To WILMETTA as she passes)* Girl, don't stare so. I'm human. Born with seven veils over my face, that's all. Tell me your name—I know it before you open your mouth.

WILMETTA: Wilmetta Logan.

MADAM: Um-hum. Who's your mother?

WILMETTA: She's dead.

MADAM: I'll get her for you from the spirit world tonight. What's her name.

WILMETTA: Essiebelle.

MADAM: Brown?

WILMETTA: No, ma'am, Johnson. She divorced my first step-father and married the other one.

MADAM: So you got two step-fathers. And your real father's name wasn't Logan, either. It were Jackson.

WILMETTA: How did you know?

MADAM: Your mother's maiden name was Smith.

WILMETTA: It sure were, Madam Klinkscale.

MADAM: I'm wonderful! That's all. See me tonight and I'll get you in touch with the spirit world. A dollar's all I'll charge—*for you*.

WILMETTA: Oh, Madam, that's so nice.

MADAM: That's Madam's way. Just a dollar—to you. Five to everybody else, honey. See me tonight right yonder in the alcove. Seance from Nine to Twelve. If you don't make the first one, make the second.

WILMETTA: Yes, Madam Klinkscale.

(MADAM proceeds to the alcove and opens her large handbag, taking therefrom incense, black candles, a crystal globe, and a silk wall-hanging of esoteric insignia which she places impressively on the wall. Meanwhile, the elevator comes down loaded with BUS-TER and his new-found friends, now including PRINCE ALI, all talking loudly)

TOO-TIGHT: *(Bounding out before the guests)* Boy, this man's a wizard. Won on three horses out of five. And betted one for me and I won, too! He's as lucky as a dog!

ROTATION: Come on, everybody, we're gonna have a drink.

SHEBA: I got a fist full of money.

BIG DOG: The deuces will run wild tonight.

BUSTER: I ain't seen nary a horse, but I sure made money.

ROTATION: Beginners luck, that's what. See what you can do shootin' pool by and by.

BIG DOG: He belongs to me next.

ROTATION: *(Angrily)* Don't try to muscle in on this! I had him first.

BIG DOG: *(Threateningly)* Boy, I'll shuck your ears off your head directly, Rotation.

BUSTER: Where is this White Horse you-all been talkin' about?

BIG DOG: That Scotch Horse? He's right in here at the bar.

BUSTER: *(Pausing beside WILMETTA)* You can't go with us, can you?

WILMETTA: I'm sorry but I'm working today.

SHEBA: *(Grabbing him)* Aw, come on, Buster! Let's go blase a little!
      (They exit into Bar)

BIG DOG: *(As he exits)* Let's have some music. Put a nickel on Louis Armstrong, somebody.
      (Records are heard playing shortly)

CLERK: I wish I could get out from behind this desk.

WILMETTA: It's a shame the way they're doing that poor boy. He won't have a penny directly.

CLERK: Not if I get off in time to invite him to a little black jack game tonight.

WILMETTA: Somebody ought to tell him.

CLERK: Don't bother, sister. This hotel was never meant to be a church. You ought to get hip to yourself, girl, all the fathers you got to take care of. *(Pointing)* Here comes old step-father Johnson now to hit you for a ball.
      (Enter an OLD MAN, strutting grandly)

WILMETTA: *(As the OLD MAN approaches)* Hello, Dad.

JOHNSON: Wilmetta, honey!

WILMETTA: Yes, Dad.

JOHNSON: Your poor old Father Johnson ain't had no luck today. Lend me a dollar so's I can play my numbers back.

WILMETTA: But, Daddy . . . . . .

JOHNSON: Now, now! I've got a good hunch, 335. If I hit I'll pay you back every cent I owe you and more, too. Besides, I needs some hash. It's suppertime.

WILMETTA: Daddy, I ain't got but ten cents to my name.

JOHNSON: Well, take ninety more out of the cash register and let the boss take it out of your pay. He won't care.

(*Elevator bell*)

WILMETTA: Oh, I couldn't do that.

JOHNSON: You'd do it for that other step-papa of yours, old Brown.

WILMETTA: No, I wouldn't neither. I couldn't do that for nobody.

JOHNSON: Would you see me starve?

WILMETTA: No, dad. Here, take this dime. But eat, don't play no numbers.

JOHNSON: No sense in just playing a dime.

WILMETTA: Come back by and by, maybe I'll have some more.

JOHNSON: I hope you will. (*Exits*) You's a sweet step-child, but I can't eat on no dime.

(*Switchboard buzzer*)

CLERK: Yes? Yes?. . . . What you want? . . . . . . The elevator? I ain't the elevator boy! Well, all right, I'll see if I can call him.

(*Enter TWO LADY SPHINXES who go to the elevator. CLERK bangs on desk bell as elevator and buzzer both ring violently at the same time. TOO-TIGHT comes from the bar*)

TOO-TIGHT: Man, don't bother me when I'm busy. Who wants what?

CLERK: Princess Bootoo wants to come down, that's what!

TOO-TIGHT: Tell her to slide down. I'm busy.

CLERK: She says she's gonna raise hell if she don't get some service around here. She's mad about her ice cream.

TOO-TIGHT: Well, she ain't never seen Too-Tight mad, is she?

CLERK: You better not fool with that little woman, boy. She's a bad actor when she gets started. I know.

TOO-TIGHT: I'll tame her down. (*He goes up in elevator*)

CLERK: That's a fresh old elevator boy. If he wasn't the boss's nephew he'd be fired sure.

WILMETTA: You're the boss's cousin, ain't you?

CLERK: Just by marriage, that's all. You see how hard I have to work.

(*Switchboard buzzes*)

WILMETTA: Terrible.

CLERK: (*In phone*) Yes! Grand Hotel! Oh, yes, Miss Bailey!. . . . Yes, m'am, Mr. Whitehead is here. Just a minute, I'll call him. (*Bangs on desk bell*) Front! Damn that Too-Tight! He's never here when you need him! Wilmetta, go yonder to the bar and call Mr. Whitehead, will you? Tell him (*Exaggerating*) Miss Suzanne de Bailey is on the phone, his fiancee.

WILMETTA: All right. *(She goes to bar door and calls)* Mr. Whitehead! *(Louder)* Ooooooo-ooooo! Mr. Whitehead. Miss Sheba, please tell Mr. Whitehead he's wanted on the phone.
    (Music stops)

BUSTER: *(Emerging, slightly drunk)* Me? I don't know how to talk on no phone. You say it's Suzanne? I sure do want to hear her voice. I wonder what do a Lonely Heart sound like. *(Taking desk phone and putting wrong end to his ear)* It don't say nothing! *(CLERK helps him)* Suzanne, is that you? . . . . . . Yes, this is me, Buster! . . . . . . You say I sound like a little boy? I is a boy. But I ain't *so* little. Ain't you a girl? Well, all right then. Suzanne, where you at?. . . . Way out in the Bronx? You just got my telegram? You comin' right away? Well, come on. Meantime, I'm going up to Big Dog's room. Huh? No, I don't gamble. I don't know how. . . . I won't . . . . . . I will. All right, sweetheart. *(Smacking a great big kiss over the phone as he hangs up)* Goodbye!. . . . She say she's coming right away. Ain't that swell?

CLERK: Just grand!

BUSTER: Gee, I wish she was here now. I'm kinder tired of waiting. *(Approaching WILMETTA)* You got some chewing gum?

WILMETTA: Any kind you want, Mr. Whitehead.

BUSTER: I wish you'd call me Buster. I ain't never been called Mr. Whitehead so much in my life.

WILMETTA: I will, Buster.

BUSTER: I wish I'd met you before I met Sheba. You coulda had that ten dollars I give her.

WILMETTA: Oh, Mr. Whitehead, I mean Buster, I wouldn't have taken it.

BUSTER: Everybody else around here's taking my money. I'd kinder like to give you something, too.

WILMETTA: *(Whispering)* Listen, Buster, keep your money. They don't mean you no good. They're just hustlers.

BUSTER: Hustlers? They said they was friends of mine.

WILMETTA: They're not. Keep your money.

SHEBA: *(Emerging from the bar followed by the others)* Come on, let's deal a little poker. Whoopee! I feel so good! *(Ringing elevator bell)*

BIG DOG: No use waiting for that crate. Let's walk up. Only one flight.

SHEBA: Come on, Whitehead, tear yourself away. Don't bother with that stuck-up old girl. Just because she was in school once, she won't have nothing to do with nobody. She jumped salty.

WILMETTA: Why, Sheba, that's not so. I just don't drink, that's all.

SHEBA: Learn, baby! Men'll like you better. Nobody likes you now but your step-fathers.

BUSTER: I like her.

SHEBA: *(Jealously)* Oh, come on, Shadow Gut! *(Cooing)* Sweetness! Sugar-Pie! You gonna like me.

> *(They exit, SHEBA pushing BUSTER up the stairs)*

WILMETTA: *(To the CLERK)* You know, I believe I like that boy myself!

> *(Elevator arrives and BOOTOO enters, looks around and goes toward MADAM's alcove)*

MADAM: *(Rising)* Bootoo, you darling! How many years since I've seen you!

BOOTOO: Vera Klinkscale! The Madam! Honey, stoop down and kiss me!

MADAM: Last time we met were in New Orleans during the Mardi Gras, were it not?

BOOTOO: It were! You sure looking well.

MADAM: You, too, and just as cute as ever. What're you doing here, Bootoo?

BOOTOO: Come for the Sphinx convention, same as you. Child, we ought to make money.

MADAM: Ought to is right. Negroes from every which a where'll be here.

BOOTOO: I'm doing an Oriental dance, and girl, I can really dance down. *(She hums a few strains and shakes her hips seductively)*

MADAM: Bootoo, you stop! Well, you ain't lost no ground since I seed you last. Who's your manager now?

BOOTOO: Some old joker calls his self Prince Ali Ali! But his real name is J. C. Jones . . . . . .

MADAM: Huh?

BOOTOO: I say his real name is J. C. Jones.

MADAM: J. C. Jones? Why, he's one of my first husbands! You don't mean big old fat J. C. Jones?

BOOTOO: That's him.

MADAM: The one that's been following circuses for the last forty years?

BOOTOO: The very one.

MADAM: Bootoo, do he treat you right?

BOOTOO: Naw!

MADAM: I knowed he wouldn't.

BOOTOO: And that's what I want to see you about, Vera. I wants you to consult them spirits o' yourn and tell me how to get my back pay.

MADAM: An old cheat! He's owing me money, too, right now. He's the one that started me out in 1901 at the World's Fair in Buffalo, New York. I were just a young girl then, and he had me out reading minds. Bootoo, he's low.

BOOTOO: Lower'n a snake's belly.

MADAM: Well, we'll fix him! Now, you wants your money?

BOOTOO: Yes, I wants it.

MADAM: Then I'll have to charge you a little something in front, honey, even if we is friends. I got to call on my Indian controls and Indians won't open they mouths for nothing for nobody.

BOOTOO: I'm geared to pay, Vera.

MADAM: Gimme Five. That's all I'll make it to you, Bootoo. And you'll get back Five Hundred.

BOOTOO: *(Handing her the money)* I believes you. You sure did help me out once before down in Memphis.

MADAM: Shssssss-sss! The past is past, Bootoo. We looks toward the future now. *(Beginning her act)* Shet your eyes and don't say a word.

BOOTOO: I won't.

MADAM: Then don't.

BOOTOO: I won't.

MADAM: Then hush! Please!

BOOTOO: I will.

MADAM: How's I gonna concentrate and you "I willin" and "I wontin" all over the place? Shut up, now.

BOOTOO: Yes, ma'am. I sure will.

MADAM: *(Going into a trance)* Shssssss-sssss-sss-sss-ss! *(A long period of silence, then MADAM begins to mutter in an unknown tongue while BOOTOO clutches the edge of her chair)* Bully-goo! Bully-goo! Molly-goo! Bully-goo, goo! Minnie, Minnie! Ha, ha! Aw-aaa! Minnie-ha-ha! *(Chanting)* Come here, you Indian maid so fair, with your long and jet black hair, come here, come here! . . . . Bully-goo! Bully-goo! Aw! *(She begins to talk in a high falsetto voice, ostensibly the voice of her Indian control, Minnehaha)* Out here by the laughing waters, I can see the world so clear. I see Princess Bootoo, sitting here. Bootoo! Bootoo! What you want, my dear?

BOOTOO: I wants money!

MADAM: Shsss-sss-ss! Bootoo, speak no word. I know your every need.

I am Minnehaha, Minnehaha, ha-ha, Minnehaha . . . . . . *(In a low voice)* You've been going around, Bootoo, with an old Negro by the name of J. C. Jones, but he don't mean you no good. He owes you money what he done held back from you after he hired you out from circus to circus and fair to fair, and made you dance forty-five times a night at the Shriners Conclave. He even much owes you Five Hundred Dollars right now.

BOOTOO: Yes, he do.

MADAM: And you wants it. Listen, I'm gonna tell you how to get it, Bootoo. But I got to whisper in your ear. Laughing Water, Minnehaha, don't want nobody else to hear. Come near, come near.

> *(As BOOTOO draws near MADAM to receive her whispered message, TOO-TIGHT comes out of the elevator and crosses toward the bar)*

TOO-TIGHT: Man, they got that Whitehead chump up there just losing money ever time the deal goes round. Ten and twenty dollars at a time. And Sheba's done persuaded him to buy two great big quarts of Scotch whiskey at Ten Dollars a quart! They gonna pick that rascal clean before I get a chance to start my dice game.

WILMETTA: I just think it's awful the way they're doing that poor boy.

CLERK: You should worry. You ain't smart, Wilmetta, or you'd get on that gravy train, too.

WILMETTA: I don't want nothing I don't come by honest. I just can't scuffle so rough.

> *(BUSTER comes down the steps looking sad and bewildered)*

CLERK: There's Mr. Whitehead now. What can we do for you, Mr. Whitehead?

BUSTER: I reckon I'll just wait down here for Suzanne. Them folks upstairs don't want to do nothing but play cards, and everytime they deal, I lose. *(At desk)* Say, can I send a telegram?

CLERK: *(Handing him a blank)* Sure, write it out and I'll send it for you.

BUSTER: *(Taking the blank and looking around helplessly. He sees Wilmetta and goes toward her)* Could you write it out for me? It's to my Pa.

WILMETTA: Course, I will. What you want to say?

BUSTER: Well, tell him I got here. *(Shamefacedly)* And—that I ain't got no money, to send me some.

WILMETTA: How much?

BUSTER: That don't make no difference. Pa's generous with money. He ain't got nothing else to do with it, nohow.

WILMETTA: What's his name, your father?

BUSTER: Same as mine, except for *Big*. Just put Big Buster Whitehead, Shadow Gut, Texas. Got that?

WILMETTA: I got that.

BUSTER: Tell him, Pa, I'm here. I ain't seed my fiancee yet but I'm gonna see her. And to send me some money cause I ain't got none . . . . . . Little Buster.

WILMETTA: There you are!

BUSTER: Thank you, Miss-er-er . . .

WILMETTA: Just call me Wilmetta.

BUSTER: Wilmetta. *(Hesitant about leaving)* Say, you got some more chewing gum?

> *(TOO-TIGHT entering with bottles on a tray)*

TOO-TIGHT: Here goes your Scotch, Mr. Whitehead. You better come on.

BUSTER: I'm busy buying gum.

TOO-TIGHT: Excuse me, sir! *(Exits via elevator)* Excuse me!

WILMETTA: Have you chewed up a whole package of gum already, Mr. Whitehead?

BUSTER: I gived it away. Everybody's got the gimmes, I do believe.

WILMETTA: Why don't you stay here and talk with me? I don't want a thing.

BUSTER: I wish I'd stayed with you first when I comed in. *(Shyly)* You're the kind of girl I dream about.

WILMETTA: Aw, gee, Mr. Whitehead.

BUSTER: And I'm scared I'm gonna keep on dreaming about you— even after I get married.

WILMETTA: You mustn't do that, Mr. Whitehead.

BUSTER: I can't help it. I been thinking about you all the time upstairs playing cards—until I got hungry. I ain't et today.

WILMETTA: Here's your gum.

BUSTER: *(Taking her hand)* Can I eat supper with you?

WILMETTA: Sure you can. I cooked some greens at home. *(Remembering)* But, oh! Miss Bailey'll be here, won't she?

BUSTER: Shaw! I forgot about her.

> *(Suddenly in the alcove, MADAM gives a loud Indian scream)*

MADAM: Wha-hoo-oo-o! *(She throws back her head, stiffens out her body, and begins again to speak in tongues)* Bugley-boo! Bugley-boo,

bugley-boo! *(Then sweetly)* Goodbye, goodbye, goodbye, Minne-
ha-ha, good-bye.

BOOTOO: Goodbye!

MADAM: *(Suddenly sitting up and being herself)* Bootoo! Are you here?
That's right, you're here! Madam . . . . . has been away off . . . . . .
in the spirit land, away off with Minnehaha. Did Minnehaha speak
to you? Shss-sss! Don't tell me what she said. I'll never know. I'm
only the medium through which the spirit speaks. Did you hear her,
Bootoo?

BOOTOO: I sure did, and I'm gonna do what you say.

MADAM: Shsss! Not a word. Quiet, quiet!

BOOTOO: You's wonderful, Madam.

MADAM: Wonderful! Seven veils over my face at birth. When you get
that Five Hundred, you owe me twenty more, Bootoo. Now let us
retire to our suites. I has a public seance tonight.

BOOTOO: And I got to work out the plan.

(They go into the lobby and MADAM presses the elevator bell)

BUSTER: *(Seeing BOOTOO)* I reckon I'm really drunk now sure
enough. What's that?

WILMETTA: No, you aren't drunk, Buster. That's a real little lady.
That's Princess Bootoo.

BUSTER: Made that way?

BOOTOO: *(Strutting)* The only brownskin midget in existence. I usually gets a quarter from folks to look at me.

BUSTER: Well, for a dollar could I look at you a long time?

BOOTOO: Long as you want to, baby, long as you want to.

*(The elevator arrives and from it pour all of BUSTER's friends,
ALI, SHEBA, ROTATION, BIG DOG, and several others. Down
the stairs and from the bar enter several KNIGHTS as TOO-
TIGHT in great excitement announces the news)*

TOO-TIGHT: She's coming! She's coming! We just seed her from the
third floor window, getting off the bus. His fiancee is coming.

WILMETTA: Buster, Miss Bailey's coming.

BIG DOG: It won't be long now.

BUSTER: Boy, I hope she'll like me. Somebody lend me a comb, quick!

ROTATION: Here, I got one. *(Hands him a pocket comb)* Do you want
my nail file, too?

BUSTER: No, there ain't no time for no filing.

*(The street door opens and a very large, ugly, overdressed woman
twice BUSTER's age enters in a cloud of out-moded feathers and*

laces. It is SUZANNE DE BAILEY prancing like a war-horse, her gold teeth gleaming)

SUZY: Where is he? Where is my sugar lump? Where's my brown baby? I means sweet papa Whitehead! Where's he at?

TOO-TIGHT: Yonder he is!

SUZY: *(Rushing with open arms toward BUSTER)* Buster! Baby! Honey! Here's your lonesome heart at last. *(She holds out her arms, but as she approaches, BUSTER bucks his eyes, opens his mouth, and slumps slowly to the floor in a dead faint. WILMETTA, SHEBA, BOOTOO, and MADAM rush to help him, but SUZY glares at them so ferociously that they back away. She bends over BUSTER and announces to the world:)* This here is my man! And I mean for everybody else to lay off.

CURTAIN

Act II, Scene 1

The same.

TIME: *That evening.*

AT RISE: *WILMETTA is still at the tobacco stand. TOO-TIGHT is still on the elevator. The only change in staff is that at the desk the MAN-AGER himself now presides, Mr. Lighthouse, a portly and important gentleman with a diamond tie-pin. TWO KNIGHTS stroll through the lobby and go upstairs carrying packages from the liquor store. ALI ALI and SHEBA sit holding hands in the alcove. Everyone in this scene is dressed in his best, ready for the night life of the hotel. The elevator door opens and TOO-TIGHT enters the lobby.*

TOO-TIGHT: *(Going toward the desk)* Mr. Whitehead wants to know if there's an answer to that telegram he sent his papa yet?

MANAGER: Tell him not yet, no answer a-tall. But he'd better get one to pay his room rent with tomorrow.

TOO-TIGHT: He sure is a fool. Ain't got by two dollars left out of two hundred. Cards, horses, and Sheba!

MANAGER: A country-jake for fair.

TOO-TIGHT: I bet he lives so far back in the woods they use hootin' owls for roosters and 'possums for house-cats.

MANAGER: People like that ought not come worrying us city folks a-tall.

TOO-TIGHT: What worries me is I didn't get none of that gravy. If I was *your* cousin, I wouldn't give you no such confinement job like running a elevator.

MANAGER: I'm just trying to help you make some money, Too-Tight. You can't do nothing else.

TOO-TIGHT: Then why don't you give me a job doing nothing then, like them look-out men you has posted outside to signal when the dicks is coming to raid the bookie joint?

MANAGER: Man, you have to have pull with the racketeers to get those kind of jobs. Besides, you have to be a man. You ain't nothin' but a pup.

TOO-TIGHT: Pup, your eye! I've seed more in fifteen years than you'll see in fifty.

MANAGER: Well, don't tell me about it now. Go take those cigarettes up to Big Dog in 311, they phoned for 'em an hour ago. If the game's good, he might chuck you out a dime.

TOO-TIGHT: I don't want no dime. I want a quarter. *(To WILMET-TA)* Baby, gimme three packs of Camels and one Piedmont.

WILMETTA: How is poor Mr. Whitehead getting along?

TOO-TIGHT: Pretty well, considering who's holding his head.

WILMETTA: Is she still with him?

TOO-TIGHT: You know old lady Bailey ain't gonna leave that young boy. Sick or well, she's gonna marry him tomorrow. And she's giving a party in the cafe tonight to announce their engagement.

WILMETTA: Poor Buster! What room's he in?

TOO-TIGHT: 407, right next to Suzy's, with the bath between.

WILMETTA: I wish I could go up and see him.

TOO-TIGHT: You better wear a sword and shield if you do. Or else take both your step-fathers with you. Yonder comes one of them now, as usual. *(He exits via the elevator as the bell rings)*

(Old man BROWN enters from the street and approaches WIL-METTA, stepping importantly. WILMETTA looks worried)

WILMETTA: Hello, Daddy. What you want now?

BROWN: Wilmetta, listen! I didn't come to ask you for a thing this time. Not a thing. I just made a dollar. Somebody across the street in Tiger's gimme this note to deliver to Mr. Ali in person.

WILMETTA: Why, Daddy, that's fine! It must be a powerful important note.

BROWN: Where'll I find this here Ali Ali?

WILMETTA: I saw him going in the alcove yonder with Miss Sheba a while back. Step over there and look.

(As BROWN approaches the alcove, ALI ALI and SHEBA are embracing amorously)

BROWN: Is you Mr. Ali Ali?

ALI: I am. And why?

BROWN: I was told to give you this note right now.

ALI: Aw, I see. Thank you.

BROWN: Any answer?

ALI: Step aside a moment till I read it. *(To SHEBA)* Probably just a mash note from some woman. They're crazy about me. I get so many of 'em in my business. Lemme see. *(Tears it open and reads. Suddenly he leaps from the settee and screams)* Ohooooo-oo! Allah! Allah! *(He clutches his heart)* Somebody's done stole the Princess!

> *(The MANAGER, TOO-TIGHT, WILMETTA, and several others come running. SHEBA screams. BROWN exits hurriedly)*

MANAGER: Mr. Ali! Mr. Ali! What's the trouble, Mr. Ali?

SHEBA: That sweet little midget is gone!

ALI: Somebody's kidnapped my midget!

MANAGER: Kidnapped the midget?

WILMETTA: Princess Bootoo?

ALI: Yes, Bootoo! And that's not the worst of it!

SHEBA: What?

ALI: They wants Five Hundred Dollars to bring her back.

MANAGER: Five hundred dollars?

SHEBA: For that, you could have me.

ALI: *(Wailing)* Bootoo! My Princess! My poor little Princess! Five hundred dollars. *(He almost swoons)*

MANAGER: Shall I get the police?

ALI: No, no! Wait a minute! No! Who brought this note! *(He turns around to look for BROWN, but he has gone)* Where is the man who brought this note?

WILMETTA: It was my step-father.

MANAGER: Your step-father? That won't go so well with you, my girl.

WILMETTA: But I don't know a thing about it.

MANAGER: No, but it was your step-father. *(To ALI)* Mr. Ali, I'll get the police.

ALI: Not yet, not yet. Wait! Look what she says.

MANAGER: Who says?

ALI: Bootoo. It's written in her own handwriting. Here, read it. I can't. I'm too weak. Five hundred dollars! *(He sinks into a chair)*

MANAGER: *(Reading)* "Prince Ali, old J.C.—send and get me out of here at once, if not sooner. I have been kidnapped and am being held for ransom. FIVE HUNDRED DOLLARS. Give it to the man who brought this note and don't bother him because he don't know a thing about it and is supposed to hand the money to another man sent by a man who's sent by the man who kidnapped me. And don't tell the police, because if you do, these kidnappers will spank me till I can't set down. They think I am a child, but I told them I was thirty-five years old. I lied. I am really forty. Ali, send that money right away, so I can get out of here and eat my supper. If you don't they're gonna kill me. I am hungry. FIVE HUNDRED DOLLARS RANSOM. Yours truly, Princess Bootoo." Ain't that awful! Poor Princess!

ALI: Five hundred dollars! That's what's awful! *(Musing)* I wonder do I want her back that bad.

SHEBA: Well, you don't know where to send the money now. The man that brought the note is gone.

ALI: Aw-oo! That's right! Oh, Lord! Dear Allah! Poor Bootoo!

MANAGER: And if we call the police, they'll hurt the Princess! And we might never find old Brown that brought this note now. Wilmetta, where'd that trifling step-father of yours go?

WILMETTA: I don't know.

MANAGER: You better find out or you'll be in jail, too!

WILMETTA: Oh, Mr. Lighthouse!

ALI: But what shall I do?

MANAGER: I know. Consult Madam Klinkscale.

ALI: Who is she?

MANAGER: The medium. She knows everything, man. She can tell you all.

ALI: *All* would be too much. I just want to know how to get my midget back—if I decide I want her. Five hundred dollars! The evil little varmint.

MANAGER: But she's a good money-maker, ain't she?

ALI: No, a devil. I lost forty pounds since I've been managing that little wretch and ain't made but $20,000. Just lemme get her back, and I'll take every penny of this out of her salary.

SHEBA: Why, Mr. Ali!

ALI: Get me that medium if she don't charge too much!

MANAGER: I'll phone up for Madam Klinkscale now. *(As he crosses to the desk, to WILMETTA)* And as for you, young lady, mixed up with kidnappers is a serious offense. It's liable to mean your job.

WILMETTA: Please Mr. Lighthouse!

MANAGER: Unless—

WILMETTA: *(Frightened)* Unless what?

MANAGER: Unless—*(Reaching for her hand)*—you let me be your friend. You know I like you, Wilmetta.

WILMETTA: But, Mr. Lighthouse, I'm a good girl.

MANAGER: Don't let that worry you. I'm a good man.

WILMETTA: I couldn't, Mr. Lighthouse.

MANAGER: Wilmetta. *(Commanding)* Gimme your hand, else I'll have your step-father and you both put in jail.

WILMETTA: *(Giving him her hand and bowing her head in shame)* Please, Mr. Lighthouse!

> *(There is a roll of drums outside. Through the street door, in full regalia, purple capes swinging, march the LADIES DRILL CORPS of the Society of the Royal Sphinx. Headed by their HIGH WORTHY DAUGHTER in a shaggy drum major's hat, they strut in swing formation up to the desk. From the bar and stairway come various guests to watch the procession)*

HIGH WORTHY: Ladies, halt! *(Announcing)* I'm the High Worthy Daughter Ruler, Camp Number Ten from Louisville. I brings with me our National State-wide Prize Drill Corps, Number 53. Ladies! Do your stuff! Mark time, Mark! Sister Bulldozer, put your drum down and go beat out a march on that piano in that cafe yonder. *(Exit Sister BULLDOZER)* Ladies! Double time, mark! *(As the music begins)* Let's show Cleveland what we can do! Forward, march! . . . . . Double wheel, turn! . . . . . . Aw, my! . . . . . . Left by twos, march! . . . . . . Butterfly's wing, by twos, march! . . . . . . Yes, yes, yes! . . . . . . Now! The May Pole swing, circle, swing, march!. . . . Left by twos, march . . . . . . Ladies, halt! *(As they draw up before the desk again, there is great applause from all present. Enter MADAM)* Just a sample, just a sample! We is here to take the prize! Manager, is you got our reservations?

MANAGER: Indeed I have, ladies! Welcome to the Grand Hotel. Too-Tight, the keys! Show these ladies to their rooms.

TOO-TIGHT: How'm I gonna get this army in my elevator? They'll break it down.

HIGH WORTHY: Everywhere we goes we marches, son. We don't need no elevator.

TOO-TIGHT: Then let's take the steps. *(Commanding)* High Grand Worthy, give your orders! Ladies, follow me.

HIGH WORTHY: Forward, march!
> *(The music strikes up again and they exit by way of the steps, led by TOO-TIGHT, as MADAM approaches ALI)*

MADAM: Ali, Ali, I got your call. Didn't nobody need to tell me you wanted me. I knowed it beforehand. Somebody's done stole Bootoo. *(As ALI is about to open his mouth)* Don't say a word! Let the spirits talk. They's talking through me now, 'cause you ain't worthy to come into their presence. Get thee behind me, Satan! And get thee before me, Ali Ali, and set down in that alcove. *(ALI backs into the alcove, followed by MADAM)* I know you, Negro. You ain't from no Cairo, Egypt in Arabia. You's from Mound Bayou, Mississippi. Your name is J. C. Jones. Now gimme Five dollars before I tell you any more! *(ALI ALI gives her five dollars)* I's seed you before in the crystal globe. I's seed your ma and your grandma. They told me to tell you, *beware*, J. C. Jones. *Beware* of how you does your women.

ALI: But I ain't done nothing wrong to Bootoo.

MADAM: You ain't done her right, that's why she's been taken away, kidnapped out of your reach, held for ransom. Five hundred dollars. Pay it, J. C. Jones.

ALI: Pay it to who?

MADAM: To me.

ALI: Oh, no, that note didn't say nothing about pay it to you.

MADAM: Pay it to me or else I'll tell you things about yourself that your own self don't want to know.

ALI: Now, listen, Madam who-ever-you-is. I'm a showman, too. Fact is, I'se handles mediums myself. Now what can you tell me?

MADAM: I can tell you about that time when you stole Two Thousand Dollars from the box office at the World's Fair in Buffalo and went off with it and ain't been heard of since. That's what I can tell you!

ALI: Huh?

MADAM: I can tell you about the time you took a poor little innocent colored girl named Vera Mae Strode and taught her how to trick people out of their money by acting like a mind-reader. Then you tricked her out of hers and went off and left her without a penny to her name and you with Two Thousand Dollars.

ALI: Hush, hush, hush!

MADAM: Hush, nothing! I ain't told you all. I can look back into the past and see when you left little Vera Mae in that Buffalo hotel with the bills unpaid, and a trail of bogus checks behind you from here to yonder. You's a cheater, J. C. Jones! And you know it!

ALI: *(Rising)* Woman, I denies the allegation and I defies the alligator.

MADAM: *(Also rising)* You can't defy me, J.C. 'cause I'll turn you in to the law. I sees you in the penitentiary now. I sees bars, I sees guards, I sees shackles on your legs.

ALI: You mean you'd turn me over to the law?

MADAM: Quicker'n a snake can put his belly to the ground.

ALI: *(Sinking down in despair)* Aw-ooo! Madam, please don't.

MADAM: Furthermore, I can look into the future and see what's on your mind tonight.

ALI: I don't want to know! I don't want to know!

MADAM: Yes, you will know, too. I ain't gived you Five dollars worth yet. I sees you right now getting ready to trick a poor little Georgia midget out of her money. I sees you getting ready to go on and let her stay kidnapped, and you take up with some old gal named Sheba what used to dance in the Brown Skin Scandals. I know you done told Sheba you gonna make her another Sally Rand—soon as you can buy some fans.³ J.C., gimme five hundred dollars to get Bootoo out of ransom before I expose you to the world.

ALI: Madam, you just ain't natural. You ain't no natural medium. You knows too much. How you know all that?

MADAM: Seven veils at birth, that's how. Do I get that money for the Princess? *(Silence)* Or do I give my revelations to the law?

ALI: I reckon you gets the money. I ain't got *but* Five Hundred. Here! *(He gives her the money)*

MADAM: Then how you gonna get them fans for Sheba?

ALI: She'll have to dance without fans. But, Madam, I wish you'd let Bootoo stay where she's at. She ain't no good to me no more. Everybody's seen her. She ain't no attraction.

MADAM: So you want to get rid of her and take up with Sheba, heh? Well, you'll never do it, J.C.

ALI: But what you care who I take up with, Madam?

MADAM: Look at me and see, J.C. *(She lifts her veil)* Look at me!

ALI: *(Amazed)* Vera! My first wife!

MADAM: You mean your *only* wife. Since when we've been divorced?

ALI: I reckon we ain't!

MADAM: Then it's bigamist I got on you, too!

ALI: *(Still amazed)* Vera Mae Strode from Mississippi!

MADAM: By way of Buffalo. Mrs. Jones to you. *(Sentimentally)* J.C., I still wears your wedding ring, even after the way you did me.

ALI: Vera, I always loved you—even if I did quit you.

MADAM: And I loved you.

ALI: Did you?

MADAM: Of course I did. You was the first man that ruint me.

ALI: Vera, honey!

MADAM: Now you see why I ain't gonna let you take up with no high-yellow fan-dancer in your old age. And why you're gonna get rid of that Midget, too, J.C. I needs you back in my business. You's a good trickster. And that chauffeur I got ain't worth a dime.

ALI: Is he your present husband?

MADAM: In the sight of God only—'cause he ain't never bought me no ring.

ALI: Have you always used my ring, ever' time you got married?

MADAM: Ever' time, J.C.

ALI: *(Happy)* Now, ain't that sweet of you?

MADAM: Oh, I loved you, J.C., even if you did leave me.

ALI: And I adored you, Vera, little and cute as you was.

MADAM: Then come on back to me now—even if I is fat and over thirty.

ALI: I will. I'm kinder fat, too.

MADAM: And do right from today.

ALI: I always does right now. Since I joined the Free Wheeling Baptist Church in Memphis last year, I ain't sinned since. And don't intend to. I'm holy and sanctified now.

MADAM: Thank God! I always wanted you to be a Baptist. Listen, with your talent and my brains, and all I's learned about mediumology since the days when I was just a little blindfolded child-wonder and you was Professor Jones, who held up the watch and said, "What is this?" Since them days, J.C., I's really made something out o' myself. I's studied the science of numbers, I's studied the crystal ball, I's studied astrology and Black Magic, and Marie Laveau. I's slept all night in the French graveyard in New Orleans, and I's gone into the silences with Hiawatha and Minnehaha. J.C., I's a medium now.

ALI: Vera, since I's seen you I's made something of myself, too. Why, now I don't have to steal money no more a-tall. I just talks people out of it honest. I can sell anything from snake oil to midgets. I's been everything from a Indian herb doctor to a Sheik from Cairo, Arabia. Vera, with my brains and your talents, we can clean up. You're right. We ought to be back together. Honey, I feels my love come down again. Lemme kiss you.

MADAM: J.C., darling!

(They kiss)

ALI: How much is Bootoo gonna give you for getting that Five Hundred Dollars out of me? I know it's a frame up.

MADAM: Twenty.

ALI: That ain't enough. Gimme the Five Hundred back and I'll give *you* fifty of it for yourself.

MADAM: You will? What'll we do about Bootoo?

ALI: Let her stay kidnapped.

MADAM: But suppose she showed up here.

ALI: How is she gonna show up here if she's kidnapped?

MADAM: She ain't kidnapped. Bootoo ain't nowhere but at the movies looking at TARZAN OF THE APES.

ALI: Well, let her stay. I don't want her.

MADAM: She's crazy about Tarzan, but she's liable to get tired sometime, and come out before we leave town. Besides, I got a seance tonight, gonna make plenty of money. I want you to help me.

ALI: Then if Bootoo shows up, just leave her to me. I'll scare her till she shrinks up like her shadow.

MADAM: I used to think Bootoo was my friend, but since I seen the way she's tried to trick you out of Five Hundred Dollars, she ain't nothing to me no more.

ALI: That's right, Vera. Now gimme back all my money.

MADAM: *(Handing him a roll of bills)* Here! But don't let me catch you going around with no other womens from now on. Understand!

ALI: I won't, baby. *(Counting)* But where's the Five Dollars I paid you when I come in here? This is only Five Hundred.

MADAM: That's down in my stocking. I can keep that Five, can't I, honey?

ALI: Naw! Get it out.

MADAM: *(Handing it to him)* Here, darling.

ALI: And I want you to fire that chauffeur right away.

MADAM: I'll get rid of him now, J.C.

ALI: As for Bootoo, if she ever comes out of that show while I'm in town, I'll have her locked up for extortion and murder.

MADAM: Murder?

ALI: Yes. She knows I got a weak heart. Then she goes and writes me a note to scare me to death. Five Hundred Dollars! I ought to spank her good.

MADAM: J.C., from now on, if you ever whips any other woman but me, I'm gonna throw your ring away. I'm your wife. Spank me!

ALI: I will, don't worry.

MADAM: But we got work to do now. You go and tell everybody Madam Klinkscale's seance is about to begin. If they wants to meet their husbands or their wives, papas or mamas in the spirit world, to see me.

ALI: Rick.

MADAM: If they want to know the number for tomorrow, see me.

ALI: Um-hum!

MADAM: Tell the lodge folks if they want to know who's gonna be elected HIGH GRAND OFFICERS of the Knights and Ladies of the Royal Sphinx, see me.

ALI: I'll tell 'em.

MADAM: Whatever anybody anywhere wants to know, see me.

ALI: Yes, indeedy! *(Worried)* But say, listen, Vera, is we paid off the police to hold any seance yet?

MADAM: Damn the police! We're paying off the hotel, and they got look-out mens stationed outside. But ain't no cops likely to come in here tonight. If they do, the signal to raise up is when the lights flash twice.

ALI: When the lights flash twice?

MADAM: That means everybody for his self.

ALI: I got you. Now I'm going out and bring the crowd so we can make some money. *(Sternly)* You hurry up and fire that chauffeur.
    (He begins to circulate about he lobby and eventually disappears into the bar. MADAM tidies up the alcove as JULIUS, the Chauffeur, enters with both arms full of folding chairs)

JULIUS: Madam, here's the chairs for the seance.

MADAM: *(As she arranges them)* Looks like all you can do is carry chairs. You ain't brought me a bit of information of no kind tonight. What's the dope on the lodge election day after tomorrow? Who's the inside click going to put through? How much money that oil man got?

JULIUS: Well, you see, Madam, I ain't . . . . . .

MADAM: You ain't found out nothing, that's all I see.

JULIUS: Well, you know, the first day, it's kinder hard to get any dope on a new town. You can't just walk up to people and ask 'em about their business, 'cause they'll figger you a detective or something. I been trying to get you news.

MADAM: I might as well get it out of the newspapers for all the good you do me. Julius, I think I'll fire you.

JULIUS: Huh! See if I care! Maybe I'd get paid something, then. Ever since I been your husband, anyhow, you've treated me like a dog.

MADAM: Don't get personal with me, Julius. You ain't my husband. You just my private secretary.

JULIUS: Well, I will get personal, Vera. I'm tired o' wearing this uniform, and carrying chairs, and Madaming you around, and you making all the money and won't give me none. Private secretary, hell!

MADAM: That'll do, Julius.

JULIUS: Dressing me up like a chauffeur and we ain't even got a car! Fooling the public, talking about your fish-tail Cadillac in the garage getting the hub-caps polished. If I got to be a chauffeur I don't want to ride no Greyhound busses.

MADAM: Julius, you had better stop disclosing my secrets so loud. I has got a Cadillac—in my mind.

JULIUS: Yes, and I *ain't* got no salary in my pocket. Fire me, but pay me first.

MADAM: Julius, you know we didn't make hardly nothing in Cincinnati.

JULIUS: I don't care what we made, I wants mine.

MADAM: Now, don't get tough, or I'll get tough, too. I'm gonna give you twenty dollars. Here! Enough to get back to Chicago, where you come from.

JULIUS: You owes me ninety-five.

MADAM: Take the uniform. That cost fifty dollars.

JULIUS: Fifty and twenty ain't but eighty. I don't want this uniform, no how. Gimme me money.

MADAM: Julius, you better get out of here before I concentrate on you.

JULIUS: *(Backing away)* I'm gonna call the cops!

MADAM: The cops! Huh! What do Madam care about the cops? Get out of here and leave me with my spirits. Be gone!

> *(Exit JULIUS via street door.*
> *(The elevator arrives and from it come two KNIGHTS and a LADY, also BUSTER, with SUZY on his arm. SUZY is dressed and powdered anew, but BUSTER is looking very woebegone. As she parades across the lobby with him toward the cafe, he gives one sorrowful look at WILMETTA)*

SUZY: Buster, you's got the strongest arm I's ever held.

BUSTER: It feels like it's gonna give out tonight.

SUZY: Soon's you get a little Cream of Kentucky under your belt, you'll be all right.

> *(Exit SUZY and BUSTER into bar)*

WILMETTA: *(Sighing)* Oh!

KNIGHT: *(Peering into the alcove)* Madam, is you about to begin your spirituals?

MADAM: Step in! Step right in, you and your friends. The seance commences directly. Set down and hold your silence.

(They tiptoe into alcove and sit down)

LADY: Madam, shall we pay now?

MADAM: The spirits'll tell you when to pay, daughter, in due time.

LADY: Oh!

(Enter SHEBA LANE and ALI ALI from the bar)

SHEBA: Now, you're going around racking up business for that old medium. First a midget, then a medium. Looks like to me you just going from one freak to another. What's the matter, don't I appeal to you?

ALI: *(Trying to talk quietly)* It's not that, Sheba, darling. It's just I don't see my way clear to manage no fan-dancer now. You see, I got to survey the field first and find out what the prospects are. Then I'll write you.

SHEBA: You didn't have to survey no field this afternoon.

ALI: But afternoon and evening is different. Besides, I thought you had a date with that young oil fellow tonight.

SHEBA: I don't go around with children. I like married men.

ALI: Well, honey, I can't do you no good now. Excuse me, *please*. Ali has work to do. *(He bows himself away from her and goes upstairs)*

SHEBA: Huh! I might as well go and see what Madam Houdini plans to pull off. She must be a power. *(She goes into alcove and sits down besides one of the KNIGHTS)* What's the price of admittance to this shindig, may I ask?

MADAM: The spirits is in no mood for shindigs, Sheba Lane. Sit down or else retire.

SHEBA: How'd you know my name?

MADAM: I knows all, sees all, hears all. You leave Ali Ali alone. You hear me?

SHEBA: That old fat African!

MADAM: Silence! I does the talking here. All who ain't come to listen to Madam Klinkscale, keep silent. We commune with the mystic Sphinx tonight. Silence all! And wait.

(A murmur among the LODGE FOLKS.

(Enter MISS KING, of the First Act, shuffling along in her big shoes)

MISS KING: I just didn't play the right numbers, that's all.

TOO-TIGHT: You sure ain't.

MISS KING: Look at 235. Right bang up. I had it in my mind to play it. Instead of that, I played Black Dog.

TOO-TIGHT: Too bad. But there's a woman here now can give numbers that're sure to come, and you don't have to dream 'em.

MISS KING: What's her name? Where's she at?

TOO-TIGHT: Right over yonder, about to start a seance.

MISS KING: Shaw! Lemme get over there and see. Here, take these bones upstairs and put 'em in my room for Peewee. I know she's hungry as a dog.

TOO-TIGHT: Peewee is a dog.

MISS KING: She ain't no cat. I hates a cat that never barks and don't care if you get robbed or roped or not. I wants some pertection around me. *(As she enters the alcove)* Excuse me for talking so loud. I didn't know the silence done commenced. Excuse me.

OTHERS: Sh-sss-sss!

(Down the stairs, in single file, come the LADIES DRILL CORPS, headed by the HIGH WORTHY and ALI)

HIGH WORTHY: Column right, march! *(As the LEADER reaches the alcove)* Invade the alcove, march! And take your seats.

(Enter BUSTER, SUZY, and ROTATION from the bar)

SUZY: Thank you Mr. Rotation, thank you!

ROTATION: And just as I congratulates you, Miss Suzy, so now on your handsome groom, Mr. Whitehead, I congratulate yourself on your most beautiful bride-to-be! *(He shakes hands with BUSTER)*

SUZY: *(Giggling and delighted)* Oh, how nice! And you will come to our little party later on tonight in the cafe, won't you? Buster and me'd be glad to have you. Lots of folks are coming. We just invited everybody, 'cause this is our first wedding.

ROTATION: I'll be there with bells on, ringing!

BUSTER: *(Backing away)* You-all excuse me a minute. *(He approaches the desk)* Is any telegram come here yet from my papa?

MANAGER: Not yet, Mr. Whitehead. None at all.

BUSTER: I hope it comes directly.

MANAGER: It better come, or else who'll take care of that party bill tonight?

BUSTER: We just won't have none, that's all. It ain't my idea. That's Suzanne's. Damn if I want a party.

MANAGER: Mr. Whitehead, no profanity. This is a decent hotel!

BUSTER: Excuse me! But damn if I do.

MANAGER: But to announce your engagement, you must have a party. Is the wedding to be soon?

BUSTER: Tomorrow morning, early. Suzanne says we gonna drive out of town tonight right after the party, where you don't have to wait a-tall to get married.

MANAGER: That's right. You just pay for the license and get tied up. Miss Bailey has ordered a car to be outside a little after midnight, driver and all, so you won't have to do nothing but hug as you ride.

BUSTER: But suppose my money don't come? How much does he charge to drive us to that marrying place?

MANAGER: Oh, fifty dollars or so, that's all.

BUSTER: Well, I hope it don't come.

MANAGER: Why, Mr. Whitehead! Think of what you'll owe me—a party, a honeymoon suite, a car.

BUSTER: I'm thinking about home, now, not you. I ain't never been away from home before. Shadow Gut! Dear old Shadow Gut!

MANAGER: Aw, don't feel homesick. Just make yourself at home here. This is a nice home-like hotel with everything you want, slot machines, nickel jukebox, restaurant, bar. Enjoy yourself, young man.

BUSTER: I'll try, but it ain't like my home.

MADAM: *(Muttering and moaning in the alcove)* Bullygoo! Bullygoo!

SUZY: *(Calling)* Buster, come on. Honey, we wants to hear the seance.

MANAGER: I'll have you paged, Mr. Whitehead, if your wire comes.

BUSTER: What you mean, *paged*?

MANAGER: *(As SUZY takes BUSTER away)* Called! Called! Called!

ALI: *(Tiptoeing about the lobby, whispering in Guests' ears)* Seance! Seance! Come in now, all who's coming. Madam is about to start.
> *(He holds back the curtain and BUSTER, SUZY, ROTATION and others enter the alcove. During the seance, ALI stands just inside the curtains. MADAM begins to breathe heavily, then to rock and moan, then to speak softly in foreign tongues, as before, gradually growing louder and louder)*

MADAM: Bully-goo, bully-goo, bully-goo! Paglimeeno, paglinona, bully-goo! Jay See! Bully-goo, bully-goo! *Dol*-bully-goo-*lar*! J.C., collect. *Dol*-bully-goo-*lar*! J.C. *(She begins to moan again)*

ALI: The spirits say the contribution'll be a dollar tonight. All who want to commune with the spirits, one dollar tonight. *(As one man rises to approach the table)* I'll take it, brother. Just give it to me, sister. *(He passes among them, collecting the dollars)*

MADAM: *(Suddenly giving a loud halloo)* Hal-looo! Hal-looo, Minnehaha, calling Hiawatha, hal-loooo! *(Then, in a bass voice)* Hello,
Minnehaha, Laughing Water, what does my little Indian maiden
wish to know tonight? *(Falsetto)* She wants, oh, Hiawatha, to know
all about the friends whose names she's going to call. Those friends
must answer her. Is there, is there a Mary in the house? Mary, answer
me.

MISS KING: Mary who?

MADAM: *(Falsetto)* Mary J—no, K. That's right, Mary K.

MISS KING: Mary King, that's me. You got that much right.

MADAM: Laughing Water gets all right. Listen, Mary King, I see away
out in the Spirit world, I see your husband, Johnny King.

MISS KING: Uh-oh! You wrong there. I ain't never had no husband.

MADAM: Laughing Water sees your husband.

MISS KING: Well, she's just lying then.

VOICES: Sh-sss! Tsh! Tch! Tch!

ALI: Sister, sister!

MISS KING: I'm *Miss* King, and I ain't never been married.

MADAM: Laughing Water's calling, calling, trying to find Johnny J. . . .
Johnny J. . . . He was loving Mary King.

MISS KING: Wrong, too. Johnny Jenkins never did care nothing about
me. He were my sister's husband.

(General murmurs)

MADAM: Laughing Water's frightened, frightened. She no like to be
called a lie. *(Very deep bass)* Hiawatha's here to help you. Silence!
Silence in the universe . . . Now, Mary King, what in the —— on
earth do you want for your dollar?

MISS KING: I wants the number for tomorrow, that's all I want. Don't
bring me no spirits.

MADAM: Aw, the number! Later, later! Now, we roam the world of
spirits. Quiet, quiet, wait on numbers. *(Falsetto)* I see, I see, I see
Suzy.

SUZY: That's me.

MADAM: With a question in her mind. Ask it, Suzy.

SUZY: I really wants to know, Laughing Water, is—is—is . . . . . . Say, is
you ever been married?

MADAM: Never, never, never!

SUZY: Then you can't tell me what I wants to know.

MADAM: *(Bassing)* Try Hiawatha, try Hiawatha.

SUZY: I'm scared o' Hiawatha. He might be like Buster.

MADAM: Hiawatha know no Buster. Who is Buster?

SUZY: Stand up, Buster.

> *(BUSTER rises)*

MADAM: Aw, a tall young man is Buster, looks like Indian, looks like Blackfoot. Are you Blackfoot?

BUSTER: Naw, I'm Whitehead, naw, I'm Whitehead.

TOO-TIGHT: *(Paging BUSTER)* Telegram! Telegram for Mr. Whitehead.

MADAM: I hear voices not of spirit! Ugh! Spoil seance! Ugh! Spoil seance! Calling, calling Mr. Whitehead.

BUSTER: *(To SUZY)* Excuse me. I'll be back.

> *(He leaves alcove, and opens wire. A smile of joy spreads over his face. He rushes to WILMETTA)*

MADAM: Hiawatha now is going. Madam now will give out numbers.

VOICES: *(Murmuring)* Aw! Numbers! Um-hum! Yes!

MADAM: *(Murmuring and counting in a chant)* One-two-three-four! One-two-three-four! Listen now, I'll give a number! One-two, etc.

BUSTER: *(Excitedly)* Wilmetta! Look-ahere! My pa's done dug another oil well and listen what he says: Son, new well is geyser, ten thousand barrels a day, we ain't millionaires no more, but billionaires! Here's ten thousand dollars to finish up your wedding trip with. Send for more if you need it. Your pa, Big Buster.

WILMETTA: Why, Buster, that's wonderful.

BUSTER: I'm going down now and cash it. Wilmetta, what you want for a present?

WILMETTA: Buster, honey, I don't want anything! I'm just glad for you.

BUSTER: Don't you want a automobile? I seed a big red one down the street.

WILMETTA: That must-a been the hook and ladder down at the fire-station.

BUSTER: Well, does you want one?

WILMETTA: No, Buster.

> *(Enter a SCRUBWOMAN who puts her bucket down near the alcove and begins to roll up her sleeves. She goes across to the desk and gets a box of soap powders)*

BUSTER: Wilmetta, you never want nothing, does you? But I want something from you.

WILMETTA: What, Mr. Whitehead?

BUSTER: I wants help. I don't want to marry Suzanne. I ain't the only fish she's been fishing for. I just bit first, that's all.

WILMETTA: What?

BUSTER: She's got a whole trunk full of letters upstairs. Looks like she done wrote every Lonesome Heart on the list.

WILMETTA: Why, she's a regular old heart-hunter, ain't she?

BUSTER: Seems like she is. Anyhow, I know she's *old*! Do you think she really ain't but 25?

WILMETTA: I always thought she was about 45.

BUSTER: And do you think she really loves me like she says?

WILMETTA: Not like you ought to be loved, Buster.

BUSTER: Wilmetta, I ain't gonna marry her.

WILMETTA: How're you gonna get out of it?

BUSTER: I don't know. What could I do? Think for me, will you?

(Long pause while they think)

WILMETTA: You could marry somebody else first, maybe.

BUSTER: That's an idea! Then I couldn't marry her, could I?

WILMETTA: No, you couldn't.

BUSTER: 'Cause if you got one wife, can't nobody make you have two.

WILMETTA: That's right.

BUSTER: But I'd have to marry right away, quick.

WILMETTA: You sure would.

BUSTER: I wonder who I could marry right away?

(WILMETTA and BUSTER gaze questioningly at one another, while in the alcove MADAM's voice is heard loudly giving out numbers as two uniformed POLICEMEN enter and calmly look around)

MADAM: 216, 972, 344, 850 . . . . *(Suddenly the MANAGER sees the POLICE and presses a button under his desk. Immediately the lights blink twice. A second of complete and petrified silence. Then a quick commotion as MADAM cries in her Indian voice)* Raise up! Take you chairs and walk! Hiawatha is gone!

(There is general scattering, but everyone attempts to appear natural and casual before the cops)

HIGH WORTHY: *(Rising)* Ladies Drill Corps, forward, March!

(The DRILL CORPS, each with a chair, marches in a hurried procession up the stairs. Hidden by the crowd as it rises, MADAM tucks up her skirt around her waist, removes her veil, hides her paraphernalia, and gets down on her knees. ALI throws his turban away and reveals for the first time his bald head. In no time at

all everybody has disappeared in the bar, up the stairs, or into *the elevator which immediately ascends, leaving only BUSTER standing beside the empty tobacco stand, the MANAGER behind the desk, ALI reading a newspaper, SHEBA and a KNIGHT in the alcove, and MADAM revealed with her arms deep in the bucket. The COPS look around)*

SERGEANT: Nothing wrong here. That must have been a false message we got, heh, Pat? I don't see no seance around. *(To the MANAGER)* Nobody's running a fortune-telling place in here, are they?

MANAGER: Not at all, Mr. O'Grady, of course not. This is a family hotel. Nothing like that, nothing like that here.

SERGEANT: I thought you wouldn't be engaged in such a business, Mr. Lighthouse.

MANAGER: I should say not. No! No! This is a respectable hotel.
(Enter PRINCESS BOOTOO)

BOOTOO: Yes, there is something wrong, too. I wants my money.

SERGEANT: What money, little lady?

BOOTOO: The money that big pot-bellied rhinoceros over there owes me. Where is it? *(To MADAM)* I thought you told me that plan of yours would work? Ain't you got it out of him yet? I done set through five showings of TARZAN and you ain't sent that ransom yet. I'm tired, hungry, and thirsty, both.
(One COP approaches ALI, the OTHER goes toward MADAM. Calmly, the MANAGER files his nails)

MADAM: *(Hastily)* J.C., give her the money.

ALI: *(Pulling out a roll of bills)* Here! Here's all I owe you. Take it now, you're fired.

BOOTOO: Fired, nothing. I quit.

ALI: You don't! You're fired!

BOOTOO: You kiss my foot! I'm gonna take a vacation.

BUSTER: You can come home to Shadow Gut with me if you want to.

BOOTOO: I'm liable to accept. *(To the POLICE)* Boys, everything is rick. You-all can go. I'm going in the bar and get myself a drink.
(Exit COPS and BOOTOO)

MADAM: J.C., come and get me up off my knees.

ALI: *(Helping her up)* Vera, you're a smart woman.

MADAM: Oh, course I'm smart, J.C. We're gonna be the best fortune telling team in the business now.

ALI: You told that right, Vera. We're gonna stick together, too, from now on.

MADAM: Ignited we stand, divided we fall, J.C.

ALI: Kiss me!

> *(THEY embrace. At the cigar counter, WILMETTA and BUS-TER gaze at one another as before. In the alcove, SHEBA and KNIGHT kiss, too. The elevator door opens and SUZY emerges)*

SUZY: Buster! Oh, Buster, baby. *(Seeing him)* Oh, there you is! Honey, I thought them cops got you and taken you to jail. Come here, baby, and kiss me. You's joy to my soul!

> *(She goes to BUSTER and grabs him around the neck. All the couples kiss again)*

TOO-TIGHT: *(In the elevator car)* Going up!

CURTAIN

ACT II, Scene 2

SETTING: *The same. Midnight.*

AT RISE: *Lights are low. Piano music off stage in the bar, a slow drag tempo. Sounds of dancing feet. The lobby is empty, save for WILMETTA still at the cigar stand. She is weeping. The elevator door is open, and the bell rings unheeded. The switchboard buzzes unattended. Everybody is at the party. COCO enters limping and heavily bandaged, followed by HEAVY.*

HEAVY: Hello, Wilmetta.

WILMETTA: Hello, Heavy.

HEAVY: What you doin' looking so sad tonight?

WILMETTA: I just feel bad, that's all. Did you-all win?

HEAVY: We come near winning—up until Coco got knocked out.

COCO: Aw, man, I would-a won by a long shot, if that old referee hadn't kept on getting in my way.

HEAVY: He sure did, boy! You had to fight Big Rocky and the referee too!

COCO: Nobody could stand up under that. I'm a lightweight. That referee weighs more'n Primo Carnera.

WILMETTA: I'm so sorry you lost, Coco. Now you can't pay Buster.

COCO: Buster who?

WILMETTA: That boy who lent you the money to go.

HEAVY: Lent? He ain't lent nothing. He betted it.

COCO: And he lost.

WILMETTA: You mean you lost.

COCO: Well, we lost. But all Buster lost is money. Look at me. *(He hobbles toward the bar)*

HEAVY: Maybe if we go in and get a drink, we'll feel better.

COCO: How we gonna pay for it?

HEAVY: Damn if I know. Maybe Sheba's in there.

WILMETTA: Everything's free tonight, so you don't need any money. Mr. Whitehead's fiancee's giving a party, to announce the engagement.

COCO: To who?

WILMETTA: Suzy Bailey.

HEAVY: Is that who that boy come way up here from Texas to marry? Well, dog-bit-my-soul!

COCO: *(Losing his limp)* Come on, Heavy, let's go see.
     (They disappear into the bar. Enter MISS KING down the stairs)

MISS KING: Wilmetta, what on earth's the matter with that elevator? I been ringing my arm off, tired as I am.

WILMETTA: Too-Tight's at the party I guess.

MISS KING: Must be a good party from the sound of it! *(She hobbles across the lobby)* I'm gonna try and go in but, chile, my dogs is barking.

WILMETTA: Waiting table is hard on the feet, ain't it Miss King?

MISS KING: Hard is right. But maybe that music'll liven 'em up. See you later, girlie. *(Limping)* Oh, Lawd!
     (Enter STEP-FATHER JOHNSON peering quickly around, as he struts up to WILMETTA)

JOHNSON: Listen, Wilmetta, lend me a dime, will you?

WILMETTA: Daddy, you know I ain't got a cent. You took the last penny I had, when you was here before.

JOHNSON: Aw, Wilmetta, listen, I know for sure 546 is bound to come out in the morning.

WILMETTA: What makes you think so?

JOHNSON: I was sitting over there asleep in the pool hall, and I dreamed it just as plain. And a voice say to me, Joe Johnson, go get a dime and play it straight, just as sure as the world. 546. And so I said to myself, now I know Wilmetta'll want to be in on this, and I'll just go get a dime from her now—and we'll split the winnings.

WILMETTA: I wish I had it, Daddy Johnson. But between you and Daddy Brown, I can't keep a thing. Besides, I got bad news to tell you, awful bad news.

JOHNSON: What is it, Wilmetta? I hope you ain't sick.

WILMETTA: Worse'n that. I lost my job.

JOHNSON: You lose your job?

WILMETTA: Yes, the manager fired me tonight. This is my last go round.

JOHNSON: Ain't that awful! Now what am *I* gonna do?

WILMETTA: He got mad cause I wouldn't let him kiss me, and him a married man!

JOHNSON: So now you's fired.

WILMETTA: *(Sniffling)* Yes, Daddy Johnson.

JOHNSON: After all the trouble I went to, to get you this job, too.

WILMETTA: I'm so sorry, Daddy. Now, where'll I go? What'll I do?

JOHNSON: Well, you could-a kissed him once.

WILMETTA: But if I'd of kissed him once, no telling how many more he might want.

JOHNSON: If your mother knew you'd lost this job, she'd turn over in her grave, crazy as she was about me. Wilmetta, I got to eat. Fact is I'm hungry right now.

WILMETTA: Go on over yonder in the bar, and get you some sandwiches.

JOHNSON: With what?

WILMETTA: It's a party. Everybody is invited, free.

JOHNSON: A freeby?

WILMETTA: Yes, a freeby, to announce Buster's engagement. *(Weeping louder)*

JOHNSON: I don't care what it's to announce, if it's free. See you later, daughter.

> *(He exits in the bar, as MADAM KLINKSCALE and ALI ALI come grandly down the stairs. MADAM is in a black and trailing evening gown, ALI in a tail-coat and gorgeous red silk turban. They go toward the bar)*

MADAM: It sure were nice of that young couple to invite us old folks to their party.

ALI: Miss Bailey's might near as old as you, Vera, if you ask me.

MADAM: What is age, Ali, in love?

ALI: Nothing a-tall, dear, nothing a-tall!

> *(They exit into the bar, as two flashy young gamblers come down the stairs, and stop at the tobacco counter to purchase cigars. SHEBA and her KNIGHT, obviously intoxicated, enter from the bar, and stagger gaily across to the alcove)*

1ST GAMBLER: *(Pulling out roll of bills)* Give us a couple Corona Coronas, Little Girl.

2ND GAMBLER: *(Also pulling out bills)* Naw, make it Havana super-specials, baby. We got all the money in the world.

1ST GAMBLER: Just busted the bank. Who said old Big-Dog could play poker? Here, kid, is a tip for you. *(Hands WILMETTA a coin)*

WILMETTA: Thanks a lot, Sammy. I sure need it.

> *(The GAMBLERS exit laughing, putting rolls of bills back into their pockets, as BIG-DOG enters turning his pants inside out, looking for a dime)*

BIG-DOG: Wilmetta, you got any loose cigarette I can get for a penny? They done broke me upstairs. Flat! And in my own game, too. I sure must-a used a *good* deck for once by mistake.

WILMETTA: Oh, Big-Dog, that's too bad. I'll buy a pack of cigarettes. I feel like smoking myself. *(Hysterically)* I feel like taking a drink. I feel like doing something desperate. I lost my job.

> *(The crowd in the bar overflows in the lobby. Noise, laughter, and chatter as the KNIGHTS and LADIES and other guests come out. ROTATION SLIM and MADAM KLINKSCALE are arm in arm. BUSTER carries BOOTOO on his shoulder. Everyone is elegantly dressed except BUSTER, who still wears his same old clothes. The MANAGER bustles about)*

MANAGER: Just enjoy yourselves, folks. It's kinder crowded in there, so come on out where you can dance and have your fun! The stuff is here and it's mellow! The house is Mr. Whitehead's.

> *(The PIANIST in the bar begins to play the BLUES, and everybody starts to stomp. TOO-TIGHT dances with the stout MISS KING. As they approach the elevator, the bell rings loudly)*

MISS KING: Baby, ain't you supposed to run that car?

TOO-TIGHT: Damn that car!

> *(They sway gaily to the music. SHEBA hugs her KNIGHT. Old ragged STEP-FATHER JOHNSON prances with a LADY of the Drill Corps. The HIGH WORTHY herself is in the arms of a tall feathered KNIGHT with a golden sword at his side. ALI ALI holds a beautiful young GIRL close to his bosom. SUZY dances with ADOLPHUS, the desk CLERK. As the HIGH WORTHY nears the center of the lobby, she begins to sing the blues, in a deep hoarse voice)*

HIGH WORTHY: *(Singing, as she dances)*
> I hate to see

That evening sun go down.
Hate to see that
Evening sun go down.
The man I love, Lawd,
He has done left this town.
Feelin' tomorrow
Like I feel today.
Feeling tomorrow
Just like I feel today,
Gonna pack my grip
And make my get-away.

VOICES: *(All join in chorus)*
Got the St. Louis Blues,
Just as blue as I can be.
The one that I loves got a heart
Like a rock cast in the sea.
Or else he never would-a gone
So far away from me.

> *(Feathers sway, capes switch, feet stomp. Suddenly when the singing ceases, a lone dancer takes the center of the floor and begins to Mambo. The music whips up its tempo. Couples gradually separate, and stand aside to watch the dancer)*

DANCER: Folks, let my feet get loose! . . . . . . And my soul get happy!

BOOTOO: Aw, do it, boy!

BIG-DOG: Whip that piano, Miss Lucy!

DANCER: Yes, cause I'm a dancing stud!

ROTATION: Swing, gate, swing!

> *(Various dancers, including SHEBA, BOOTOO, ROTATION, and SUZY do their steps, and mambo off toward the bar. Everyone is danced out, and thirsty as the music ceases. There is a general exodus to the bar)*

VOICES:
Whee, it's hot!
Let's get some nice cool beer.
I wants a highball, myself.
Uh! I'm thirsty as a goat!
Me, too, boy!
Come on, let's collate that collation!

SHEBA: *(To a feathered KNIGHT)* Baby, lend me your feather to fan with.

ALI: *(Wiping his face on the tail end of his turban)* UH! I can't hardly stand this turban.

WOMAN: Lawd, have mercy! These shoes!

> *(As the crowd returns to the bar, BUSTER is revealed leaning on the tobacco stand talking to WILMETTA. Both look very sad and woebegone)*

BUSTER: I sure feels bad. Don't none of this here make me feel good.

WILMETTA: Nor me. I feels awful, too, Buster.

BUSTER: What's the matter with you?

WILMETTA: I lost my job.

BUSTER: You did? How come?

WILMETTA: Cause I wouldn't let old Lighthouse kiss me tonight.

BUSTER: Did he ever kiss you before?

WILMETTA: Of course not.

BUSTER: You don't let any and everybody kiss you, do you, Wilmetta?

WILMETTA: No, I don't.

BUSTER: You's the kind of girl I like.

WILMETTA: I wish you really did like me, Buster.

BUSTER: I just told you I really do. Gee, I hate to see you crying about your old job.

WILMETTA: I ain't crying about losing my job. I'm crying cause you're going away *(wailing)* tomorrow!

BUSTER: Don't cry about that, Wilmetta. I don't care about going away, I'm tired o' Harlem, really I am.

WILMETTA: Then what's the matter with you?

BUSTER: I feels bad because I have to marry Suzy.

WILMETTA: Oh!

BUSTER: Wilmetta, I——I——

WILMETTA: Yes, Buster?

BUSTER: Say, listen Wilmetta, ——I——there's something I want to ask you.

WILMETTA: What is it, Buster?

> *(Enter SUZY from the bar looking for BUSTER)*

SUZY: Buster! Buster! Come on, darling, they're fixing to give a toast to the bride and groom. Just think, all them people in there fixing to give us a toast! *(She drags him toward the bar)*

BUSTER: *(To SUZY)* Wait, I ain't got my gum yet.

SUZY: Come on, now, honey. You don't need no chewing gum.

BUSTER: Wilmetta, I—I—

> *(They exit into bar as STEP-FATHER JOHNSON emerges with*

his hands full of sandwiches. Behind him come ROTATION SLIM,
BIG-DOG, and HEAVY, who gather in a group near the alcove)

JOHNSON: *(To WILMETTA)* Wilmetta, here, have a sandwich.

WILMETTA: *(Handkerchief to her eyes)* I don't want any, Daddy.

JOHNSON: Better eat today, you might not tomorrow.

WILMETTA: I know it, Daddy.

JOHNSON: It's a wonder that old no-good-for-nothing Step-Father Brown of yours, ain't been around here tonight. Looks like he would-a smelt this freeby.

WILMETTA: He got all mixed up with Bootoo's kidnapping. I guess he don't know it's over now and settled.

JOHNSON: Well, don't let his path cross mine, tonight nor never! I hates his guts.

WILMETTA: I wish you-all would like each other. I likes you both.

JOHNSON: You's too much like your mother, Wilmetta. You loves everybody! *(Stuffing the last morsel into his mouth)* I'm going and get myself another sandwich. *(He exits as HEAVY begins to talk)*

HEAVY: That Buster's got entirely too much money—a thousand dollars—and we all here broke.

BIG-DOG: You told that right, boy. I'm broker'n a he-hant in a empty pawn shop.

ROTATION: And I'm the he-hant's partner. We got to get some of that kale out of that country joker.

HEAVY: He just won't get drunk and pass out.

BIG-DOG: No! But say, I got an idea! Does he smoke?

HEAVY: Yes, I gave him a Lucky awhile ago. He smokes.

BIG-DOG: Then next time, give him a reefer.

ROTATION: Big-Dog, go to the head of the class! You is the brightest little colored boy in the Grand Hotel.

HEAVY: Man, that's just it. Dope him up on tea.

ROTATION: Good old marihuana! Make him blow his top! Why didn't I think of that before. Who's got some?

HEAVY: I carries them all the time. *(Pulling out reefers)* Coco smokes the hell out of 'em.

BIG-DOG: No wonder he got his brains beat out tonight.

HEAVY: Huh! Rocky smokes 'em more'n him. It was that referee, I tell you. Every time Coco backed up, there was the referee right in his way.

ROTATION: All right, all right! Can the jive! But how're we gonna get young Shadow Gut out here?

HEAVY: Just go call him, go call him!

ROTATION: Suzy ain't gonna let him come.

BIG-DOG: Tell Miss Suzanne Dorine de Bailey that us boys have got a little secret information to impart to him, about what every young man ought to know on the night of his wedding. Old Miss Bailey'll want to know it, too, so she'll let Buster come and find out.

ROTATION: That's just what we'll do. I'll go get him.

HEAVY: Make it soon, cause my palm is itching.

(As ROTATION starts for BUSTER, BUSTER himself emerges from the bar, and hurries toward WILMETTA)

BUSTER: Wilmetta, I just want to ask you——

(ROTATION grabs him by the arm)

ROTATION: Come on over here a minute, buddy, with us boys. We want to tell you something you ought to know.

BUSTER: *(Stopping reluctantly)* What you want to tell me?

ROTATION: Just some friendly advice, fellow, that's all, seeing as how you're a young man, about to be married for the first time, we old married men—

BUSTER: *(To WILMETTA)* Wilmetta, maybe I ought to hear this. I'll be right back.

(He goes with ROTATION to the alcove, where they all sit down on the settee)

BIG-DOG: Now, Buster, son, listen. I been married four times and—

HEAVY: Here, take a cigarette to steady your nerves while Big-Dog talks.

(They all take reefers)

BUSTER: It ain't that bad, is it?

HEAVY: I'm tellin' you, marriage is something!

ROTATION: The first time I got married, buddy— Here, have a light.

(They all light reefers, and draw deeply on them. TOO-TIGHT enters escorting BOOTOO to the cigar-stand)

BUSTER: What kind o' cigarette is this? It taste mighty kinder sweet to me.

HEAVY: That's pure Arabian tobacco. I got 'em from a man what's been over there.

BIG-DOG: These cigarettes is swell, Buster. Just inhale real deep—and hold it for awhile. That's the way to catch the aroma.

BUSTER: It does make you feel kinder good, don't it?

BIG-DOG: Good is right! Now, as I were saying about this wedding. . . .

BUSTER: I don't need to know about no wedding, man. My pa breeds razor backed hogs.

BIG-DOG: Me and Rotation and Heavy, we was thinkin', you could give us 20 or 30 dollars maybe to put you wise.

HEAVY: Yeah—to what you jokers in Shadow Gut ain't heard of yet.

BUSTER: *(Draws deeply on the reefer again)* Good as I feel now! I ain't in need of nothin', man. I believe I could beat Coco, tonight.

ROTATION: Aw, sit down, fellow, Coco's all beat up already. He ain't no trouble.

BUSTER: Then I'll take you, Heavy. *(He draws back a fist)*

HEAVY: Nobody wants to fight, fellow, we want to teach you something. Sit down.

BUSTER: I don't want to fight neither, I just want to play. I feel like a yearling calf, when the grass is green. *(Imitating a calf)* Baaa-aaaaa!

ROTATION: Well, suppose you lend us a couple hundred bucks, pal, just to make you feel better. What do you say?

BUSTER: *(Pulling out bill after bill)* Sure, pal, I'll give you two hundred dollars . . . . . . if you'll eat your hat like a goat.

BIG-DOG: Now, Buster, don't be funny.

ROTATION: No, cause we might get tough on your hands.

BUSTER: That ain't funny, unless you eat the hat. Then you won't need the two hundred dollars.

BIG-DOG: *(Angrily)* We ain't joking, son. *(Pulling his knife out)* You see this here?

HEAVY: And this here? *(Pulls his knife)*

ROTATION: *(Also pulling a knife)* And this here?

BUSTER: What you gonna do, play mumble-peg?
> *(Enter CHAUFFEUR as TOO-TIGHT completes buying some gum for PRINCESS BOOTOO, which they chew violently)*

CHAUFFEUR: The car's outside for Whitehead and Bailey. Tell 'em, will you?

TOO-TIGHT: O.K. pal, I'll page 'em. *(To BOOTOO)* Come on, let's go get the bride and groom. *(They skip gaily across the lobby)* Miss Bailey, Miss Bailey, the wedding car's outside. Mr. Whitehead, Mr. Buster Whitehead, car outside!
> *(From the bar pour a crowd of people, glasses in hand, following the excited SUZY)*

SUZY: Where is my little sugar lump, my sweet baby mine?

TOO-TIGHT: *(Circling around)* Mr. Whitehead, Mr. Whitehead! Car outside!

BUSTER: *(In the alcove)* What you want, you sweet little old Lonesome Heart, you? Come here!
> *(The men quickly hide their knives, frustrated)*

SUZY: *(Looking into the alcove)* The auto's come to take us to get married. Is you all ready, darling?

BUSTER: Solid ready, dear! *(Offering his arm)*

SUZY: *(As BUSTER escorts her to the elevator)* Then just lemme run upstairs and get my coat and hat. I'll be right down . . . . . . Too-Tight!

TOO-TIGHT: Yes, Ma'm, Miss Bailey!
> *(TOO-TIGHT and SUZY exit into the elevator)*

BUSTER: *(Turning around and taking a final draw on his reefer)* Whee-hoo!! I feel like Tarzan! Wilmetta, here I come! Everybody else, scat! *(He gallops across the lobby and stops at the cigar-stand)* Chick, get your coat on.

WILMETTA: *(Astonished)* For what, Buster?

BUSTER: We gonna get married, gal.

WILMETTA: But you ain't asked me yet.

BUSTER: Ain't I tried to ask you fifty times? *(Commandingly)* Fetch your bahootney on out of here!!

WILMETTA: Where're we going?

BUSTER: We gonna elope.

WILMETTA: But do you love me, Buster?

BUSTER: Much as I love myself. Come on! *(As WILMETTA hesitates)* Don't you love *me*?

WILMETTA: Sure, I do.

BUSTER: Then bring it, baby! *(Snapping his fingers)* Bring it!

WILMETTA: *(Looking at her wrist watch)* But I have ten more minutes to work.

BUSTER: To hell with work. You ain't far from bein' Mrs. Buster White-head.

WILMETTA: But what about my step-fathers?

BUSTER: Come on. Damn a step-father! *(He pulls her toward the door)*

WILMETTA: My nose! My nose! I ain't powdered my nose!

BUSTER: Neither have I. Come on!
> *(She drops her coat under their feet. Both stoop to get it, and bump their heads soundly together. They rise laughing, and fall into one another's arms with a loud kiss. The crowd cheers and begins to throw confetti. The manager holds the door open)*

VOICES:

> Good luck!
>
> God bless you!
>
> Enjoy yourselves!
>
> Oh, the sweet souls!
>
> Praise the Lord!

WILMETTA: Goodbye! Goodbye!

BUSTER: Goodbye, everybody! See you tomorrow!

> *(Exit BUSTER and WILMETTA amid the shouts of the crowd. The elevator door opens and SUZY emerges, white veil flowing and carrying flowers)*

SUZY: I'm ready, Buster, baby! Come on, dear! *(Dead silence, except for the honk of an auto horn, and the purr of the car pulling away outside. Nobody moves)* What's the matter? Ain't he here? Is he gone to the men's room? *(SUZY darts about the crowd looking for BUSTER, her veil flying, her eyes rolling wildly. Suddenly she stops)* Where's he at? Where's my baby at?

HIGH WORTHY: *(Gently)* Honey, your baby's gone.

SUZY: *(Dashing to the door)* Gone? . . . . . . But where's the car?

BIG-DOG: He took the car, too

SHEBA: *(Cattily)* And that ain't all!

SUZY: What else?

SHEBA: *(With relish)* Wilmetta!

> *(SUZY faints into the arms of two large lodge LADIES, who help her to a chair, as the piano in the bar softly plays the BLUES. SUZY looks wildly about, and clutches the arms of her chair)*

SUZY: *(Moaning)* Aw-ooo-oo! My baby's gone! *(Crazily, she stares into space, as the music in the bar is loud)*

CURTAIN

Act III

SETTING: *The same. Noon, the next day.*

AT RISE: *Everything is as in Act I, ADOLPHUS is at the desk talking to ROTATION, and TOO-TIGHT mans the elevator, except that at the tobacco stand, SHEBA now presides instead of WILMETTA. Insistent buzzing of the switchboard finally causes the CLERK to answer it. The elevator door opens and two KNIGHTS emerge, their swords swinging at their hips, their plumes waving. One carries a banner of silk and gold. Behind them hobbles the STOUT WOMAN, MISS KING, in high-heeled slippers, carrying a folding chair. The two KNIGHTS hurry through the lobby on their way to the parade.*

TOO-TIGHT: You ain't going to work today, Miss King?

MISS KING: No, indeedy, baby. I'm gonna see the parade. With all them Knights and Ladies marching, string bands and brass bands, you know I ain't gonna miss it.

TOO-TIGHT: What time's it due to pass?

MISS KING: It ought to be soon. They due to leave 145th and Lenox at noon.

TOO-TIGHT: By C.P. time that'll be one o'clock.

MISS KING: Well, whatever time it is, I'm gonna be out on Seventh Avenue, watching 'em swing by. Got my chair to set down, if my feet don't hold me.

> *(She hobbles out the street door and exits, as a tall bewildered-looking OLD MAID enters with a hand bag, and approaches the desk. The CLERK turns from the switchboard to bang the bell for TOO-TIGHT)*

CLERK: Boy! Princess Bootoo says bring up her breakfast.

TOO-TIGHT: What's that little runt want to eat?

CLERK: *(Reading)* Oatmeal, bananas and cream, fried potatoes, ham omelette and sausage, wheat cakes, and a cup of coffee. Hurry up!

TOO-TIGHT: You better call Mr. Lighthouse to help me carry it.

CLERK: *(Ignoring the OLD MAID, who stands at the desk)* Now, Rotation, as I was telling you before that buzzer cut me off, I walked that chick all the way home last night—that pretty chick Ali Ali kept dancing with at the party.

ROTATION: I know you was mellow.

CLERK: Mellow as Four Roses! But listen! After I got her way up there on Sugar Hill, you know what she did?

ROTATION: No, what did she do?

CLERK: Come holding out her hand and saying *goodbye*.

ROTATION: Not even a kiss nor nothin'?

CLERK: *(As buzzer rings)* Not even nothing!

ROTATION: I know you was burnt up.

CLERK: Damn right! You know what I told her? Boy, I says . . . . . . *(Insistent buzzing)* Doggone this switchboard! Everytime I get busy! *(He answers it as the OLD MAID waits)* Hello! Yes, yes! . . . . . . Mrs. Ricks told me to tell you, she says, she's not in . . . . . . I don't know where she's at. She just tole me she's not in . . . . . . You say you're

Mr. Ricks, her husband? *(Carelessly)* Oh well, I expects you's the last person she wants to be connected up with . . . . . . What? You say you gonna shoot me, if I don't connect you with her room? You'd have to shoot a mighty long ways to shoot through this phone! . . . . . . Huh? What's that? *(In consternation)* You say you're across the street at the drug store? Uh-oh! Here! *(Jiggling the connection)* I'll connect you up right away. *(Frightened)* Oh, Lawd, he's done hung up! *(He turns back to the desk mopping the sweat from his brow)*

OLD MAID: Young man, I want a room.

CLERK: *(Gulping)* Yes, ma'm, single or double?

OLD MAID: I'm single.

CLERK: *(Pushing her the register)* Well, just sign here.

OLD MAID: Write it down for me, will you? That train's wore me to a frazzle.

CLERK: Yes, ma'm! *(Gazing nervously in all directions)* What's the name?

OLD MAID: Miss Marietta Maxwell Graham.

CLERK: *(Writing as his hand shakes)* Miss . . . . . . Marietta . . . . . . *(He sees the irate HUSBAND enter, and hurriedly approach the desk, his eyes gleaming)* Oh, Lawd!

HUSBAND: So you're the butt-end of the cheap five-cent cigar, that's trying to keep me from talking to my wife, are you? I've a good mind to try your chops! Where is she? She can't leave me!

CLERK: *(His teeth chattering)* In 317, Mr. Ricks.

ROTATION: *(Writing it down)* I'll play that today.

HUSBAND: I'm going up.

> *(He rings for the elevator. TOO-TIGHT is missing)*

CLERK: *(Rushing to switchboard, and ringing)* Mrs. Ricks? . . . . . . 317? This Mrs. Ricks? Your husband's just starting up to your room on the elevator. You better leave quick. *(A suppressed scream over the wires. HUSBAND continues to ring impatiently for the elevator boy. CLERK turns again to the OLD MAID)* Now what did you say your name was, ma'm?

OLD MAID: Miss Marietta . . . . . . Maxwell . . . . . . Graham, young man!

> *(At that moment WIFE rushes down the stairs, and collides with HUSBAND, at the elevator entrance. Both step back and scream. WIFE reverses her footsteps hastily up the stairs again, with the HUSBAND in full chase behind her)*

ROTATION: Looks like he's gonna string her up a little, don't it, boy?

CLERK: Man, these wives is awful!

OLD MAID: *(Tapping her foot)* Young man, do things like that go on here often?

CLERK: Well, seems like I 'members something like it once before, lady.

OLD MAID: Then this ain't a decent place for me. Where is the women's Y.M.C.A.

CLERK: 'Bout three blocks up the avenue.

OLD MAID: *(Picking up her handbag in a huff)* Then I'll go there.
       (She exits as TOO-TIGHT comes from the bar with a tray loaded with food, and crosses to the elevator)

TOO-TIGHT: What about Mr. and Mrs. Whitehead? Ain't they ordered breakfast yet?

CLERK: You know we never get no calls for breakfast from the honeymoon suite.

TOO-TIGHT: Well, looks to me, even newlyweds is got to eat! As broke as Wilmetta's been around here, I know she's hungry.

ROTATION: She's living on love from now on.

TOO-TIGHT: Well, I'm gonna knock on their door and see.

CLERK: You sure is anxious to hustle up on a tip. You must be broke.

TOO-TIGHT: *(Exits into elevator)* I is. *(Car goes up)*

SHEBA: *(Calling from the cigar-stand)* Rotation, come on over here, and keep me company. I don't see what fun two mens has talking together all the time.

ROTATION: You's soundin' kinda peevish, baby.

SHEBA: I think I'll get married, then I won't have to work.

ROTATION: Work? I ain't never seen you working before. How come you're holdin' down the tobacco works?

SHEBA: Oh, I just took this job to help Mr. Lighthouse out, till after the Conclave's over. The way Wilmetta went and got married on him, is awful.

ROTATION: If you got a chance to marry a rich oil man, I'll bet you'd snatch it up, quicker'n a hen grabs corn.

SHEBA: Why, I wouldn't be that grasping. Besides, I don't want no baby like Buster. *(Eyeing him and sighing)* Rotation, I wants a man.
       (Loud screams as the WIFE dashes out through the lobby. Down the stairs comes the HUSBAND behind her, panting like a bull. Both exit into the street. The CLERK, SHEBA, and ROTATION all peek out from behind their respective hiding places. MISS SUZY BAILEY comes grimly from the elevator, and goes toward an armchair)

CLERK: Good morning, Miss Bailey, how are you?

SUZY: *(shortly)* I don't feel good.

CLERK: Anything I can get for you?

SUZY: No! *(Pause)* They're back, ain't they?

CLERK: *(Feigning ignorance)* Who, Miss Bailey?

SUZY: You know who I mean.

CLERK: Yes'm, they're back. Been back since about eight o'clock. The chauffeur says, they woke up the Justice of the Peace, and got married before daybreak.

SUZY: It ain't decent to be all that anxious.

CLERK: It sure ain't, Miss Bailey. Er-have you had your breakfast yet?

SUZY: *(Sitting down)* Don't want none.

CLERK: You ain't going to work today?

SUZY: Naw! *(A long pause)* Where are they at?

CLERK: In the honeymoon suite, asleep, I reckon.

SUZY: Hum-m-mm! I'm gonna set right here—if it's till doomsday!

CLERK: You're gonna set right there? For what, Miss Bailey?

SUZY: To kill 'em, when they come down.

CLERK: Huh?

SUZY: And don't you try to warn 'em neither. Do, and I'll shoot you.
(She opens her purse, and displays a large pistol, holding it up for the CLERK to see)

CLERK: *(Wiping his brow)* It ain't none of my affair, Miss Bailey.

SUZY: Don't let it be.

CLERK: No'm, I sure won't.

SUZY: I'm gonna set right here and watch that elevator, until they come out.
(The elevator door opens. The CLERK jumps, as SUZY puts her hand in her bag. TOO-TIGHT walks out carrying an empty plate)

TOO-TIGHT: That midget wants another order of pancakes! *(As he crosses to the bar)* Miss Suzy, are you gonna see the parade?

SUZY: Naw.

TOO-TIGHT: I reckon I ain't either, with this old confinement job I got.
(Exits into bar. STEP-FATHER BROWN enters, and looks around the lobby. Goes to the cigar-stand, surprised at not seeing WILMETTA)

BROWN: Pardon, Miss, but is you working here?

SHEBA: *(As ROTATION steps aside)* I am.

BROWN: Then, where is my step-daughter, Wilmetta?

SHEBA: Why, she's married! Ain't you heard?

BROWN: Married? And left me, her poor old father? To who?

SHEBA: Oh, she made a good catch, all right! To some rich young oil lummucks from Texas, named Whitehead.

BROWN: Where they're at?

SHEBA: Upstairs in the honeymoon suite, sleeping.

BROWN: I'm gonna wake 'em up.

SHEBA: You better ask the desk clerk about that.

BROWN: *(To the desk CLERK)* I want to see Wilmetta.

CLERK: *(Grandly)* You mean Mrs. Whitehead? I don't know as she wants to be disturbed.

BROWN: But I'm her step-father, you know that.

CLERK: I'll see if I can get her on the phone.

> *(As CLERK works switchboard, a DELIVERY BOY enters)*

BOY: Packages for Mr. and Mrs. Whitehead.

CLERK: Take 'em upstairs. The elevator boy'll show you.

> *(The BOY enters the elevator. Shortly TOO-TIGHT emerges from the bar with a plate of pancakes and crosses to elevator. Exit BOY and TOO-TIGHT)*

BROWN: Can't you get 'em on the phone?

CLERK: I'm trying.

BROWN: Must be sleeping like logs.

CLERK: Yes, here's somebody . . . . . . Hello! Mrs. Whitehead? . . . . . . Your step-father Brown's down here, and wants to come up . . . . . . Yes'm . . . . . . Yes . . . . . . All right, I'll tell him . . . . . . Thank you! *(Turning to BROWN)* She says you can't come up now, but they'll both be down in a little while. They're leaving for Shadow Gut on the two o'clock train, so just have a seat.

BROWN: *(Angrily)* You just call right back up there, and tell Wilmetta, I ain't had my breakfast yet, to send me down fifty cents to eat on.

CLERK: She said she doesn't want to be disturbed, so I can't.

BROWN: *(Muttering)* Now, ain't that something! Her own step-father, too.

> *(He takes a seat in the alcove, and opens a paper. As the elevator is heard approaching, SUZY opens her purse for her gun. The CLERK becomes tense. The door opens, and the DELIVERY BOY emerges)*

BOY: *(Grinning)* Gee-zus! They gave me a good tip.

ROTATION: What'd you bring 'em?

BOY: Swell clothes, man, ordered by phone this morning from our store. They gonna be all dressed out.

> *(He exits. Bell rings, and TOO-TIGHT ascends)*

SHEBA: That lucky hussy, Wilmetta!

ROTATION: I wish I could get that chump of a Buster in just *one* game of pool!

CLERK: Or better yet, blackjack!

SUZY: *(Ominously)* All I wants is to get him where I can see him. That's all!

> *(Dead silence. Then in the distance the sound of a band playing afar off)*

ROTATION: Uh-oh! The parade's coming. I'll see you later, Sheba. Gimme a pack of Camels before I go.

SHEBA: *(Handing him the cigarettes)* I wish I could see that parade.

ROTATION: I'll pay you for these later.

SHEBA: Huh?

> *(ROTATION exits. Again the hum of the elevator, and SUZY prepares to shoot. The CLERK puts his fingers to his ear, crouching. The elevator door opens, and BIG-DOG, HEAVY, and COCO dodge back into the elevator, as SUZY waves her gun. As she puts it away, they emerge on the way to the street. The CLERK breathes a sigh of relief)*

BIG-DOG: *(To SUZY)* Hello, Miss Suzy! You better come with us and see that parade. The Knights and Ladies are strutting their stuff. Come on.

SUZY: I will not.

> *(Elevator bell. TOO-TIGHT goes up)*

HEAVY: Old Coco here's got one eye closed, and can't but half-see the procession. Look, Miss Suzy!

COCO: *(Laughing)* One eye's better'n none, ain't it?

SUZY: *(Grimly)* I ain't laughing!

COCO: *(Breaking away)* Excuse me! Come on, boys, let's go.

SHEBA: *(Calling)* Big-Dog, I ain't never seen you up this early in the morning.

BIG-DOG: How could you, when you ain't been up yourself. Throw me a cigar there, will you?

SHEBA: *(Throwing him a cigar)* Enjoy yourself, boy.

> *(Exit BIG-DOG, HEAVY, and COCO to the street. The sound of music is nearer)*

CLERK: That band music sounds right good, don't it, Miss Bailey?

SUZY: Not to me!

> *(SUZY rolls her eyes at him and he hushes, pulls out his handker-*
> *chief, and begins to wipe and rewipe his brow. He grows more and*
> *more excited as voices are heard in the elevator, a woman's femi-*
> *nine chatter, then gay laughter. SUZY rises, and gets behind her*
> *chair with pistol drawn. The door opens. From the elevator comes*
> *ALI ALI with MADAM KLINKSCALE. SUZY sits down again)*

MADAM: J.C., the signs of Agitarius are with us.

ALI: Vera, I ain't never studied no Zodiac, but that kiss you just gimme
in the elevator, felt like I was being slapped in the face with honey!

MADAM: J.C., you's a mess! I know I ain't that sweet.

> *(Loud giggling, as they exit out the door. SHEBA leaves her stand,*
> *and goes to the door also)*

SHEBA: I'll be John Browned if I'm gonna miss all the excitement. I'm
at least gonna stand here in the door, and look out.

TOO-TIGHT: *(Also going to the door)* Me, too.

CLERK: Better not let the manager catch you?

SHEBA: Who, old Lighthouse? All I'd have to do is to pinch his cheek,
and he'd melt into my arms. You must not know I'm sweet Mama
Sheba Lane.

CLERK: Who ever you is, you better not go out to see that parade—if
you workin' in here.

TOO-TIGHT: Aw, you must mad because you can't go.

SHEBA: That's all.

> *(Cheering is heard without, and the roll of drums)*

TOO-TIGHT: Just look at them uniforms.

SHEBA: That's the Ladies Drill Corps, ain't it?

TOO-TIGHT: It sure is. *(To the CLERK)* Boy, you ought to come here
and see our High Grand Worthy, just a stepping!

SHEBA: Hot dog! I'm sure proud of my sex. Can't nobody else swing
it like that.

TOO-TIGHT: Men's ain't so far back.

SHEBA: No, but look at the women! *(Imitating them as the band breaks*
into a syncopated march) Capes just a-switching!

TOO-TIGHT: My, my, my!

> *(He pays no mind to the elevator bell ringing constantly. Suddenly*
> *the buzzer begins too)*

CLERK: Hello! Hello! *(Then very politely)* Oh, yes, Mr. Lighthouse.
You say you're in the honeymoon suite now, helping Mr. Whitehead
dress? Yes, sir? Yes, indeed! Yes, sir! And I'll make out the bill. Yes,

sir! *(He turns excitedly toward the front)* Too-Tight, Sheba, you-all come here!

TOO-TIGHT: You go to grass!

SHEBA: You must be crazy, Adolphus! I ain't gonna miss this for nothing.

CLERK: *(Coming out from behind the desk, circling cautiously around SUZY, as he goes to the door to whisper to TOO-TIGHT and SHEBA)* It's Mr. Whitehead, you dumbbells, and the boss. Don't you want them good tips he's liable to shell out? Him and Wilmetta are about to leave for Texas, and they want their baggage down right away.

TOO-TIGHT: Why didn't you tell me that, man?

(TOO-TIGHT and SHEBA leave the door excitedly)

SHEBA: *(Powdering her nose behind the counter)* Oh, that sweet man, Mr. Whitehead! The first Negro I ever met with an oil well.

CLERK: *(Looking up from his figures)* Several oil wells, darling.

TOO-TIGHT: Going up!

(Exits in elevator. SUZY rises and begins to pace the floor, much to the distress of the CLERK. She walks a short distance, then turns suddenly to eye the elevator. In the street, the bands play gaily. Drums roll, feet march. SUZY takes out her pistol, and inspects it calmly. SHEBA sees her and stops petrified, her powder-puff posed in mid-air. From then on SHEBA's eyes follow SUZY, her head turns as SUZY walks, as if by a magnet. Both SHEBA and the CLERK are jittery with fear. The CLERK keeps trying to add up figures)

CLERK: I wonder how much we should charge for that honeymoon suite by the hour? Charges vary. *(As no one answers him)* I guess five dollars an hour. . . . Now, that's $35 right there. Now, add Seventy-two for the hire of the car last night. . . . Thirty-five and Seventy-two makes Ninety-five. Now, plus the party . . . . . . *(SHEBA attempting to leave her stand, closes the gate with a bang. The CLERK jumps and yells out loud)* Oh!

SUZY: *(To SHEBA)* Where are you going?

SHEBA: To the—to the——the——

SUZY: Get back and set down. *(Muttering)* Running around here loose, liable to get in my way.

(SHEBA returns behind the tobacco stand. The CLERK writes with trembling fingers. The bands play in the street, suddenly the elevator begins to hum. SUZY stops behind her chair, her pistol in hand. SHEBA and the CLERK are petrified. Voices in the elevator,

as it comes to a stop. The door opens. A mass of moving baggage is revealed)

TOO-TIGHT: *(Calling unseen behind the baggage)* Taxi for Mr. White-head!

CLERK: *(Repeating)* Taxi for Mr. Whitehead!

(SUZY raises her pistol. For a fleeting moment, she stands irreso-lute, then fires point blank, all the bullets in the gun at the barri-cade of baggage)

SHEBA: *(Screaming)* Aw—oooooo!

(Both the CLERK and SHEBA disappear behind their respective barriers. STEP-FATHER BROWN flees into the bar. Baggage tumbles everywhere into the center of the lobby, and in the midst of it all, the black box of PRINCESS BOOTOO flies open, and out of it steps BOOTOO herself, knife in hand, blade drawn)

BOOTOO: What's going on here? *(Behind her on the floor, beneath the baggage, sprawl TOO-TIGHT and the MANAGER. BOOTOO advances with the knife)* Don't you shoot me, you evil-looking —

(SUZY, backing up, clicks the trigger of her now empty gun. Finally TOO-TIGHT, the MANAGER, and the CLERK, realizing that the danger is over, all rush forward and grab SUZY, while TOO-TIGHT holds BOOTOO, still waving her knife)

SUZY: I thought—I thought—you all was— Where is *Buster* and *Wil-metta*?

TOO-TIGHT: Aw, woman, the elevator was full of baggage, so they're coming down the steps.

BOOTOO: Don't try to kill me! I'll peel your head!

MANAGER: Miss Bailey, you know we don't allow no shooting in the Grand Hotel.

(MANAGER and CLERK release her)

SUZY: I got the wrong target that time. *(Ashamed)* Mr. Lighthouse, really, shooting at you—I'm mortified!! *(She puts her gun away)*

MANAGER: Oh, that's all right, Miss Bailey. Only please don't do it again.

SUZY: I won't. I sure won't. *(Sinks down in the chair quite broken)* Looks like nothing I ever do turns out right, nohow. Something always goes wrong.

BOOTOO: After all this here go around, I need another plate of pan-cakes.

(BOOTOO exits. TOO-TIGHT picks up the baggage to stack it near the desk. The CLERK, the MANAGER add up the bills, while SUZY muses her fate)

SUZY: All I can ever do is just work, work, work. Cook and scrub for the white folks! Wash and iron! Dry babies! Answer somebody else's doorbell . . . . . . I wants a house of my own. That's what I want. I wants me a husband. I wants a couple of little brown-skin babies. How come I can't have nothing? I know I ain't so good-lookin', and I know I'm not so young, but here's Buster just a-running from me, like I were a varmint! Poor boy! He made out in his letters, he were a full growed man. How did I know he were just a puppy, twenty-one years old!. . . . Lonesome Hearts, huh! *(Calling)* Sheba, which one of us do you think is the foolishester—Buster or me?

SHEBA: To tell the truth, Miss Bailey, ain't neither one of you foolish. Things just don't turn out right, that's all.

SUZY: Just don't turn out right, do they? *(Rising)* Well, I reckon I might just as well go on back to work. *(To the CLERK)* Adolphus, get me Mrs. Vanderzant on the phone. I'm gonna tell her I'm coming on back out there and get dinner.

CLERK: *(Adding)* Nine and five is thirteen, and seven is twenty-two. . . . Just a minute, Miss Bailey. We got to get this bill ready. . . . Eight and six is . . . . . .

SUZY: *(Musing)* Things just didn't turn out right.

(BUSTER and WILMETTA come tripping gaily down the stairs, dressed in new spring clothes and sport-model shoes, looking very smart and happy, hand in hand)

TOO-TIGHT: What took you-all so long Wilmetta?

WILMETTA: Buster stopped to kiss me on every floor.

BUSTER: Say, what was that noise we heard down here. Sounded like a shootin' match.

MANAGER: Oh, that was just some fire-crackers going off in the parade outside.

SUZY: You're wrong! That were my heart-a-breaking, that's what it was!

BUSTER: *(Embarrassed)* Oh! Hello, Suzanne!. . . . I . . . . . . er-re. . . . I'm . . . . . I . . . . . .

WILMETTA: Suzy! I. . . . We . . . Oh, Suzy. . . .

SUZY: My heart is broke, that's all.

BUSTER: You know, I'm sorry, Suzanne.

SUZY: I ain't no Suzanne, neither. Just plain old Suzy Bailey, with a lonesome heart.

    (WILMETTA motions to BUSTER)

BUSTER: *(Approaching SUZY)* Suzy, me and Wilmetta, we been thinkin' we owes you something pretty nice—you gettin' us together and all, and—well, here's the papers I fixed up for you—Read it. *(BUSTER hands her a deed which he takes from his pocket)*

SUZY: *(Reading)* To Suzanne Dorine de Bailey, Well No. 3. . . . Buster, what do this mean?

BUSTER: Old No. 3, that's the oil well over in the West Field, down by the Pike, and it sure will make you a good livin' too.

SUZY: A oil well for me? For ole Suzy Bailey? No, lawd, I don't believe it.

WILMETTA: It's true, Miss Bailey. Look, it's all signed too. Buster and me had it fixed up this morning.

SUZY: Huh? Suzy Bailey got a oil well? Suzy Bailey a oil well—Suzy Bailey got a oil well—

BUSTER: Sure, Suzy Bailey got a oil well—Glad I saw you to give it to you, 'stead of sendin' it to you.

SUZY: Huh! Well, lemme go over here and read it. *(She retires to the alcove)*

MANAGER: Now, Mr. Whitehead, here's your bill all made out.

CLERK: And here's quite a little mail came for you this morning.

BUSTER: Mail? How come I got mail? Who know I'm here?

CLERK: Everybody in Harlem's heard about you by now. We don't have a rich oil man around often.

BUSTER: *(Taking the letters)* Lemme see what they say. *(Putting his arm around WILMETTA)* Let's read 'em, darling.

WILMETTA: I'll open 'em and you read 'em, honey. They look like invitations.

BUSTER: O.K. *(Reading)* Um-hum! That's just what they is—invitations. Listen! *(Reading)* "Mr. Buster Whitehead, Grand Hotel: The Eleven Brownskins of the Evening Shadow Club invites you to a Chitterling Strut tomorrow, Thursday evening at 80 West 133rd St. from eight until—!" *(Puzzled)* Until what? *(Reading)* "Fried Chitterlings, Ten cents. Free Beer."

WILMETTA: Frances, my best girl friend is a member of that club. They give nice functions.

BUSTER: Does you want to stay over for it, honey?

WILMETTA: No, Buster, I wants to see Shadow Gut. *(Handing him another)* Read this one.

BUSTER: This ain't nothing but a card. *(Reading)*
  If you want to dance
  Your dinner down
  Come around to Mamie's
  Tonight and clown.
  2419 Eighth Avenue, Suite 3
  For Mr. Buster Whitehead in his honor.
  Signed by, Mrs. Floretta Lloyd, and Little Mama Lucas
  Do you think we ought to go Wilmetta?

WILMETTA: No, baby! Let's catch our train right now.

BUSTER: Then lemme pay this bill. Is the taxi outside?

CLERK: Right around the corner. We can't get any nearer, because the parade's going by.

BUSTER: *(Pulling out a roll of bills)* And where is Princess Bootoo? Won't Pa be tickled when he sees her!

WILMETTA: It sure is nice of Bootoo to give herself to us for a wedding present.

BUSTER: Sure is. We gonna feed her good, long as she wants to stay. Too-Tight, go see where she's at.

TOO-TIGHT: She yonder in the bar eatin' pancakes. *(He exits into bar)*

MANAGER: *(Receiving money for bill)* Thank you, Mr. Whitehead! Thank you! Any time a-tall, you're welcome at the Grand Hotel.

CLERK: Welcome as the flowers in May.

SHEBA: Or Santa Claus in December.

BUSTER: Is we got plenty of time to make that train?

MANAGER: Plenty. Fact is, you can follow the parade a little while, if you want to.

BUSTER: It would be kinda fun, wouldn't it, Wilmetta?

WILMETTA: It sure would, Buster!

BUSTER: Come on, baby, let's go. *(Enter TOO-TIGHT with BOOTOO, followed by STEP-FATHER BROWN in an angry mood)* Princess, we're ready.

BOOTOO: *(Getting in her box)* Me too.

TOO-TIGHT: Lemme call somebody to help me carry these boxes. *(Exits)*

BROWN: *(Whining)* Uh-hum! Going off and leave me without a word, wasn't you, Wilmetta?

WILMETTA: But I was going to write you a letter.

BROWN: A letter! And me ain't had my breakfast yet, not a mouthful.

BOOTOO: Naw, but you had a snout-full.

BROWN: *(Crying)* Wilmetta, it's a shame the way you's doing me.

WILMETTA: Oh, Daddy Brown, please don't take it so hard.

> *(Enter TOO-TIGHT from the street with STEP-FATHER JOHNSON)*

TOO-TIGHT: They liable to give you a quarter, if you help me carry them bags.

JOHNSON: A quarter! And she's married to a rich oil man. *(Approaching)* Wilmetta, ain't you got no heart a-tall? Married and leaving, and didn't even tell me.

BROWN: *(Angrily)* You get away from here! I'm gonna carry these bags.

JOHNSON: No, you ain't. This is my job! She's *my* step-daughter.

BROWN: And mine, too.

JOHNSON: Yes, but her mama liked me better'n she did you.

BROWN: That's a lie. You just bit me in the back, that's all.

JOHNSON: *(Exasperated)* Brown, I'll knock you eye-balls out.

BROWN: Well, if you do, you better put 'em back, before I sees they's out.

WILMETTA: *(Going between them)* Oh, Daddy Brown! Please, Daddy Johnson! On my wedding day, don't fight!

MANAGER: Not in here! This is a respectable hotel, men! You can't fight here.

BUSTER: What do they want, Wilmetta?

BROWN and JOHNSON: *(Together)* Money!

BUSTER: Here! Here's fifty dollars apiece. Maybe that'll hold you till you can find some kind of jobs.

WILMETTA: Oh, Buster, you're too generous.

BUSTER: What's mine's yours, darling, and what's yours's mine, even your step-fathers!

BROWN: I sure am glad we got a son-in-law!

JOHNSON: Yes, sir! And I bet there's gonna be some grandson?

BROWN: Name the first chile after me, Wilmetta!

JOHNSON: No! After me, Wilmetta.

WILMETTA: *(Taking her husband's arm)* No, after Buster.

TOO-TIGHT: *(Picking up baggage)* Come on! Cause I ain't got all day.

> *(The STEP-FATHERS fill their arms with bags. The CLERK pushes BOOTOO's box, now closed. The MANAGER opens the*

*street door. Strains of music pour in as BUSTER and WILMETTA
shout goodbyes)*

SHEBA: Goodbye, Mr. Whitehead!

SUZY: Goodbye, Buster!

SHEBA: So long, Wilmetta! *(Under her breath)* You hussy!

SUZY: Goodbye, and thank you.

BUSTER: Goodbye, all! We'll be back next summer for the Exposition.
Suzy, I'll bring you a razor-backed hog.

WILMETTA: Sheba, I'll bring you a diamond-backed rattler.

ALL: Goodbye, goodbye, goodbye!

*(Exit BUSTER, WILMETTA, TOO-TIGHT, the STEP-
FATHERS, and the MANAGER)*

SUZY: I don't know which I'd rather have, an oil well or a man.

SHEBA: The oil well, honey! Think what that'll mean in your old age.
Money's what counts all the time.

SUZY: Maybe so. But you need a man and money both, to really bring
joy to your soul.

SHEBA: I never did care much for *just* men, myself!

*(MANAGER, CLERK, and TOO-TIGHT return, followed by
ROTATION)*

MANAGER: Miss Bailey, I want to offer you the best room in the house.
And no more rent than the $2.50 a week you're paying now. Just
keep on writing letters, that's all. The more Lonesome Hearts you
bring to Cleveland, the better. You're great for business!

TOO-TIGHT: This is the first $5 tip, I've had since I been born!

CLERK: And nobody ever gave the Clerk a tip before!

MANAGER: Miss Bailey, your friends is all right. Whitehead was a
thoroughbred.

SUZY: That he was!

ROTATION: The parade's over! Too bad you had to miss it, Miss Bailey.
But I guess you don't care since you got an oil well? *(SUZY smiles)*
Say, ain't you kinder hungry? Wouldn't you like to ride up to the
Big Apple with me, and let me treat you to a wimpy?

SUZY: Rotation, you know I picks my men by mail!

ROTATION: Oh, excuse me!

*(He crosses to SHEBA, and they light cigarettes, and talk softly.
Violent ringing of elevator bell, and at the same time, loud buzzing
at the switchboard)*

TOO-TIGHT: *(Starting for the elevator)* Dog-gone that ding-busted bell. *(Exits)*

CLERK: Everytime I get busy! *(He goes to the switchboard)*

MANAGER: Is there anything I can do for you, Miss Bailey?

SUZY: Nothing that I knows of. I'm gonna get up from here, and go to work in a minute.

MANAGER: To work? And you got a oil well?

SUZY: You don't think I'm gonna let Mrs. Vanderzant starve, do you? I'm just gonna set here a minute more, and get myself together, that's all.

MANAGER: Lemme bring you a little drink from the bar. That might be just what you need.

SUZY: No, it ain't just what I need neither. I needs something for my soul. Here, Mr. Lighthouse, take this nickel, and put it on Count Basie. He always did ease my mind. Play "April in Paris" cause I might go over there next year, and pick me out a French husband.

MANAGER: Yes, Miss Bailey. *(He exits into bar)*

    ("April in Paris" floats in from the jukebox. SUZY sighs deeply, as she takes a picture from her purse, and looks at it)

SUZY: Buster Whitehead, Lonesome Heart No. 72! *(Gently)* He do look kinder like a black Frenchman.

CURTAIN

Front Porch

1938

In the midst of a variety of theatrical projects in the fall of 1938, Hughes rashly promised a new play, *Front Porch,* to the Gilpin Players of Karamu House, who promptly scheduled it for a November opening. With rehearsals already underway, the play arrived bit by bit. The final scene of Act III was so delayed that director Rowena Jelliffe wrote an "alternative ending" herself just before opening night, November 19, 1938. Unlike Hughes's version, Jelliffe's ending was a happy one, which averted problems caused by the similarity of the story to events in the life of the person she had cast in the leading role.

This is Hughes's only play depicting the world of a black middle class, and his critique of their repressed respectability, intraracial class prejudices, and reactionary politics is thoroughgoing. The response to the play was tepid. On November 17, 1938, the *Cleveland Plain Dealer* commented on its "unique hewing to Caucasian standards." Yet *Front Porch* is suggestive in its intimation of the blues reality of Mrs. Harper, whose life with her husband had been grim, and in its several references to the deep discouragement and frequent shiftlessness of many black men, unable to find meaningful and rewarding labor. The final gesture with which the play closes in Hughes's version is perhaps an allusion to Eugene O'Neill's *Mourning Becomes Electra.* The text reproduced here is the only complete version in the Langston Hughes Papers.

Characters

MRS. PAULINE HARPER, mother, a school teacher
HARRIETT, daughter, a typist
CANTWELL, son, in high school
LUCIA, daughter, in junior high school
J. DONALD BUTLER, graduate student in psychology
KENNETH, warehouse attendant
MRS. KLEIN, a Jewish lady (voice offstage)
TAXI DRIVER (voice offstage)

Act I, Scene 1

PLACE: *The United States. An outer residential area in any large city in the North.*

TIME: *The Present.*

SETTING: *The front porch of a rather pretentious Negro home. Grassy lawn. Flowers. Trees. But the houses are close together, close enough to talk from one porch to another. It is Saturday afternoon in the early spring. Tulips in the window boxes.*

ACTION: *As the curtain rises, MRS. HARPER stands talking to her Jewish neighbor. Within, a child practices monotonously on a piano.*

MOTHER: Yes, Mrs. Klein, it's just awful, awful the various and sundry ways the working people are taking advantage of us now-a-days. Why, this morning there were no fresh vegetables at all on the market. The trucking strike—

MRS. KLEIN: *(Offstage on own porch)* It's terrible vat they are doink! Why, Mrs. Harper, my husband, he tells me the clerks down at the store now, they're wanting all Saturday off free, this coming summer, not just half a day—vich ought to be enough for anybody.

MOTHER: True, Mrs. Klein! I don't know what they're thinking. I really don't. And you and me pay for their union whims.

MRS. KLEIN: My husband, he pays! All the time, Mr. Klein, he pays. He pays good. But the workers, never satisfied. And they all Jewish workers, too. But even some Jews there are won't stick mit other Jews!

MOTHER: I know, Mrs. Klein. We leading colored people, sometimes have to struggle with our folks, too. Why even one or two of the colored teachers at our school want to join that red teachers union the radicals are trying to get up. But I'll have nothing to do with it, myself!

MRS. KLEIN: You been teaching now a long time, Mrs. Harper?

MOTHER: Twelve years, Mrs. Klein! I'm in line for an assistant principalship. I've passed the exams twice now. And when I'm appointed, I'll be the first colored woman in the entire state to hold such a position.

MRS. KLEIN: Well, I hope you're soon appointed, Mrs. Harper. But if you fool with that union, you won't be.

MOTHER: When I was a child, nobody thought about unions and strikes and demonstrations. They make so much trouble for our government now-a-days.

(LUCIA stops playing the piano within and comes to the door)

MRS. KLEIN: Vell, in the old country we had plenty trouble. But I didn't think here in America, I would live to see the day when a 10 cents clerk could stand up and sass my husband, and my husband couldn't even fire him, without consulting mit a union! Vat ist dis?

MOTHER: Awful! Awful, awful! *(Turning away a moment)* Lucia! You haven't practiced an hour yet. Keep on with those exercises, dear! Keep on now!

LUCIA: *(In doorway)* All right, mother, but my fingers are tired.

MOTHER: Not half as tired as they'll be later in life, unless you learn to be a lady.

LUCIA: You can't make much money playing a piano, mother, can you?

MOTHER: But if you marry a decent man—as you no doubt will— your husband might enjoy a little music when he gets home from the office.

LUCIA: How many colored men've got offices, mother? I'm going to marry a Spaniard.

MOTHER: Lucia! Get back to your music now!

LUCIA: Yes, mother. *(Exits to inside)*

MOTHER: Are you going in, Mrs. Klein?

MRS. KLEIN: Yes, goink in now! By and by, my children be home for supper.

MOTHER: It is getting along, isn't it? Well, until later!

MRS. KLEIN: Later, yes, maybe this evening I be on porch.

MOTHER: Perhaps I shall, too. Anyway, until the Philharmonic comes on the air.

MRS. KLEIN: Vell, till later.

MOTHER: Yes, Mrs. Klein. *(Turns to her flowerpots. Her son, CANT-WELL, a boy in his late teens, enters, baseball bat in hand, clothes awry)* A pretty sight you are, Cantwell! For a boy your age, out playing like a ragamuffin with all the vagabonds in the neighborhood.

CANTWELL: Aw, mother!

MOTHER: Besides, that Latin test is due on Monday, and you certainly aren't much on your parsing.

CANTWELL: I don't want to go to any college that has Latin for an entrance requirement anyhow.

MOTHER: You'll learn that Latin, young man, and pass it, or I'll know the reason why! You and Lucia try my soul sometimes. Why don't you be like Harriett, always at the top of the honor roll all through school and college.

CANTWELL: Big sister again! *(Hugging his mother)* Model of intelligence and virtue, huh, mother, Harriett is?

MOTHER: I'm perfectly serious, Cantwell.

CANTWELL: Where is big sis, ma?

MOTHER: Don't *ma* me! I can't appreciate your would-be jokes. Harriett's delivering some typing she did this morning for Attorney Brooks.

CANTWELL: That fat old jigaboo with the big Packard?

MOTHER: Cantwell! He's the only colored lawyer with an office downtown.

CANTWELL: I don't care where his office is, he doesn't pay Sis half enough for her work. Always wants something typed in a hurry, too. Then pays half price.

MOTHER: But maybe if Harriett's work pleases Mr. Brooks, he'll hire her permanently in his office.

CANTWELL: Not hardly! Mr. Brooks likes flashy office girls with lots of jive. I've been down there.

MOTHER: He might like an intelligent one for a change.

CANTWELL: Why don't you let Harriett go on and take that job with the Belt Brothers in their Real Estate Office?

MOTHER: I would if it were a genuine *real estate* office. But no member of this family'll ever work for that set of numbers writers. Real estate, just a blind!

CANTWELL: They pay good wages to the folks who work for them. One of the fellows in my class works for Belt's after school and earns nearly twenty dollars a week.

MOTHER: Well, you'll never work for them, nor Harriett, if I can help it.

CANTWELL: Where am I going to work this summer, then, Mother?

MOTHER: I don't know, but it won't be for a set of colored racketeers. I didn't move out here to a decent neighborhood to have my children running down on Boyle Avenue to the rats for a job.

CANTWELL: No, but we have to work somewhere. You've got this house to pay for yet. And I want to go to college next year, so if I get a good summer job, it'd help a lot. Sam Belt needs some young fellows, he says, in his restaurant, or in the office.

MOTHER: Restaurant? You call Belt's Bar a restaurant?

CANTWELL: Well, it the biggest colored business in town. You're always talking about colored folks doing something first class. He's

even got a crystal dance floor in the back. *(Dancing)* Hey! Hey! Aw!
    Boogie!

MOTHER: Cantwell, I think that's enough! You have an hour before
    supper. Put it in on your Latin, son.

CANTWELL: Aw, mom, I told Jerry Weinstein I'd be back down to the
    corner in a few minutes.

MOTHER: For what?

CANTWELL: Oh, just to talk over those sandlot games we're getting
    up the Saturday before graduation, before all the boys get summer
    jobs.

MOTHER: You couldn't have talked that over this afternoon?

CANTWELL: Might've, but I didn't!

MOTHER: That corner's getting awfully attractive to you lately! Mrs.
    Klein tells me the boys who congregate there have made insulting
    remarks to her daughter as she goes by, the young ruffians!

CANTWELL: Some of her own Jewish boyfriends flirting with her!
    Certainly wasn't me.

MOTHER: I trust not. You've been reared better.

CANTWELL: Besides, there're no colored girls out here for me to flirt
    with anyhow! That's the trouble with this old neighborhood. Not
    enough colored folks around.

MOTHER: You prefer Boyle Avenue, I suppose?

CANTWELL: Well, at least I don't have to learn Yiddish down there,
    or some other foreign brogue.

MOTHER: Cantwell, these are the very best of white people out here!

CANTWELL: Sure, I like 'em alright. But I don't ever remember any
    of these neighbors of ours inviting us over.

MOTHER: I trust we're not seeking their invitations?

CANTWELL: No, but when we lived downtown with the colored folks,
    we had more fun.

MOTHER: And less culture! Go study your Latin, Cantwell. We'll have
    supper soon as Harriett gets home.

CANTWELL: O.K. But I'm going out tonight.

MOTHER: Where?

CANTWELL: Just out!

    (Goes inside house. MOTHER shakes her head. The piano inside
    stops as the Big Brother passes)

LUCIA: *(Within)* Hy, heavy lover!

CANTWELL: Hy, Toots!

MOTHER: Children! Such vulgarity!

LUCIA: Oh, mother, that's just slang! I learned it from Cantwell.
>   (*Plays her exercises very loudly. MRS. HARPER plucks geranium leaves from the pots. From the street, HARRIETT enters*)

HARRIET: Hello, Mother!

MOTHER: Harriett, Honey!

HARRIETT: Here's some lovely lettuce for supper! The strike didn't seem to affect the downtown stores.

MOTHER: Thank God for that!

HARRIETT: But they're being picketed. When I came out, the nicest colored fellow stopped me and asked me why I went in.

MOTHER: The nerve of him stopping you!

HARRIETT: Well, I don't know—after he explained to me what it was all about! You see, the big wholesalers haven't lived up to their contract.

MOTHER: You mean this stranger told you this? You stopped and talked to him?

HARRIETT: Yes. . . . . . .

MOTHER: But suppose the police had come. Picketing's a crime, isn't it?

HARRIETT: No mother, not at all! It's legal, he said. The police have no right to break it up.

MOTHER: But they do. And they might've then.

HARRIETT: I know it. But those pickets are brave, mother. He had a scar on his arm from a police club yesterday.

MOTHER: Negroes are taking part in this strike, too, then?

HARRIETT: Yes! Lots of the warehouse helpers are colored. He said out of three thousand on strike, four or five hundred are colored.

MOTHER: Who is this *he* you keep speaking of?

HARRIETT: Well, he's a representative on the strike committee from his warehouse. He represents both colored and white men, mother! Isn't that wonderful? His union draws no color line. And they picket together.

MOTHER: Is he a communist?

HARRIETT: He doesn't look like one. He's a nice fellow, mother. He asked me to go with him to a public meeting tonight—the strikers are having.

MOTHER: He what?

HARRIETT: He asked me to go with him—so I said yes. I want to learn what it's all about, this strike.

MOTHER: You mean to say you're going out at night with a total stranger, Harriett?

HARRIETT: Mother! After all, I'm grown up. And he's perfectly charming to talk to—a gentleman.

MOTHER: That's what you think! Young lady, you'll remain home this evening. Mr. Butler's coming over to see you.

HARRIETT: *Us,* not me, mother! You know J. Donald's just like home folks, anyway, he comes so often. You two schoolteachers have a lot in common.

MOTHER: It's not me, darling. He's fond of *you,* Harriett. In fact he's in love with you.

HARRIETT: Oh, Mother!

MOTHER: He's just a shy young man afraid to ask you to marry him, that's all.

HARRIETT: He may be shy, but he's not so young. He taught eight years, didn't he tell us, before he came up here to graduate school to get his Ph.D. in psychology. So he can't be a baby!

MOTHER: He's just the right age for a man to marry and make a good husband. I know that! He's sowed his wild oats by now.

HARRIETT: If he ever had any!

MOTHER: Harriett! Mr. Butler's going to amount to something. In a few years more he may be dean of Tennessee State. And who knows, in due time president? His wife wouldn't have to worry, so think of that.

HARRIETT: But you do think she'd have much fun?

MOTHER: Fun?

HARRIETT: I don't think I'd like to be J. Donald's wife.

MOTHER: Why not?

HARRIETT: He's too—too, I don't know! Too smart, I guess. Besides, he dances like a white man.

MOTHER: You mean he doesn't go through all those vulgar convolutions you call the jitterbug! No. And I don't blame him. J. Donald's a gentleman, if there ever was one.

HARRIETT: And a scholar!

MOTHER: Honey, don't be sarcastic! You know what's in my mind?

HARRIETT: Yes, I know. A good marriage. You've talked so much about that, mother.

MOTHER: Well, hasn't it made an impression? Here's a young man coming every night to see you, so he must like you. He's well fixed. His college has given him a sabbatical scholarship. He has his career cut out for him. He'd give you a comfortable home, the best society. He's of a good family,—father a doctor in Nashville, mother of the Virginia Crawfords.

HARRIETT: But I'm not interested.

MOTHER: Do you want to be a typist all your life? Your chances, or anyone else's now, of getting in the school system here are pretty low, even with a Master's degree. They're laying off teachers, not hiring them. And colored teachers . . . . . .

HARRIETT: Are few in number anyway, I know. But I'm not afraid of work. I'll find something. Or maybe somebody that I love to marry not just *like,* like J. Donald.

MOTHER: But do you like him a little?

HARRIETT: Not much, to tell the truth.

MOTHER: You haven't talked with him as I have. He really has fine ideals, that man! He's a true servant of education. Those southern boys and girls must be proud to have him for a teacher.

HARRIETT: I don't doubt it, but I don't want him for a husband, mother!

MOTHER: *(Angrily)* Very well! But you needn't invite strange young men off the streets here to this house. Especially radicals with signs.

HARRIETT: You don't think he'd bring his sign with him, do you?

MOTHER: He might. I'll talk to him when he comes.

HARRIETT: We'll both talk to him. He'll do us all good.

MOTHER: You'll remain inside, young lady.

HARRIETT: You mean we won't ask him in?

MOTHER: He'll get no farther than this porch. And I'll talk to him.

HARRIETT: Oh, mother! Our house is surely not that exclusive, is it?

MOTHER: I'll meet him here.

HARRIETT: But I'll ask him in.

MOTHER: This is my house, Harriett!

CANTWELL: *(Calling)* Ma, when're we gonna eat? My Latin's done.

MOTHER: I'll go over it with you after supper, line by line. We'll fix the food now. Lucia, set the table darling! *(Opening the door)* Harriett, wash the salad. The beans are done. Come on, let's slice the bread.

> *(They go inside. A young MAN enters, searching for a house number. He is a heavy-set, muscular young man, dressed in what might be a cross between a working suit and his Sunday-best. He wears no tie. He is good-looking and strong. He rings the bell. HARRIETT comes to the door)*

KENNETH: Howdy-do!

HARRIETT: Oh! I wasn't expecting you so soon. I—I—we haven't had supper yet.

KENNETH: Neither have I, but I thought we'd grab a sandwich on the run. I meant to tell you the meeting's early, and if we don't get there beforehand, we might not get a seat.

HARRIETT: You mean that great big Convention Hall will be full?

KENNETH: Sure, all the union workers in town'll turn out. It'll be a solid sender of a meeting. Irving speaking! And Granich! And some of the big officials.

HARRIETT: Any colored speakers?

KENNETH: I don't think so. But some might speak from the floor. I might even say a few words myself!

HARRIETT: You wouldn't be afraid?

KENNETH: Naw, I ain't afraid. I can holler as loud as any of the rest of 'em. And I got something to holler for, too. I'm gonna tell 'em if they'd just organize all the colored workers all over town, and the unemployed too, then there wouldn't be these colored strike-breakers coming in on us—even if they are offering them eight dollars a day.

HARRIETT: Are they trying to break your strike? That wasn't in the papers.

KENNETH: The papers don't print half of what they know. The bosses'll try anything to win—even to hiring Negroes where a Negro never worked before!

HARRIETT: Then there might be fights—even riots.

KENNETH: Might be. But there won't be race riots this time. The white workers know that not all Negroes are scabs. Besides, they've got plenty white scabs of their own. But come on, get yourself together, Miss—er—

HARRIETT: Harper.

KENNETH: Harper, and let's go!

HARRIETT: Sit down just a minute there in the porch swing. It's so hot inside. I'll see if I can arrange it.

KENNETH: You mean you might not go?

HARRIETT: Well, you see, it's so early. And supper's waiting. I'll see my mother. *(Enter CANTWELL)* Cantwell, this is Mr. er—er—

KENNETH: Mason.

HARRIETT: Mr. Mason, my brother, Cantwell Harper. *(Exits inside.)*

CANTWELL: Glad to know you, Mr. Mason. What do you think about the new baseball season?

KENNETH: Well, I haven't thought much. You see, we're on strike.

CANTWELL: Gee, you're one of those reds?

KENNETH: What do you mean, red?

CANTWELL: I mean, well—er—er, striking and things like that, the papers always say red . . . . . .

KENNETH: Sure, but who owns the papers?

CANTWELL: Who?

KENNETH: The big guys who live off the things we make, and pack, and load—but don't own. The boss pays for the ads, so the papers side with the bosses, not with us.

CANTWELL: Oh!

KENNETH: You see? They call us reds just to kid the people into thinking we're a lot of old time Russian bomb throwers. Do I look like an old time Russian?

CANTWELL: You don't look like an old time, or a new time Russian, either, Mr.—er—er—

KENNETH: Mason. No, I'm just a Boyle Avenue jig. But I'm one jig with a union label.

CANTWELL: Which union?

KENNETH: Warehouse and Truckmen's Union.

CANTWELL: What do you do?

KENNETH: When I'm working I carry hundred-pound boxes around all day from the packing room to the loading platform.

CANTWELL: Boxes of what?

KENNETH: Radio parts, where I work now.

CANTWELL: No wonder you look like an athlete! You'd make a good football blocker.

KENNETH: Used to play in high school. But I had to quit and go to work.

CANTWELL: Too bad. You might have made All-American.

KENNETH: Yeah, but if you ain't got no people, it's hard staying in school.

CANTWELL: I guess it is. My old man's dead, so I know a little about it, trying to get through, and go to college.

KENNETH: Who helps you?

CANTWELL: My mother. She's a school teacher. Say, you know where I can get a job this summer?

KENNETH: Things is pretty tight, fellow! I don't know.

CANTWELL: That editorial last night on the front page of the STAR said your strike wouldn't help things any, either. Said it made 'em worse.

KENNETH: Aw, the papers! Sure, *they* say strikes make depressions, even. But it's the other way around. Don't they teach you anything about causes and effect in school?

CANTWELL: Sure, in physics, but not about strikes. Say, er. . . .

(MOTHER appears, followed by HARRIETT)

MOTHER: Cantwell, your supper's on the table. You and Lucia go ahead and eat. Harriett and I'll be there.

CANTWELL: O. K., mom. What I like is food and more food. I'd have an even better appetite if it wasn't for Latin. *(Exits)*

HARRIETT: Mother, this is Mr. Mason!. . . . Mrs. Harper!

KENNETH: Glad to know you. *(Offers hand. Gingerly received)*

MOTHER: How-do-you-do, Mr. Mason? My daughter tells me you've come to take her to some kind of meeting tonight.

KENNETH: Yes, Mrs. Harper, I'd like to take her.

MOTHER: But I think otherwise, Mr. Mason.

KENNETH: Oh! I'm sorry! But I thought she was grown, I mean old enough, I—

HARRIETT: He means he thought I was a grown woman, mother, as I am!

MOTHER: You're in my house, Harriett, and under my care until you marry, if it's fifty years from now. Now, Mr. Mason, since my daughter is not going out with a person she's just met a few hours ago in the street and personally I don't know why you should presume to ask her—I must request you to excuse us while we have our supper.

KENNETH: Oh, all right!

(He starts to leave. HARRIETT stops him)

HARRIETT: But it's not all right, Mr. Mason! Wait! I am going with you! I want to attend that union meeting. I want to learn something about what's going on. *(In a low voice)* I don't want to be bossed around forever, mother. I'm going with Mr. Mason.

MOTHER: Harriett! Go in the house!

KENNETH: Jimmynee! Wait a minute. I don't want to break up your home life, Miss Harper. Maybe your mother don't understand. Listen, I'm not a dangerous guy, Mrs. Harper. I'm just a young fellow who works for a living like all the rest—that have jobs. I saw your daughter coming out of that big food store downtown that's trying to break the union. So I said to myself, gee, us colored folks sure ought to be in favor of better working conditions, if anybody is,—so maybe she just don't understand, which she didn't! So I went up to her and told her in a nice way what it was we was striking for, didn't I, Miss—er—er—Harper?

HARRIETT: That's right! You were perfectly polite.

KENNETH: And we got into a little conversation, and I saw that she was a nice girl. If I might say it, meaning no freshness, Mrs. Harper—just the nice kind of fine girl I've always been wanting to meet.

MOTHER: And by that, you mean just what?

KENNETH: Well, you see, Mrs. Harper, down where I live on Boyle Avenue—

HARRIETT: We lived there too, once!

MOTHER: Twelve years ago! Then it was different.

KENNETH: Down there, you see, well, it's mostly poor people and they don't have a chance to teach their girls nothing. I don't mean they aren't nice, sometimes, but well, anyhow, *(Embarrassed, hurriedly)* what I mean is, Mrs. Harper, I think you've got a daughter any mother would be proud to have. That's what I think.

MOTHER: Thank you for your opinion, Mr. Mason. That still doesn't change my mind about the proprieties.

KENNETH: The what?

MOTHER: The proprieties.

KENNETH: Oh! *(Puzzled)* Well, I certainly will respect your daughter, Mrs. Mason, if that's what you mean. We couldn't go wrong in a public meeting, anyhow, could we?

MOTHER: We?

KENNETH: I mean me!

HARRIETT: *(Taking KENNETH's arm)* Mother, I'll be back early. By eleven surely . . . . . . Let's go!

MOTHER: Harriett! You'll not go a step!

HARRIETT: Come on, Mr. Mason?

> *(KENNETH turns and looks appealingly at the mother. HARRI-ETT takes his arms and almost pulls him away. They exit. MRS. HARPER stands blazing with fury. LUCIA and CANTWELL appear at the door)*

MOTHER: Harriett! Harriett! . . . . . . Harriett!

LUCIA: *(Maliciously)* So the angel of the family's doing wrong for once!

MOTHER: Go in that house and eat your supper.

> *(THEY disappear within. MRS. HARPER looks off down the street)*

CURTAIN

Act I, Scene 2

SETTING: *The same. Late evening.*

ACTION: *MRS. HARPER sits in the porch swing talking to J. DONALD BUTLER who occupies a chair near the lighted window.*

DONALD: It's God, Mrs. Harper! It's God that's lacking in all these modern theories of education. And that's where the white folks up North fall short. They don't have anything about God in their text books.

MOTHER: That's true, J. Donald. But up here where we have so many different nationalities and creeds in our schools . . . . . .

DONALD: That doesn't matter, Mrs. Harper. In the final analysis, we all have the same God. In our Southern Colleges, we teach Him, too. We don't get so modern down there, we can't teach Him and His Word.

MOTHER: That should be done.

DONALD: You know, when I was younger, I really wanted to be a preacher. I rather liked to hear myself talk. And I've always been clean in character, mind, and body.

MOTHER: Why didn't you take up the ministry, J. Donald?

DONALD: Well, I realized, to tell the truth, that there's no money in it—unless you're a Baptist.

MOTHER: And your family's Presbyterian.

DONALD: Yes. For me to be a Baptist minister would break my mother's heart. She never did like the Baptists.

MOTHER: The Presbyterian services are simpler, purer, more dignified, of course.

DONALD: That's right. But perhaps it's all for the best I went into teaching instead. I couldn't be going out to dances, as I do from time to time if I were a minister.

MOTHER: Certainly not in the Baptist church!

DONALD: And especially since I've been up North here, and met your daughter, I find dancing quite a pleasure.

MOTHER: In moderation, it is a pleasure. Tell me, what formal is it you're asking Harriett to attend next week?

DONALD: The Kappa's annual Spring dance—if she'll go with me.

MOTHER: Of course she will. She enjoys going out with you. Why don't you ask her more often, J. Donald?

DONALD: My studies, Mrs. Harper. It certainly isn't that I've been going out with anyone else.

MOTHER: There are so few nice girls in town!

DONALD: Ordinary, ordinary, most of them! Loud, uncultured, wild! That's what I like about Harriett, she's not that way.

MOTHER: She's a home girl. I keep my children close to me.

DONALD: That's right.

MOTHER: *(Proudly)* Then we have the advantage of this neighborhood. I moved out here for the sake of them.

DONALD: You've done a wonderful thing buying this house, and putting three children through school all by yourself.

MOTHER: It's been a struggle, J. Donald! But I've done it! Thirteen years next month, my husband's been dead.

DONALD: That long?

MOTHER: That long! But I was determined to bring up my children right. To tell the truth, I've mothered and fathered them both, fed them, clothed them, taught them, prayed with them—now I'm proud of them. Harriett through college—if this depression hadn't come on, she would have had a position! Cantwell graduating from High School next month. Lucia, her last year in Junior High, bright as a dollar, excellent at the piano, too.

DONALD: You're a remarkable woman, Mrs. Harper, a remarkable woman.

MOTHER: And I'm not selfish about them, either. I want my children to marry, have homes of their own—but I want them to marry well.

DONALD: They owe it to you, and themselves.

MOTHER: A doctor, a lawyer, a teacher like yourself. That's why I keep them off of Boyle Avenue, out of that district full of common Negroes.

DONALD: Your children would hardly find associates among that group.

MOTHER: You'd be surprised how indiscriminating young people are, especially now-a-days. They seem to be bored with nice people, nice music, nice anything. Of course, I can't say I have that trouble with mine, J. Donald, especially not Harriett.

DONALD: She's pure gold.

MOTHER: Although she's a bit strange at times. Harriett's a dreamer, that's what she is. She used to love fairy stories, knights on a white horse, Romeo and Juliet, J. Donald, she needs someone to bring her back to earth.

DONALD: I could do that.

MOTHER: Sometimes she doesn't seem to understand where her place is as a young girl from a good family. Today she got so terribly interested in the strike situation, for instance, that she felt she just had to learn more about it—so she's gone to a strike meeting! Now, we all know that's no field for a well-bred young lady. But the child's trying to find an outlet for herself, some way to help humanity, J. Donald. I wish the city schools were employing new teachers. That would solve all this.

DONALD: She ought to go South. The colored race needs her down there—and they pay well, too, on some campuses.

MOTHER: Why don't you suggest that to her? If she could get a good teaching position in the South . . . . . .

DONALD: I'll take her back with me next year.

MOTHER: Take her back with you! Why, J. Donald!

DONALD: I mean, marry her, if she'll let me. Then she could teach at my college. $2,000 a year, eventually—maybe! I'll be Dean of Men, shortly, no doubt, $3,000 a year. In no time at all we'd be prosperous, no time at all.

MOTHER: You'd make an excellent couple, J. Donald, you two!

DONALD: I think so myself. But every time I mention love to Harriett, she seems to feel it's funny.

MOTHER: She's just embarrassed, being a pure girl.

DONALD: She giggles.

MOTHER: Oh, J. Donald! Girls do giggle when they don't know what else to do. But you know, faint heart never won fair lady! Press the question.

DONALD: I'll ask her again tonight—if she ever gets home.

MOTHER: She'll be here directly, I'm sure. She ought to be here now. You don't think those workers could've started a riot?

DONALD: I don't know anything about workers, Mrs. Harper. But I do know I've got to get back to the "Y" and do some studying. Quiz in Educational Psychology IV Monday. And since that course cost me $65, I can't afford to flunk it.

MOTHER: *(Rising and looking down the street)* Suppose you step in and have a cup of chocolate. It's still a little cool for porches. Come on out in the kitchen with me while I make it.

DONALD: We college men are always hungry.

MOTHER: Maybe we can get a symphony on the radio later. Between the static and the strike news, I had to turn the philharmonic off just before you came. Beethoven's Ninth, too!

DONALD: I'm fond of the "Poet and Peasant," aren't you, Mrs. Harper? It's a lovely piece.

MOTHER: Lovely! Lovely! I adore classical music, but I can't abide jam! Nothing later than the waltz, really, for dancing for me.

DONALD: Swing, no doubt, is all right in its place—which isn't in the home, however.

MOTHER: That's what I try to tell Cantwell, but he's always tuning in on Count Basie—annoying Lucia.

DONALD: Where is Lucia?

MOTHER: Upstairs crying because I wouldn't allow her to go to some birthday party a girl I've never heard of is having. Lucia's usually more selective in her associates.

DONALD: She's just at that age, where the brook and river meet.

MOTHER: Yes, but she appreciates my control. Come in, let's make the chocolate.

(DONALD holds the door open as MOTHER exits. He looks at his wristwatch)

DONALD: I'll have to eat and run! It's late. Nearly ten-thirty.

(Also exits into house. Their voices fade away within)

MOTHER: Early to bed, early to rise, make a man healthy, wealthy and . . .

(Slowly down the street come KENNETH and HARRIETT. They stop at the steps. HARRIETT offers her hand. KENNETH holds it as he talks)

HARRIETT: It was wonderful Kenneth. I've never been so excited in my life, all those working people, so sincere, so vast, so. . . .

KENNETH: I'm glad you went with me, Harriett. But do you have to go in now? We could sit here a while on the porch, couldn't we, and talk?

HARRIETT: Not tonight, Kenneth! It's late. My mother says it doesn't look right to the neighbors sitting on the porch so late.

KENNETH: Gee, I'm glad I met you! Listen, I'll be out tomorrow. We don't picket on Sundays, so we'll go. . . . If I just had some money, say, we'd rent a boat and go rowing in the park!

HARRIETT: I've got enough to rent a boat, if that's all.

KENNETH: Hell! I don't want to take a girl out on her own money, the first time.

HARRIET: Well, let's just go and walk in the park. All the buds are coming out. It's spring!

(THEY sit on the steps in the moonlight)

KENNETH: Yes, it's spring . . . . . . Gee, Harriett, you're pretty!

HARRIETT: Do you think so?

KENNETH: Yes, I do.

HARRIETT: *(Slowly)* Kenneth, you're like something out of a book to me. The way I met you and all. It doesn't seem real!

KENNETH: Like the movies?

HARRIETT: Yes, like the movies. Or a dream!

KENNETH: What do you mean, a dream? I'm real! I'm no ghost.

HARRIETT: No, not a ghost—but you're like a knight in armour, a big strong knight coming to a damsel in distress, right out of English literature—like Lancelot, Kenneth!

KENNETH: I don't what you're talking about . . . . . . But kiss me!

HARRIETT: Not now! Not tonight!

KENNETH: Then stop calling me names! What do you mean, Lancelot? Who'd he pitch for?

HARRIETT: Tennyson! Like in the old days when knights rode white horses, and the women in cold castles waved at them from high windows. You see, Kenneth, I'm like one of those women—believe it or not—lost in a big lonely house, who doesn't know what to do. Now, here you come opening up a new world for me—the world you showed me tonight, where a battle's to be fought and won. At least, I can stand on the sidelines and cheer.

KENNETH: That sounds like football. But come on, kiss me, kid!

HARRIETT: You see, we live way out here in this white neighborhood, sort of marooned like, and proper, and lonesome . . . . . . I'm glad I met you, Kenneth.

KENNETH: Then kiss me.

> *(She resists a moment. Then a long kiss at the foot of the steps. In the doorway MRS. HARPER appears with DONALD. She drops her cup of chocolate in amazement)*

MOTHER: Harriett!

> *(They come on to the porch)*

HARRIETT: Yes, mother?

DONALD: Who is that man?

KENNETH: Good evening!

MOTHER: Harriett, I'll speak to you in the parlor. *(She holds door open)*

HARRIETT: Yes, mother. Goodnight, Kenneth.

KENNETH: *(Reluctantly releasing her hand)* Goodnight! I'll see you tomorrow.

HARRIETT: Yes! At three, tomorrow.

KENNETH: At three.

MOTHER: You're not welcome here again, young man!

DONALD: You certainly are not!

MOTHER: Neither tomorrow, nor any other time.

HARRIETT: I'll be waiting for you, Kenneth.

KENNETH: Then I'll be here, tomorrow! Goodnight, everybody.
>   *(He exits. HARRIETT goes up the steps to the porch)*

DONALD: No telling what disease you can catch—kissing strangers! Harriett, who is that man?

HARRIETT: My knight on a white horse!

DONALD: Your knight?

HARRIETT: Yes, my brownskin knight—with a picket sign!

MOTHER: Rubbish! Come in this house, Harriett!
>   *(MOTHER holds the door open as HARRIETT exits within, followed by the MOTHER)*

HARRIETT: Goodnight, J. Donald

Donald grabs his hat angrily as the

CURTAIN FALLS

Act II, Scene 1

SETTING: *The same. Sunset. Fourth of July. The flag is out. MRS. HARPER, dressed for a garden party, comes onto the porch and looks anxiously up and down. She has a wicker basket and a package in her arms. Her neighbor's door is heard closing. The voice of MRS. KLEIN comes across the yard.*

MRS. KLEIN: Goink out, Mrs. Harper?

MOTHER: Yes, Mrs. Klein. Our club's annual Fourth of July supper's this evening, on Dr. Hawkins' lawn.

MRS. KLEIN: Oh, out-doors supper? That's nice! It's too hot to be in house tonight. My husband, he just made up mind to take me for little ride. It's so hot.

MOTHER: You ought to ride by and see Dr. Hawkins' lawn. It's beautifully hung with Japanese lanterns, and we're having special fireworks a little later.

MRS. KLEIN: Wonderful! Maybe me and Mr. Klein ride past and look.

MOTHER: Dr. Hawkins has the most beautiful Negro home in the city!

MRS. KLEIN: My! I would like to see it. *(Sputtering of car is heard)* There comes Mr. Klein now backing out garage. Maybe we can give you lift where you are goink?

MOTHER: Now, that would be nice, Mrs. Klein, but I was just trying to wait and see if any of my children would get home before I leave. Lucia's to play a piano solo on the program tonight.

MRS. KLEIN: All your children out enjoyink holiday, I suppose?

MOTHER: At some picnic the young folks have at Riverdale Park. One of the church clubs. But certainly they ought to be home by now, or else I'll have to go on without them.

MRS. KLEIN: Don't they know to come?

MOTHER: Oh, yes, no doubt they'll be along later. There's no food for them here, so they'll have to come to the party for supper.

MRS. KLEIN: Then why don't you let us give you a lift? We ain't goink no place special, just ridink.

MOTHER: Thank you, I believe I will! I've so much to carry. I'm lending them my silver and some dishes tonight. Just let me lock my door. *(She locks door)*

MRS. KLEIN: I believe in neighbors beink neighbors, like in old country.

MOTHER: I do, too, Mrs. Klein.

MRS. KLEIN: I always say, no matter what color, a human is a human.

MOTHER: You're right, Mrs. Klein.

MRS. KLEIN: *(To her husband)* Herman, open that back door. Mrs. Harper is goink with us a piece. And don't back no further up on my nasturtiums. What's matter, you don't see good?

MOTHER: *(As she exits)* How kind of you, Mr. Klein! It's not far, but to walk in this heat . . . .

MRS. KLEIN: Just get right in, Mrs. Harper. . . .

> *(Car doors close. Noise of motor, dying in the distance. Enter CAN-TWELL and LUCIA)*

CANTWELL: Looks like nobody home. I guess mama's gone.

LUCIA: She'll be mad, too, if we don't get over there soon.

CANTWELL: Aw, who wants to go to any old lawn supper, anyway? Lots of old dicties!

LUCIA: Why, Cantwell! We've got to go, it's a nice supper. Anyhow, so we might as well wash up a little and go on. Let me just sit here a minute in the swing and cool off. *(LUCIA sits in the porch swing, CANTWELL on the steps)* Say, you don't think Harriett'll bring that warehouse boy-friend of hers to the lawn party, do you?

CANTWELL: Wouldn't Mom raise sand, if she did? Oh, boy!

LUCIA: Anyway, J. Donald'll be there.

CANTWELL: Be there? He's supposed to call for Harriett right here at eight. I heard her tell him *yes* the other day.

LUCIA: Oh, so you've been listening in on your sister's conversations! Well, she'd better hurry up and get here, and leave Kenneth at the picnic.

CANTWELL: I'd like to see those two bozos meet—Kenneth and Donald! I bet there'd be a nice argument.

LUCIA: J. Donald's no trouble.

CANTWELL: But he does get to roaring pretty loud sometimes around here when he and Mother get together on the subject of who isn't who in colored society.

LUCIA: You mean on who *is* who—because J. Donald's from one of the best families in the South.

CANTWELL: So are we, on Mother's side, but who cares?

LUCIA: Cantwell! I agree with mother. After all, Harriett has no business going around with a fellow like Kenneth, even if he is nice looking.

CANTWELL: Boy! But can that guy play baseball? Did you see him pitching this afternoon out at the picnic? Man, I wish I had his curves.

LUCIA: I don't like baseball.

CANTWELL: Harriett does.

LUCIA: You mean she likes the pitcher. But if she's got any sense, she'll listen to mother and forget all about Kenneth—on vacation so long—or strike as he calls it—he hasn't even got fifty cents to pay for a taxi from the end of the carline to the park.

CANTWELL: Aw, if you were in love, you'd rather walk, too, and get there slow.

LUCIA: I may *be* in love, for all you know. But somebody in this family has to be discreet!

CANTWELL: Well, well, well!

LUCIA: If I was a boy, I certainly wouldn't be seen mooning around that funny-looking old girl you were with this afternoon—even if you did graduate in the same class.

CANTWELL: Say, you and mother both make me sick sometimes. That girl's all right! Just because she don't belong in the colored blue-book. . . . . . .

LUCIA: O.K. Go ahead! Let her lead you around by the nose if you want to, for all I care. I bet you'd better not bring her home though.

CANTWELL: Don't worry, I won't. We can find better places than home to go.

LUCIA: Why, Cantwell! That's not a very nice thing to say.

CANTWELL: I wish we lived back down on Boyle Avenue, anyhow.

LUCIA: I'm going to tell Mother!

CANTWELL: Oh, go on in and wash your nose! We might as well start out to the Hawkins' party and get it over with. I got a date by and by. *(Rising)* I'm going down to the corner and get a pack of butts.

LUCIA: If mother ever finds out you're smoking . . . . .

CANTWELL: Maybe she'll find out tonight. I'm liable to show up on Dr. Hawkins' lawn with a firecracker in my mouth.

LUCIA: *(In doorway)* Say, Cantwell, should I wear my little blue dimity or the dotted Swiss? Which do you like best?

CANTWELL: Wear a Russian blouse!

LUCIA: You're not funny! *(Exits into house)*

CANTWELL: *(Searching in his pockets and counting his change)* Whee! I need a quarter more!

(He empties all his pockets as KENNETH and HARRIETT enter)

KENNETH: Look at old home-run Cantwell! How many did you make, man?

CANTWELL: Wouldn't't've made one if you'd been pitching on their side. Boy! The way you fanned them out!

KENNETH: Just fooling around with you guys today! You ought to see me when I'm really warmed up, man!

CANTWELL: Hey, when that tall yellow boy hit that two-bagger and you . . . . .

HARRIETT: Say, listen! Once you two start baseball, you'll never hush. Mother's expecting you at the party, isn't she, Cantwell? Has Lucia gone?

CANTWELL: Upstairs primping! I'm going down the street a minute. Phone call to make.

HARRIETT: Your phone calls take hours. Don't forget, mother wants you two kids there early—you to help out with the tables and Lucia to arrange the music or something. I'll be there later. Hurry on, will you, Cantwell?

CANTWELL: All right, Sis, don't get excited! I'll be back in a little while. See you later, Kenneth!

(CANTWELL exits. HARRIETT and KENNETH sit on the steps. The sunset fades to dusk)

KENNETH: Do you just have to go to that lawn party? We've been on a picnic all day! You ought to have enough fresh air.

HARRIETT: I've got to go, Kenneth! It's mother's favorite club.

KENNETH: You wouldn't ask me to go with you, would you?

HARRIETT: Please, Kenneth! I'd let you take me anywhere—but you know you and mother don't get along two minutes.

KENNETH: I don't mind your mother. I treat her like a lady, and always will. But that so-and-so of a J. Donald—I'll punch him in his snout!

HARRIETT: What did you promise me, Kenneth? That you wouldn't start a row with any of mother's friends, didn't you?

KENNETH: I won't. Not with your mother's friends.

HARRIETT: Meaning . . . . . . ?

KENNETH: Meaning, your *mother's* friends.

HARRIETT: J. Donald's nothing to me, Kenneth. You know that.

KENNETH: But he's always around.

HARRIETT: That's more than can be said about you. I know you're busy with your strike, and union meetings, and all—but I could stand a little more of you.

KENNETH: When I *am* around, all I get's the porch swing. But J. Donald's always inside, like somebody's house dog.

HARRIETT: Let's not start that again, Kenneth, dear! After all, this is mother's house, and until we get the money to get married and have a home of our own . . . . .

KENNETH: We could start out in a furnished room, Harriett, right now.

HARRIETT: I'd be willing. Your room's big enough for me. But, I guess—at least, I always did think a girl owed something to her mother, too. And my mother's worked so hard, Kenneth, all alone since my father died, to bring us up. She's almost paid for this house. I want to work and help her until it is paid for.

KENNETH: We could both help her, and be together, too! I'll start making good money again, once this strike is settled, and we've won.

HARRIETT: But it looks like you won't win.

KENNETH: We won't go back until we do win. Our demands are just enough!

HARRIETT: I know that, but the Mayor doesn't think so, nor the city council. They're going to break the strike with troops, if they have to. It was on the radio this morning.

KENNETH: I know! The radio called us all kinds of un-American names today—in honor of the Fourth. But if they send a mob of thugs and strike-breakers into our warehouse, well—this arm's good for something else besides throwing a baseball.

HARRIETT: Kenneth, honey, don't get in trouble! Don't get hurt!

KENNETH: Hurt? Trouble? Don't you call being on strike three months trouble enough already? And don't you think I've ever been hurt? I didn't come up easy, kid. I'm not afraid.

HARRIETT: But I don't want you to be hurt, Kenneth! If something happens to you, I couldn't bear it.

KENNETH: You mean—you love me that much?

HARRIETT: I love you that much, besides . . . . . .

KENNETH: Golly! Then I've got to look out for myself! Come on, kiss me!

HARRIETT: For what?

KENNETH: For fun!

HARRIETT: Is being in love fun?

KENNETH: Don't you think so?

HARRIETT: *(Slowly)* Yes! I think so.

KENNETH: Then kiss me.

HARRIETT: Not here on the front porch.

KENNETH: Shall we go inside?

HARRIETT: I have to go, Kenneth, in no time at all.

KENNETH: Right this minute?

HARRIETT: Well, no, not exactly. Not right this minute, but . . . . . .

KENNETH: Then . . .

HARRIETT: Let's go sit under the apple trees in the back yard. You haven't seen our back yard, have you? Mother's pretty proud of it— rustic bench, grape arbor, three big fruit trees, nice green grass—not at all like ordinary back yards.

KENNETH: Never seen it, but I'd like to see it.

HARRIETT: Come on, I'll show it to you.

> *(They exit around the house. CANTWELL enters smoking a ciga-rette glowing in the dark. He sits on the steps and counts his change again. Shrugs his shoulders and lies down, his back on the porch. He hums a tune from a popular song between puffs of his cigarette. Suddenly there is a girl's scream within. Hasty footsteps on the stairs. LUCIA comes running through the screen door)*

LUCIA: Oh! Oh—oo-o! Cantwell! There's somebody in the back yard. I hear a man in the garden. Some robber's trying to get in the house! Oh! I'm scared to death! O-oo-o!

CANTWELL: Calm down! What would he get if he got in? He wouldn't want you!

LUCIA: There's really somebody out there! Go, look quick, brother!

CANTWELL: Trying to put me on the spot, huh?

LUCIA: Don't play, Cantwell! Go see what it is! Please!

CANTWELL: Probably just Harriett and her star pitcher playing ball.

LUCIA: *(Indignantly)* Harriett wouldn't be in the back garden with a man at night. You know she wouldn't. She isn't home yet anyway.

CANTWELL: Yes, she is home, too. I'll bet they're trying out that little old rustic love-seat. Anyhow, I'll go see.

LUCIA: *(Half crying)* Be careful, Cantwell! Call if you need me.
   (LUCIA walks nervously back and forth across the porch. Suddenly there is a burst of laughter from the rear of the house. LUCIA pauses in her tracks. CANTWELL re-enters through the house)

CANTWELL: I told you, just your big sister and her sepia knight, Mr. Mason!

LUCIA: *(Shocked)* Oh! Isn't that awful!

CANTWELL: What's so awful about it? The moon's shining.

LUCIA: Mother would die if she knew.

CANTWELL: Who's going to tell her?

LUCIA: Don't look at me like that, Cantwell. You haven't any sense of the proprieties at all!

CANTWELL: Whee! *(As footsteps are heard)* Look who's coming!
   (Enter J. DONALD in a white suit, carrying a panama. His eye-glasses gleam in the moonlight)

DONALD: Hello! Ready for the lawn party, Lucia?

CANTWELL: Where'd you get the ice-cream suit, J. Donald? Let me turn on the light and look at you, man!
   (CANTWELL switches on porch light and reveals J. DONALD in all his summer splendor)

DONALD: Just got a report on my exams the other day. I came out so well—all A's but one—so I thought I'd treat myself to a suit.

CANTWELL: Looks swell, fellow! What kind of material is that?

DONALD: Gabardine, white gabardine.

CANTWELL: *(Obviously manufacturing conversation as he opens door)* That sort of material costs a lot, doesn't it, J. Donald? Come on in and sit down.

DONALD: Well, it's not cheap, gabardine! Say, where's. . . .

CANTWELL: I hear an all white suit's hard to keep clean, too.

DONALD: Yes, rather, I believe. Say, where is Harriett?

LUCIA: *(Bursting)* She's. . . . . . .

CANTWELL: She's upstairs dressing. I'll go tell her you're here. Come on inside.

LUCIA: She's not dressing, J. Donald! She's out in the back yard with a— a—

DONALD: What?

LUCIA: With a man!

DONALD: A man? What man?

LUCIA: Kenneth! And you ought to stop it!

DONALD: That—that red trouble maker? He must know your mother's away, to come sneaking around like this. I'll get him out of here. Hold my hat, Lucia.

> *(LUCIA takes his hat. Exit DONALD inside through house. CANTWELL looks at his sister in disgust)*

CANTWELL: What did you have to blab that for? You stupid little dope! *(Exits within)*

LUCIA: Cantwell Harper!

> *(Laughter and voices approach. LUCIA goes nervously to side railing and listens. She draws back. HARRIETT and KENNETH enter around the house)*

HARRIETT: . . . . great big hard apples on that biggest tree! When they're ripe, we'll shake 'em down and make cider, just for us.

LUCIA: Mr. Butler's looking for you, Harriett!

HARRIETT: Where?

LUCIA: In the back yard.

HARRIETT: What's J. Donald doing looking for me out there?

LUCIA: That's where you were, isn't it?

KENNETH: What's J. Donald doing *living*, I'd like to know? He's always here.

HARRIETT: I told you he was escorting me to the lawn party tonight, Kenneth.

KENNETH: *(Joking)* Huh! I just *take* you places—but he "escorts" you.

HARRIETT: Run along, Kenneth, darling! You know there's nothing between J. Donald and I. And there is between us.

KENNETH: Sure, I know it! I'm just kidding. Guess I've had enough of the sweetest girl in the world, for one day, anyhow. And after what you've just told me! Boy! You couldn't kiss me again, could you?

HARRIETT: *(Brushing his lips lightly)* Sure, there now, run along. I've got to dress.

KENNETH: Goodnight!

HARRIETT: Goodnight, Ken, dear! *(KENNETH exits)* Lucia, aren't you going to mother's party?

LUCIA: Yes, I'm going.

(DONALD comes to the door within and stops)

HARRIETT: Then you'd better run ahead! You and Cantwell, or else you'll be too late to be of any use. I'll be along directly. I must go in and dress. *(HARRIETT starts into house and runs face to face with J. DONALD in doorway, coming out)* Hello, J. Donald!

DONALD: Where's that fellow?

HARRIETT: You mean Kenneth? He's just gone!

DONALD: Must be afraid! Running away from me, heh?

HARRIETT: He didn't even know you were here, J. Donald.

DONALD: Harriett! I want to talk to you, please, before we go.

HARRIETT: Lucia, dear, would you mind? You ought to go now, anyway.

(LUCIA exits within)

DONALD: That's one way of trying to hurt me, isn't it, Harriett—telling me Kenneth isn't aware of my existence?

HARRIETT: It's not that, J. Donald. Of course he knows you . . . But he didn't know you were here now.

DONALD: Well, maybe he didn't, but I am here anyway. And *I'm* in love with you, too, Harriett. I've told you so before, and I've tried to prove it to you—but maybe you don't understand. Or maybe you don't care.

HARRIETT: But I—I'm . . .

DONALD: If you don't understand, I'll tell you all over again, plainer than I did before—because if you don't care now, maybe I can. . . . make you care. I'll try, for I'm too much in love to give you up to somebody else—especially when that somebody else couldn't possibly help you, or do your life any good. . . . . . .

HARRIETT: J. Donald, listen! Mother's led you on about me. I know, but that hasn't been my fault, has it? I like you. You're good company to go out with, sometimes, some places. But I don't love you, and I've said that before. We might as well start understanding each other clearly, very clearly. We have to now. I like you, and I don't want to hurt you, but maybe if you realized how I feel . . .

DONALD: I do realize. You think you love Kenneth . . . .

HARRIETT: I know I love Kenneth!

DONALD: How do you know?

HARRIETT: Love is something you don't have to *know*, Donald. You only have to feel it here in your heart, and all through your body. You feel it, like—like—moonlight in your blood, like sunshine in the morning.

DONALD: I feel like that toward you, Harriett. Only you express it better than I know how to.

HARRIETT: I'm sorry you're in love with me, Donald.

DONALD: I'm not sorry. Even if I did get a B in that lab exam, my only B in a straight A record, I got it because all that day when the quiz was held, I kept thinking about you instead. I couldn't get my mind off you. *(Meekly)* And my body felt like sunshine and moonlight, too.

(CANTWELL and LUCIA enter from the house)

CANTWELL: Cut out the poetry! We're off to the lawn fete.

LUCIA: You two had better come on, too, Harriett, right now.

HARRIETT: We'll be there, soon as I can change my dress.

CANTWELL: We'll dig you!

(He and LUCIA exit down the street)

HARRIETT: *(Kindly)* Don't be in love with me, J. Donald.

DONALD: I am! And when a person's sun and moon has no world to shine on, then what?

HARRIETT: I don't know then what, J. Donald.

DONALD: Anyway, I wanted to tell you, Harriett—I just want to tell you that if—that when—well, I mean if—you're young, this is the first time you've been in love maybe—you'll get over it! Five or six months, and ended. I'll wait for you. I'll be right here.

HARRIETT: You mean you think I'll get over being in love with Kenneth? No, I won't, J. Donald—not even after we've been married fifty years.

DONALD: Married? You're not planning on marrying that fellow?

HARRIETT: Soon as the strike is over, and he can find a house for us. Anyway, it won't be long.

DONALD: Married! Have you told your mother?

HARRIETT: No, I've just decided tonight, just said, *yes.* But I can still work and help mother pay for this house.

DONALD: It's not that! Your mother won't be thinking of that! It's you—you—not making a good marriage, that'll be so—so—indecent! That man has nothing to give you, Harriett.

HARRIETT: *(Rising and opening the door)* He can give me all I want, J. Donald. *(DONALD is silent)* I'll run upstairs and get dressed now. We'll go to mother's party. *(She exits)* Perhaps in time for the Roman candles.

> *(DONALD starts to speak, but does not. He remains seated on the porch, staring straight ahead. Then he takes off his glasses and wipes them slowly with a large white handkerchief. Then he wipes his brow. Finally he blows his nose)*

CURTAIN

Act II, Scene 2

SETTING: *The same. Midnight.*

ACTION: *CANTWELL and LUCIA enter carrying baskets. CAN- TWELL unlocks the door, goes in, and allows it to slam in his sister's face, as MOTHER and HARRIETT enter.*

LUCIA: Cantwell, you might hold the door for a lady.

CANTWELL: *(Within)* Aw, go to the devil!

MOTHER: *(As LUCIA opens door)* Cantwell, there's no need of you being rude and ungentlemanly to your sister! Come here and take these things for me. *(He returns)* Just because I wouldn't let you leave the lawn supper and go on a date with that girl you've been butting your brains out about lately, is no reason for you to act like a four year old!

CANTWELL: *(Taking packages)* I'm sorry!

MOTHER: I really don't know what's getting into you and Harriett.

CANTWELL: Is that all, Mother?

MOTHER: Yes, that's all. You and Lucia go upstairs to bed now. I want to sit here in the cool and talk to your sister.

LUCIA: Mother! I hope you'll . . . . .

MOTHER: No advice from you, Lucia! Thank you! Goodnight.

LUCIA: Goodnight!

CANTWELL: Goodnight, Harriett.

HARRIETT: Goodnight, brother.

> *(Exit LUCIA and CANTWELL)*

MOTHER: It's after midnight, but you know why I've got to talk to you, Harriett.

HARRIETT: Yes, I know, Mother.

MOTHER: Let's sit down, right here on the steps, where the moon's shining, so I can see your face. Nothing's ever hurt me more in my life. *(They sit)* I have to ask you why—why is it I must learn of your—your—this engagement from somebody else, not from you?

HARRIETT: J. Donald told you?

MOTHER: He told me—but I can't believe it. If it's true, why didn't you tell me? But it's not true! I know it's not true! It can't be.

HARRIETT: It is true, Mother!

MOTHER: No!

HARRIETT: I didn't tell you because—I know you don't like him.

MOTHER: You mean you've promised to marry him?

HARRIETT: He asked me.

MOTHER: And you said, *yes?*

HARRIETT: I said, *yes,* Mother.

MOTHER: To a man who's never been welcome in this house—though you've brought him in against my will. Without J. Donald I might never have been told . . . . . I suppose.

HARRIETT: Mother, I always dreamed when I got engaged I'd come and tell you first. And I would've told you tonight, even, but I couldn't—with you behind a table full of cakes and lemonade. So J. Donald beat me to it. It's my engagement—but he beat me to it.

MOTHER: Your engagement? By what right do you engage yourself to a no-good young radical who hasn't even the courtesy to respect me?

HARRIETT: Mother! He does respect you, but you don't give him a chance to like you.

MOTHER: Six months ago, you didn't know he was in the world.

HARRIETT: No, but I know now! And he is my world.

MOTHER: What kind of spell has he got over you—a nice girl, a decent educated girl, that he can presume to take you away from me? Here, I've worked my fingers to the bone, studied, taught school and summer school without a vacation, to make something of you children, to give you culture, this home. And now you think so little of me that you announce your engagement to a Boyle Avenue ruffian without even the thoughtfulness of letting your mother know first.

HARRIETT: I didn't announce it, Mother! J. Donald proposed to me again, so I told him about it. That's all. Kenneth and I just made up our minds tonight, out there under the apple trees.

MOTHER: In my garden?

HARRIETT: Yes, in the garden.

MOTHER: Well, you're not going through with it! Not at all! A man without so much as a roof over his head, no job, lazing around on strike with a gang of thugs! A decent Negro'd have something better to do than that.

HARRIETT: Mother, you don't understand, or you won't understand, why those men're on strike. But strike or no strike, I love Kenneth. And I'm going to marry him.

MOTHER: Do you know anything about him—his background? Who his people are?

HARRIETT: He has no people. But his parents were poor working folks before they died—just like we used to be.

MOTHER: Used to be? You mean *your* father. I'm from the Cantwells of Cincinnati, caterers and business folks for the last three generations. Your great grandmother owned pearls from Tiffany's.

HARRIETT: Yes, but my father worked as a bell-hop, and died in a hotel locker room, didn't he?

MOTHER: That's nothing to be proud of. Your father. . . . . .

HARRIETT: I loved father though. I remember how he used to take me walking in the evening down Boyle Avenue, crowded with colored folks just up from the South, and we used to stop in front of the phonograph shops and listen to the records playing, and watch the little barefooted kids dancing in the streets.

MOTHER: Your father never knew right from wrong, Harriett. If he'd lived, we'd still be down there on Boyle Avenue, in the slums.

HARRIETT: *You* must have loved father. You married him.

MOTHER: Yes, I married him. That's why I don't want you to marry Kenneth—why I won't let you marry Kenneth! I never spoke to you about your father much—I wanted you to remember him kindly— but I will speak now. Listen, Harriett! You think it's because Kenneth's from Boyle Avenue that I don't like him? You think it's because we live out here in this white neighborhood that I'm a snob, trying to make snobs out of you? Well, listen, daughter! Listen! It's because I married a man like Kenneth—and went through hell with that man until he died—that I don't want you to go through the same hell! That's why I won't let you marry Kenneth. I won't let you! I won't let you!

HARRIETT: Didn't you love my father?

MOTHER: That's what made it worse, because I loved him. Then I didn't know what a man's like who's never been used to anything, who comes out of a family that has nothing, and who doesn't care.

HARRIETT: Kenneth's not like that. He does care.

MOTHER: If he cared, wouldn't he be working, instead of lazing up and down the street, with a picket sign? And if he cared would he ask you to marry him—on nothing?

HARRIETT: But. . . .

MOTHER: Don't tell me! There're no *buts*. Men always find some excuse not to work, to quit their jobs, to give up, to lay around and live on a woman. With your father, always, his job was no good, the boss was prejudiced, in another town he'd find better work! We married in Cincinnati, against my grandmother's wishes. He was a waiter for my grandfather, but no sooner were we married than he threw up everything, went to Lexington, and took me with him. You were born in Louisville. Cantwell born in Chicago! Lucia born in Buffalo! We lived in ten towns in twelve years. And never got anywhere! I cooked, I worked out, I sewed, I tried to help him. No! Always dissatisfied! Always on the move. If there'd been strikes in those days for colored folks, he'd have been a perpetual striker. It wasn't until after he died that I owned any furniture of my own. Always renting furnished rooms with you children, or else buying furniture on credit and never getting it paid for before we moved. Always behind, and in debt. No! When he died, I decided my duty was to you children, that I had to make *for you* the kind of life he failed to make. You remember—I went back to college at nights, passed my teacher's exams, got appointed, and took you out of Boyle Avenue. I bought this house, gave you an education! And now do you want us to go back where we started from? Do you? Do you?

HARRIETT: But, mother, I love him!

MOTHER: You love him? Bah! Hunger and rooming houses, and stopped-up sinks and no money, and roaches and bedbugs and worry, and children a man can't feed—can kill love! A future of poverty, and more poverty and nothing but poverty—can kill love.

HARRIETT: I'd work, too. I'd help him.

MOTHER: I said that, too, when I married your father. My family pleaded with me not to go with him, but I thought I knew best, so I went. Now I know better. I'm getting to be an old woman, Harriett—and still an unpaid roof over my head, and two children yet to go to college.

HARRIETT: But, mother, is a house and an education everything?

MOTHER: It's not everything, but it's the basis of everything. A man or a woman has to know something to live in this competitive world—

most of all, a colored man or women. They have to have a roof of their own to be their own masters. Your Kenneth has neither—an eighth grade education and a furnished room!

HARRIETT: But strength, and intelligence! And a job when the strike's over.

MOTHER: He had a job before the strike, didn't he? But what has he saved? Look at his clothes! Look at him! When a man like J. Donald wants you, a clean-cut, intelligent man—what you see in Kenneth is more than I can understand.

HARRIETT: What did you see in father?

MOTHER: I was raised by my grandmother, I've told you. Me—young, innocent, foolish! She was an old woman. I had nobody to talk to, nobody to tell me. She tried, but she didn't know how to tell me. Now I know from experience. I've been through it all. I won't let you marry Kenneth Mason.

HARRIETT: I'm a grown women, Mother, twenty-four years old.

MOTHER: You can be thirty, forty—but if you've been sheltered all your life as I've tried to shelter you, and if you don't remember— since you didn't really know when we had next to nothing to eat because I gave my share to you children—I didn't whine in front of you—I was proud—I hid your father's failings—I cried in bed at night alone when he was in the pool halls. *(Sobbing)* When he got discouraged and began to drink, I tried to hide it from my children. It's hard for a man with nothing to ever amount to anything. They're not like a woman! They don't fight on through to the end! They get discouraged and give up. They give up easily. *(Almost hysterically)* You don't know! You can't know! But I'm telling you now. I don't want you to marry a man with nothing. No! When you marry, it shan't be Kenneth Mason. Harriett, for my sake, marry J. Donald. Marry somebody who'll give you a chance to live, to grow—or I couldn't bear it. Honey, I couldn't bear it.

HARRIETT: *(Softly)* Listen, Mother. I've got to marry Kenneth.

MOTHER: *(The MOTHER's sobs cease abruptly)* You've got to marry Kenneth? . . . . What do you mean by that?

HARRIETT: I mean, I'm going to have a child, Mother!

MOTHER: *(Backing away)* What? What?

HARRIETT: Kenneth's child.

MOTHER: *(Rising. With a broken sob)* Oh, my God! How . . . . . What? . . . . . . *(The MOTHER walks across the porch, wringing her hands)*

HARRIETT: I tell you, he came into my life like a whirlwind, Mother! He held me! And it was like the sun holding me! I don't know how! I don't know why! I only know—I loved him! I love him!

MOTHER: Love! Love! You try to tell me about love. You don't know what it is. But I know! I know. *(She turns with sudden fury on her daughter who has risen and stands there pale against the railing. She cries aloud)* You won't have that child! You won't! You won't have that child! Harriett! You won't have that child!

HARRIETT: *(Quietly)* Mother, the neighbors will hear you. It's late.

MOTHER: *(In a tense whisper)* I said, you won't . . . . . . have . . . . . that child!

CURTAIN

Act II, Scene 3

SETTING: *The same. A week later. Afternoon.*

ACTION: *There are two bags sitting on the porch, an umbrella, and a little pile of books. HARRIETT is in the porch swing. CANTWELL on the steps.*

CANTWELL: Tough break, Sis, getting sick this way just when you go and get yourself engaged. But Kenneth's getting arrested—and having to listen to Mother all day on the subject—is enough to get you excited.

HARRIETT: I guess the poet's right when he says, the course of true love never did run smooth.

CANTWELL: Must be right. Geez, I'd hate to have a mother-in-law, wouldn't you?

HARRIETT: I sometimes think it's pretty hard just having a mother.

CANTWELL: Mother means well. Gee! I feel sorry for her having to teach all summer in this heat! But she's got so much on her mind . . . I'm going to stay out of college this year and get a job that'll bring in enough to help her with this house.

HARRIETT: I'll keep on working, too, and add my part. Even if I was married, I'd do that.

CANTWELL: Well, you can't marry Ken now with him in jail, can you?

HARRIETT: Not when they won't even let anybody see him. I've been down there four times.

CANTWELL: The papers have worked up such a lot of prejudice against the strikers.

HARRIETT: But it isn't legal to hold prisoners more than three days incommunicado! Lawyer Brooks says it isn't legal.

CANTWELL: But Lawyer Brooks won't touch their cases with a ten foot pole.

HARRIETT: No! He says he's out to make money, not to defend "radicals," as he calls them, even if they are under false arrest.

CANTWELL: Brooks defends racketeers and number writers, though.

HARRIETT: And reefer-vendors.

CANTWELL: But how can they hold Kenneth and the others as accomplices to a murder, if they weren't anywhere near the place where that strike-breaker fell off the truck?

HARRIETT: Because they claim the truck was stoned. And they say the strike committee incited the strikers to violence. Kenneth was on the strike committee.

CANTWELL: Brooks says it's a serious charge and they can hold them without bail for months if they want to.

HARRIETT: It's a frame-up to keep the strike committee in jail and break the strike quicker.

CANTWELL: The strike is broken. All the trucks are running again and the warehouses are open. The scabs are in, and the union's lost.

HARRIETT: Kenneth always said workers lose every battle but the last battle.

CANTWELL: What did he mean by that?

HARRIETT: That the workers have to take the world—before they can control it, I guess.

CANTWELL: Do you think so?

HARRIETT: I don't know. I only know they've taken my world and put it there behind prison walls where they won't let me pass. And all my dreams have come tumbling down like bricks on my head. I don't know what to do.

CANTWELL: It's tough, Sis. But why is Mother sending you to Cincinnati? If your nerves are bad, why couldn't you just stay home here and rest?

HARRIETT: That second cousin of ours in Cinci that's a doctor—mother seems to think he can do me more good than anybody here. She's hammered at me so hard, I haven't any mind of my own left.

CANTWELL: Don't know, but I thought that doctor-cousin of mother's specialized in babies and consumption. I guess Mother just wants to get you out of town for awhile. She's ashamed of having you engaged to a guy in jail.

HARRIETT: But if I could just see Kenneth! I'm lost without him.

CANTWELL: The last time you saw him was Fourth of July, the day of the picnic, heh?

HARRIETT: Yes.

CANTWELL: And that lawn party. Boy! Was Mother hot when J. Donald told her you were engaged.

HARRIETT: Poor Mother!

CANTWELL: Gee! She had to stop cutting cake and sit down.

HARRIETT: I didn't mean to hurt her, Cantwell. But she's determined to always treat me like a little girl.

CANTWELL: What makes parents so dead-set against their kids all the time? They never seem to want you to do anything you want to do, or like anybody you want to like. I wonder if father would've been that way?

HARRIETT: Father was different. He did what he wanted to do, and I think he believed in everybody else doing the same way.

CANTWELL: I just barely remember him. He was a swell guy! I wish father had lived. He was teaching me to play ball in the alley when I could barely walk. Remember?

HARRIETT: Mother says he would've still been down on Boyle Avenue, if he'd lived.

CANTWELL: Well, we might have had more fun. Out here's all right, but folks limit their sociability to conversations from porch to porch. Even foreign white folks, when they get to America, start acting like the natives and drawing the color-line.

HARRIETT: That's the good thing about Kenneth's union—they don't draw any color line.

CANTWELL: But look at them now—in jail!

HARRIETT: I don't care. I respect them for standing up for their rights.

CANTWELL: Even the colored folks are against them, though. The colored paper this week says a young fellow like Kenneth had no business being mixed up with them anyhow.

HARRIETT: Cheap politicians own that colored paper, no wonder! They print whatever they're paid to print.

CANTWELL: Money talks! And how!

(Enter LUCIA with a newspaper)

LUCIA: Hello!

HARRIETT: Hello, Lucia!

LUCIA: I brought an evening paper, Harriett, so you can read about your boy-friend.

HARRIETT: Let's see! *(Rises)*

LUCIA: *(Reading with relish)* There's a big headline tonight. STRIK-ERS BOUND OVER TO THE GRAND JURY. Face Ten to Sixty Years. Seven accused of inciting to. . . .

    (As she reads, HARRIETT sinks back into the swing. Puts her hand to her head, almost faints. CANTWELL runs to her. He snatches the paper from Lucia)

CANTWELL: What's the matter with you, Lucia? Harriett, listen! *(To Lucia)* Run and get her a glass of water. Don't take it so hard. Those old papers don't know everything.

HARRIETT: I'll be all right. Just a little dizzy, I guess. I'll be all right, brother.

CANTWELL: Straighten up, Sis. Here comes J. Donald! Don't give him a chance to crow over you.

HARRIETT: *(Wearily)* I guess I don't care much, Cantwell. What's the use, anyhow? J. Donald'll start it all over again—Kenneth's no good—a nobody—no family—no money! *(Tears in her eyes)* I know they're making putty out of me. I hate myself—but they've convinced me. After a week of browbeating and prayers and persuasion, I'm beginning to believe mother now.

    (Enter J. DONALD)

DONALD: Good afternoon, Harriett, Cantwell!

CANTWELL: Hello!

HARRIETT: Hello, J. Donald!

DONALD: I've come to help you get down to the station.

HARRIETT: That's nice of you, J. Donald. But the train's not till five. Mother isn't home from school yet.

DONALD: I cut a lab to be here early. Too hot on the campus today, anyhow. You look rather pale, Harriett. Feeling bad?

HARRIETT: I guess the heat's got me. Or the idea of the trip. *(Enter LUCIA with water)* Thank you, Lucia.

LUCIA: You're welcome! Why, hello, J. Donald!

DONALD: Hello! How's the music coming on?

LUCIA: I'm learning one of the *Nocturnes* now. Want to hear me play it?

DONALD: I'd rather like to.

CANTWELL: I wouldn't!

LUCIA: I'll play it for you, J. Donald.

CANTWELL: I'm going down to the corner, then!

(Exit LUCIA within, and CANTWELL down the street. The piano is heard shortly)

DONALD: So you're leaving today. I hope the trip'll do you good and get your mind off of everything unpleasant, dear girl.

HARRIETT: You and mother think it's awfully important getting me out of town, don't you?

DONALD: Travel is a cure for many ills, Harriett. I told your mother that if she thought it wise that you went even farther, maybe to the seashore, I had a little money I could let her have. A loan she might call it.

HARRIETT: That's kind of you, J. Donald, but I guess Cincinnati's far enough.

DONALD: Too far—but you have relatives there. So if you don't mind, I'll run down and see you as soon as my summer semester is over.

HARRIETT: I wouldn't mind, if you wanted to come.

DONALD: Of course, I want to come. I want to see you get well. I know how it upsets you, that boy's arrest. But God works in mysterious ways His wonders to perform, Harriett. Perhaps it was all for the best. Who knows?

HARRIETT: If suffering is good, J. Donald, then perhaps it is for the best. We've suffered. I know Kenneth's suffering now, poor boy!

DONALD: Always thinking about others! But it's you I'm thinking of. And your mother! What she's gone through this last week!

HARRIETT: I know it's hard for mother. That's what wears me down! She's always kept me so afraid of her. But she relies a great deal on you, J. Donald.

DONALD: I wish you'd rely on me, too, Harriett. Tell me, it's all off, isn't it? Don't you agree with your mother? Don't you see how a man like Kenneth would drag you from pillar to post? Worry to worry? Don't you want a home and a family? Don't you want what I can give you? Don't you see what your mother means?

HARRIETT: I suppose I do, J. Donald, and I'm going away, as mother wishes. But I don't know where I am! I don't know what I want to do! But I can't do any good by staying. The union has the money for Kenneth's defense. And I can't see him. So I might as well go away.

DONALD: And get well.

HARRIETT: And get well. I'm afraid you and mother have won. And my knight is gone!

DONALD: We could get married this fall, darling—and you'd be with
    me while I finish my graduate work. Then we'd teach together down
    South. And pay off the debt on this house. And build a house of our
    own. And raise a family!

HARRIETT: It all sounds very wise, and very good, J. Donald. But
    don't ask me now! Please don't ask me now!

DONALD: Your mother'd be happy, so happy. And my mother, too.

HARRIETT: I'd like everybody to be happy—like I want to be happy.

DONALD: You'd be happy, darling! I'll make you happy. I'll . . . . .

    (The door slams next door. MRS. KLEIN speaks)

MRS. KLEIN: Harriett! Harriett! Your mother, she just telephone me
    from the school. She says she's gonna be little late. Teacher's
    meetink. For you and Cantwell to take taxi and meet her at the
    station.

HARRIETT: Yes, Mrs. Klein.

MRS. KLEIN: So when I see you on the porch talking, I call already you
    a taxi by phone. It'll be here in a minute. And I fixed you nice lunch
    to carry in train, too.

    (Piano stops)

HARRIETT: Oh, how good of you, Mrs. Klein! Thank you!

MRS. KLEIN: You just send one of children over for lunch. Pumper-
    nickel and whole big chicken, Jewish style. And apple cake.

HARRIETT: That sounds awfully good, Mrs. Klein.

LUCIA: *(Coming out)* I'll go for it. *(Exits across yard)*

MRS. KLEIN: Just carry the box, top side up.

HARRIETT: I'll be careful with it. Thank you.

MRS. KLEIN: And have a good trip. Come back well and smilink.

HARRIETT: I'll try to. Say goodbye to your daughter for me.

MRS. KLEIN: Yes, I will. Well, goodbye! I've got bread in oven. I must
    go back in house now. Goodbye.

HARRIETT: Goodbye, Mrs. Klein.

    (Door closes on opposite porch)

DONALD: A friendly neighbor. Everybody respects your mother.

HARRIETT: Yes, they do!

LUCIA: *(Returning with the box)* Give me a piece of the apple cake, will
    you, Harriett? You won't eat it all on the train.

HARRIETT: Help yourself! But leave the crumbs, greedy.

LUCIA: I will . . . . . . *(Goes into house)*

HARRIETT: I'd better run in and powder my face. *(Looking at baggage)*
    Oh, yes, and get my coat!

DONALD: I'll call you when the taxi comes, darling.

HARRIETT: I'll be right down—I think I see it now, turning the corner.

DONALD: *(Taking her hand)* Say, would you kiss me on the way to the station, Harriett?

HARRIETT: *(In doorway)* If you want me to, J. Donald!

DONALD: I want you to, Harriett! *(Drawing her to him)* Now! Right now! *(His lips touch hers, but suddenly she turns her head away and buries her face on his shoulder, shaking with sobs. The taxi horn sounds. HARRIETT enters the house. J. DONALD picks up her bags and smiles broadly as he starts down the steps)* I think she loves me! Gee! She hates to leave me! She loves me! She loves me!

CURTAIN

Act III, Scene 1

SETTING: *Autumn now. The leaves are falling. The flowers are gone and the plants are turning yellow. The screen door has been taken down. It is early morning. There are milk bottles on the steps.*

ACTION: *KENNETH enters. His clothes are frayed. His coat collar is turned up. He has no top coat. It is cold. He looks at the house, walks past as though he is afraid to enter, then returns. LUCIA comes out hurriedly, a house dress and apron on, starts toward the milk bottles and suddenly sees Kenneth.*

LUCIA: Oh! So you're out!

KENNETH: Yes, they turned me loose this morning. Lack of evidence so their frame-up fell through. But I've come to see Harriett.

LUCIA: You can't see her.

KENNETH: I can't see her?

LUCIA: The doctor says she's too sick to see anybody, except the family.

KENNETH: Too sick? But I'm the family. I. . . .

LUCIA: No one thinks you're the family but you.

KENNETH: But I've got to see her. How is she? What's the matter?

LUCIA: Something she got in Cincinnati, some kind of infection. She's pretty sick.

KENNETH: Then let me in. I've got to be with her.

LUCIA: Oh, no you don't! *(Barring the door)* I'll call mother!

KENNETH: You mean I can't come in?

LUCIA: We don't want you in this house again.

    (LUCIA goes in quickly and closes the door. KENNETH stands

*there for a moment, walks slowly down the steps and stops, unde-
cided what to do. CANTWELL comes out hurriedly, his overcoat
on)*

CANTWELL: *(Seeing Kenneth)* Kenneth!

KENNETH: Cantwell! What's the matter with Harriett?

CANTWELL: She's sick, awfully sick. She wants you.

KENNETH: Then I've got to go in, to see her.

CANTWELL: Wait a minute! You don't know what's happened, do you?

KENNETH: How could I know?

CANTWELL: You never got her letters in jail?

KENNETH: No, I never got her letters.

CANTWELL: She never heard from you, either.

KENNETH: I wrote her. What happened to my letters?

CANTWELL: I don't know. You see, mother sent her to Cincinnati,
after you got locked up. And down there she got sick. And kept
getting worse and worse. Until finally she came back home last week,
so thin I hardly knew her.

KENNETH: But what's the matter?

CANTWELL: It's you, Kenneth. You see, listen, old man, mother and
J. Donald talked her out of marrying you. Now she's going to marry
J. Donald, when she gets well.

KENNETH: What?

CANTWELL: But I'm afraid she's not going to get well this way. She
talks about you all the time. Then mother scolds her, and she cries.
And when I come home from work every day, it's the same old
story—J. Donald sitting there looking like a sad dog, and Harriett
with her face to the wall trying to shut out the sight of him. I think
the thought of marrying him's what's killing her.

KENNETH: She won't marry him. Poor kid! She won't have to marry
him now. I'll take her away, and make her well again, and marry her
myself.

CANTWELL: She's pretty weak, Kenneth, but maybe if you did take her
out of this house, where nothing's honest and healthy any more—
she'd get well.

KENNETH: I'll take her to my room, and nurse her, and keep her there
with me. She's mine, Cantwell, and I want her. I want her.

CANTWELL: *(Holding him back)* Don't try to go in now. There'd only
be a row. Wait until mother goes to school. She'll be leaving in a few
minutes. Then go upstairs and talk to her. Pay Lucia no mind. Come
on, walk with me to the carline. I'm late to work. *(Starting off as he*

lights a cigarette) I've got to go way downtown. *(As KENNETH hesitates)* Come on. You can come back. On the way I'll tell you more about it.

> *(The two men exit. LUCIA comes out with a broom and begins to sweep the dry leaves off the porch. MOTHER emerges on her way to school)*

MOTHER: I have a feeling I shouldn't go to school. Harriett is worse. Lucia, if she gets restless, or has an attack of hysteria or anything of the sort, call me up at once. Run next door. Mrs. Klein will let you use the phone.

LUCIA: Yes, mother, I will. The doctor comes at eleven, doesn't he?

MOTHER: Yes, at eleven. And if J. Donald comes, tell him not to sit with her too long. Visitors only make her restless. As for that other fellow! Lucia, maybe I'd better stay here today! Do you think he'll come back?

LUCIA: I won't let him in, mother. I'll keep the door locked, and look out first if the bell rings.

MOTHER: If it weren't that I'm in charge of the rhetorical program today, I'd stay at home. But I can't afford to miss many more days. We need the money so badly.

LUCIA: If I don't get back to school, too, I'll get so far behind in algebra . . .

MOTHER: I know, dear. We'll have to make some arrangements, if your sister doesn't get better soon. I'll have to hire someone to stay with her, some old woman perhaps in need of a home.

LUCIA: Yes, mother . . . . . Should I tell J. Donald about Kenneth's being out?

MOTHER: Yes, I'll tell him. We can't let that jail-bird get to Harriett again.

LUCIA: I'll tell him soon as he comes. J. Donald'll be mad.

MOTHER: But be careful about the door. I must hurry. It's nearly eight.

LUCIA: Goodbye, mother.

MOTHER: Goodbye, Lucia. I don't know what I'd do without you. You're the only one of my children who seems to understand what I'm striving for, the only one who likes me anymore.

LUCIA: I'm with you, mother. Goodbye.

MOTHER: Goodbye.

> *(She exits. LUCIA continues sweeping. HARRIETT is heard calling)*

HARRIETT: *(Voice upstairs)* Mother! Mother!

LUCIA: I'm coming, Harriett! *(She exits within. In a moment, KEN-NETH appears. He looks around, hesitates, then enters quietly. Suddenly, LUCIA screams. Their voices are heard within)* Get out! Get out!

KENNETH: I must see Harriett, Lucia. I must see her.

LUCIA: No! No! Get out!

HARRIETT: *(Upstairs)* Kenneth! Kenneth! Oh, Kenneth, are you here?

KENNETH: I'm coming, Honey!

LUCIA: *(At the door now)* I'll call the police! I'll call mother! I'll have you put out! *(LUCIA exits excitedly. Runs next door to Mrs. Klein's, is heard knocking on the door)* Mrs. Klein! Oh, Mrs. Klein!

MRS. KLEIN: Vat is it? Vat? Vat's matter?

LUCIA: Oh, Mrs. Klein, let me in quick, to the phone. There's a man in our house who has no right to be there. Let me in.

MRS. KLEIN: A robber? Vat is it? Come in! Come in!

   (The neighbor's door closes. In a moment, Kenneth emerges. He looks anxiously down the street)

HARRIETT: *(Within)* I can walk, Kenneth. I can walk to the carline.

KENNETH: No, darling! A cab will pass in a minute. There's lots of them pass in the mornings taking people to work. I'll whistle—there's one now. Just get your coat. *(KENNETH goes down and whistles for the cab. Motor is heard approaching. KENNETH calls to the cab driver)* Just a minute, we'll be ready.

DRIVER: *(Voice offstage)* O. K. I'll be right here.

   (KENNETH exits within house. J. DONALD enters as KEN-NETH emerges with HARRIETT in his arms, her gown hanging beneath her coat, a scarf on her head)

DONALD: What's happening? Is she going to the hospital? *(Recognizing Kenneth)* Oh! So you're back! Where're you taking Harriett?

KENNETH: I'm taking her with me.

DONALD: What?

HARRIETT: Go on, Kenneth! Go on! Please, let's go on!

DONALD: Just a minute! Put that girl down! Let me get the straight of this. Where is Mrs. Harper? Where is your mother, Harriett?

   (Door opens next door. LUCIA appears, calling loudly)

LUCIA: J. Donald! Oh, J. Donald, I'm so glad you've come! He's trying to take my sister away, and mother isn't here, and I've been calling trying to get someone to help me.

DONALD: Take her back in the house. *(He blocks Kenneth's way by force)*

MRS. KLEIN: You will kill that poor girl, taking her out in the cold like this.

HARRIETT: Don't let them stop you, Kenneth! Don't let them stop you!

LUCIA: *(Seizing KENNETH)* Put my sister down! Put her down!

KENNETH: Let me go!

> *(He breaks away, but J.DONALD calls to the cab-driver)*

DONALD: Don't let that man in that cab! You do and you're a kidnapper!

DRIVER: *(Starting motor)* I don't want no parts of this myself. Get another cab, Mister. I don't handle this kind of business. I'm gone.

> *(Motor sounds disappear in the distance)*
> *(KENNETH stands on steps with HARRIETT in his arms)*

HARRIETT: I'll walk! I'll walk away from this house, with the man I love. *(She struggles to be free)* Nobody'll stop me now. I'll go with him, J. Donald. You nor mother nor anyone else'll stop me.

KENNETH: Darling, wait! I'll get another cab. *(He puts her on steps)*

HARRIETT: *(Holding him)* They'll take me back inside that house. I'll die inside there. Oh, Kenneth, honey, take me with you, now!

DONALD: The girl's lost her mind! She's weak and sick. Leave her alone. Why did you have to come back anyhow? Why did they let you out of jail?

LUCIA: Mother'll have him locked up again.

HARRIETT: No, No! Go away, J. Donald! Let us be! Lucia, go away, inside. All of you, leave me alone! Leave me alone!

DONALD: You won't go with that jail-bird, Harriett. . . . You can't.

LUCIA: Carry her back upstairs, Donald. Please, make her go upstairs.

KENNETH: Don't touch her! And don't touch me!

> *(As KENNETH faces J. Donald, HARRIETT rises and leaves steps)*

HARRIETT: Come on, Kenneth!

> *(KENNETH turns to help her. Suddenly, with a little cry she sinks down among the dry leaves on the sidewalk. LUCIA runs to her)*

LUCIA: OH-oo-ooo-oo!

MRS. KLEIN: Mein Gott! I go call doctor, quick! *(Door slams)*

DONALD: Now, see what you've done.

KENNETH: *(Kneeling over her)* Harriett! Harriett! Harriett, honey! Harriett!

LUCIA: Oh! Take her up! One of you men, take her up, and bring her in out of the cold.

KENNETH: I'll bring her in. Out of the cold.

> (*Very gently KENNETH lifts her up and turns toward the house. LUCIA opens the door. J. DONALD turns to follow*)

CURTAIN

Act III, Scene 2

SETTING: *The same. A few days later. Afternoon. Bright sunshine.*

ACTION: *KENNETH and J. DONALD sit on opposite sides of the porch.*

KENNETH: I can't bear it, Donald, I can't bear it.

DONALD: It seems to be the Lord's will, Kenneth. The Lord giveth and the Lord taketh away.

KENNETH: The Lord? J. Donald, they've prayed to the Lord, but she keeps on getting weaker and weaker.

DONALD: He knows best, Kenneth.

KENNETH: I've given two quarts of blood, but she's weaker and weaker.

DONALD: Not even your blood made her rally. Strange, I offered my blood, too, but it was yours the doctor chose.

KENNETH: I'd give my life for Harriett.

DONALD: I'd give my life, too.

> (*The door opens. LUCIA speaks*)

LUCIA: The nurse wants someone to run down to the drug store and get a bottle of alcohol.

KENNETH: I'll go.

DONALD: I'll go.

LUCIA: Suppose you go, J. Donald. Charge it to mother's bill.

DONALD: Yes, Lucia.

> (*He exits. LUCIA goes back into the house. KENNETH buries his head in his hands. CANTWELL enters*)

KENNETH: Off from work so early?

CANTWELL: I came home. I thought maybe Harriett might want me.

KENNETH: She's no better.

CANTWELL: Is mother with her?

KENNETH: Yes, and the nurse.

CANTWELL: Poor kid!

> (*Pause*)

KENNETH: Cantwell, do they think—do they think that I—that I'm to blame?

CANTWELL: Mother never liked you, Kenneth—not so much *you,* as what she thinks you stand for.

KENNETH: Why? Why?

CANTWELL: Mother's world's built on a different dream, Kenneth— to escape from Boyle Avenue—not to change it. She doesn't realize that her dream and her whole world's crumbling, for white folks as well as Negroes. She thinks we're safe in this house out here in a decent neighborhood, safe—and saved.

KENNETH: She never wanted Harriett to know me, did she, to go with me?

CANTWELL: No, she didn't, Kenneth.

KENNETH: But I tried to do right, Cantwell. I never tried to put anything over on her. When I asked Harriett to marry me, I didn't know that the whole strike committee'd be locked up. I couldn't foresee that.

CANTWELL: I know you couldn't, Kenneth.

KENNETH: But if I could've, it would've been just the same for me.

CANTWELL: Yes, but mother'll never understand that it was just a frame-up to get the whole committee out of the way until the strike was broken. She thought you really were a criminal—according to the papers.

KENNETH: Yes, I know. Lots of people don't understand.

CANTWELL: Then, she was afraid maybe you'd be like my father.

KENNETH: Like your father?

CANTWELL: Yes, never anything more than just a working man—not getting ahead in life.

KENNETH: How do you mean—your father never got ahead?

CANTWELL: Father was restless. Always moving from town to town. But I know why he kept on moving. I've begun to understand lots of things lately since I've been out of school, working. I see what we colored men are up against now—all the worst jobs at the lowest wages. So I don't blame them for quitting sometimes, and moving on to another town, and getting another job of the same kind—since that's the best there is for us. At least, we get a change of scenery.

KENNETH: Or we stay and fight.

CANTWELL: In father's day they didn't know what to fight—so, I guess, they took it out in restlessness and drink.

KENNETH: But now we can organize.

CANTWELL: And that's moving too slow. I'm working as a elevator-boy and we're not organized.

KENNETH: And I'm locked out of a job since we lost the strike. But we'll keep on fighting. We must keep on trying.

CANTWELL: We've got to join up with others, I know. If I open my mouth alone, I'm fired.

KENNETH: Nobody can fight alone.

CANTWELL: But mother doesn't understand that. Unions are radical to her. She and J. Donald believe in culture and God.

KENNETH: But Harriett understands.

CANTWELL: Yes, Harriett understands. That's why she wants to get out of this house that's closed against the winds of tomorrow, this house that tries to be a little narrow island of its own in a big sea of strange currents and mighty undertows—this house that tries to keep away from the great stream of Boyle Avenue where the Negro life of this town centers—this house that I wish my mother'd never bought out here with the respectable folks that break strikes and vote down relief for the hungry. No, Kenneth, Harriett understands. She'd go with you, even to prison.

KENNETH: She's got to get well!

CANTWELL: Another blood transfusion today?

KENNETH: Yes, but she doesn't rally.

(Enter J. DONALD with a package)

DONALD: I have the alcohol.

CANTWELL: I'm going upstairs. I'll take it.

DONALD: Ask if there's anything else I can do.

CANTWELL: I will, Donald. *(He exits with package into house)*

DONALD: In times like this, there's so little, so little! The time to do good's before the crucial moment arises, not after. Oh that poor girl's mother, losing her oldest child after so many years of work and struggle to educate her.

KENNETH: Don't talk like that! Harriett's not dead yet. She might live. She's got to live. She's got to live.

DONALD: Don't shout.

KENNETH: I'm sorry. I'm almost to the point where I don't know what I'm doing, what I'm saying. But I do know Harriett wanted to come with me, and you tried to keep her from me. Why didn't you stay out of her life, why didn't you leave her alone?

DONALD: Why didn't you?

KENNETH: Because I love her.

DONALD: I love her, too.

KENNETH: *(Anguished pause)* Then what are we sitting here quarreling about? We both wanted her to be happy, I guess. But my path led one way and yours another, that's all. And you took advantage. . . . No, I mustn't.

DONALD: Mustn't what?

KENNETH: Mustn't talk about it any more now. She would have been mine, that's sure, had the way been clear.

(CANTWELL emerges)

CANTWELL: She doesn't know me.

DONALD: Is she asleep?

CANTWELL: No, not asleep. She's just looking straight ahead. But when I bent over and took her hand, she thought it was you, Kenneth. She called your name, so soft I could hardly hear it. She wants you, Kenneth.

KENNETH: Then I'll go—and stay there beside her.

(He goes into the house. CANTWELL lights a cigarette)

CANTWELL: She's breathing awfully fast now!

DONALD: She won't know him, either, so why does he go?

CANTWELL: Maybe she'll know him, Donald. She loved him better than anybody else in the world.

DONALD: I would have given my blood for her, too, but the doctor wouldn't take it. I offered it, but the doctor wouldn't take it. *(Tears come, so he takes off his glasses, and wipes his eyes)*

CANTWELL: I know it, old man . . . Say! Come on! Don't cry, fellow.

DONALD: *(Changing the subject)* It's warm to be so late in the year, isn't it? But the leaves are falling.

CANTWELL: Yes, the leaves are falling.

DONALD: Down South, this time of year the flowers are still blooming. Even roses, big red roses.

CANTWELL: How do you like the South, J. Donald?

DONALD: It's my home. I was brought up there. I'm used to its ways.

CANTWELL: But how do you like it?

DONALD: It's where I live. And somebody's got to stay there and help our people. Harriett and I, we could've founded our own school.

CANTWELL: What would you teach if you had a school?

DONALD: English, and Latin, and trigonometry, philosophy, psychology.

CANTWELL: And would you teach a man to be a man?

DONALD: You can't go too far down South, Cantwell. We're not radicals there yet.

CANTWELL: Not yet?

DONALD: No, not yet . . . . . Listen! I hear someone crying.

CANTWELL: *(Rising)* It's Lucia! They're moving about upstairs.

DONALD: Someone's coming down.

> *(The door bursts open and KENNETH comes out, his face distorted with grief)*

CANTWELL: Kenneth! *(But he does reply. KENNETH goes blindly down the steps and out into the street)* Kenneth!

> *(The MOTHER comes to the door and speaks very slowly and calmly)*

MOTHER: Cantwell, Donald! Harriett is gone. Come in, children. We'll draw the curtains now, and lower the shades. Come in, J. Donald. *(DONALD enters. CANTWELL remains standing on the steps looking down the street)* Come in, son. Help me close the windows.

> *(CANTWELL does not move. He stands with the sunlight in his face, looking down the street where KENNETH has gone into the distance)*

CANTWELL: Mother, leave the windows open! Leave the windows open!

> *(MRS. HARPER closes the door and leaves him standing there)*

CURTAIN

ACT III, Scene 1

Alternative ending which may be used instead of preceding 3rd Act—for those preferring a happy conclusion.

An hour later—LUCIA sits on the steps reading the funnies and eating an apple. CANTWELL comes running in.

CANTWELL: Where's Harriett? Has she gone to the train already? *(LUCIA doesn't answer)* Well, dope, can't you get your trap open? This is serious. I say has Sis gone to the train. *(Pulling paper away)* Listen to me, will you? Can't you see I've got something important on my hands?

LUCIA: *(Chewing her apple)* Ladies don't converse during the process of mastication. Want me to choke on this apple just because you're all lathered up about something or other? You might learn poise, Cantwell.

CANTWELL: Is she gone, I said?

LUCIA: *(Taking a bite and talking as she chews)* Yes, she's gone. What do you think? You didn't come back to say goodbye.

CANTWELL: I know it. I had an idea. When did she leave? How long ago?

LUCIA: Oh, a half hour or more. Stop acting so important. I hope you notice, Cantwell, that I'm unmoved by all this heavy mystery.

CANTWELL: If you knew what I do—I've just begun to put two and two together around here. But, of course, you're too young to suspect what it's all about.

LUCIA: Too young! Oh, dear me! Why you're a mere child, Cantwell. Look at you, letting yourself get in such a stew? You're so naive.

CANTWELL: What time does the train leave?

LUCIA: Wouldn't you like to know? Huh! Well, I might tell you—if you'll tell me what this two and two is that you're being so smart about.

CANTWELL: Well, it isn't the kind of thing little girls should know about, see?

LUCIA: Cantwell Harper, have you been smoking again? *(Sniffing)* Well, if you must—

CANTWELL: Now look here. I've got to find Harriet. I've just been down to the jail, see? And—

LUCIA: The jail? What will Mother say? Did you see Kenneth?

CANTWELL: No, I didn't. But I saw one of those union guys—one of the officials. And he said that Kenneth was sitting pretty. He said—

LUCIA: Sitting pretty. In a jail? Really, Cantwell, if the Harpers have started calling on their friends in jail.

CANTWELL: Oh, shut your gap. Can't you see that Mother's going to make an awful mess of Harriett's life?

LUCIA: Oh, so somebody's been listening at doors!

CANTWELL: Well, if you'd been listening at doors you'd know that Harriett shouldn't be sent off down there to that doctor cousin of Mother's. It isn't decent. What time does the train leave for Cincinnati?

LUCIA: At five o'clock, Mr. Harper. *(Looks at watch)* And it's twelve-of now. Well, he is still in jail, isn't he?

CANTWELL: Yes, he's still in jail, but maybe if Harriett knew—
      (He dashes off down the street and LUCIA looks puzzled. She recovers paper, watches down the street, then settles down again to apple and funnies, when MRS. KLEIN's screen door bangs)

MRS. KLEIN: Lucia! Lucia!

LUCIA: Yes, Mrs. Klein?

MRS. KLEIN: Your mama, she just call on telephone to ask where is Harriett.

LUCIA: Harriett? Why, she's gone to the train. She left in a taxi with Mr. Butler, oh, over half an hour ago.

MRS. KLEIN: That's just like I tell her. But she is lookink all over station and ain't find her any place. My! My! What's a matter, you think?

LUCIA: Oh, it's all right. Mother's just nervous. They'll find each other.

MRS. KLEIN: Vell, maybe you right. I'll tell her look again.

LUCIA: Oh, is she still on the wire? Well, tell her to ask that nice Mr. Carter—he's a red cap there—a friend of Mother's. He knows everybody. He's sure to see Harriett buying her ticket.

MRS. KLEIN: That's good idea. I tell her. Mr. Carter, you say?

LUCIA: Yes. Mr. Carter—he's a red cap.

MRS. KLEIN: O.K. Lucia. I tell her.

LUCIA: Thank you, Mrs. Klein.

MRS. KLEIN: That's nothing. Nothing. I like to help out neighbors.

> (*LUCIA puts apple core in flower box, resumes her funnies, when sound of taxi makes her look down the street. Her look changes to amazement as she sees J. DONALD and HARRIETT step from taxi*)

DONALD: This is all a mistake, Harriett. You're being so—so impulsive—What will your mother say? She'll be so upset again. She—

LUCIA: Why, Harriett! Mother won't like this. Mother just telephoned—

HARRIETT: I'm not going, Lucia! I've changed my mind. I'm going to stay right here.

LUCIA: Did Cantwell find you?

HARRIETT: Cantwell! Why, no. Why?

LUCIA: Well, he went dashing out of here acting awfully high and mighty about something or other. Thought he had to tell you something.

HARRIETT: Well, it doesn't matter now.

LUCIA: Harriett, Mother's going to be awfully—

HARRIETT: Oh, I can't help it if Mother doesn't like it. It's Mother—mother—always mother,—this will make mother unhappy—that might upset mother—But I tell you I can't live that way. I've got to think about me—

DONALD: There now. Don't get excited, dear. We'll sit here quietly and—

HARRIETT: You leave us alone, now for a little while, will you, Lucia? That's a dear. I want to talk to J. Donald alone.

DONALD: Yes, Lucia, please.

LUCIA: Oh, all right—but I must say, I don't think you're very appreciative of all Mother's done for you.

DONALD: Please, Lucia. *(Exit into house LUCIA)* Now then! Let's sit down right here in the swing and talk it all over. Just the two of us. I think if you'll just trust me, Harriett, that I can help you see things more clearly. Maybe—

HARRIETT: But I see things so clearly now, J. Donald. I've never in my life—I've never been so sure. And I feel strong. Oh, I can manage now. I know I can. And I can make mother see. Well, no, maybe I can't do that—but if I can't I can stand my ground—yes, and I can keep my head high, too.

DONALD: But your mother knows best, Harriett. She's planned this trip because—

HARRIETT: Oh, no—no—Mother can't know—Oh, I know how hard things have been for her. She's been so hurt—and she's afraid—truly afraid—that I shall be hurt too. But she can't hang her fears all over me—She can't tie me with them hand and foot. Why I was running away—I was running away from Kenneth—from myself—my own self—and something else too—something I can't tell you about, J. Donald.

DONALD: But what has come over you, Harriett? Why just an hour ago you were so sensible—and—

HARRIETT: It was when the taxi was stopped at that corner—do you remember—when we were blocked by the strikers' victory parade. Something I saw in their faces as they passed by—So brave they were—and believing in themselves and each other. They were like Kenneth and me. Didn't you see them? All those faces—black faces—white faces—streaming past—looking up—

DONALD: They were just poor unfortunate working men, Harriett, not blessed as you and I are. Oh, doing the best they can, no doubt.

HARRIETT: But didn't you look at them?

DONALD: Yes. To tell the truth I felt sorry for them. In comparison with those of us who are in the professions, they're rough, uncultured.

HARRIETT: Oh, you weren't looking at them. You were looking at their clothes. They've been on strike—This whole town had been against them—from the mayor—down to—well—to you.

DONALD: They're always getting into rows—making trouble—getting in the papers—in jail. But let's not bother about all that now. Let's talk about—

HARRIETT: I know they're right. They looked so right—And I felt ashamed—and then—then I felt strong. And I want to live gaily and bravely as they do. Oh, I know you won't understand—you can't. But I've seen them at their meetings. They know how to keep each other strong—though alone they would just be poor lost people—like my father. I belong with them. It's my way.

DONALD: But remembering your father should make you understand why your Mother isn't willing to risk your happiness to a man like Kenneth.

HARRIETT: Listen, J. Donald. As I watched those men go by—I understood my father's life so clearly. He needed men like that to make him steady—to make him strong. No common working man can stand alone. Father couldn't. And mother never knew what he was up against. But what could he do? If there'd been a union then—but there wasn't. He had to fumble through his life. He might have walked proudly and bravely down the street as they did. All the tangles straightened out for me—in that one moment.

DONALD: But you're all up in the clouds, Harriett. This man—and these working people that interest you so much—they've cast some kind of spell over you. You're not yourself.

HARRIETT: Oh yes, I am. I'm really Harriett now. I haven't known her very well before this. She was always sliding around the corner from me. And we've got such a lot to do.

DONALD: We?

HARRIETT: Yes. Kenneth and I.

DONALD: But you've got to face the facts, Harriett. Kenneth is in jail. The papers said—

HARRIETT: Yes, I know. But Kenneth always said you couldn't believe the papers. And the strikers have won—You saw the parade yourself.

DONALD: Well, I don't know what to think, Harriett. I thought I had a good deal to offer a woman, but—I don't know.

HARRIETT: There's never really been anything between us, J. Donald. As I sat there in the taxi beside you, I knew that all my life I'd be wanting Kenneth there—not you. You think I'd grow to love you—It seems so reasonable that I should. But I wouldn't. I'd come to hate you. Oh yes, I would. And that wouldn't be fair because you've been so good and kind—in your way, to me—to mother—to all of us.

DONALD: If you'd only give me a chance, Harriett—

HARRIETT: We couldn't make each other happy. Don't you see? We'd always be seeking different things—liking different people. There's a new world waiting for me.

DONALD: You believe in yourself, Harriett. I see that. You almost make me believe in you, too, when I see your face like this—a light shining through from the inside. *(Cleans glasses, rising)* You've hurt me, Harriett. But you've got to have your way. That's all right. I won't stand in your way any longer.

HARRIETT: That's pretty swell of you. Could you—would you be willing to try to make Mother see too?

DONALD: That won't be so easy. But I'll have a talk with her tomorrow. Goodbye now, Harriett. I'll be getting back to the lab. I can still get an hour in.

HARRIETT: It's better than I thought. I thought I'd have you all against me—all but Cantwell. But you're being willing to help—

DONALD: You need your rest—Goodbye now—

HARRIETT: Goodbye, Donald. *(She exits into house)*

> *(DONALD wipes his brow. Starts down steps when CANTWELL and MOTHER enter)*

MOTHER: I don't understand this. What's happened? Why didn't Harriett take that train? Tell me!

DONALD: She's in the house, Mrs. Harper.

CANTWELL: Gee! So she's here? Put a star in my crown! *(He goes to the door, then turns and listens)*

DONALD: I've just said goodbye to her—I'm not going to bother her any more. It isn't fair. I've said goodbye.

MOTHER: Are you out of your senses? Why didn't you bring her to the station? I trusted you.

DONALD: It's no use. Harriett's changed. We were on the way to the station, down near that big warehouse—when we had to stop in a traffic jam. Those strikers—it seems they've won their strike.

CANTWELL: That's what I told you, Mom. Whoopee!

DONALD: They were having a victory parade and they all came streaming by us as we stood there—And something just came over Harriett. She'd been so quiet up to then. But as they went past, their banners almost touching us—well, she changed. That's all. And she said, "I'm not going to run away. Kenneth needs me now. He's won. I can't run away. He'll be free."

CANTWELL: Just like that Union guy said!

DONALD: What union guy?

CANTWELL: The one I saw at the jail. You see I went down there and tried to see Kenneth—to tell him you were sending Harriett away and all.

MOTHER: Cantwell! I can't even trust my own family. What's come over you all? I don't see. I don't see! *(She sobs)*

CANTWELL: Well—But Mom—they are engaged—and everybody else was against 'em—so I thought—well, after all, I'm her brother.

MOTHER: So she's back here again. After all my plans.

DONALD: Yes. She told the taxi driver to turn around . . . that she wasn't going to the station—that she wanted to come back here. I was helpless—

MOTHER: We're all helpless. Why won't they let me help them. I love them so—But now it's disgrace—and shame—

CANTWELL: It's not that bad, Mother. Honest, won't you listen to what I've been telling you? I tell you that guy at the jail—that union official that was down there, he said their union had taken their case before the Regional N.L.R.B. or N.L.R.D. or N.L., something like that, and the committee chances looked pretty good—the strikers too.

DONALD: But the papers said—

CANTWELL: Phooey with the papers—that's ancient history.

MOTHER: And am I to rejoice that this lazy striking good for nothing is about to get out of jail so that he can marry my daughter?

DONALD: But, Mrs. Harper, maybe after all, well, you see Harriett loves him. And maybe we've all been—

MOTHER: I don't know what's come over you all—And you too, J. Donald—

CANTWELL: But honest, Mom, Ken's a swell guy. You've never really given him a chance. And he's important. The union guy said he's slated for a promotion in the Union Council. You see, he, Kenneth, might have sold 'em out—and he didn't. And that takes guts, believe me, especially when you know you might go to jail for standing by your guns. He's a prince.

MOTHER: That's enough, Cantwell. Take your sister's bags, please, and carry them to her room. I want to sit alone a minute.

CANTWELL: All right, Mom. But don't let it get you down. I'm right here, you know. *(Hugging her)* I'll be seeing you.

> *(CANTWELL takes bags into the house. MOTHER turns to Donald)*

DONALD: It's hard, Mrs. Harper. I wish I could help you. Send for me if you need me. I won't be coming so often now. Harriett and I have said goodbye.

MOTHER: You've been a loyal friend, J. Donald. Closer than my own children even. Goodbye. I'm going to sit alone here—for a moment. *(He seats her in a swing)*

DONALD: You're a brave woman. Goodbye.

HARRIETT: *(Coming out)* Oh, Mother, look at me. And forgive me! It's so hard for you to understand, isn't it? And I seem so ungrateful—and we've said such hard things to each other. Come in to supper and see what I've made. A surprise for you.

MOTHER: Harriett. What are you going to make of yourself?

HARRIETT: Oh, let's not bother about that now. Tonight we'll have a long talk and I'll make it all as clear to you as it is to me. But hurry now. I have to go someplace right after supper. I'm in an awful hurry.

MOTHER: Where are you going, Harriett?

HARRIETT: Now don't get cross again. You're being so nice now. I really ought not tell you.

MOTHER: My Harriett is happy again—Something's happened.

HARRIETT: Yes, something's happened. I'll try to tell you tonight.

MOTHER: Where are you hurrying to after supper?

HARRIETT: Careful now. To jail—to try and see Kenneth—I've got to.

MOTHER: Yes, I thought so—Well, let's see what you've got for supper. *(They rise and move toward door)*

HARRIETT: Everything you like. It isn't half good enough for you. *(As they enter the house, KENNETH comes up the walk. He is unshaven, but neat and clean. He rings the bell. CANTWELL come to door)*

CANTWELL: Count me blessed! How are you, man?

KENNETH: Old Home-Run Cantwell!

CANTWELL: Gee, I've been hanging around that old jail house for three days trying to get to see you. Couldn't get past the guard for nothing. Somebody got you out—or did you jump out the window?

KENNETH: Released and how!

CANTWELL: Somebody go your bail?

KENNETH: Bail, nothing. I'm out, man. Out for good. The union officials took our case to the Labor Board—you know the N.L.R.B.

CANTWELL: Say it again—that's something I got to learn. N.L.—

KENNETH: N.L.R.B.—National Labor Relations Board.

CANTWELL: N.L.R.B. ———— Go on.

KENNETH: Well, the Regional investigator of the Board, he got the facts together, went to the company guys and they, the company, agreed to take us back and pay us our back wages. Didn't even have to file a complaint against the company.

CANTWELL: Boy, that's mellow! And are you something!

KENNETH: Seems like I'm getting places all right!

CANTWELL: Yes, that union fellow I talked to down at the jail, he said you'd more than likely get a promotion in the union council— because you made the men to stick when they were getting kinda wobbly—

KENNETH: Yeah. Got it in my pocket. See this? "In recognition of good judgment and loyal service displayed in the recent strike crisis, we hereby ask your permission to nominate you in the forthcoming election for the Presidency of Bristol Warehouse Local #982 of the Packers' and Truckers' Union." Swell, huh! Doesn't mean any money, but it's the kind of thing makes a man feel good!

CANTWELL: You said it. But I know you didn't come here to pay me a call. Want to see somebody?

KENNETH: You bet. Can you fix it?

CANTWELL: Man, I'm a fixer. Watch me! *(He turns and goes indoors, calling)* Harriett! Fuller Brush man on the front porch—wants to give you a nice little brush.

(HARRIETT comes to the door)

HARRIETT: Oh, Kenneth, you're free—you're free.

(Embraces her)

KENNETH: But you're not. I've got you locked up here—and just you try to get away.

HARRIETT: Oh, it's so good, Kenneth—And you're so good to feel— to look at.

KENNETH: Aw, Harriett honey, I know I look like a tramp. Haven't had a shave for three days—but I couldn't wait. Honest. So here I am looking like a grizzly.

HARRIETT: Dear grisley! But how did you get here?

KENNETH: Company settled with the N.L.R.B. without even having to file a complaint against them. What do you know about that? Back to work with all my back pay too.

HARRIETT: Oh, Ken. And now we'll find a nice little house and— Kenneth—

KENNETH: Yes—

HARRIETT: It will have to be a very nice little house.

KENNETH: Sure it will—nice and clean and plenty cozy.

HARRIETT: And one room at least must be full of sunshine, Kenneth.

KENNETH: That's right. But wait a minute—what do you mean?

HARRIETT: I mean the baby's room, Kenneth.

KENNETH: You're sure! Golly! I'll say it's got to have sunshine. A baby!

HARRIETT: Yes, Ken—ours!

MOTHER: *(Calling from within)* Harriett!

HARRIETT: *(KENNETH and HARRIETT separate. KENNETH gets ready to meet Mother. MOTHER appears at the door)* Yes, Mother.

MOTHER: I was just thinking, dear. If the workers are going to run the town, I think I'll call up Mr. Sims and join that Teachers' Union!

> *(HARRIETT staggers, KENNETH catches her, picks her up, carries her to swing, folds her in his arms, just as CANTWELL turns on the light within. CANTWELL looks out window, sees Kenneth and Harriet in each others arms. LUCIA comes to door)*

CANTWELL: Whoopee!

LUCIA: I think I'll play a little Mendelssohn.

CANTWELL: Try and swing it, will you?

Mendelssohn's Wedding March, slightly syncopated is heard within as the
CURTAIN FALLS

Don't You Want to Be Free?

A Poetry Play

From Slavery
Through the Blues
To Now—and then some!
With Singing, Music, and Dancing

1938

In 1938, just back from Spain, Hughes wanted a theater of his own. His friend Louise Thompson obtained the backing of the International Workers Order, which provided space and sponsorship for the theater, and all of its first members were I.W.O. workers. The theater was affiliated with the leftist New Theatre League. Louise Thompson also proposed that Hughes provide for the theater a play linking together his best poetry. Taking up her suggestion, Hughes wrote *Don't You Want to Be Free?* drawing both on his own poetry and on many of the radical theater techniques he had employed in *Scottsboro, Limited*. As his Production Notes insist, *Don't You Want to Be Free?* was to be performed in the "modern manner."

Premiering on April 21, 1938, in a loft on 125th Street in Harlem, *Don't You Want to Be Free?* was a resounding success, running for 135 performances, on weekends only. In the second, and final, season of the Harlem Suitcase Theatre, *Don't You Want to Be Free?* was preceded by short satirical pieces, selected from among those included here as "Six Satires."

In 1952, Hughes wrote to his friends Rowena and Russell Jelliffe that *Don't You Want to Be Free?* was "probably the most performed Negro play of our time, having had 135 performances in Harlem when it was done in 1937–38, and some 200 or more in various cities and at most of the Negro Colleges throughout the country, Wilberforce, Howard, Talledega, Dillard, Atlanta University, etc."

In *Don't You Want to Be Free?* Hughes worked out a form perfectly suited for popular theater, and one to which he was to return frequently; perhaps its best known successor is Hughes's civil rights play, *Jericho–Jim Crow* (1963). He also adapted the form of *Don't You Want to Be Free?*

to a variety of themes: for voting drives (*The Ballot and Me,* 1956), for freedom rallies (*For This We Fight,* 1943), and for a play on the occasion of the sixtieth anniversary of St. James Cathedral in Harlem (*St. James: Sixty Years Young,* 1955). He regularly updated the play itself, changing especially its concluding sections to reflect the political situation and idiom of the day. For example, in the "War Version" (1944), the white worker supports the Young Man (factory worker/machinist) when he is attacked by the white foreman, and the play concludes with black and white workers insisting on enlisting together. The end of World War II is reflected in the 1946 conclusion: instead of "Harlem is tired," the Young Man says: "All sensible Americans are tired of the old out-moded prejudiced ways of living with one race pitted against the other." In 1952, the Overseer figure accuses the Young Man of being a "black red," and warns he is building a concentration camp for "Negra leaders." In 1963, mention is made of freedom rides, sit-ins, and other landmark events of the civil rights movement.

This text of *Don't You Want to Be Free?* is as published in *One Act Play Magazine* in October 1938. The Production Notes are in the Langston Hughes Papers.

Characters

A YOUNG MAN
A BOY
A GIRL
A WOMAN
A MAN
AN OLD WOMAN
AN OLD MAN
AN OVERSEER
A MULATTO GIRL
A WIFE
A HUSBAND
A LAUNDRY WORKER
A MEMBER OF THE AUDIENCE
TWO NEWSBOYS
VOICES
A CHORUS

SETTING: *A bare stage, except for a lynch rope and an auction block. No scenery and very few props. No special lighting. Only actors needed— and an audience. There is no curtain, so a YOUNG MAN simply comes forward and begins to speak.*

YOUNG MAN: Listen folks! I'm one of the members of this group, and I want to tell you about our theatre. This is it right here! We haven't got any scenery, or painted curtains, because we haven't got any money to buy them. But we've got something you can't buy with money, anyway. We've got faith in ourselves. And in you. So we're going to put on a show. Maybe you'll like it because it's about you, and about us. This show is for you. And you can act in it too, if you want to. This is your show, as well as ours.

Now I'll tell you what this show is about. It's about me, except that it's not just about me now standing here talking to you—but it's about me yesterday, and about me tomorrow. I'm colored! I guess you can see that. Well, this show is about what it means to be colored in America. Listen:

(Crash of cymbals)

I am a Negro:
   Black as the night is black,
   Black like the depths of my Africa.

I've been a slave:
   Caesar told me to keep his door-steps clean.
   I brushed the boots of Washington.

I've been a worker:
   Under my hand the pyramids arose.
   I made mortar for the Woolworth Building.

I've been a singer:
   All the way from Africa to Georgia
   I carried my sorrow songs.
   I made ragtime.

I've been a victim:
   The Belgians cut off my hands in the Congo.
   They lynch me now in Texas.

I am a Negro:
   Black as the night is black,
   Black like the depths of my Africa.

(Tom-toms)
(From either side come an African BOY, Left, and a GIRL, Right, dressed in clothes of bright colors. The GIRL begins to dance in the African manner, whirling slowly to the beating of the drums.)

BOY:

> The low beating of the tom-toms,
> The slow beating of the tom-toms,
>> Low . . . slow
>> Slow . . . low—
>> Stirs your blood.
>> Dance!
> A night-veiled girl
>> Whirls softly into a
>> Circle of light.
>> Whirls softly . . . slowly,
> Like a wisp of smoke around the fire—
>> And the tom-toms beat,
>> And the tom-toms beat,
> And the low beating of the tom-toms
>> Stirs your blood.

(Cool music like rippling water. Lifting her arms to the sun, the GIRL speaks.)

GIRL:

> To fling my arms wide
> In some place of the sun,
> To whirl and to dance
> Till the white day is done.
> Then rest at cool evening
> Beneath a tall tree
> While night comes on gently,
>> Dark like me—

> That is my dream!

> To fling my arms wide
> In the face of the sun,
> Dance! whirl! whirl!
> Till the quick day is done.
> Rest at pale evening . . .
> A tall slim tree,

Night coming tenderly
Dark like me.

(The BOY has drawn near the GIRL and stands before her. She looks at him, takes his hands, and they gaze into each other's eyes.)

YOUNG MAN: I guess I was like that boy a long time ago, when we lived in Africa, and the sun was our friend. I guess I was crazy about that girl that I met at night in the moonlight under the palm trees. *(Roll of drums, like thunder! The BOY and GIRL run away, Right. The YOUNG MAN speaks to the audience.)*

I was Africa then
But the white men came.
I was in my own land, then.
But the white men came.

They drove me out of the forest
They took me away from the jungles.
I lost my trees.
I lost my silver moons.

Now they've caged me
in their circus of civilization.
Now I'm in a cage
In their circus of civilization.

In 1619 the first slaves came to Jamestown, brought in chains in sailing vessels to America.

(Enter Right four slaves: GIRL, BOY, OLD MAN, and WIFE chained by the wrists together. They walk in a straight line, moaning musically across the stage. The YOUNG MAN joins them. They are followed by an OVERSEER with a whip. All exit Left except the GIRL and the OVERSEER. The GIRL mounts the slave-block, wild-eyed and frightened.)

OVERSEER: Get along now! Get on! Step along there! *(Approaching auction block.)* Folks, look here what I got! A nice healthy black gal, folks. Wild! Ain't trained, but a little of this will break her in. *(Holds up his whip.)* Congo women can't be beat for working, and she's a Congo woman. Good for house or fields. Look at them legs, wiry and strong. *(Feels her legs.)* Look at them hands. Long fingers, just right for pickin' cotton. *(To the GIRL.)* Open your mouth, gal!

(Punches her with the whipstock.) Open your mouth. *(GIRL opens her mouth.)* See! Healthy! Nice white teeth! *(With a leer.)* This girl's all right for most anything. What am I offered for her, gentlemen? Speak up! Make your bids. What am I offered for her?

VOICE: One hundred dollars.

OVERSEER: Heh! One hundred dollars! What? That ain't a starter! What am I offered for this gal, gentlemen? I got a hundred.

VOICE: One hundred fifty!

OVERSEER: One hundred fifty! Hundred fifty! Good for cooking, washing, hoeing, anything you want.

VOICE: Two hundred!

OVERSEER: That's more like it! Two hundred! Two . . .

VOICE: Two hundred ten.

VOICE: Two hundred twenty.

VOICE: Two hundred fifty.

OVERSEER: Two hundred fifty! Two hundred fifty . . .

VOICE: Three hundred!

OVERSEER: Three hundred! Do I hear another? What? Three hundred dollars worth of black gal! Going! Going! Gone! *(Strikes the floor with his whip. There is a loud scream from the GIRL.)* Gone for three hundred dollars! Here, take her. Make her work now. *(He pushes the GIRL off the block and she goes aside sobbing, Right. Dark voices are heard chanting.)*

VOICES:

> Cook them white folks dinner,
> Wash them white folks clothes,
> Be them white folks slave-gal,
> That is all she knows.
> Be them white folks slave-gal,
> That is all she knows.

(OLD MAN enters Left in the overalls and ragged shirt of a slave. He mounts the block.)

OVERSEER: Kinder old, folks, but still got plenty in him. Nothing like an old work-horse. He's well broke in. Something of a preacher, too. Helps keep the other slaves out o' mischief o' Sundays. What am I offered? Fifty? . . . Hundred fifty. Going, going, gone! For a hundred and fifty! Get off the block, you old ape! Get off the block and lemme get somebody up here I can make some money off of. *(He pushes the OLD MAN away. He goes aside, muttering.)*

VOICES:

> Whip done broke his spirit,
> Plow done broke his back.
> All they wants a slave, that's all,
> When a man is black.
> Nothin' but a slave, that's all,
> If a man is black.

OLD MAN: No, no! No, no!

> *(The YOUNG MAN enters Left. The OVERSEER's face glows.*
> *He rubs his hands.)*

OVERSEER:

> Ah! Here's a nice fine black buck!
> Strong's you'd want to see
> Boy, get up on that block
> And make some dough for me!

YOUNG MAN:

> No!

OVERSEER:

> What? No!
> Who're you talkin' to?

YOUNG MAN:

> You!

OVERSEER:

> You must've gone crazy
> Talking like that to me.
> Get up on that block!

YOUNG MAN:

> No! I want to be free! *(Kicks block off stage.)*

OVERSEER:

> Free?

YOUNG MAN:

> Yes, free!
> Not sold like a slave.
> Before I'll be sold again
> I'll go down to my grave.

> *(The OVERSEER strikes him with his whip.)*

GIRL: Oh!

YOUNG MAN: No! no! no! *(As he backs away and falls before the blows of the OVERSEER's whip.)*

OVERSEER: I'll teach you to want to be free! To talk back to me! *(Lashing him. YOUNG MAN falls.)*

GIRL: Oh! . . . Oh! . . . Oh!

OLD MAN: *(Begins to sing.)*
> Go down, Moses,
> Way down in Egypt land,
> And tell ole Pharaoh

CHORUS:
> To let my people go.

OVERSEER: *(Turns to OLD MAN and strikes him with his whip.)* Shut up, you dog!

(As the OLD MAN falls, the GIRL takes up the song.)

GIRL:
> Go down, Moses,
> Way down in Egypt land,
> And tell ole Pharaoh

CHORUS:
> To let my people go!

OVERSEER: *(In wild confusion, rushes to the GIRL and strikes her.)* Shut up, you god-damned dogs! Shut up!

(But then the YOUNG MAN rises and takes up the song.)

YOUNG MAN:
> Go down, Moses,
> Way down in Egypt land,
> And tell ole Pharaoh
> To let my people go.

CHORUS:
> And tell ole Pharaoh
> To let my people go.

(A great wave of revolt rises disguised as a song. The OVERSEER is powerless against it. He calls for troops, for arms. He pulls a gun.)

OVERSEER: Send soldiers! Get out the militia! Shoot these dogs!

(Shots are heard. The OLD MAN falls prone. The GIRL falls. An OLD WOMAN enters Right and kneels over the dead.)

OVERSEER: *(As he shoots.)* Shut up! Shut up! Shut up! *(He exits Left.)*

YOUNG MAN: *(Coming forward toward the audience.)* But we didn't shut up! We were never wholly quiet! Some of us always carried on our fight and kept alive the seeds of revolt. Nat Turner was one. Denmark Vesey was another who tried to lead the slaves to freedom.

Harriet Tubman was another who sought roads to escape. Sojourner Truth another. Some they beat to death. Some they killed. But some of us always kept on, even though the way looked dark.

OLD WOMAN: So dark! So dark! *(Sings over the bodies of her dead.)*

> Oh, nobody knows
> The trouble I've seen!
> Nobody knows but Jesus.
> Nobody knows
> The trouble I've seen.
> Glory, Hallelujah!
>
> Sometimes I'm up,
> Sometimes I'm down.
> Oh, yes, Lawd!
> Sometimes I'm almost
> To the ground.
> O, yes, Lawd!

CHORUS:

> Oh, nobody knows
> The trouble I've seen . . .

OLD WOMAN: *(As the CHORUS hums.)* Children scattered. Home gone. Sons and daughters sold away. I don't know where they are. *(Rises.)* But I look at the stars and they look at the stars. And somehow I feels better. And now I walks the world lookin' for truth. I'se a so-journer lookin' for truth.

YOUNG MAN: Sojourner Truth!

OLD WOMAN: Yes, son.

YOUNG MAN: Is we ever gonna be free?

OLD WOMAN: Son, we gonna be free. Ain't you heard them names?

YOUNG MAN: What names?

OLD WOMAN: Black names and white names in the air. Listen! *(Flag rises.)*

VOICES: Douglass! Douglass! Frederick Douglass! William Lloyd Garrison!   Emerson! . . . Whittier! . . . Lowell! . . . Douglass! John Brown! Lincoln! John Brown! Abraham Lincoln. *(Roll of drums. Bugle calls.)*

OLD WOMAN: The Civil War! And freedom!

YOUNG MAN: *(Takes flag.)* White soldiers and black soldiers fighting for our freedom.

OLD MAN: *(Rising.)* Slaves rising from the dead for freedom.
GIRL: *(Rising.)* Women lifting up their heads for freedom.
CHORUS:

>Glory! Glory! Hallelujah!
>Glory! Glory! Hallelujah!
>Glory! Glory! Hallelujah!

YOUNG MAN: Everybody sing! *(He starts the verse.)*
CHORUS:

>John Brown's body
>Lies a-mouldering in his grave . . .
>>*(Repeat Chorus.)*

>*(As they sing, all exit, Right. Enter the MAN and the WOMAN in old clothes, Left, cross Right. They begin to hoe in a field.)*

WOMAN: John, this ain't no freedom.
MAN: Free, to work and get no pay. Lucy, how come we's

>Just a herd of Negroes
>Driven to the field,
>Plowing, planting, hoeing,
>To make the cotton yield.

>When the cotton's picked
>And the work is done
>Boss man takes the money
>And we get none.

>Leaves us hungry, ragged
>As we were before.
>Year by year goes by
>And we are nothing more

>Than a herd of Negroes
>Driven to the field—
>Plowing life away
>To make the cotton yield.

WOMAN: Yes, honey, all you say is true, 'cause

>There stands the white man,
>Boss of the fields—
>Lord of the land
>And all that it yields.

And here bend the black folks,
Hands to the soil—
Bosses of nothing,
Not even our toil.

MAN: The South! Honey, the South's so pretty, magnolia trees and cotton, but sometimes it's bad, too. So evil and bad!
    (Enter OVERSEER bringing chair.)
WOMAN: The white folks won't pay us nothing, that's the trouble. Besides the Jim Crow cars, the Jim Crow schools, and the lynchings—when you work, they don't pay you nothing.
MAN: That's what happened to Wilbur, to our boy! All over a little mite o' money.
WOMAN: Yes, that's what happened to Wilbur. He went to ask the man for his money—and they killed him.
    (On the Left, the OVERSEER sits in a chair tilted back, smoking a big cigar. Enter the YOUNG MAN, Right, crosses Left.)
YOUNG MAN: Mr. Mallory, the crops all sold, ain't it? Can you gimme my part now?
OVERSEER: Your part? What you mean, your part, George?
YOUNG MAN: I mean my money that you owe me.
OVERSEER: You better be careful how you use that work *owe*, boy. I don't owe you nothing.
YOUNG MAN: *(Trying to restrain himself.)* But I raised nine bales, Mr. Mallory. And my contract calls . . .
OVERSEER: Your contract? Hell! What about my bills? What about the commissary store? What about that sow belly and corn meal I been advancing you all the year for you and your lazy old woman, and them kids of yours that you thinks too good to work in the cotton fields. Trying to send pickaninnies to school! Huh! You're an uppity black boy, anyhow. Talkin' about what I owe you! Why even after the nine bales was sold, you owed me more'n a hundred dollars. Why, you ungrateful scoundrel. Get on back there in that field and start plowin' for next year's crop.
YOUNG MAN: Mr. Mallory, I ain't goin'. Not till I see the figures.
OVERSEER: You ain't going? What you mean, you ain't going? Don't talk back to me!
YOUNG MAN: I ain't going. I'm tired o' workin' for nothing.
OVERSEER: *(Rising.)* Are you trying to say I don't pay my field hands? Get out o' here. You impudent black cuss, you! Get out o' here!

YOUNG MAN: No, sir, Mr. Mallory, not without my money.

OVERSEER: You impudent dog! Get out o' here before I beat the hell out of you.

YOUNG MAN: No!

> *(The OVERSEER walks up to the YOUNG MAN and hits him in the mouth. The YOUNG MAN stands as if in a daze, then he suddenly deals the OVERSEER a blow that sends him reeling unconscious to the floor. There is a crash of cymbals. Whistles. The far-off cry of a mob. The MOTHER and FATHER are terror-stricken. The YOUNG MAN looks for a place to hide. There is no hiding place.)*

MAN: Hurry, son, hurry! They gonna kill you!

WOMAN: Run, Wilbur! Oh, honey, run! Go the swamp way, so's the dogs can't smell no tracks. Run!

MAN: Hurry! Hurry! Hurry! Son, hurry!

YOUNG MAN *(Darting wildly about.)* There ain't no place to run. I hit the white man. I done hit the boss! And there ain't no place to run. Nobody helps me. Nobody to protect me. *(He approaches the lynch rope that dangles from the sky and puts his head into the noose.)* I know it! You got me! All you crackers got me. Dead! I'm dead!

> *(His body slumps as if dead. NEWSBOYS enter selling papers.)*

NEWSBOYS: Negro lynched in Alabama! Big Lynching Near Selma! Read all about it! Read about the lynching! Negro accused of rape! Big lynching!

WOMAN: *(Standing before the hanging youth.)* My boy is dead!

MAN: *(Bitterly.)* Damn the ones what kilt him! Damn their souls to hell!

WOMAN: John, my boy is dead, I'm all alone—and my boy is dead!

> *(Begins to sing.)*

> I couldn't hear nobody pray.
> Oh, Lawdy! Couldn't hear nobody pray.
> Way down yonder by myself,
> I couldn't hear nobody pray!

> *(Enter a young MULATTO GIRL, who sits down beside the hanging body, Center, and begins to recite.)*

MULATTO GIRL:

> Way down South in Dixie,
> (Break the heart of me!)
> They hung my dark young lover
> To a cross road's tree.

Way down South in Dixie,
(Bruised body high in air)
I asked the white Lord Jesus
What was the use of prayer.

Way down South in Dixie
(Break the heart of me)
Love is a naked shadow
On a gnarled and naked tree.

OVERSEER: *(Left—Rising and shouting.)*
　　　Pull at the rope! O!
　　　Pull it high!
　　　Let the white folks live
　　　And the black man die.
MAN:
　　　Yes, pull, it then,
　　　With a bloody cry!
　　　Let the black boy swing
　　　But the *white folks* die.
OVERSEER:
　　　The white folks die?
　　　What do you mean—
　　　The white folks die?
MAN:
　　　That black boy's
　　　Still body says:
YOUNG MAN:
　　　Not I!
MAN:
　　　Not I!
VOICES:
　　　Not I! Not I! Not I!
　　　　(The OVERSEER sneaks away.)
YOUNG MAN: They killed Christ, didn't they, when he tried to change
　　the world?
WOMAN: But did he die?
EVERYBODY: *No!*
YOUNG MAN: They killed John Brown, didn't they, when he tried to
　　free the slaves?

WOMAN: But did he die?

VOICES: No!

YOUNG MAN: What did Angelo Herndon say when they had him in prison for trying to help the poor? What did Herndon say?

VOICE: Let them kill Herndon, if they will, but a million more will rise to take my place.

YOUNG MAN: You can't kill the working class, he said. And when we rise . . .

WOMAN: *(Begins to sing.)*
> In that great gettin' up mornin'
> Fare you well! Fare you well!
>> *(Repeat.)*

CHORUS:
> There's a better day a-comin'! etc.
>> *(The old spiritual rises triumphally as the YOUNG MAN takes his head from lynch rope. He comes with tramp's bundle on stick and stands before the MULATTO GIRL. The MAN and WOMAN exit Right as the singing dies down.)*

YOUNG MAN: So many things is wrong in this world, honey, but the wrongest thing of all is poverty. Being poor. You're the girl I loved once, now look at you! All painted and powdered, and wrong. But I know what happened. I don't blame you for it. You was young and beautiful once, and golden like the sunshine that warmed your body. But because you was colored, honey, this town had no place for you, nothing for you to do.

MULATTO GIRL: So one day, sitting on old Mrs. Latham's back porch polishing the silver, working for two dollars a week, I asked myself two questions. They ran something like this: What can a colored girl do on the money from a white woman's kitchen?

VOICE: Two dollars a week.

MULATTO GIRL: And ain't there any joy in this town?

VOICE: Two dollars a week.

YOUNG MAN: Now the streets down by the river are your streets. *(Turning away.)* And the sinister shuttered houses of the bottoms hold a yellow girl seeking an answer to her questions.

VOICE: *(Softly.)* Two dollars a week.

MULATTO GIRL: The good church folks won't even mention my name any more.

YOUNG MAN: But the white men who visit those houses . . .

MULATTO GIRL: *(Triumphantly.)* Pay more money to me now than they ever did before when I worked in their kitchens. *(Distant laughter.)*

YOUNG MAN: *(Bitterly.)* I'm going away. I got to go away.

MULATTO GIRL: Goodbye, Wilbur.

YOUNG MAN: *(Without looking back.)* I'm going up North. *(As he walks left.)* I'm going far away.

MULATTO GIRL: Goodbye, Wilbur! *(She powders her face and begins to recite:)*

> My old man's a white old man!
> My old mother's black!
> But if ever I cursed my white old man
> I take my curses back.
>
> If I ever cursed my black old mother
> And wished she were in hell,
> I'm sorry for that evil wish
> And now I wish her well.
>
> My old man died in a fine big house.
> My ma died in a shack.
> I wonder where I'm gonna die,
> Being neither white nor black?

> *(As she walks away, a piano begins to play the Blues, the sad old Negro blues. She exits Right.)*
> *(The YOUNG MAN sings as he picks up his pack and begins to trudge the road.)*

YOUNG MAN:

> Goin' down de road, Lawd,
> Goin' down de road,
> Down de road, Lawd,
> Way, way down de road.
> Got to find somebody
> To help me carry dis load.
> Sun's a-settin',
> This is what I'm gonna sing.
> Sun's a-settin'
> This is what I'm gonna sing:
> I feel de blues a-comin'
> Wonder what de blues 'll bring?

Road, Road, Road, O!
Road, road . . . road . . . road, road!
Road, road, road, O!
On de No'thern road.
These Mississippi towns ain't
Fit fer a hoppin' toad.

> *(The YOUNG MAN sits down beside the road. Enter WIFE, Right, and BOY, Left.)*

Gee, but I got the blues.

> *(The piano sings with the sad weary notes of the Blues.)*

Do you-all know what the blues is?

WIFE:

The blues ain't nothin'
But the dog-goned heart's disease.
I say, blues ain't nothin' but
The dog-gone heart's disease.
When you got the blues, you
Sho can't find no ease.
(Sighs.)

I got the blues. Reckon I'll run down the street a minute, see if I can walk 'em off!

> *(She dresses and powders to exit later from her dreary flat. At Left, undressing in a dark hall bedroom, the BOY answers, too.)*

BOY: I got the blues. Guess I'll go to bed. Maybe I can sleep 'em off.

YOUNG MAN: The blues is songs folks make up when their heart hurts. That's what the blues is. Sad funny songs. Too sad to be funny, and too funny to be sad. *(Exit WOMAN.)* Colored folks made up the blues! Listen!

> *(Loudly, the piano player beats out his Blues.)*

BOY:

I got the Weary Blues
And I can't be satisfied.
Got the Weary Blues
And can't be satisfied—
I ain't happy no mo'
And I wish that I had died.
(But the player keeps on playing softly in the night.)

YOUNG MAN: You see, that's the blues.

(At Right, a HUSBAND comes home from work and throws his hat and dinner pail on the table.)

Sometimes there's the family blues.

HUSBAND: God-dog it!

I works all day
Wid a pick an' a shovel
Comes home at night,—
It ain't nothin' but a hovel.

I calls for ma woman
When I opens de door.
She's out in de street,—
Ain't no good no more.

I done her swell
An' I treats her fine,
But she don't gimme no lovin'
Cause she ain't de right kind.

I'm a hard workin' man—
But I sho pays double.
I tries to be good but
Gets nothin' but trouble.

(He sits down at the table and begins to sing.)

Trouble, trouble, I has 'em all my days.
Trouble, trouble, has 'em all my days.
Seems like trouble's gonna drive me to my grave.

(He snatches up his hat and leaves.) I'm gonna get drunk.

YOUNG MAN: And sometimes there's the loveless blues—when all you got left is a picture of the one you care for.

(At left, the BOY who has been looking at his girl's picture begins to sing.)

BOY:

All I want is your picture,
Must be in a frame.
All I want is your picture,
Must be in a frame—
So when you're gone
I can see you just the same!

(He stops and begins to talk to the picture.)

Cause you don't love me, baby,
Is awful awful hard.
Gypsy done showed me
My bad luck card.

There ain't no good left
In this world for me.
Gypsy done tole me,—
Unlucky as can be.

   (Throws down picture.)

I don't know what
Po' weary me can do.
Gypsy says I'd kill ma self
If I was you.

   (The BOY gets up, puts on his coat, and begins to sing.)

I'm goin' down to the railroad
And lay my head on the track,
Goin' down to the railroad,
Lay my head on the track,
If I see the train a-comin',
I'm gonna jerk it back.

   *(He exits, Left. At Right, WOMAN enters, looks around anxiously
   and begins to cry.)*

YOUNG MAN: And then there is them left-lonesome blues.
WIFE: Oh, Lawd! Looks like Jackson done left me. And I wasn't gone
   nowhere but to put my numbers in. Jackson, you done broke my
   heart this evenin'.

I ain't got no heart no mo'
Next time a man comes near me
Gonna shut and lock my door,
Cause they treats me mean—
The ones I love.
They always treats me mean.

   (She begins to sing.)
Oh, you mens treats women
Just like a old pair o'shoes.
You mens treats women

Just like a old pair o'shoes.
You kicks 'em round and
Does 'em like you choose.

*(She goes and stands beside the piano on the opposite side from the
HUSBAND.)*

YOUNG MAN: And then there is those morning after blues.

HUSBAND: It's the next day now. *(Begins to sing.)*

I was so sick last night I
Didn't hardly know my mind.
So sick last night I
Didn't know my mind.
I drunk some bad licker that
Almost made me blind.

Had a dream last night I
Thought I was in hell.
I drempt last night I
Thought I was in hell.
Woke up and looked around me—
Babe, your mouth was open like a well.

I said, Baby, baby,
Please don't snore so loud.
Baby! Please don't snore so loud.
You jest a little bit o' woman but you
Sound like a great big crowd.

WIFE: *(Replies in song.)*

Now, listen, Mr. Jackson,
Don't say that to me.
Listen, Mr. Jackson,
Don't say that to me,
Cause if you do,
We is bound to disagree.

HUSBAND: Baby, you ain't gonna leave me, is you? You all I got.

WIFE: Yes, I'm gonna leave you. You all I got, too, but I sure can get
along without you. So, goodbye!

ALL: *(Singing.)*

Blues, blues, blues!
Blues, blues . . . blues, blues, blues!

Blues is what's the matter
When you loses all you got to lose.
(Exit HUSBAND Right, WIFE Left.)

YOUNG MAN: Colored folks made the blues! Now everybody sings 'em. We made 'em out of being poor and lonely. And homes busted up, and desperate and broke. *(Rises.)* But me, I haven't got any blues! I got a little job, not much. *(Leans against wall.)* Got a little time to stand on the corner at night and watch the girls go by! Boy, these Harlem girls'ye sure got it! Looky yonder! *(Enter, Right, the GIRL, beautiful in a red dress. As she passes, he recites):*
Man alive! When Susanna Jones wears red
Her face is like an ancient cameo
Turned brown by the ages.

VOICE:
Come with a blast of trumpets,
    Jesus!

YOUNG MAN:
When Susanna Jones wears red
A queen from some time-dead Egyptian night
Walks once again.

VOICE:
Blow trumpets, Jesus!

YOUNG MAN:
And the beauty of Susanna Jones in red
Burns in my heart a love-fire sharp link pain.

VOICE:
Sweet silver trumpets,
    Jesus!

(The GIRL exists Left and the YOUNG MAN takes off his coat and starts polishing a brass spittoon. As he works he talks to himself.)

YOUNG MAN: Gee, if I just had a little money, I think I'd get married. But I kinder hate to start out with nothing. Suppose we had a kid? Well, I'd want my kid to have a decent break, that's what. At least a chance to go to high school. I didn't even have that. Had to start work soon as I was big enough. My folks never did get ahead. There ain't many decent jobs a colored boy can get nohow. Here I am polishing spittoons in a hotel. But I've travelled around plenty, been all over America mighty near. And most towns, there just ain't nothin' much for a colored boy to do. Lots of factories won't even hire colored men. Lots of places I can't join unions. Anyhow this old

spittoon looks right good. *(He holds up the shining spittoon proudly.)*
When a thing's clean, it always looks better, no matter what. But,
gee! Have *I* always got to do the cleaning? Always the dirty work?
Me! Always? *(He recites as he polishes.)*

Clean the spittoons, boy.
    Detroit,
    Chicago,
    Atlantic City,
    Palm Beach.
Clean the spittoons.
The steam in hotel kitchens,
And the smoke in hotel lobbies,
And the slime in hotel spittoons:
Part of my life.
    Hey, boy!
    A nickel,
    A dime,
    A dollar,
Two dollars a day.
    Hey, boy!
    A nickel,
    A dime,
    A dollar,
    Two dollars
Buys smokes, shoes,
A ticket to the movies.
House rent to pay,
Gin on Saturday,
Church on Sunday.
    My God!
Movies and church
and women and Sunday
all mixed up with dimes and
dollars and clean spittoons
and house rent to pay.
    Hey, boy!
A bright bowl of brass is beautiful to the Lord.
Bright polished brass like the cymbals
Of King David's dancers,

Like the wine cups of Solomon.
　Hey, boy!
A clean spittoon on the altar of the Lord.
A clean bright spittoon all newly polished,—
At least I can offer that.

　　(The BOSS enters, Left, crosses Right.)
OVERSEER: Com'mere, Boy!
YOUNG MAN: Yes, sir.
OVERSEER: Listen, George.
YOUNG MAN: Wilbur's my name.
OVERSEER: Well, whatever your name is, listen. I'm the boss and I
　　got to cut down expenses. You know, that bank crash—folks ain't
　　spending money. I'm gonna let the bell-boys do the house man's
　　work from now on. You can get your check and go.
YOUNG MAN: *(Stunned.)* Yes, sir, Mister Mallory, but . . .
　　*(The OVERSEER walks to the other side, and seats himself for a
　　shine. He calls to the OLD MAN who enters, Right.)*
OVERSEER: Hey, George!
OLD MAN: Yes, sir! Yes, sir!
OVERSEER: Gimme a shine!
　　(As he shines his shoes, WOMAN enters Left and begins to dust.)
OLD MAN: Yes, sir! Yes, sir!

I must say yes, sir.
To *you* all the time.
Yes, sir! Yes, sir!
All my days
Climbing up a great big mountain
Of yes, sirs.

Rich old white man
Owns the world.

Gimme your shoes
To shine.
Yes, sir, boss,
Yes, sir!

YOUNG MAN: *(Pointing at the OLD MAN.)* That was my grandfather.
　　(On the left, the WOMAN in a maid's apron is working.) And my

mother, out working for the white folks. When I was a kid, never nobody home to take care of me. I don't want my kids to grow up that away. Look at my mother.

WOMAN:

>All day, subdued, polite—
>Thoughtful to the faces that are white.

OLD MAN:

>Oh, tribal dance!
>Oh, drums!
>Oh, veldt at night!

YOUNG MAN:

>Forgotten watch-fires on a hill somewhere!

OLD MAN:

>Oh, songs that do not care!

WOMAN:

>At six o'clock, or seven, or eight, you're through
>You've worked all day,
>Then Harlem waits for you.
>The el, the sub, a taxi through the park.

YOUNG MAN:

>Oh, drums of life in Harlem after dark.

WOMAN:

>Oh, dreams! Oh, songs!

OLD MAN:

>A little rest at night.

WOMAN:

>Oh, sweet relief from faces that are white!
>   *(Takes off her apron, puts on her coat and hat, and goes home, crossing Right, to her son, the YOUNG MAN.)*

OVERSEER: Say, George! Be careful of my corns!

OLD MAN: Yes, sir, Mr. Mallory, yes, sir!

OVERSEER: And polish those shoes good now! I want to see my face in 'em when you get through. *(The OLD MAN bends over his task.)*

WOMAN: Good evening, son!

YOUNG MAN: Mom, I lost my job!

WOMAN: You lost your job?

YOUNG MAN: Yes! They laid me off tonight.

WOMAN: Well, honey, you'll find another one. Maybe.

YOUNG MAN: I don't know, mom. Things is so tight, I done lost heart! Look how long I been a man now, and ain't never had a job that amounted to nothing. I've been all over, and everywhere just the same. The dirty work for colored folks, the cheap work, underpaid work! I'm tired, mom. Soon as I come here to be with you a while and we get this little flat, first thing I do is lose my job. And the landlord's just sent us a notice about raising the rent, too. Mom, I'm about ready to give up. I swear I am!

WOMAN: Son, you ain't gonna give up no such a thing. Listen! You gonna keep right on just like I been keeping on. Did you ever stop to think about it, honey, about your mother, and all the rest of us colored women—what we been up against all through history, son. Sit down and lemme tell you, for

> *(Piano music.)*
>
> I'm standing here today
> Like a living story of that long dark way
> That I had to climb, that I had to know
> In order that our race might live and grow.
> Look at my face, boy, dark as the night,
> Yet shining like the sun with hope and light.
> I'm the child they stole from the sand
> Three hundred years ago in Africa's land.
> I'm the dark girl who crossed the wide sea
> Carrying in my body the seed of the Free.
> I'm the woman who worked in the field,
> Bringing the cotton and corn to yield.
> I'm the one who labored as a slave,
> Beaten and mistreated for the work that I gave—
> Children sold away from me, husband sold, too.
> No safety, no love, no respect was I due.
> Three hundred years in the deepest South,
> But love put a song and a prayer in my mouth.
> Love put a dream like steel in my soul.
> Now through my children, we're reaching the goal.
> I couldn't read then. I couldn't write.
> I had nothing back there in the night.
> Sometimes the valley was filled with tears,
> But I kept trudging on through the lonely years.
> Sometimes the road was hot with sun.
> But I had to keep on till my work was done.
> I *had* to keep on! No stopping for me—
> I was the seed of the coming Free.

I nourished our dream that nothing could smother
Deep in the breast—the Negro Mother.
I had only hope then, but now through you,
Dark child of today, my dreams must come true.
All you dark children in the world out there,
Remember my sweat, my pain, my despair.
Remember my years heavy with sorrow—
And make of those years a torch for tomorrow,
Make of my past a road to the light,
Out of the darkness, the ignorance, the night.
Lift high my banner out of the dust.
Stand like free men supporting my trust.
Believe in the right, let none push you back.
Remember the whip and the slaver's track.
Remember how the strong in struggle and strife
Still bar you the way, and deny you life—
But march ever forward, breaking down bars.
Look ever upward at the sun and the stars.
Oh, my dark children, may my dreams and my prayers
Impel you forever up the great stairs—
For I will be with you till no white brother
Dares keep down the children of the Negro Mother.

OVERSEER: *(Who is now a Landlord, coming to knock at their door, Right.)* Madam, did you get my notice about raising your rent, ten dollars a month more?

WOMAN: Yes, sir, I got the notice, but I am tired of that. I ain't gonna pay no more. We're paying enough.

OVERSEER: You'll pay it or move, and no smart talk about it, neither.

YOUNG MAN: *(Rising.)* Say, listen here! Who're you to speak to my mother like that?

OVERSEER: I'm the landlord. If you don't like it, get out of my place.

YOUNG MAN: Lemme see you get instead!

OVERSEER: What? This is my house!

YOUNG MAN: Yes, but you don't live in it! We live here! *(He towers above the Landlord.)* This is Harlem.

> *(The OVERSEER backs away and puts on a waiter's apron. WO-MAN begins to peel potatoes, YOUNG MAN to study. At the left a BOY holding a menu calls.)*

BOY: Say, waiter! Where is that waiter? . . . Hey, waiter! Give me an order of spaghetti and a bottle of beer, please.

OVERSEER: Sorry! We don't serve colored here.

BOY: What? You mean on a 125th Street, and don't serve colored?

OVERSEER: Sure, this is a white place.

BOY: *(Rising.)* And you don't serve colored people?

OVERSEER: You heard me, big boy.

BOY: I might of heard you, but this is Harlem speaking now. Get me that spaghetti. I'm tired of this stuff! Talking about you don't serve colored people. Ain't I an American?

> *(OVERSEER backs away. OLD WOMAN enters Left as a picket carrying a sign that reads:)*
> *DON'T BUY HERE!*
> *THIS STORE DOES NOT*
> *EMPLOY NEGRO CLERKS*
> *(Slowly she walks back and forth in front of a store bearing the sign: MEAT MARKET. The OVERSEER rushes out in the white apron of a Butcher.)*

OVERSEER: What you doing in front of my store? What I done to you? What for you walking up and down with that sign, destructing my business? Long as you trade with me, what is this?

OLD WOMAN: You know what it is Mr. Schultz! You know how long I been trading with you, don't you?

OVERSEER: More'n ten years, Mrs. Brown.

OLD WOMAN: And all that time, I ain't never seen a colored clerk in this store, not one. My boy growed up and went through high school, and to college, and got more education than you ever had, but when one of your clerks died, and my boy come here to ask you for a job, you said: "No, you might give him a little janitor's job, but you got to have a *white* clerk." *(Loudly.)* That's why I'm picketing out here, Mr. Schultz. Harlem is tired! No work! No money! I tell you, Harlem's tired!

> *(OLD WOMAN brandishes her sign and the BUTCHER flees, to take off his apron and put on a coat and pair of pince-nez glasses with a flowing black ribbon. He is the EDITOR of a daily paper and carries a handful of proofs. The YOUNG MAN enters.)*

YOUNG MAN: You're the editor of the DAILY SCRIBE?

OVERSEER: I am.

YOUNG MAN: I wrote a letter to your paper more'n two weeks ago

about the hard times we colored folks've been having, and you didn't
print it. I wish you'd tell me how come?

OVERSEER: Ah, yes! I remember that letter. I'll tell you, boy, why we
didn't print it. That letter would stir up trouble. I know times are
hard, but you colored people have always been good citizens, peaceful and nice. Why get excited now? Just wait. Times'll be better—the
Republicans will be in again soon. Believe in God, boy, and in the
good old stars and stripes, and be loyal to your country.

YOUNG MAN:

But, Mr. Editor,
I've been loyal to my country
A long time, don't you see?
Now how about my country
Being loyal to me?

I fought in 1812 and 1863,
San Juan Hill in Cuba,
And for Democracy—
And fighting's not the only thing
I've done for liberty:
I've worked and worked a plenty,
Slave and free.

So when I pledge allegiance
To our flag so fair,
I keep looking at the stars and stripes
A-waving there,
And I'm wishing every star
Would *really* be a star for me,
And not just half a star
Like Jim Crow Tennessee—
And no false convict's stripes such as
Scottsboro's put on me.

I want that red and white and blue,
Mr. Editor,
To mean the same thing to me
As it does to you—
For I've been just as loyal
To my country as you have,
Don't you see?

Now, how about my country
Being loyal to me?

OVERSEER: Why—er—uh—you're a radical!
> *(Enter a WHITE WORKER.)*

WHITE WORKER: I don't think so!

OVERSEER: Who're you?

WHITE WORKER: A white worker. You don't have to be colored to know what hard times are. Or to want a square deal. I can tell you that!

OVERSEER: Well, what do you want?

WHITE WORKER: A world where there won't be no hard times. And no color line—labor with a white skin'll never be free as long a labor with a black skin's enslaved.

OVERSEER: By God, you're a radical, too!
> *(WHITE WORKER and YOUNG MAN shake hands.)*

YOUNG MAN: Friend, you understand!

WHITE WORKER: I understand!

OVERSEER: Radicals! Radicals! Lock 'em up! Lock 'em up! Radicals! Lock 'em up! Radicals! Radicals! *(Exits, yelling loudly.)*

YOUNG MAN: Quiet, please—cause Harlem is tired!

WHITE WORKER: *(As he leaves with YOUNG MAN.)* We're all tired!
> *(WIFE enters Left, broom in hand.)*

WIFE: Yes, we're tired! Tired as we can be! *(WIFE sweeps. OVERSEER removes glasses, puts on dark hat, carries a brief case, and is now an INSURANCE MAN: Goes to WIFE and knocks.)* Yes?

OVERSEER: *(Cockily.)* Insurance man! Got your book ready?

WIFE: You want me to pay you?

OVERSEER: Of course. It's due, isn't it?

WIFE: Um-hum! You from the Cosmopolitan Company, ain't you?

OVERSEER: I am.

WIFE: And you don't hire no colored folks in your office, do you?

OVERSEER: Not so far as I know. Why?

WIFE: You won't give colored people certain kinds of policies you carries, neither, will you?

OVERSEER: Well, you see, in some cases your people are bad risks.

WIFE: But my money's *good* money, ain't it?

OVERSEER: Of course, it is.

WIFE: And you want my money, don't you?

OVERSEER: Why, yes. Of course, I do.

WIFE: Well, you ain't gonna get it! *(Fiercely.)* A company that won't hire none of my people, what won't half insure us, and then sends a man to Harlem to collect from me that keeps his hat on in the house! *(OVERSEER, frightened, snatches off his hat.)* Well, you ain't gonna get nary a penny of mine! Get out of here. Go on back downtown to your Jim Crow office. Tell 'em Harlem is tired. *(She shoos him out.)* I'm gonna join a colored insurance company myself.

> *(The OVERSEER flees. Panting, he sits down in a chair Right and is now a LAUNDRY BOSS. He begins to pay out money, while several girls pass before him.)*

MULATTO GIRL: Chile, you better wrap up good. It's kinder chilly out there.

LAUNDRY WORKER: Catch your death o' pneumonia, working all day in this steaming oven.

GIRL: You told that right.

MULATTO GIRL: I sure am glad it's pay day. Let's get in line here and get our money.

OVERSEER: Here, Dorothy Mae! Here's your wages. Now don't get drunk tonight! . . . Here, Miss Lizzie, something for your preacher tomorrow. Now, behave yourself in church! Here! *(As a good looking LAUNDRY WORKER approaches him for her wages.)* Say, Toots, uh, listen . . .

LAUNDRY WORKER: Toots, who?

OVERSEER: Why, er . . .

LAUNDRY WORKER: Is this six dollars all you're giving me for a whole week's work in your laundry?

OVERSEER: That's all you earned, girlie.

LAUNDRY WORKER: Sixty hours in this steaming hole, and that's all I've earned? You must be crazy. I've ironed six hundred shirts this week, at least.

OVERSEER: Well, six dollars is your salary.

LAUNDRY WORKER: Then you take that salary and stick it on back in your drawer, from now on, cause I am tired of working for nothing. Harlem is tired. You're living in a big house up in White Plains, and me slaving all day for nothing in your laundry. You making all your money off of colored folks, and taking every dollar of it out of Harlem to spend. I'm tired.

OVERSEER: *(Jumping up.)* You must belong to the union. You move on before I call the police. You're an agitator!

LAUNDRY WORKER: What police? Some of these days *you're* going to have to move on, because Harlem is tired. Fact is, I think you ought to move now.

WIFE: Yes, you ought to move!

BOY: Get going!

> *(OVERSEER clutches his money and rushes away. But he is surrounded by people, threatening him and crying in anger. The Harlem riots of March 19, 1935 begin.)*

WOMAN: Gouging me for rent!

BOY: You won't serve colored people!

YOUNG MAN: Won't gimme a job!

LAUNDRY WORKER: Working us like slaves!

OLD MAN: Living on Harlem!

WOMAN: Getting rich off black people.

YOUNG MAN: Jim Crow landlord!

WOMAN: Won't rent us a house downtown.

OLD MAN: Starving my children!

LAUNDRY WORKER: Get out of Harlem!

WIFE: Yes, get out of Harlem!

OVERSEER: *(Trying to escape.)* Help! Help me! Help! What have I done? Help me! *(Blows police whistle.)* Help! Help! Help! Help!

NEWSBOYS: *(From all directions, enter NEWSBOYS shouting.)* Riot in Harlem! Negroes running riot! Riot! Read all about it! Riot! Riot! Riot! MARCH 19th RIOT IN HARLEM! RIOT IN HARLEM. Read all about it. HARLEM IS TIRED! Harlem's tired!

WOMAN: *(As the siren dies down. Quietly:)* Harlem is tired.

BOY: Yes, Harlem's tired.

LAUNDRY WORKER: Harlem is tired!

YOUNG MAN: You understand, folks? Harlem's tired.

MEMBER OF THE AUDIENCE: *(Rising.)* But say?

YOUNG MAN: Yes?

MEMBER OF AUDIENCE: Riots won't solve anything, will they, brother?

YOUNG MAN: No, riots won't solve anything.

MEMBER OF AUDIENCE: Then what must we do?

YOUNG MAN: Organize.

MEMBER OF AUDIENCE: With who?

YOUNG MAN: With the others who suffer like me and you.

LAUNDRY WORKER: Organize with the laundry workers, then.

WOMAN: Organize with the tenants' leagues.

BOY: Organize with the students' unions.

YOUNG MAN: Colored and white unions to lift us all up together.

MEMBER OF AUDIENCE: You mean organize with white folks, too?

YOUNG MAN: That's what I mean! We're all in the same boat! This is America, isn't it? It's not all colored. Not all white. It's both.

MEMBER OF AUDIENCE: You mean organize with that white waiter who won't serve you? Organize with him?

YOUNG MAN: Yes, I mean with that waiter, too. His problem's the same as ours—if he only knew it.

MEMBER OF AUDIENCE: Well, they ought to hurry up and find out then! Some of 'em won't even let us in their unions. Yet we're all workers! Let the white workers learn to stop discriminating against us, if they want us with 'em.

YOUNG MAN: Right! They've got to learn. And we must teach them. But when they do learn, and black and white really get together, what power in the world can stop us from getting what we want?

BOY: Nothing!

WOMAN: That's right!

WIFE: You tell 'em!

YOUNG MAN: Right! They've got to learn—but there are some who know already, and they've organized unions that are strong and growing.

MEMBER OF AUDIENCE: Who are they?

YOUNG MAN: The Auto Workers of Detroit. *(Enter a Negro and a white, AUTO WORKERS.)* The Sharecroppers of the South. *(Enter a white and black SHARECROPPER.)* The Miners of Birmingham. *(Enter two MINERS, one white and one colored.)* The Stevedores of the West Coast. *(Enter a black STEVEDORE and a white STEVEDORE.)* And others, too. I know—not yet enough, but they are learning. And when we do learn, and black and white really get together, what power in the world can stop us from getting what we want?

BOY: Nothing!

WOMAN: That's right!

WIFE: You tell 'em!

YOUNG MAN: Tomorrow belongs to the workers, and I'm a worker!

WOMAN: I am, too!

OLD MAN: And me!

LAUNDRY WORKER: Me, too!

MEMBER OF AUDIENCE: And me! I get your point. *(Sits down.)*

YOUNG MAN: Good! We're Negro workers. Listen! This is what we're going to say to all other workers, just this: I, a Negro, offer you my hand. I offer you my strength and power. Together, we can make America a land where all of us are free from poverty and oppression and where no man or woman need ever be hungry, cold, or kept down again. White worker, here is my hand. Today we're man to man.

MAN: White worker, here's my hand.

BOY: Here's my hand.

LAUNDRY WORKER: *(Speaking.)*

Who want to come and join hands with me?
Who wants to make one great unity?
Who wants to say no more black or white?
Then let's get together, folks,
And fight, fight, fight!

ENTIRE CAST: *(Singing.)*

Who wants to come and join hands with me?
Who wants to make one great unity?
Who wants to say no more black or white?
Then let's get together, folks,
And fight, fight, fight!

Who wants to make America a land
Where opportunity is free to every man?
Who wants to test the power of the worker's might?
Then let's get together, folks,
And fight, fight, fight!

Who wants to make Harlem great and fine?
Make New York City a guiding light to shine?
Who wants, to lead the workers toward the light?
Then let's get together, folks,
And fight, fight, fight!

(As they sing the audience joins with them, and various members of the audience, workers, doctors, nurses, professional men, teachers, white and black, come forward to link hands with the characters in the play until the players and the audience are one.)

Oh, who wants to come and join hands with me?
Who wants to make one great unity?
Who wants to say, no more black or white?

> Then let's get together, folks,
> And fight, fight, fight!

THE END

Production Notes[1]

Don't You Want to Be Free? is an impressionistic play endeavouring to capture within the space of an hour the entire scope of Negro history from Africa to America. It should move swiftly from one scene to another with no waits other than those indicated by the action. It should be presented in a modern manner with no curtains or stage effects other than a lynch rope which hangs at the back, center, throughout the entire performance, and serves as a symbol of Negro oppression. This rope is used actively only in the lynching scene when the YOUNG MAN puts his head into the noose on the words, "All you crackers got me." He takes his head from the noose on the words, "Not I." Symbolic of the eternal resurrection of hope of an oppressed people.

This play may be produced on any sort of stage or platform, with or without wings or exits. In cases where the stage or platform has no back-stage exits, the entire cast may be seated on the front rows of the auditorium just before the performance, and may make their entrance into the scene from there, exiting back into the audience as well. Whatever form of staging is used, audience-space should still be employed for much of the action of the play, since the idea behind this type of production is to cause the audience to feel that they, as well as the actors, are participating in the drama—and not simply sitting inactively looking at a show. For instance, the YOUNG MAN should begin the play by entering without any previous signal, with all the house lights on, down the center aisle of the auditorium, delivering his first speech from the floor in front of the stage, very simply, as though he were making an announcement. He then steps upon the stage for the beginning of the play—the poem "I Am a Negro."

The SLAVES, driven by the OVERSEER, may also enter directly from the audience, either from the seats in the front row, or down one of the aisles, moaning and crying as they run. . . . The bidding of those for the SLAVES should come from BIDDERS scattered throughout the audience. . . . The VOICE speaking the lines, "Cook them white folks' dinner," etc., should also be in the audience, with a megaphone if the auditorium is a large one. . . . The CHORUS OF SINGERS should occupy a front section of the audience and sing directly from their seats without rising. . . . The NEWSBOYS should shout their papers up and down the aisles. . . . When the YOUNG MAN exits after his scene with the MULATTO GIRL, he should exit down the steps from the stage and up the center aisle to the back of the auditorium. There he should pick up his tramp's pack—bandanna handkerchief containing his belongings tied on a stick—and make his entrance again, singing the blues as he comes slowly down the aisle, with the CHORUS humming as an undercurrent to his song. . . . The GIRL IN RED may also make her entrance down the center aisle, pausing at the front to powder her nose, perhaps, before walking proudly across the stage as the YOUNG MAN's eyes follow her. . . . The Harlem riots may use the front of the auditorium as well as the stage on the opposite side. Then into a huddle as though beating someone. OLD WOMAN faints at the edge of the crowd. The GIRL rushes to revive her. Members of the CHOIR, the VOICES, and the BIDDERS should be provided with ad lib lines to shout during the riot, and several should have police whistles to blow, thus contributing to the general excitement . . . THE MAN IN THE AUDIENCE should speak from the eighth or tenth row. . . . It is thoroughly permissible for the audience to sing the songs along with the cast, if they spontaneously wish to do so, or to come up and join hands with the cast during the song at the end of the play.

CASTING NOTES: In the casting of this play, an attempt should be make to choose actors representing an appearance in complete accord with a cross-section of all the types to be found in any Negro community, ranging from the very dark in complexion to the very light. The YOUNG MAN should be a strong, husky, brownskin fellow, not over the age of 25 in appearance, possessing a wholesome, likeable personality and a deep manly voice. Since the entire play revolves around him, he must typ-ify the finest type of hard-working youth of the Negro race, not highly educated, but seeking always the path toward education, light, and free-dom. . . . The OVERSEER may be played by an actor of light complex-ion who can make up easily as a white man. . . . The OLD WOMAN, who may be listed on the program as SOJOURNER TRUTH, should in costuming resemble as much as possible, especially in her first scene, photographs of SOJOURNER TRUTH. . . . The NEWSBOYS should be between 14 and 16 years of age—if they are too young, they amuse the audience and cause laughter at a serious point in the play. . . . The blues sequence may be cast as an entire unit in itself, with singing-actors who need take no part in the rest of the play, except to come in as part of the riot crowd, remaining on the stage for the finale, when the entire cast comes forward in the final song.

MUSIC: All of the songs in this production should be sung with the richness, fervor and rhythm so characteristic of Negro music at its best. In no case should polished arrangements of the spirituals be used, but they should have the natural, simple, mellifluous and rhythmic quality to be heard in the singing of any humble NEGRO church. *Go Down Moses, In That Great Gettin' Up Mornin'*, and *John Brown's Body*, especially should be sung with great spirit, gusto, and very stirringly. All of the spirituals may be sung by the entire chorus, except in cases where an exceptional singing-actor is able to carry his part in the song alone. The blues sequence should be accompanied by an expert, old-time, stomp-down blues-piano player who should continue the same rhythm throughout the entire sequence, playing softly but steadily through the spoken portions. The action of the blues sequence should be in time to the music, the characters walking and moving in tempo. . . . The spirituals, *Sometimes I Feel Like a Motherless Child,* may be used as background music on the piano for the MOTHER's long poem concerning her trials and tribulations, going into the strong chords of *GO DOWN, MOSES* at the end.

COSTUMES: The AFRICAN BOY should wear only a bright loin cloth, the AFRICAN GIRL a sarong of a darker flowered material with ivory or wooden bracelets, and perhaps a barbaric necklace. The OVERSEER in his early scenes wears a Simon Legree coat, a black string tie, and a wide Panama hat; as a plantation master, he may be in his shirt sleeves; for his various other scenes, he may change only a coat, a hat, a butcher's apron, etc., as the case demands. The MULATTO GIRL should wear a bright and attractive, but over-gaudy costume, too much rouge, and cheap jewelry. The YOUNG MAN can wear an ordinary dark suit, a blue work shirt and a tie which he removes when he enters for the scene with the PLANTATION MASTER.

SOUND: A good loud cymbal is needed. A drum may be used to accompany the more stirring spirituals. Two sound effects records are required, those of the barking dogs for the lynch scene, and army bugle calls to be used for the Civil War. These may be played on any victrola backstage with a loud needle. Police whistles and a siren are needed for the riot scene, and other sound effects such as breaking glass, rattling of tin cans, ambulance and fire bells may be used.

LIGHT EFFECTS: The light effects for the play may be as simple or as elaborate as the acting group can afford. If spotlights are used, the various scenes may be picked out with the spots as the scenes occur, blacking out as the scenes end—but this is not necessary; and if blackouts are used, immediately one scene is blacked out, another should be lighted, so that there is no wait, *not even the slightest* between scenes—since the success of this play depends upon a rapid moving-picture technique of one scene flowing directly into another. Since, with amateur groups, elaborate lighting usually creates a problem and often proves spotty and distracting when awkwardly handled, *very simple* lighting effects are urged for this production. If spotlights are available, a straw-amber or steel-blue need be the only gelatin slides used to vary the lighting. For the lynching, a complete blackout may be used with just a small handspot to form a flashlight in the first row, focused on the face of the dead boy while the NEWSBOYS shout their papers. In case no special lighting is available the entire play may be performed in the ordinary light of any church or hall.

GROUPS TO BE CONTACTED FOR PROMOTION: This play should appeal especially to Negro History groups, labor unions, social workers, and liberal and progressive organizations of all types, as well as Negro fraternal groups. It is suggested that the play be performed in a small auditorium, perhaps two performances a week over a period of several weeks, rather than performing the play just once in a large auditorium—since this is the type of play which catches on by word of mouth advertising, so people should be given a chance to hear about it. Also, a small hall packed to the doors is much more encouraging to actors than a large hall partially filled. Then, too, several performances of the same play help greatly in perfecting the acting technique of the group.

FINALE: The music of the final song may be secured from Langston Hughes, 20 East 127th Street, New York 35, New York; or from the composer, Sammy Heyward, 2265 Fifth Avenue, New York 37, New York.

Six Satires

1938

For the second season of the Harlem Suitcase Theatre, Hughes provided a series of skits to precede *Don't You Want to Be Free?* It seems that three were performed on any given evening. Pointedly satirical, these slight pieces take on sacrosanct cultural icons. *Colonel Tom's Cabin* turns the tables on Harriet Beecher Stowe's American classic, *Uncle Tom's Cabin. The Em-Fuehrer Jones* takes on Eugene O'Neill's *The Emperor Jones* (1920), whose use of "the Negro" as its central character cast such a long shadow on subsequent stage representations of African American men. *Limitations of Life* lampoons the 1934 film adaptation of Fannie Hurst's popular novel *Imitation of Life. Scarlet Sister Barry* mocks Ethel Barrymore's insistence on playing the lead in *Scarlet Sister Mary* (1931) in blackface, despite the availability of outstanding African American performers and her avowed respect for the great African American actor Rose McClendon. *Young as We Is* and *America Hurrah* take up a range of contradictions emanating from American racism. A cover sheet to one collection of these skits credits the plays to Langston Hughes, Louis Douglas (an actor who joined the group in the second season), and the Valise Collective.

Colonel Tom's Cabin

PLACE: *The South*
TIME: *Relative*
CHARACTERS:
    Uncle Tom
    Mars Sinclair
    Little Eva
SCENE: *Pillars of a mansion. Honeysuckle. Cotton stalks in flower.*
NOTE: *The two men are brightly costumed in the manner of the old South.*
    UNCLE TOM has a halo of snow white hair circling a bald pate.
    MARS SINCLAIR is fair and upright. Only LITTLE EVA is abnormal. She is an overgrown adult in child's clothes, frills and ribbons.

Also, alas, she is colored, with blond curls. She is petulant and naughty. As the curtain rises, MARS SINCLAIR contemplates the beauties of the South.

MARS SINCLAIR: Ah, the beautiful South! *(Scratching)* Sunshine, cotton, *(hands in pockets)* mammies and moonlight. But where is Uncle Tom and Little Eva? A little light on my dark subjects.

TOM and EVA: *(Bound into view)* Here we is, Mars Sinclair!

SINCLAIR: Tom, damn you! I own you, body and soul.

TOM: My body may belong to you, Mars Sinclair! *(Switching)* But, oh! My soul!

EVA: *(To the white man)* I ain't for no stuff from you, myself. *(Histing dress.)*

TOM: Why, little Eva, you mustn't talk to Mars Sinclair like that.

SINCLAIR: *(Loud)* Why, little Eva! *(Soft)* You must be bright and sunny, *(up Lights)* keep your soul *([show] sole of shoe)* as clean as our fair Southern skies, be a gentle lady.

EVA: Aw, nuts!

TOM: Why, Miss Eva! You'll never go to heaven that away. God don't love ugly.

EVA: Has he seen you?

SINCLAIR: Respect your Uncle Tom, Little Eva, even if you don't respect me. After all, he's a perfect slave *(Side kick)* and I'm a perfect master.

EVA: Neither one of you's nothing to me. I like Benny Goodman. Hot cha! Aw, swing it!

TOM: Why, Miss Eva, don't you be a nice little girl, *(Pause)* like Topsy?

EVA: I don't have to. I'm white.

SINCLAIR: Now, Eva, don't sass your poor old Uncle Tom.

TOM: Oh!

SINCLAIR: After all, he may not be white outside, *(kick)* but he's at least yellow within.

EVA: *(Singing)*
> A tisket! A tasket!
> I lost my yellow basket!
> And if that girlie don't return it
> I don't know what I'll do.
> Oh, me!
> I wonder where my
> Basket can be!
> *(Pecking)* A tisket! A tasket!

TOM and SINCLAIR: So do we! So do we! So do we!

SINCLAIR: Oh, how beautiful these old Southern songs are. Mammy! Mammy! *(On knees)* Tom, you sing us one.

TOM: I can't, Mars Sinclair. I's tongue-tied.

EVA: You ought to be hog-tied, you old handkerchief-head, you!

SINCLAIR: Just one song, Uncle Tom.

TOM: Well, I'll try an aria from PORGY AND BESS, Mars Sinclair.

SINCLAIR: Never mind, Uncle Tom. I meant a spiritual.

EVA: *(Cut in)* Like the St. Louis Blues, man! Swing it, Jack!

TOM: *(Singing)*

> *I hate to see that evening sun go down.*
> *I hate to see that evening sun go down.*
> *cause the man I loves . . . .*
>   *(Little Eva starts to switch and hop to the music.)*

SINCLAIR: Why, little Eva, don't tell me you've been collecting jitterbugs.

EVA: I'd rather be a jitterbug than a Southern belle any day—*(To Tom)* a dumb belle.

SINCLAIR: Eva, when you grow up, I want you to be a member of the Junior League.

EVA: Naw, I want to be a D. A. R.

SINCLAIR: And I want you to go to church.

EVA: Naw, I want to go to the Cotton Club. *(crying)*

SINCLAIR: And I want you to always vote my way like your dear old Uncle Tom here.

TOM: *(Suddenly)* No, no, Mr. Sinclair, you got me wrong there. I don't vote your way, sir.

SINCLAIR: What!

TOM: No sir, not me!

SINCLAIR: But you would vote my way for my sake, wouldn't you, Uncle Tom?

TOM: No! No! I may chop your cotton and cut your cane, but when I votes, *(to the audience)* I votes for Roosevelt.

EVA: Red! Red! Red! Red! Look at him! He's a red!

SINCLAIR: Why, Uncle Tom! I'm hurt.

TOM: While I'm struttin' ma stuff, Mr. Sinclair, I might as well tell you—Uncle Tom is Mister Thomas now!

SINCLAIR: Oh, all your sweetness is gone!

EVA: Hee! Hee! Hee! Hee!

TOM: And now, folks, I'm gonna do something else I been wantin' to

do ever since the Civil War—*(Calls Eva)* Come here, honey! and
that is slap Little Eva smack down.

> *(He slaps LITTLE EVA down. SINCLAIR cries aloud, palm to
> his cheek. Exit TOM wiping his hands.)*

SINCLAIR: Tom! *(Calling after TOM)* You've broken Little Eva's
wings. Look at them on the grass.

EVA: *(Bawling loudly)* Waw—aaa—aa—a!

CURTAIN

The Em-Fuehrer Jones

PLACE: *The Black Forest.*
TIME: *Maybe Someday.*
CHARACTERS:
> *The Em-Fuehrer*
> *A Boxer*
> *Voices*

SCENE: *A forest at night. Quite dark except for a will-o'-the-wisp light
that follows the Em-Fuehrer.*

NOTE: *The EM-FUEHRER has a little mustache, and a bang of hair
over his forehead. He is Aryan (so he says). He wears a uniform, a
few medals, an officer's cap, and high boots. He goosesteps. He heils! He
doesn't want the world or himself to know that he is afraid but, to tell
the truth, he is lost in a great black forest.*

EM-FUEHRER: *(Goose-stepping)* Heil!

VOICES: *(Echoing very faintly)* Heel!

EM-FUEHRER: Heil!

VOICES: Heel! Heel!

EM-FUEHRER: *(Angrily)* Heil! Ich habe gesagt, Heil!

VOICES: *(Clearly now)* Heel! Heel! Heel!

EM-FUEHRER: Vas ist das? Dat can't be Aryan voices! Dat can't be my
crowd. Vere is dis anyhow? Heil!

VOICES: Heel! Heel! Heel! Heel! Heel!
> *(Tom-toms begin to beat)*

EM-FUEHRER: Mussolini! Cut out that Ethiopian racket! *(Tom-toms
louder)* I don't like it! That's non-Aryan! Heil!
> *(The VOICES chuckle in savage joy)*

VOICES: Heel! Heel! Heel! Heel!

EM-FUEHRER: Vat is dis? How come I hear dose voices? Shut up! Shut up! . . . . . I must be off mein road to Roumania. I must be off. Vere ist the road? *(He goose-steps and sights)*

VOICES: He's off! He's off! He's off! . . . . . Rou-maniac! Rou-maniac! Maniac!

(Sudden footsteps running, like the crunching of track shoes)

EM-FUEHRER: Ah-ha! I know! I'm at the Olympics! Heil! . . . . . But who's that running? I can't see. It's too dark . . . . . Who's that in the dark?

VOICES: Jessee! Jessee! Jessee!

EM-FUEHRER: Jessee who? Jessee vat?

VOICES: Jessee Owens! Jessee Owens! Owens! Owens! Owens!

EM-FUEHRER: Ach! Non-aryan! Stop him! Non-aryan!

(Footsteps and tom-toms grow louder)

VOICES: Heel! Heel! Heel! Heel!

EM-FUEHRER: Heil! Stop him, I say! *(Pleading)* Jessee, vat you doing running after me? You got your laurel wreath, so stop it, I say! *(Footsteps continue)* I don't want to race with you. These boots hurt my feet. Oh! Wait a minute! Lemme take them off! *(Sits on ground and removes boots)* What's this I'm Schmelling? Something's Schmelling! *(Sniffs his boots)*

VOICES: Joe Louis! Joe Louis! Joe Louis!

(Leaps up and throws his boots aside)

EM-FUEHRER: Mein Gott! Non-aryan! Schmelling, heil!

VOICES: Heel! Heel! Heel! Heel!

(Loud laughter)

EM-FUEHRER: Lemme get away from here? Vat way is Berlin? It must be there. *(Begins to goose-step, then to trot, later to run)*

VOICES: Gefullterfish! Gefullterfish! Gefullterfish!

EM-FUEHRER: *(Drawing back)* Mein Gott! I can't go there! That's the Bronx! *(Unbuttons coat)* A map! A map! My reich for a map! *(Finds a map in his inner pocket)* Where is Yorkville? Where is the Bund Hall? Where is Mein Kampf?

VOICES: Camp! Kampf! Camp! Kampf!

EM-FUEHRER: Stop it! Stop it! Vait till I get my gang together. *(Calling)* Chamberlin! Chamberlin! Oh, Chamberlin! *(Tom-toms louder and louder)* Daladier! Daladier! Hey, Dala-dier. . . . . . .

VOICES: Hey! Hey! . . . . . Hey! Hey!

(The tom-toms fall into a syncopated rhythm)

EM-FUEHRER: Mein Gott! Where ist Mein Kampf?

(He begins to take off his clothes piece by piece as he runs and cast them away. First his cap, then his coat, then his shirt, and undershirt. He has a swastica tattooed on his back and on his chest, very large, blue-black. The tom-toms and the mocking voices continue.)

VOICES: Oi-yoi-yoi! Oi-yoi-yoi! Oi-yoi-yoi! Oi-yoi-yoi!

EM-FUEHRER: *(Stopping with sudden command)* Em-Fuehrer! Hold on to yourself! An Aryan never gets scared! Be proud! Proud! Vat's the matter? Are you lost? My map's no good—but maybe I'll try the stars. *(Looks up)* Oh, no! I mustn't look at the stars! Einstein invented the stars. They're Non-aryan!

VOICES: Oi-yoi-yoi! Oi-yoi-yoi!

EM-FUEHRER: Shut up! If you don't, I'll hold a plebescite and get even with you! Whee, it's so hot! Lemme get off this shirt! If the sun would just come up, maybe even a dictator could see. *(A red sun rises in the East)* Mein Gott! Not that sun! That's red! *(Suddenly screams)* Ow-oo-o! The Bolshevike! Bolsheviki! *(Backs hastily up against a cactus and yells in pain)* Aw-wwww-www-ww-w! *(Turns and salutes the cactus)* Heil! *(Suddenly drooping)* Oh, I thought it was Goering! Where's Goering, Goebbles, Goering? Don't lemme go primitive! Heil! Lemme pray! Oh! Lemme pray! *(Falls on knees)* Wotan! Wotan! Oh-oo-o-o, Wotan!

VOICES: Ave Maria! Ave Maria!

(He leaps to his feet)

EM-FUEHRER: Catholics! Catholics! Innitzer! Oh! Lemme out of here!

VOICES: Go! Go! Go! Go!

EM-FUEHRER: Go where? Go where? Go where?

VOICES: Goebbles! Goebbles! Goebbles!

EM-FUEHRER: Lemme out of this black forest! Black! Black! Wah! Black! Fritz Kahn, I'm coming! I'm coming to America! *(Pistol shots. Loud drums. Fire and flares. The EM-FUEHRER leaves the stage and runs wildly into the audience—an average New York audience. Suddenly the house lights come on. The drum stops. He looks around and collapses in the aisle.)* Mein Gott! Pennsylvania Avenue! Non-aryan!

(An enormous Negro youth in boxing togs with a Joe Louis ribbon across his chest comes down the aisle, picks the EM-FUEHRER up by the seat of his pants, and drags him back across the stage in full light. At the wings, the colored boy stops and speaks triumphantly into a microphone.)

BOXER: Ah guess it was dat punch to de ribs dat got him!
BLACKOUT

Hurrah, America!
(Jersey City Justice)
With Louis Douglas

PLACE: *Jersey City.*
TIME: *Now.*
CHARACTERS:
> *A German-America*
> *An Italian-American*
> *A Negro American*
> *A Policeman*

NOTE: *The GERMAN-AMERICAN wears a large Swastica in his but-
ton-hole, the ITALIAN-AMERICAN a fasces. They both speak with
accents, look slightly foreign but well-dressed, evidently have jobs. The
NEGRO is unemployed. The POLICEMAN might be Irish. The scene,
a street corner.*

GERMAN: Vat dis country needs is a good Hitler.
BOTH: Heil, Hitler!
ITALIAN: Or either a good Mussolini.
BOTH: Viva, Il Duce!
> *(Enter a little Negro. Stops meekly and looks on)*
GERMAN: Vat we need is keep down labor unions.
ITALIAN: Like Il Duce! And take over a few more black colonies.
GERMAN: Like Abyssinia! And put the Jews in concentration camps.
ITALIAN: Like Hitler! And give guns to babies.
GERMAN: Like Mussolini! And burn books.
ITALIAN: Like Hitler! And send troops to General Franco.
GERMAN: Like Mussolini! And purify the white race.
ITALIAN: Like Hitler! Then America would amount to something.
> Democracy's no good, no how!
GERMAN: Heil, Hitler!
ITALIAN: Heil!!. . . . Viva, Mussolini!
GERMAN: Viva!
ITALIAN: Heil!
GERMAN: Heil!

ITALIAN: Viva!

> *(Joyfully taking part in the excitement, too, the NEGRO suddenly comes to life.)*

NEGRO: Hurrah, America!

> *(The others turn on him in astonishment)*

GERMAN: Vat?

ITALIAN: What?

NEGRO: Hurrah, America!

ITALIAN: What-a you say?

GERMAN: Who told you should butt in anyhow?

NEGRO: But I-I—

GERMAN: You, nothing!

ITALIAN: This for you!

> *(They both light in on the poor NEGRO and begin to beat him right and left. Police whistles blow. A COP comes running. The COP grabs the NEGRO by the collar.)*

COP: What the hell are you doing to these white men?

NEGRO: I was just saying, Hurrah, A——

> *(Before he can finish)*

COP: Shut up!

GERMAN: He attacked me.

ITALIAN: He insulted us.

GERMAN: He got fresh mit me.

ITALIAN: He hit me, socko!

COP: He did, huh? You black scoundrel! What's getting into you dark-ies, anyhow?

NEGRO: All I said was, Hurrah, A——

COP: Shut up! Don't talk back to me. We got to have a little law and order in this town. You'll go to jail. *(Twisting the NEGRO's coat collar until he chokes)*

GERMAN: Dat's right! Heil, Hitler! Dat's right!

ITALIAN: That's right! Viva, Mussolini! Lock him up!

COP: That's right! Long live Mayor Hague! *(To NEGRO)* Come on, you!

> *(The GERMAN and the ITALIAN give the Fascist salute as the COP roughly drags the little NEGRO out by the neck. Weakly, the little NEGRO shouts.)*

NEGRO: Hurrah, America! Hurrah, America! Hurrah, Amer——.

Limitations of Life
A satire on the movie *Imitation of Life*

PLACE: *Harlem.*
TIME: *Right now.*
CHARACTERS:
>*Mammy Weavers*
>*Audette Aubert*
>*Ed Starks*

SCENE: *A luxurious living room, swell couch and footstool. At the right, electric stove, griddle, pancake turner, box of pancake flour (only Aunt Jemima's picture is white) and a pile of paper plates. Also a loaf of white bread.*

NOTE: *AUDETTE AUBERT, pretty blond maid, is busy making pancakes on the stove. Enter MAMMY WEAVERS, a colored lady, in trailing evening gown, with tiara and large Metropolitan Opera Program, speaking perfect English with Oxford accent.*

AUDETTE: *(Taking Mammy's ermine)* Mammy Weavers, ah been waiting up for you-all. Ah thought you might like some nice hot pancakes before you-all went to bed.

MAMMY: You shouldn't have waited up for me, my dear.

AUDETTE: Aw, chile!

MAMMY: Besides, I don't wish any pancakes, Audette. I've just had lobster a la Newburg at the Palm Tavern.

AUDETTE: Well, now! How did you-all like the opera, Mammy Weavers?

MAMMY: Lily Pons was divine tonight, but Tibbett was a wee bit hoarse.

AUDETTE: Oh, Ah'ms so sorry, Mammy Weavers! Maybe Tibbett ought to use Vicks like Nelson Eddy.

MAMMY: *(sighing)* I'm just a wee bit tired, Audette.

AUDETTE: Oh, Mammy Weavers, set right down and rest your feet. *(Brings footstool)* I'll run fetch your slippers, honey. *(Fools with earrings)*

MAMMY: I don't know what I'd do without you, Audette.

AUDETTE: I'll never leave you, Mammy Weavers. *(Runs and gets slippers)* Just lemme put your carpet slippers on. *(Kneels)* I'll rub your feet a little first.

MAMMY: *(Relaxing)* Oh, that feels so good!

AUDETTE: *(Looking up like a faithful dog)* Do it, Mammy Weavers??

MAMMY: Tell me, Audette, where is your little Riola tonight?

AUDETTE: Lawd, Mammy Weavers, ma little Riola's tryin' so hard to be colored. She just loves Harlem. She's lying out in de back yard in de sun all day long *tannin'* herself, ever day, tryin' so hard to be colored.

MAMMY: What a shame, the darling's so fair and blue-eyed! Even though her father *was* an Eskimo, you'd never know it. *Never.*

AUDETTE: He wooed me on a dogsled when I were on that Resettlement Project in Alaska. How romantic it were! But he melted away after Riola were born. Then I started workin' for you, Mammy Weavers.

> *(Enter ED STARKS, a sleek-haired jigaboo in evening clothes.)*

ED: Delilah, here's your car keys, my dear. *(To the maid)* Audette, why don't you go to bed?

AUDETTE: I can't sleep till Mammy Weavers gets home.

MAMMY: Darling Audette! I want to do something nice for you, my sweet. Try to think of something you want more than anything else in the world.

AUDETTE: All I wants, Mammy Weavers, is a grand funeral when I die.

MAMMY: Darling! But don't you want a nice home of your own?

AUDETTE: NO, Mammy Weavers, that little room down in your basement is all right for me.

MAMMY: Wouldn't you like a fur coat then?

AUDETTE: Lawd, Mammy Weavers, hush your mouth! All I wants is just to work for you. *(Jumping up)* I gwine make Mr. Ed. Starks some nice hot pancakes right now. Don't you want some, Mr. Ed?

ED: You know I like your pancakes, Audette. But if its all the same with you tonight, give me some of that fine white bread.

MAMMY: *(Indignant)* No, Ed! No! Pancakes will do. I got a patent on that flour. We get it free. Bread's too high.

ED: O.K., Delilah!

AUDETTE: *(Turning pancakes)* Does you all want butter, 'lasses, or honey on your pancakes, Mr. Ed?

ED: I wan jelly on mine!

AUDETTE: Jelly? . . . . Then I'll run downstairs to the pantry and fetch some for you, Mr. Ed.

MAMMY: Oh, Audette you shouldn't do so much for us.

AUDETTE: I'll never get tired of doin' for you and Mr. Ed, Mammy Weavers. I just love colored folks.

MAMMY: I like white folks too, my dear. *(Musing)* I was raised by the sweetest old white mammy! When I remember all my dear old New England mammy did for me, I want to do something for you, Audette. Something you'll never forget. Come here, darling sweetheart! *(With great generosity)* Dear, maybe, you'd like a day off?

AUDETTE: A day off?

MAMMY: Yes, dear, a day off.

AUDETTE: *(Flipping a pancake)* Not even a day off, Mammy Weavers! Ah wouldn't know what to do with it.

ED: *(Throwing up his hands)* Once a pancake, always a pancake! *(Picks up Jemima box with white auntie on it, and shakes his head.)*

CURTAIN

Scarlet Sister Barry

PLACE: *Realm of Art.*
TIME: *Oh!*
CHARACTERS: *One Actress and her Voices.*
SCENE: *A velvet back drop.*
NOTE: *The ACTRESS, who is blond and pale on one side, brown-skin and colored on the other, in race and make-up half and half, emerges from the center folds of the curtain, her white side foremost. She strikes a posture.*

ACTRESS:

Dear public: In my time
I've played everything
From Juliette to the Twelve Pound Look—
Now I want to play a Negress
From a Pulitzer Prize book.
Of course, you know it runs the danger
Of being slightly declasse,
But the First Lady of Our Theatre
Has a right to do just what she may.
I've visited the South, of course,
A day or two at a time—
So my Negro dialect naturally
Is perfectly sublime.
Thus, as Scarlet Sister Mary,

I now propose to show
How the First Lady of this Stage portrays
Even a Negro.
Listen:
(Singing as she turns her dark side to the audience.)
Way down upon de Swanee Ribber
(Steamboat whistle)
Oh, river! Ah hear his gentle voice calling me, Lula Mae! —
Cherio, Lula Mae!—His voice says, Lula Mae, Lula Mae, here's July!
July de 4th, says I.
Naw, your husband, July.
What do you want, July? Says I.
You know what I want, honey.
Un-huh! You been gwine—gone—going-go—gone too long,
July.
Ah ain't been no whar but down de ribber, honey.
(Steamboat whistle. She sings.)
Way down upon de Swanee Ribber!
But July, me, your little Bright Skin's been waitin' for you.
You got a dark way of showing it.
(As she half turns around)
You two-faced hussy!
Oh, July!
You betrayed me while I been away, Lula Mae!
(Whistle)
But you left too soon, July. You didn't even wait to see if our
chile would be a little blond or a little brunette.
What did you name our chile, Lula Mae?
I didn't name it after you, that's shure!
Who did you name it after, then?
I name him after his father.
Who was his father?
You think I'd a-named him what I did if I'd a-knowed who his
father were?
What did you name him, Lula Mae?
I named him—Mark.
Mark who?
Question Mark!
(Cymbals)
Lawd-a-mercy, Lula Mae! I'm going away again.

(Whistle)
Cheerio, July!
    (Singing)

You're old Man Ribber,
So jest keep rollin' along!

    (She waves farewell. The curtain falls and rises to great applause
    off stage. The actress finishes acting and turns her white side to the
    audience again. She bows profusely.)
Thank you folks! Thank you! The Greatest Lady of Our Theatre
thanks you.
    (Moving toward the wings she recites)
Now, in my role of Scarlet Sister Barry,
I've proven I could show
How a great artiste like me portrays
Even the Negro!

    Goodbye! . . . . . Goodbye!
CURTAIN

Young as We Is

PLACE: *A big city.*
TIME: *Any time.*
SETTING: *The street.*
CHARACTERS:
    Shineboy
    Newsboy
    Dancing Boy
    Voices
NOTE: *Typical little Negro boys of the city streets. The SHINEBOY is the*
    raggedist. They are clean, but poor, brave and funny. Beginning to earn
    their own living in the world. The SHINEBOY sits on his little box
    calling to all passers-by.
SHINEBOY: Shine? Shine, Mister? Shine?
    (Enter a NEWSBOY)
NEWSBOY: You know I don't want no shine. What you ask me for?
SHINEBOY: Had to ask somebody. That's my business.
NEWSBOY: Paper?
SHINEBOY: Naw, you know I can't buy no paper. Can that jive!

NEWSBOY: What you mean, can that jive? That's *my* business.

SHINEBOY: What paper you selling?

NEWSBOY: Amsterdam News.

SHINEBOY: What you doin' sellin' a colored paper in a white neighborhood?

NEWSBOY: Why not? Colored folks reads white papers. How come white folks ought'n ter read colored papers?

SHINEBOY: They ought to. But they ain't. You can't sell nary one here.

NEWSBOY: Don't be so pessumistical.

SHINEBOY: Boy, where you hear that word?

NEWSBOY: That's what my mama always say to my papa when the pay check ain't come.

SHINEBOY: Your papa gets paid in checks?

NEWSBOY: Yes, sir.

SHINEBOY: What he do?

NEWSBOY: WPA work. What's your papa do?

SHINEBOY: He don't do nothing. He's dead.

NEWSBOY: What your mama do?

SHINEBOY: Works out.

NEWSBOY: Who takes care o' you then?

SHINEBOY: Nobody. I don't need nobody to take care o' me.

NEWSBOY: Yes, you do, too. Where you eat?

SHINEBOY: Anywhere I can. I just had a hotdog.

NEWSBOY: Boy, you must have money.

SHINEBOY: I made a nickel this morning.

NEWSBOY: Whee! I ain't made but three cents all day. And this a Saturday, too.

SHINEBOY: No wonder! You's trying to sell colored papers in a white neighborhood.

NEWSBOY: Aw, don't be so pessumistical.

SHINEBOY: You got somebody home to feed you! I has to make my own eatin' money, I does.

NEWSBOY: I *does*! I *does*! Where was you borned?

SHINEBOY: Mississippi.

NEWSBOY: I thought it. Don't say *I does*.

SHINEBOY: What must I say?

NEWSBOY: Say *I do's*.

SHINEBOY: Oh! I do's. Well, anyhow . . . . . .

VOICE: You little colored boys get on out from in front of my window. I'm trying to sleep.

NEWSBOY: O.K. ma'm. Want an Amsterdam News?

VOICE: No! You got the whole street to talk in. Move on, will you, please?

SHINEBOY: Yes, ma'm.

NEWSBOY: Yes, ma'm.

SHINEBOY: Always being bossed around. It's a shame to be young as we is.

NEWSBOY: There you go again. Young as we *is*! Why don't you talk right?

SHINEBOY: I'm tryin'. What must I say, Booke Carter?

NEWSBOY: Say young as we -er-are.

SHINEBOY: O.K. But what I mean is, kids is always being bossed around. Home, and school, and everywhere. Anyhow, I wish I was back in school.

NEWSBOY: You ain't in school? Young as you is—are?

SHINEBOY: Naw, I used to was in school, but I ain't now.

NEWSBOY: You used to *was*?

SHINEBOY: Yes, I used to was.

NEWSBOY: *(In disgust)* Aw, man!

SHINEBOY: What's the matter now?

NEWSBOY: I see where I got to take you in hand. And *one* day ain't enough.

SHINEBOY: Is I said something wrong?

NEWSBOY: Is you? You sure are!

SHINEBOY: What?

NEWSBOY: You said—aw, skip it! I guess you too young to know. You just a juvenile.

SHINEBOY: Juvenile? What's a juvenile?

NEWSBOY: A juvenile! That means when you too young to know. That's what the judge told Buster's mama, who lives across the hall from us.

SHINEBOY: What the judge tell her?

NEWSBOY: Buster stole some apples from in front of the store, and the cops took Buster, but the judge turned him loose, and bawled Buster's mama out something terrible. Old judge said to Buster's mama, you got no business letting your child run the streets, young as he is, cause he don't know right from wrong yet. He's just a juvenile.

SHINEBOY: OH! Say, I know a big word, too.

NEWSBOY: You does? What is it?

SHINEBOY: It's a riddle. You got to guess it.

NEWSBOY: I got to guess it?

SHINEBOY: Yes! Listen! If a tree was to get blowed down in a hurricane, and fall on a house and break the window, what would the window say?

NEWSBOY: Dog-gone if I know what the window would say!

SHINEBOY: You ought to know. You's so smart!

NEWSBOY: What would the window say?

SHINEBOY: Guess.

NEWSBOY: Would it cuss?

SHINEBOY: No, that window too nice to cuss.

NEWSBOY: Would it pray?

SHINEBOY: How can a window pray and it ain't got no knees?

NEWSBOY: Then what would it say?

SHINEBOY: A great big word! Guess one more time.

NEWSBOY: I ain't never guessed a-tall yet. You say, if a tree was to get blowed down during a hurricane, and fall on a window, what would the window say?

SHINEBOY: That's right? What would it say?

NEWSBOY: What would it say?

SHINEBOY: Aw, man! *TRE-mendous,* that's what it would say.

NEWSBOY: That sure is a big word!

    (Terrific noise)

VOICE: Scat from in front my store! Git!

NEWSBOY: Aw, dry up.

VOICE: Git! Git!

    (Loud racket)

SHINEBOY: If we wasn't kids, you wouldn't yell at us that away!

NEWSBOY: Ain't this awful! I'm goin' home.

SHINEBOY: Wait a minute! Here comes my pal.

    (Enter dancer)

DANCER: What you know, Jack.

SHINEBOY: I ain't got 'em, Bo. Is you jangled today?

DANCER: Man, I ain't jangled a drop! Ain't been nobody stopped longed enough for me to get started to jangling.

NEWSBOY: What you-all mean, jangled?

SHINEBOY: Shaw! This here man's a dancer like Bojangles!

NEWSBOY: OH! He can dance?

SHINEBOY: Sure, he can dance!

DANCER: You got a dime?

NEWSBOY: No!

DANCER: Well, how you gonna see then? I dances for money.

NEWSBOY: OH! I thought maybe you'd dance for nothing.

DANCER: You gonna gimme one of your papers for nothing.

NEWSBOY: No, that's my business.

DANCER: Dancing is my business, so what?

NEWSBOY: I thought folks dances for fun.

DANCER: I do when I ain't working.

NEWSBOY: Ain't none of us working right now, so come on, hit up a tune.

DANCER: Well, I reckon I might think about it.

SHINEBOY: Go ahead, start thinking, Jack.

DANCER: O.K. *(Begins to sing and dance)*
>   Flat foot floogie
>   With the floy-floy!
>   Hey! Hey! . . . . . Hey! Hey!
>   *(All three take part in the singing and dancing until the street is filled with noise. Suddenly a cop's voice breaks the silence.)*

VOICE: What are you kids doing there, begorra? Break it up! Get going! Go on!

KIDS: The cop! The cop! The cop!

VOICE: Beat it! Go on! Clear out o' here!
>   *(The KIDS grab their things and run.)*

SHINEBOY: I guess we might as well give up.

DANCER: This must be a hincty old neighborhood. Can't nobody have no fun.

NEWSBOY: Everybody done jumped salty this morning. Let's go home to Harlem.

DANCER: Let's go.

SHINEBOY: Shine, Mister? Shine? Shine? Shine?

NEWSBOY: Papers! Papers! Papers! Amsterdam News! Papers.

DANCER:
>   Flat foot floogie
>   With the floy-floy! . . .
>   Hey! Hey!
>   *(They exit down the aisles giving vocal vent to the wares they have to sell.)*

PIANO CURTAIN—"Up Town, Downtown. All Around the Town."

The Sun Do Move
A Music-Play

1942

Hughes wrote this play for the second theater company that he founded, the Skyloft Players, who performed it at the Good Shepherd Community Center in Chicago. Premiering on April 24, 1942, *The Sun Do
Move* played Thursdays and Fridays for the month of May. Perhaps re-
flecting his recent Hollywood experience in writing the film script for
Way Down South (1939) with the actor Clarence Muse, Hughes envi-
sioned this play as running without break, with music providing transitions between the scenes. *The Sun Do Move* is the first of his religious
plays, and its stirring conclusion reflects also his involvement in writing
for the war effort. As in *Don't You Want to Be Free?* Hughes here retells
African American history, this time personifying the characters whose
determination and many sorrows are celebrated in a triumphant conclusion. While *Don't You Want to Be Free?* is primarily a blues piece,
the dominant mood and mode of *The Sun Do Move* is the spirituals.
Both works reflect Hughes's increasing interest in incorporating African
American music into his dramatic work, bringing to the stage experimentation that had long been part of his poetry.

The text is that of a mimeograph published by the Publications Department of the International Workers Order and located in the Slichter
Industrial Relations Collection in Littauer Library of the Social Sciences
Program, Harvard College Library, Harvard University. There are pho-
tocopies of this text in the Langston Hughes Papers, Beinecke Library.

TIME: *1800 to the Civil War.*
PLACE: *The Deep South.*
MUSIC: *The Spirituals.*
Production without scenery in the simplified manner of OUR TOWN
    or WAITING FOR LEFTY. The play may be done in the style of
    a motion picture or radio drama with no break in continuity and
    no intermissions, the spirituals between scenes serving as transition
    music during blackouts.

Prologue

SETTING: *A bare stage. Enter a young man in a porter's cap, sweat shirt, and trousers who begins to sweep with a broom of straw. Enter another young man, JOE, in a drape modern suit who looks puzzled.*

JOE: What you doing, Jack?

SWEEPER: I'm sweeping away Monday.

JOE: I don't dig you.

SWEEPER: Sweeping away Tuesday, Wednesday, Thursday, Friday.

JOE: Saturday, too?

SWEEPER: Yep! Even much Sunday.

JOE: Um-mum-hum!

SWEEPER: Also June, July, and August.

JOE: Just listen to that cat! Labor Day, too?

SWEEPER: Sure! *All* of September! Sweeping away October, November—

JOE: And even Christmas?

SWEEPER: Um-hum! Christmas.

JOE: Then there won't be nothing left?

SWEEPER: Nothing but yesterday.

JOE: Yesterday?

SWEEPER: Yep, yesterday.

JOE: You're going to sweep away everything?

SWEEPER: Everything—but yesterday.

    (Lights dim to sunset)

JOE: Then I guess I got to take off these drapes cause they won't be stylish.

SWEEPER: Sure, we both got to lay these clothes away.

JOE: I just got through making the last payment too.

SWEEPER: Don't worry. You don't need no drapes in Africa.

    (A distant tom tom begins to beat as the two boys strip to loin cloths of African weave)

JOE: Africa?

SWEEPER: That's what I said. A hundred years ago in Africa.

    (Sunset dims to an eerie darkness. Into the scene, hidden by great painted shields, float hooded dancers in the straw masks of an African ceremony. The women, who are not masked, are dark and beautiful as the Congo dusk. An Ashanti war song is sung. Enter the KING)

JOE: Who are you anyway, fellow?

KING: Ebewe of Ashanti. *(He takes his spear)*

MEN: Rock of the forest.

> *(A feathered crown is placed upon his head)*

KING: EBEWE!

CHORUS: Rock!

KING: Ebewe!

CHORUS: King!

KING: Ebewe!

CHORUS: King! King! King! King!

> *(He mounts his throne and stands worshipped by his people. A beautiful girl draws near and he puts one arm protectively about her. His other hand clutches a spear.)*

KING: Melanthie!

CHORUS: Queen!

KING: Queen Melanthie!

CHORUS: Queen Melanthie!

MEN: Rulers of Ashanti.

> *(The drums rise to a crescendo that suddenly slows to the heavy boom of cannon. The people fall away startled as a messenger rushes in.)*

MESSENGER: The slave traders come! The Portuguese come! The English, the Spanish, the Dutch! The slavers come.

KING: Warriors to arms! To arms! Men of Ashanti! To arms!

> *(The women withdraw into the background. The men to battle, stylized ballet. Exit JOE and SWEEPER.)*

VOICE: But we have no guns! We have no guns! We have no guns!

KING: We have our strength and we have our spears.

VOICE: But we have no guns. We have no guns. So they steal us, and enchain us, and enslave us—because we have no guns.

> *(The cannon booms ever louder. The KING, his WIFE beside him, flings his spear into the night as his warriors fall around him. A SLAVER rushes in bringing with him a rope that is like a chain. They struggle but the rope is put about their necks and those of the fallen warriors. Defeated they are taken prisoners.)*

SLAVER: Ebewe! Rock!

VOICES: Ha, ha, ha, ha, ha!

SLAVER: Ebewe! King!

VOICES: Ha, ha, ha, ha, ha, ha, ha, ha, ha!

> *(The rope extends on and on into the darkness with many other Negroes in the toils. Driven by the SLAVER's whip, they march to*

the slave ship, whose rocking mast and sail appear behind them in the center. They lie down side by side as their KING is chained to the mast. EBEWE will not lie down. He stands defiant against the mast singing an Ashanti war song. The SLAVER strikes him with a whip. He falls only to rise again as the slaves join him in song. Their voices are almost drowned in the roar of wind and sea as the sail rocks and creaks and the voyage to the New World is begun.)

SLAVER: Stop it! Stop it, I say! That's no slave song! Stop it! Stop it! To the ships! Get on to the slave ships! Get on! Get on!

(The SLAVER pulls his pistol and fires. Abruptly the song is cut. EBEWE sinks slowly to the deck. The light picks out now only ME-LANTHIE, his Queen, standing above him. She takes up the theme of the song and carries it on joined by a chorus of women's voices above the roar of wind and sea. Blackout. Lights up, downstage as two young Negroes in rags—the same as before but dressed now in cast off clothing of the style of 1800—enter from opposite directions. One is sweeping vigorously with a broom of straw.)

JOE: Boy, what you doing?

SWEEPER: Sweeping, Joe.

JOE: You raising a might lot of dust, that's all.

SWEEPER: I reckon you can't see. Tain't just dust I'm raising. I'm sweeping away blood and tears.

JOE: You think maybe you might find a gold piece somewhere in that dust?

SWEEPER: Sure, I maybe might. They had an auction here yesterday—sold two hundred slaves. And today they gonna sell two hundred more—cause a ship just came in from Afriky.

JOE: Did?

SWEEPER: That's why I'm sweeping away the blood and tears. The white folks don't like to walk in that stuff—not here in New Orleans.

JOE: The mens don't care. But the fine ladies might get blood—

SWEEPER: And tears—

JOE: On they slippers. Hey!

(Suddenly the SLAVER's voice is heard dilating on the virtues of the human stock offered for sale. He enters, pushing before him, MELANTHIE, Ebewe's wife, who mounts the auction block.)

SLAVER: Look at her, folks! Just off the Flying Queen from Africa! A fresh cargo of slaves, folks. Ashantis—from one of the best tribes in Africa. Full grown slaves, enough to last a long time. Big bargains for your money! Look what's on the block now—a lovely young heifer—about to bear a calf. A queen—Melanthie, they call her—with child by the king of the tribe. King—ha, ha, ha! The Africans like titles, too. But we didn't bring the king—ashore. We left him in the sea—too impudent. You can have this woman and child—approximately for the price of one. What am I bid, ladies and gentlemen? What am I bid?

VOICES:

Two hundred!

Three hundred!

Four hundred!

Five hundred!

Six! Seven! Eight!

Nine hundred!

One thousand!

(*The auctioneer's hammer sounds. Gold pieces clink.*)

SLAVER: Going! Going! Gone! To Mr. Pritchard for one thousand dollars—gold! (*Giving her push*) Teach her to pick cotton, man. She's a Queen. She's ignorant. Ha-haw-haw-haw-ha! She never seen cotton. Ha-haw-haw-ha! Cotton!

(*Crude voices everywhere shout "Cotton! Cotton!"*)

VOICES:

Cotton!

Cotton!

Cotton!

(*Their cries blend into a distant song that grows louder as ME-LANTHIE exits driven by the SLAVER.*)

CHORUS: (*Singing*)

Cotton needs picking so bad!

So bad! So bad!

Cotton needs picking so bad!

Gonna kick all over this field.

(*JOE and the SWEEPER join the pickers as the scene brightens into a cotton.*)

Act I

Field in full boll. At left, on stage extension, the porch of a plantation mansion with chairs out of doors. It is about the year 1830 in the slavery-

time South. The sun is shining. The front porch is empty. But in the field the slaves are at work, picking cotton. They sing the cotton picking song. Suddenly the young woman, MARY, feels ill. She puts her hand to her head, is about to fall. A young man, ROCK, very tall and dark, hurries to her. He takes her sack from her shoulder. She leans on his body. He is very gentle with her. (At left OLD MASTER enters to sit on porch. SERVANT brings him a fan.)

JOSH: You-all better keep on picking this cotton. Overseer see you stopping, he whip you good.

REVEREND: Better keep singing, too, so's he can tell what part de field we in.

CLARA: He sure will whip you, Rock, standing up there like a statue.

ROCK: Mary's sick.

JOSH: Ain't no black woman got no call to be sick.

MAMMY: Her time's most come.

CLARA: Even if her time is come, she can't stop work.

　　　(ROCK is visibly agitated)

JOSH: Rock act like he gonna have a baby. He ain't sick, too, is he?

ROCK: No, I ain't sick—but this here's gonna be my baby when it come, just like it's Mary's.

CLARA: You made it—and Mary gwine bear it. But it gwine be Old Master's chile, not your'n. We's slaves.

JOSH: Don't even belong to ourselves.

　　　(MARY buries her head on ROCK's chest)

MARY: Rock, we's slaves!

ROCK: What you cryin' for, honey? We's always been slaves.

JOSH: That sure ain't nothin' new.

MARY: My baby gonna be a slave-child, too.

JOSH: So what? Can anybody here tell us how it feels to be free?

MAMMY: Can't nobody tell you—cause we always been slaves out here in this cotton field in the hot sun, like now. But any bird knows its good to be free.

REVEREND: Even much any varmint knows that.

ROCK: Sometimes slaves run away—and get free.

JOSH: Um-hum! But which away is freedom?

ROCK: They say it's in de North.

JOSH: Where is the North?

ROCK: Someday I'm gonna find out.

JOSH: You gwine find out what a good whippin' is if you don't get back to work. De Overseer be down here by and by, and *(sings)*
   Dis cotton needs pickin' so bad!

CHORUS: So bad! So bad! Etc. . . .

ROCK: Honey, can you make it now?

MARY: Rock! Oh, Rock! I's scared! Sometimes I feels something awful coming over me. Rock! Rock!

ROCK: Women's always feels bad when they's carrying a baby, and worse'r if it's gonna be a boy child, Mary.

MARY: Rock, suppose Old Master—suppose Old Master sold you away?

ROCK: Sold *me* away?

MARY: Liza what cooks at the Big House say she heard Old Master talking 'bout how times is hard, how money's tight, and maybe he sell some of his slaves.

MAMMY: They ain't gonna sell no *old* slaves! That's sure. We don't fetch no fancy prices.

JOSH: If Old Master sell anybody, it'll be young ones like Rock.

MARY: Not Rock! I couldn't stand it! No!

ROCK: If Old Master sell me, Mary, I'll come back. I'll run away and come back and get you. And both of us, all three of us, run off to de North.

CLARA: You can't find de North. Can't none of us find de North.

ROCK: I'll find my way back to the woman I love, though.

MARY: Else I'll find my way to you. *(She turns to go to picking)*

JOSH: But suppose they sold you away down the river?

ROCK: Down the river?

MARY: Down the river?

JOSH: Away far off—down de Mississippi River.

MARY: Down de Mississippi River?

JOSH: Yes, down de river.
   (The MASTER sits rocking with his palm leaf fan. POMPEY, a slave in livery, enters.)

POMPEY: It's the slave trader, Massa. He done come!

MASTER: Show him up! Show him up!
   (The SLAVER pauses at the foot of the steps)

MASTER: So you're from down the river, Mr. Clay?

SLAVER: From down the river where the sun is hot, Mr. Pritchard. Where the fields are rich—and we treat every slave like a son-of-a-bitch!

MASTER: Down the river—where the slaves think hell is located.

SLAVER: They ain't far from wrong, neither, Mr. Pritchard. We work 'em hard down there. They die off quick. But we produce crops, and we pay good prices for strong hands. You got any strong black bucks here?

MASTER: I've got one strong one. *(Calling servant)* Pompey! Oh, Pompey! Go tell the Overseer to send me—ROCK.

> *(MARY faints in the field. Women gather around her. An old woman's voice humming the melody of the African song is heard.)*

POMPEY: Yes, Sir, Massa, yes, sir!

> *(Blackout left as light switches to right where, in the doorway of a slave hut sits LANTHIE, shelling peas. She hums the Ashanti song. Into the scene rushes ROCK.)*

ROCK: Grandma Lanthie! Grandma Lanthie! Mary's time done come. She's calling for you in the field.

LANTHIE: Lawdy mercy! Lemme go! That's the first chile she ever birthed—and it's liable to be hard.

ROCK: Hurry, granny! Hurry! She ain't been able to pick no cotton hardly all day long. I been picking for her.

LANTHIE: Just lemme get some clean rags and wash my hands. I'm coming, son, I'm coming.

ROCK: This gonna be your first great-grand-chile, Grandma Lanthie.

LANTHIE: Just like you was my first grand-chile.

ROCK: You reckon this gonna be a boy-chile, too?

LANTHIE: If it do, we name it Little Rock—after you—and your father.

ROCK: And my grand-father—Ebewe—Rock—who was a king in Africa.

LANTHIE: Yes, after him, who was a king in Africa. Come on, son, let's we hurry.

> *(They start to exit as POMPEY enters.)*

POMPEY: You Rock! Hey, you Rock! What you doin' out of that field?

ROCK: What you want, Pompey?

POMPEY: *I* don't want nothing. It's Old Massa want you, that's who. Overseer look all over that cotton field for you.

ROCK: Massa want me now?

POMPEY: Yah, he want you—now. *(Softening)* Son, the slave trader done come.

> *(Blackout. Softly the chorus begins, "Oh, Mary doncha weep, doncha moan" as the light shifts to the porch of the mansion house again where the MASTER sits talking to the TRADER.)*

SLAVER: So you only sell 'em, one at a time, heh, Mr. Pritchard?

MASTER: Only one at a time—as I need the money.

SLAVER: You think you'll have another one or two for me next time I make the trip up country?

MASTER: Very probably, Mr. Clay. You see, I don't mind admitting I'm a bad manager—and a worse gambler. I lose more than I win. Besides, in another year or so, I'm thinking of closing out this plantation, moving into town.

SLAVER: It's right nice in town, Mr. Pritchard. I never was much myself for country life. Now, you take Memphis *(kisses his finger tips)*—it's fine! Wine, women, song! And New Orleans—
  (POMPEY enters with ROCK)

POMPEY: Massa, here's Rock.

SLAVER: Ah! So this is the buck?

MASTER: This is the one. Strong as an ox.

SLAVER: As stubborn?

MASTER: No, pretty good worker. Fells trees, clears land, picks cotton, drives mules.

SLAVER: I'll give you Five Hundred.

MASTER: Don't make me laugh! He's the best of the lot—but I need the money.

SLAVER: *(To ROCK)* Open your mouth, buck . . . Hum! Sound teeth. Turn around. *(Feels his muscles)* Mr. Pritchard, I'll give you Six Hundred.

MASTER: Mr. Clay!

SLAVER: Can he breed?

MASTER: His woman's got a child on the way.

SLAVER: How's his temper?

MASTER: Good.

SLAVER: I still say Six.

MASTER: He'll fetch a thousand on the market. You may have him for Eight.

SLAVER: Six Fifty and we'll call it a deal. *(As PRITCHARD hesitates)* Cash, you know.

MASTER: Immediately?

SLAVER: Immediately.

MASTER: I'll compromise for Seven.

SLAVER: Do you realize I'm in business, Mr. Pritchard?

MASTER: I'm in business, too, Mr. Clay. I'll let him go. But not at cheatery.

SLAVER: Seven, you say?

MASTER: Seven.

SLAVER: I'll take the buck.

MASTER: Cash, Mr. Clay.

SLAVER: Cash, Mr. Pritchard. Make out the papers. I've another slave to pick up in the neighborhood—so I'll call for this one in the morning.

ROCK: Massa?

MASTER: No complaining now, Rock.

ROCK: Mary's time done come. She birthing a baby in the field. If you're through with me, can I go to her?

SLAVER: Just a minute! Just a minute! *(Takes a pair of leg irons from his belt)* With these on your legs, you can go, Rastus. You're Mr. Clay's property now, and I'll have no run-aways to worry about. *(He shackles his legs in a chain)* Now go see about your wench. I'll get you at sun-up in the morning, so be ready . . . Go on! Get!

   (ROCK exits stumbling toward the field)

MASTER: Next time you're by, you might take his woman off my hands, too.

SLAVER: His woman? Sure, I'll buy her, but he'll never see her again. Rock's going down the Delta. Women, I sell them in Memphis for house maids and cooks.

MASTER: Want to buy any old ones?

SLAVER: No old ones. Why?

MASTER: I got one hanging on, name's Lanthie, about eighty. But she can still shell peas, and midwife.

SLAVER: Huh!

MASTER: My grandfather bought her once—right off a slave ship from Africa. King's wife, he said.

SLAVER: Keep her, Mr. Pritchard. Too old for me. Gimme pretty white women—and young black ones.

MASTER: And your whiskey?

SLAVER: Straight.

MASTER: Hey, Pompey! A drink for me and Mr. Clay.

POMPEY: Yes, sir, Massa, yes sir. . . .

   (Blackout. Song comes up strong "Oh, Mary, doncha weep, doncha moan." The light center stage reveals the cotton field again, a corner under a tree where a group of women are gathered around MARY, unseen on the ground. Above the diminishing song of the women her moans are heard. They sing softly:)

WOMEN:

   Oh, Mary, don't you weep, don't you moan.

Oh, Mary, don't you weep, don't you moan.
Pharaoh's army got drowned.
Oh, Mary, don't you weep.

> *(Two women, CLARA and MAMMY draw aside and speak above the song)*

MAMMY: It's her first child. She's having it hard.

CLARA: But Old Lanthie'll bring her through.

MAMMY: In a minute you gonna hear that child cry.

CLARA: And de breath o' life'll be breathed once more.

MAMMY: Bless God! Praise his name!

CLARA: This gonna be a strong chile. Rock's a strong man. And Mary, a strong woman!

MAMMY: Where is Rock? He never did come back after he went for Lanthie a hour ago.

CLARA: Many a strong man gets scared when it comes to this.

MAMMY: Mighty brave when it comes to courting though.

CLARA: But 'nother story when the reckoning comes.

MAMMY: Shaw! A man ain't got the guts to birth no chile.

CLARA: Uh-hum! Takes we womens for that. Yonder comes Rock now.

MAMMY: Lawd-a-mercy! What's them on his feet?

CLARA: Looks like slavery chains I seed on the auction gang. Mammy! *(With a cry)* They's selling Rock away!

MAMMY: Sh-sss-ss-s! Don't say nothing now, Clara. Let Mary have her baby in peace. *(Rock enters stumbling)* You Rock, stay where you is!

ROCK: Mary? How is she? How is she?

MAMMY: She doing well's to be expected—doing what she's doing.

CLARA: Lanthie's there, Rock. Everything's all right. But what's them?

ROCK: Massa done sold me.

MAMMY: Just when your chile is borned.

ROCK: Is he borned yet? Lemme go see.

MAMMY: No, stand right here, Rock! Them things is for women.

CLARA: 'Sides, do you want Mary to see you with them chains on your feet?

ROCK: But she's calling! She's moaning! She's crying!

> *(He takes a step, but the women stop him.)*

MAMMY: Stand still, son. She don't need to know *yet* you's being sold away. *(There is a piercing scream.)* Stand here. *(A pause. Then a baby's cry is heard.)* Lanthie'll bring your baby to you.

> *(Joy breaks out among the women as, from their midst, LANTHIE rises with a babe in swaddling clothes. She begins to sing:)*

LANTHIE:

> Go tell it on de mountain,
> Over the hills and everywhere!
> Go tell it on de mountain,
> A little chile is born!
>> *(In full volume the chorus repeats her song. The male cotton pickers enter jubilantly. ROCK stands as though transfixed. LANTHIE brings the child to him and lays it in his arms. ROCK begins to sing:)*

ROCK:

> Go tell it on de mountain,
> Over the hills and everywhere!
> Go tell it on de mountain,
> A little chile is born!
>> *(Together they look down at the child as the song rises in full chorus. Blackout. In the darkness, footsteps are heard—the running and darting of slaves whispering a frightful message.)*

VOICES:

> Rock, he done sold Rock.
> Reckon he gonna sell us?
> Is Massa gonna sell me?
> He gonna sell us all.
> One at a time, one at a time.
> Why he want to sell me? I's old.
> Where he gonna sell me to?
> Slave trader pass every week, every day.
> Slave trader! Slave trader! OOO-ooo-o!
> Away from my chillun! Away! Away!
> Away from my mother! Oh!—OO-ooo-o! Mother! Mother!
>> *(As the light comes up it reveals the slave quarters at night where slaves sit dejected in doorways or squat on the ground. Friends surround ROCK. All sing:)*

CHORUS:

> Oh, is Massa gwine sell us tomorrow?
> Yes, yes, yes! Etc.
> Oh, watch and pray.
> Farewell, mother, I must leave you. Etc.
> Oh, watch and pray.
>> *(In hut at left MARY lies on her cot with the child. As the singing continues, LANTHIE, who sits besides her, rises)*

LANTHIE: Lemme go quiet my chillun out there, daughter. Old Massa gonna hear 'em by and by, then de Overseer come with his lash. Stay still, Mary, I be back. *(LANTHIE exits to full stage)*

CLARA: Lanthie! Grandma Lanthie! What we gonna do? They done sold Rock. Maybe my man next. Maybe my child be next.

JOSH: Lanthie, what you think happening? Old Massa broke? Is he gonna sell us all?

LANTHIE: Chillun, hide your troubles in your heart—tonight. Mary's sick in here from bearing child. Don't make her burden no heavier. Our hearts is like stones already. They taking my only grandchile from me—Rock—but I gwine to care for his wife and for his son—till he gets 'em back. Grandma Lanthie gwine look after them, son.

(The song comes up again as ROCK sings)

ROCK:
> Granny, don't you grieve after me.
> No, no, no, etc.

LANTHIE: Son, watch and pray! Watch and pray!

(Inside the hut MARY has risen on her arms in bed. In anguish, high and clear, her voice rises)

MARY: *(Singing)*
> Lord, I cannot stay here by myself.
> Lord, I cannot stay here by myself.
> I'm gonna weep like a willow and moan like a dove.
> Oh, Lord, I cannot stay here by myself . . . . .

(Stumbling in his chains, ROCK goes toward her. He enters the cabin and kneels at her bed. The light fades so that only the two lovers are seen in the hut.)

ROCK: Mary, honey, don't cry. Don't worry.

MARY: I can't help it, Rock. I can't help it. Why do Old Massa have to sell you now? Why, now? Just when our baby born, our little family starting to grow. Ain't we worked good for him? Don't he care nothing about us?

ROCK: He don't care nothing about us. We just slaves to him.

MARY: It's breaking my heart, Rock. Breaking my heart. *(She sobs)*

ROCK: But you know I love you, don't you, Mary? You know I'm gonna be thinking about you every day, gonna be true to you, spite of all, don't you?

MARY: I believe you, Rock. I know you will.

ROCK: Look up at me then—and don't be 'fraid. I'm gonna pass the night here with you. In the morning—I'll be taken away. But I'm gonna find you again—if it takes me my whole life long. I'll be back—be back and get you—and we'll run away to the North together. I don't care where Old Massa sell me, don't care how far down the river it is—I'm gonna break these slavery chains from my legs, wherever I be. I don't care how many overseers they got with guns, nor how many dogs, Mary, I'm gonna run away, come back and find you, and take you and this baby with me. *(He leans over and picks up the child. As he speaks he rises to his feet.)* This here's our first son, Mary. He gonna be—free!

(Chorus comes up strong)

CHORUS:

Oh, Mary, don't you weep,
Don't you moan.
Pharaoh's army got drowned.
Oh, Mary, don't you moan.
(Blackout)

Act II

A log by a roadside. Enter the SLAVER dragging two slaves, ROCK and FROG, chained together before him.

SLAVER: You-all slaves set right here on this road till I go down to yonder spring and wash and cool myself off. Mind you, don't you try to move, cause I got my Winchester.

(They sit on a log. SLAVER exits.)

ROCK: I reckon old man Clay don't think we hot and dirty, too.

FROG: You know Massa Clay ain't gonna let you wash up in that spring he wash and drink in. You must not know these white folks down here in the Delta. Where you from, boy?

ROCK: Tennessee.

FROG: How come you got sold?

ROCK: Ol Massa gambles. He always needs money.

FROG: I got sold cause I wouldn't work. Whoever bought me done get the no-workingest slave alive.

ROCK: These drivers down here, they tell me, knows how to make anybody work.

FROG: You mean they whips you? Huh! I'm tough to that. Just raise up my shirt and look at my back.

(ROCK lifts up his shirt)

ROCK: Hum! Looks like a checker board!

FROG: I been whipped so much I don't feel it no more. And I done been sold so much, they calls me "Traveller." I got a bad reputation as a slave.

ROCK: That one reason they sold you so far off this time, I reckon.

FROG: Down the river where they ain't never heard of me. We's bound for hell, boy. Whee! It's sure hot as hell on this road, and am I thirsty? Wish I could go down to that spring and get me some cool water.

ROCK: Me, too.

FROG: Say, wouldn't it be fun to be free?

ROCK: What would you do?

FROG: Run down to that spring and drink and drink.

ROCK: Then what?

FROG: Take myself to New Orleans, marry the prettiest brownskin I could find, and go to balls and dances every night. What would you do?

ROCK: I'd go back and find my wife and boy. Then go up North and work and have a home.

FROG: It sure would be fun to be free! But I ain't got no wife, man. Neither no child. They sells me so fast from one plantation to another, I don't have time for no love making.

ROCK: Travelling slave, huh?

FROG: Have to catch my kisses on the fly. You know, Rock, I kissed a girl up yonder at old Jeep's Plantation last night and her kisses ran right down to my heels.

ROCK: Then what happened?

FROG: Old Jeep say, "The slave trader's come after you Frog. Get ready, go with him." When I left that girl, she were standing at the front fence crying. You seed her, didn't you?

ROCK: I saw her.

FROG: She said, "Goodbye, Frog! Goodbye!" and she wove her hand.

ROCK: Pretty, too.

FROG: Man, wouldn't it be fun to be free?

ROCK: I'd go right back and get my wife and baby.

FROG: Wife and a baby! Who else you leave behind?

ROCK: Grandma Lanthie. How about you?

FROG: I lost track o' my family so long ago, no use talking. Brother sold here, sister sold there. And I never did see my father.

ROCK: How come?

FROG: He was sold away from my mother two years before I was born.

ROCK: *My* father run away. Died with Nat Turner.

FROG: You mean when all them slaves riz up?

ROCK: He was there.

FROG: Your father was a brave man, Rock. *(Cautiously)* Say, listen, does you ever have any ideas like that yourself—of running away? Of rising up fighting for your freedom? Does you?

ROCK: Does you?

FROG: Does you?

> *(They move away from each other as far as the chains permit, suspicious, afraid. Then suddenly begin to laugh.)*

ROCK: You're afraid of me!

FROG: You afraid of me!

ROCK: Ain't that something!

FROG: Two slaves afraid of each other.

ROCK: Cause they both want to be free.

FROG: It sure wouldn't be me would tell no master.

ROCK: Nor me.

FROG: Is you got any such idea?

ROCK: I got the idea—and I mean to carry it out.

FROG: I got the idea, too. We'll run off together. When?

ROCK: I don't know when. Nor how?

FROG: Nor from where?

ROCK: But we got the idea.

FROG: Rock, you and me gonna be pals.

ROCK: We gonna be partners, Frog.

FROG: We gonna be more than that, we gonna be brothers.

ROCK: And stick together.

FROG: Till we get to be free.

ROCK: That's our secret. You swear to keep it?

FROG: I swears to keep it.

ROCK: Then you and me—and freedom—is friends.

> *(They shake hands)*

FROG: And ain't nothing gonna come between us. Rock, you know what?

ROCK: What?

FROG: When we get on that Northern road—it's cold up there, ain't it?

ROCK: They say it is.

FROG: I'm gonna take my coat and cover you up at night if you need it.

ROCK: You sound like a sure-enough friend, Frog.

FROG: And Rock, listen, if you get hongry, you know what I'm gonna do?

ROCK: What?

FROG: I'm gonna sneak out of our hiding place and beg some bread from cook-house to cook-house long the road. And even if I don't get nothing but *one* biscuit, hongry as I is, partner, I'm gonna take that biscuit and put it in my pocket and keep it till I get back to you. Then I'll break it in half— *(Rock reaches out his hand)* And eat both halves myself!

    (Loud laughter from both. SLAVE DRIVER enters)

SLAVER: Here! Here! Cut out all that racket! Get up on your feet and let's go. Ten miles yet to walk—and it's sunset nearly now.

FROG: Mister Clay, did you bring us a little water?

SLAVER: I ought to bust you cross your head! Water? There'll be a trough full for you at the slave pen tonight. Come on, get them ten miles behind you—then you can drink.

FROG: It sure would be fun—to have a little water!

ROCK: It sure would be fun—

FROG: To have a biscuit.

    (TRADER cracks his whip)

SLAVER: Come on! Get on! Get on! Get on!

    (They exit as the sun sets. Blackout. Light at left reveals a cabin doorstep in the evening glow. MARY sits on the stoop singing to her child.)

MARY:

> Go to sleep,
> Baby-chile,
> Go to sleepy, mama's baby,
> When you wake
> You will have
> All de pretty lit'le horses.

> Black and blue,
> And sorrel, too,
> All de pretty lit'le horses.
> Hush-a-bye,
> Don't you cry,
> Go to sleep, my lit'le baby-bye!

    (Enter GRANDMA LANTHIE)

MARY: The winter's almost gone, Grandma Lanthie. And we had no kind of word from Rock.

LANTHIE: They taken Rock way far away—down the river—to Mister Clay's own plantation, they tell me. Rock just about got there by now. It's a long way to walk. He got to look around a little and make his plans. Don't worry, honey. Just nurse that chile and take care of it so it be a big strong boy—and able to travel—when Rock comes back to get you. I wish I was gonna be here to go with you.

MARY: Don't say that, Grandma Lanthie!

LANTHIE: No use hiding it, chile. I can't stand these aches and pains much longer, leastwise not those aches that in my heart. But don't worry, Mary, wait for Rock, and care for that baby so he'll be a big strong man to help fight for the new day.

MARY: You mean the freedom? You think it'll ever come?

LANTHIE: I know it'll come, chile, sure as the sun do move.

> (*The old woman hobbles into her cabin as, in the deepening sunset, MARY resumes her lullaby.*)

MARY:

> Hush-a-bye,
> Hush-a-bye!
> Go to sleepy, mama's baby
> Hush-a-bye,
> Don't you cry!
> Go to sleep, my lit'le baby-bye!

> (*The evening light fades to a moonglow on MARY's cabin, as it comes up on a distant slave hut far away in the delta at right stage. There MR. CLAY, the slaver, is removing the chains from ROCK's arms.*)

SLAVER: Rock, this is your stopping place. You gonna work in my rice fields from sun-up to sun-down every day. But at night—just to show you my heart's in the right place—you can sleep here with Belinda. (*He calls to a woman within the hut*) Belinda! Belinda! I got a man for you.

> (*Belinda emerges*)

BELINDA: Yes, Massa Clay.

SLAVER: Rock, this is your wife.

ROCK: I got a wife back where I come from, sir.

SLAVER: Well, you gonna have another one here, two or three of 'em, maybe—according to how many wenches I want to breed this year. I'm gonna start you with this gal, Belinda. Belinda, here's your man.

BELINDA: I likes him, Massa.

SLAVER: Now, I'm gonna leave you two alone, but be up with the sun in the morning. If you don't, you'll taste a little of this. *(He brandishes his whip)*

BELINDA: Massa, we'll be up at dawnin'.

SLAVER: Rock, I got guards, and I got hounds. Don't run away.

ROCK: Yes, sir, Mr. Clay.

>*(The SLAVER exits. The man and woman stare at one another)*

BELINDA: Come in.

ROCK: I want to set here on this stump and get my mind together.

BELINDA: You don't need to get your mind together to be with me. You a fine looking man. I'm gonna love you Rock.

ROCK: I told you, I *got* a wife.

BELINDA: Yes, but she's far away. You might even much never see her again. Being's as we're slaves, we got to look out for now. Rock, come on in my house.

ROCK: I just want to set here awhile.

BELINDA: Then set there! Dog-gone it! Set there!

>*(Angrily she enters the cabin leaving ROCK alone. Miles away on another doorstep MARY sings to their child. In his soul he hears her voice. But he hears another voice, too, as the SLAVER—a carica-tured Simon Legree—with a big cigar in his mouth—tilts his chair back center stage and says:)*

SLAVER:

>Down on the Delta where the land is rich
>We treat our slaves like a son-of-a-bitch.
>Down on the Delta they die like flies,
>So we're always on the look-out for fresh supplies.
>We need 'em in the cotton, we need 'em in the cane.
>The auction block supplies that need for a modest gain.
>Now you take that healthy young bastard, Rock,
>One of the best, pure bred stock.
>Strong black buck for house, for field.
>Use him for breeding and watch his yield.
>But if he gets sassy, tries to run away,
>*We* know how to deal with 'em down this way.
>I got whips, I got guns, I got guards, I got dogs,
>And swamps all around—with snake-filled bogs.
>Just let a slave try to run away—
>He'll remember the cure for many a day!

Down here in the Delta where the land is rich
We treat our slaves like a son-of-a-bitch.
    (BELINDA calls peevishly from the cabin)
BELINDA: I'm waiting for you, Rock.
ROCK: My mind is troubled. I just want to set here.
BELINDA: Maybe you's hongry. I got some corn pone in the ashes. And some nice cool water in the bucket.
ROCK: No, I ain't hongry.
BELINDA: Then if you don't want to eat nor drink, I's waiting for you—in the bed.
ROCK: Woman, I'm setting here looking one thousand miles away—and I ain't studying you. I sees another cabin and another woman with a boy child in her arms. I want to get to her, where she is, be where she's at. That's all I want.
BELINDA: Rock, you better come in here with me, setting out there talking like a fool. How you gonna get one thousand miles away? Huh? Answer me that? *(She emerges to sit beside him rubbing her cheek against his)* What's the matter, honeyman? Don't you like me?
ROCK: No.
BELINDA: What?
ROCK: I said, no.
BELINDA: Then you ain't gonna stay with me?
ROCK: I sure ain't.
BELINDA: Then I'm gonna go right now and tell Master.
ROCK: You gonna do which? *(Blocking her way)*
BELINDA: Gonna go—
ROCK: Go where? *(Backing her into the house)*
BELINDA: In the house here, so you can be with me.
ROCK: That ain't what you said.
BELINDA: I didn't mean it.
    (ROCK threatens her with serio-comic gesture)
ROCK: You said you was gonna go tell Old Massa.
BELINDA: But I didn't mean it.
ROCK: But you said, it, didn't you? *(He draws his hand back)*
BELINDA: Yes.
ROCK: Then go and tell him! Go on! Go tell him! *(He runs her out of the house)*
BELINDA: No, I ain't gonna tell him! I didn't mean that! Rock, lemme back in my house.
ROCK: No, no! You don't come back in here. You gonna tell Old Massa.

BELINDA: No, I ain't. Rock, please lemme back in. The mosquitoes is something awful out here.

(ROCK sinks down on the bed as she batters the door.)

ROCK: I don't care nothing about the mosquitoes nor you, either. I done told you, Belinda, my mind is one thousand miles away.

BELINDA: *(Sobbing)* Oh, Lawd! Massa Clay done brought a crazy slave here to stay with me! I don't like it! I don't like it! Drat these mosquitoes. *(Slapping at the insects)* I don't like no man like that. All the chilluns I done bored on this plantation, ain't nary one of 'em had no uppity papa like that—what won't even let me in my own house. Lemme in! Lemme in! Lemme in!

(FROG enters and squats on his haunches looking)

FROG: 'Scuse me, Miss.

BELINDA: *(With a startled scream)* Who's you?

FROG: I'm Frog. Is you seen a new-come slave anywhere around here named Rock?

BELINDA: What you want with Rock?

FROG: I'm his partner.

BELINDA: Well, no wonder Rock ain't got no sense—having a partner like you.

FROG: I wouldn't talk that way about your friends, Miss.

BELINDA: What's your name, you say?

FROG: Frog. And who might you be?

BELINDA: Belinda.

FROG: You're a sweet looking woman.

BELINDA: You think so, Mr. Frog?

FROG: I really do.

BELINDA: Then you got more sense than your friend is.

FROG: Now, don't say that. There ain't nothing the matter with Rock.

BELINDA: He's just a fool! Been setting out here all evening talking about he's looking one thousand miles away.

FROG: I reckon he sees his family in his mind's eye.

BELINDA: Mind's eye, my foot! Massa gived Rock to me.

FROG: Wished he'd give *me* to *you* instead. *(FROG embraces her hand shyly)*

BELINDA: Huh! I believes this little old sawed-off man do like me, after all.

FROG: Like you? Honey if you was to kiss me, it would tickle me all de way from pillar to post.

BELINDA: Lemme see!

(She grabs FROG and kisses him. FROG hollers out loud)

FROG: Ye—hoo-eoo-oo-o! Miss Heavy-sot, what's that you got—makes me like you so? Belinda I warn't looking for Rock. I were looking for *you*. Let's we inspect this pecan grove.

BELINDA: Uh-hum! Too many stickers down there.

FROG: I could wallow all over them stickers if I was with you. I wouldn't even know it.

BELINDA: Well, I would. Let's we got this away, honey, down by the mill-stream—where the soft moss is.

FROG: Let's go!

(BELINDA leads FROG away in the moonlight. Blackout. At center stage, miles off on the Pritchard plantation, GRANDMA LANTHIE totters forward. Friends bring a cot for her and place it under a tree. But the old woman stands, as if hearing a voice. She sings at first as though to herself supported by the hum of the chorus.)

LANTHIE:

Hush, Oh, hush, somebody's callin' me.
Hush, Oh, hush, somebody's callin' me.
Hush, Oh, hush, somebody's callin' me.
Oh, ma Lord, Oh, ma Lord, what shall I do?

I think, I think, de angels callin' me.
I think, I think, de angels callin' me.
I think, I think, de angels callin' me.
Oh, ma Lord, Oh, ma Lord, what shall I do?

MARY: Come on Grandma Lanthie, lay down out here in the cool, it's so hot in the cabin. Lay down and take your rest, 'fore the pain come and cut you in two again. You been up walking around all day.

(The women gather round her as LANTHIE lies down on her cot. A tall slave, the minister, enters and appeals to death to come down easy.)

REVEREND:

O de sperit say
I want yuh fo' to go down, death, easy.
I want yuh go down, death easy.
I want yuh go down, death, easy.
An' bring ma servan' home.

O de sperit say
Creep to de bedside easy,

I want yuh creep to de bedside easy
An' bring my servan' home.

March up in de kingdom easy,
March up in de kingdom easy,
I want yuh march up in de kingdom easy,
An' bring my servan' home.
   *(To the hum and moan of the assembled slaves a MAMMY prays
   in a high voice)*

MAMMY: Oh, hear me this evening, Lord, as you take Sister Lanthie home to thy bosom. She's labored long in the heat of thy vineyard, Lord. Now she's ready to go home. Take her where she can see her children, Lord, what's gone before her. Take her where she can see her friends gone long ago. Take her where she can see them what was with her in her homeland in Africa, Lord, where the gods had other names, and not your name. But they was gods, too, Lord. Take her this evening, into a kingdom where the Overseer don't call no more, neither does the slavery chain rattle, nor the trader come to sell you away, and the only river flowing there is Jordan, and the only master reigning there is Jesus. She's ready now, Lord, to rest, in your bosom. She knows you understand. She's got her East roots in the rising sun and her West roots in the morning star. She's ready, ready now to put on her starry crown, put on her snow white robe, and walk with Michael through the pearly gates down the streets that shine like the setting sun. Oh-ooo-oo-o! Lord! Friend Lanthie's ready now to say Gabriel, Gabriel, Gabriel— *(Talks into the song)*

WOMEN:
   Where shall I be when de first trumpet sound?
   Where shall I be when it sound so loud?
   When it sound so loud till it wake up de dead,
   Where shall I be when it sound?
      (Women support LANTHIE as she reaches out her hand to MARY.)
   Gwine to try on ma wings when de first trumpet sound.
   Gwine to try on ma wings when it sound so loud.
   When it sound so loud till it wake up de dead,
   Where shall I be when it sound?

LANTHIE: Mary, honey, tell Rock—tell him—I couldn't wait till he come back. Tell him I had to steal away. But when you-all gets to de freedom—think of me. *(She smiles gently)*

WOMEN:

> Steal away, steal away, steal away to Jesus.
>
> Steal away, steal away home.
>
> I ain't got long to stay here.
>
> *(MARY sobs)*

REVEREND: Sister Lanthie was a Queen in Africa! Lord God Jesus—
and all the gods of Africa—guide her on her way.

> *(LANTHIE is dead. The light fades . . . Blackout . . . The late af-
> ternoon sun reveals a path along a dike with the green of rice plants
> below. Slaves from the rice field are passing with their trousers rolled
> up and bare legs wet. They carry hoes, forks, and other implements
> of toil. FROG is among them. He sits down on the edge of the dike.
> Chatter of slaves.)*

SLAVES:

> Huh! Sho am hongry!
>
> That sun were a scorcher today.
>
> Wonder how my baby is? Believe it got de smallpox.
>
> Tain't nothing but mosquitoes got it all bit up.

FROG: Whee-ee-e! I sho am tired. *(Sits down)*

SLAVE: You Frog, you better come on here, else the eating trough be
empty.

FROG: I ain't worried. Belinda'll save me something.

SLAVE: De scraps all she'll be able to save, hongry as I is.

> *(All pass by and exit save FROG. He sits there rubbing the mud
> off his toes and sings a little song.)*

FROG:

> Dat old black sow, she can root in de mud,
>
> She can tumble and roll in de slime.
>
> But dat big red cow, she get all mired up,
>
> So dat cow need a tail in fly-time.

> Now, where you reckon that buddy o' mine at? He's sho due to
> pass this way.

> Yes, de cow need a tail in fly-time. . . .
>
> *(ROCK enters wearily)*

ROCK: How yuh, Frog?

FROG: Tolerable po'ly, cause I swear they getting too much work out
o' me down here. Every time I raise up to take a breath, I look into
a shotgun or de overseer boss's mouth.

ROCK: They got us covered, all right, all right.

FROG: They don't mind shooting neither.

ROCK: Nor throwing you in de bayou—

FROG: Wid de snakes—

ROCK: After you's shot.

FROG: And nobody likes to be buried in muddy water.

ROCK: Um-hum!

FROG: Massa say a run away slave's same as a thief—he steal his labor from his master. He say we his cattles.

ROCK: *Chattels,* Frog.

FROG: Chattels and cattles all de same here. Say, Rock, what's on your mind?

> *(They look around carefully)*

ROCK: To leave.

FROG: To run away?

ROCK: To get out of here soon as we can.

FROG: In spite o' the guns?

ROCK: In spite o' the dogs.

FROG: In spite o' the swamps?

ROCK: Spite of everything. If I can't be free, I can sure die trying.

FROG: And me.

ROCK: I done found a island in the Big Swamp, Frog. A little island with a high-up place where crocodiles ain't likely to come, and a tree to climb for a look out post.

FROG: We gonna hide on that island?

ROCK: Till they give up looking for us.

FROG: Then—

ROCK: We gonna make it to the highway by night—and to the North.

FROG: *(Hilariously snapping his fingers and singing:)*

> Oh, freedom!
> Freedom over me!
> Before I'd be a slave—

ROCK: Quiet, pal!

FROG: Dumb and mum, partner! *(They shake hands)* Till Saturday—

ROCK: When we go hunting.

FROG: In the Big Swamp—

ROCK: For freedom.

> *(Blackout. They exit. Simultaneously at left MARY approaches her doorway calling within to a child, as BELINDA approaches her doorway at right)*

MARY: Little Rock, Little Rock, if you don't stop scampering all over that floor and get in bed! It's long ago time for all little chilluns to be in bed.

    (CLARA enters)

CHILD: *(Within)* Mama, come sing to me about de pretty lit'le horses.

MARY: You got to sleep. Mama wants to talk to Miss Clara a while.

CHILD: Then tell me about King David.

    (At opposite side in the Delta, BELINDA)

BELINDA: Frog, you little Frog, stop that crawling all under that bed and everywhere. Dog-gone if you ain't might nigh bad as your father. Massa gwine sell you if you keep on being so previous. *(Turning)* Frog! Big Frog! Come in here, let's we go to bed. Setting out under the chinaberry tree all night telling big ole lies and neglecting me. You Frog. I say come here—'fore I peal your head with a stone.

    (FROG enters dragging his feet)

FROG: Oh, Lawd! A man can't have no peace. If it tain't de Overseer, it's his wife.

BELINDA: You and your friend, Rock, you-all is the tall-tale-tellingest Negroes I ever did see. And you, you jest jokes and lies by the hour.

FROG: Ain't no lies in it. Every tale I tell is true.

BELINDA: Then come in this cabin and tell me some, too. I likes to be entertained once in awhile.

    (BELINDA drags FROG off. On the opposite stoop CLARA sits smoking her pipe and talking with MARY)

CLARA: Looks like Old Massa done lost all he had gambling, Mary. Every penny. Now he gonna sell what few slaves he got left.

MARY: How Rock ever gonna find me again?

CLARA: You still hopes?

MARY: He's brave—ain't scared to run away. But where'll I be when he gets the chance?

CLARA: Pompey say Old Massa gonna sell you, Mammy and me to a female relation of his'n in Memphis what's just got a lot of money from somewhere, wants to put on de dog and have herself two or three cooks and mammies and maids. You'd make a good lady's maid—all the training you had in de Big House when Old Mistis was living.

MARY: Somehow I'd rather work in de fields, Clara, in the air and the sun.

CLARA: Than to be in the house, and have hot biscuits out of the kitchen if Mistis don't eat all of her'n?

MARY: Grandma Lanthie worked all her life in de fields and didn't care nothing about Mistress' hot biscuits. I's scared I won't get along in the house.

CLARA: Maybe Mistis slap you once in awhile, but she won't use no whip like the Overseer.

MARY: A slap can hurt much as a whip, Clara.

(*Blackout . . . Delicate laughter of fine white ladies is heard. Between columns of smilax a beautiful southern belle appears in hoops of white lace. Before her stand three slave women, CLARA, MAMMY, and MARY. Mary holds a child.*)

MISTRESS: So these are my new slaves. How kind of my cousin, Mr. Pritchard, to send them so promptly. A cook, a mammy, a maid. And a little boy! Hum! Take them around the back, put them in a tub, and give all of them a good scrubbing. . . . Caesar! Caesar! Some more tea for the ladies!

(*SLAVES exit left, MISTRESS right, as light fades to an ominous darkness in which frightened voices are heard whispering, repeating, calling:*)

SLAVES:

Rock gone! Frog gone!

Runs away! Oh, my Lord!

They gonna beat us! Beat us all!

Rock run away! Frog gone!

Nobody's seed 'em! White folks asking.

Overseer's looking! Oh, my Lord!

Rock gone! Frog gone!

Frog! Rock! Rock! Frog! Gone! Gone!

(*OVERSEER enters with whip and pistol. Shouting loudly, frightening and intimidating everyone.*)

OVERSEER: Where are they? Where's Rock? Where's Frog? You know, where are they?

SLAVE: (*Being choked*) Oh, Massa, I don't know, I don't know, I don't know—don't—know—ooo-oo-o . . .

OVERSEER: Tell me, or I'll beat you within an inch of your life! Where are they?

OLD MAN: Boss, I never seed 'em go! I never seed 'em! No, suh, truly, suh, I never seed 'em.

OVERSEER: Belinda! You Belinda! Come out of there.

(*BELINDA emerges to stand on the doorstep*)

BELINDA: Yes, Massa Clay?

OVERSEER: Where're them bastards? Did Frog stay here last night?

BELINDA: He better not stay no where else, suh!

OVERSEER: When did he leave? When did you last see him?

BELINDA: Bout noon, suh! He say he might go to the meadow yonder hunting for rabbits with stones.

OVERSEER: He didn't say the swamp?

BELINDA: No, suh!

OVERSEER: You sure? Lie to me—and I'll beat you within an inch of your life.

BELINDA: I wouldn't lie to you, Mr. Clay, no suh. Frog scared o' de swamp—they's snakes there.

OVERSEER: Albert, get the hounds ready. Mayberry, saddle my horse. Ivory, go call Mr. Crips, call Mr. Dunham, call all the white men around here. We'll catch them runaways and we'll bring them back with their skin dripping off their backs. Sound the alarm, blow the horn. Two slaves have run away.

> *(Great noise of alarm, horses hooves, cries. But over and beneath it all softly, persistently the chorus begins to sing:)*

CHORUS:

> Freedom! Freedom!
> Freedom over me!
> Before I'd be a slave—
> *(Fades out here to a faint hum. As the hub-bub continues. Creeping down the aisle of auditorium come the two fugitives, hunted, panting, tired)*

FROG: I can't run another inch . . . Neither can I wade . . . Neither walk.

ROCK: It ain't far now. I know de island ain't far now.

FROG: This dark, and all this water, full of cold things, roots, and slimy reeds like—

ROCK: Frog! There you go getting yourself all scared.

FROG: Getting scared? I ain't *getting* scared, I am scared. But not of dogs nor guns.

ROCK: I know. You're scared of moccasins. But they don't bite in the water, and they don't bite at night. So shut up.

FROG: Don't tell me they don't. . . .

ROCK: I said, shut up!

> *(Afar off the baying of hounds. Cries)*

FROG: You hear them dogs?

ROCK: Long ways off—but they'll find no scent in water. No tracks in this ooze. Frog, here's our island.

FROG: Let's sit down and rest. Whee-ee-o! This is the first time in my life I ever been free.

ROCK: Fun?

FROG: *(Wryly)* Yeh, it's fun. *(Then more jubilantly)* It is kind of fun. Just to look up at the stars and not see 'em from a slave yard is fun. Just to know you don't have to look the Overseer in the face tomorrow morning, that's fun. Rock, it is fun! Partner, even in all this water—being free is fun.

ROCK: But we got a long road to go, boy. This is just the starting point. When we hit the highway, that's when we got to be smart, darting, dodging, hiding, like a fox.

FROG: How long we gonna stay in this swamp, Rock?

ROCK: Maybe a week, maybe two, till we don't hear the hounds baying no more. Till we know they done give up looking for us.

FROG: Then I just as well settle down and make myself real comfortable. Say, Rock, you reckon Belinda gonna miss me?

ROCK: Sure, she's gonna miss you.

FROG: And little Frog, he's the cutest devil.

ROCK: When you free, you can work and buy 'em out of slavery. That's what I'm gonna do for Mary and my son—if I finds it's too hard to carry 'em with me.

FROG: Carry 'em with you? You aims to pass by your Old Mass's place on the way North?

ROCK: That's what I aim to do.

FROG: Then we ain't goin' right straight to freedom?

ROCK: You can go. I got a stop to make.

FROG: Then I'll make it with you. Partner, we stick together.

ROCK: All right, Frog. We stick together.

(An owl beings to hoot. FROG jumps up)

FROG: What's that?

ROCK: Tain't nothin' but an owl. Set down, man.

FROG: That's bad luck.

ROCK: You're crazy. Owls holler every night. Don't mean nothin'!

FROG: It just mean somebody's gonna die.

ROCK: Shut up!

FROG: I hope it tain't me.

ROCK: You want it to be me, then?

FROG: I don't want it to be one nor to'other. But with all these snakes and varmints around—

ROCK: Frog, I said shut up! Would you rather be here on the road to freedom or back in the fields behind a mule?
FROG: I sure don't like mules. Say, Rock, ever hear about Sam Johnson?
ROCK: No.
FROG:

> He were a man with a cruel mind.
> Drove his mule till de mule went blind.
> Drove his hoss till de hoss said, "Whoa!"
> Beat his wife till she fell on de flo!

> Don't you like that Rock.

ROCK: You know I don't beat no womens. *(ROCK stretches out on the ground and yawns.)*
FROG: I felt like hitting Belinda once. Fact is, I raised my hand to her. All she said was, "Um-huh!" And my whole arm got paralyzed.
ROCK: Big and strong as Belinda is, she'd throw you out de door like a sack o' meal.
FROG: That female *is* got a whole lot o' meat on her bones, ain't she? I wonder do she miss me tonight?
ROCK: She didn't have no idea your going, did she?
FROG: You know how womens is. She kinder suspected something. 'Sides she heard me singing the other day when Old Massa passed.
ROCK: Singing what?
FROG:

> When I'm gone,
> When I'm gone,
> When I'm gone,
> Lord, when I'm gone—
> Massa, you goin' to miss me,
> When I'm gone.

ROCK: Frog, you lying.
FROG: If I'm lying, I'm dying.
ROCK: You know you wasn't singing that in front of Old Massa. Lemme go to sleep—'fore I knock your eyes out.
FROG: If you do knock 'em out, you better put 'em back before I sees they out. Man, I was singing to Belinda, too:

> You goin' to miss me for my walk,
> Miss me for my talk . . . . . .

> *(As he sings ROCK begins to snore. FROG looks down at him, takes his old coat and puts it over him, then lies down himself.*

The owl hoots again. FROG looks up disturbed. He moves over very close to ROCK. Both begin to snore. . . . Blackout. . . . Roll of thunder. Lightning. Sound of heavy rain in darkness. Running water. When the lights come up, it is many days later. The clothes of FROG and ROCK hang from tree limbs drying. ROCK is in a tree, his lookout post. FROG sits dejected on the ground.)

FROG: Rock, what you see from up yonder in that tree. You mighty quiet.

ROCK: Seem like I see peoples moving way off on the edge of the swamp.

FROG: Black peoples or white peoples?

ROCK: White peoples.

FROG: Then I don't feel so good. Is they got boats?

ROCK: I don't know. I can't tell.

FROG: Much rain as we been having all these days we been out here, bayous, creeks, ponds, bogs, everything all full of water. This swamp's full of water just like a lake. No way to get out now, if they comes, cept to dive in de water wid the snakes and crocodiles—and get et.

ROCK: We sure didn't figure on all this rain.

FROG: And I sure didn't figure on starving to death before I got free. My belly's rubbing my backbone right now. *(Bird chirps)* What's that?

ROCK: A cat bird. See how pretty it fly?

FROG: Hell with it! Hongry as I is, I wants a cat-fish. Say, when you reckon the sun's gonna come out and dry these clothes of our'n? I gets cold at night sleeping naked.

ROCK: Reckon we'll just have to sleep in wet clothes—if we sleep at all this night.

FROG: What you mean, *if* we sleep?

ROCK: I see peoples all around this swamp, Frog. I see 'em unloading rowboats from the ox carts over on the field road.

FROG: What you think that means, Rock?

ROCK: They gonna search this swamp for us—and we got to get out.

FROG: How can we get out—and the water done riz over our heads?

ROCK: Swim where it's deep, wade where it ain't, swing from the trees, crawl through muck—anyway to make Bayou Seco and the slave quarters on Old Man Kingsley's plantation. Maybe the slaves'll hide us there. Maybe.

FROG: And won't give us away?

ROCK: Maybe they won't. We got to take that chance, Frog. It's our only chance. Say! They coming into the swamp. I see 'em starting into the swamp. (*ROCK comes down out of the tree as distant cries and echoes are heard. They knot their shirts about their necks and prepare to flee.*) Come on! We got to swim for it, Frog.

FROG: Crocodiles, get out my way! Alligators, run—here I come.

CHORUS:

> When I'm gone,
> When I'm gone,
> When I'm gone,
> Lord, when I'm gone—
> Somebody's goin' miss me
> When I'm gone!
>
> (*Blackout . . . Water sounds, distant oars, crackle of underbrush, far off shouts and cries. Then, at another point in the swamp, in a glimmer of light, ROCK and FROG are seen emerging from the water, panting.*)

FROG: I hear 'em rowing, hear their oars, but I can't tell which way it is—noises all round in this swamp! They coming, coming, and we ain't got not even a weapon to defend ourselves.

ROCK: David killed Goliath with a stone.

FROG: We ain't even got a stone.

ROCK: Look around, gather up some—stones, sticks, clubs anything— in case we have to make a fight for it.

> (*They gather up stones and broken trunks of trees which they throw on a pile.*)

FROG: Here's a big rock. Here's a stick.

ROCK: They won't get us easy, that's one sure thing.

FROG: If I'd just get hold of one of their guns! . . . Man, look at this boulder. Kill a giant sure. (*FROG goes to opposite side to pull a boulder from the water's edge. He stoops down. Suddenly he leaps back terrified with a loud cry:*) Moccasins! (*He reaches for a stick on the ground and raises it to crush the snake's head when there is a hiss, a sharp cry, and the stick stops in mid-air. FROG is bitten. He grabs his ankle.*) Rock! Rock! Rock!

> (*FROG limps toward center. ROCK comes running.*)

ROCK: What's the matter, boy?

FROG: I'm snake-bit! Snake!

> (*ROCK sees the snake gliding away into the water*)

ROCK: Gone!

(FROG sinks down in fear and pain as ROCK rips away a piece of his trouser leg to tightly tie it above FROG's wound.)

FROG: I went to lift that stone—and right there coiled beside it! I didn't see it, so dark in this swamp. Didn't see it till it sprung! Aw! Rock, I feel cold all over.

ROCK: Keep quiet, Frog. Lemme tie this. Then I'll suck the poison out.

FROG: Ain't gonna do no good, Rock. I feel it all through my veins. Like ice and fire, running all through my veins. It's getting dark. Too dark. I can't hardly see you, partner. But seems like I still hear them oars. Do you hear them oars, Rock?

ROCK: Yes, I hear 'em.

FROG: Then run! Get away! Go on, partner. We won't never see the North together now. But go on, partner—quick. Leave me here.

ROCK: You my friend, ain't you?

FROG: Yes.

ROCK: And we agreed to stick together, didn't we?

FROG: But I can't run, Rock. I can't swim no more. That snake—

ROCK: I ain't gonna leave you now, Frog.

FROG: Don't be no fool! They coming, the slavers coming. And I can't run—neither can I fight—but you fight for me. Take that stone and throw it at Goliath! Take that stone!

ROCK: I'll fight, Frog! You lay here quiet.

FROG: Oh-ooo-o! Cold, Rock! So cold—all this dampness! I told you 'bout that owl, didn't I, Rock? I told you when I heard it hoot. I see great big old dark wings closing down, closing down on me, closing down. Hear 'em beating—now—beating . . . . . *(the sound of the oars drawing near)* beating, beating . . . . . *(ROCK looks around anxiously as he draws FROG's head into his lap)* beating . . . . . chariot's wings, Rock . . . . . Look! I'm gonna be free! . . . . . Only—tain't like we planned, Rock.

ROCK: No, Frog, tain't like we planned.

FROG: But I'm gonna be a man, partner, not a cattle no more. You hear me, partner? A man! A man! Frog's gonna stand up and be a man, not a slave, never no more! I feel it over me—like ice, like fire, like a mighty wind, like de lightning, like a cyclone storm. It's freedom, partner! Freedom— *(sings)*

Oh, freedom! Oh, freedom!
Freedom over me!
Before I'd be a slave
I'd be buried in my grave

And go home to my Lord
And be free!

Partner, you sing it for me. I can't get my breath no more.
(FROG sinks down, his dying head in ROCK's lap. Softly, ROCK
begins to sing:)
ROCK:
Oh, freedom!
Freedom over me!
Before I'd be a slave
I'd be buried in my grave
And go home to my Lord
And be free!
(Suddenly a shot rings out. There are shouts, cries, and the splashing
of water. Gently ROCK lays FROG on the ground and reaches
behind him for a stone. He rises and lifts the stone to throw it.
Another shot strikes his wrist. The stone falls from his useless arm. He
crouches, runs, at bay. Exits only to meet a wave of exultant sound.)
VOICES:
Get him! Get him! There he goes!
We got him! We got him! Whee!
Hit him! Beat him! Got him!
(ROCK is flung violently back into the scene, sprawling on his face
in the mud. The SLAVER leaps on his back and begins to bind his
arms behind him.)
SLAVER: So you will run away, will you? I'll teach you! Get up! Get up!
You bastard! Get up! *(Amid the triumphant shouts of the crowd in the*
boats, ROCK rises to his feet, panting, bleeding, bound. The SLAVER
wipes his hands.) We caught the big buck alive, folks! This dead slave
on the ground ain't worth nothing nohow. Get in that boat, Rock.
A hundred lashes due you tonight—and once a month for the next
year! I'll teach you to run away, you black dog, you! Get!
(He slashes at him with his whip as the voices from the boats roar
approval. ROCK exits. The SLAVER gives a final kick to FROG's
body as he leaves. Sound of oars as the voices retreat in the distance.
Softly, then rises to a crescendo, the CHORUS sings:)
CHORUS:
Oh, freedom!
Freedom over me!
Before I'd be a slave

I'd be buried in my grave
And go home to my Lord
And be free!
(*Light fades to a single glow on FROG's face . . . Blackout . . .
Suddenly, the gay tinkle of Christmas bells are heard. Happy voice
shouting greetings. Music boxes play. A blaze of light reveals a huge
life-sized calendar. A slave boy struts past and tears away the leaf
marked "November". The remaining sheet is "December—1858."
The boy exits dancing. At left a slave women enters, at right MARY
crosses with her son, LITTLE ROCK, now seven years old.*)

MAUM: Merry Christmas, Mary! Merry Christmas, Little Rock.

MARY: Merry Christmas, Maum Dorsey.

CHILD: Merry Christmas, Mam.

MAUM: Nippy weather, we having, heh, Mary?

MARY: Right sharp, but good. I like it.

MAUM: I do, too. Coming to the party in slave row tonight?

MARY: Don't know. If Mistress don't need me, maybe. I got to dress
her hair for the ball. And Baby Rock's got to deliver some presents.

MAUM: You Big House folks has to work *too* hard, *all* the time, everyday. We country women's has it easier in that respect.

MARY: House or field, we works—if we's slaves. Good evening, Maum
Dorsey.

MAUM: Good evening, chile! Good evening!
(*They exit in opposite directions. Light goes up full stage to reveal
the MISTRESS beautiful in lace negligee polishing her nails before
her mirror. A knock. MARY enters with LITTLE ROCK.*)

MISTRESS: Mary, you're late.

MARY: I had to stop by the confectioners, then leave the note you gave
me for—

MISTRESS: I'm in no mood for explanations. I said, you're late returning.

MARY: Yes'm, but I—
(*The MISTRESS gives her a resounding slap*)

MISTRESS: That's your "*but*"—
(*LITTLE ROCK dashes between them to protect his mother*)

MARY: Rock! (*She pulls him toward her*)

MISTRESS: You little brat! If you dare—If it weren't Christmas, I'd
order you both thrashed. But I can't upset my nerves anymore
tonight. I've more than I can put up with now—to weary me!
Waiting an hour for you to get back to dress me for the ball. My

sister-in-law'll be furious if I'm late. Look, Rock, the parcels are there. Deliver them at Mrs. Winstead's house on the next corner and, mind you, come directly back. On the way, tell the coachman I'll have the carriage in five minutes.

CHILD: Yes, Mistress.

MISTRESS: Then go! Go! What are you standing there for? *(LITTLE ROCK takes the parcels and runs out)* Mary, that child of yours irritates me no end. There's something sassy about him, impudent in the very way he looks at me.

MARY: I'm sorry, Mistress.

MISTRESS: Perhaps up country where you came from, slave children are permitted to grow up wild, disrespectful, but not here in Memphis. You've been under me five years now. You should know.

MARY: I do know, Mistress. And I tries to raise him to your liking.

MISTRESS: He acted just now as if he never saw a slave-wench slapped before.

MARY: Rock just a little child, Mistress. I tries not to let him see things like that.

MISTRESS: Well, since I don't intend to stop slapping you whenever you need it, perhaps we'd better send Little Rock where he won't be able to see "things like that."

MARY: Oh, I didn't mean in that way, Mistress. You don't mean . . . you wouldn't . . . you wouldn't sell my child?

MISTRESS: No, I don't need money. But I think I'll give him away. I've been feeling all day these presents stacked there for my sister, the governor's wife, are most insufficient. They honor Memphis so seldom with a visit. I want them to go away feeling we're at least hospitable—and prosperous . . . Don't pull my hair now. A little black page boy as a gift—I think she might like that. Anita has a way of handling slaves, too, that might be good for Little Rock . . . Be careful, Mary, you know I don't like my hair combed down that way. *(A knock)* Yes?

CHILD: Me, Mistress.

MISTRESS: Come in, boy. Mary, bring me that big red ribbon from the chest . . . Hurry! . . . Little Rock, come here! Let me see . . . Hum-m-m! Yes, a big red bow right on your neck. Fine! As gay as Christmas. This'll amuse my sister. She'll tell everybody in Kentucky about it when she gets back with you . . . Stand still so I can tie it . . . Meanwhile, Mary, take the rest of my presents out in the hall for the coachman to pick up. You, Rock, will sit on the box with him to the ball. *(With terror in her eyes MARY exits)* So put your coat on.

CHILD: I'm going to the ball with you, Mistress?

MISTRESS: You're going to Kentucky with my sister and the governor tonight—along with the rest of my Christmas gifts. *(MARY returns)* My wrap, Mary.

CHILD: Mistress, you're giving me away?

> *(Furiously she shouts)*

MISTRESS: Yes, you little brat, I'm giving you away! . . . There's dust on my slippers, Mary.

> *(MARY stoops down and wipes the dust from her mistress' shoes. Still on her knees. She holds hold her arms to her son. He comes to her.)*

CHILD: Mama?

MARY: Be a man, son! You remember what I told you about Little David, the giant-killer?

CHILD: Who played on his harp?

MARY: Yes, who played on his harp. Tell yourself that story sometimes and think of your mama.

MISTRESS: I'm waiting, Mary!

MARY: Goodbye, son.

CHILD: Goodbye, mama.

> *(MARY opens the door)*

MISTRESS: Hang up these things before I get back, Mary—and have a fire going. Come on, Rock. Get going. A Christmas gift! Ha! Ha! Ha! Ha! A Christmas gift!

> *(She exits laughing gaily with the child behind her. MARY hurries to the window to watch her son until he is out of sight. Then she begins to sing:)*

MARY:

> I am a poor pilgrim of sorrow
> Out in this wide world alone.
> I've heard of a city called heaven.
> I've started to make it my home.
>
> Sometimes I am tossed and driven, Lord,
> Sometimes I know not where to roam—
> I've heard of a city called heaven.
> I've started to make it my home.
>
> *(MARY bows her head on the dressing table and sobs. Blackout.)*

Act III

SETTING: *A stone quarry.*
ACTION: *A group of men slaves naked to the waist are breaking rock. They are a tough looking lot. Among them is ROCK. Across his back the scars of many beatings. They sing, letting the hammer fall on each, "Huh."*
SLAVES:

>I been hammerin—huh!
>In dis mountain—huh!
>>Four long years—huh!
>>Four long years!

>Dese old rocks in—huh!
>Dis yere mountain—huh!
>>Hurts ma side—huh!
>>Hurts ma side!

>Ain't no use to—huh!
>Send for doctor—huh!
>>Water boy's daid—huh!
>>Water boy's daid!

OVERSEER: *(Voice off stage)* Time out! Let 'em have some water! Mighty hot day! Water-boy, give 'em a drink.
>*(The men rest their hammers and wipe their brows as WATER-BOY passes among them with pail and dipper. ROCK and another fellow talk.)*

FELLOW: So this is where they sends the tough slaves—to the rock quarry! Us—they can't break in no other way.
ROCK: This is where they *tries* to break you—but it jest makes me meaner and stronger.
FELLOW: You been in this quarry long time, heh, Rock?
ROCK: Five-six years—since I tried to run away.
FELLOW: And you ain't never tried to run away no more?
ROCK: You see these marks on my back, don't you?
FELLOW: You ain't tried lately—cause I been here two-three years, myself. Ain't nobody tried lately.
ROCK: No, but I been thinkin'.
OVERSEER: Time up! Fall in! Grab them hammers!
FELLOW: What you been thinkin'?
ROCK: I been thinkin'— *(Sings)*
>Take ma hammer—huh!

Give it to Jonah—huh!
>Say I'm gone—huh!
>Say I'm gone!
>
>*(Men look around apprehensively. Another answers)*

He jest foolin'—huh!
He jest foolin'—huh!
>That's a lie—huh!
>That's a lie!
>
>*(But ROCK replies:)*

Did you ever—huh!
Stand on mountain—huh!
>In a cloud—huh!
>In a cloud!
>
>*(Full chorus comes up strong:)*

Did you ever—huh!
Stand on mountain—huh!
>In a cloud—huh!
>In a cloud!
>
>*(Blackout. . . . As the light comes up it reveals dimly the men drag-ging old quilts and sacks into the corner of a shack to sleep. ROCK lies down. A guard faces without, then sits on a log.)*

ROCK: I can't sleep, fellow. Can't rest.

FELLOW: Shut up! You ain't talking to me. You know Overseer'll beat us for talking at night.

ROCK: I can't sleep! Troubled in mind. I don't know, but feel like something's happening to folks I love—something happening one thousand miles away.

FELLOW: Hush! Shut up, Rock. Keep your thoughts to yourself.

ROCK: Jest talking to myself anyhow! Talking to myself.

>*(Light comes up center stage revealing MARY at an ironing board, while gradually at left the interior of a slave hut housing two or three Negro boys is revealed, among them LITTLE ROCK.)*

MARY: Too long! The time's too long! Rock said he'd be back. But maybe he couldn't run away! Maybe they caught him and beat him—killed him. I don't know. Maybe he couldn't find me—but I ain't so far from the old plantation. Anybody up there could tell him where I'm at. Maybe he—forgot! No. No! he couldn't do that! He ain't forgot me, nor his child. But somehow I can't sleep at night no more—might as well be up yere working, ironing Mistress' things. Seven years now, ain't seen him, ain't heard tell of him since they sold him away. Now my child's gone, too. Little Rock gone. Got nobody, got nobody!

> *(In the cabin right the three slave children lie on their pallets and talk. LITTLE ROCK speaks:)*

CHILD: My mama used to tell me a story about a little boy way back in Bible times what took a stone and kilt a great big giant.

BOY: What were that boy's name?

CHILD: Name David. And the giant were Goliath.

BOY: How he kill a great big giant with one little stone?

CHILD: Cause he were strong and good—and the giant were bad—and Lil' David just hauled off and throwed that stone and kilt him dead.

BIG BOY: Shut up, you two, and let a man sleep. I got to work in de field and all you little squirts go to do is hang around the stable and polish harness and run errands and set up on the box with the coachmen and look cute. Shut up, lemme sleep!

BOY: All right, Rufus.

CHILD: But I can't sleep, Rufus! It's strange here. I can't sleep.

> *(On pallet at left BIG ROCK, tossing, speaks:)*

ROCK: Can't sleep! Can't sleep! A stone's hung round my neck.

> *(At ironing board in center MARY speaks:)*

MARY: So tired—but I can't rest! No use going to bed. Trouble! Worry in my mind! My child needs me! My man needs me! I knows it! I feels it! Can't rest! Can't sleep. . . .

> *(LITTLE ROCK sits up on his pallet of rags:)*

CHILD: My mama told me, in the Bible, says they were a little boy like me, named David, took hisself a great big rock—went and kilt a giant.

BIG BOY: Go kill yourself one then—and shut up!

CHILD: I can't find the giant, Rufus! Can't find the right giant.

BOY: Old Massa's a giant.

BIG BOY: You crazy! De Overseer's de giant.

CHILD: They's all giants! They's too many of 'em—all around, every-where—every plantation—they's so many of 'em. I can't find no stones to kill all them giants. *(Pause)* 'Sides I ain't brave like David was. I's scared, Rufus. And I's here all by myself, and I want my mother. I want to go back where my mama's at. I wants to go home. I's by myself.

BIG BOY: Huh! He's gonna cry! What's the matter, Little Rock? You acts like you the only chile ever been sold away! Shut up boy, or else I'll come over there and beat your hide! Go to sleep, both you little monkeys! Ain't nobody by they selves, with me and Len here. So shut up, Rock, and go to sleep.

CHILD: All right. *(Silence, save for LITTLE ROCK's sobbing. Then he sits up and looks around but the others have begun to snore. He whispers:)* But I can't sleep! And I can't stand it! And I ain't gonna stay here— cause there ain't no stones nowhere 'round big enough to kill all these old giants. I reckon I ain't no little David! Mama, I ain't David! I wish I was, but I ain't no David. I gonna wrap myself up tight, tight, tight, in these dirty old sacks and I ain't gonna breath no more. I ain't gonna breath no more.

> *(He lies down, wraps all sacks and coverings about him, head and all, and rolls into a corner—in the opposite hut, BIG ROCK speaks)*

ROCK: Can't sleep, thinking about my child. I know he must be a big boy now, seven, eight years old.

> *(At the ironing board, MARY:)*

MARY: I know that chile wish he were here with his mama so's she could tell him about King David, and sing that song with them pretty little horses. He always did like to hear that. Little Rock, go to sleep, honey—

> Go to sleep,
> Baby-chile,
>
> Go to sleepy, mama's baby.
> When you wake
> You will have
>
> All de pretty lit'le horses.

> *(She takes a piece of her ironing in her arms as if it were a child)*

ROCK: Mary—Mary's been waiting for me all this time. Too long to wait. She must think I done died. She must believe I done forgot about her. But the road still runs back to the river. The road still runs to the Pritchard Plantation—and from there to the North. It's better to be dead than to be a slave. I can't wait no more. Can't hold back no longer. They's always guards. They's always dogs. And they's always guns. Guns! A gun! A man needs a gun. But the guard's got the gun. Sometimes a guard—turns his back. David killed the giant with just a stone. This here quarry's full of nothing but stones. . . . Nothing but stones. *(ROCK begins to creep toward the door. He looks about. The guard sits on a log with his back turned. ROCK picks up a stone. Swiftly he brings it down full on the guard's head, takes the pistol from the prone figure's holster and looks at it triumphantly.)* This time they won't catch me—and if they do—they won't catch *me*. They'll catch a dead man—maybe—or die themselves. I reckon there ain't no chance but the desperate chance. I'm gonna take it. *(He looks carefully at the pistol and inspects its load)* I got to take all the bullets he's got. *(He removes the guard's ammunition belt and puts it on himself. As he straps it he beings to sing softly:)*

> Oh, Freedom!
> Freedom over me!

> *(The light fades as ROCK walks slowly and surely away. Exits. The morning sun comes up on the cabin at left where the slave boys sleep. The big one sits up and shakes the other two.)*

> Before I'd be a slave
> I'd be buried in my grave
> And go home to my Jesus
> And be free!

> *(The song continues as the boy sits up)*

BIG BOY: Wake up that other little cry baby there, Len. I got to get out to the field. Daylight's dawning—and I don't want no whipping today. *(The big boy exits)*

BOY: I'll wake him up . . . Hey! Hey!

> *(Singing)*

> No more moaning, no more moaning,
> No more moaning over me. . . . .

> *(The younger boy tries to waken LITTLE ROCK)*

BOY: Roll out, sleepy colored boy! Come on, get up. It's time to go polish them brass bits and harness rings, and all them other pretty do-dads on them horses for Missis' fine carriage. Come on, hurry up, sleepy boy! Else we all get whipped. I ain't got no time to wake you up. Hey! I ain't you pappy no how. . . . Come on, Little Rock! Get up, man! Get up! Get up! Get up! *(He succeeds in uncovering the child's face and realizes he is dead.)* Aw! He cold! This boy cold! Lawdy mercy! Aw-ooo-oo-o! He dead! Little Rock's dead! Dead! Dead!

> *(The BOY backs away terror stricken. A ray of sunshine falls through the door on LITTLE ROCK. The CHORUS comes up strong:)*

CHORUS:

> Freedom! Freedom!
> Freedom over me!
> Before I'd be a slave

I'd be buried in my grave
And go home to my Jesus
And be free!

> *(Blackout. . . . In the darkness the running and panting of a man is heard. He knocks softly at a door right. A startled woman's voice answers)*

WOMAN: Who dat?

ROCK: Open the door.

WOMAN: For what? Who're you?

ROCK: A man. And I'm hongry.

WOMAN: Huh?

ROCK: Just crack the door, you'll see. I'm black. I'm a slave.

WOMAN: *(Cracking the door)* A runaway slave?

ROCK: Yes, I'm taking that chance—to find the North.

WOMAN: This a bad plantation. What you want?

ROCK: Something to eat.

WOMAN: Wait . . . Here, son, here! Take this corn pone quick and go. I ain't seed you, and I ain't heard you, and I don't know nothing, and go! God bless you! Go!

> *(Blackout as he hurries away in the night. . . . Sound of horses' hooves at slow trot in pitch darkness)*

ROCK: Hey! Stop that horse, black boy! Where you going?

> *(Answers in slow drawl.)*

VOICE: Back to the plantation from the mill. They was late grinding Massa's corn.

ROCK: I'm going your way, too. I'm too tired. Lemme ride behind you in the meal sacks.

VOICE: Who is you?

ROCK: A slave like you. Lemme ride.

VOICE: You don't belong round here I never seed—I mean heard you before.

ROCK: No, I don't belong round here. And I ain't staying round here, neither. I'm going on up the road—North.

VOICE: Get on this horse. But if anybody pass, don't be on this horse.

ROCK: I'm like a ghost, partner! Don't worry. I been disappearing into trees, into ground, into air for three-four weeks now. By day hiding in holes like a fox. Don't nobody ever see me clear—and won't—'cept Mary—till I see freedom's border line behind.

VOICE: Get up, Old Ned! Schk! Schk! Get 'long. You riding a ghost, and a man, and two bags of meal tonight. Get 'long! Get up!

*(Horses hooves retreat in distance. Moonlight on a path in woods.
Two slaves are passing)*

FESS: Lucious, I never did like to come through these woods in the
dark.

LUCIOUS: Better'n going round by the grave yard.

FESS: True! This is what comes o' having gal friends on 'nother plantation from where we's owned.

LUCIOUS: Our Old Massa don't own no pretty gals. You know that
Fess?

FESS: Nothing but mule-womens—chop more cotton than me. Hey,
what's that?

LUCIOUS: What's what?

FESS: I heard a noise.

LUCIOUS: You jest scared, Fess. You ain't heard a thing.

FESS: Aw-ooo-oo-o! Look! Lucious, there's a bear!

ROCK: If I am a bear, then I'm a talking bear!

FESS: He's a . . . . talking. . . . bear!

LUCIOUS: Fool! That ain't no bear! He's a man! What you want,
fellow?

ROCK: Where's the old Pritchard Plantation? Ain't this here part of it?

LUCIOUS: This here's part—but it's according to what part you's
looking for. It's all divided up now, and rented out to mostly poor
white trash.

ROCK: I'm looking for the slave quarters by the stable.

LUCIOUS: Who you want there?

ROCK: Grandma Lanthie, Mary—

FESS: Lord have mercy! He's a ghost! Grandma Lanthie's dead too long
ago. Is you dead, too?

ROCK: No, I ain't dead! I'm her grandson, Rock!

FESS: Rock—what were sold away when I were a child?

LUCIOUS: Sho enough! It is great big old Rock! I remember you. Man,
your grandma's gone! And your wife been sold away going on four
or five years.

ROCK: Sold away? Where?

LUCIOUS: Tain't far! Just to Memphis to Old Man Pritchard's cousin's
wife. They rich folks. Anybody can tell you where they lives in Memphis. But how'd you get here? You was sold too long ago down the
river.

ROCK: I told Mary I'd be back. Here I am. I'm a runaway.

FESS: Runaway? Don't come near me then! I don't want to be beat nor shot for seeing you.

ROCK: You haven't seen me.

LUCIOUS: No Rock, Fess ain't seed you. If he is, I'll brain him 'fore he tells it. Ain't neither one of us seed you. Man, go on your way and find your woman—and make it to Canaan if you can.

FESS: All I seed out here in these woods, man, was a ghost and a bear.

ROCK: Thank you! *(He exits)*

FESS: Lucious! Where that there ghost-bear I just seed go by?

LUCIOUS: Fess, what's the matter wid you? You ain't seed neither man, nor ghost, nor bear, less'n you seed it in your mind—and you ain't got no mind.

FESS: So I must ain't seed a thing.

LUCIOUS: No, sir, ain't neither one of us seed a thing!

FESS: Then come on here, Lucious, let's at least go see these gals!

> *(Blackout. . . . The rising moon reveals ROCK peering cautiously about in the slave yard of a Memphis house. The gruff voice of a Negro watchman with a lantern assails him.)*

WATCHMAN: Hey! What you want?

ROCK: Is this Mis' Pritchard Dean's place?

WATCHMAN: Yes! What you desires, ragmuffin?

ROCK: Is there—is there a girl named Mary here?

WATCHMAN: Mary? What you want with any Mary?

ROCK: Is she here?

WATCHMAN: She Mis' Dean's personal maid. She don't stay in no slave row.

ROCK: Where she stay at?

WATCHMAN: In de shed at the back of the Big House. Why? She don't have no truck wid no roustabouts like you. You look like you jest come off de levee.

ROCK: I did. I seed Miss Mary one day down in the market place—and I kinder fancied her looks.

WATCHMAN: A back door creep, huh? Well, Mary stick close to herself. She don't take up no loose time with no rounders. She say she been married once long time ago. She's still waiting for her man to come back. So, buddy, you jest losing your time. Get on back to de levee and load them steamboats. Go on, get!

ROCK: She see me, she might like me.

WATCHMAN: Then keep on sneaking round the white folk's house—
and get your black hide beat. Mary's sleep now anyhow.

ROCK: Which away—I go see?

WATCHMAN: That a way. *(Exit ROCK)* Um-huh! What a man won't
do for a little lovin'! Now, when I were young, used to creep around
like that myself. Had me a pretty Creole woman . . . . .

> *(He exits talking to himself. ROCK taps at a door right. MARY
> sits up in her bed within)*

MARY: Who that?

ROCK: Me?

> *(Instantly she catches his voice, rises. Then almost faints. Fear and
> doubt overcome her.)*

MARY: Who? Me? What me? *(She almost screams)* Who's that?

ROCK: Mary, it's me.

> *(She rushes to the door and flings it open.)*

MARY: Thank God! Rock! Rock! Rock!

ROCK: Mary! My wife! Mary!

> *(They embrace. CHORUS bursts forth strongly:)*
> Pharaoh's army got drowned!
> Oh, Mary don't you moan!

MARY: I hoped, I prayed, I waited, I cried! Now, here you is, here you
is! Here you is!

ROCK: And we ain't never gonna be separated no more, Mary. We
gonna take the desperate chance. We gonna be free. Where our son?
Get ready to come with me.

MARY: Rock, I's ready. I'll come with you anywhere—even if we die.
But, honey, we ain't got no son. He gone. He dead.

ROCK: Dead? Little Rock is dead?

MARY: Mistress given him away last Christmas time. She given him away
to Kentucky—and they writ back he died. He wasn't sick never.

ROCK: I reckon his little heart broke.

MARY: And he died.

ROCK: Our next child be born free. Mary, how I been longing for you,
wanting you! Is you ready to come with me? We'll make it up the
river to Illinois, or Ohio, and on to the North. I's found out all
about the way. And maybe the underground folks'll help us. Is you
ready?

MARY: I's ready Rock. Now. Just lemme get my clothes on.

> *(MAMMY appears outside in the moonlight. She calls:)*

MAMMY: Mary! You, Mary!

MARY: Hide here, Rock, behind the door. Lemme see what she wants. . . . Yes, Mammy, what you want?

MAMMY: Mistress just taken one her spells indigestion. She say for you to come there quick. And to tell Lemuel to saddle a horse and go for the doctor, and to wake up Lucy to make her a mustard poultice. She taken right painful like.

MARY: Tell her I'll be there right away. *(Mammy exits)* Rock, we'll have to wait. Too many folks awake round here now. Come on, follow me. I knows a good place to hide you—in Mistress' woodbox to which I carries the key. Come on.

ROCK: I no sooner sees you than you's got to leave me. Master, Mistress always calling. But it won't be long now. *(They kiss)* I'll hide in that box—but you come back and let me out.

> *(They go outside toward a long covered box)*

MARY: I got something to tell you, too, 'bout a underground man, a white Yankee man, I knows. He's a peddlar, he sells things and he knows which way is freedom—and how to get there.

ROCK: Can black folks really trust him?

MARY: Two or three slaves done escaped—and sent word back he's faithful. But I don't never talk with him. I waited for you to come for me. I don't want to be free by myself. Here get in this box, and lemme lock you up. If the peddlar man come in the morning, I send him to talk to you right here.

ROCK: Ain't you coming back till morning?

MARY: It's most daybreak now, honey. But I'll come back if I can.

> *(ROCK gets in the box. She closes and locks it. Exits. Blackout. CHORUS sings:)*

> Pharaoh's army got drowned!

> Oh, Mary, don't you moan.

> *(Suddenly the sun comes up brightly and reveals the backyard full of activity. MAMMY is hanging out clothes. A chimney sweep passes with his contraptions. A dog frolics with a bone. Children play.)*

[SWEEP:] Old soot's onery!

> Old soot's mean!

> Clean your chimneys!

> Clean 'em clean!

MAMMY: Old dirty black chimney-sweep, get on away from here. Didn't nobody send for you.

SWEEP: Yes, they did, too! I'm going in this house this morn and clean that flu—so's my Old Master can draw *his* pay—for *my* work.

MAMMY: Better stop talking so sassy 'bout your Old Master. Pat-terollers hear you and beat the tar out of you.

SWEEP: Sure is plenty of 'em guarding, up and down, and all over Memphis. Must be scared some us slaves run away.

MAMMY: I ain't interested in talking with you! Get on out here with your soot—and me hanging up these nice clean clothes—'fore I shuck yo' ears.

SWEEP: Kiss my foot, old woman!

(Exit CHIMNEY SWEEP as MAMMY threatens him with the wash stick. Enter MARY.)

MAMMY: How Mistress this morning?

MARY: She resting easy. I got her all surrounded with hot water bottles.

MAMMY: She ought to rest easy. She never do nothing.

MARY: She say she don't know if it's her stomach or her nerves.

MAMMY: Nerves, huh! Nobody but white folks got no nerves. I has to die to get a hot water bottle on me. What you doing, girl, sitting on that old wood box?

MARY: Oh, I jest likes to sit here. It so nice and warm this morning.

(MARY taps twice on box. Gets answering rap from ROCK as WOMAN talks.)

MAMMY: Don't feel so warm to me. Not warm enough to be jest idling and sitting round out doors. . . . Looky there! There comes that old Yankee peddlar man walking like his back is broke.

MARY: Oh, I want to see him. I been saving my few pennies Mistress throw me to buy a piece of silk for a scarf-shawl.

MAMMY: I ain't never knowed you to buy no silk before. You better beware that Yankee anyhow. White folks don't like to see us talking to him.

MARY: He sell to slaves all the time.

MAMMY: Yes, but the patterollers keep they eye on all Yankees down this way. I ain't even gonna greet him, myself. I values my hide.

(Enter the PEDDLAR. MAMMY does not speak.)

PEDDLAR: Good morning! You-all got any coppers to dispense with today? I got wool pieces, silk pieces, knit caps, baby clothes—cheap. What the white folks don't buy, I sell to slaves, or whoever. Good morning!

MARY: Good morning! I want to see some stripped silk, please sir.

PEDDLAR: Yes, indeed!

MARY: Spread it here, on this box here.

PEDDLAR: Is it clean?

MAMMY: I tells you now, *no*, tain't clean! (*She picks up her clothes basket and exits*)

PEDDLAR: What's the matter with her?

MARY: Jealous cause I got a coin to spend.

(*The PEDDLAR and MARY both look around carefully*)

PEDDLAR: I have other wares, too, I don't speak much about, Mary.

MARY: I know. You're the freedom man.

PEDDLAR: They say you had the thought a long time in your mind.

MARY: But I was waiting! I was waiting for—

(*A slave passes carrying two pots from the house*)

PEDDLAR: Now this silk here, it's the finest from New— As I was saying, I'm here to help on things like that. Are you still waiting to make up your mind?

MARY: My mind been made up. I was waiting for my husband. Now he's here; from the Delta.

PEDDLAR: Where is your husband, Mary?

MARY: In this box. Rock! You there?

(*She taps on the box. ROCK answers*)

ROCK: What's left of me. This wood sure ain't no soft bed.

MARY: Here's the peddlar man, Rock.

ROCK: What he look like? White?

PEDDLAR: Yes, Rock, and old, and bent—but straight inside. And by God's will, I believe in freedom.

ROCK: I believes in it, too.

PEDDLAR: I take a chance. Do you?

ROCK: I done took my chance. I'm taking it now talking to you.

PEDDLAR: Mary, watch the gate there. Rock, where're you from?

ROCK: Clay's stone quarry way down in the Delta.

PEDDLAR: I've heard about that place. It's where they break men, so I'm told.

ROCK: Only they don't call us men.

PEDDLAR: You escaped from there?

ROCK: Yes, sir!

PEDDLAR: Just, "yes," Rock. Then I know you're brave—and worthy of the band of freedom. This is the year 1858, Rock, and all over this country there's mighty forces moving for freedom. Every day now on the underground, our train is running.

ROCK: Um-hum! Well, I want to know when this freedom train's gonna start—cause I can't spend the rest of my life cramped up in this box.

PEDDLAR: It leaves tonight, Rock. Your wife is ready?

ROCK: She's ready—too long ago! And I'm ready, too.

PEDDLAR: Then meet me at Jenkin's Cross Roads on the pike, four miles south of town, an hour after the moon goes down.

ROCK: An hour after the moon goes down.

PEDDLAR: But I want to warn you—our train don't carry no cowards, and it don't carry none that can ever turn back. Either you go through—or you don't. It's a dangerous train to ride, Rock. If it's overtaken by the enemy, all is lost. If some passenger wants to turn around, nothing to do but stop him in his tracks. I mean—*kill him,* Rock, so he won't tell no tales. This freedom business is not easy. It's not for the faint-hearted.

ROCK: But it's for me.

PEDDLAR: Then you won't be in this box much longer. Now— *(Enter a slave woman with two chickens)* These silks, as I was saying, Mary, now these silks, as I said—you couldn't invest those few pennies your mistress gave you in a better bargain. Just look here and feel. None today? All right, then I'm on my way. Goodbye, Mary!

MARY: Goodbye!

> *(The yard fills with slaves going to and fro. MARY exits. The PEDDLAR exits. The CHIMNEY SWEEP leaves the house humming:)*

By and by, when de morning comes . . .

> *(He gives a sweep at the clothes on the line with his dirty broom and hurries out laughing. Then sings again in the distance. MARY returns with a big ham bone in her hands. She looks around nervously, takes her keys and opens the box.)*

MARY: Rock! Rock! Quick, here's something for you to eat, honey.

> *(But just as ROCK's hand reaches up to snatch it, MAMMY enters to take down her clothes. MARY quickly closes the box and begins to nibble off the bone herself.)*

MAMMY: You sure likes this backyard today, Mary. You must think spring done come for sure.

MARY: It's too warm in Mistress sick room! I near bout smother!

MAMMY: Delicate as you is, nibbling off a ham bone. I never seed you do nothing like that before. You acting like a field hand.

MARY: I'm awful hongry, Mammy.

MAMMY: I jest knowed that old chimney sweep gonna dirty up my clothes with his soot. Jest looky here! Ain't that awful! If Mistress weren't sick, I'd go right straight and tell her.

MARY: That's sure too bad.

MAMMY: I might as well go now and fix up the tub agin for washing.
  (*Exit WOMAN. MARY again attempts to get the bone to ROCK when a slave child runs by.*)
MARY: Rock, I knows you near about starved.
ROCK: And near about daid in this hot old box. But gimme that ham bone.
MARY: Here! Quick! (*Slams box shut.*)
ROCK: Mary, you done throwed that bone to my feet—and I can't reach it.
MARY: Oh, my! Wait! Sss-ss-s!
ROCK: I ain't got no teeth in my heels.
MARY: Just a minute, honey! (*Opens box*) Here 'tis. Now you stay there till the darkness come. I'll bring plenty to eat then.
ROCK: And tonight—
MARY: Yes!
ROCK: We takes the chance.
MARY: We takes the chance!
  (*WASHWOMAN returns with basket and begins taking down the clothes. MARY helps her.*)
MAMMY: If I catch that old chimney sweep here agin, I sure gonna beat his head myself, so help me Jesus!
MARY: I'm gonna help you beat him, Mammy! I'm gonna help you.
MAMMY: Where your ham bone at, Mary?
MARY: Oh, I done throwed that to an old dog.
  (*ROCK growls like a dog . . . Blackout . . . In the darkness the voice of the PEDDLAR is heard as the CHORUS hums softly, then sings:*)
CHORUS:
  Deep river, Lord!
  My home is over Jordan.
  Deep river! Oh!
  I want to cross over
  Into camp ground.
PEDDLAR: Rock . . . Mary . . . Phineas . . . Jane! This wagon is in the hands of our friend and driver, Conductor John Andrews—but above all, it is in the hands of God! Get in. Keep quiet. Don't say a word. Answer to no voice ever should any call. God bless you! And pray in your hearts.
JANE: Chillun, pray! God, this is the freedom train. Keep it, God, on de Northern track. We knows you will. Amen!

PHINEAS: Amen!

ROCK: Amen!

MARY: Amen!

PEDDLAR: God speed you all!

DRIVER: Sck! Sck! Get up! Get on!

> (*Sound of horses hooves and a heavy wagon creaking away into the night. The footsteps of the PEDDLAR retreat in the distance. When the light comes up it reveals at dawn the interior of an old fashioned parlor in an Illinois farm house—a secret station of the underground railway. A Quaker couple, DAVID and MARTHA, man and wife, in their quaint garb are anxiously awaiting someone.*)

MARTHA: It's sun-up, David, and they aren't here yet. I wonder has something happened to that load of corn?

DAVID: Corn? Thou needst not talk thus—with just us here, Martha.

MARTHA: I'm always afraid the slave catchers will hear, David. I'm so nervous I can hardly stand it.

DAVID: Is the hot coffee ready, and the food? Those poor souls will be cold and famished.

MARTHA: It's ready, David.

DAVID: And the blankets and cots are in the cellar?

MARTHA: They're there.

DAVID: It's a double bottomed wagon—but crowded—four or five blacks this time—and they'll be stiff as a board from the jolting.

MARTHA: Thou hast no fear, David, that they'll be held up at the ferry?

DAVID: The toll-man is one of us today, Martha. Everything is fixed.

MARTHA: Is little Dave keeping a good look-out at the upstairs window?

DAVID: He is.

MARTHA: David, God gave me a good *man* when he gave thee to me. I always did believe in every human creature being free, but I was at a loss to know how to help freedom's cause until I married thee. Now, I thank Him, he has made of this house a station on the underground road to freedom. Just a station, but many a black soul has found the threshold to a new life here. Sometimes I wish they could stay, live with us, and know our ways and learn our love of Christ.

DAVID: The slaves have love in their hearts. If they didn't, they'd have risen up long ago and killed and slaughtered.

MARTHA: It looks as if killing and slaughter's about to break out in the

land anyhow, David. Lincoln's appealing for union—and the South
is shouting back defiance of God and Lincoln, both.

DAVID: God works in a mysterious way his wonders to perform,
Martha. He sometimes takes. . . .

> (*A child's voice is heard upstairs*)

BOY: Dad! Mother! The wagon load of corn is crossing the ferry.

DAVID: Thank the Lord! More souls are crossing the river they've
waited so long to cross. The border line of freedom is now water
beneath them. Bring them safely over, Lord.

MARTHA: Bring them safely over! David, I hear the horses.

DAVID: I'll go into the stable yard and unload that corn.

MARTHA: I'll go with thee.

> (*Blackout . . . Light comes up revealing the back of a wagon piled
> high with corn in the shuck. The driver is heard whoaing the horses
> as they champ and rattle their harness. DAVID and his wife are
> busy unfastening the chains that support the back of the wagon. The
> driver's voice is heard.*)

DRIVER: Goodmorrow, friends! I'm safely here again.

DAVID: Goodmorrow, John Andrews!

MARTHA: God bless thee!

DRIVER: These horses are pretty tired. I'll unhitch and water them
while you look after the corn.

DAVID: Come in to breakfast when they're stabled, John Andrews.

DRIVER: Thank ye, I will.

> (*Clank of harness and sound of horses hooves as they are led away.
> The wagon back falls and reveals within the heads of MARY and
> another slave woman, JANE, covered with shucks and straw.*)

DAVID: In God's name, friends, I welcome thee!

MARTHA: Welcome! Welcome!

> (*The Quakers pull the women out. Then ROCK and a man,
> PHINEAS. In the gray dawn the slaves stand stiff and dazed but
> gradually come to life as they stretch and beat their arms about.*)

MARY: God bless, you, Mistress, sir! Where is we at?

DAVID: In Illinois! With Quakers. You're on freedom's soil.

MARY: At last, Rock, at last—we's on freedom's soil. Thank God-A-
Mighty! We's free at last!

ROCK: Free at last! Free at last!

CHORUS:

> Thank God-A-Mighty!
> I'm free at last!

Free at last! Free at last!

Thank God-A-Mighty!

Free at last!

> *(There is a great burst of song as the slaves and chorus join in. All then, as the sun rises, shake hands, fall on their knees and sing:)*
> *(Rising)*

FELICIA: Free! Free! Free! Free!

JOSIAH: Praise God, chillun, the sun do move!

ROCK: Yes, the sun do move!

WOMAN: Friends, I've got food for you, and drink, and beds to sleep. Come now. Come and eat.

ROCK: Can't eat! Can't sleep!

MARY: Can't drink! Too happy!

FELICIA: Can't lay down! Can't rest! Too happy!

JOSIAH: Praise God, chillun! The sun do move!

ROCK: Yes, the sun do move! Slavery chain done broke at last!

CHORUS:

> Broke at last, broke at last!
>
> Slavery chain done broke at last!
>
> Gonna praise God till I die!
>
> *(Blackout as all dance and shout. . . . ROCK walks forward into the spot light singing alone:)*

ROCK:

> I did tell him how I suffer
>
> In de dungeon and de chain.
>
> All my days with head bowed down,
>
> And my broken flesh and pain—
>
> But brethren—
>
> Slavery chain done broke at last,
>
> Broke at last, broke at last.
>
> Slavery chain done broke at last!
>
> Thank God till I die.
>
> *(Blackout. . . . Sound of running train. A seat in a day coach)*

ROCK: Boston! Wonder how many stations off that is?

MARY: Here we's riding in a train just like free, white, and quality folks!

ROCK: We *is* free! I got papers here to prove it.

MARY: The abolitionists gived us these papers—but we ain't really free till we gets where we going, and you get a job, and we gets our home and is settled, and can't nobody find us nor lay hands on us to take us back where we come from.

ROCK: Won't nobody bother us now, Mary. We in friendly territory. These folks up here in Massachusetts believe in freedom. I hears 'em say they'd go fight—if Lincoln calls them—to free *everybody* and preserve the Union.

MARY: I hope he calls 'em.

ROCK: A year or two back, you and me, we wouldn't believe there was any good white folks nowhere on earth.

MARY: But we knows it now. That peddlar! Them Quakers! And all these people here that believes in being free. Rock, I'm so happy I want to sing—

> In my heart,
> In my heart
> Oh, I feel so very happy
> In my heart.

> *(The light fades to blackout. Above the roar of the train, there is a bugle call, then the roll of drums in march time, and the distant sound of the tramp of soldiers. When the light comes up it reveals the interior of a modest home in Boston, MARY is laying the table for supper, she sings:)*

CHORUS:

> There's a little wheel a-turnin'
>   In my heart.
> There's a little wheel a-turnin'
>   In my heart,
>   In my heart,
>   In my heart,
> There's a little wheel a-turnin'
>   In my heart

MARY: Rock, you better come on home here from that blacksmith shop for your supper. What makes a man be always late, come eating time? I just bet he's off somewhere's watching the soldiers pass. They say they's organizing black troops, too, to go fight for freedom. I hopes they is! Black and white together! I hopes they is! But Rock, I'd kinder hate to see him go. We ain't had but hardly a year together—but that year in freedom's sure been sweet. I wish everybody could enjoy freedom. If Rock want to go fight so everybody can enjoy it—and I mean sure enough freedom—then I want him to go. Yes, I want him to go. It's a struggle—this world—but somehow I don't feel no ways tired— *(Her talk merges into song)*

CHORUS:

> In my heart,
> In my heart,
> I don't feel no ways tired
> In my heart.
>
> *(CHORUS continues with song as MARY goes to the door)*

[MARY:] Wonder where is that man? Lemme go to the door and see do I see him. Might as well sweep off the doorstep while I'm there. *(She exits to full stage with broom)*

CHORUS:

> Oh, I feel so very happy
> In my heart,
> I feel so very happy
> In my heart.
> In my heart,
> In my heart,
> I feel so very happy
> In my heart.
>
> *(While she is sweeping, ROCK enters unseen behind her. He has on the uniform of the Union army, but still carries his dinner pail. He puts his arms tightly around MARY from behind so she is unable to see him. Kisses her playfully on the neck.)*

MARY: Oh!

ROCK: Mary!

> *(She struggles to get loose)*

MARY: Rock! I been waiting for you to come home to eat your supper. You're late! And here you come carrying on some foolishness!

> *(He releases her)*

ROCK: Look!

MARY: You've joined the army!

ROCK: The 54th under Colonel Shaw—we're leaving tonight.

MARY: You're going to fight for freedom.

ROCK: For freedom, Mary.

MARY: Then go, Rock! I wants everybody to be free, and Lincoln done called! Here, gimme that dinner bucket and go take your gun. While you're gone, I'll keep the doorstep clean, I'll sweep away yesterday. There won't be no more slavery time sorrows nowhere when you come back. We got Fred Douglass now, and Harriet Tubman, and

Sojourner Truth—and Abe Lincoln. And more than that, honey, we got the Lord! Go, husband! Go, Rock—to that mighty army of the free!

>*(They embrace to the sound of marching feet. ROCK exits as MARY waves from the doorstep)*

CHORUS:

>Glory! Glory! Halleluiah!
>Glory! Glory! Halleluiah!
>Glory! Glory! Halleluiah!
>His truth is marching on.

>*(As the CHORUS continues softly, MARY speaks)*

MARY: Yes, He's marching on! The Lord's marching on with me. Marching on with my people—with all the people that believes in being free. I look back and I see all the miseries of slavery time— the Overseer with his whip, Old Massa with his dogs. But I see the good people, too—the Yankee Peddlar, and the folks who believed in every slave being free. *(As she speaks each character enters until the entire cast is on the stage)* Then I see Lanthie out of Africa, Frog in that lonesome swamp, my child sold away, Clara, Josh, Maum Dorsey, Phineas, Jane—all my friends out of yesterday. Then I look ahead—and I see my race blossoming like the rose. I see schools and churches everywhere. I see love and life everywhere. I see colored men and women, fine men and women, teachers, preachers, doctors, lawyers, masons, mechanics, singers, dancers, voters, statemens in the congress—I see my people everywhere, all over America, all over the world taking part in the making of a new life. Folks, the sun do move! I see you—black and white together, standing with me, working with me, singing with me. Come on! Everybody! Shout! March! Sing!

CHORUS:

>Glory! Glory! Halleluiah!
>Glory! Glory! Halleluiah!
>Glory! Glory! Halleluiah!
>His truth goes marching on.

>>*(ROCK enters proudly bearing the American flag and marches to center between MARY and LANTHIE. Entire cast and choir comes forward to footlights, while, in silhouette in the background, the Union army marches to the roll of drums and the call of bugles. Finale.)*

>As he died to make men holy

Let us die to make men free—
While His truth goes marching on!
   (At the third curtain call, cast leads audience in "The Star Span-
   gled Banner.")[1]

Notes

Mulatto

1. Hughes to Webster Smalley, July 31, 1961, Langston Hughes Papers.
2. Prohibition ended in 1933; Mississippian Theodore G. Bilbo was elected to the U.S. Senate in 1934; John Rankin, from the same state, served in the U.S. House from 1921 to 1953. This speech suggests that some of this version of the play was written prior to the end of prohibition.

Mule Bone

1. Specifically, Gates writes: "Several drafts of *Mule Bone* exist, housed at Howard and at Yale. The most complete draft, however, and the only one containing two scenes in Act Two, is that dated 'Cleveland, 1931.' It is this draft that we have published here. Since the manuscript for *Mule Bone* was never copyedited during the authors' lifetimes, there are some apparent inconsistencies in characters' names and relationships to one another. For instance, Daisy Taylor is the daughter of Mrs. Blunt, and is seemingly unrelated to Mrs. Taylor. We have noted any name changes in the text" (*Mule Bone: A Comedy of Negro Life* [New York: HarperPerennial, 1991], 43).
2. A few corrections of obvious typographical errors have been made to Gates's text.
3. At this point in the original manuscript, for unknown reasons, the name *Childers* changed to *Singletary*. We have kept *Childers* for consistency.
4. At this point in the original manuscript, for unknown reasons, Daisy *Taylor* is referred to as Daisy *Blunt*. We have kept *Taylor* for consistency. Likewise, just below *Dilcie* Anderson is referred to as *Becky*, and we have kept *Dilcie*.

Harvest

1. Susan Duffy, *The Political Plays of Langston Hughes* (Carbondale: Southern Illinois University Press, 2000), 56.

2. Ibid.; Leslie Sanders, "Interesting Ways of Staging Plays: Hughes and Russian Theatre," *Langston Hughes Review* 15:1 (spring 1997): 4–12.

3. There is no scene 5 in the script in the Langston Hughes Papers.

4. There are two Act IIs in the most complete draft in the Langston Hughes papers. This one is marked "Act II"; it incorporates conversations and information in the other Act II (called "Act II, Scene One") and adds new information.

5. This seems to be a note from one collaborator to another. It has been retained in keeping with the general editorial principles governing this volume.

Little Ham

1. Bloomington: Indiana University Press, 1963.

2. "Hambone n. (1890s–1940s) probably a reference to the human thigh and the hip; word used in children's jingles ('Hambone, Hambone, where you been?'); from the late nineteenth century through the thirties, an all-purpose metaphor for black cultural experience; variously known to refer to rhythm, the penis, hard times" (*Juba to Jive: A Dictionary of American-American Slang*, ed. Clarence Major [New York: Penguin Books, 1994]).

Soul Gone Home

1. Hughes to Ulysses Kay, May 31, 1954, Langston Hughes Papers.

Emperor of Haiti

1. Arnold Rampersad, *The Life of Langston Hughes, Volume 1, 1902–1941: "I, Too, Sing America"* (New York: Oxford University Press, 1986), 165.

2. François Mackandal, who in 1751 fled to the mountains, is said to have killed six thousand whites before his capture in 1758 and execution at the stake.

When the Jack Hollers

1. Probably a typographical error.

2. Perhaps what is meant is "ary a plate."

Joy to My Soul

1. Jack Warfel, *Cleveland Press,* May 25, 1939.
2. Langston Hughes, *The Big Sea* (1940; New York: Hill and Wang, 1963), 274.
3. In the 1930s, Sally Rand popularized a form of the Japanese fan dance in which she used huge Ostrich feathers and danced apparently in the nude.

Don't You Want to Be Free

1. This is the only play for which Hughes wrote elaborate production notes. The version here is a later revision by Hughes of his original notes.

The Sun Do Move

1. Hughes detailed the music in *The Sun Do Move* as follows:
ACT I: Cotton Needs Pickin'—Full Chorus
      Oh, Mary, Don't you Weep—Full Chorus, women first, then men
      Go Tell It On De Mountain—Soloists: LANTHIE, ROCK, Chorus
      Is Massa Gwine Sell Us Tomorrow?—Full Chorus, ROCK, solo
      Lord, I Cannot Stay Here By Myself—Solo, MARY. Chorus hums
ACT II: Lullabye—Solo, MARY. Female Chorus
      Somebody's Callin' Me—Solo, LANTHIE, Chorus hums
      Deep River—Chorus hums behind sermon and prayer
      Steal Away To Jesus—Full Chorus, women first, then men
      Cow Need a Tail in Fly Time—Solo, FROG
      Oh, Freedom—Solo, FROG, ROCK, Full Chorus
      When I'm Gone—Solo, FROG
      City Called Heaven—Solo, MARY. Chorus
ACT III: Hammerin' Song—Male Chorus. Solo, ROCK
      Free At Last—ROCK, MARY, Full Chorus
      Let Us Break Bread Together—Full Chorus
      Slavery Chain Done Broke At Last—Full Chorus
      Little Wheel A-Turnin'—MARY. Chorus hums.
      Battle Hymn of the Republic—Full Chorus

Sources: RELIGIOUS FOLK SONGS OF THE NEGRO (Hampton)
BEFO' DE WAR SPIRITUALS
NEGRO FOLK SONGS, Book 4, Curtis-Burlin
BOOK OF AMERICAN NEGRO SPIRITUALS, Johnson